A Computer
and Communications
Network Performance
Analysis Primer

Prentice-Hall Software Series

Brian W. Kernighan, advisor

A Computer and Communications Network Performance Analysis Primer

B. W. Stuck

E. Arthurs

Bell Laboratories
Murray Hill, New Jersey

PRENTICE-HALL, INC.
Englewood Cliffs, New Jersey

Library of Congress Cataloging in Publication Data

Stuck, B. W.
    A computer and communications network performance
analysis primer.

    (Prentice-Hall software series)
    Includes bibliographical references and indexes.
    1. Electronic digital computers—Evaluation.
2. Computer networks—Evaluation.   I. Arthurs, E.
II. Title.   III. Series.
QA76.9.E94S78 1984   001.64   84-8283
ISBN 0-13-163981-1

This book was typeset in Times Roman and Courier by the authors, using a Autologic APS-5 phototypesetter driven by a DEC PDP/VAX-11/780 running the UNIX operating system release System V.

Unix is a trademark of Bell Laboratories. DEC, PDP and VAX are trademarks of Digital Equipment Corporation.

Printed in the United States of America

10 9 8 7 6 5 4 3 2 1

ISBN 0-13-163981-1 01

Prentice-Hall International, Inc., *London*

Prentice-Hall of Australia Pty. Limited, *Sydney*

Editora Prentice-Hall do Brasil, Ltda., *Rio de Janeiro*

Prentice-Hall Canada Inc., *Toronto*

Prentice-Hall of India Private Limited, *New Delhi*

Prentice-Hall of Japan, Inc., *Tokyo*

Prentice-Hall of Southeast Asia Pte. Ltd., *Singapore*

Whitehall Books Limited, *Wellington, New Zealand*

Dedicated To

Mary-Jane and Alberta

PREFACE: **WHY THIS BOOK**

This book is an outgrowth of a course taught within Bell Laboratories by the authors entitled **Performance Evaluation of Computing Systems and Networks.** The students had completed an integrated seven course sequence of internal education courses comparable to current graduate computer science courses at colleges and universities in the United States of America; this material was a candidate for a final eighth course in that sequence.

Methodology

The intent of the course was to introduce fundamental notions associated with performance analysis of digital computing systems and digital communication networks to an audience not familiar with this area. Where the line is drawn between computers and communications we leave for others to decide. Because of the wide variety of phenomena that could be dealt with in such a course, the background of the students, and the time available, the currently widely used approach of stressing techniques for deriving fundamental results was *not* used. Instead, the approach adopted was to teach by example or case study. First, we would present an operational description of a computer communication system showing the flow of control and data for each step of each job, followed by a minimum list of measurements (both inputs and outputs) that would be needed to quantify performance, then present the *results* of a performance analysis for that problem, discuss the significance of the results and illustrate it with numerical studies, and spend virtually *no* time at all deriving the results. Our reason for doing so was that the students are primarily interesting in *doing* performance analysis, in being able to relate concepts in class to situations arising in their own work, and being able to do so quickly and in a timely manner. We feel it is much more important for the students to understand the variety of approaches available, the strengths and shortcomings, than to spend classroom time on derivations. Remember, our students are full time employees with their own work assignments. Many of them are simply not interested in derivations. The present version does contain a limited number of derivations of key results, in order for this work to be self contained. For those interested, suitable references are provided to the technical literature to derivations and additional related topics.

The lecture topics also reflect the needs of audience. We began with a complete description of relatively simple computer communication systems where all the work is present at an initial time and must be executed to meet some optimality criterion. If the number of jobs becomes larger and larger, the time required to execute the jobs grows, and it is appropriate to examine mean value performance measures such as throughput rate and delay because in our experience this has proven to have the greatest most immediate practical value. This is complemented with measurement, data analysis and simulation, because it is essential to relate models to reality as early as practicable, in order to motivate and hold the attention of students. Jackson queueing network analysis followed next because this is a natural refinement of the mean value analysis concepts. In either mean value analysis or Jackson queueing network analysis, a bottleneck or single point of congestion arises, which leads us into our next topic, congestion and queueing analysis of a single serially reusable resource. Each two hour lecture consisted of working exercises in class that were handed out the previous lecture, and introducing new material. The exercises are the crux of this material, and are really an integral part of the course. In our experience, it is more important to have the students work the problems in order to be capable of doing performance analysis of actual computer and communication systems than it is to read the text alone. Again, the students are *engineers* and the crux of engineering, in our opinion, is manipulating numbers in a great variety of ways to gain *qualitative* insight into design issues via *quantitative* methods. Many of the exercises worked here arose in the course of our own work at Bell Laboratories on over one hundred distinct computer based communications systems; the diverse demands and variety of phenomena coupled with the realization that the same tools could be applied again and again, with suitable modifications, led us to teaching and to this book. Students were encouraged to participate in class discussion, and to carry out projects on analyzing performance of systems encountered in work.

Supplementary Texts

This document was supplemented with other texts:

- H.Lorin, **Parallelism in Hardware and Software,** Prentice-Hall, Englewood Cliffs, NJ, 1972.

- L.Kleinrock, **Queueing Systems, Volume II: Computer Applications,** Wiley, New York, 1976.

- A.Tanenbaum, **Computer Networks,** Prentice-Hall, Englewood Cliffs, NJ, 1981.

- P.Seaman, **Analysis of Some Queuing Models in Real-Time Systems,** IBM Data Processing Division, GF20-0007-1, 1971.

- R.W.Conway, W.L.Maxwell, L.W.Miller, **Theory of Scheduling,** Addison Wesley, Reading, Massachusetts, 1967.

Numerous other texts were consulted and used as appropriate, but these texts were the ones that shaped our approach to the greatest extent.

Philosophy

Two problems are encountered by the pedagogue in teaching this material. First, the material must be motivated via examples from actual applications that may boggle the purist in complexity while being much too simplified for the practitioner. Second, general unifying principles must be explained to allow students to systematically attack wholly new systems, and this may alienate the practitioner while being too loose and lacking rigor for the purist. The role of judgement, of what is appropriate and what is not, cannot be learned, in our opinion, except by *doing,* by having close association and interactions with systems such as are described here. Any laboratory or controlled experimentation with an actual computer or communications system is highly recommended to supplement this book.

Several features are worth keeping in mind in presenting this material:

- Digital systems are intrinsically *complex* in that the number of possible *states* a system can be in can easily exceed trillions of trillions. This appears to be in the nature of the beast, and no amount of chicanery will allow us to forget that *details matter!*

- Although the systems are complex, they possess *structure* at every turn: Any digital system consists of hardware or logical abstractions embodied in software of processing, storage, and communications between processing, storage, and the external world. In our experience, this structure helps to guide the performance analyst in making judgements at every step of the job. The structure suggests what data should be gathered, how to develop cause and effect inferences, what changes might or might not be feasible.

- The realm of *analysis* is concerned with exploring the consequences of various hypotheses or mathematical models. This draws on combinatorics for enumerating and aggregating system states in order to manage complexity, algebraic techniques for deducing canonical structures or models, probability theory for explaining how the different likelihoods of system operation interact and evolve, and optimization for attempting to achieve a satisfactory design with a given set of constraints.

The Emphasis in the Material

The material is broken into three areas, progressing from basic to advanced concepts: basic or mandatory material, Jackson queueing networks, and priority scheduling of a single serially reusable resource. The basic material demands a clear functional step by step description of system operation, followed by a statement of performance goals, measurements of inputs and outputs, and mean value analysis. This material could easily occupy a one semester course, drawing on the examples and references provided. The Jackson queueing networks are a refinement of the mean value analysis, and provide the opportunity to introduce a wide variety of tractable models of actual computer communication systems. The material on priority scheduling is the most mathematically sophisticated, and requires the greatest intellectual maturity.

We feel it is more important to capture *all* of the relevant phenomena in performance analysis to *some* extent rather than being *exhaustive* in some subset of all the relevant factors and perhaps *ignoring* other factors entirely; in our own experience, this has come back to haunt us on numerous occasions. For this reason, we have focused on what we feel are *simple* analytic models in the presentation of the material, that can be successively refined in a hierarchical manner as data is gathered, rather than beginning with simulation models. The attempt is to avoid modeling *complexity* at much too early a stage, before the data in fact warrants this. Because of this, the first four chapters by themselves are intended to form the core for a one semester course on performance analysis. These chapters contain virtually *all* the requisite concepts and techniques needed for practicing performance analysis engineering.

Our approach has been slanted toward analysis and away from rote. Simulation forces a systematic attack on a problem: what are the inputs? what are the outputs? what can be measured? Unfortunately, in our experience, all too often *none* of these issues are clearly articulated, and this has driven us toward paper and pencil simulation models, or analysis, as a first step in problem solving. Analytic methods can often allow a rough sizing or bounds on regions of acceptable throughput rate and delay within hours, while months may elapse before a more complicated simulation model shows comparable insight. Clearly not all simulations are complex, and simulation models are in fact developed in a hierarchical manner, but we would rather have students *think* first about the nature of the problem before jumping into techniques for modeling. This is *not* to say that simulation should *not* be done: on the contrary, in the course of our work we demand, as professionals, that models and hypotheses be vindicated with measurement and controlled experimentation, in order to gain confidence in predictions and extrapolations to new regions of operation. However, this controlled experimentation may often occur late in the development and system integration and testing phase of a product, when it may be too late to reverse earlier design decisions in the areas of data base management, application program structuring, operating system, and hardware. We feel it is better to carry out this process in an ongoing manner throughout development and deployment, through the complete life cycle of a product, and this means starting with simple analytically tractable models and then refining them via analysis and simulation. Finally, how can a simulation be checked? Via special cases, such as the analytically tractable models presented in the bulk of this book: it is difficult enough to check the logical correctness of a deterministic program, let alone a program whose behavior is unknown (such as is often the case with simulation) and having checks such as provided by analysis is often invaluable. Again, we *do* favor simulation, when properly applied: in our (admittedly limited) experience, and with the students we have taught, we have found the present approach most fruitful. For all these reasons, we have chosen to slant our presentation in its present direction.

Pacing the Presentation

One comment we have received repeatedly from students is that they must *think* to work the exercises. This course demands the integration of a great many concepts encountered in several different courses over a period of years. A month into the course, many students are apparently conceptually overloaded. The students had little difficulty with any of the numerical studies: no derivations are required, only the ability to correctly substitute into formulae involving addition, subtraction, multiplication and division. Those students who stick with the material do extremely well, as shown by an upward progression in test scores from start to finish of the course: what we chose to teach the students in fact learned. All of this very strongly suggests that the pacing and course organization is very important.

One alternative is to present the introductory material as part of other courses, e.g., in a course on operating systems or communication protocols, to lessen the shock. The actual course could then begin with Jackson network analysis and progress to priority scheduling. Two variants are possible, doing this all over one semester, or, by drawing on the references for additional material, doing this over two semesters, one on Jackson networks and one on priority scheduling.

We did not have the luxury of presenting the introductory material as part of other courses, and only had one semester available. Spending roughly four weeks on deterministic or static scheduling and mean value analysis in our experience exposes the students to virtually all the fundamental concepts of performance analysis and data analysis, and is an appropriate point for an exam. The intent is to expose the students to as many diverse examples and concepts as possible, hopefully familiar from other courses, jobs, trade magazines (algorithms, digital hardware, operating systems, compilers, editors, communications protocols), to motivate the material, while demanding *quantification* of system performance, not simply a functional description of correct logical operation of a computer communication system. Four to five weeks on Jackson networks (with mean value analysis being presented first, then Jackson network analysis) is an appropriate time interval for students to get caught up with the concepts, and is an appropriate point for an exam. Again, many examples can be introduced here to motivate the material, while the concepts need not be nearly as challenging as in the first part. The remainder of the course can be spent on new topics associated with priority scheduling of a bottleneck serially reusable resource, and is an appropriate point for a final test. Our goal was to present as many examples as possible, to allow browsing, to give as much freedom of presentation, so as not to confine the teaching and learning.

Finally, those interested may wish to draw on the references and readings, to present this material over two semesters. The first semester might deal with a more detailed treatment of static scheduling (multiple processor algorithms for sorting, for numerical analysis, for signal processing) and mean value analysis leading into Jackson networks. The second semester might be a systematic exploration of Jackson network models and static priority scheduling.

Acknowledgement

We are indebted to the Bell Telephone Laboratories for providing a stimulating environment for carrying out this work, for giving us the freedom to pursue in as much detail as was felt required understanding of numerous diverse systems, and for allowing that material to coalesce into this present form.

We are indebted to the Computer Science Department at Columbia University for allowing us to teach a course based on this material in the fall of 1983. A great deal of constructive criticism was received from the students over a fifteen week period for which we are greatly appreciative. The present book has benefited immensely from these comments.

Murray Hill, New Jersey, USA

Additional Reading

[1]   R.Hinderliter, S.D.Shapiro, *A Program of Continuing Education in Applied Computer Science,* Computer, **14** (10), 76-80 (1981).

TABLE OF CONTENTS

LIST OF FIGURES

CHAPTER THREE: DATA ANALYSIS AND SIMULATION   **93**

CHAPTER FOUR: MEAN VALUE ANALYSIS   **140**

A Computer
and Communications
Network Performance
Analysis Primer

Why do performance analysis? There are two basic reasons:

[1] To improve productivity: more work is accomplished in the same amount of time.

[2] To add functionality: totally new functions will be performed that offer the potential for new productivity gains or new revenue.

Productivity has two components:

[1] Comparisons of different configurations of an existing system doing an established set of functions. Here are some illustrative examples:

  • A file system is stored on a disk. Where should the files physically be located to provide acceptable access times for typical usage?

  • An office contains three groups. Should there be one secretary per group, or a pool of three secretaries for all the groups?

[2] Changing the configuration of an existing system doing an established set of functions to improve performance. Here are some examples to illustrate this point:

  • A computer system for program development is configured with one megabyte of memory. What information is needed to determine how much memory is really needed?

  • A file system for billing inquiries is stored on two disk spindles. A single controller governs access to the two spindles. What information is needed to determine if a third disk spindle is needed? What about adding another controller?

  • An application program that generates management reports reads one file repeatedly. What information is needed to determine if this file should be replicated and stored on more than one disk spindle, to improve performance?

  • A packet switch has four communication links. Should there be a pool of buffers for all messages on all links, or should buffers be dedicated to different types of packets (e.g., control packets versus data packets, or so many buffers per line)

  • A telephone switching system is controlled by a single processor. What information is needed to determine if this processor should be replaced by a single faster processor, or two processors of the same speed, in order to handle fifty per cent more telephone calls per hour?

Here are some examples of added functionality:

- An office already owns a computer controlled word processing system. What information is needed to determine if this system can support electronic mail?

- A bank wishes to install a network of automatic teller machines. What information is needed to determine what type of computer will be needed to handle this work?

- A CATV franchise wishes to supply voice communications over TV channels not used for entertainment. What type of computer system will be needed to handle billing for this purpose?

Coupled with any performance analysis must be an economic analysis to quantify benefits and costs. All too often costs are ignored altogether, for a variety of reasons. If costs are ignored, then, *de facto,* costs are assumed negligible. However, *costs are lost benefits.* If costs are studied, then the outcome must be worse than before the study, because now costs are **not** negligible. Costs quantify the benefits of different alternatives, which is one aspect of decision making.

Remember, issues of computer performance evaluation cannot be answered absolutely. They must be addressed relative to other factors, such as economic issues, political considerations, and many more. The aspects of performance dealt with here are still only a subset of all the factors that must be considered in evaluating a total system to determine if it is suitable for a given application.

Although we focus on performance analysis here, we can be more specific, and list some of these other considerations:

- Economic: What is the cost to the user and the provider for a set of services?

- Marketing: What are the long term strategies or goals? What products attempt to meet those goals?

- Service: What service must be provided by the vendor, and by the purchaser? At what cost?

- Human engineering and psychological: What do human beings see and hear and feel when they interact with the system?

- Logical correctness and functionality: What functions should the system perform? How do we know these functions are being correctly executed?

- Systems engineering: Should products be leased or purchased? From what vendors? What hardware configuration is cost effective? What software configuration?

1.1 An Example

The figure below shows a representative hardware block diagram of a computer system.

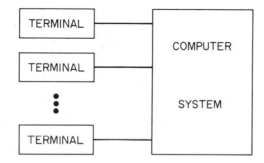

Figure 1.1.Computer System Hardware Block Diagram

Operators at terminals spend some time reading, thinking and entering commands. The commands are fed into the computer system, and executed, and the cycle repeats itself. In order to say *anything* at all quantitative concerning performance, we must describe *how* the system works. The simplest script for describing this would be to have only one type of job done by every operator. The script that each operator would follow might be

- Read, think and enter a command

- Wait for the response to the command

The process then repeats itself, again and again and again. This is summarized in the flow chart below. We measure the average time to do each step. There are two entities, an operator (at a terminal) and a computer system. The table below is a summary of what entities are needed at each step, and the average time per step:

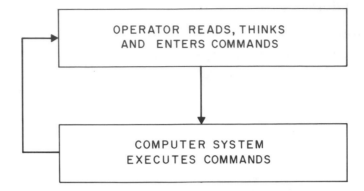

Figure 1.2.Operator Interaction With Computer System Flow Chart

Table 1.1.Steps, Entities and Mean Time per Step

Step	Operator	Computer	Time
Read,Think,Type	1	0	T_{think}
Wait for Response	0	1	T_{system}

The times that are tabulated are measured with *no* contention, i.e., with only one operator at one terminal using the computer system. We will use the *no* contention measurements to extrapolate to system behavior *with* contention. But before doing so, we must take a diversion.

1.2 What Is a Resource?

The entities in the example above are concrete examples of what we call *resources*. In order to understand the performance of a computer or communication system, we must understand what *state* the system is in at any instant of time. It is often useful to summarize the system state by what jobs are holding what resources at each step of execution. What is a *resource?* **A resource is anything that can block subsequent execution of a job.** A job requires one or more resources at each stage of execution, and if it does not have them all, it is blocked from execution until the necessary resources are available. What are the resources in the previous example?

- Each operator is a resource

- Each terminal is a resource

- Each command is executed on a computer system, so the computer system is a resource

We could aggregate this set of resources in different ways. For example, in order for an operator to interact with the system, an operator needs a terminal, so we might combine these two resources and talk about operators and terminals interchangeably. We could disaggregate this set of resources in different ways. For example, we might look inside the computer system, and find a processor, memory, a disk controller handling one or more disk spindles, and so on, as well as operating system software and application programs, each of which might usefully be thought of as resources. Whatever description is most useful in a given situation will determine what level of aggregation and disaggregation is needed.

The *state* of the system at any instant of time is given by the number of operators at terminals actively reading, thinking, and typing, and hence holding a terminal resource, and the number of jobs inside the system in execution or waiting to be executed. More formally, $J_{operator}$ denotes the number of operators reading, thinking and typing, while J_{system} denotes the number of jobs inside the system. Each of these can take on integer values ranging from zero to N, the total number of terminals with operators, but there is a constraint that every job must be *somewhere,* either with an operator or inside the system, and hence

$$J_{operator} + J_{system} = N$$

The state space Ω is given by all ordered pairs $(J_{operator}, J_{system})$ such that the total number of jobs equals the total number of active operators:

$$\Omega = \{(J_{operator}, J_{system}) \mid J_{operator}, J_{system} = 0, 1, \ldots, N; J_{operator} + J_{system} = N\}$$

A useful picture of the system state is a *queueing network* block diagram. For our earlier example of terminals connected to a single system this is shown in the figure below:

We see two queues, represented by a box with an open left end. Resources are shown by circles or servers: each terminal is represented by a circle, while the system is represented by one circle. Jobs circulate from the terminals into the system and back again.

Both physical and logical resources are required at each stage of execution of computer programs, and we must know these in order to say anything about performance. Resources can be

- Serially reusable--one job at a time can use a processor, a data link, a given secondary storage device, a protected file, a critical region of operating system code

- Shared concurrently--multiple buffers in an operating system allow different jobs to share the buffer resource concurrently

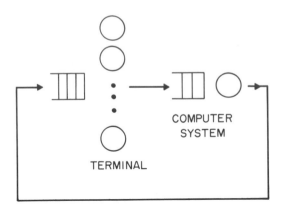

Figure 1.3.Queueing Network Block Diagram

- Consumable--messages between software modules exemplify this resource type

In our previous example, the system is serially reusable, while the terminal resource can be thought of as shared concurrently: there is a pool of terminals, and we are not distinguishing anything about the work going on at each terminal (if we did, then each terminal would be a serially reusable resource). Because the notion of resource is essential to performance analysis, we will motivate this basic concept with additional examples in later sections.

1.3 Resource Allocation Policy

The choice of *policy* or *schedule* for allocation of resources is central to performance evaluation. We will focus on a variety of policies to allocate resources throughout this book, because the central issue in modern digital system design is the ability to allocate resource as demands change with time in a cost effective and flexible manner. Any scheduler will execute the highest priority job in the system at any one time. An illustrative flow chart of a scheduler is shown on page seven.

The details of *how* to set the *priorities* will concern us throughout the rest of this book. Again, we only have *finite* resources, due to economic concerns, that must be allocated amongst competing tasks in order to meet diverse and perhaps conflicting goals.

1.4 Likelihoods and Statistics

One problem with characterizing performance of computer communication systems is their *intrinsic* complexity. Even if we could know the state of every logic gate, which could be billions upon billions of states, what would we do

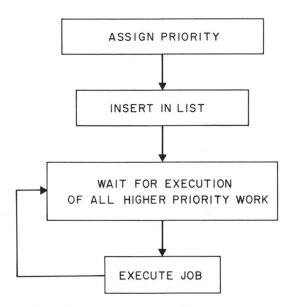

Figure 1.4.Scheduler Flow Chart

with the information: it is simply too difficult to track and comprehend. On the one hand, for logically correct operation, we are interested in knowing *all* the states: is the system in a working state, or is it in an unacceptable state? On the other hand, for performance, we are not always interested in *all* the states, but only the most *likely* that the system would be operating in. Statistics are a natural way of summarizing this type of complexity. Statistics allow us to quickly draw cause and effect inferences. Computer communications systems do not operate in a *random* manner, which is one aspect of statistics. Our purpose in using statistics is to study the most *likely* behavior, averaged over a suitably long time interval. Finally, how long is long? This is a relative notion: we are assuming that the measurements and statistics we gather stabilize, and are well characterized by an average value or mean. Transients will be ignored until later.

1.5 Performance Measures

Our intent is to focus on some of the many facets of what is called *performance* of a computer or communication system. This had its origin in voice telephony, determining how many voice telephones could be connected to a switching system to provide acceptable service. The demands placed on such systems can generate *traffic* or *congestion* for different resources. We will refer to performance interchangeably with *traffic handling characteristics* of such systems from this point on.

Traffic handling measures are either quantitative or qualitative. Two types of measures arise: those oriented toward *customers* or *users* of the system, and those oriented toward the *system* as a whole. Each of these measures has its own costs.

1.5.1 Customer Oriented Goals, Inputs and Outputs From the point of view of a customer or user of a system, we might be interested in the time delay (both execution and waiting) for each step of each job: from arrival, to the initial wait for service, through service, and the final clean up prior to completion. Service might involve some work to set up a job (e.g., handle an appropriate interrupt of a processor), followed by execution of the job (e.g., processing followed by input/output to secondary storage followed by processing and so forth), followed by clean up (e.g., handle an appropriate interrupt of a processor). The time epochs of interest are the arrival or ready time of a job, the job completion time, the desired completion time or due time or window or deadline.

From these statistics we could compute for each job its

- queueing or flow time--time from arrival until completion

- waiting or ready time--time to start processing less arrival time

- lateness--actual completion time minus desired completion time

- tardiness--maximum of zero and lateness

Can you think of any more? These are summarized in the figure below:

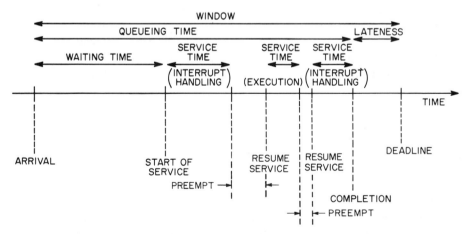

Figure 1.5.Illustrative Time Epochs for Processing a Job

For each measure or time interval, there would be a cost attached, which would reflect economic criteria. We could compute these for each step of each job submitted by each user. This can be quite complex, and instead we might compute a statistic, such as the *average* cost, averaged over all jobs by all users over time.

1.5.2 System Oriented Goals, Inputs and Outputs From the point of view of the system as a whole, we might wish to record over a given time interval

- The fraction of time each resource is busy doing work

- The mean throughput rate of executing jobs: the mean number of jobs executed in a given time interval

- The fraction of time two resources are simultaneously busy (in order to see how many steps are being executed concurrently)

In our previous example, we would be interested in

- The fraction of time each operator is reading, thinking and typing

- The fraction of time the system is busy executing work

- The mean throughput rate of executing jobs

- The fraction of time at least two operators are busy

- The fraction of time the system plus at least one operator is busy

For each resource, we could attach a cost for being idle, and compute the cost per resource for each user, or compute a statistic such as the average cost due to a resource being idle, averaged over all jobs and all users and over time.

1.6 An Example (Revisited)

Let's calculate as many performance measures as possible for our previous example: operators at terminals only doing one type of job, reading and thinking and typing followed by waiting for a response for the system. We will compute these *exactly* for one operator using the system, and then use this to *bound* performance with more than one operator, which is really the region of interest.

1.6.1 One Operator What is the response time for one operator? This is given by

$$\textit{mean response time for one terminal} = T_{response} = T_{system}$$

The rate at which work is executed by the system is the reciprocal of the mean time to completely cycle through a job. There are only two steps, and hence the mean throughput rate is given by

$$\textit{mean throughput rate for one terminal} = \frac{1}{T_{think} + T_{system}}$$

For example, if the mean time spent reading, thinking, and typing is fifteen seconds, while the mean response time is one second, then we see

$$mean\ response\ time\ for\ one\ terminal = T_{system} = 1\ second$$

$$mean\ throughput\ rate\ for\ one\ terminal = \frac{1}{T_{think} + T_{system}}$$

$$= \frac{1}{15\ sec + 1\ sec} = 1\ command\ every\ 16\ seconds$$

What is the utilization of the operator, the fraction of time an operator is busy?

$$operator\ utilization = \frac{T_{think}}{T_{think} + T_{system}} = \frac{15\ sec}{15\ sec + 1\ sec} = \frac{15}{16}$$

What is the utilization of the system, the fraction of time the system is busy?

$$system\ utilization = \frac{T_{system}}{T_{think} + T_{system}} = \frac{1\ sec}{15\ sec + 1\ sec} = \frac{1}{15}$$

What is the fraction of time both the operator and the system are simultaneously busy? *Zero!*

1.6.2 Two Operators   If two operators were using this system for command execution, what changes? The best the mean response time could ever be would be as if each operator were using the system separately. Hence, we see a *lower* bound on mean response time given by

$$mean\ response\ time\ with\ two\ terminals \geqslant T_{system} = 1\ sec$$

The worst the mean response time could ever be would be to have one operator submit a job and immediately thereafter have the other job submitted, which gives us a *upper* bound on mean response time:

$$mean\ response\ time\ with\ two\ terminals \leqslant 2T_{system} = 2\ sec$$

If we summarize all this, we find

$$T_{system} \leqslant T_{response} \leqslant 2T_{system} \quad two\ terminals$$

The definition of mean throughput rate is simply the rate at which each operator is doing work, multiplied by the total number of operators. Each operator spends some time reading, thinking, and typing, and then waits for a response, so the mean throughput rate for each operator is

$$mean\ throughput\ rate\ per\ operator = \frac{1}{T_{think} + T_{response}}$$

The upper bound on mean response time gives us a lower bound on mean throughput rate:

$$mean \ throughput \ rate \ per \ operator \geqslant \frac{1}{T_{think} + 2T_{system}}$$

The lower bound on mean response time gives us an upper bound on mean throughput rate:

$$mean \ throughput \ rate \ per \ operator \leqslant \frac{1}{T_{think} + T_{system}}$$

For the total system, with two operators we have twice the mean throughput rate of one operator:

$$\lambda_{lower} \leqslant total \ system \ mean \ throughput \ rate \leqslant \lambda_{upper}$$

$$\lambda_{lower} = \frac{2}{T_{think} + 2T_{system}} = 2 \ commands \ every \ 17 \ seconds$$

$$\lambda_{upper} = \frac{2}{T_{think} + T_{system}} = 2 \ commands \ every \ 16 \ seconds$$

What is the utilization of each operator? The fraction of time each operator is busy is the mean rate each operator does work multiplied by the mean time spent reading, thinking and typing:

$$operator \ utilization = mean \ throughput \ rate \ per \ operator \times T_{think}$$

Since we have upper and lower bounds on mean throughput rate, we have upper and lower bounds on operator utilization. What is the system utilization?

$$system \ utilization = total \ mean \ throughput \ rate \times T_{response}$$

Since we have upper and lower bounds on mean throughput rate and response time, we have upper and lower bounds on system utilization.

What about bounding other measures of concurrency?

- The fraction of time both operators are busy reading, thinking and typing and the system is idle

- The fraction of time one operator is reading, thinking and typing and the other operator is waiting for the system to respond

- The fraction of time both operators are waiting for the system to respond

EXERCISE: Explicitly calculate bounds on each of these measures.

1.6.3 N>2 Operators What happens if we increase the number of operators more and more? At some point the system will be completely busy doing work, and this will occur at

$$total\ mean\ throughput\ rate = \frac{1}{T_{system}} = 1\ command\ every\ second \quad N \rightarrow \infty$$

This is a *different* upper bound from the upper bound on mean throughput rate we just found. Our first upper bound was due to *how* the system was used by operators, while this upper bound is *intrinsic* to the system. One way to measure this is to *always* have a command ready to be executed. Once a command finishes execution, another command is immediately started in execution. Every system will have a maximum rate at which it can execute jobs, and this is a *key* performance measure. We combine both upper bounds in one expression:

$$mean\ throughput\ rate \leqslant \lambda_{upper} = \min\left[\frac{1}{T_{system}}, \frac{N}{T_{think} + T_{response}}\right]$$

As we vary the number of active operators or terminals, $N=1,2..$, the upper bound on mean throughput rate exhibits a *breakpoint* (denoted $N_{breakpoint}$ terminals or users) as a function of N, moving from an *operator limited* regime to a *system limited* regime. The breakpoint marks that value of N for which the two upper bounds equal one another:

$$\frac{N_{breakpoint}}{T_{think} + T_{system}} = \frac{1}{T_{system}} \quad N_{breakpoint} = \frac{T_{think} + T_{system}}{T_{system}}$$

Below this breakpoint, the terminals and operators cannot generate enough work to drive the system to continuously execute commands. Above this breakpoint, the system is continuously busy, and the operators are experiencing delays. This suggests the notion of a *bottleneck:* a resource that is completely busy. The terminals and operators are a bottleneck, provided the number is less than the breakpoint, and otherwise the system is a bottleneck. This breakpoint is a different measure of *concurrency*.

The mean response time is related to the mean throughput rate via the *definition* of mean throughput rate. A job is either with an operator (who is thinking) or inside the system (being executed):

$$total\ mean\ throughput\ rate = \frac{N}{T_{think} + T_{response}}$$

If we solve for the mean response time (which is a function of the number of terminals, among other things), we find

$$T_{response} = \frac{N}{total\ mean\ throughput\ rate} - T_{think}$$

On the one hand, the worst the mean response time could be is to be the last job to be done, after all the other operators submit jobs:

$$T_{response} \leqslant NT_{system}$$

This gives us a *lower* bound on mean throughput rate:

$$total\ mean\ throughput\ rate \geqslant \frac{N}{T_{think} + NT_{system}}$$

On the other hand, the best the mean response time could be is to be equal to the response time for one terminal:

$$T_{response} \geqslant T_{system}$$

Since the mean throughput rate can be upper bounded by two different expressions, we have two possible *lower* bounds on mean response time, and we will choose the larger of the two:

$$T_{response} \geqslant \max\left[T_{system}, NT_{system} - T_{think}\right]$$

These upper and lower bounds on mean throughput rate are plotted in the figure below versus number of active operators.

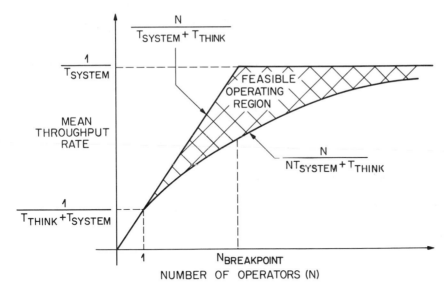

Figure 1.6. Upper and Lower Bounds on Mean Throughput Rate

Figure 1.7 plots upper and lower bounds on mean response time versus number of active operators.

1.6.4 Stretching Factor Ideally, as we increase the number of terminals, the mean throughput rate increases, while the mean response time stays low. Unfortunately, at some point the mean response time will grow, and the mean throughput rate will saturate. This suggests writing the mean throughput rate

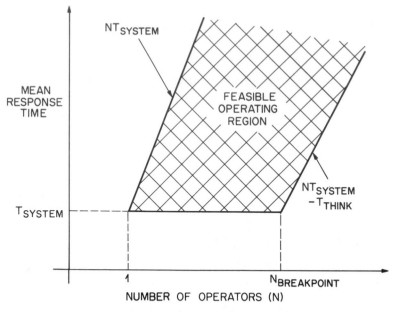

Figure 1.7. Upper and Lower Bounds on Mean Response Time

as the product of two factors, one that is a dimensionless *stretching factor* and one that is the ideal mean throughput rate, N times the mean throughput rate for one terminal:

$$mean\ throughput\ rate = \frac{N}{T_{think} + T_{response}}$$

$$= stretching\ factor \times \frac{mean\ throughput\ rate\ for\ N > 1}{N\ mean\ throughput\ for\ N = 1}$$

By definition, we see

$$stretching\ factor = \frac{N\ mean\ throughput\ rate\ for\ N = 1}{mean\ throughput\ rate\ for\ N \geqslant 1}$$

The upper and lower bounds on mean throughput rate for the system give us upper and lower bounds on the stretching factor:

$$stretching\ factor \geqslant \frac{NT_{system}}{T_{think} + NT_{system}}$$

$$stretching\ factor \leqslant \begin{cases} 1 & N \leqslant N_{breakpoint} \\ \dfrac{NT_{system}}{T_{think} + T_{system}} & N \geqslant N_{breakpoint} \end{cases}$$

The upper bound on stretching factor grows *linearly* with the number of active terminals, i.e., it stretches proportional to N. Ideally, we want *no* stretching, i.e., a stretching factor of unity.

1.6.5 Additional Reading

[1]   E.Arthurs, B.W.Stuck, *Upper and Lower Bounds on Mean Throughput Rate and Mean Delay in Queueing Networks with Memory Constraints,* Bell System Technical Journal, **62** (2), 541-581 (1983).

[2]   H.Hellerman, T.F.Conroy, **Computer System Performance,** McGraw Hill, NY, 1975.

1.7 The Two Fundamental Approaches to Achieving Desirable Performance

The previous example shows the following: there are only two *fundamental* approaches to achieve a desired level of performance in a computer communication system.

1.7.1 Execution Time Speeding up one or more steps of a job, or reducing the execution time of one or more steps, is one way to impact performance. Recoding an application program, reducing the amount of disk input/output or terminal character input/output are examples of application program speed changes. Replacing a processor with a faster processor, or a data link with a faster data link are examples of hardware speed changes.

1.7.2 Concurrency and Parallelism At a given instant of time, there are a given number of jobs in the system that are partially executed, which are said to be *concurrently* in execution. In particular, a certain number of the jobs concurrently in execution can in fact be *actively* in execution, and these jobs are said to be executing *in parallel*. The greater the number of jobs *actively* in execution, the greater the impact on performance. This will be the central theme for the remainder of the book. Note that the execution time of each step of a job need *not* be reduced, so the total time to complete a job is the same, but the *total* number of jobs per unit time that can be executed can be increased. A single processor handling multiple terminals doing program development is an example of *logically* concurrent execution of multiple jobs: at any instant of time, only one job is running on the processor, but there can be many jobs partially executed in the system. An operating system that can support multiple disk spindles off multiple controllers doing independent *parallel* data transfers is an example of *parallelism* or *physical* simultaneous execution of multiple jobs.

1.8 Layered Models of Computer and Communication Systems

Layers accomplish two things:

- They allow us to deal with a subsystem internals in one way, and design this to meet a set of goals

- They allow us to deal with a subsystem externals (for handling input and output to other subsystems) in a different way from the internals and design this to meet a different set of goals

What layers and resources lie inside the box labeled *system?* One way to answer this is hierarchically, as a series of *layers* that are peeled away, with resources residing in each layer. Figure 1.8 shows an illustrative layered model of the computer system described earlier:

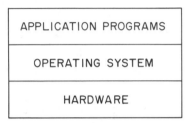

Figure 1.8.Layered Model of Computer System

In this model we see subsystems labeled

- Hardware--Terminals, processor, memory, input/output handlers, disk controller, disks, tape drives, printers and so forth

- Operating system--A set of programs that control the hardware and make use of it (i.e., the operating system programs reside in secondary disk storage and in main memory and require processor time to run, and so forth)

- Application programs--A set of programs that make use of operating system functions to accomplish a specific application

What are the resources here? Examples might be

- Hardware resources--Processors, memory, disk controller, disk spindle, printer, input/output handler, terminal, cache, floating point accelerator, communications bus

- Operating system resources--Tables, files, events, signals, semaphores, messages, objects, processes, capabilities, pages, segments, partitions

- Application resources--Data base manager, application level transaction manager, communications manager, front end terminal manager, compilers, editors, report generators

Ultimately a resource involves using up *hardware,* but remember that *anything* that can block execution of a job is a resource. Many viewpoints of the same thing are often useful here.

1.9 Layers and Performance

Each layer is a candidate for performance analysis. First, we might wish to speed up each:

- Hardware might be too slow for certain jobs and can be replaced with faster hardware with little or no changes to the operating system and application software

- Operating system software might be too slow for certain jobs, and might be changed to speed up certain system calls that demand a lot of resources (either because they are called frequently or because they demand a lot or both)

- Application software might be too slow for certain jobs, and might be recoded to speed up certain areas, to take better advantage of the operating system and hardware

At present, application programs are typically done with serial flow of control, while operating system programs typically handle concurrent flow of control: to take better advantage of concurrency of the hardware and software resources, the application programs might be recoded to take better advantage of the operating system and hardware.

To improve performance, we might

- Keep the operating system and application software, and replace hardware with faster hardware

- Keep the operating system and hardware, and recode the application to take best advantage of the operating system with its hardware

- Keep the application software and hardware, and change the operating system (adding more file space, changing the scheduling algorithm, changing the buffering strategy)

We can aggregate and combine these different layers in talking about performance evaluation. At the hardware level, we might be interested in the maximum mean instruction execution rate, the memory access time per word, and so forth. At the operating system level we might be interested in system functions and time required to execute each on a given hardware configuration. At the application level, we might be interested in taking best advantage of operating system call implemented on a given hardware configuration.

We have fixed the evaluation interface and the subsystems underneath it in describing performance. This structures our data analysis and allows us to quickly draw cause and effect inferences about performance problems. There is also a need to evaluate each layer by itself, or to evaluate sets of layers together: this realm of testing and diagnostics is worthy of independent study by itself, and can be the subject of more than one book. Here we are suggesting a methodology for representing total system state for different purposes: many such state representations are fruitful.

1.10 An Application Program Development View

The figure below shows a flow chart of the types of activities involved in application program development.

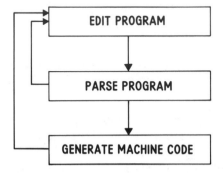

Figure 1.9.Application Program Development Flowchart

First, a program is entered into a computer system using an interactive editor. Next, the program is parsed to see if the syntax matches the rules of the language. If errors are reported, the program is rewritten, and parsed again, until the program successfully passes this stage. Next, machine code is generated, and this may produce a variety of new error messages that were not checked by the parser. The program is rewritten, and now this may introduce parsing errors. If the program successfully is parsed and generates executable code, we may wish to make use of optimizing features of the compiler (to reduce the amount of storage and execution time). Again, this step may generate a variety of errors, and cause the program to be rewritten. Finally, we have a program that passes all the rules of parsing, code generation, and optimization. We still might have to rewrite this program, because although it does what we *say*, it might not do what we *mean*.

Figure 1.10 is a block diagram summarizing all of these actions.

1.10.1 Steps and Resources We can construct a step resource table for each activity outlined above.

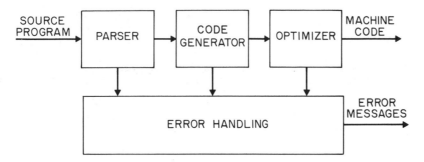

Figure 1.10. Program Development Block Diagram

Table 1.2. Step/Resource Table

Step Type	Programmer Required	Processor Required	Time Symbol	Value
Read, Think	1	0	T_{think}	15 sec
Edit Code	0	1	T_{edit}	1 sec
Parse Code	0	1	T_{parse}	1 sec
Generate Code	0	1	$T_{generate}$	30 sec
Optimize Code	0	1	$T_{optimize}$	30 sec

Illustrative values of time for each step are shown in the table. Note the great discrepancy between the time required to handle simple edits and parsing versus to handle code generation and optimization. To simplify our analysis, we will aggregate together the steps for parsing, code generation and optimization. Together we call these steps *compilation* with a total mean time of $T_{compile}$.

1.10.2 Resource Allocation We want to examine the consequences of different schedules or resource allocation policies about performance measures. We will study

• Executing jobs in the order of submission

• Round robin quantum scheduling

1.10.3 Execution in Order of Arrival There are two different job types, edits and compilations. We have a total of N terminals, so the following cases *might* occur:

• There are *no* jobs in the system, and so once a job is submitted it immediately runs to completion

• Every other terminal has submitted a job, and we are the last in line.

For the first case, the mean queueing time is simply T_{edit} or $T_{generate}$ or $T_{optimize}$, depending upon what type of job was submitted. For the second case, the mean queueing time is as small as NT_{edit} if all jobs are edits, or as big as $NT_{generate}$ if all jobs are compilations.

The variation in response time can be huge: if an edit command was last in line, and all the other commands were compilations, a relatively quickly executing command would have to wait for many very long commands, and this might be unacceptable!

1.10.4 Execution via Quantum Round Robin Scheduling This schedule executes a job for a maximum amount of time called a *quantum,* and either the job finishes or it goes to the end of the queue where it will get another shot, until eventually it finishes. This is shown in the queueing network block diagram below:

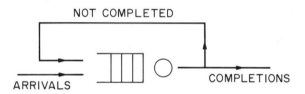

Figure 1.11.Round Robin Queueing Network Block Diagram

Let's look at two cases, as before:

- There are *no* other jobs in the system, and provided nothing more arrives, a job will run until it is executed

- All the other terminals have submitted commands, and we are last in line

For the first case, the mean response time is T_{edit} or $T_{compile}$, depending upon the command type. For the second case, caution is needed. If the quantum is set equal to T_{edit}, then if we have submitted an edit, it will complete at NT_{edit}, *even* if all the other commands were compilations; each of the other commands would only get one quantum of time. On the other hand, if the quantum is set to $T_{compile}$, then if we had an edit command and all the other commands were compilations we would wait for $(N-1)T_{compile} + T_{edit}$ for a response, much much greater than for our first choice of quantum.

1.10.5 Summary For this particular example, where we have a *huge* variation in the execution time of jobs, with short jobs being much more urgent than long jobs, and where we do *not* know whether a command will be short or long, quantum round robin scheduling with the quantum set at T_{edit} can offer short response to short commands, while long commands take a long time.

If we set the quantum to $T_{compile}$, then we are executing jobs in order of arrival, and encounter *huge* variations in response time.

Note that if all jobs took the *same* amount of time, then we would set the quantum equal to that amount, and execute jobs in order of arrival.

1.10.6 Additional Reading

[1] A.V.Aho, J.D.Ullman **Principles of Compiler Design,** Addison Wesley, Reading, Massachusetts, 1977.

[2] L.Kleinrock, **Queueing Systems, Volume II: Computer Applications,** Wiley, NY, 1976.

1.11 Local Area Network Interfaces

The hardware block diagram below shows one design for a *local area network interface* between a *local area network* and a *work station.* The interface resources are a local bus that interconnects the work station interface (called here the *bus interface unit* or *BIU)* to the network interface unit *(NIU),* a bus controller to determine which device gains access to the bus, plus a local processor with memory for buffering bursts of data (either from the work station to the network or vice versa).

The steps involved in transferring data from the work station out over the local area network are summarized in the figure below.

The steps involved in data transfer are summarized in the table below:

Table 1.3.Work Station/Local Network Data Transfer

| Step | Resources | | | | | Time |
Number	Bus	Processor	Memory	NIU	BIU	Interval
WS->BIU	1	0	0	0	1	$T_{WS \to BIU}$
BIU->MEM	1	0	1	0	1	$T_{BIU \to MEM}$
Process	1	1	1	0	0	$T_{process}$
MEM->NIU	1	0	1	1	0	$T_{MEM \to NIU}$

As is evident, more than one resource must be held at each step of execution of this type of job.

What is the maximum rate of executing network accesses?

• If the work station is completely busy transferring data to the bus interface unit, then

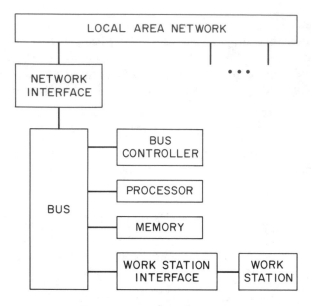

Figure 1.12.Local Area Network Hardware Interface Block Diagram

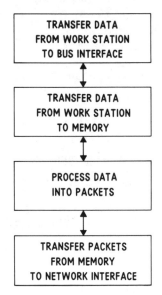

Figure 1.13.Work Station to Local Area Network Data Transfer

$$maximum\ mean\ throughput\ rate\ =\ \frac{1}{T_{WS \rightarrow BIU}}$$

• If memory is completely busy, then

$$maximum\ mean\ throughput\ rate = \frac{1}{T_{BIU \rightarrow MEM} + T_{MEM \rightarrow NIU}}$$

- If the processor is completely busy, then

$$maximum\ mean\ throughput\ rate = \frac{1}{T_{processor}}$$

- If the network is completely busy, then

$$maximum\ mean\ throughput\ rate = \frac{1}{T_{MEM \rightarrow NIU}}$$

The smallest of these, the one that becomes completely busy first, we call the *bottleneck* resource. In any system, there will be *some* bottleneck; the design question is to *choose* where it should be, while the analysis question is to *find* it.

1.12 A Communications System Example

A different type of layering model that is being widely used is the *Open Systems Interconnection (OSI)* architecture of the *International Standards Organization,* shown in the figure below.

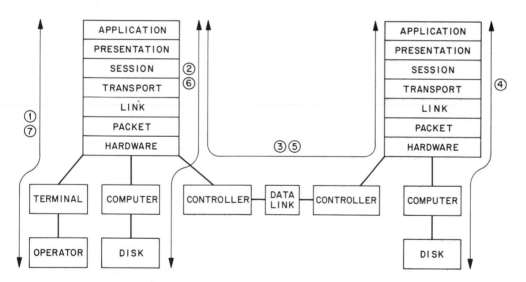

Figure 1.14.Open Systems Interconnection Architecture

In the figure, we show the seven layers of the model, plus an illustrative example of the flow of control and data to move a file from one system to another. The layers are as follows:

[1]   Hardware level--Specifications of voltages, currents, media, waveforms, timing, and packaging.

[2]   Frame or message level--Specifications of the meaning of each bit within a frame or packet of bits, signifying either control (source and destination address, priority, error detecting or correcting code) and data.

[3]   Link level--Multiple transmitters and receivers send frames to one another over a logical abstraction of a *physical* circuit called a *virtual* circuit.

[4]   Transport level--Multiple transmitters and receivers send packets or frames to one another over one or more logical circuits.

[5]   Session level--Controlling initiation, data transfer, and completion clean up of a communication session.

[6]   Presentation level--Conversion of an application program protocol to a session level protocol.

[7]   Application level--Description of application program behavior.

In the illustrative example, a file is transferred from one system to another as follows:

[1]   An application program is accessed from a terminal to begin the process

[2]   A chain of commands is retrieved from a local disk to control communication over a link

[3]   Communications software controls initial access to the link and sends a request over the link to the appropriate application in the other system

[4]   The desired file is retrieved from secondary storage

[5]   The file is transferred from one application to another via the link

[6]   The application program notifies the operator the file has been retrieved

[7]   The application program stores the file in local disk space

At each step, in order to say *anything* concerning performance, we would need to specify what resources, software and hardware, are required for each step, for what time interval, along with a policy for arbitrating contention for shared resources. Questions concerning the physical location of text and data can only be answered by describing both the system operation and the staff or people operations.

What are the resources for this system?

[1]   Hardware Level--Processor, memory, and bus time

[2]   Frame or message level--Source and destination address tables

[3]   Link level--Packet sequence numbers with associated priorities

[4]   Transport level--Network name tables, virtual circuit tables

[5]   Session level--Number of sessions outstanding

[6]   Presentation level--Table of each protocol conversion in progress

[7]   Application level--Table of number of in progress communications

To be explicit, we suppose that there are two different computer systems, labeled A and B each with their own processor and disk for handling this scenario. The table below is a summary of the steps and resources required for the file transfer shown earlier:

Table 1.4.Step/Resource Summary

Step	CPU A	DISK A	LINK	CPU B	DISK B	Time
Start	1	0	0	0	0	T_{start}
Load	1	1	0	0	0	T_{load}
Request	1	0	1	1	0	$T_{request}$
Retrieve	0	0	0	1	1	$T_{retrieve}$
Transmit	1	1	1	1	1	$T_{transmit}$
Notify	1	0	0	0	0	T_{notify}
Store	1	1	0	0	0	T_{store}

What is the maximum mean throughput rate, denoted by λ_{upper}, of doing file transfers?

- If CPU A is a bottleneck, then the maximum mean throughput rate is given by

$$\lambda_{upper} = \frac{1}{T_{start} + T_{load} + T_{request} + T_{transmit} + T_{notify} + T_{store}}$$

- If disk A is a bottleneck, then the maximum mean throughput rate is given by

$$\lambda_{upper} = \frac{1}{T_{load} + T_{transmit} + T_{store}}$$

- If the link is a bottleneck, then the maximum mean throughput rate is given by

$$\lambda_{upper} = \frac{1}{T_{request} + T_{transmit}}$$

- If CPU B is a bottleneck, then the maximum mean throughput rate is given by

$$\lambda_{upper} = \frac{1}{T_{request} + T_{retrieve} + T_{transmit}}$$

- If disk B is a bottleneck, then the maximum mean throughput rate is given by

$$\lambda_{upper} = \frac{1}{T_{retrieve} + T_{transmit}}$$

Communication link data rates are only *one* component in controlling the *maximum* mean throughput rate: the processors and disks at either end can also be important.

EXERCISE: What happens if we have only *one* processor and *one* disk?

1.12.1 Additional Reading

[1] A.Tanenbaum, **Computer Networks,** pp.15-21, Prentice-Hall, Englewood Cliffs, New Jersey, 1981.

[2] F.D.Smith, C.H.West, *Technologies for Network Architecture and Implementation,* IBM J.Research and Development, **27** (1) 68-78 (1983).

1.13 Operating System Performance

An *operating system* is a set of *logically* concurrently executing programs. An operating system runs on a given hardware configuration and provides services to application programs.

1.13.1 Hardware Configuration We assume that the hardware configuration consists of one processor with a fixed amount of memory, a set of terminals that are connected to the processor via a terminal handler, and one disk. The disk is used for two purposes, to store programs and data that the programs access, and for holding programs that cannot be held in main memory, so called *swapped* programs.

1.13.2 Application Programs The operating system hides the details of the hardware operations of the processor, disk input/output, terminal input/output, and memory administration or management, from the application programs, by presenting a set of interfaces called *system calls* that allow these programs to interact without knowing the details of the system call implementation. The operating system *schedules* or manages or administers the physical and logical resources, which is the crux of performance. The programs are *virtual* processors, and for short are called *processes*. Each process can be in the following states: ready to run except that the processor is busy with higher priority work, idle, executing or running on the processor, blocked on terminal input/output (waiting for a terminal to respond), blocked on disk input/output (waiting for a disk to respond), or blocked on memory (waiting for memory to

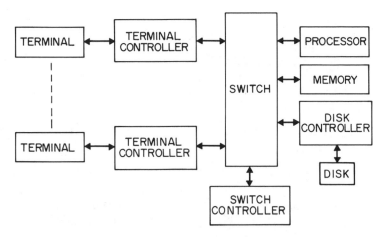

Figure 1.15.Hardware Block Diagram

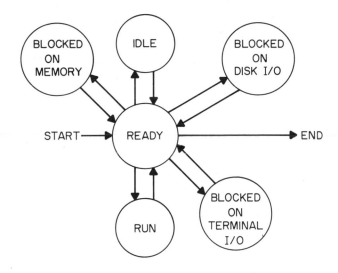

Figure 1.16.States of a Process

become available). This is summarized in Figure 1.17. The operating system, as it schedules each step of each job, would migrate or move each program or process around, from one state to another, in the course of execution. The figure below shows one set of processes that might be managed by the operating system: For each state of a process, we can list the resources required:

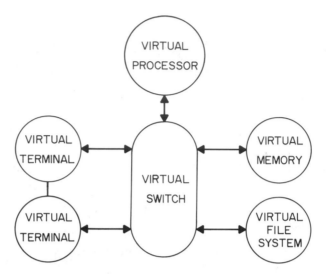

Figure 1.17.Illustrative Set of Processes Managed by Operating System

Table 1.5.State/Resource Summary

State	Processor	Memory	Disk	Terminal	Mean Time
Idle	0	0	0	0	T_{idle}
Run	1	1	0	0	T_{cpu}
Blocked:					
On Disk I/O	0	1	1	0	T_{disk}
On Terminal I/O	0	1	0	1	T_{term}
On Memory	0	0	0	0	T_{memory}

Different resources are held at different steps. Each job migrates through a network of queues, as shown in Figure 1.18.

The resources of memory and processor time are allocated sequentially: a process must first be loaded into memory, and holds this while waiting for the processor, or while waiting for input/output from the disk.

Processes that are resident in main memory are candidates for being swapped to secondary disk storage. Processes that are swapped out of main memory are candidates for being loaded into main memory.

The policy for determining which processes are resident in main memory and which are not, and for determining which processes are executed by the processor and by the disk, are *separate* from the logically correct execution of each step of each program.

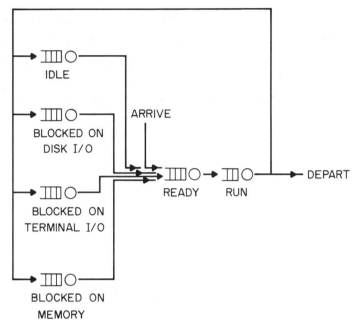

Figure 1.18.Operating System Network of Queues

The maximum mean throughput rate of executing processes can be limited by memory, disk input/output, terminal input/output, or processor time. Suppose we gathered measurements on the *total* time the system processes were in each state over a given time interval.

- If memory is the bottleneck, then the time spent in the memory blocked state would be the greatest

- If the disk is the bottleneck, then the time spent in the disk blocked state would be the greatest

- If terminal handling is the bottleneck, then the time spent in the terminal blocked state would be the greatest

- If the processor is the bottleneck, then the time spent in the processor running state would be the greatest

EXERCISE: Suppose an operating system table contains a list of all active processes. What data should be gathered to determine if this is limiting performance by simply being set too small?

1.13.3 Additional Reading

[1] A.L.Shaw, **Principles of Operating Systems,** Prentice-Hall, Englewood Cliffs, NJ, 1974

[2]   D.M.Ritchie, K.Thompson, *The UNIX^{TM} * Time-Sharing System,* Communications of the ACM, **17** (7), 365-374 (1974).

[3]   K.Thompson, *UNIX Implementation,* Bell System Technical Journal, **57** (6), 1931-1946 (1978).

[4]   D.M.Ritchie, *UNIX Retrospective,* Bell System Technical Journal, **57** (6), 1947-1870 (1978).

1.14 Processor Design

Many actual processors are made up of networks of smaller processors, as shown in the figure below:

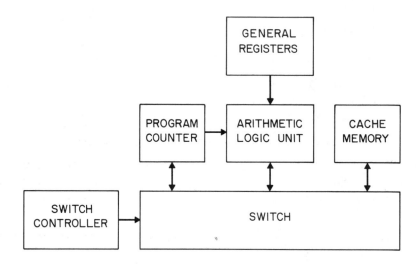

Figure 1.19.Processor Block Diagram

A processor might consist of an arithmetic logic unit, that has three types of memory connected to it:

• General register or so called *scratch pad* memory connected via a special dedicated bus

• Program counter processor connected via both a special dedicated bus to the processor and via a general purpose switch to cache memory

---

*   UNIX is a trademark of Bell Laboratories

• Cache memory that is much higher speed memory than main memory for hiding recently used segments of text and data on the assumption that it is highly likely they will be executed in the immediate future

The resources here are the arithmetic logic unit, the program counter and general registers, and cache memory, with the switch and switch controller necessary to allow communications between these different devices.

The flow chart below illustrates how the processor would execute an instruction.

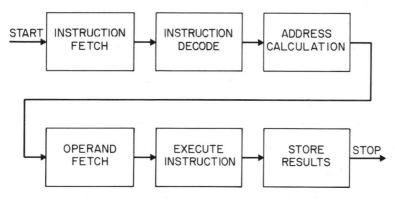

Figure 1.20. Processor Instruction Execution Flow Chart

The steps and resources required are summarized in the table below:

Table 1.6. Steps/Resource Summary

Step	PC	ALU	GR	Cache	Switch	Time
Load PC	1	0	0	0	1	T_{PC}
Fetch Instruction	0	1	1	0	1	T_{fetch}
Decode Instruction	1	1	1	1	0	T_{decode}
Fetch Data	0	1	1	1	1	T_{data}
Execute Instruction	1	1	1	1	1	$T_{execute}$
Store Results	0	1	1	1	1	T_{store}

Each of these resources can execute at a maximum rate. The total system mean throughput rate is upper bounded by λ_{upper}: As we raise the number of executing programs, one resource will become completely busy first, which will be called the *bottleneck*.

- If the program counter is a bottleneck, then the maximum mean throughput rate is

$$\lambda_{upper} = \frac{1}{T_{PC} + T_{decode} + T_{execute}}$$

- If the ALU is a bottleneck, then the maximum mean throughput rate is

$$\lambda_{upper} = \frac{1}{T_{fetch} + T_{decode} + T_{data} + T_{execute} + T_{store}}$$

- The maximum rate at which the general registers can load and unload instructions is

$$\lambda_{upper} = \frac{1}{T_{fetch} + T_{decode} + T_{operand} + T_{execute} + T_{store}}$$

- The maximum rate at which the switch can transfer instructions is

$$\lambda_{upper} = \frac{1}{T_{PC} + T_{fetch} + T_{data} + T_{execute} + T_{store}}$$

Based on this analysis, we see that the bottleneck is the *switch*. This is because the switch is held for the long time per instruction execution.

EXERCISE: What can be changed to move the bottleneck to the ALU?

1.14.1 Additional Reading

[1] G.Radin, *The 801 Minicomputer,* IBM J.Research and Development, **27** (3), 237-246 (1983).

[2] G.J.Myers, **Advances in Computer Architecture, Second Edition,** Wiley, NY, 1982.

[3] H.Lorin, **Introduction to Computer Architecture and Organization,** Wiley, NY, 1982.

1.15 Text Outline

The problems and chapters in the text are organized along the lines described in the preface.

1.15.1 Introductory Material First, we survey results from *deterministic* or *static* scheduling theory. All of the work that must be executed is present at an initial time; we wish to study different configurations and schedules to see how long it takes to finish all the work. The intent is to get used to systematically described computer communication system operation: for each step, what resources are required, for how long. This occurs in practice in telephone call processing, discrete manufacturing, and data communications: a list of work is scanned at the start of a clock cycle and all the work must be finished before the clock begins its next cycle.

Following this, data analysis and simulation is surveyed. This is a mandatory step in verifying self consistency and having credibility in performance analysis. In order to summarize data with a model, measurements must be gathered, and evidence presented showing how well the data fits the model. Many would argue the issue of data interpretation is the crux of performance analysis.

Next, we study the long term time averaged behavior of systems that execute jobs requiring *multiple resources* at each step of execution. An example would be a job that requires both a processor and a given amount of memory and a given set of files. Both the mean throughput and mean delay per job are studied for different hardware and software configurations and for different scheduling policies. The concluding section reinforces this analysis with a series of examples drawn from office communication systems: case studies, starting from models of simple everyday situations and building up to more realistic and complex situations.

1.15.2 Jackson Networks Next additional modeling assumptions or restrictions are made beyond just means or averages, which lead to so called *Jackson* queueing network models. These assumptions yield sharper performance bounds on computer communication systems than mean values. Case studies are studied, starting from the simple and proceeding to the more realistic and complicated. Each case is analyzed first via mean values alone, and then refined using Jackson network models.

1.15.3 Priority Scheduling In a computer communication system typically one resource is limiting the maximum mean throughput rate of completing work, and this is called the *bottleneck*. Here we study in detail how to effectively schedule work at the bottleneck resource in order to ameliorate delay, using priority arbitration. We will make much stronger assumptions about the system statistical behavior here than we did in earlier sections, and we will display much greater variety and accuracy (not just means but variances and even statistical distributions) in the phenomena we will deal with.

1.16 Additional Reading

[1] D.Ferrari, **Computer System Performance Evaluation,** Prentice-Hall, Englewood Cliffs, N.J., 1978.

[2] U.Grenander, R.F.Tsao, *Quantitative Methods for Evaluating Computer System Performance: A Review and Proposals,* in **Statistical Computer Performance Evaluation,** W.Freiberger (editor), Academic Press, NY, 1972.

[3] H.Lorin, **Parallelism in Hardware and Software,** pp.3-44, Prentice-Hall, Englewood Cliffs, NJ, 1972.

[4] M.Phister, Jr., **Data Processing Technology and Economics, Second Edition,** Digital Press, 1979.

Problems

1) A data communications system consists of a single transmitter, a noisy link, and a single receiver. The transmitter sends ones and zeros (bits) over the link. Each bit is equally likely to be transmitted correctly a given fraction of time, $1-P$, and to be incorrectly transmitted a given fraction of time P, due to noise corrupting the transmission. The diagram below summarizes all this:

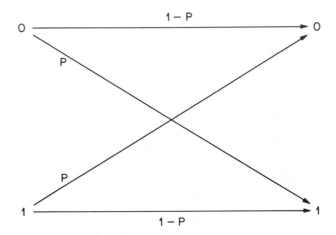

Figure 1.21.Bit Transmission Probabilities

Determine the data transmission rate, measured in successfully transmitted bits per second, of each of the following communications systems

A. A three hundred bit per second data link that requires retransmission of one bit in every ten thousand (P=0.0001) due to noise; repeat for retransmission of one bit in every one hundred due to noise

B. A ninety six hundred bit per second data link that requires retransmission of one bit in every ten thousand due to noise; repeat for retransmission of one bit in every one hundred due to noise

C. A courier delivery service that takes a twenty four hundred foot magnetic tape containing sixteen hundred bits per inch of tape and will deliver it five thousand miles away in twenty four hours; repeat if the tape contains six thousand two hundred and fifty bits per inch

D. A courier delivery service that takes a one hundred megabyte magnetic disk pack and will deliver it five thousand miles away in twenty four hours; repeat for a five hundred megabyte magnetic disk pack

2)* Imagine you have trained your St.Bernard, Bernie, to carry a box of three floppy disks, each containing a quarter of a million bytes. The dog can travel to your side, wherever you are, at eighteen kilometers per hour. For what range of distances does Bernie have a higher data rate than a twelve hundred bit per second noiseless data link? Repeat for the case where Bernie can carry a single ten megabyte disk pack.

3) A computer system consists of three identical processors, each processor being capable of executing a one second job in one second. The system must execute nine jobs, with the execution times for these jobs as follows: (3, 2, 2, 4, 4, 2, 9, 4, 4).

   A.   If the jobs are selected for execution in the above order, how long does it take to completely execute all jobs?

   B.   Can you find an order of execution which reduces the time to completely execute all the jobs? If so, how long is it?

4) A computer system consists of a pipeline of N identical processors, with the input job stream going into the first processor, the output of the first processor feeding the input of the second processor, and so on:

Figure 1.22. Three Stage (N=3) Processor Pipeline

$T(K)$ denotes the time, which is constant, required to complete the Kth step of executing a job. Derive the following results:

A) The time required to completely process one job, T_1:

$$T_1 = \sum_{K=1}^{N} T(K)$$

B) The time required to completely process M jobs, T_M:

---

*   A.S.Tanenbaum, **Computer Networks,** p.30, Prentice-Hall, Englewood Cliffs, NJ, 1981.

$$T_M = \sum_{K=1}^{N} T(K) + (M-1)\max_K T(K) = T_1 + (M-1)T_{\max} \quad T_{\max} \equiv \max_K T(K)$$

C) The mean throughput rate of executing or processing M jobs in time T_M:

$$mean\ throughput\ rate = \frac{M}{T_M}$$

D) The long term time averaged mean throughput rate $M \rightarrow \infty$:

$$long\ term\ time\ averaged\ mean\ throughput\ rate \equiv$$

$$\lim_{M \rightarrow \infty} mean\ throughput\ rate\ \text{for}\ M\ jobs = \frac{M}{T_M}$$

5) The figure below is a hardware block diagram of a multiple processor multiple memory computer system:

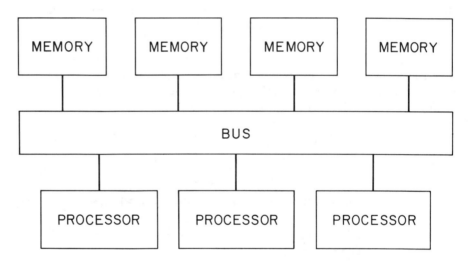

Figure 1.23.Multiple Processor Multiple Memory Hardware Block Diagram

Two steps occur for each job:

[1]   A processor executes code

[2]   Data is fetched from memory

This is summarized in the table below:

Table 1.7.Job Step/Resource Summary

Step	Processor	Memory	Time
1	1	0	$T_{execute}$
2	0	1	T_{fetch}

The hardware configuration for this system consists of three processors and four memories.

A. Draw a queueing network block diagram of this system

B. A total of M jobs can be held in the system at any one time. Plot upper and lower bounds on mean throughput rate and mean delay versus M for $T_{execute} = T_{fetch} = 1$

C. Repeat the above for $T_{execute} = 3T_{fetch} = 1$

D. What is the stretching factor for both cases?

6) The hardware configuration for a word processing system consists of four terminals, a central processor, a disk controller, two disks, a high speed printer and a low speed printer. One terminal is dedicated to express or rush jobs, and uses the high speed printer. The other terminals are dedicated to normal jobs, and use the low speed printer or, if available, the high speed printer.

A. What are the hardware resources in this system?

B. Make a flow chart for each step required for a normal job. Repeat for a rush job.

C. What are the resources required for each step of a normal job? A rush job?

D. With no contention, what is the mean time to execute a normal job? A rush job?

E. What is the maximum mean throughput rate to execute J normal jobs? J rush jobs?

F. Suppose there are only normal jobs. Plot upper and lower bounds on mean throughput rate and mean delay versus the total number of normal jobs. Repeat if there are only rush jobs.

G. Suppose we fix the *mix* or fraction of jobs of each type, rush and normal, that the system can execute at any one time: F_{rush} and F_{normal} are the fraction of rush and normal jobs. If we submit J total jobs and allow $J \rightarrow \infty$, what resource will become completely busy first?

H. Suppose jobs are executed either in order of arrival or with a quantum round robin scheduler. What are the ranges on mean response time and mean throughput rate for each schedule?

7) The hardware configuration for an order entry system consists of sixteen terminals, four cluster controllers (one for each four terminals), a dedicated link to a computer, and a computer. The computer hardware configuration consists of a processor, memory, a disk controller, two disks connected to the disk controller, a printer, and an interface to a data link to a second inventory control computer system. The system operates as follows:

- Clerks enter orders at terminals and then wait for the system to respond

- The order is sent by the cluster controller over the data link to the computer

- The computer does some initial processing on the order, and if it is valid, stores it in the secondary disk storage

- The computer returns control to the operator at the terminal

- At a later point in time, the orders stored in secondary disk storage are retrieved and sent over a communications line to the inventory control system

Answer the following questions:

A. Make a flow chart of this job work flow

B. Make a table showing the resources required at each step of execution

C. If we ignore the last step of retrieving orders from disk and communicating them to an inventory control system, what is the fastest rate at which orders can be executed?

8) We want to study electronic mail pending performance at the hardware level in more detail. An operator at a terminal submits a query, making use of the hardware configuration shown in Figure 1.24. The steps involved in mail query are as follows:

- The terminal controller seizes the switch and alerts the processor

- The processor transfers the query from the terminal via the terminal controller through the switch to memory

- The processor executes the commands associated with mail pending on the data in memory via the switch

- The processor seizes the switch and accesses the mail pending information which is stored on secondary storage in a moving head disk

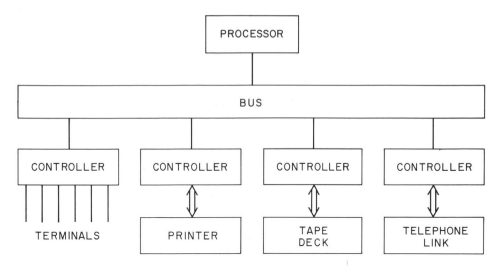

Figure 1.24.Hardware Block Diagram

- The processor executes the code associated with this mail pending activity while holding the bus and memory

- The terminal is notified of the mail pending by the processor seizing the switch and demanding the information be transferred from memory to the terminal controller

- The tape controller is seized by the processor via the bus in order to transfer information logging the mail pending activity

- At a later point in time the processor will transfer data from the tape to memory via the switch

- The processor will generate a management report on mail activity and transfer this to the printer via the switch from memory

Answer the following questions:

A. What are the hardware resources?

B. Make a table showing what resources are required at each step and for how long.

C. What is the maximum rate at which mail pending can be executed, assuming nothing else is executed?

9) We want to study electronic mail pending performance at a higher level in more detail. The steps involved in checking to see if electronic mail is pending are summarized in the figure below. In words, these steps are:

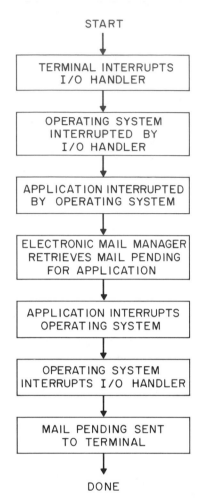

START

TERMINAL INTERRUPTS
I/O HANDLER

OPERATING SYSTEM
INTERRUPTED BY
I/O HANDLER

APPLICATION INTERRUPTED
BY OPERATING SYSTEM

ELECTRONIC MAIL MANAGER
RETRIEVES MAIL PENDING
FOR APPLICATION

APPLICATION INTERRUPTS
OPERATING SYSTEM

OPERATING SYSTEM
INTERRUPTS I/O HANDLER

MAIL PENDING SENT
TO TERMINAL

DONE

Figure 1.25. Electronic Mail Pending Flow Chart

[1]   The terminal interacts with the input/output handling routines to generate operating system activity

[2]   The operating system generates application program activity in turn

[3]   The application program retrieves the mail pending from the data base manager

[4]   The operating system is fed the list of outstanding mail items

[5]   The input/output handling routines generate the list of outstanding mail items on the terminal

Answer the following questions:

A.   Make up a flow chart for mail pending.

40

B. The resources available here are hardware, operating system, data base management, and application. Verify that the table below is a candidate for showing the resources held at each step:

Table 1.8.Mail Pending Step Resource Summary

Step Number	Resource				Time Interval
	Hardware	Op Sys	Data Base	Application	
1	1	0	0	0	$T_{hardware}$
2	0	1	0	0	$T_{op\ sys}$
3	0	0	0	1	T_{applic}
4	0	0	1	0	$T_{data\ base}$
5	0	0	0	1	T_{applic}
6	0	1	0	0	$T_{op\ sys}$
7	1	0	0	0	$T_{hardware}$

C. What is the mean response time with only one terminal using the system? What is the mean throughput rate with only one terminal using the system?

D. Assuming only mail pending queries are made, what is the maximum mean throughput rate for executing this command?

CHAPTER 2: **CONCURRENCY AND PARALLELISM**

In this chapter our goal is to explicitly calculate bounds on the mean throughput rate of executing a single transaction type or a given transaction workload mix for a particular class of models of computer communication systems. In many instances, this provides a *fundamental* limitation on system performance: if a packet switch can only switch one hundred packets per second, then no amount of chicanery (e.g., clever scheduling, increasing the degree of multiprogramming, adopting a new paging strategy, and so forth) will allow this packet switch to switch two hundred packets per second. On the other hand, we must ask ourselves what is the *best* that we might do: is there any intrinsic reason why the packet switch can switch at most one hundred packets per second, or is it possible to increase this to five hundred packets per second by judicious changes in hardware, operating system kernel, data base manager, and application code?

The crux of performance analysis is describing *how* a computer communication system processes each step of a job. The models described here require as inputs a detailed description of the step by step processing of a job, and give as outputs bounds on system performance. By dealing with examples or tractable models of *parallelism* and *concurrency* for computer systems, we hope to build up *intuition* about the benefits of different approaches. A disclaimer is in order: systems that improve performance via added concurrency are in many ways more sensitive to the workload than systems that improve performance via raw speed, because in order to take advantage of concurrency some knowledge of the workload must be used. What happens when the workload changes? Caveat emptor!

2.1 General Approaches

Figure 2.1 shows the two fundamental approaches to parallelism in computer communication systems. The hardware configuration and operating system are fixed: a group of processors interconnected by a high speed bus, with a network operating system to coordinate resource allocation. How do we structure a set of application programs to take advantage of this type of system?

At one extreme of parallelism, the group of processors operates in parallel (i.e., fed by a single queue or work stream) Each processor does all the work for each job. As more processors are added, more work can be done. The total delay will be approximately the processing time of a job, because if we have sufficiently many processors it is highly likely that one will always be available to handle a job.

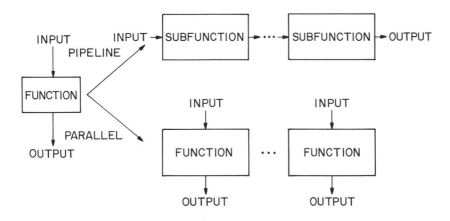

Figure 2.1.Pipeline and Parallel Configurations

At the other extreme of parallelism, processors are functionally dedicated to doing a given step of a job. Each step of a job is done sequentially, or in tandem, like a bucket brigade or pipeline of processors. All the input is handled at one stage and all the output at another stage. The pipeline has a great deal of interaction between adjacent stages, unlike the purely parallel case, and hence the potential benefits may not be nearly as great with the pipeline as with the parallel processor case, even though both systems attempt to take advantage of concurrency in the workload.

Finally, we might have an arbitrary network of processors that jobs migrate amongst, which would be a combination of the purely parallel and purely pipeline cases. We will discuss in more detail the two simple cases of parallel and pipeline processing because we can gain insight into the more complicated but realistic situation of the general network.

2.1.1 An Arithmetic Logic Unit An arithmetic logic unit must perform three jobs

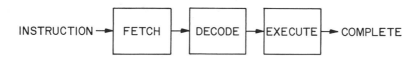

Figure 2.2.Arithmetic Logic Unit Block Diagram

[1] Fetch an instruction from memory

[2] Decode the instruction

[3] Execute the instruction

This is an example of a pipeline with three distinct functions.

2.1.2 Floating Point Accelerator A floating point accelerator is a special purpose processor that can accelerate or assist general purpose processors to perform floating point operations at high speed. Here the steps that must be carried out are

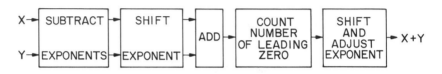

Figure 2.3. Floating Point Accelerator Block Diagram

[1] Subtraction of the exponents

[2] Shifting right the fraction from the number with the smaller exponent by an amount corresponding to the difference in exponents

[3] Addition of the other fractions to the shifted one

[4] Counting the number of leading zeroes in the sum

[5] Shifting left the sum by the number of leading zeroes and adjusting the exponent accordingly

Although this partitioning is typical, there are variations in practice to account for overflow and underflow detection, representation of zero, and other number bases.

2.1.3 Additional Reading

[1] P.M.Kogge, **The Architecture of Pipelined Computers,** Hemisphere Publishing, Washington, DC, 1981

2.2 An Example: Printing Ten Jobs

Ten jobs are present at an initial time, say zero. Each job requires $L_K, K = 1, ..., 10$ lines to be printed. These number are given in the table below:

Table 2.1.Lines for Each Job

Job	Lines	Job	Lines
A	L_A=2,000	F	L_F=1,000
B	L_B=1,000	G	L_G=1,000
C	L_C=1,000	H	L_H=2,000
D	L_D=1,000	I	L_I=2,000
E	L_E=2,000	J	L_J=1,000

We see six jobs need one thousand lines to be printed, and four jobs need two thousand lines to be printed. The mean number of lines that must be printed is:

$$L_{average} = \frac{1}{10} \sum_{K=1}^{10} L_K = 1,400 \; lines$$

The average is a useful statistic if most jobs require roughly the average (same) number of lines to be printed. That *is* the case here; in fact, six jobs require less than the average, while four require more than the average.

We want to compare the performance of the following configurations

- A single printer that can print one thousand lines per minute

- Two printers that are fed from a common buffer, each of which can print one thousand lines per minute

- A single printer that can print two thousand lines per minute

We will measure total system performance via *mean throughput rate* which is defined as the total number of jobs (denoted by N=10 here) divided by the total time to execute these jobs, denoted by T_{finish}, called the *make span:*

$$mean \; throughput \; rate = \frac{N}{T_{finish}} \; jobs/minute$$

We will measure job oriented performance by the mean time a job, say job K, spends in the system, either waiting to be printed or being printed, until it is completed. We will call this time interval for job K its *flow time* and denote it by $F_K, K=1,...,N=10$. The total mean flow time is the flow time averaged over all jobs:

$$mean \; flow \; time = \frac{1}{N} \sum_{K=1}^{N} F_K = \frac{1}{10} \sum_{K=1}^{10} F_K \equiv E(F)$$

2.2.1 A Single Printer The single printer case gives us a baseline or benchmark for measuring performance against. It is a natural starting point for virtually any investigation. No matter what order is used to execute jobs, the total number of lines printed for this set of jobs is:

$$L_{finish,single\ printer} = \sum_{K=1}^{10} L_K = 14,000\ lines$$

The mean throughput rate is simply the total number of jobs divided by the mean time to print all the jobs:

$$mean\ throughput\ rate\ for\ one\ printer = \frac{N}{T_{finish}} = \frac{1}{T_{average}} \qquad T_{average} = \frac{T_{finish}}{N}$$

If a single printer can print one thousand lines per minute, then

$$mean\ throughput\ rate = 10\ jobs\ in\ 14\ minutes$$

while if a single printer can print two thousand lines per minute, then

$$mean\ throughput\ rate = 10\ jobs\ in\ (14/2){=}7\ minutes$$

Suppose that we print the job stream according to a priority schedule. How will this impact the flow time or time in system statistics? Let's try two special cases to gain insight. The first priority schedule operates as follows: job K is said to have higher priority than job J if $L_K \leqslant L_J; K,J{=}1,...,N{=}10$. In other words, the fewer the lines, the shorter the printing time of a job, the higher its priority. The motivation is to let short jobs get printed quickly, so that they will not have to wait for long jobs, which take a long time anyway. Shortest processing time first scheduling attempts to minimize *job* delay or flow time statistics.

Two additional rules will be used:

* Once a job begins printing, it runs to completion, and cannot be preempted by any other job

* No job can be printed in parallel with itself. For one printer this is no problem, but for two printers this would allow us to split a job, and we do not allow this

We will refer to this schedule as *SPT/NP* (shortest processing time has highest priority, with no preemption) in what follows. The schedule for this case is shown below:

Figure 2.4. SPT/NP Single Slow Printer Schedule

The mean flow time for this schedule for a single one thousand line per minute printer is given by

$$E\,(F_{SPT/NP}) \;=\; \frac{1}{10}[1+2+3+4+5+6+8+10+12+14] \;=\; 6.5 \;\; minutes$$

For a single two thousand line per minute printer, the mean flow time is simply half this.

The second priority schedule operates as follows: job K is said to have higher priority than job J if $L_K \geqslant L_J; K,J=1,...,N=10$. In other words, the longer the printing time of a job, the higher its priority. We will refer to this schedule as *LPT/NP* (longest processing time has highest priority, with no preemption) in what follows. The idea for choosing this schedule is that long jobs will take a long time to print, so we might as well begin printing them as soon as possible in order to finish *all* the work as soon as possible. The longest processing time first rule is oriented toward optimizing a *system* performance measure, the fraction of time the system is busy doing work. The schedule for this case is shown below:

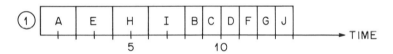

Figure 2.5. LPT/NP Single Slow Printer Schedule

The mean flow time for this schedule for a single one thousand line per minute printer is given by

$$E\,(F_{LPT/NP}) \;=\; \frac{1}{10}[2+4+6+8+9+10+11+12+13+14] \;=\; 8.9 \;\; minutes$$

For a single printer capable of two thousand lines per minute, the mean flow time is half this.

Each schedule results in the same total system mean throughput rate, but radically different mean flow time statistics.

2.2.2 Two Parallel Printers For the second case, two parallel printers, the worst we could do would be to never use one processor. One alternative is to schedule the jobs, with the shortest execution time jobs having the highest priority:

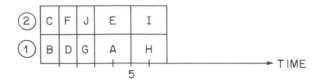

Figure 2.6. SPT/NP Two Slow Printer Schedule

This means the shortest amount of time to execute all ten jobs is $T_{finish}=7$.

The mean throughput rate is given by

$$\textit{mean throughput rate for two parallel printers}_{SPT/NP} = \frac{10}{7} = \frac{1}{0.7 \; minute}$$

The speedup compared with a single processor is given by comparing the time to finish all jobs on one processor versus the time to finish all jobs on two processors:

$$speedup_{SPT/NP} = \frac{T_{finish}(P=1)}{T_{finish}(P=2)} = \frac{14}{7} = 2$$

The mean flow time is given by

$$E(F_{SPT/NP}) = \frac{1}{10}[1+1+2+2+3+3+5+5+7+7] = 3.6 \; minutes$$

On the other hand, we might print jobs with the longest processing time jobs having the highest priority:

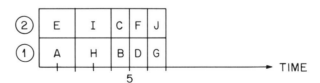

Figure 2.7. LPT/NP Two Slow Printer Schedule

The mean throughput rate for printing jobs is given by

$$\textit{mean throughput rate for two parallel printers}_{LPT/NP} = \frac{10}{7} = \frac{1}{0.7 \; minutes}$$

The speedup over a single printer is given by

$$speedup_{LPT/NP} = \frac{T_{finish}(P=1)}{T_{finish}(P=2)} = \frac{14}{7} = 2$$

Note that the mean throughput rate and the speedup depend upon the scheduling algorithm. The best possible speedup would be to do all the jobs in half the time of a single processor, while the worst would be to just use one processor (and ignore the other):

$$1 \leqslant speedup \leqslant 2$$

Finally, the mean flow time per job for this schedule is given by

$$E(F_{LPT/NP}) = \frac{1}{10}[2+2+4+4+5+5+6+6+7+7] = 4.8 \; minutes$$

The mean flow time for scheduling longest jobs first is radically larger than the mean flow time for scheduling shortest jobs first.

2.2.3 Summary We summarize all these findings in the table below:

Table 2.2. Performance Measure Summary

Configuration	Schedule	Mean Throughput Rate	Mean Flow Time
One Slow Printer	SPT/NP	1 job every 1.4 min	6.5 minutes
One Slow Printer	LPT/NP	1 job every 1.4 min	8.9 minutes
Two Slow Printers	SPT/NP	1 job every 0.7 min	3.6 minutes
Two Slow Printers	LPT/NP	1 job every 0.7 min	4.8 minutes
One Fast Printer	SPT/NP	1 job every 0.7 min	3.25 minutes
One Fast Printer	LPT/NP	1 job every 0.7 min	4.45 minutes

What conclusions do we draw?

- Using one fast vs two slow printers has no impact on mean throughput rate

- One fast printer offers slightly better mean flow time compared with two slow printers

- Shortest processing time scheduling results in a lower mean flow time compared with longest processing time scheduling

We will see these lessons repeated later.

2.2.4 Sensitivity One of the primary reasons for carrying out performance analysis studies is to determine the *sensitivity* of the conclusions to parameters. We might not know the number of lines that must be printed for each job, and are only using guesses or estimates. Two types of studies can be done:

- Changing all the numbers by a small amount. For example, we might change the number of lines printed for each job up or down by ten lines or less, and see what changes in mean throughput rate and mean flow time.

- Changing a small set of numbers by a large amount. For example, we might change job J from one thousand lines to *ten* thousand lines.

Let's pursue the second type of study, changing job J from one to ten thousand lines of printing, and study the consequences.

First, what about a single slow printer? The SPT/NP schedule is shown below:

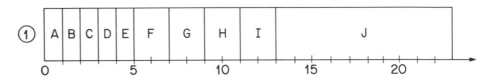

Figure 2.8.SPT/NP Schedule for One Slow Printer (10,000 Lines for Job J)

The *make span* is the time required to completely execute all the work. The make span for this schedule is twenty three minutes, and hence the mean throughput rate is

$$mean\ throughput\ rate\ =\ \frac{N}{T_{finish,SPT/NP}}\ =\ 1\ job\ every\ 2.3\ minutes$$

The mean flow time for SPT/NP is

$$E\left(F_{SPT/NP}\right)\ =\ \frac{1}{10}\ [1+2+3+4+5+7+9+11+13+23]\ =\ 7.8\ minutes$$

For a single high speed printer, the mean flow time is simply half of this, and the mean throughput rate is twice as high.

On the other hand, for LPT/NP scheduling on a single slow printer, we see the make span is identical with SPT/NP, as shown in the figure below:

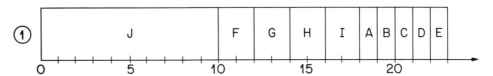

Figure 2.9.LPT/NP Schedule for One Slow Printer (10,000 Lines for Job J)

By inspection from this figure, the mean flow time is

$$E\left(F_{LPT/NP}\right)\ =\ \frac{1}{10}\ [10+12+14+16+18+19+20+21+22+23]\ =\ 17.5\ minutes$$

For a single high speed printer, the flow time is half of this, while the mean throughput rate is twice as big.

Next, for two parallel printers, the SPT/NP schedule is shown below:

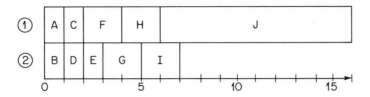

Figure 2.10.SPT/NP Schedule for Two Slow Printers (10,000 Lines for Job J)

The mean throughput rate is simply

$$mean\ throughput\ rate = \frac{N}{T_{finish,LPT/NP}} = \frac{10}{16\ minutes}$$

while the mean flow time is

$$E(F_{SPT/NP}) = \frac{1}{10}[1+1+2+2+3+4+5+6+7+16] = 4.7\ minutes$$

Finally, for two parallel printers, the LPT/NP schedule is shown below:

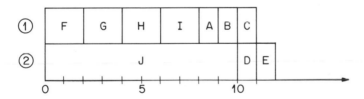

Figure 2.11.LPT/NP Schedule for Two Slow Printers (10,000 Lines for Job J)

The mean throughput rate is simply

$$mean\ throughput\ rate_{LPT/NP} = \frac{N}{T_{finish,LPT/NP}} = \frac{10}{12\ minutes}$$

while the mean flow time is

$$E(F_{LPT/NP}) = \frac{1}{10}[10+2+4+6+8+9+10+11+11+12] = 8.3\ minutes$$

All these calculations are summarized in the table below:

Table 2.3.Performance Measures(10,000 Lines for Job J)

Configuration	Schedule	Mean Throughput Rate	Mean Flow Time
One Slow Printer	SPT/NP	1 job every 2.3 minutes	6.5 minutes
One Slow Printer	LPT/NP	1 job every 2.3 minutes	17.5 minutes
Two Slow Printers	SPT/NP	1 job every 1.6 minutes	4.7 minutes
Two Slow Printers	LPT/NP	1 job every 1.2 minutes	8.3 minutes
One Fast Printer	SPT/NP	1 job every 1.15 minutes	3.9 minutes
One Fast Printer	LPT/NP	1 job every 1.15 minutes	8.75 minutes

2.2.5 Summary   What lessons have we learned?

- A single printer mean throughput rate is less insensitive to scheduling compared with a distributed two printer system

- In order to achieve greater mean throughput rate, either we speed up a single printer or we add printers; how many and where depend upon the workload

- Responsiveness or mean flow time is critically influenced for any of these examples by the workload and the configuration

- One large job can impact the performance of the two printer system much more adversely than the single high speed printer system

2.3 A More General Example

N jobs are present at some initial time, say zero, and are executed on P identical processors. The execution times for the jobs are denoted by $T_K, K=1,...,N$. The jobs are independent of one another: there is no precedence ordering among the jobs. How long does it take to execute all the jobs? One way to answer this is to calculate the total execution time, T_{finish} or T_F, required for each possible ordering of the jobs; since there are N jobs, there are $N!$ schedules, and we will find out for moderate values of N such as 20 to 30 that even trying out one schedule a second can take us centuries to investigate all possible schedules. Our approach here is to find upper and lower *bounds* on the total time required to execute all N jobs on P processors without investigating all possible scheduling rules.

2.3.1 One Processor Used   First, suppose we had P processors, but only used *one* processor. This is the *worst* we might do: it gives an upper bound on T_F equal to the sum of the execution times for all the jobs.

$$T_F \leqslant \sum_{K=1}^{N} T_K$$

Furthermore, this gives us a *lower* bound on mean throughput rate:

$$mean\ throughput\ rate \geqslant \frac{N}{T_F} = \frac{N}{\sum\limits_{K=1}^{N} T_K} = \frac{1}{T_{average}} \qquad T_{average} = \frac{\sum\limits_{K=1}^{N} T_K}{N}$$

While this is an example of one type of *upper* bound on the total make span or an equivalent *lower* bound on mean throughput rate, it is *not* the best possible set of bounds. How can we do better? A digression is needed.

2.3.2 The Geometry of Static Scheduling   The figure below shows an illustrative mode of operation for this system: the number of busy processors versus time is plotted. Initially all processors are busy, until one by one they become idle and all the work is completed at T_F.

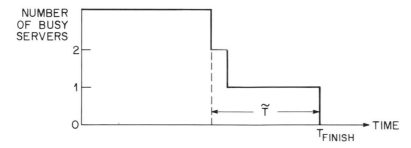

Figure 2.12.Illustrative Operation: Number of Busy Servers vs Time

We denote by $S(t)$ the number of busy servers at time t. The area under the curve formed by $S(t)$ is simply the total amount of processor time all the jobs require:

$$\int_0^{T_F} S(t)dt = \sum_{K=1}^{N} T_K$$

In the figure above, we have denoted by $\tilde{T}$ the duration of time from the last instant when all the processors are busy until all processors are first idle. Our program is to relate the model ingredients, i.e., the area under the curve $S(t)$, the number of processors, the job processing times, and T_F, by bounding $\tilde{T}$.

2.3.3 A Lower Bound on Makespan   What is the *shortest* total execution time? Since we have P processors, they could all start execution at the same time and finish at the same time:

$$\frac{\sum_{K=1}^{N} T_K}{P} \leqslant T_F$$

On the other hand, if one job requires more execution time than the average amount of processor time per job, then this one job will determine the shortest possible make span:

$$\max_{K} T_K = T_{\max} \leqslant T_F$$

We can combine all these bounds:

$$\max \left[T_{\max}, \frac{\sum_{K=1}^{N} T_K}{P} \right] \leqslant T_F$$

If no one job requires significantly more execution time than any other job, then

$$T_{\max} << \frac{\sum_{K=1}^{N} T_K}{P}$$

and hence all processors are simultaneously executing work.

On the other hand, if one job requires significantly more execution time than any other job, then

$$T_{\max} \approx \sum_{K=1}^{N} T_K$$

and effectively only one processor is busy executing work.

2.3.4 An Upper Bound on Makespan The largest that $\tilde{T}$ might be is the largest time required to run any single job:

$$\tilde{T} <= \max_{K} T_K = T_{\max}$$

On the one hand, we can *lower* bound the total area under this curve by demanding that all but one of the processors finish all their work at the same time, and the final processor is busy executing one job for $\tilde{T}$:

$$P[T_F - \tilde{T}] + \tilde{T} \leqslant \sum_{K=1}^{N} T_K$$

If we rearrange this, we see that

$$T_F \leqslant \frac{\sum\limits_{K=1}^{N} T_K}{P} + \frac{P-1}{P} \, \tilde{T} \leqslant \frac{\sum\limits_{K=1}^{N} T_K}{P} + \frac{P-1}{P} \, T_{\max}$$

We can rewrite this as

$$T_F \leqslant \frac{\sum\limits_{K=1}^{N} T_K}{P} \left[1 + \frac{(P-1)\, T_{\max}}{\sum\limits_{K=1}^{N} P_K} \right]$$

The first term is simply the average time per processor to execute jobs. If no one job requires much more processing time than any other job, i.e., if

$$(P-1)\, T_{\max} << \sum\limits_{K=1}^{N} T_K$$

then the total time to execute all the jobs is roughly the total execution time per processor:

$$T_F \approx \frac{\sum\limits_{K=1}^{N} T_K}{P}$$

If one job requires much more processing time than any other job, i.e., if

$$T_{\max} \approx \sum\limits_{K=1}^{N} T_K$$

then the total time to execute all the jobs is roughly equal to the single processor execution time:

$$T_F \approx \sum\limits_{K=1}^{N} T_K$$

On the other hand, if one job takes virtually all the time, then effectively only one processor can be used, so this should not be that surprising.

2.3.5 Speedup At any given instant of time there are $J_E(t)$ jobs *in execution* on P processors. Since job K requires T_K time units to be executed, the total execution time of jobs must equal the *integral* or *area* of $J_E(t)$ from the initial time $t=0$ to the end of execution of all jobs T_F:

$$\sum\limits_{K=1}^{N} T_K = \int\limits_{0}^{T_F} J_E(t)\, dt$$

On the one hand, the total time required to execute all jobs with one processor $P=1$ is simply the sum of all the job execution times:

$$T_F(P{=}1) = \sum_{K=1}^{N} T_K$$

On the other hand, the definition of speedup in going from $P{=}1$ to $P{>}1$ processors is simply

$$speedup = \frac{T_F(P{=}1)}{T_F(P{>}1)}$$

Combining all of the above, the speedup can be written as

$$speedup = \frac{1}{T_F}\int_0^{T_F} J_E(t)\,dt = E[J_E]$$

mean number of jobs in execution $= E[J_E] = speedup$

This result is fundamental: if there is *one* resource (such as a single processor), there is *no* opportunity for speedup. If there are *multiple* resources (one processor, one disk, one printer, one terminal), there can be as many opportunities for multiplying the mean throughput rate as there are resources.

2.4 Preemptive vs Nonpreemptive Scheduling

What about *preemptive* versus *nonpreemptive* scheduling? Here we see that we can in fact *achieve* the lower bound on make span. Two cases arise: either there is one job that takes longer than the average time per processor of all the jobs, i.e.,

$$T_{finish} = \max_K T_K = T_{max}$$

or there is no job that takes longer than the average time per processor:

$$T_{finish} = \frac{\sum_{K=1}^{N} T_K}{P}$$

Combining all this, we see

$$T_{finish} = \max\left[\max_K T_K, \frac{\sum_{K=1}^{N} T_K}{P}\right]$$

The figure below shows a *nonpreemptive* schedule for three processors with a fixed workload to make this concrete.

Preemption will allow us to achieve the *smaller* of these two bounds. How can this be achieved? One way is to assign jobs to the first processor until T_{finish} is passed, and then assign the overlap plus other jobs to the next processor until T_{finish} is passed, and so on until we assign all the work.

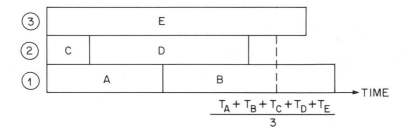

Figure 2.13A.Three Processor Nonpreemptive Schedule

EXERCISE: How in fact can we achieve this schedule? It appears that we run the end of the job before we run its beginning.

EXERCISE: How do we circumvent the problem that no job can execute in parallel with itself?

In fact this bound is achievable if there is no precedence ordering among the jobs, i.e., some jobs must be done earlier than others.

The figure below illustrates a preemptive schedule, and shows that the make span for the preemptive schedule equals the average processor time.

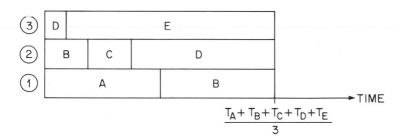

Figure 2.13B.A Preemptive Schedule for Three Processors

2.5 Impact of Partial Ordering and Fluctuations

Suppose we have a list of N jobs, and for convenience we suppose $N=2P$. We break the list of jobs into two lists, $J_1,...,J_P,J'_1,...,J'_P$. The jobs are not independent: some jobs must be executed before other jobs. We denote by $J'_K < J_K, K=1,...,P$ the constraint that J'_K must be executed before J_K can begin execution. Each unprimed job requires one unit of memory to be executed; each primed job requires P units of memory to be executed. The execution time for the unprimed jobs are all identical and equal to one; the execution time for each of the primed jobs is identical and equal to ϵ which we will make very small compared to one:

$$T_K = 1 \gg T'_K = \epsilon \quad K=1,...,M$$

We have a total of P units of memory and P processors. We wish to investigate two different schedules:

- Schedule one: $J'_1,...,J'_M,J_1,...,J_M$

- Schedule two: $J_1,...,J_M,J'_1,...,J'_M$

For the first schedule, in order to satisfy the partial order constraint, we execute the primed jobs in order, and then execute in parallel on the M processors all the unprimed jobs:

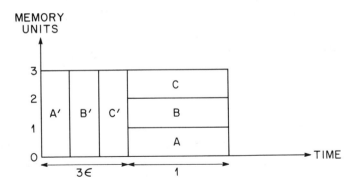

Figure 2.14. Schedule One for Three Processors

The make span or total time to finish all the jobs is

$$T_{finish} = P\epsilon + 1 \quad schedule\ one$$

For the second schedule, in order to satisfy the partial order constraint, we execute a primed job and then an unprimed job in pairs until we execute all the jobs: The make span or total time to finish all the jobs is

$$T_{finish} = P(1 + \epsilon) \quad schedule\ two$$

The ratio of these two can vary immensely. For example if $\epsilon=1$ then

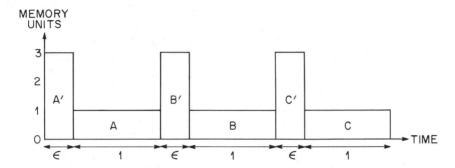

Figure 2.15.Schedule Two for Three Processors

$$\frac{T_{finish,I}}{T_{finish,II}} = \frac{P(1+\epsilon)}{1+P\epsilon}\Big|_{\epsilon=1} = \frac{2P}{P+1}\underset{P\to\infty}{\to}2$$

and hence we can be off by no more than a factor of *two* with these two schedules. On the other hand, if $\epsilon \ll 1$, then

$$\frac{T_{finish,I}}{T_{finish,II}}\Big|_{\epsilon\ll1} = \frac{P(1+\epsilon)}{1+P\epsilon}\underset{\epsilon\to0}{\to}P$$

and hence we can be off by a factor of P which could be *much* greater than just a factor of two!

2.6 Polynomial Evaluation

Job precedence constraints arise in evaluation of polynomials, which is frequently done in practice in signal processing. These give us additional concrete examples to build intuition concerning the performance of parallel processors. Our problem is to evaluate a polynomial Y:

$$Y = \sum_{K=0}^{N}A_KX^K$$

The inputs are the coefficients $A_K, K=0,...,N$ and the value of X, while the output is the scalar Y. Given P processors, we want to understand what is the *minimum* time required to completely evaluate one such polynomial. We will do so in special cases, to build insight.

2.6.1 Addition We begin with the case where all the coefficients are arbitrary, but $X=1$. We must evaluate Y where

$$Y = \sum_{K=1}^{N}A_K$$

Each addition is assumed to take one time unit. If we had one processor, this would require $N-1$ additions, and hence $N-1$ time units. Given four processors, and $N=15$, the table below shows the operations of each step of the evaluation.

Table 2.4.Summation Evaluation with Four Processors

Time	Processor 1	Processor 2	Processor 3	Processor 4
1	$Z_1=A_0+A_1$	$Z_2=A_2+A_3$	$Z_3=A_4+A_5$	$Z_4=A_6+A_7$
2	$Z_5=A_8+A_9$	$Z_6=A_{10}+A_{11}$	$Z_7=A_{12}+A_{13}$	$Z_8=A_{14}+Z_1$
3	$Z_9=Z_2+Z_3$	$Z_{10}=Z_4+Z_5$	$Z_{11}=Z_6+Z_7$	IDLE
4	$Z_{12}=Z_8+Z_9$	$Z_{13}=Z_{10}+Z_{11}$	IDLE	IDLE
5	$Y=Z_{12}+Z_{13}$	IDLE	IDLE	IDLE

For four processors, the total time required to sum fifteen coefficients is now five, while for one processor the total time was fourteen. The speedup is the ratio of these two:

$$speedup = \frac{T_{finish}(P=1)}{T_{finish}(P>1)} = \frac{14}{5} = 2.8 \quad N=15$$

The best possible speedup would be to keep all processors busy, and hence this would be a factor of four. Effectively, we have $4-2.8=1.2$ idle processors.

What happens as $N\rightarrow\infty$? Now all four processors are continuously busy, and hence

$$speedup = \frac{T_{finish}(P=1)}{T_{finish}(P>1)} = P=4 \quad N\rightarrow\infty$$

What happens as $P\rightarrow\infty$? At the first step, each processor will add one term to another term, reducing the total number of items by a factor of two. This can be repeated, until $\log_2(N)$ time steps elapse for summing all terms together.

Combining all these ideas, it can be shown that

$$T_{finish} \geqslant \left\lceil \frac{N}{P} \right\rceil - 1 + \left\lceil \log_2[min(P,N)] \right\rceil$$

where $\lceil X \rceil$ is the smallest integer greater than or equal to X.

EXERCISE: Show that for $P=4, N=15$ this lower bound on T_{finish} is achieved.

2.6.2 Powers Suppose that $A_N=1, A_K=0, K\neq N$, so we wish to evaluate $Y=X^N$. If one processor is available, and multiplication requires one unit of time, then to evaluate Y worst case would require $N-1$ time steps. However, we can do better! Suppose that $N=2^5$, i.e., N is a power of two. Instead of taking thirty one time steps to evaluate Y, consider the following procedure:

Table 2.5. Steps for Evaluating $Y = X^{32}$

Step	Value
1	$Z_1 = X^2$
2	$Z_2 = Z_1^2 = X^4$
3	$Z_3 = Z_2 Z_2 = X^8$
4	$Z_4 = Z_3 Z_3 = X^{16}$
5	$Y = Z_4 Z_4 = X^{32}$

If $N \to \infty$, it can be shown in general that even if N is not a power of two a single processor can evaluate X^N in $\log_2(N)$ multiplications:

$$T_{finish} \approx \log_2(N) \qquad N \to \infty, P = 1$$

On the other hand, for $P \to \infty$, i.e., with an infinite number of processors, P processors can evaluate X^N in $\log_2(N)$ multiplications:

$$T_{finish} \approx \log_2(N) \qquad P \to \infty$$

Hence, *one* processor can evaluate X^N as quickly as an *infinite* number of processors, and we can gain *nothing* by parallelism.

2.6.3 General Case In general, we wish to evaluate Y where

$$Y = \sum_{K=0}^{N} A_K X^K$$

For $P = 1$, a single processor, one algorithm for evaluating Y is given by

$$Y = ((..((A_N X + A_{N-1})X + A_{N-2})X + A_{N-3})...)X + A_0$$

For $N = 22$ this requires twenty five additions and multiplications for $P = 1$.

On the other hand, for $P = 2$, one algorithm for evaluating Y is given by

$$Y = \sum_{K=0}^{N/2} A_{2K} X^{2K} + X \sum_{K=0}^{N/2-1} A_{2K+1} X^{2K+1}$$

and hence we must evaluate two polynomials in X^2. For $N = 22$ and $P = 2$ this requires twenty four additions and multiplications.

For $P = 3$, one algorithm for evaluating Y involves writing Y as the sum of three polynomials in X^3, and using all three processors.

Combining all these items, it can be shown that

$$\frac{2N}{P} \log_2(P) \leqslant T_{finish} \leqslant \frac{2N}{P} \log_2(P) + o(\log_2(P))$$

The final term, $o(\log_2(P))$, is negligible as $P \to \infty$, in the sense that

$$\lim_{P \to \infty} \frac{o(\log_2(P))}{P} = 0$$

Hence, the speedup, measured in the time required to evaluate this expression with P processors versus $P=1$ is roughly given by

$$speedup = \frac{T_{finish}(P=1)}{T_{finish}(P>1)} \approx \frac{P}{\log_2(P)} \quad P \to \infty$$

2.6.4 Summary We have shown that

- Evaluating roughly N binary operations with P processors can lead to a speedup approaching P

- Evaluating X^N with P processors leads to *no* speedup over a single processor

- Evaluating a polynomial in N terms with P processors leads to a speedup of $P/log_2(P)$ over a single processor, which is in between the other two cases.

The lesson here: the workload can significantly impact the actual benefit of using multiple processors.

2.6.5 Additional Reading

[1]   I.Munro, M.Paterson, *Optimal Algorithms for Parallel Polynomial Evaluation,* Journal of Computer System Science, **7,** 189 (1973).

[2]   A.H.Sameh, *Numerical Parallel Algorithms--A Survey,* in **High Speed Computer and Algorithm Organization,** D.J.Kuck, D.H.Lawrie, A.H.Sameh (editors), pp.207-228, Academic Press, NY, 1977.

2.7 Critical Path Scheduling

P parallel processors are available for executing jobs fed from a single queue. First, suppose there is no precedence ordering among jobs, i.e., no job need be done before any other job. One scheduling rule called *critical path* scheduling is to execute tasks according to their processing time, with longest tasks first. The intuitive notion is that the longest jobs are *critical* in determining how short the make span can be, and hence it is essential to be operating on the critical path schedule for shortest make span or highest mean throughput rate. A different way of thinking about this is to allow the number of processors P to become infinite: each job will be assigned to one processor, and the make span equals the time to do the longest job. With a finite number of processors the make span will be longer than with an infinite number of processors, and hence we have a *lower* bound on the total time to finish a workload.

If there is a precedence ordering of jobs, then we sort times required for each job *stream* longest to shortest, and schedule the first job as the job that is the start of the longest critical path or longest stream that must be executed, and having scheduled this first job we now repeat this exercise with one less job, until all jobs are scheduled.

EXERCISE: Construct a flowchart for critical path scheduling, and exhibit pseudo code for implementing the flow chart.

Again, a different way of thinking about this is to allow the number of processors P to become infinite: each job will be assigned to one processor, and the make span equals the time to do the longest path of jobs. Viewed in this way, we see that

$$\max \left[T_{critical\ path}, \frac{1}{P} \sum_{K=1}^{N} T_K \right] \leqslant T_{finish}(N)$$

where $T_{critical\ path}$ is the make span for a critical path schedule.

$$T_{finish}(N) \leqslant \frac{1}{P} \sum_{K=1}^{N} T_K \left[1 + \frac{(P-1)\,T_{critical\ path}}{\sum_{K=1}^{N} T_K} \right]$$

If the make span for a critical path schedule is much less than the average time each processor is busy, then

$$T_{finish}(N) \approx \frac{1}{P} \sum_{K=1}^{N} T_K$$

and hence the make span is reduced by P or the mean throughput rate increases by P.

On the other hand, if the make span for a critical path schedule is much more than the average time each processor is busy, then

$$T_{finish}(N) \approx T_{critical\ path}$$

and effectively there is no gain with more than one processor.

In a different vein, it can be shown that

$$\frac{T_{finish,CRITICAL\ PATH}}{\min_{SCHEDULE} T_{finish,SCHEDULE}} \leqslant \frac{4}{3} - \frac{1}{3P}$$

In other words, critical path scheduling is no worse than any other single processor $(P=1)$ scheduling rule in minimizing T_{finish}, is 1/6 longer than the *best* (in terms of minimizing T_{finish}) two processor scheduling rule, and is 1/3 longer than the best infinite processor scheduling rule!

2.8 P Identical Parallel Processors

In practice, the execution times of the jobs are not often known with any precision. This occurs for a variety of reasons: the data to be manipulated varies from job to job, the text program executes different branches depending upon the data, and so forth. Here we attempt to capture this phenomenon by fixing the mean or average execution time of a job, and modeling the fluctuations of job execution times as non negative random variables drawn from the same distribution.

A more precise statement of the problem is as follows: N jobs must be executed by P servers or processors. The jobs are all present at an initial time, say zero. The time to execute job $K=1,...,N$ is denoted by T_K. We will assume that the sequence of job execution times are non negative random variables, with the same marginal distribution:

$$PROB[T_K \leqslant X] = G(X) \quad K=1,2,...,N$$

The mean time to execute a job is denoted by $E[T]$ where

$$E[T] = \int_0^\infty X dG(X) = \int_0^\infty [1 - G(X)]dX < \infty$$

The time to completely execute all N jobs is denoted by C_N.

The mean throughput rate of completing jobs is given by the ratio of the total number of jobs divided by the mean time required to complete all the jobs:

$$mean\ throughput\ rate = \frac{N}{E[C_N]}$$

The shortest that C_N could be is

$$C_N \geqslant \frac{1}{S} \sum_{K=1}^N T_K$$

The longest that C_N could be is

$$C_N \leqslant max[T_{max}, \frac{1}{S} \sum_{K=1}^N T_K]$$

where

$$T_{max} = \max_{K=1,...,N} T_K$$

The mean throughput rate is the ratio of the total number of jobs divided by the mean time to complete these jobs:

$$mean\ throughput\ rate \equiv \lambda_N = \frac{N}{E[C_N]}$$

Our goal is to allow the number of jobs to become larger and larger, $N \to \infty$, such that the mean throughput rate stabilizes at an average or limiting value. In fact, this limit is

$$\lim_{N \to \infty} \lambda_N = \frac{P}{E[T]}$$

In words, each job requires a mean execution time of $E(T)$, and we will realize a *speedup* of P because all the processors will be busy. As a bonus, the upper and lower bounds on mean throughput rate will also approach this limit under these conditions. This shows that the *details* of the workload may not matter nearly so much as might be expected.

2.8.1 Analysis For any real number, say Y, we will use the following trick:

$$T_{max} \leqslant Y + \sum_{K=1}^{N} U_{-1}[T_K - Y]$$

where $U_{-1}(X) = 0$ $X<0$, $= 1$ $X>0$ is a so called generalized unit step function. This allows us to write

$$T_{max} \leqslant Y + N \int_{Y}^{\infty} [1 - G(X)]dX$$

We denote by ω the small value of X such that $1 - G(X)=0$:

$$\omega = \inf_{X} \{X| \ 1 - G(X) = 0\}$$

Two cases arise:

2.8.2 ω finite For this case, $\omega<\infty$, we see that

$$T_{max} \leqslant \omega \quad \rightarrow \quad E[T_{max}] \leqslant \omega$$

and hence

$$\frac{P}{E[T]} \ \frac{1}{1 + \dfrac{(P-1)\omega}{NE(T_{max})}} \leqslant \lambda_N \leqslant \frac{P}{E[T]}$$

As the number of jobs becomes larger and larger, $N \rightarrow \infty$, the mean throughput rate as well as upper and lower bounds approach the desired result:

$$\lim_{N \rightarrow \infty} \lambda_N = \frac{P}{E[T]}$$

2.8.3 ω infinite For this case, we find it useful to define a related quantity μ_N:

$$\mu_N = \inf_{X>0} \left\{X| 1 - G(X) \leqslant \frac{1}{N}\right\}$$

Because $\omega=\infty$, it is clear that $\lim_{N \rightarrow \infty} \mu_N = \infty$.

On the other hand, we see that

$$E[T_{max}] \leqslant \mu_N + N\int_{\mu_N}^{\infty} [1 - G(X)]dX$$

Because

$$\lim_{N \to \infty} \int_{\mu_N}^{\infty} [1 - G(X)]dX = 0$$

we see that

$$N \int_{\mu_N}^{\infty} [1 - G(X)]dX = o(N)$$

This implies that

$$1 - F(\mu_N) \leqslant \frac{1}{N} \quad \rightarrow \quad 1 - G(X) = o\left(\frac{1}{X}\right)$$

This in turn implies

$$o\left(\frac{1}{\mu_N}\right) \leqslant \frac{1}{N}$$

and in turn that

$$\mu_N = o(N)$$

Finally, we see that

$$E[T_{\max}] = o(N)$$

and this allows us to show that

$$\lim_{N \to \infty} \lambda_N = \frac{P}{E[T]}$$

as in the previous case.

2.8.4 An Example Suppose we examine a particular $G(X)$:

$$G(X) = 1 - Q exp[-QX/E[T]] \quad 0 < Q \leqslant 1$$

This has a mean at $E[T]$ and a great deal of fluctuation about the mean, with the fluctuations increasing as $Q \rightarrow 0$.

The trick here is to fix $1 - G(\mu_N)$ at $1/N$:

$$1 - G(\mu_N) = Q exp[-Q\mu_N/E[T]] = \frac{1}{N}$$

This in turn fixes μ_n:

$$\mu_N = \frac{E[T] \, ln(NQ)}{Q}$$

Now if we substitute into the earlier expressions, we see

$$E[T_{max}] \leqslant E[T] \left[\frac{ln(NQ)}{Q} + \frac{1}{Q} \right]$$

Finally, the mean throughput rate is upper and lower bounded by

$$\frac{P}{E[T]} \frac{1}{1 + \dfrac{(P-1)[1+ln(NQ)]}{NQ}} \leqslant \lambda_N \leqslant \frac{P}{E[T]}$$

2.8.5 Bounds The longest possible completion time C_N occurs when we execute all jobs but one, and the remaining job requires the largest amount of processing time of all jobs:

$$C_N \leqslant \frac{1}{P} \sum_{K=1}^{N-1} T_K + (T_N = T_{max}) \equiv C_{max}$$

The shortest possible completion time C_N occurs when either all jobs finish execution at the same instant of time on all P processors, or all but one job are executed on $P-1$ processors and the remaining job executes on one processor and has the largest processing time:

$$C_N \geqslant \max[T_{max}, \frac{1}{P} \sum_{K=1}^{N} T_K] = C_{min}$$

The ratio of the longest to the shortest completion times is upper bounded by

$$\frac{C_{max}}{C_{min}} \leqslant 2 - \frac{1}{P}$$

In other words, as we go from P=1 to P=2 processors, the greatest *relative* change in the mean completion time for *any* scheduling policy is $2 - 1/2 = 1.5$, while going from P=2 to P=3 processors gives a maximum gain due to scheduling of $2 - 1/3 = 5/3$.

2.9 Single Processor Deadline Scheduling

In deadline scheduling, different classes of tasks have different urgencies; we denote by W_K the allowable queueing time window that we can tolerate for job $K=1,...,N$. At the arrival epoch of a job, say job K, that arrives at time A_K we look up its window in a table, add the window to its arrival time, and call the result the *deadline* or priority or urgency number for that task:

deadline for job K $\equiv D_K = A_K + W_K$ $K=1,2,...,N$

That job is inserted in a queue in priority order or deadline order, most urgent jobs first, with jobs executed in deadline order. Note that windows need not be positive! We compare performance via queueing time statistics and via a different pair of quantities. If we have two classes of jobs, each with its own window, and we fix the *difference* between the two windows but allow the *smaller* (or larger) window to become infinite in size, then we approach *static* priority scheduling. Very roughly speaking, static priority scheduling allows control over first moments of queueing times of tasks, while deadline and other dynamic scheduling policies allow control of asymptotic distributions of queueing and waiting times. The measures of performance of interest are

- *lateness*-- the lateness of job K is defined as its completion time minus its deadline;

$$L_K = C_K - D_K \quad K = 1,2,...$$

Negative lateness implies the job queueing time was less than its deadline, while positive lateness means the job queueing time exceeded its deadline.

- *tardiness*-- the tardiness of job K is zero if the job is finished by its deadline, and equals the lateness otherwise; put differently, the tardiness is the maximum of zero and the lateness

$$T_K = max[0,L_K] \quad K = 1,2,...$$

What are desirable properties of deadline scheduling? One is that deadline scheduling minimizes the *maximum* lateness or *maximum* tardiness over *any* scheduling policy. This suggests that deadline scheduling will be useful in time critical jobs, which is perhaps not so surprising! How do we show this property? Suppose we had a schedule that violated deadline scheduling ordering yet had a smaller maximum lateness than deadline scheduling. This means that there is at least one time interval where one job, say job J, is waiting and another job, say job I, is executing, even though the deadline for job J is less than the deadline for job I. We denote the non deadline schedule by S' while the deadline schedule is denoted by S. Since the maximum lateness is smaller using S' we see

$$max[L(S')] \leqslant max[max[L(S)],L(S')]$$

Since the completion time of job I under schedule S' is given by

$$C_I(S') = max[C_J(S),C_I(S)]$$

we see that

$$max[L(S')] \leqslant max[max[L(S),C_J(S)-D_I,L_I(S)]$$

Finally, since the deadline for I is greater than that for J, we see

$$max[L(S')] \leqslant max[max(L(S)),L_J(S),L_I(S)] = max[L(S)]$$

This is precisely what we wanted to show.

Several consequences follow immediately:

- Even knowing the arrival pattern in advance cannot help minimize the maximum lateness better than deadline scheduling

- If the windows are equal to the service times for the respective jobs, then deadline scheduling minimizes the maximum waiting time

- If all the windows are equal to one another, then deadline scheduling is equivalent to service in order of arrival

Suppose we have two types of jobs, A and B, with processing times and windows as shown:

Table 2.6.Job Statistics Summary

Job Type	Service	Window
A	$T_A=3$ seconds	$W_A=5$ seconds
B	$T_B=2$ seconds	$W_B=3$ seconds

The figure below shows an arrival pattern consisting of one type A arrival at time t=0 followed by a type B arrival at time t=1 and t=4, with the resulting work pattern for deadline scheduling, and static priority scheduling (A higher priority than B, B higher priority than A). Note that *neither* static priority schedule can meet *all* deadlines, while the deadline schedule can. Hence the need for *dynamic* rather than *static* priority scheduling!

Suppose we had N distinct types of jobs, with each job type having its own service time T_K with associated window W_K and maximum storage for job K of B_K bytes, where K=1,...,N. A natural measure of utilization is given by U where U is defined to be the storage multiplied by the service time, and divided by the window, summed over all job types:

$$U = \sum_{K=1}^{N} \frac{B_K T_K}{W_K}$$

If $U<1$ then we want to show that all deadlines can be met. Let's examine the worst case, where the maximum number of requests are always present and the service time is the largest possible. This implies that server is busy handling type K requests at a rate of B_K/W_K. Since the requests are absorbing the maximum possible processing times, the utilization of the server will equal U; but for the entire system to keep up with its work, we must demand $U<1$.

Example: Suppose we had a set of sources (memory boards, disk controller boards, terminal controller boards, processor boards, and so on) that each demand access to a shared bus. If each source can only have one request outstanding at one time, and we choose the window equal to the service time for each type of bus access request, and all the service demands will be met if and only if

$$\sum_{K=1}^{N} \frac{1}{T_K} \leqslant 1$$

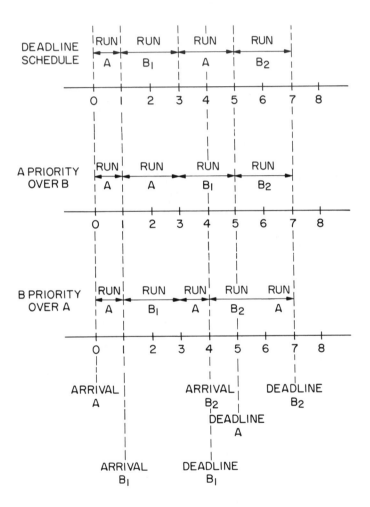

Figure 2.16.Illustrative Comparison of Deadline vs Static Priority Scheduling

2.10 Pipelining

Suppose that each processor is dedicated to executing a given function. One special case of this is to construct a *pipeline* of processors, where the input of one processor is the output of another processor, and so forth:

Figure 2.17.Three Stage Pipeline

Each job consists of a series of steps, that must be done in exactly this order.

2.10.1 An Example Six jobs each require the following processing at each of three steps:

Table 2.7.Execution Times for Six Jobs

Job	Step 1	Step 2	Step 3
1	3	2	4
2	2	4	1
3	1	5	2
4	3	2	2
5	1	1	1
6	2	1	4

The schedule for this set of jobs is (1,2,3,4,5,6), i.e., execute the jobs in the order of job number. A schedule is shown in the figure below:

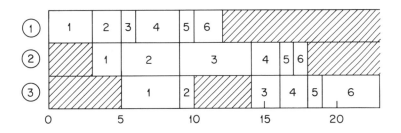

Figure 2.18.Three Stage Pipeline Schedule For Six Jobs

2.10.2 A More Sophisticated Example Suppose N jobs must be executed on a $P=N$ stage pipeline. The execution times of job step I for job $K=1,...,N$ is denoted by T_{IK}. Suppose that the execution times are given by

$$T_{IK} = \epsilon, \quad I \neq K \quad T_{IK} = 1, \quad I = K$$

Two different schedules are of interest:

- Schedule one: $(1,2,...,N)$

- Schedule two: $(N,N-1,...,1)$

For schedule one, the figure below shows an illustrative plot of the activity of each processor:

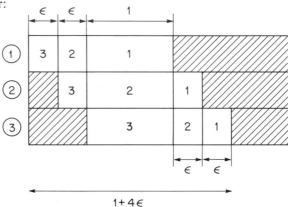

Figure 2.19. Schedule One Processor Activity ($P=3, N=3$)

The total time required to execute all the work for P processors is

$$T_{finish,I} = P + (P-1)\epsilon$$

For schedule two, the figure below shows an illustrative plot of processor activity:

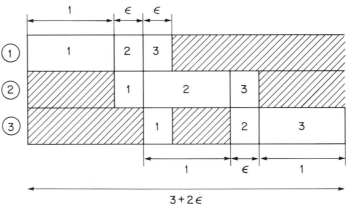

Figure 2.20. Schedule Two Processor Activity ($P=3, N=3$)

The total time required to execute all the work for P processors is

$$T_{finish,II} = 1 + (P+1)\epsilon$$

There are two cases of interest: $\epsilon=1$ so all jobs take the same amount of time, and hence

$$T_{finish,I} = T_{finish,II} = P$$

and $\epsilon \ll 1$, so that only stage K of job J_K requires one time unit of processing, and hence

$$T_{finish,I} \approx P \quad T_{finish,II} \approx 1 \quad \epsilon \rightarrow 0$$

If there is radical imbalance, the time required to execute all the work can differ by the number of processors!

2.11 Bounding The Make Span for Pipelines of Single Processors

Our goal in this section is to find upper and lower bounds on the make span for a pipeline of single processors, much as we did earlier for parallel processors.

Suppose a list or schedule of N jobs is to be followed, with the jobs ordered $(1,2,...,N)$. P processors are available. Each job consists of $S=P$ steps. Each processor is dedicated to executing one and only one step. The time required to execute step $I=1,...,S$ of job $K=1,...,N$ is denoted by T_{IK}.

2.11.1 Upper Bound on Make Span One immediate upper bound on the total time required to execute all jobs is to simply execute the jobs one at a time:

$$T_{finish} \leqslant \sum_{K=1}^{N} \sum_{I=1}^{S} T_{IK}$$

EXERCISE: Can you find a *sharper* upper bound that is less than or equal to this upper bound and includes the same model parameters?

2.11.2 Lower Bound on Make Span In order to lower bound the make span, the total time required to execute all jobs, we realize that there are three possible contributions to the make span:

- The time required to execute job one from step one through step $J-1$:
$$\sum_{S=1}^{J-1} T_{1S}$$

- The time required to execute every job at step J: $\sum_{K=1}^{N} T_{KJ}$

- The time required to execute job N from step $J+1$ through step S:
$$\sum_{I=J+1}^{S} T_{NI}$$

Combining all these, we see that for one particular step in the pipeline, J,

$$\sum_{I=1}^{J-1} T_{1I} + \sum_{K=1}^{N} T_{KJ} + \sum_{I=J+1}^{S} T_{NI} \leq T_{finish}(J)$$

To get the best possible lower bound, we should look for the largest this set of lower bounds could be, for all steps:

$$\max_{1 \leq J \leq S} \left[\sum_{I=1}^{J-1} T_{1I} + \sum_{K=1}^{N} T_{KJ} + \sum_{I=J+1}^{S} T_{NI} \right] \leq T_{finish}$$

This development can be made more formal as follows. Suppose that C_{KJ} denotes the completion time of job step $J=1,...,S$ for job $K=1,...,N$. For convenience, we assume there is a fictitious initial stage, labeled zero, with $C_{K0}=0$ for all K. The completion times of step J of job one obey the following recursion:

$$C_{J1} = C_{J-1,1} + T_{J1} \quad J=1,...,S$$

The completion times of step J of job K obey the following recursions:

$$C_{KJ} = \max[C_{K,J-1}, C_{K-1,J}] + T_{KJ} \quad J=1,...,S$$

If we use the inequalities $X < max[X,Y]$ and $Y < max[X,Y]$ then we see

$$C_{KJ} \geq C_{K-1,J} + T_{KJ}$$

The completion time of step J of job N is similarly given by

$$C_{NJ} \geq C_{N,J-1} + T_{NJ}$$

Combining all of these bounds, we obtain the result sketched earlier.

2.12 Johnson's Rule

Now we turn to a two stage pipeline.

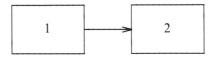

Figure 2.21.Two Stage Pipeline

N jobs have associated processing times $T_{1,K}$ at stage one and $T_{2,K}$ at stage two, $K=1,...,N$. Our goal is to minimize the total system busy time to completely execute all this work.

As an example, suppose we have five jobs (A, B, C, D, E) that must each be executed in two stages, with the execution times for each job summarized as follows:

Table 2.8. Job Execution Times

Job	Stage 1	Stage 2
A	6	3
B	0	2
C	3	4
D	8	6
E	2	1

The jobs are executed according to an alphabetical priority ordering. The total time to execute all the jobs according to this schedule, the make span, is 22.

Can you find a priority list schedule that achieves this?

The principal result here, due to Johnson, is

- Execute tasks on the second stage in the same order as on the first stage

- J_K is executed before J_I if

$$\min[T_{K,1}, T_{I,2}] \leqslant \min[T_{K,2}, T_{I,1}]$$

An algorithm for finding a scheduling that does this is

- Find the minimum $T_{I,K}$ where $I=1,2$ and $K=1,...,N$

- If I=1 put this at the head of the schedule; if I=2 put it at the end of the schedule

- Delete this task from the schedule and repeat the above procedure until no tasks remain

Roughly speaking, we want to put tasks requiring big processing times at the start of the schedule and small processing time tasks at the end of the schedule. Now, how bad can we do? It can be shown that

$$\frac{T_{finish,SCHEDULE}}{\min_{SCHEDULE} T_{finish,SCHEDULE}} \leqslant P$$

or in other words, we could be off by the total number of processors in the pipeline!

2.13 S Stage Pipeline

Earlier, when we were analyzing parallel processor groups, we remarked that the workload is not precisely known in practice. We modeled that by allowing the mean execution time for each job to be fixed, and the fluctuations about the mean were modeled by random variables. Here we carry out exactly the same exercise.

2.13.1 Problem Statement N jobs must be executed by a system of P processors. Each job consists of S steps that must be done one after another; each step consists of execution of a given amount of text code operating upon a different amount of data, depending on the nature of the job. The system consists of a pipeline of stages: stage K consists of P_K processors fed from a single queue. Each processor can execute only one job at a time. The execution time for step K is denoted by $T_K, K=1,...,S$.

The completion time for all N jobs is denoted by C_N. The mean throughput rate is the number of jobs divided by the mean completion time:

$$\lambda_N = \frac{N}{E[C_N]}$$

Our goal is to show that the mean throughput rate approaches a limit as the number of jobs becomes larger and larger:

$$\lim_{N \to \infty} \lambda_N = \min_K \left[\frac{P_K}{E(T_K)} \right]$$

In words, the stage with the lowest maximum mean throughput rate, the so called *bottleneck* stage, will determine the *system* total maximum mean throughput rate. Furthermore, the upper and lower bounds on mean throughput rate approach this value. Hence, the details of the workload do not matter as much as might be expected.

2.13.2 Upper Bound on Mean Throughput Rate One upper bound on mean throughput rate is given by the number of jobs in the system:

$$\lambda_N = \frac{N}{\sum\limits_{K=1}^{N} E[T_K]}$$

A second upper bound on mean throughput rate is given by all the processors at a given stage being completely busy:

$$\lambda_N = \min_{K=1,...,S} \frac{P_K}{E[T_K]}$$

Combining all this, we see

$$\lambda_N \leqslant \min \left[\min_{K=1,...,S} \frac{P_K}{E[T_K]} , \frac{N}{\sum\limits_{K=1}^{N} E[T_K]} \right]$$

If the processing time at each stage has *no* fluctuations about the mean processing time, i.e., the processing times are deterministic, then we claim that this upper bound is *achievable*. Finally, as $N \to \infty$ we obtain the desired result.

2.13.3 Lower Bound on Mean Throughput Rate The longest completion time, and hence the lowest mean throughput rate, is given by executing only one job at a time:

$$E[C_N] \leq N \sum_{K=1}^{S} \frac{E[T_K]}{P_K} + o(N)$$

If each service time is assumed to be an independent random variable, with

$$PROB[T_K \leq X] = 1 - \alpha\exp\left[-\alpha X/E[T_K]\right] \quad K=1,...,S; X>0$$

so that the mean service time at stage K is fixed at $E(T_K), K=1,...,S$ but $\alpha \to 0$ results in greater and greater fluctuations about the mean.

In order to obtain our desired result, we must show that for any positive number, say $\epsilon>0$, that

$$\lim_{\alpha \to 0} E[C_N] \geq N \sum_{K=1}^{S} \frac{E[T_K]}{P_K} - \epsilon$$

To see this, we need introduce additional notation and machinery.

Let $X_1,...,X_N$ be nonnegative independent random variables with distribution functions given by $G_1(),..,G_N()$ respectively. We define X_{max} as the maximum of these random variables:

$$X_{max} = \max[X_1,...,X_N]$$

Let E_K be the event that $X_K>Y$. The probability that the maximum X_{max} exceeds Y is given by

$$PROB[X_{max}>Y] = PROB[\bigcup_{J=1}^{N} E_J]$$

This can be upper and lower bounded as follows:

$$PROB[\bigcup_{J=1}^{N} E_J] \leq \sum_{J=1}^{N} PROB[E_J]$$

$$PROB[\bigcup_{J=1}^{N} E_J] \geq \sum_{J=1}^{N} PROB[E_J] - \sum_{J<K} PROB[E_J \cap E_K]$$

If we substitute in, we see

$$\sum_{J=1}^{N}[1 - G_J(Y)] - \sum_{J<K}[1 - G_J(Y)][1 - G_K(Y)] \leq PROB[X_{max}>Y]$$

$$PROB[X_{max}>Y] \leq \sum_{J=1}^{N}[1 - G_J(Y)]$$

An alternate way of computing this event is to define Y_K as the total time that stage $K=1,..,S$ is not empty, and hence

$$C_N \geqslant max[Y_1,...,Y_S]$$

On the other hand, each Y_K can be lower bounded by the total service time at stage K over the total number of processors at stage K

$$Y_K \geqslant \tilde{Y}_K \equiv \frac{total\ stage\ K\ service\ time}{P_K}$$

Now we realize that

$$PROB[\tilde{Y}_K \leqslant X] = G_K(X) = \sum_{J=0}^{N} \binom{N}{J} \alpha^J (1-\alpha)^{N-J} \left[1 - \sum_{K=0}^{J-1} \tilde{E}_K \right]$$

$$\tilde{E}_K \equiv \frac{X^K}{K!} exp[-X] \quad X = P_K \alpha X / E[T_K]$$

Hence, we see that

$$1 - G_K(X) = \sum_{J=1}^{N} \binom{N}{J} \alpha^J (1-\alpha)^{N-J} \sum_{K=0}^{J-1} \tilde{E}_K$$

The mean of $\tilde{Y}_K$ is given by

$$E[\tilde{Y}_K] = \frac{NE[T_K]}{P_K}$$

while

$$1 - G_K(X) \leqslant constant(K) \, [1 - (1 - \alpha)^N]$$

We see that

$$\lim_{\alpha \to 0} \sup_{X > 0} [1 - G_K(X)] = 0$$

so that

$$E[C_N] \geqslant E[max(\tilde{Y}_1, \dots, \tilde{Y}_S)]$$

$$\geqslant N \sum_{K=1}^{S} \frac{E(T_K)}{P_K} - \sum_{J < K} \int_0^{\infty} [1 - G_J(X)][1 - G_K(X)]dX$$

However, the last term can be made as small as possible by choosing α as close to zero as needed.

Finally, as we allow $N \to \infty$, we obtain the desired result for the mean throughput rate.

2.14 General Problem Classification

Suppose that N jobs, labeled $J_K, K = 1,...,N$ are to be executed. Each job can be processed on at most one processor at a time. This means that if a job can be processed on more than one processor at a time, we will break it up into one or more distinct jobs, each of which can be processed on only one processor at a time. Furthermore, each processor can execute at most one job at any instant of time.

2.14.1 Job Data Each job has its *release* time or *arrival* time, the earliest time it can begin execution, denoted by $A_K, K=1,...,N$. Each job has its *deadline* denoted by $D_K, K=1,...,N$ which is the time by which it should *ideally* be completed.

Each job requires a number of steps, with $S_K, K=1,...,N$ denoting the number of steps for $J_K, K=1,..,N$.

A *precedence relation* denoted by $<$ between jobs may exist. We denote by $J_I < J_K$ the requirement that J_I is to complete before J_K can start. One way to show all of these is via a table, showing for each job step all the job steps that must be completed before that job step can be executed. A second way to show all of these is via a block diagram or *graph:* each job is a node in a graph, with arrows into each node emanating from job step nodes that must be completed *prior* to that job step. This is a *directed* graph: the arrows have direction. This graph has no *cycles:* there is no chain of arrows that completes a closed chain or cycle. This is an *acyclic* graph.

Example: Consider the following set of six jobs with a given precedence relationship:

Table 2.9.Six Job Precedence Relationships

This Job	Must Be Preceded By	This Job
2		1
3		1
4		3
5		2,6
7		4,5

The precedence relationships are summarized in the directed acyclic graph shown in Figure 2.22.

Each job can have its own *weight* to reflect the relative importance of a job: $W_K, K=1,...,N$. A nondecreasing real valued *cost* function, $F_K(t)$, measuring the cost incurred if J_K is completed at time t.

2.14.2 Resource Configuration There are P processors, with each processor being capable of executing a job step at a *different* rate. Each step of each job will require a given amount of processing time. Let T_{IKM} denote the amount of processing time required at step $I=1,...,S_K$ for job $K=1,...,N$ on processor $M=1,...,P$. If all processors are identical, we will *ignore* or suppress the subscript M due to different types of processors. If $T_{IKM}=\infty$ then we assume

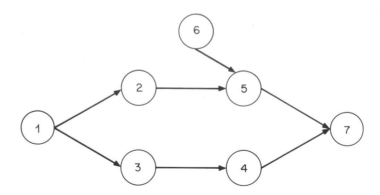

Figure 2.22.Precedence Constraints for Six Jobs

this step of this job will *never* by convention be executed on that processor (because it will take forever).

Each job will require one processor, which may be thought of as an *active* resource, and zero or more *passive* resources, such as memory or storage, an operating system file, and so forth. R_{IKL} denotes the amount of passive resources $L=0,...,\tilde{R}$ (possibly zero) required by job $J_K, K=1,...,N$ at step $I=1,...,S_K$. We assume that the total amount of resource type L available will not be exceeded by any one step of any one job.

2.14.3 Scheduling Policy The scheduling policy determines which job is executed at any given instant of time with a given set of resources. Competition for resources occurs *implicitly* via scheduling of resources, and *explicitly* via cooperation and precedence ordering between jobs.

We assume that if work is ready to be executed, that it will immediately be assigned to an idle processor (this rules out a variety of pathological situations from this point on).

Schedules can be *nonpreemptive* where once a job begins execution it runs to completion, or *preemptive* where once a job begins execution it can be interrupted by more urgent jobs. Preemptive scheduling can involve *resuming* execution at the point of interruption (and hence we call these schedules *preemptive resume)* or *repeating* execution anew (and hence we call these schedules *preemptive repeat)* The total amount of resource L available, $\tilde{R}_L, L=0,...,M$, cannot be exceeded at any instant of time by any allowable scheduling rule.

2.14.4 Performance Measures We will focus on a variety of performance measures for jobs.

Here are some examples of job oriented performance measures:

- The *completion time* for job J_K, denoted C_K

- The *lateness* for job J_K, denoted $L_K \equiv C_K - D_K$

- The *tardiness* for job J_K, denoted $T_K \equiv max[0, L_K]$

Here are some examples of system oriented performance measures:

- The total time required to execute all the jobs, T_{finish}, assuming all the ready times are *zero,* i.e., the jobs are all present at the same initial time. This is called the *make span* because it is the span of time it takes to make or execute all jobs

- The mean throughput rate, which is the total number of jobs executed divided by the total time interval

$$mean \ throughput \ rate = \frac{N}{T_{finish}}$$

- The fraction of time each processor is busy *at all* or its *utilization*

- The fraction of time two different processors are *simultaneously* busy

EXERCISE: Can you think of any more?

2.14.5 Parallelism and Concurrency Two jobs are said to be executing *concurrently* at a given time t if both started execution before time t and *neither* has completed execution. An example might be two programs that have been submitted by different people to be link edited and compiled on the same processor and are waiting for the compilation to be completed: the processor is *concurrently* executing each job, but at any given instant of time *one* job is using the single processor. This is called *logical* concurrency.

Two jobs are said to be executing in *parallel* at a given time t if both are actively being executed or moving to completion at time t. An example would be a computer system with a single processor and a single secondary storage unit: two units can be executing in parallel, one using the processor and one using the secondary storage unit, at the same instant of time, providing the operating system supports this mode of operation. This is called *physical* concurrency.

2.14.6 Additional Reading

[1] R.L.Graham, E.L.Lawler, J.K.Lenstra, A.H.G.Rinnooy Kan, *Optimization and Approximation in Deterministic Sequencing and Scheduling: A Survey,* Annals of Discrete Mathematics, **5,** 287-

326(1979).

[2]   E.G.Coffman, Jr. (editor), **Computer and Job Shop Scheduling Theory,** Wiley, NY, 1976.

[3]   M.S.Bakshi, S.R.Arora, *The Sequencing Problem,* Management Science, **16,** B247-263 (1969).

2.15 A Packet Switching System

A computer communication system receives packets from any of L lines and transmits packets over the same L lines. Two types of packets can be received: data packets and control packets. Control packets are required to set up a communication session between a transmitter and receiver pair, to acknowledge proper receipt of W data packets, and to conclude a communication session between a transmitter and receiver pair. Data packets are made up of pieces of a message stream between a transmitter and receiver. Each transmitter and receiver session demands one logical or passive resource, a *virtual circuit* that will be set up over a single *physical circuit* to allow time division multiplexing or sharing of the physical circuit among multiple pairs of transmitters and receivers. Two types of processors are available called slow and fast: the slow processor requires less buffering for each data packet than the fast processor, and is less expensive. For simplicity, the ready time of each control and data packet is assumed to be zero, i.e., all packets are available at time zero. Control packets have a deadline or urgency of ten milliseconds, while data packets have a deadline or urgency of one hundred milliseconds. A nonpreemptive schedule is used: once execution is begun, a packet is processed to completion. The table below summarizes the information needed to specify the performance of this system:

Table 2.10.Job Steps

Step	Job	Type	Can Be Preempted By
1	Control	Startup	Step 2
2	Control	Takedown	No Job
3	Data	Transmit	Step 1,2

The resources required are summarized below:

Table 2.11.Job Step Resource Requirements

Job Step	Slow Processor		Fast Processor		Passive Resources	
	Time	Buffer	Time	Buffer	VC	Packet ID
1	5 msec	32 Bytes	2 msec	64 Bytes	1	1
2	7 msec	32 Bytes	4 msec	64 Bytes	1	1
3	10 msec	512 Bytes	5 msec	1024 Bytes	1	1

The following information is available concerning the performance *goals* of the system:

Table 2.12.Packet Switching System Performance Goals

Step	Criterion	Normal Business Hour	Peak Business Hour
1	Window	50 msec	200 msec
2	Window	25 msec	100 msec
3	Window	100 msec	500 msec
1	Weight	10	100
2	Weight	20	500
3	Weight	1	10
1	Cost	1	5
2	Cost	2	10
3	Cost	2	8

Finally, the precedence ordering for jobs is as follows

Table 2.13.Job Step Precedence Ordering

This Step	Must Be Preceded By	This Step
2		1,3
3		1

EXERCISE: Compare the performance during a normal and peak business hour of a static priority schedule with priority ordering (2,1,3) with a deadline priority schedule.

2.15.1 Additional Reading

[1] R.W.Conway, W.L.Maxwell, L.W.Miller, **Theory of Scheduling,** Chapters 1-7, Addison Wesley, Reading, Mass., 1967.

[2] E.G.Coffman (editor); J.L.Bruno, E.G.Coffman, Jr., R.L.Graham, W.H.Kohler, R.Sethi, K.Steiglitz, J.D.Ullman (coauthors), **Computer and Job-Shop Scheduling Theory,** Wiley, New York, 1976.

[3] R.L.Graham, *Combinatorial Scheduling Theory,* pp.183-211, in **Mathematics Today: Twelve Informal Essays,** edited by L.A.Steen, Springer-Verlag, NY, 1978.

[4] M.R.Garey, R.L.Graham, *Bounds for Multiprocessor Scheduling with Resource Constraints,* SIAM J.Computing, **4,** 187-200 (1975).

[5] M.R.Garey, R.L.Graham, D.S.Johnson, *Performance Guarantees for Scheduling Algorithms,* Operations Research, **26,** 3-21 (1978).

[6] D.J.Kuck, *A Survey of Parallel Machine Organization and Programming,* Computing Surveys, **9** (1), 29-59 (1977).

[7] J.T.Schwartz, *Ultracomputers,* ACM Transactions on Programming Languages and Systems, **2** (4), 484-521 (1980).

[8]   G.R.Andrews, F.B.Schneider, *Concepts and Notations for Concurrent Programming,* Computing Surveys, **15** (1), 3-43 (1983).

Problems

1) Two N tuples denoted by $\underline{X}=(X_1,...,X_N)$ and $\underline{Y}=(Y_1,...,Y_N)$ are inputs to a computer system. The output of the system is the scalar inner product, denoted $<\underline{X},\underline{Y}>$, of the two inputs:

$$<\underline{X},\underline{Y}> = \sum_{K=1}^{N} X_K Y_K$$

P identical processors are used to evaluate the inner product expression. Each processor is capable of executing one addition or one multiplication in one second.

A. For $P=1$ and $N=16$ find a schedule that minimizes the total time, T_{finish}, required to evaluate one inner product $<\underline{X},\underline{Y}>$.

B. For $P=4$ processors and $N=16$ find a schedule that minimizes T_{finish} to evaluate one inner product $<\underline{X},\underline{Y}>$. Compute the speedup in going from one to four processors.

C. Repeat all the above for $N=17$

D. If the number of inputs is a power of two, i.e., $N=2^J, J=1,2,...$ and the number of processors is a power of two, i.e., $P=2^K, K=1,2,...$, show that the total time T_{finish} required to evaluate an inner product need not exceed

$$\left\lceil \frac{2N}{P} \right\rceil - 1 + \left\lceil \log_2(P) \right\rceil$$

where

$$\lceil X \rceil = \textit{smallest integer greater than or equal to } X$$

2) A computer system takes as input a sixteen tuple $(A_1,..,A_{16})$ and generates a scalar output X:

$$X = A_1(A_2 + A_3(A_4 + A_5(A_6 +.. + A_{13}(A_{14} + A_{15}A_{16}))))))$$

A. One processor is used to evaluate X. The binary operations of operations of addition and multiplication each take one unit of time to perform. How long does it take to evaluate X?

B. With two processors, show that it is possible to evaluate X in ten units of time.

3) Nine jobs are present at time zero. Each job requires one processor for the amount of time shown below:

Table 2.14.Job Execution Time

Job	Time	Job	Time	Job	Time
1	3	4	2	7	4
2	2	5	4	8	4
3	2	6	4	9	9

Each job requires one processor for execution; no job can execute in parallel with itself. Nonpreemptive scheduling is used: once a job begins execution, it runs to completion. These jobs are not independent, but have a precedence ordering:

Table 2.15.Job Precedence

This Job	Must Be Preceeded By	This Job
9		1
5,6,7,8		4

A. Construct a schedule for three processors. What is the minimum time required to complete all nine jobs?

B. Repeat part (A) for two processors

C. Repeat part (A) for four processors

D. Repeat part (A) with three processors but all the execution times reduced by one

E. Repeat part (A) with three processors but the precedence constraint is now weakened as shown in the table below:

Table 2.16.Job Precedence Summary

This Job	Must Be Preceeded By	This Job
9		1
7,8		4

4) You have just been put in charge of an assembly line for bicycle manufacturing. The first thing you learn is that assembling a bicycle is broken up into a number of specific smaller jobs:

- **FP--** Frame preparation, including installation of the front fork and fenders

- **FW--** Mounting and front wheel alignment

- **BW--** Mounting and back wheel alignment

- **DE--** Attaching the derailleur to the frame

- **GC--** Attaching the gear cluster

- **CW--** Attaching the chain wheel to the crank

- **CR--** Attaching the crank and chain wheel to the frame

- **RP--** Mounting right pedal and toe clip

- **LP--** Mounting left pedal and toe clip

- **FA--** Final attachments (including mounting and adjustment of handlebars, seat, brakes)

Each step takes a person a given number of minutes, summarized in the table below:

Table 2.17. Job Step Summary

Job	FP	FW	BW	DE	GC	CW	CR	RP	LP	FA
Time(Minutes)	7	7	7	2	3	2	2	8	8	18

Certain jobs must be done before others: try mounting the front fork to the bicycle frame if the brake cables are already attached! The table below summarizes which jobs must precede which others during assembly:

Table 2.18. Job Precedence Summary

This Job	Must Be Preceded By	These Jobs
FA		FP,FW,BW,GC,DE
BW		GC,DE,FP
FW		FP
GC,CW		DE
LP,RP		CR,CW,GC
CR		CW

Because of space and equipment constraints, the twenty assemblers are paired into ten teams of two people each. The goal is to have each team assemble fifteen bicycles in one eight hour shift. The factory quota is one hundred fifty bicycles assembled in one eight hour shift. For a team of two assemblers, the standard priority schedule has been FP, DE, CW, CR, GC, FW, BW, LP, FA, RP. This means that each assembler scans this list of work, highest priority on down, until a job is found that can be done while meeting the precedence constraints. The assembler will work on this job until it is finished, with no interruptions.

A.   Plot the activity of each assembler on a team versus time for each bicycle. Will the factory meet its quota?

B.   You rent all electric power tools for all assemblers. This reduces the time to do each job by one minute. For the standard schedule plot the activity of each assembler versus time for one bicycle. Will the factory meet its quota?

C.   You return the rented tools, and hire a third assembler for each team. For the standard schedule, plot the activity of each assembler versus time for one bicycle. Will the factory meet its quota?

D.   For two assemblers per team, using a critical path schedule, plot the activity of each assembler versus time for one bicycle. Will the factory meet its quota?

E.   **BONUS:** Repeat B),C) using a critical path schedule. Will the factory meet its quota?

5) Four processors are arranged in a pipeline to execute a stream of jobs.

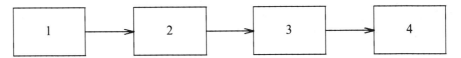

Four Stage Processor Pipeline

Six jobs are executed on this system, and require the following processing at each step:

Table 2.19.Processing Times per Step

Job	Step 1	Step 2	Step 3	Step 4
1	4	4	5	4
2	2	5	8	2
3	3	6	7	4
4	1	7	5	3
5	4	4	5	3
6	2	5	5	1

A.   Construct a schedule for executing the six jobs on this processor pipeline.

B.   Compute the mean flow time for the above schedule:

$$E(F) = \frac{1}{N}\sum_{K=1}^{N} F_K \quad N=6$$

C. Let $J(t)$ denote the number of jobs in the system, either waiting to be executed or in execution, at time t. Calculate the mean number of jobs in the system, $E(N)$:

$$E(N) = \frac{1}{T_F} \int_0^{T_F} J(t)\,dt$$

D. Show that

$$E(N) = \frac{N}{T_F} E(F)$$

6) During passage through a computer system, a job is processed by two different processors in sequence. We denote by the ordered pair (T_1, T_2) the processing time required at the first stage T_1 and at the second stage T_2 by each job. Assume that six (6) jobs arrive simultaneously for service. The processing times for this workload are given by (4,2), (2,3), (3,1), (3,1), (6,4), (2,4). Construct a schedule which processes the six jobs in the minimum time.

7) A system consists of P identical processors, each of which can execute *IPS* maximum assembly language instructions per second. This system must execute N identical tasks, all present at an initial time say zero, and each of which comprises N_{inst} assembly language instructions. The time to execute one task on one processor is $T_{P=1}$ and is given by

$$N_{inst} = T_{P=1}\, IPS \quad \rightarrow \quad T_{P=1} = \frac{N_{inst}}{IPS}$$

With P processors, the time required to execute a single task is T_P. The *speedup* is defined as the ratio of the single to multiple processor (single task) execution times:

$$speedup = \frac{T_{P=1}}{T_P}$$

A. If $\pi(K), K=1,\ldots,P$ denotes the fraction of time K processors are simultaneously active executing work, show that

$$speedup = mean\ number\ of\ busy\ processors = \sum_{K=1}^{P} \pi(K)K$$

B. Let $N_{inst}(K)$ denote the number of instructions executed by K simultaneously active processors. Show that

$$N_{inst}(K) = \pi(K)T_P\,[K\ IPS] \quad K=1,2,\ldots,P$$

C. With P processors, F(K), K=1,...,P, denotes the fraction of assembly language instructions that are executed concurrently or in parallel on K processors. Show that

$$F(K) = \frac{N_{inst}(K)}{\sum_{J=1}^{P} N_{inst}(J)} \quad K=1,2,..,P$$

D. Show that

$$speedup = \frac{1}{\sum_{K=1}^{P} \frac{F(K)}{K}}$$

E. We wish to evaluate repetitively sums consisting of fifteen terms:

$$Y = A_1 + \cdots + A_{15}$$

for different choices of $A_K, K=1,...,15$. We have four processors, (P=4); each processor can evaluate one partial sum at a time. The total sum can be evaluated in five steps as follows:

Table 2.20. Four Processor Evaluation of Fifteen Term Summations

Step	Processor One	Processor Two	Processor Three	Processor Four
1	$B_1=A_1+A_2$	$B_2=A_3+A_4$	$B_3=A_5+A_6$	$B_4=A_7+A_8$
2	$B_5=A_9+A_{10}$	$B_6=A_{11}+A_{12}$	$B_7=A_{13}+A_{14}$	$B_8=A_{15}+B_1$
3	$C_1=B_2+B_3$	$C_2=B_4+B_5$	$C_3=B_6+B_7$	IDLE
4	$D_1=B_8+C_1$	$D_2=C_2+C_3$	IDLE	IDLE
5	$Y=D_1+D_2$	IDLE	IDLE	IDLE

The intermediate scratch values are denoted by $B_1,...,B_8,C_1,...,C_3$ and D_1,D_2 in the steps above. Find $\pi(K),F(K);K=1,2,3,4$. Compute the speedup factor directly from the table above, and from $\pi(K)$ and $F(K)$ directly.

F. For F(K)=1/P, show that

$$speedup = \frac{P}{\sum_{K=1}^{P} \frac{1}{K}} \approx \frac{P}{ln(P+1)+\gamma} \quad as \ P \rightarrow \infty$$

$$where \ \gamma = Euler's \ constant = 0.5772156649$$

G. Verify that the algorithm for evaluating fifteen term summations with four processors obeys the following formula:

$$maximum\ speedup = \cfrac{P}{\cfrac{P}{N-1}\left\lceil\cfrac{N}{P}\right\rceil - \cfrac{P}{N-1} + \cfrac{P\log_2[min(N,P)]}{N-1}}$$

$$\lceil x \rceil = smallest\ integer\ greater\ than\ or\ equal\ to\ x$$

It can be shown* that if we wish to evaluate N degree polynomials on P processors,

$$Y = \sum_{K=0}^{N} A_K\ X^K$$

$$maximum\ speedup = \frac{P}{\log_2 P}\ \cfrac{1}{1 + \cfrac{P\ F(P)}{2N\log_2 P}} \qquad \lim_{P\to\infty}\frac{F(P)}{\log_2 P} \to 0$$

8) Messages are processed by a transmitter and then a receiver. The order of processing messages at the transmitter and receiver is identical. The processing time for message K by the transmitter is denoted by T_K, and by the receiver is denoted by R_K. There are a total of N messages to be transmitted at time zero. We define $T_{N+1}=0$, $R_0=0$ for simplicity. The receiver can buffer at most two messages at any one time; once the receiver has two messages, the transmitter stops processing messages until the receiver only has one message.

A. What are the precedence relations for processing N messages?

B. Show that the total time or make span to process all N messages is given by

$$make\ span = T_F = \sum_{K=0}^{N}\max\left[T_{K+1}, R_K\right]$$

C. Show that the total time or make span to process all N messages can be written as

$$make\ span = T_{finish} = \sum_{K=1}^{N}(T_K + R_K) - \sum_{K=1}^{N-1}\min\left[T_{K+1}, R_K\right]$$

D. The mean throughput rate is defined as

---

* I.Munro, M.Paterson, *Optimal Algorithms for Parallel Polynomial Evaluation,* Journal of Computer System Science, **7,** 189 (1973).

$$mean\ throughput\ rate\ =\ \lim_{N \to \infty} \frac{N}{T_{finish}}$$

Show that

$$mean\ throughput\ rate\ =\ \frac{1}{E[\max(T,R)]}$$

$$E[max\,(T,R)] \equiv \lim_{N \to \infty} \frac{1}{N} \sum_{K=1}^{N} max\,(T_{K+1},R_K)$$

where $E[max\,(T,R)]$ is the average of the maximum of the transmitter and receiver time per message. For $T_K=T=constant$, $R_K=R=constant$, explicitly evaluate this expression. For $R=1$ and $T=1,0.5,0.2$ what is the mean throughput rate?

E. Show that

$$T_{finish} \geqslant max\left[R_N + \sum_{K=1}^{N} T_K, T_1 + \sum_{K=1}^{N} R_K\right]$$

F. What changes if the receiver can buffer an infinite number of messages?

CHAPTER 3: **DATA ANALYSIS AND SIMULATION**

The widespread availability of inexpensive computing power is having a major impact on data analysis. In times to come, greater volumes of data be collected and analyzed than ever before, and the complexity of the data will mushroom. Computers allow us to carry out calculations and displays of data that were literally *unthinkable* only a decade ago. This will have a profound impact on the design of computer systems: an integral part of the design will be data gathering and analysis tools to determine system performance. As more and more data is gathered on each design, iterations will be carried out based on inferences from data.

Because so much data can be gathered (literally millions of items per day), it is essential that the data be stored and displayed in a manner that guides someone in drawing cause and effect inferences quickly. This means imposing *some* structure at the outset on the data gathering, storage and display. This structure is a *model*. All models imposed on the data should be checked against both *analytic* or *simulation* models. This could occur at any point in a product life cycle of a computer communication system: during initial conception, during development, during manufacturing, and on into installation, operations, maintenance, repair and salvage. Digital simulation provides a useful and effective adjunct to direct analytical evaluation of communication system performance. Indeed, there are many situations where explicit performance evaluation defies analysis and meaningful results can be obtained only through either actual prototype hardware and software evaluation or digital computer simulations. The former approach is generally cumbersome, expensive, time-consuming, and relatively inflexible. These are considerations which typically weigh heavily in favor of digital simulation.

Simulation also frees the analyst from a great deal of repetitive work involved in substituting numbers into formulae and tables and enables the analyst to concentrate on results. Another advantage is the insight into system performance provided, both by the modeling process itself and by the experience gained from simulation experiments. Again, computers can assist us: it may be quite difficult or expensive to gather data or measurements, so computer assisted analysis can quantify the importance of the data gathering and analysis procedures.

3.1 Methodology

There are two stages in this methodology. The first is a collection of techniques that together are called *exploratory data analysis* to determine if any patterns arise. For example, if we have one hundred items of data, and ninety nine of them are between zero and one, and one is at five hundred, what do we do: Do we assume the ninety nine are fine and discard the one outlying value? Do we assume none of the hundred data are valid because the one outlying value uncovered a fundamental flaw in the measurement technique? Our point is that a great deal of judgement is required at this stage, intuition built upon practice, hours and hours of checks and cross checks to ascertain that in fact the data gathered are valid, hold together, and tell a story. Put differently, exploratory data analysis is an art, and some people are better artists than others.

A second stage is to summarize the data using a small number of parameters that comprise a *model* which must be tested on the data and then used to *predict* wholly new operations. The model can be based on a mathematical *analysis* or it can be *algorithmic* in nature, a *simulation* model. In this chapter we focus on exploratory data analysis, and on simulation models, while the remainder of the book focuses on analytic models for the second stage.

This is an iterative process: gathering data, analyzing, and modeling, followed by more data gathering, analysis, and modeling. The trick is really knowing when to stop!

3.1.1 Additional Reading

[1]   B.Efron, *Computers and the Theory of Statistics: Thinking the Unthinkable,* SIAM Review, **21,** 460-480 (1979).

[2]   U. Grenander, R. F. Tsao, *Quantitative Methods for Evaluating Computer System Performance:A Review and Proposals,* in **Statistical Computer Performance Evaluation,** W. Freiberger (editor), Academic Press, NY, 1972.

[3]   F.Hartwig, B.E.Dearing, **Exploratory Data Analysis,** Sage Publications, Beverly Hills, 1979.

[4]   F.Mosteller, J.W.Tukey, **Data Analysis and Regression,** Addison-Wesley, Reading, Mass, 1977.

3.2 Statistics

Three types of statistics will concern us here:

- *First* order statistics such as averages or mean values

- *Second* order statistics that measure *fluctuations* about averages and *correlation* with time of the same thing or two different things

- *Distributions* or fractions of time that a given event is true

We now will examine each of these in more detail.

3.2.1 First Order Statistics Computer communication systems have *states*. This suggests we should *count* the number of times each state is entered or left, and measure the *time* the system is in each state.

Suppose that N observations are made. For example, the data might be the time intervals that a system is in a given state, say K, or the number of times a transition is made from state K to state J. Let $X_I, I=1,...,N$ denote the *Ith* observation. The mean of these observations, denoted $E(X)$, is given by

$$E(X) = \frac{1}{N} \sum_{I=1}^{N} X_I$$

For example, consider a job that goes through two steps: submission from a terminal by an operator and processing. This cycle is repeated again and again. Typical types of data that might be gathered would be

- The time spent reading and thinking and entering each job in

- The time an operator spends waiting for a response to a submission

- The time intervals the system is busy processing jobs which infers the fraction of time the system is busy at all, its *utilization,* or equivalently, the fraction of time the system is idle at all, its *idleness*

- The number of jobs submitted to the system from operators, which should be checked against the number of jobs actually executed by the system. This would infer the mean throughput rate: the number of jobs executed over the observation time interval.

EXERCISE: Can you think of any more?

3.2.2 Second Order Statistics Two types of measures are of interest here: the *fluctuations* about the mean or average, and the *correlation* between different events.

For our computer system model, we might look at the number of transitions from one state to another state, or we might measure the time the system spends in a pair of states. The measure of fluctuation is called the *variance,* denoted by σ_{XX}^2 and given by

$$\sigma_{XX}^2 = E\left[\sum_{I=1}^{N} (X_I - E(X))^2 \right]$$

The subscript XX emphasizes that this is the average of the *square* of each value of X from the total mean. A related measure of interest is its *square root* which is denoted by σ_{XX} and called the *standard deviation.* Often it will be clear from the context what the underlying variable is, such as X here, and this subscript will be dropped.

A related measure of interest is the so called *squared coefficient of variation* which is defined as the variance over the mean squared:

$$squared\ coefficient\ of\ variation\ = \frac{\sigma_{XX}^{2}}{E^2(X)}$$

In words, this measures the standard deviation in units of the mean or average. If the squared coefficient of variation is much less than one, then there is little fluctuation about the mean. The squared coefficient of variation will be *zero* when there is no fluctuation. When the squared coefficient of variation is much greater than one, there is significant variability about the mean.

The measure of correlation called the *cross-variance* is denoted by σ_{XY}^2 and is given by

$$\sigma_{XY}^2 = E\left[\sum_{I=1}^{N}(X_I - E(X))(Y_I - E(Y))\right]$$

The subscript *XY* emphasizes that this is the product of two measures of distance from the mean. Because of our definition, the variance is also called the *covariance,* because it is a special type of cross variance, one that is crossed with itself.

3.2.3 Examples In a computer system, what type of data might be aggregated into these statistics?

- The fraction of time terminals four, seven, and thirteen are busy submitting work.

- The fraction of time terminals one, five, and eight are busy submitting work *and* the system is busy executing jobs, to get a quantitative measure of *concurrency.*

- The mean response time at terminal two

- The standard deviation and squared coefficient of variation of response times for terminal five

3.2.4 Distributions The final type of statistic we will examine is the fraction of time a given event takes place, which is also the *distribution* of an event. For example, we might ask what fraction of data are less than a given threshold:

$$PROB[X_I \leqslant Y] = \textit{fraction of data less than or equal Y}$$

One example is the datum for which half the data are bigger and half are smaller, called the *median.* This would be similar to an *average* or first order statistic.

A second example is the fraction of time X per cent of the data is below a given point, such as the twenty fifth percentile (also called the first quartile) and denoted by $P_{0.25}$, or seventy fifth percentile (also called the third quartile) and denoted by $P_{0.75}$. The difference between the twenty fifth and seventy fifth percentile would be a measure of spread or fluctuation about the *median*.

A third example would be the *minimum* or *maximum*. These show the *worst* or *most atypical* pieces of data. Often these uncover errors in underlying software and hardware, and should be in every measurement package.

A fourth example would be the fifth percentile, denoted $P_{0.05}$, or the ninety fifth percentile, denoted $P_{0.95}$. These also give a measure of the *extremes* or *atypical* patterns present in the data. On the other hand, because the final five per cent of the data is being rejected or trimmed (in this sense of asking where ninety five per cent of the data lies), this statistic can test the *sensitivity* or *robustness* to extreme values of the minimum and maximum. This is like an insurance policy, that checks to see if the minimum and maximum really are telling what we think they are. Similar statements hold for the tenth percentile, $P_{0.10}$, and the ninetieth percentile, $P_{0.90}$.

All of these measures are summarized in the figure below:

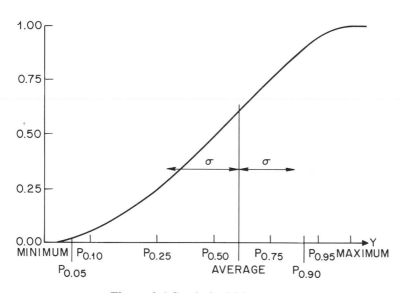

Figure 3.1.Statistical Measures

3.2.5 Sensitivity of Statistics to Assumptions Certain statistics are quite sensitive to two different phenomena:

- A small number of values may be quite different from the majority of the data, and distort the statistic

- Most of the data may be slightly off from the exact true measure, due to timing or rounding

We wish to have quantitative measures as well as heuristic measures to test to see if a statistic is in fact *robust* or insensitive to either phenomenon.

In our example in the previous chapter, ten jobs had to be printed, with one job requiring ten thousand lines to be printed, four jobs requiring two thousand lines each to be printed, and five jobs requiring one thousand lines each to be printed. The mean or average number of lines per job was

$$\text{mean number of lines per job} = \frac{1}{10} \sum_{K=1}^{10} L_K = 2{,}300 \text{ lines}$$

On the other hand, the median is simply

$$P_{0.50} = \text{median} = \tfrac{1}{2}(1{,}000 + 2{,}000) \text{ lines} = 1{,}500 \text{ lines}$$

and nine of the ten jobs are within five hundred lines of the median.

A different way of seeing this is to deal with a *trimmed* mean, where we discard an equal number of extreme values. This tests the *sensitivity* of our analysis to extreme values. If we discard the highest and lowest data, we find

$$\text{trimmed mean} = \frac{1}{8} \sum_{K=1}^{8} L_K = 1{,}500 \text{ lines}$$

which is much smaller than the total mean. If we trim two more extreme values off, we find

$$\text{trimmed mean} = \frac{1}{6} \sum_{K=1}^{6} L_K = 1{,}500 \text{ lines}$$

and hence this is stable or robust to trimming thresholds.

What about fluctuations about the mean? The variance about this mean is given by

$$\sigma_L^2 = \frac{1}{10} \sum_{K=1}^{10} [L_K - E(L)]^2 = 6{,}810{,}000 \text{ lines}^2 \quad \sigma_L = 2{,}610 \text{ lines}$$

Note that the standard deviation, which is one measure of fluctuation about the mean, is *larger* than the data for all jobs but one. Again, this suggests the job that requires much more processing than the other jobs is causing these problems. This can be seen by using the difference between the twenty fifth and seventy fifth percentiles as a measure of spread about the mean:

$$P_{0.75} = 2,000 \; lines \quad P_{0.25} = 1,000 \; lines \quad P_{0.75} - P_{0.25} = 1,000 \; lines$$

EXERCISE: Can you think of any more tests for showing if data is anomalous?

EXERCISE: Can you construct a flowchart for automating this?

3.3 Measurement Criteria

Earlier we observed that there are two types of measurement criteria: first, user oriented criteria, such as delay statistics for different transaction types, with examples being

- Arrival time to start of service, or waiting time

- Arrival time to end of service, or queueing time

- Arrival time to end of execution of a given step of a job

- Completion time minus deadline, or lateness

- The larger of zero and lateness, or tardiness

Second, system oriented criteria, such as utilization of different system resources with examples being

- Fraction of time a given single resource is busy, e.g., the fraction of time a processor is busy, or the fraction of time a disk is busy

- Fraction of time two given resources are busy, e.g., the fraction of time both the processor and the disk are simultaneously busy

- Fraction of time three given resources are busy, e.g., the fraction of time the processor, the disk, and the terminal input/output handler are simultaneously busy

- Mean rate of execution of a given type of job, or mean throughput rate

Measurements should be designed to directly measure criteria such as these, so that a direct assessment can be made: is the system in fact meeting its goals? what goals are reasonable?

The majority of measurement tools in the field at the present time are system oriented; it is quite rare to directly measure delay statistics and throughput rates for different transaction types. Why is this so? In some systems, the load placed on the system software to gather data will be comparable (or greater than!) the load we wish to measure; this is dependent on the software and hardware technology employed, and may well change in the future.

3.3.1 Additional Reading

[1] D.Ferrari, G.Serazzi, A.Zeigner, **Measurement and Tuning of Computer Systems,** Prentice-Hall, Englewood Cliffs, NJ, 1983.

3.4 An Example: Report Generation on Two Printers

As an example, consider the statistics associated with printing a set of reports using two printers attached to a computer system. First, we summarize the reports and how long each will take to print, plus the desired time interval or *window* we can tolerate for printing each report:

Table 3.1.Report Execution Time Summary

Report	Print Time	Window Time
A	3 minutes	5 minutes
B	2 minutes	3 minutes
C	10 minutes	15 minutes
D	2 minute	4 minutes
E	1 minutes	2 minutes

All reports arrive at once, i.e., all reports are ready to be executed at time *zero*. The figure below shows the completion times for one schedule where the priority is chosen according to the job letter: job A has higher priority than job B, and so forth.

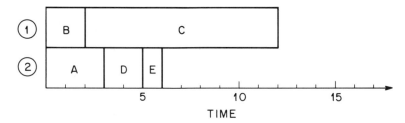

Figure 3.2.Printer Activity Using Alphabetic Priorities

All jobs are completely executed at twelve minutes past zero. For each job, we can tabulate delay statistics, and find:

Table 3.2.Alphabetic Priority Delay Statistics

Report	Completion	Waiting	Queueing	Lateness	Tardiness
A	3	0	3	-2	0
B	2	0	2	-1	0
C	12	2	12	-3	0
D	5	3	5	1	1
E	6	5	6	4	4

A variety of companion statistical measures, averaged over all jobs, are summarized below:

Here is one interpretation of this summary: The average time in system consists of an average waiting time of 2 plus an average service time of 3.6,

Table 3.3.Alphabetic Priority Job Performance Measures

Statistic	Completion	Waiting	Queueing	Lateness	Tardiness
Average	5.6	2.0	5.6	-0.2	1.0
σ	3.5	1.9	3.5	2.5	1.6
$P_{0.75}-P_{0.25}$	2.0	3.0	2.0	3.0	1.0
Minimum	2	0	2	-3	0
Maximum	12	5	12	4	4

equaling the average time in system of 5.6. The maximum tardiness is four, while the average tardiness is one. Inspection reveals that twice the standard deviation does *not* approximately equal the difference between the third and first quartile, which suggests that the one long job has significantly skewed the statistics.

What about system oriented performance criteria? These are summarized below:

Table 3.4.Alphabetic Priority System Performance Measures

Statistic	Value
Mean Throughput	5 jobs in 12 minutes
Fraction of Time Printer 1 Busy	50.0%
Fraction of Time Printer 2 Busy	100.0%
Fraction of Time Both Printers Busy	50.0%

The lack of balance in utilization between the two printers makes it evident that the one long job has significantly skewed the utilizations away from equality.

In contrast to this, we assign priorities such that the shorter the processing time of a job, the higher its priority. This attempts to let the short jobs run quickly at the expense of the long job that will take a long time anyway. The execution pattern for this schedule is shown in Figure 3.3.

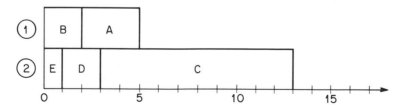

Figure 3.3.Shortest Processing Time Priority Arbitration

As above, the same statistics are tabulated for each job in Table 3.5.

Table 3.5.Shortest Processing Time Priority Delay Statistics

Report	Completion	Waiting	Queueing	Lateness	Tardiness
A	5	2	5	0	0
B	2	0	2	-1	0
C	13	3	13	-2	0
D	3	1	3	-1	0
E	1	0	1	-1	0

As before, the same job oriented statistical performance measures, averaged over all jobs, are summarized below in Table 3.6.

Table 3.6.Shortest Processing Time Job Performance Statistics

Statistic	Completion	Waiting	Queueing	Lateness	Tardiness
Average	4.8	1.2	4.8	-1	0
σ	4.3	1.2	4.3	0.6	0.0
$P_{0.75}-P_{0.25}$	1.0	2.0	1.0	0.0	0.0
Minimum	1	0	1	-2	0
Maximum	13	3	13	0	0

Here is one interpretation of this data: Each job has a mean waiting time of 1.2 plus a mean service time of 3.6, resulting in a mean queueing time of 4.8. This is smaller than the first priority arbitration rule. As with the alphabetic schedule, the one long job has skewed the standard deviation significantly more than would be expected from the difference of the two quartiles.

What about system oriented performance measures? These are summarized below:

Table 3.7.Shortest Processing Time System Performance Statistics

Statistic	Value
Mean Throughput Rate	5 jobs in 13 minutes
Fraction of Time Printer 1 Busy	38.46%
Fraction of Time Printer 2 Busy	100.0%
Fraction of Time Both Printers Busy	38.46%

The one long job has skewed the utilization of the two printers far away from equal loading.

A second point to keep in mind is that *all* five jobs are being printed, but some are printed ahead of others. This means that *logically* all jobs are being printed concurrently (actually only one job at a time can use a printer), but the choice of priorities can control the *delay* or *responsiveness* (waiting time or completion time) of a job, with the amount dependent on the workload. For these two priority arbitration rules, these differences are summarized as follows:

Judged on these measures alone, the shortest processing time arbitration rules offer superior performance to the alphabetic arbitration rules.

Table 3.8. Job Delay Statistics Summary

Performance Measure	Alphabetic Priority	Shortest Processing Time Priority
Average Completion	5.6	4.8
Average Waiting	2.0	1.2
Average Queueing	5.6	4.8
Average Lateness	-0.2	-1.0
Average Tardiness	1	0

Finally, what about system oriented performance measures:

Table 3.9. System Utilization Statistics Summary

Performance Measure	Alphabetic Priority	Shortest Processing Time Priority
Mean Throughput Rate	5 jobs/12 min	5 jobs/13 min
Fraction of Time Printer 1 Busy	50.0%	38.46%
Fraction of Time Printer 2 Busy	100.0%	100.0%
Fraction of Time Both Printers Busy	50.0%	38.46%

From the system operations point of view, it looks like a wash: neither priority scheme offers significant benefits over the other.

3.4.1 Summary Our intent here was to take two printers and five jobs and walk through a data analysis exercise of performance, from the point of view of each job and its delay, and from the point of view of the system and its operations. We did not even begin to exhaust the list of statistics that we could in fact generate for such a *simple* system. Our intent was not to bury you, the reader, with numbers, but rather to show that the key ingredients are understanding the workload (look at how the one long job impacted everything), understanding how the system executed jobs (for different schedules), and to develop techniques for making judgements. The job delay statistics carried the day for shortest processing time scheduling: the system performance statistics appeared to be comparable. Take from this the *methodology* of data analysis, and *not* the conclusions per se.

3.5 Modeling

We impose structure at the outset on the data gathered for two reasons: first, there is simply too much data so findings must be summarized in a small number of parameters; second, there are only a limited number of actions that a performance analyst can suggest. Remember that the possible changes dealt with application code, operating system, and hardware, with different costs associated with each type of change: why not focus at the outset on these three topics? what types of models or structures could we impose on the data at the outset that would suggest fruitful cause and effect changes in system performance?

Here is one such model: different types of transactions require different amounts of hardware resources (terminal processing time, data link transmission time, data base processing time, data retrieval access time, and so forth) and operating system resources (files, tables, messages, processes), and application program resources (input handler, data base manager, scheduler, communications controller). For each transaction we would log or measure the amount of each resource actually used, on a per process basis, i.e., a transaction is executed by a set of processes.

Here is a typical example of a model of a computer communication system. The system resources consist of

Table 3.10.Computer System Resources

Hardware	Amount	Operating System	Amount
Processors	3	Processes	298
Disks	7	Files	365
Links	15	Buffers	149
Disk Controllers	3	Virtual Circuits	487
Terminals	29	Semaphores	732
Terminal Controllers	5		
Tape Drive	1		

How do logical resources arise? They arise from attempting to *control* the flow of *data* through a computer communication system. Each physical and logical resource has a *name*. Each resource must be assigned to a given *location*. There is a policy for interconnecting or *routing* data and control information among the different resources: disks are connected to disk controllers, terminals to terminal controllers, and so forth. Conceptually, the logical resources are tables associated with these entities: these tables must be accessed and contention arbitrated just as with physical resources. The reason logical resources are often ignored is that a system administrator configures the system when it is initially powered up so that these resources *hopefully* will never be bottlenecks. This must be examined on a case by case basis.

Each job will be holding one or more resources at each step of execution. One possible representation of state of the system at any instant of time is what jobs hold what resources. A second possible state representation is what jobs are holding what resources and are queued waiting for other resources to become available. One system statistic related to this is the fraction of time each resource is busy and idle. One job statistic related to this is to determine what processes are busy and idle.

EXERCISE: What about the workload imposed on this system? How does this impact the measurements?

3.5.1 Additional Reading

[1]   G.E.P.Box, W.G.Hunter, J.S.Hunter, **Statistics for Experimenters,** Wiley, NY, 1978.

[2]   D.Freedman, R.Pisani, R.Purves, **Statistics,** Norton, New York, 1978.

3.6 An Illustrative Example: Directory Assistance Operator Work Times

When directory assistance operators handle queries, two steps are involved: listening to the query, typing it into a terminal, and perhaps the reading the terminal, followed by waiting for the response to the query. What is the distribution of time to listen and enter the query?

Two stages are involved in answering this question: examining a variety of nonparametric statistics which suggest naturally what distributions are reasonable candidates for what models, and a model fitting.

3.6.1 Description of the Data The times for a directory assistance operator to answer a query were measured. This was done by a stop watch and the results recorded on a paper by pencil. The 597 data were aggregated into classes or bins, with the total width of the bin being five seconds, beginning with zero. A visual inspection of the data gathered did not reveal any apparent outlying or spurious or erroneous values. The data are summarized below:

Table 3.11.Directory Assistance Operator Work Time Histogram

Number of Observations		Total	Number of Observations		Total
Greater Than	*But Less Than*	*Observed*	*Greater Than*	*But Less Than*	*Observed*
0 sec	5 sec	0	50 sec	55 sec	16
5 sec	10 sec	0	55 sec	60 sec	16
10 sec	15 sec	18	60 sec	65 sec	14
15 sec	20 sec	85	65 sec	70 sec	6
20 sec	25 sec	112	70 sec	75 sec	4
25 sec	30 sec	110	75 sec	80 sec	6
30 sec	35 sec	82	80 sec	85 sec	4
35 sec	40 sec	51	85 sec	90 sec	2
40 sec	45 sec	36	90 sec	95 sec	2
45 sec	50 sec	30	95 sec	---	3

3.6.2 Nonparametric Exploratory Data Analysis The figure below shows an empirical distribution for the data, while the next figure shows a histogram. The table below summarizes a variety of statistics computed from the observations:

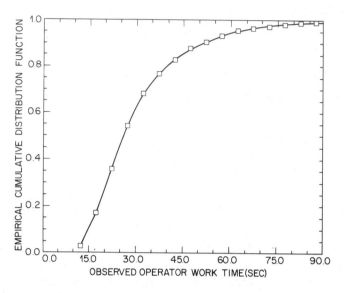

Figure 3.4. Empirical Distribution Function

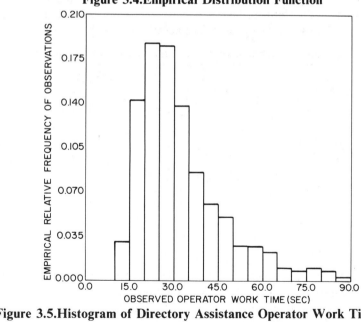

Figure 3.5. Histogram of Directory Assistance Operator Work Time Data

Table 3.12. Moment Estimates

Mean	32.77 sec
Variance	238.99 sec^2
Variance/(Mean^2)	0.2224

On the other hand, the percentile order statistics are summarized below:

Table 3.13. Order Statistics

1%	12.5 sec	75%	37.5 sec
5%	17.5 sec	90%	52.5 sec
10%	17.5 sec	95%	62.5 sec
25%	22.5 sec	99%	87.5 sec
50%	27.5 sec		

It is of interest to compare the square root of the variance, or the standard deviation, with the difference between the twenty fifth and seventy fifth percentiles:

standard deviation = 15.46 sec   *75th to 25th percentile* = 15 sec

This shows that the standard deviation significantly *underestimates* the actual fluctuation about the mean compared with the differences in the third and first quartiles.

3.6.3 Model Fitting We choose to fit the data with a gamma distribution with integer parameter. These are also called *Erlang-K* distributions, so called because each distribution is the K fold convolution of identical exponential distributions. If we let $G(X)$ denote the fraction of time an observation is less than or equal to X, then its moment generating function is given by

$$\hat{G}(z) = \int_0^\infty e^{-zX} dG(X) = \left[\frac{1}{1 + \tau z} \right]^K$$

The first two moments of this distribution are given by

$$\int_0^\infty X \, dG(X) = K\tau$$

$$\int_0^\infty X^2 \, dG(X) = K(K+1)\tau^2$$

We have already computed the first two moments of this distribution, so let's see what type of distribution might fit these moments. One way to investigate this is to examine the *ratio* of the variance to the mean squared. This is dimensionless, and in fact equals the reciprocal of the degree of the distribution:

$$\frac{variance}{(mean)^2} = \frac{1}{K}$$

The data suggests this ratio is 0.224, so an Erlang-4 or Erlang-5 might be an adequate fit.

A quantile quantile plot is used to fit the data to the model. On the horizontal axis sorted observations are plotted. For each observation, there is a corresponding quantile Q, i.e., that fraction of the data that is less than or equal to that observation. We now ask what quantile in the model distribution yields the same value of Q, and choose that for the vertical axis. If the model quantiles and observed quantiles are identical, the plot should be a straight line with slope unity. We will tune the model parameters until we have a visual straight line fit!

The figures below show different quantile quantile plots for an Erlang K distribution, where K=1,2,3,4,5.

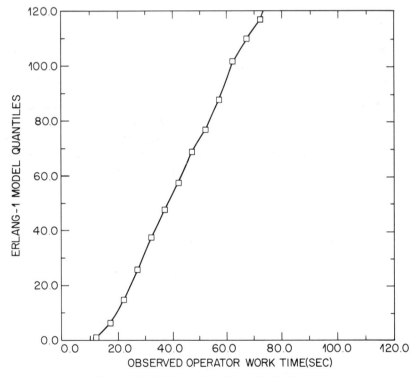

Figure 3.6.Erlang 1 vs Data Q-Q Plot

As is evident, an Erlang 1 or exponential distribution does *not* match the data very well.

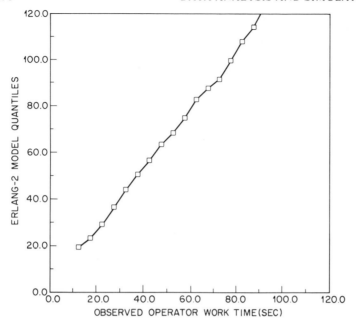

Figure 3.7.Erlang 2 vs Data Q-Q Plot

An Erlang 2 does much better than an Erlang 1 at fitting the data, but the match is still not very good.

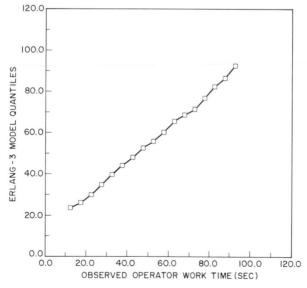

Figure 3.8.Erlang 3 vs Data Q-Q Plot

An Erlang 3 appears to do an excellent job of fitting the data.

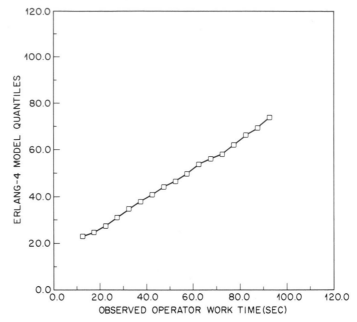

Figure 3.9.Erlang 4 vs Data Q-Q Plot

An Erlang 4 does not do as well as an Erlang 3 at fitting the data.

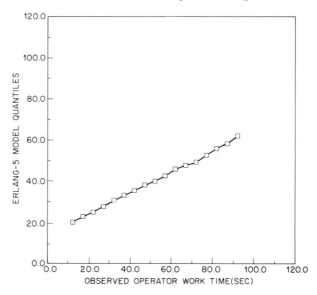

Figure 3.10.Erlang 5 vs Data Q-Q Plot

An Erlang 5 does worse than an Erlang 4 in fitting the data.

The Erlang 3 comes closest to fitting the data over the *entire* range.

One way to quantify goodness of fit of model to data besides eye ball is to check an error measure. We define *local* error as $e_K = |q_{model,K} - q_{data,K}|$ where $q_{model,K}$ is the Kth model quantile, and $q_{data,K}$ is the Kth data quantile, and K=1,...,N. The first measure we will use is the mean absolute deviation of data from the model, denoted E_1:

$$E_1 = \frac{1}{N} \sum_{K=1}^{N} e_K$$

The second measure is the square root of the mean square deviation, denoted E_2:

$$E_2 = \left[\frac{1}{N} \sum_{K=1}^{N} e_K^2 \right]^{1/2}$$

The third measure is the maximum deviation of the data from the model, denoted E_{max}:

$$E_{max} = \max_{K=1,...,N} e_K$$

The table below summarizes the calculations for each measure of error:

Table 3.14. Error Criterion Summary

Model	E_1	E_2	E_{max}
Erlang 1	29.5	38.1	81.0
Erlang 2	15.6	17.5	31.3
Erlang 3	4.0	5.2	11.1
Erlang 4	8.3	10.2	18.4
Erlang 5	13.1	16.5	30.3

This suggests the Erlang 3 is the best model, confirming the graphical test.

3.6.4 Additional Reading

[1] M.B.Wilk, R.Gnanadesikan, *Probability Plotting Methods for the Analysis of Data,* Biometrika, **55**, 1-17 (1968).

3.7 Measurement Tools

There are two types of tools for measuring system traffic handling characteristics, hardware monitors and software monitors.

3.7.1 Hardware Monitors A hardware monitor might consist of a set of high impedance probes (much as are found in high performance oscilloscopes), a logic plugboard, a set of counters, and a display or recorder of some sort. The probes are attached to memory locations, registers, bus connectors, and so forth, as wished, and interface to the logic plugboard. The logic plugboard is used to count the number of transitions of a given type that a probe measures: number of clock cycles that the processor or disk controller is busy, number of clock cycles that both the processor and disk controller are busy, and so forth. The display or recorder presents this information to a human in a useful manner, or records it for processing elsewhere. One trend today is to build the hardware performance monitoring capabilities directly into the computer communication system hardware, and to allow remote diagnostic capabilities to also be built in. The value of this in field service and support can be immense: a remote site can notify a central repair bureau site of a failure (either transient or permanent), the central site with trained personnel can carry out specialized tests, and take an appropriate action, often without intervention of the remote site personnel.

3.7.2 Software Monitors A software monitor makes use of physical resources, unlike the hardware monitor, and thus can place some load on the system. How much of a load depends upon a variety of factors: how frequently is the monitor invoked, how many resources are consumed per invocation, and so forth. In practice the load placed on any one device by the measurement tool should be negligible, but in point of fact for current systems it is difficult to drop the measurement load utilization below ten per cent. On the other hand, a great deal of flexibility is gained in software versus hardware monitoring, and the timeliness of the information can be invaluable. One approach to the problem of measurement load is to simply insert software modules at the outset of system design that consume resources but do no useful work: as the system software monitor is installed, more and more of these extraneous modules are removed, and no one knows the difference!

3.7.3 Putting It All Together How do we use these tools? First, we must start up the system with a controlled load, and then determine that the measurements being gathered have stabilized. Second, we must examine the data to determine if the system behavior is stationary: do certain events occur at five or ten or sixty minute time intervals that will impact performance? Put differently, when do we stop the measurements? The measurements can be either event driven, i.e., gathered only at those time instants when certain events have occurred, e.g., after one thousand transactions have been processed, or clock driven, i.e., gathered at evenly spaced time instants. The load placed on the system by event driven monitors is often much greater than clock driven monitors, but the event driven monitor may be more useful and flexible for interpreting data.

3.7.4 Example Here is an illustrative set of measurements that might be gathered on a computer communication system:

- Processors--Busy (application, monitor, system) or idle (blocked or true idle), system buffer hit rate, cache hit rate, time from when a process is ready to run until it runs

- Disks--Busy (seeking, transferring) or idle, number of requests per unit time, number of reads, number of writes, number of swaps, number of characters in/out

- Disk Controllers--Busy or idle, number of characters in/out, number of reads, number of writes

- Links--Busy or idle, number of characters in/out, number of reads, number of writes

- Terminals--Busy or idle, number of characters in/out, number of reads, number of writes, time from last character input until first character output

- Terminal controllers--Busy or idle, number of characters in/out, number of reads, number of writes

- Process--Busy or idle (blocked or true idle), number of context switches per unit time, number of characters in/out, number of page faults, number of active pages per unit time, number of messages in/out, number of files opened/closed, number of reads, number of writes

- Files--Busy or idle (locked or true idle), number of reads, number of writes, number of changes, number of characters in/out

EXERCISE: Can you think of any more?

3.7.5 Additional Reading

[1] D.Ferrari, G.Serazzi, Λ.Zeigner, **Measurement and Tuning of Computer Systems,** Prentice-Hall, Englewood Cliffs, NJ, 1983.

[2] P.A.W.Lewis, G.S.Shedler, *Empirically Derived Micromodels for Sequences of Page Exceptions,* IBM J.Research and Development, **12,** 86-100 (1973).

[3] S.Sherman, F.Baskett III, J.C.Browne, *Trace-Driven Modeling and Analysis of CPU Scheduling in a Multiprogramming System* Communications of the ACM, **15** (12), 1063-1069 (1972).

[4] D.W.Clark, *Cache Performance in the VAX-11/780,* ACM Transactions on Computer Systems, **1** (1), 24-37 (1983).

3.8 Data Analysis and Interpretation

How do we interpret data? With great care! Data can be aggregated in a variety of ways: the utilization of a given hardware device can be found by simply measuring the total time it is busy and then dividing by the total measurement time interval. What good is this? Bottlenecks, hardware resources that are completely utilized can be spotted quickly, and a variety of secondary avenues can now be explored. Why is the hardware device busy? Is it intrinsic to the task it must do, i.e., more resources of that type are needed?

Is it a software error, e.g., a print statement was inadvertently left in the code? Is it a structural problem of the operating system or application code using some logical resource, e.g., a file, again and again when in fact the application or operating system could be changed and this problem would simply not occur? Again, the consequences of each of these avenues must be quantified before choosing one.

How can we aid this process? By graphically plotting utilization of one or more devices versus time: this will show, first of all, which devices are bottlenecks, and second of all the correlation between the utilization of different devices. A picture here is worth everything! Next, we can repeat this procedure for different processes versus time. Does this picture of what is actually taking place match what should take place: is there an error in the software? This approach can help to uncover it.

How do we do this in practice? First, we develop a clear picture of how control and data interact for each step of each job. Second, we examine the utilization of each resource: which resources are close to complete utilization, which are not?

Third, we examine which processes and files are associated with those resources that are generating this load, and attempt to see which of these entities are generating the majority of the load on the bottleneck

Fourth, we ask ourselves if this is reasonable: maybe there is an error, maybe there is no reason for this to be so, yet it is! If this is reasonable, we go to the next step.

Fifth, the evaluation of alternatives, either hardware or operating system or application software. In any event, there is a bottleneck in the system: if it is not acceptable, the bottleneck should be moved to some other resource. If it cannot be moved to some other resource, then perhaps scheduling of the bottleneck to meet delay goals is possible.

3.9 Simulation

What are the stages in doing a simulation?

- Model Formulation--Gathering a precise description of the arrival statistics and resources consumed for each transaction type, along with the policies for ameliorating contention for resources

- Model Implementation--Programming the model in a language (e.g., assembler, BASIC, FORTRAN, GPSS, and so forth) to match the formulation

- Model Validation--Generating controlled loads with known behavior on subsystems or modules, then on aggregations of modules, and finally on the whole system, and matching that behavior against expectations with negligible discrepancy

- Experimental Design--Creating a variety of controlled loads with unknown behavior; often the time required to carry out all experiments can prove prohibitive, and systematic techniques must be employed

- Data Analysis--Displaying the measurements using the tools described earlier in order to gather cause and effect inferences concerning behavior

The figure below shows a time line of a simulation. We note three distinct items there:

- Event--Change in state of system entity

- Activity--Collection of operations that change state of entity

- Process--Sequence of events ordered in time

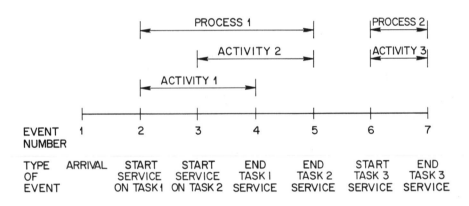

Figure 3.11.Representative Timing Diagram of a Simulation

In this figure the latter portion of activity I and the first portion of activity II can be executed concurrently, but activity III must be done serially.

The table below summarizes some simulation languages that are in widespread use and the method they use for timing control.

Table 3.15.Examples of Simulation Languages

Event Scheduling	Activity Scanning	Process Interaction
GASP	CSL	GPSS
SIMSCRIPT		SIMULA

Any simulation must present evidence of

- Stationarity--Are initial start up transients still in evidence? What about shut down transients? How repeatable is the experiment? Or are the transients really what is of interest?

- Variability--Are fluctuations severe? What types of confidence intervals or error brackets are present?

- Correlation--What types of time scales are evident? Do all events occur on the same time scale or are some short relative to others: what impact might this have? Is there coupling between events, activities, processes?

A wealth of information on these topics is found in the reading, and elsewhere.

3.9.1 Additional Reading

[1] G.S.Fishman, **Concepts and Methods in Discrete Event Digital Simulation,** Wiley, NY, 1973.

[2] S.H.Fuller, *Performance Evaluation,* in **Introduction to Computer Architecture,** H.Stone (editor), Science Research Associates, Chicago, Illinois, 1975.

[3] H.Kobayashi, **Modeling and Analysis: An Introduction to System Performance Evaluation Methodology,** Addison Wesley, Reading, Mass., 1978.

3.10 The Structure and Mechanics of Simulation

In order to provide a maximum flexibility, simulation software packages used to aid communication systems analysis and design should have a modular structure. Most of the software packages that are in use now are made up of four major components:

- model library

- system configuration tools

- simulation exercise tools

- post processor tools

The system configuration tools select a set of models of functional blocks from the model library and connect them in the desired topology as specified by the block diagram of the system being designed. Parameters of various functional blocks are specified either when the system is being configured or during the execution of the simulation which is supervised by the simulation exercise tools. Time histories of events at various points in the system are generated and stored by the simulation exercise tools. These time histories are examined by the post processing tools at the conclusion of the simulation run, and performance measures are computed from the time histories. At the end of a simulation, the design engineer uses the post processor output to verify if the performance requirements and design constraints are met. If the design objectives are not met, then several iterations are made until a suitable design is found.

3.10.1 Simulation and Programming Languages Software should be written in a higher level (than assembly language) *programming* language such as FORTRAN, PASCAL or C. Unfortunately, these languages do *not* allow input via block diagrams, which requires a preprocessor *simulation* language description of the system being analyzed or designed. This approach lends itself to portability and frees the user from having to know the details of the underlying operating system and hardware configuration of the simulation facility. For discrete event simulation, three widely used languages are GPSS, SIMSCRIPT and GASP. Each of these are preprocessors to a lower level language. For additional flexibility the simulation software may permit the intermixing of statements written in the simulation and programming languages. This will result in a minor restriction of the free format input of blocks, namely the models will have to appear in the order of their precedence in the description of the simulated system.

3.10.2 Topological Configuration The model configuration tools in the simulation package should permit the design engineer to connect the functional blocks in any desired topological interconnection. While this free topological requirement may complicate the simulation software structure, it provides the maximum flexibility.

3.10.3 Model Library The usefulness of a simulation package depends heavily on the availability of a model library that contains a large number of models of various functional blocks that make up transmission systems and networks. Computer routines that model functional blocks should be reentrant so that functional blocks may be used at multiple and arbitrary instances in the simulation of a transmission system. The model configuration tools should permit unlimited nesting of models such that subsystem models may be built using library models. It is also desirable to make provisions to enable user to write his own models, use it in the simulation directly, and/or enter it into the model library.

3.10.4 Time and Event Driven Simulation A simulator can be designed to be time driven where processing is initiated at every "tick" of the simulation clock, or event driven where processing takes place only when an event of interest (such as the arrival of a message) takes place. For maximum flexibility, provisions should be made for both modes of processing such that some blocks in the system are event driven whereas others could be time driven.

3.10.5 Testing for Stationarity The reason for checking the status of the simulation is to gather a variety of either transient or long term time averaged statistics. If long term time averaged statistics are of interest, then the question of how much data to gather at each sample point, and with what degree of confidence, will influence the simulation parameters. This monitoring feature can be very useful in long Monte-Carlo Simulations. As an aside, we note that just because one million separate pieces of data have been collected does *not* guarantee we have a statistically significant sample: only if the samples are uncorrelated from one another can we say that we have some confidence that the data set may be sufficient.

3.10.6 Post Processor The postprocessing routines are an important part of a simulation package since these routines are the ones that enable the design engineer to view the results of the simulation. The model configuration tools and the simulation exercise tools should be designed to allow a designer to draw direct cause and effect inferences about system operation. As a minimum, the postprocessor package should have routines that perform the functions of common laboratory test equipment, (load generators, profilers of resource utilization for each job step and for time delays of each job step). Statistical analysis routines as well as graphics display routines are also essential.

3.10.7 User Interface Finally, the whole simulation package should be made user friendly. This includes both online and offline documentation and help. Two currently popular approaches here are using menus to trace a tree of commands or actions, and using key words (which appears to offer certain advantages for sophisticated users) by allowing menus to be bypassed if need be. This is currently an area of active research, encompassing novel interactive graphics and mouse controls, among other approaches. The simulation software should also have the following provisions to aid the user: symbolic debugging, run-time diagnostics, parameter checking and online error control for inputing.

3.10.8 Additional Reading

[1] N. R. Adam (editor), *Special Issue on Simulation Modeling and Statistical Computing,* Communications ACM, **24** (4), 1981.

[2] G.W.Furnas, T.K.Landauer, L.M.Gomez, S.T.Dumais, *Statistical Semantics: Analysis of the Potential Performance of Key-Word Information Systems,* Bell System Technical Journal, **62** (6), 1753-

1806(1983).

[3]   U. Grenander, R. F. Tsao, *Quantitative Methods for Evaluating Computer System Performance:A Review and Proposals,* in **Statistical Computer Performance Evaluation,** W. Freiberger (editor), Academic Press, NY, 1972.

[4]   L. Kleinrock, W. E. Naylor, *On Measured Behavior of the ARPA Network,* Processing AFIPS National Computer Conference, **43,** 767-780(1974).

3.11 Simulation of Link Level Flow Control

Here is a case study in doing a simulation study. A transmitter sends packets to a receiver over a channel and gets a positive acknowledgement. A hardware block diagram is shown in the figure below:

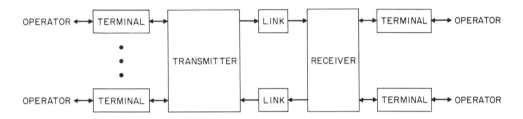

Figure 3.12.Communications Link Hardware Block Diagram

Here is a model of the operation of such a system: Each packet is processed by the transmitter, propagates through the channel to the receiver, is processed by the receiver, and leaves. An acknowledgement propagates back to the transmitter, and requires zero transmitter processing time. The receiver can only buffer a maximum of W packets. If the receiver buffer is full, the transmitter is shut down until space is available in the receiver. A queueing network block diagram of this system is shown in Figure 3.13.

An example of a simulation of such a system, done in GPSS, is shown below.

The sequence of transmitter and receiver packet processing times is constant. The channel propagation time has a given mean value; the sequence of channel propagation times is constant. The packet interarrival times are independent exponentially distributed random variables with a given mean interarrival time. The remaining parameters are the maximum number of unacknowledged packets transmitted, called the *window* size, denoted W, and the number of acknowledgements required to be received by the transmitter to start sending packets once shut down, called the *batch* size, denoted B. Flow control is used to make sure no messages are lost due to memory or buffers not being available in the receiver. This occurs for a variety of reasons, for example, when there is

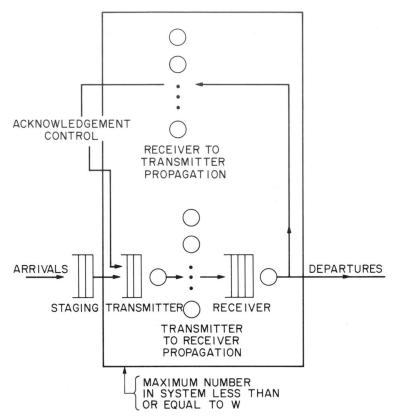

Figure 3.13.Communications Link Queueing Network Block Diagram

a mismatch in the speed of the two entities, or when the receiver must handle other work than just packet communication and is effectively slowed, and so forth.

Ideally, controlling or pacing the rate at which the transmitter sends packets should have no impact on performance. Our goal is to study not only mean throughput rate but also packet delay statistics, using this simulation as a tool to understand design tradeoffs.

3.11.1 Nonnegligible Channel Propagation Delay   First, the channel propagation delay is set to fifty times that of the processing time required by the transmitter or receiver. This is representative of what might be found in a ground to space satellite in synchronous orbit to ground data link. The first case studied set the window size equal to fifty two packets, W=52. In this regime the transmitter and receiver are the bottlenecks here, not the channel. It was suspected that the larger the window size, the better the delay

```
*LOC   OPERATION   A,B,C,D,E,F,G
*
*  FULL DUPLEX LINK LEVEL WINDOW FLOW CONTROL
*  WITH CHANNEL PROPAGATION DELAYS
*
      SIMULATE
 1     FUNCTION   RN3,C24
0         0          0.1          0.1040.20.222
0.3       0.355      0.4          0.5090.50.69
0.6       0.915      0.7          1.20.751.38
0.8       1.6        0.84         1.830.882.12
0.9       2.3        0.92         2.520.942.81
0.95      2.99       0.96         3.20.973.5
0.98      3.9        0.99         4.60.9955.3
0.998     6.2        0.999        7.00.99978.0
*
* INTERARRIVAL TIMES IID EXPONENTIAL ARRIVALS
* WITH MEAN INTERARRIVAL TIME 280
*
 1             GENERATE    280,FN1
*
*  QUEUE 1--TRANSMITTER QUEUE
*
 2             QUEUE 1
*
* LOW WATER MARK=5
*
 3             TEST E      Q3,K7,5
 4             LOGICS      1
*
* HIGH WATER MARK=7
*
 5             TEST E      Q3,K6,7
 6             LOGICR      1
 7             GATE LR     1
 8     SEIZE               1
 9             DEPART      1
10             ADVANCE     100
*
* TRANSMITTER PACKET PROCESSING TIME=100
*
11             RELEASE     1
12             TABULATE    4
*
```

```
*  QUEUE 2--FORWARD AND REVERSE CHANNEL
*
13          QUEUE       2
14          SEIZE       2
15          DEPART      2
16          ADVANCE     0
*
* CHANNEL PACKET DELAY=0
*
17          RELEASE     2
18          TABULATE    5
*
* QUEUE 3--RECEIVER
*
19          QUEUE       3
20          ADVANCE     100
*
* RECEIVER PACKET PROCESSING TIME=100
*
21          SEIZE       3
22          DEPART      3
23          RELEASE     3
24          TABULATE    6
4           TABLE       M1,100,10,40
5           TABLE       M1,100,10,10
6           TABLE       M1,200,50,40
25          TERMINATE 1
*
* GENERATE 10000 EVENTS
*
            START       1000
```

Figure 3.14.GPSS Link Flow Control Simulation

characteristics of packets. The two cases studied here were identical in their delay characteristics, to within statistical fluctuations! It may well be that the details of the simulation used here versus an actual field system may differ in critical ways that are not reflected here.

The simulation consisted of generating ten groups of packets, with each group comprising one thousand packets. The results were examined for homogeneity, to see if the system had reached statistical steady state. Statistics were gathered for ten groups of one thousand packets each; the observed variability was felt to be within statistical fluctuations, and the uniformity of the statistics across the samples suggested that long term time averaged statistics were in fact meaningful. An initial warmup of one thousand packets was used before gathering statistics. A statistical summary of results is tabulated below:

Table 3.16. Simulation Statistics--Finite Channel Propagation Delay (W = 52)

$$E\,(T_{trans})=E\,(T_{rec})=1\text{--}E\,(T_{trans-rec})=E\,(T_{rec-trans})=25$$

Mean Inter-arrival Time	Mean Arrival Rate	Mean Delay	Standard Deviation	90th Delay Percentile	95th Delay Percentile	Max Packets in Transmitter
4.00	0.25	50.169	0.375	50.730	50.934	4.3
2.20	0.45	50.443	0.741	51.369	51.927	6.6
1.80	0.56	50.654	0.985	51.855	52.584	7.9
1.50	0.67	51.056	1.402	52.785	53.805	9.9
1.30	0.77	51.748	2.053	54.625	55.955	12.4
1.10	0.91	55.140	4.564	59.314	61.593	21.3

Effectively, the system performance is dominated by the transmitter which is holding more and more packets as the load increases; this is also clear from the simulation source code. On the other hand, this may be acceptable engineering practice.

3.11.2 Negligible Channel Propagation Delay Next, the time spent in propagation from the transmitter to the receiver and back again is assumed to be negligible compared to the transmitter and receiver packet processing times. For this case, since we only have two resources, a transmitter and a receiver, we only investigate two cases: $W=1$ so that one packet at a time is handled, and $W=2$ so that two packets at a time are handled, offering the hope for keeping both the transmitter and the receiver busy, and ideally doubling the mean throughput rate for the same or better delay statistics.

Table 3.17. First Two Moments of Packet Delay Statistics

Mean Interarrival Time	Mean Arrival Rate	W=1		W=2	
		Mean Delay	Standard Deviation	Mean Delay	Standard Deviation
6.67	0.15	3.366	4.085	2.088	0.257
4.00	0.25	3.378	3.453	2.169	0.375
2.80	0.36	4.248	3.194	2.292	0.546
2.20	0.45	4.983	3.316	2.442	0.741
1.70	0.59	--	--	2.745	1.080
1.30	0.77	--	--	3.748	2.052
1.10	0.91	--	--	7.141	4.562

Table 3.18.Percentiles of Packet Delay Statistics

Mean Interarrival Time	Mean Arrival Rate	W=1		W=2	
		90th Percentile	95th Percentile	90th Percentile	95th Percentile
6.67	0.15	6.395	10.610	2.393	2.722
4.00	0.25	8.145	10.635	2.710	2.930
2.80	0.36	8.670	10.675	2.915	3.400
2.20	0.45	9.615	11.295	3.365	3.955
1.70	0.59	--	--	4.025	4.820
1.30	0.77	--	--	6.585	7.965
1.10	0.91	--	--	11.300	13.557

The above tables suggest that, to within statistical fluctuations, the delay characteristics for $W=2$ and $W=1$ appear to differ greatly. Furthermore, the delay statistics for $W=2$ and $W=7$ (which are not presented here) appear to be virtually identical, to within fluctuations. The main difference in the delay characteristics for the double buffering $W=2$ and $W=7$ case was the duration of the flow control startup transient in each: as congestion rises, both systems will always be started up, and the impact of this transient is apparently negligible for the numbers investigated above.

3.11.3 Additional Reading

[1] B.Efron, *Biased Versus Unbiased Estimation,* Advances in Mathematics, **16,** 259-277 (1975).

[2] S.H.Fuller, *Performance Evaluation,* in **Introduction to Computer Architecture,** H.Stone (editor), Science Research Associates, Chicago, 1975.

[3] L.Kleinrock, *On Flow Control,* Proc.Int.Conf.Communications, Toronto, Canada, 27.2-1--27.2-5, June 1978.

[4] L.Kleinrock, W.E.Naylor, *On Measured Behavior of the ARPA Network,* Proceedings AFIPS National Computer Conference, **43,** 767-780(1974).

[5] D.E.Knuth, *Verification of Link-Level Protocols,* BIT, **21,** 31-36 (1981).

[6] G.W.R.Luderer, H.Che, W.T.Marshall, *A Virtual Circuit Switch as the Basis for Distributed Systems,* Journal of Telecommunication Networks, **1,** 147-160 (1982).

[7] G.W.R.Luderer H.Che, J.P.Haggerty, P.A.Kirslis, W.T.Marshall, *A Distributed UNIX System Based on a Virtual Circuit Switch,* ACM Operating Systems Review, **15** (5), 160-168 (8th Symposium on Operating Systems Principles, Asilomar, 14-16 December 1981), ACM

534810.

[8] C.A.Sunshine, *Factors in Interprocess Communication Protocol Efficiency for Computer Networks,* AFIP NCC, pp.571-576(1976).

[9] K.C.Traynham, R.F.Steen, *SDLC and BSC on Satellite Links: A Performance Comparison,* Computer Communication Review, 1977

Problems

1) The figure below is the cumulative empirical distribution function for the interarrival times of twenty jobs submitted to an online computer system. The data was measured in time units of milliseconds, and was sorted smallest to largest:

Table 3.19.Interarrival Time Sorted Data (x1000)

6	6	7	9	15
24	29	32	37	39
41	42	42	68	83
84	88	97	116	134

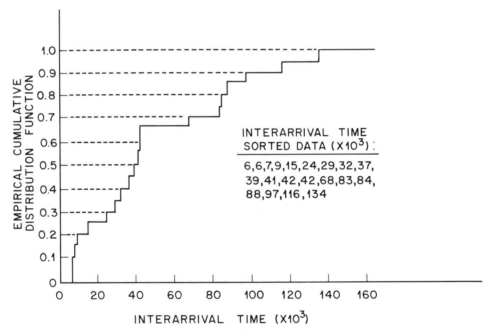

Figure 3.15.Interarrival Time Empirical Cumulative Distribution Function

A. What is the mean and median of this data?

B. What is the standard deviation and $P_{0.25}$ first quartile and $P_{0.75}$ third quartile? What is the ratio of the variance to the square of the mean?

C. What is the fifth percentile $P_{0.05}$? What is the tenth percentile $P_{0.10}$? What is the ninetieth percentile $P_{0.90}$? What is the ninety fifth percentile $P_{0.95}$?

D. What are the minimum and maximum data values?

E. **BONUS:** Construct a quantile quantile plot versus an exponential or Erlang-1 distribution. How good is the fit?

2) An online transaction processing system has the following hardware configuration:

Table 3.20. Hardware Configuration

Processor	1
Memory	4 Megabytes
Disks	2
Asynchronous Ports	32

Each disk has its own controller. The two disks are identical with one used for swapping, and the other used for retrieving text and data. Specification sheets for the disk state:

Table 3.21. Disk Specification

Velocity	3600 revolutions/minute
Transfer Rate	4 Megabytes/second
Time to Move Head One Adjacent Track	5 milliseconds
Time to Move Head Full Sweep	100 milliseconds
Average Seek Time	30 milliseconds

The operating system maintains a cache of buffers of fixed size (1024 bytes): programs first check the buffers to see if required data is there before making any physical disk accesses. All disk accesses involve transferring 1024 bytes of data per access.

The following measurements are carried out on the system in field operation during a peak busy hour:

[1] Processor measurements

- Nineteen per cent of the time spent executing application programs

- Fifty five per cent of the time spent executing operating system code

- Seventeen per cent of the time idle waiting for input/output to complete

- Nine per cent of the time idle with no work whatsoever

[2] Memory measurements

- Static text plus data requires one quarter of a megabyte

- With a desired peak busy hour load on the system, the amount of memory occupied dynamically is 1.86 megabytes

[3]   File system measurements

- Two hundred twenty four logical reads per second, with a sixty nine per cent cache hit rate (i.e., sixty nine per cent of the time the logical read did *not* generate a physical read to secondary storage)

- Seventeen logical writes per second, with a sixty seven per cent cache hit rate (i.e., sixty seven per cent of the time the logical write did *not* require the entity to be retrieved from secondary storage first, because it already was resident in main memory in a buffer; this will still generate *one* physical write to secondary storage after the system buffer contents are modified)

- Ten directory blocks per second were accessed

- Eleven accesses to file system tables per second were made

- Three name queries to the file system per second were made

[4]   Disk activity measurements

- The swap disk was busy either accessing data or transferring data to and from main memory seventy three per cent of the time; the text and data disk was busy sixty two per cent of the time

- The swap disk averaged forty accesses per second (reads and writes); the text and data disk averaged thirty nine accesses per second (reads and writes).

[5]   Asynchronous terminal measurements

- Twenty four characters per second were received by all the different ports

- Two characters per second were transmitted by all the different ports

[6]   Operating system measurements

- One hundred seventy four system calls per second were made

- Fifty one system read calls per second were made

- Four system write calls per second were made

- One process per second was created or killed

- Roughly one semaphore per second was set, unlocked, or tested

- The mean number of jobs in the run queue was three

- The fraction of time the run queue contained at least one job was seventy eight per cent

- The mean number of jobs in the swap queue was three

- The fraction of time the swap queue contained at least one job was forty six per cent

- The maximum size of the process table was eighty eight out of a maximum allowable number of two hundred

- The maximum number of simultaneously open files was one hundred thirty five out of a maximum of six hundred

[7] Swap statistics

- Roughly one and a half swaps into main memory occurred every second

- Roughly one and a half swaps out of main memory occurred every second

- One hundred and two process context switches occurred every second

Answer the following questions:

a. What are the system resources?

b. What is the state of the system at any given instant of time?

c. Which if any resource is near complete utilization?

d. What can be done to reduce congestion?

3) Additional measurements are carried out on the above system. The asynchronous ports are used to poll other computer systems. The number of ports used to poll was varied, and the duration of the polling process for a fixed number of computer systems was measured:

Table 3.22.Controlled Experiment Summary

Ports Polled	Poll Duration (Hours)	Processor Utilization	Swap Disk Utilization	Data Disk Utilization
4	5.5	0.58	0.35	0.15
6	3.6	0.74	0.45	0.20
8	2.9	0.82	0.55	0.25
10	2.9+	0.93	0.70	0.35
12	2.9+	0.97	0.90	0.35
14	2.9+	0.98	0.92	0.35
16	2.9+	0.99	0.92	0.37
18	2.9+	0.99	0.93	0.38
20	2.9+	0.99	0.93	0.38

Utilization refers to the fraction of time the processor and disks are busy doing anything whatsoever.

a. As the number of ports increases from four, the mean throughput rate goes up. Why?

b. What resource is reaching complete utilization?

c. What can be done to reduce congestion?

4) A batch processing system has the following hardware configuration:

Table 3.23.Hardware Configuration

Processor	1
Memory	2 Megabytes
Disks	4
Asynchronous Ports	32

Memory is sufficent to hold all application programs and operating system code with no swapping. The four disks are identical, with one storing system and application code, and the other three data. Specification sheets for the disk and controller state that the disk spins at 3600 revolutions per minute, can transfer data at a maximum rate of four million bytes per second, requires five milliseconds to move the head from one track to an adjacent track, and requires an average of thirty milliseconds to move the head from one point to any other point on the disk. The operating system maintains a cache of fixed size 512 byte buffers: programs first check the buffers to see if required data is there before making any physical disk accesses. All disk accesses involve transferring 512 bytes of data per access.

The following measurements are carried out on the system in field operation during a peak busy hour:

[1]   Processor measurements

- Thirty seven per cent of the time spent executing application programs

- Fifty seven per cent of the time spent executing operating system code

- Six per cent of the time idle waiting for input/output to complete

- Zero per cent of the time idle with no work whatsoever

[2]   File system measurements

- Thirty seven logical reads per second, with a seventy one per cent cache hit rate (i.e., seventy one per cent of the time the logical read did *not* generate a physical read to secondary storage)

- Six logical writes per second, with a sixty five per cent cache hit rate (i.e., sixty five per cent of the time the logical write did *not* require the entity to be retrieved from secondary storage first, because it already was resident in main memory in a buffer; this will still generate *one* physical write to secondary storage after the system buffer contents are modified)

- Forty two directory blocks per second were accessed

- Seventeen accesses to file system tables per second were made

- Seven name queries to the file system per second were made

[3]   Disk activity measurements

Table 3.24. Disk Statistics Summary

Spindle	Utilization	Accesses/Sec	Mean Waiting Time
1	41%	56	26 msec
2	41%	30	27 msec
3	9%	6	27 msec
4	25%	11	28 msec

[4]   Asynchronous terminal measurements

- Seven thousand, two hundred and forty nine characters per second were received by all the different ports

- One thousand, eight hundred and thirteen characters per second were transmitted by all the different ports

[5]   Operating system measurements

- Seventy three system calls per second were made

- Forty one system read calls per second were made

- Five system write calls per second were made

- One process per second was created or killed

- Roughly one semaphore per second was set, unlocked, or tested

- The mean number of jobs in the run queue was twenty one

- The fraction of time the run queue contained at least one job was ninety nine per cent

- The maximum size of the process table was thirty two out of a maximum allowable number of sixty nine

- The maximum number of simultaneously open files was two hundred eighty one out of a maximum of four hundred and fourteen

Answer the following questions?

a. What are the system resources?

b. What is the state of the system at any given instant of time?

c. Which if any resource is near complete utilization?

d. What can be done to reduce congestion?

5) A *full* duplex link is to be simulated. This consists of two *half* duplex or one way noiseless links, connected to a transmitter and receiver, with a dedicated microprocessor and a quarter of a megabyte of memory for the transmitter and receiver at each end of the link. Each physical link can have a maximum of five hundred and twelve virtual circuits active at any one time. The control data associated with each virtual circuit requires thirty two bytes of storage. Each virtual circuit can have a maximum number of one, two, or seven data packets unacknowledged at any one time. Control packets are used to set up virtual circuits, to acknowledge successful reception of packets, and to take down virtual circuits. Data packets are used to handle data only. The processing time and storage for each type of packet is summarized below:

Table 3.25.Packet Resources

Type of Packet	Processing	Storage
Control Packet/VC Set Up	50 msec	32 bytes
Control Packet/ACK	5 msec	32 bytes
Control Packet/VC Take Down	25 msec	32 bytes
Data Packet	100 msec	4096 bytes

A. Draw a block diagram of the hardware of this system.

B. Draw a block diagram of the steps with no contention for resources required to set up a virtual circuit, transmit a message over the link in packets, and take down the virtual circuit.

C. Control packets must be processed within one control packet transmission time. Data packets must be processed within ten data packet transmission times. Compare the performance of a static priority preemptive resume schedule with a deadline schedule assuming that there is *always* a data message consisting of five packets waiting to be transmitted.

6) The performance of a local area network is to be simulated. The hardware consists of S stations connected to a common coaxial cable or bus. Each station can send and receive packets. The stations are polled in turn to see if a packet is ready for transmission: if it is, it is transmitted, and all stations receive it. The total length of the network is such that it takes twenty microseconds for a signal to propagate from one end to the other of the cable. The stations are physically equidistant from one another on the cable. The electronics at each station require five microseconds to process signals, irrespective of whether a packet is ready for transmission or not. Each packet requires one hundred microseconds to be transmitted.

A. Draw a hardware block diagram of the system

B. Draw a flowchart showing the operation of each station

C. Code a simulation that accurately models the physical propagation characteristics of the problem, and test it for two cases

   • One station only always has a packet to transmit

   • Every station always has a packet to transmit

D. Suppose the packet transmission time is reduced to ten microseconds: what changes?

7) You telephone a colleague, the colleague is not at the telephone, and a secretary takes your message asking your colleague to return your call. Later, your colleague gets your message and telephones, but now you are not in, and a secretary takes the message that your call has been returned. You call back, and the process repeats itself, until eventually you both talk to one another via telephone. This is called *telephone tag* because you and your colleague are tagging one another with telephone messages.

A. Draw a figure summarizing the flow of messages.

B. What are the resources held at each step?

C. Write a simulation for this problem. Test it using the following numbers: each secretary can take one message every two minutes; thirty minutes elapse from when you are called and you pick up your message; each telephone call is one quarter minute to leave a message with the secretary and ten minutes when you finally talk plus each telephone call generates two tags or messages.

D. What if a voice message service is installed, so there is no need for telephone tag. This means that your message is stored for retrieval at the convenience of the callee. How does the above simulation have to be changed?

7) A paging memory management subsystem of an operating system is to be simulated. Hardware memory addressing allows the physical location of each piece of a given program to be scattered throughout main memory in units called *pages*. Logically the program appears to be resident in one contiguous area of memory. A typical program first will initialize some data and then execute data processing activities in tightly coded chunks of code that can be contained in one page before generating output that is properly formatted. A typical program will stay within a page for one hundred machine instructions on the average before switching to another page. The process repeats itself until the program finishes execution. The degree of multiprogramming refers to the number of simultaneous active programs contending for main memory.

A. Construct a flowchart showing the memory reference patterns of a typical program

B. Suppose that all programs are identical and consist of P pages each. Code a simulation that will estimate the length of time it takes to completely execute one thousand programs, assuming there is sufficient memory to hold S programs, using the following numbers:

Table 3.26. Numerical Parameters

Case I	$P=10, S=10$
Case II	$P=100, S=1$
Case III	$P=10, S=100$

C. What is gained by using paging versus simply loading programs into a contiguous area of memory from the point of view of performance?

9) A single processor must execute a given workload of jobs. Each job has three steps: interrupt handling, job execution, and cleanup. Interrupt handling and cleanup make use of serially reusable operating system tables, and cannot be preempted. Job execution can be preempted by more urgent work. Two types of jobs are executed by this system, one urgent type that has an allowable execution time window of ten milliseconds, and one less urgent type that has an allowable execution time window of fifty milliseconds. The interrupt handling is identical for each job and is one millisecond. The cleanup is identical for each job and is one half millisecond. The urgent job has an execution time of two milliseconds, the less urgent has an execution time of twenty milliseconds. The less urgent job can be preempted by the more urgent job and by interrupts and cleanup.

A. Draw a flowchart showing the steps required by each type of job

B. Code a simulation for this problem with the following two scheduling policies

  • A deadline scheduler

  • A static priority preemptive resume scheduler

Compare the simulation results. Which scheduler appears to be superior? Why?

10) One approach to speeding up performance of a computer is to attach a small *scratchpad* or *cache* of memory that is much higher speed (typically a factor of four) than main memory. The processor will load text and data into the cache, and if the cache is well designed, most of the time the next instruction to be executed will be in the cache, effectively speeding up the processor.

A. Draw a flowchart showing the flow of control and data in a program.

B. What data must be gathered as input to the simulation?

C. What types of policies can be implemented for the cache operations?

11) The performance of a telephone switching system is to be simulated. The following information is available about telephone call processing: the hardware configuration consists of one hundred telephones connected fifty each to one of two local telephone switching systems with two trunks between the local telephone switching systems. Each telephone makes one call every ten minutes on the average, and the call offhook interarrival times are independent identically distributed exponential random variables. Each telephone caller is equally likely to call any other telephone user. The talking duration of each telephone call is a sequence of independent identically distributed exponential random variables with a mean of five minutes.

The steps involved in telephone call processing are shown in the figure below:

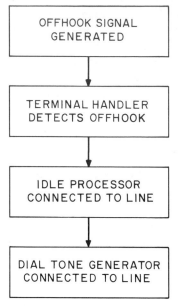

Figure 3.16.Offhook and Dial Tone Generation Steps

Assume that there is one terminal handler at each local switching system that requires ten milliseconds to detect offhook. Furthermore, assume that each local switching system has four processors for call processing, and one dial tone generator.

The steps involved in telephone call digit dialing are shown in Figure 3.17.

Assume that digit dialing requires one second for each of seven digits. The time to connect the loop to a trunk is one hundred milliseconds, the time for recording accounting data is one hundred milliseconds, and the time to generate an offhook signal on a trunk is ten milliseconds, with the dial tone generator used at the start of call processing generating the offhook signal.

The steps involved in sending digits over a trunk to the other local switching system are shown in the figure below:

Assume that the trunk handler detects an offhook in ten milliseconds, the time to connect an idle processor to the trunk is fifty milliseconds, the time to generate an offhook signal on the trunk is ten milliseconds, and the time to receive all digits is twenty milliseconds

The figure below shows the steps involved in setting up a path from the receiving local switching system back to the originating local switching system:

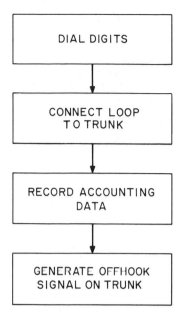

Figure 3.17. Digit Dialing and Billing

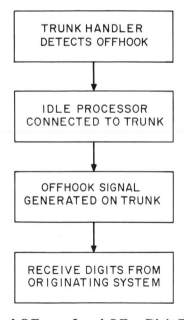

Figure 3.18. Local Office to Local Office Digit Transmission

Assume that all the steps take the same amount of time as cited above. The step of generating ringing takes two hundred milliseconds.

The final steps involved in call processing are to generate an audible ringing (taking fifty milliseconds), to stop all ringing (taking twenty milliseconds), and

137

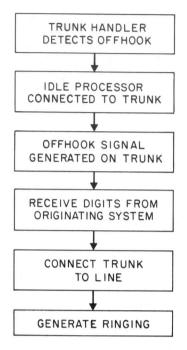

Figure 3.19.Completion of Call Path from Receiver to Transmitter

these are summarized in the figure below:

Answer all the questions:

A. Make a table showing each step of telephone call processing, the resources held at each step, and the time required with no contention for each step

B. Make a flowchart showing how control and voice information flows through this system from the time a call is originated by going offhook, to the end of a voice telephone conversation

C. What is the state of each trunk at each step of call set up processing?

D. Code a simulation program of this system. Adopt the following priority arbitration policy for contention for shared resources: step J has higher priority than step I if $J > I$. If two or more calls are contending for a shared resource at the same step of call processing, break the tie by flipping a fair coin. What is the fraction of time that dial tone delay exceeds one second for this load? What is the fraction of time that dial tone delay exceeds three seconds? What happens if time between call attempts is reduced to five minutes, and each call lasts for two minutes?

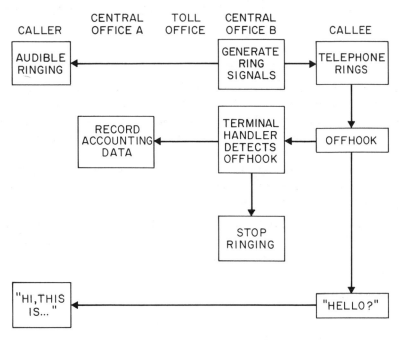

Figure 3.20.Final Steps in Call Set Up Processing

Up to this point we have examined detailed operational descriptions of models of computer communication systems. Much of the complexity in analysis *seemingly* disappears when the long term time averaged behavior of these types of computer system models is analyzed. We now focus on mean value analysis, long term time averaged behavior of mean throughput rate and mean delay. In our experience with operational systems and field experience, this is possibly the single most important fundamental result in analyzing computer communication system performance.

Our program here is to first analyze systems where there is only one type of job that takes only one step and one resource. Once we understand that case, we will generalize to systems where multiple types of jobs take multiple steps and demand multiple resources at each step.

4.1 Little's Law

In the technical literature, a key result is attributed to Little. In order to motivate the result, we return to a static model of a computer system. A system must process N jobs. All jobs are ready for processing at time $t=0$. The figure below plots the number in system process $J(t)$ versus time t for one possible scenario.

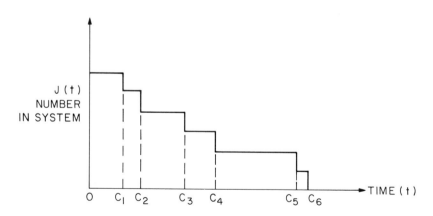

**Figure 4.1. Number in of Jobs in the System vs Time
Initial Work Present at T=0/No Arrivals for T>0**

We wish to determine the mean number of jobs in the system over the time interval starting at zero until the system becomes empty. C_K denotes the time at which the Kth job completes execution and leaves the system. Since there are a total of N jobs, the last job will leave at C_N. The area under the function $J(t)$ over the time interval $(0, C_N)$ must by definition equal the mean number of jobs in the system, denoted by $E(J)$, multiplied by the observation interval duration, C_N:

$$E(J) = \frac{1}{C_N} \int_0^{C_N} J(t)\,dt$$

Since C_K is the completion time of the Kth transaction, $K=1,\dots,N$ we see

$$E(J) = \frac{1}{C_N} [NC_1 + (N-1)(C_2 - C_1) + \cdots + (C_N - C_{N-1})]$$

$$E(J) = \frac{1}{C_N} \sum_{K=1}^{N} C_K$$

F_K denotes the total time spent in the system by job K. Since job one spends C_1 amount of time in the system, while job two spends $C_1 + C_2$ amount of time in the system, and so forth, we see that

$$E(J) = \frac{1}{C_N} \sum_{K=1}^{N} F_K$$

We now rearrange this expression, by multiplying and dividing by N, the total number of jobs:

$$E(J) = \frac{N}{C_N} \frac{1}{N} \sum_{K=1}^{N} F_K$$

We recognize the first term as the mean throughput rate, by definition the total number of jobs divided by the observation interval:

$$mean\ throughput\ rate = \frac{N}{C_N} \equiv \lambda$$

The second term is the mean time for a job to flow through the system, denoted by $E(F)$:

$$E(F) = \frac{1}{N} \sum_{K=1}^{N} F_K$$

Combining all this, we obtain the desired result:

$$\boxed{E(J) = \lambda \times E(F)}$$

The above result, that the mean number in system equals the mean throughput rate multiplied by the mean time in system, is called *Little's Law*.

We have obtained one equation in three unknowns, the mean number of jobs in system, the mean arrival rate, and the mean time in system. Our program is to *bound* each of these quantities, using the best available information. The more restrictive the information, the better the bounds; conversely, if little information is available, the bounds are still valid, but may not be as tight as desired.

4.1.1 Dynamic Arrivals Our intent is to relax the assumptions to obtain as general a result as possible. We first allow arrivals to occur at arbitrary points in time, rather than having all jobs present at time zero: A_K denotes the arrival time or ready time of the Kth job. $F_K \equiv C_K - A_K$ denotes the flow time of the Kth job, the time that elapses while job K flows through the system, from arrival (A_K) to departure (C_K). The figure below is an illustrative plot of the number of jobs in the system.

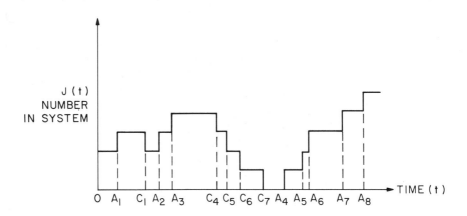

Figure 4.2. Number in System vs Time
Initial Work Present at T = 0/Arrivals for T > 0

Since each job contributes *one* unit of height for the duration of time it is in the system, since the area due to each job is its height (one) multiplied by its flow time, and since the total area is the sum of the areas contributed by each job, we see:

$$E(J) = \frac{N}{C_N} \frac{1}{N} \sum_{K=1}^{N} (F_K = C_K - A_K)$$

If we identify $\lambda \equiv N/C_N$ and $E(F)$ as before, then

$$E(J) = \lambda \times E(F)$$

What have we accomplished? We have one equation or relationship, and three parameters. In order to use this, we need to quantify two of the three parameters. An example is in order.

4.1.2 A Computer Time Sharing System One of the first applications of this type of analysis to computer systems was for time sharing program development, for MULTICS. In such a system, program developers spend some time reading and thinking and typing, with mean T_{think}, and then submit a job (an editor command, a compilation request, and so forth) that requires a mean amount of time T_{system} to be executed with no other load on the system.

With more than one request being executed, there will be contention, and hence some delay to execute each job. The mean response time for each job is measured from the time a job is submitted until the system finishes its response, denoted by R. The mean throughput rate, measured in jobs per unit time, is denoted by λ. There are a total of N program developers using the system actively at any one time. How can we use Little's Law to analyze performance?

The figure below is a hardware block diagram of this system:

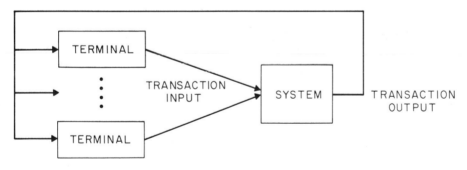

INTERACTIVE ONLINE SYSTEM BLOCK DIAGRAM

Figure 4.3. Hardware Block Diagram of Time Sharing System

The key first step in using Little's Law is to determine what the system is: is it the terminals, is it the computer, or does it include both? If we define the total system as including both terminals and the system, then the total number of jobs is fixed at N, the number of active users, with each job either being in the think state or the processing state. If we define the system as including only terminals or only the system, we do not know how many jobs are in either.

For $N=1$ user, Little's Law says the mean number of jobs equals the mean throughput rate multiplied by the mean time in the system. The mean time in the system is the sum of the thinking time plus the response time with no load:

$$N=1 = \lambda(N=1)[T_{think} + R(N=1)]$$

We have written this to stress the fact that the mean throughput rate and the mean response time depend upon the number of active terminals. We could simply rewrite this by solving for the mean throughput rate:

$$\lambda(N=1) = \frac{N=1}{T_{think} + R(N=1)}$$

Next, as $N \to \infty$, the mean throughput rate will grow no faster than linearly with N, i.e., if we put on two terminals, the mean throughput rate is at best double that of one terminal:

$$\lambda(N) \leqslant \frac{N}{T_{think} + R(N=1)} \quad N>1$$

The mean response will be no better than that for one terminal:

$$R(N) \geqslant R(N=1) \quad N>1$$

At some point, the mean throughput rate does not increase any further, but rather saturates at a limiting value characteristic of the system, denoted by λ_{max}:

$$\lambda(N) \leqslant \lambda_{max}$$

Combining both these upper bounds on mean throughput rate, we see

$$\lambda(N) \leqslant \min\left[\lambda_{max}, \frac{N}{T_{think} + R(N=1)}\right]$$

From Little's Law, the mean response time is given by

$$R(N) = \frac{N}{\lambda(N)} - T_{think}$$

Since the mean throughput rate eventually saturates at λ_{max}, the mean response time eventually grows linearly with N:

$$R(N) = \frac{N}{\lambda_{max}} - T_{think} \quad N \to \infty$$

We can combine all this in the following expression:

$$R \geqslant \max\left[R(N-1), \frac{N}{\lambda_{max}} - T_{think}\right]$$

There is a clear breakpoint here as N increases:

$$N_{breakpoint} = \lambda_{max}[T_{think} + R(N=1)]$$

For $N < N_{breakpoint}$ the terminals are unable to keep the system busy, and are a bottleneck. For $N > N_{breakpoint}$ the system is completely busy and is a bottleneck.

The worst that the mean response time could be would be to always wait for every other job to be processed immediately ahead of your execution:

$$R(N) \leqslant N\ R(N=1)$$

This in turn gives a lower bound on mean throughput rate:

$$\lambda(N) \geqslant \frac{N}{T_{think} + NR(N=1)}$$

Note that as $N \rightarrow \infty$, the lower bound on mean throughput rate approaches the rate of executing one job at a time:

$$\lambda(N) \geqslant \frac{1}{R(N=1)} \quad N \rightarrow \infty$$

This suggests defining speedup as the ratio of the mean throughput rate for executing one job at a time over the actual mean throughput rate:

$$speedup = \frac{1}{R(N=1)\lambda(N)} \rightarrow \frac{1}{\lambda_{max}R(N=1)} \quad N \rightarrow \infty$$

Figure 4.4 plots the upper and lower bounds on mean throughput rate versus number of active terminals. Figure 4.5 plots the upper and lower bounds on mean response time versus number of active terminals.

4.1.3 Additional Reading

[1] R.W.Conway, W.L.Maxwell, L.W.Miller, **Theory of Scheduling,** Addison-Wesley, Reading, Massachusetts, 1967; Little's formula, pp.18-19.

[2] J.D.C.Little, *A Proof of the Queueing Formula L = λ W,* Operations Research, **9**, 383-387 (1961).

[3] A.L.Scherr, **An Analysis of Time-Shared Computer Systems,** MIT Press, Cambridge, Mass, 1967.

4.1.4 Little's Inequality The only valid justification for *Little's Law* follows from controlled experimentation: testing the operation of a system to see how well it fits the hypothesis. Little's Law holds exactly when the system initially is empty or idle with no work, and after a period of observing its operation we stop gathering data when the system is once more entirely idle or empty. In practice, this may not be true: observations may be gathered over a finite time interval, and the state at the start of observation and the state at the end of observation may be different from the all empty or all idle state. Under a

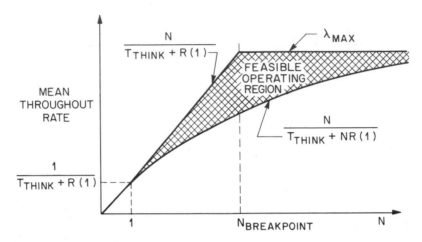

Figure 4.4.Mean Throughput Rate Bounds versus Number of Active Users

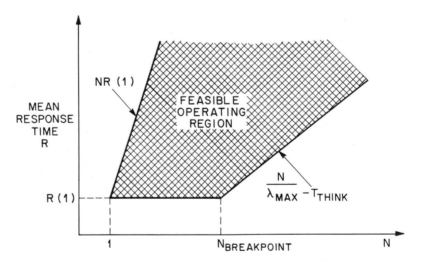

Figure 4.5.Mean Response Time Bounds versus Number of Active Users

variety of technical conditions, which must be checked in practice, Little's Law holds *in some sense*. However, there is a weaker statement that we call *Little's Inequality* that holds :

mean number in system ⩾ *mean arrival rate* × *mean time in system*

To make this precise, consider a system observed in operation from some time T to some later time $T + C_N$. We choose the interval of observation so that N jobs are observed to both start and finish; C_N is the completion instant of the Nth job. The jobs are denoted by $J_K, K=1,...,N$ with $J(.)$ denoting the total number of jobs in the system at any point in time, and $F_K, K=1,...,N$ denoting the time in system or flow time for job K. From these definitions, and following the earlier development, we see

$$\text{mean number of jobs} = E(J) = \frac{1}{C_N} \int_T^{T+C_N} J(\tau)d\tau$$

Note that a job may have entered the system prior to T but not yet left, entered prior to T and left, or entered during the measurement time but not yet left. This implies that

$$E(J) = \text{mean number in system} \geq \frac{N}{C_N} \frac{1}{N} \sum_{K=1}^{N} F_K$$

We identify the mean throughput rate with λ

$$\lambda \equiv \frac{N}{C_N}$$

while we identify the mean time in system as

$$\text{mean time in system} = \frac{1}{N} \sum_{K=1}^{N} F_K$$

If you don't believe all this, draw a picture! On the other hand, if these *end* effects are negligible (which can only be checked with controlled experimentation), then

$$\boxed{E(J) \approx \lambda \times E(F)}$$

From this point on, we assume this holds with *equality*. This has been proven to be prudent and reasonable on numerous occasions, but must always be tested for *your* particular problem!

4.1.5 Jobs With Multiple Steps What if a job has more than one step? Consider the following analysis: Each job has S types of steps, and requires one or more resources at each step for a mean time $T_K, K=1,...,S$. The system is observed over an interval with N job completions occurring at time instants $C_K, K=1,...,N$. We denote with an S tuple $\underline{J} = (J_1,...,J_S)$ the number of jobs in execution in each step, i.e., $J_K, K=1,...,S$ denotes the number of jobs in execution in step K. The state space is denoted by Ω and is the set of feasible S tuples $\underline{J}$. The fraction of time the system is in each state $\underline{J}$ over the observation interval is denoted by $\pi(\underline{J})$. From Little's Law, we can write

$$E(J_K) = \sum_{\underline{J} \in \Omega} J_K \pi(\underline{J}) \geqslant \lambda \tilde{T}_K \quad K=1,...,S$$

where the mean throughput rate is simply the total number of jobs divided by the observation time interval,

$$\lambda \equiv \frac{N}{C_N}$$

and $\tilde{T}_K$ is given by averaging T_K over the fraction of time the system is in each state:

$$\tilde{T}_K \equiv \frac{1}{N} \sum_{K=1}^{N} T_K \pi(J_K)$$

EXERCISE: Derive this for N jobs present at time zero and no further arrivals.

EXERCISE: Derive this with the system idle at some initial time, and with N arrivals and departures occurring at random points in time, so that the system is once again idle.

4.2 Scheduling a Single Processor to Minimize the Mean Flow Time

Suppose that N jobs are present at an initial time, say zero, and a single processor executes these jobs until no jobs are left. Let C_K denote the completion time of the Kth job. Let $J(t)$ denote the number of jobs still not completely executed at time t. The area under $J(t)$ is given by its integral:

$$\int_0^{C_N} J(t)dt = \sum_{K=1}^{N} C_K$$

The mean time a job spends in the system is given by

$$E(F) = \frac{1}{N} \sum_{K=1}^{N} C_K$$

Our problem is to find a schedule for a single processor that minimizes the average or mean flow time of a job. Note that the schedule cannot change C_N, the completion time of the last job, because the processor will always be busy doing *some* job until it finishes them all, but we *can* control the completion times of the jobs. Once we realize this, we see that

$$E(F) = \frac{1}{N} \int_0^{C_N} J(t)dt$$

Hence we wish to minimize the area under $J(t)$. Intuitively, we wish to drive $J(t)$ as close to zero as quickly as possible, i.e., we want to schedule jobs with the *shortest* processing time first.

To make this concrete, suppose there are two jobs, one with processing time equal to 10, and one with processing time equal to 1. One schedule is to run the short job first and then the long job, with mean time in system given by

$$E(F) = \tfrac{1}{2}(1+11) = 6$$

while a second schedule is to run the long job first and then the short job, with mean time in system given by

$$E(F)average = \tfrac{1}{2}(10+11) = 10.5$$

What we are trying to accomplish is to make sure that short jobs are not delayed by long jobs.

4.3 Telephone Traffic Engineering

Voice telephone calls are made between two locations. The only data available is that during a peak busy hour of the day, on the average $\lambda_{telephone}$ is the mean rate of calls arriving per minute that are successfully completed, with a mean holding time per successful call of $T_{telephone}$. A total of C circuits are installed. How many links L are actually needed, where one link can handle one voice telephone call?

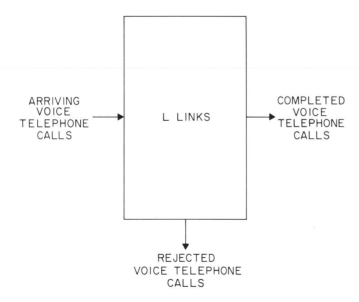

Figure 4.6. Telephone System Block Diagram

The mean number of calls in progress during this busy hour is given by Little's Law:

$$mean \ number \ of \ calls \ in \ progress \ = \lambda_{telephone} T_{telephone}$$

More formally, the number of calls in progress at any instant of time say t is denoted by $J(t)$. The state space is the set of admissible nonnegative integer values for $J(t)$ denoted by Ω. The system is observed over a time interval of duration T and the fraction of time the system is in a given state is assumed to have stabilized at $\pi(J)$. The maximum available number of circuits is C, and hence

$$E[min(J,C)] = \sum_{J \in \Omega} \pi(J) min(J,C) = \lambda_{telephone} T_{telephone}$$

Since each link can handle one call, we see that we need (roughly)

$$L \approx \lambda_{telephone} T_{telephone}$$

The units associated with the mean number of calls in progress are called *Erlangs* in honor of the Danish teletraffic engineer A.Erlang who pioneered much of the early work to quantify and answer questions such as these. In practice, we would put in more than L links as given by Little's Law because we will have fluctuations about the mean value and some call attempts will be blocked or rejected because all links are busy. We will return to this topic later.

4.4 Serially Reusable versus Concurrently Shared Resources

In many applications, some resources must be used serially, one task at a time, and others can be shared simultaneously or in parallel with many tasks. In the illustrative figure below, a job consists of two steps: the first step requires a shared resource such as reentrant application code, while the second step requires a serially reusable resource such as operating system code. Multiple simultaneous uses can be made of the shared resource, but only one job at a time may use the serially reusable resource.

For application programs executing on IBM OS/360, typically 40% of the processor time was found to be devoted to serially reusable resources, and with a great deal of effort this might be reduced to 20% of the processor time (Amdahl, 1967). This suggests that identical multiple processor configurations with one processor devoted to serial tasks and P devoted to the parallel tasks might find little benefit in going to more than two processors (60%/40% < 2) for a 1967 implementation of OS/360, while going to more than four processors (80%/20% ▬4) for an optimistic scenario. Furthermore, since the serial tasks are a fundamental bottleneck, every effort should be made to make these execute as quickly as possible.

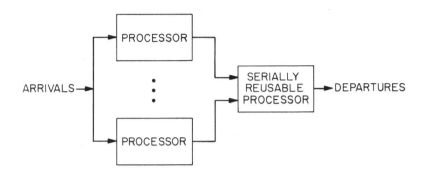

P CONCURRENTLY
SHARED PROCESSORS

Figure 4.7.Hardware Block Diagram of Serial and Concurrent Processors

Here is a somewhat more quantitative approach to these intuitive notions. A job consists of two steps. The first step must be done using a serially reusable resource (e.g., a critical region of the system), and will execute in time T_{serial}. The second step can be done concurrently, and requires $T_{concurrent}$ units of time to be executed. We might think of the serial portion being the work associated with classifying a step, readying it for subsequent execution, while the second portion might involve execution using a read only storage for example.

The system state is a pair, denoted $(J_{serial}, J_{concurrent})$, describing the number of jobs in execution on the serially reusable resource J_{serial} and on the concurrently shared resource $J_{concurrent}$.

The mean number of tasks in execution and requiring the serially reusable resource is given by

$$\lambda T_{serial} = E(J_{serial}) \leqslant 1$$

while the mean number of tasks in execution and requiring the shared resource is given by

$$\lambda T_{concurrent} = E(J_{concurrent}) \leqslant P$$

These relations give us the following upper bound on the mean throughput rate:

$$\lambda = \min\left[\frac{1}{T_{serial}}, \frac{P}{T_{concurrent}} \right]$$

A second type of upper bound arises from a limitation on the total number of jobs, denoted M, in the system. With one job, $M=1$, in the system, the mean throughput rate is given by

$$\lambda \leqslant \frac{1}{T_{serial} + T_{concurrent}} \quad J=1$$

and hence as more jobs are allowed in the system, $M>1$, the best that could be done is

$$\lambda \leqslant \frac{M}{T_{serial} + T_{concurrent}}$$

Combining this with the other upper bound, we see

$$\lambda \leqslant \min\left[\frac{M}{T_{serial} + T_{concurrent}}, \frac{1}{T_{serial}}, \frac{P}{T_{concurrent}} \right]$$

There are three types of bottleneck possible:

- The number of jobs is a bottleneck

$$\lambda_{max} = \frac{M}{T_{serial} + T_{concurrent}}$$

- The serially reusable resource is a bottleneck

$$\lambda_{max} = \frac{1}{T_{serial}}$$

- The concurrently shared resource is a bottleneck

$$\lambda_{max} = \frac{P}{T_{concurrent}}$$

Here is a different example to illustrate the importance of this phenomenon in doing tradeoffs. A processor spends 25% of its time on a representative job doing input/output over various communication links, and 75% of its time actually executing work. A front end processor is procured to offload the input/output work, and the front end processor is twice as fast as the original processor. What is the potential gain in maximum mean throughput rate? If the original system required $T_{i/o}$ seconds for each job and $T_{process}$ to execute each job, while the new front end processor requires T_{fe} seconds for each job, then the mean throughput rate is upper bounded for the old system by

$$mean\ throughput\ rate \leqslant \frac{1}{T_{i/o} + T_{process}} \quad old\ system$$

while the mean throughput rate for the new system is governed by the slower of the two subsystems

$$mean\ throughput\ rate\ \leqslant\ \frac{1}{max[T_{fe},T_{process}]}\quad new\ system$$

Suppose the front end processor is twice as fast as the original processor, so

$$T_{fe}\ =\ \tfrac{1}{2}\ T_{i/o}$$

Finally, suppose that 25% of the time the original processor is doing input/output, and 75% of the time it is doing work, so

$$T_{process}\ =\ 3\ T_{i/o}$$

Combining all this, the mean throughput rate for the old system is upper bounded by

$$mean\ throughput\ rate\ =\ \frac{1}{4T_{i/o}}\quad old\ system$$

while the mean throughput rate for the new system is upper bounded by

$$mean\ throughput\ rate\ =\ \frac{1}{max[3T_{i/o},\tfrac{1}{2}T_{i/o}]}\quad new\ system$$

and hence the maximum gain is (4/3) or thirty three per cent. In fact, as long as the front end processor is as fast or faster than the original processor, the maximum gain will be thirty three per cent. However, the delay in getting through from start to finish ignoring delays due to congestion is

$$T_{execution}\ =\ T_{i/o}\ +\ T_{process}\ =\ 4T_{i/o}\quad old\ system$$

$$T_{execution}\ =\ T_{i/o}\ +\ T_{process}\ =\ 3\tfrac{1}{2}T_{i/o}\quad new\ system$$

and this time depends directly on the speed of the original processor and the front end processor.

What if a different front end processor can be procured that is one half the speed of the original processor, but costs one third what the other front end processor cost? Now the time per job for a front end processor equals

$$T_{fe}\ =\ 2T_{i/o}\quad new\ front\ processor$$

and hence if only one front end processor is added to the system, the mean throughput rate is upper bounded by

$$mean\ throughput\ rate\ \leqslant\ \frac{1}{max[T_{fe}\ =\ 2T_{i/o},T_{process}\ =\ 3T_{i/o}]}$$

which is just as good as the more expensive front end processor, but the execution time is greater for one inexpensive but slower front end processor:

$$T_{execute}\ =\ T_{fe}\ +\ T_{process}\ =\ 5T_{i/o}$$

This is a typical finding: the mean throughput rate can be increased, at the expense of delay.

4.4.1 Additional Reading

[1]   G.M.Amdahl, *Validity of the Single Processor Approach to Achieving Large Scale Computing Capabilities,* AFIPS Conference Proceedings, **30,** 483-485, AFIPS Press, Montvale, NJ, 1967.

4.5 Packet Computer Communications Network

The block diagram below shows nodes in a packet computer communications network:

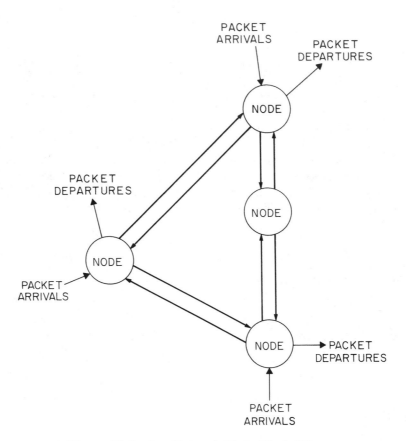

Figure 4.8.Packet Network Node Block Diagram

Messages enter or leave the network via one of N ports. There are S nodes or packet switches within the network. At node K we measure R_K packets per second for a mean throughput rate. The mean flow time of a packet, waiting plus switching time, at node K is given by $E(F_K)$. The mean flow time of a packet through the network is denoted by $E(F)$, while the total mean external arrival rate at port J is denoted by λ_J, and we denote by λ the aggregate total network throughput rate:

$$\lambda = \sum_{J=1}^{N} \lambda_J$$

From Little's Law we see

$$\lambda E(F) = \sum_{K=1}^{S} R_K E(F_K)$$

Since packets can be switched through more than one internal node, the packet throughput rate within the network can exceed the external packet arrival and departure rate:

$$R \equiv \sum_{K=1}^{S} R_K \geqslant \lambda = \sum_{J=1}^{N} \lambda_J$$

The mean flow time can be written as

$$E(F) = \sum_{K=1}^{S} \frac{R_K}{\lambda} E(F_K)$$

If we rewrite this as

$$E(F) = \frac{R}{\lambda} \sum_{K=1}^{S} \frac{R_K}{R} E(F_K)$$

then we can identify the mean number of nodes visited per packet V with

$$V = \frac{R}{\lambda}$$

while we recognize the mean flow time per node is

$$mean\ flow\ time\ per\ node = \sum_{K=1}^{S} \frac{R_K}{R} E(F_K)$$

What have we learned? The mean time a packet spends in the network equals the mean number of nodes visited per packet multiplied by the mean time per node.

4.6 A Model of a Processor and Disk System

Jobs that require more than one step are quite common. This section analyzes a model of a computer system consisting of processors and disks, with the first step of any job requiring a processor, the second a disk, the third a processor again, and so forth, until the job is completely executed.

4.6.1 Model The figure below shows a hardware block diagram of the system, while the next figure shows a queueing network block diagram. The system consists of P processors and D disks connected by a common switch. The switch is assumed to be much faster than any step of job execution involving either a processor or a disk, and is ignored from this point on. The jobs or

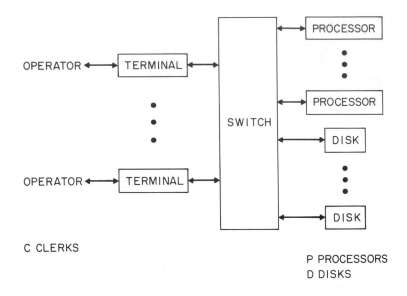

Figure 4.9.Processor and Disk Hardware Block Diagram

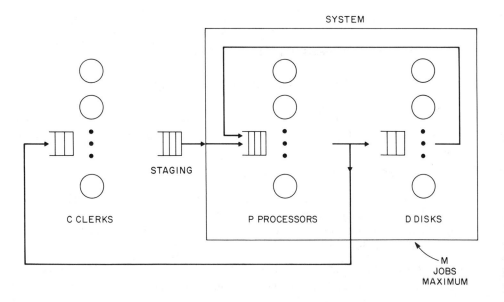

Figure 4.10.Queueing Network Block Diagram

transactions are generated from people or operators at terminals. Each operator spends a mean amount of time reading, thinking, and typing, denoted by T_{think} and then submits a job to the system and waits for a response before repeating this process. The mean response time is denoted by R and is the sum of four time intervals, due to waiting or being executed on a processor or disk.

Each job involves execution on a processor, data retrieval from disk, and so on, until the job is completely executed. Each job requires a total mean amount of time denoted by $T_{processor}$ and T_{disk} on a processor and disk respectively. No job is assumed to be capable of executing in parallel with itself. The operating system multiplexes available jobs among available processors and disks to achieve some degree of concurrent use of resources.

4.6.2 Analysis   The system state is given by a triple, where $(J_{operator}, J_{processor}, J_{disk})$ where $J_{operator}$ denotes the number of operators reading, thinking and typing, $J_{processor}$ denotes the number of jobs waiting or executing on a processor, and J_{disk} denotes the number of jobs waiting to use a disk or retrieving data from a disk.

From Little's Law, we see that the mean number of tasks executing on processors is equal to the mean arrival time multiplied by the mean time spent using a processor:

$$E(J_{processor}) = \lambda T_{processor} \leqslant P$$

Similarly, the mean number of tasks using disks is equal to the mean arrival rate multiplied by the mean time spent using a disk:

$$E(J_{disk}) = \lambda T_{disk} \leqslant D$$

From the above relations, we see that the mean throughput rate of jobs is upper bounded by

$$\lambda \leqslant \min\left[\frac{P}{T_{processor}}, \frac{D}{T_{disk}}\right]$$

A second type of upper bound arises from considering how work flows through the system: if there is only one job in the system at any time, then the mean throughput rate is simply given by

$$\lambda \leqslant \frac{1}{T_{processor} + T_{disk}} \quad \textit{one job in system}$$

and hence with J jobs in the system the mean throughput rate is upper bounded by J times that for one job:

$$\lambda \leqslant \frac{J}{T_{processor} + T_{disk}} \quad J \ jobs \ in \ system$$

Combining this upper bound with the previous upper bound we see

$$\lambda \leqslant \min\left[\frac{P}{T_{processor}}, \frac{D}{T_{disk}}, \frac{J}{T_{processor} + T_{disk}}\right]$$

Since from Little's Law or the definition of mean throughput rate the mean response time and mean throughput rate are related by

$$\lambda = \frac{J}{T_{think} + R}$$

we obtain the following lower bound on mean response time:

$$R \geqslant \max\left[T_{processor} + T_{disk}, \frac{J}{max[T_{processor}/P, T_{disk}/D]} - T_{think}\right]$$

To lower bound the mean throughput rate, we realize that the J jobs could all be waiting to run or be running on a processor, or waiting to run to be retrieving data from a disk, and hence

$$\frac{J}{T_{think} + \dfrac{JT_{processor}}{P} + \dfrac{JT_{disk}}{D}} \leqslant \lambda$$

This allows us to upper bound the mean response time:

$$R \leqslant \frac{JT_{processor}}{P} + \frac{JT_{disk}}{D}$$

These bounds define an admissible or feasible region of operation and are plotted in the figures below for the case of one processor and one disk.

4.6.3 Speedup Here are two possible scheduling policies:

- *single thread* scheduling, where one job at a time is allowed in the system and executed until completion before allowing the next job in

- *multiple thread* scheduling, where more than one job at a time is allowed in the system and executed until completion

For the first policy, we see

$$\lambda_{single\ thread} = \frac{1}{T_{processor} + T_{disk}} \quad J=1$$

The ratio of the two different upper bounds is an indication of the gain due to scheduling:

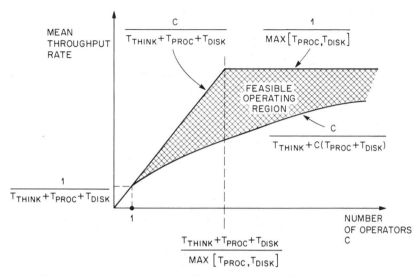

**Figure 4.11. One Processor/One Disk Mean Throughput Bounds
vs Number of Terminals.**

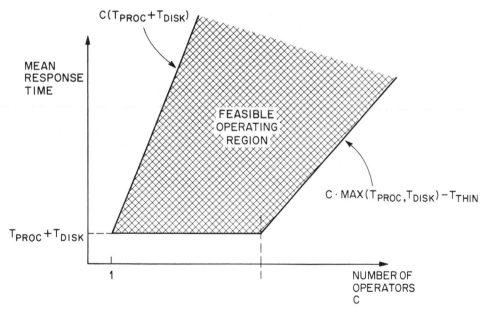

**Figure 4.12. One Processor/One Disk Mean Response Time Bounds
vs Number of Terminals.**

$$\frac{\lambda_{multiple\ thread}}{\lambda_{single\ thread}} = \frac{T_{processor} + T_{disk}}{\max\left[\dfrac{T_{processor}}{P}, \dfrac{T_{disk}}{D}, \dfrac{T_{processor} + T_{disk}}{J}\right]}$$

For one processor and one disk, this gain due to scheduling can be at most two, no matter what $T_{processor}$ or T_{disk} are! Moreover, this will only be achieved when $T_{processor}$ equals T_{disk}, but in general these two mean times will *not* be equal and hence the gain will *not* be as great as a factor of two; for example, if T_{disk} were ten times as great as $T_{processor}$, then the gain would be at most ten per cent, and other factors may swamp this *upper* bound. J is called the *degree of multiprogramming* and the two cases we have examined are degree of multiprogramming one and two, for single and multiple thread operation, respectively. If we allow multiplexing of the processor and disk amongst transactions, then $J > 1$ is allowed, but now one or the other of the two serially reusable resources will become completely utilized for J sufficiently large.

4.6.4 Bottlenecks Bottlenecks can arise from several sources:

- If the number of jobs or degree of multiprogramming is a bottleneck, then

$$\lambda_{\max} = \frac{J}{T_{processor} + T_{disk}}$$

- If the number of processors is a bottleneck, then

$$\lambda_{\max} = \frac{P}{T_{processor}}$$

- If the number of disks is a bottleneck, then

$$\lambda_{\max} = \frac{D}{T_{disk}}$$

The design problem is to choose where the bottleneck should be; remember, there will always be *some* bottleneck!

4.6.5 Asymptotics One type of asymptotic analysis is to let all parameters be fixed except one, and the final one becomes progressively larger and larger. Here a natural candidate for such a parameter is the number of operators or jobs circulating in the system J, and we see

$$\frac{1}{\dfrac{T_{processor}}{P} + \dfrac{T_{disk}}{D}} \leqslant \lambda \leqslant \frac{1}{\max\left[\dfrac{T_{processor}}{P}, \dfrac{T_{disk}}{D}\right]} \qquad J \to \infty$$

This yields the following asymptotic behavior for the mean response time:

$$T_{processor} + T_{disk} \leqslant R \leqslant \infty \qquad J \to \infty$$

This is quite instructive by itself: the mean response time can lie between a *finite* and *infinite* limit, showing how great the variation *can* be, given only mean value information.

A second type of asymptotic analysis is to fix the ratio of two parameters, and allow them both to become progressively larger, fixing all other parameters.

Here, a natural candidate is the ratio of the number of jobs divided by the mean think time per operator, which we fix at α

$$\alpha \equiv \frac{J}{T_{think}} \qquad J \rightarrow \infty \quad T_{think} \rightarrow \infty$$

which is a measure of the *total* offered rate of submitting jobs, and we allow the number of jobs or terminals to become large as well as the mean intersubmission time of jobs from each terminal, thus weakening the contribution to the total offered rate of each terminal. If we do so, we see

$$\frac{\alpha}{1 + \alpha \left[\dfrac{T_{processor}}{P} + \dfrac{T_{disk}}{D} \right]} \leqslant \lambda \leqslant \frac{1}{\max \left[\dfrac{T_{processor}}{P}, \dfrac{T_{disk}}{D} \right]}$$

$$R \geqslant \begin{cases} \infty & \alpha > \dfrac{1}{\max \left[\dfrac{T_{processor}}{P}, \dfrac{T_{disk}}{D} \right]} \\[4ex] T_{processor} + T_{disk} & \alpha < \dfrac{1}{\max \left[\dfrac{T_{processor}}{P}, \dfrac{T_{disk}}{D} \right]} \end{cases}$$

where in the above summary, we have fixed α, but allowed both $J \rightarrow \infty$ and $T_{think} \rightarrow \infty$.

Additional (distributional) information must be available to allow us to handle the case where

$$\alpha = \frac{1}{\max \left[\dfrac{T_{processor}}{P}, \dfrac{T_{disk}}{D} \right]}$$

Intuitively we see that the if the total mean arrival rate is less than the upper bound on the mean throughput rate, then the system is capable of having a *finite* lower bound on mean response time; when the total mean arrival rate is greater than the upper bound on the mean throughput rate, then the mean response time lower bound is *infinite*. The remaining case, an upper bound on the mean response time, is trivial

$$R \leqslant \infty \qquad \alpha \ fixed, J \rightarrow \infty \ T_{think} \rightarrow \infty$$

As in the first case, the mean response time can lie between a *finite* and *infinite* value, given only mean value information, i.e., the mean response time is *not* well bounded given only means but no information about fluctuations. *Mean* delay depends not only on the *mean* processing times but also *second* moments of the processing time distribution: mean value information does *not* specify the mean delay in such systems by itself.

4.7 Mean Throughput and Mean Delay Bounds in Multiple Step Single Job Networks

In this section we present the analysis that leads to *upper* as well as *lower* bounds on mean throughput and mean delay for a particular type of computer communication system that handles only one type of job. The utility is that the bounds are in fact *achievable,* and hence *sharp,* or the best possible bounds, given *only* the mean duration of each step.

4.7.1 Model Each job consists of one or more steps. At each step, a given amount of a serially reusable resource is required for a given mean time interval. Here the first step of each job involves entering the job into the system via an operator at a terminal, the second step of each job involves placing the job in a staging queue where it will wait if there are more than a given maximum number of jobs already in the system and otherwise will enter the system immediately, and one or more additional steps inside the system where the job holds a single serially reusable resource for each step of execution and then moves on, until the job is completely executed and control returns to the operator at the terminal. For each step of each job, we are given the amount of each resource and the *mean* time required to hold that set of resources. We denote by T_K the total mean time spent by a job holding resource type K, which we stress is the sum total execution time of all visits to that stage by a job.

The mathematical model consists of

- N+2 stages of stations: station 0 is associated with operators at terminals, station 1 is the staging station, and stations 2,...,N+1 (N total) are associated with a single serially reusable resource
- Stage $K=0,2,...,N+1$ has P_K identical parallel servers or processors
- A maximum of M jobs can be held at all stages $K=2,...,N+1$
- Each job moves from station to station, and requires T_K total mean amount of service time at stage $K=0,2,...,N+2$

The figure below is a queueing network block diagram of this system.

We denote by λ the total mean throughput rate of completing jobs; R denotes the total mean response time (queueing or waiting time plus execution time) per job. The system state space is denoted by Ω. Elements in the state space are denoted by $\underline{J}=(J_0, \ldots, J_{N+1})$. $J_K,K=0,2,...,N+1$ denotes the number of jobs either waiting or in execution at stage K. Feasible elements in the state space obey the following constraints:

[1]   The total number of tasks in the system is fixed at P_0

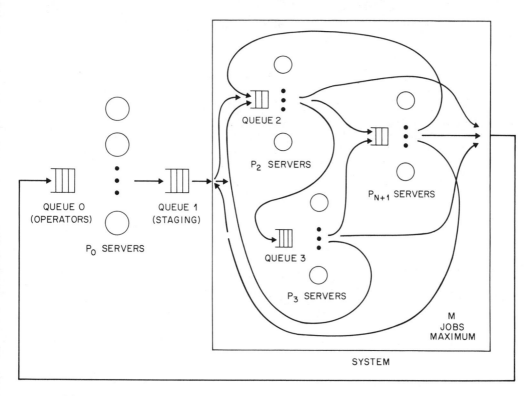

Figure 4.13.Block Diagram of Memory Constrained Queueing Network

$$P_0 = |\underline{J}| = \sum_{K=0}^{N+1} J_K$$

[2]   There can be at most a maximum of M jobs inside the system:

$$\sum_{K=2}^{N+1} J_K = \min[M, P_0 - J_0]$$

Combining all these, we see that elements $\underline{J}$ in Ω are nonnegative integer valued tuples where Ω is given by the set of all N+2 tuples $\underline{V} = (V_0, \ldots, V_{N+1})$ such that

$$V_K \geqslant 0 \ K=0,...,N+1; \ \sum_{K=0}^{N+1} V_K = P_0; \ \sum_{K=2}^{N+1} V_K = \min[M, P_0 - V_0]\}$$

The number of jobs *in execution* at stage $K=0,2,...,N+1$ is given by $\min[J_K, P_K]$ at any given instant of time. From the previous section, Little's Law allows us to write:

mean number in execution at stage $K \equiv E[\min(J_K, P_K)] = \lambda T_K$ $K=0,2,...,N+1$

where $E(.)$ denotes the time average of the argument. Our goal is to find upper and lower bounds on λ subject to the state space constraints on $J_K, K=0,...,N+1$. Since mean throughput rate and mean response time or delay

163

are related via

$$\lambda = \frac{P_0}{T_0 + R}$$

we will also obtain associated lower and upper bounds on mean delay.

4.7.2 Lower Bound on Mean Throughput Rate We first divide both sides of the following equation

$$E[min(J_0,P_0)] = \lambda T_0$$

by P_0. In like manner, we divide both sides of the following equations

$$\lambda T_K = E[min(J_K,P_K)]   K=2,...,N+1$$

by $min[M,P_0,P_K]$. Now we add up these $N+1$ equations:

$$\frac{E[min(J_0,P_0)]}{P_0} + \sum_{K=2}^{N+1} \frac{E[min(J_K,P_K)]}{min[M,P_0,P_K)]} = \lambda \left[\frac{T_0}{P_0} + \sum_{K=2}^{N+1} \frac{T_K}{min[M,P_0,P_K]} \right]$$

Now we interchange the mean value with the summation on the left hand side:

$$E \left[\frac{min[(J_0,P_0)]}{P_0} + \sum_{K=2}^{N+1} \frac{min[J_K,P_K]}{min[M,P_0,P_K]} \right] = \lambda \left[\frac{T_0}{P_0} + \sum_{K=2}^{N+1} \frac{T_K}{min[M,P_0,P_K]} \right]$$

Our goal is to lower bound the left hand side by one, which will yield a lower bound on λ.

Two cases can arise. First, there can exist one $I=2,...,N+1$ such that $P_I \leqslant J_I$. Since all the terms on the left hand side are nonnegative, we can lower bound the left hand side by ignoring all of these terms except term $I=2,...,N+1$:

$$\frac{min[J_0,P_0]}{P_0} + \sum_{K=2}^{N+1} \frac{min[J_K,P_K]}{min[M,P_0,P_K]} \geqslant \frac{min[J_I,P_I]}{min[M,P_0,P_I]} \geqslant \frac{P_I}{min[M,P_0,P_I]} \geqslant 1$$

Second, for all $K=0,2,...,N+1$, $P_K > J_K$ and hence

$$min[J_K,P_K] = J_K   K=2,...,N+1$$

Two subcases arise: if $P_0-J_0 \leqslant M$ then there is no waiting by any job in the staging queue, and

$$\frac{J_0}{P_0} + \sum_{K=2}^{N+1} \frac{J_K}{min[M,P_0,P_K]} \geqslant \frac{J_0}{P_0} + \frac{P_0 - J_0}{P_0} = 1$$

The other subcase is if $P_0-J_0 > M$ and then there is waiting in the staging queue, so

$$\frac{min[J_0,P_0]}{P_0} + \sum_{K=2}^{N+1} \frac{J_K}{min[M,P_0,P_K]} \geqslant \sum_{K=2}^{N+1} \frac{J_K}{min[M,P_0,P_K]} = \frac{M}{M} = 1$$

Hence, we see that

$$\lambda \left[\frac{T_0}{P_0} + \sum_{K=2}^{N+1} \frac{T_K}{min[M,P_0,P_K]} \right] \geq 1$$

and we obtain the desired lower bound:

$$\lambda_{lower} = \frac{P_0}{T_0 + \sum_{K=2}^{N+1} \frac{P_0}{min[M,P_0,P_K]} T_K}$$

The total mean time to execute a job at each stage in the system has been stretched from $T_K, K=2,...,N+1$ to $\tilde{T}_K, K=2,...,N+1$ where

$$\tilde{T}_K = \frac{P_0}{min[M,P_0,P_K]} T_K \geq T_K \quad K=2,...,N+1$$

$$\lambda_{lower} = \frac{P_0}{T_0 + \sum_{K=2}^{N+1} \tilde{T}_K}$$

which is one way of quantifying the slowdown at each node due to congestion.

4.7.3 Upper Bound on Mean Throughput Rate From the definition of λ we see

$$\lambda = \frac{E[min(J_K,P_K)]}{T_K} \leq \frac{min[P_K,P_0,M]}{T_K} \quad K=0,2,...,N+1$$

From this same identity, we obtain a second upper bound:

$$\lambda T_K \leq E[J_K] \quad K=0,2,...,N+1 \quad \rightarrow$$

$$\lambda[T_0 + \sum_{K=2}^{N+1} T_K] \leq E[J_0 + \sum_{K=2}^{N+1} J_K] = P_0$$

The constraint on the maximum number of jobs inside the system can be written as

$$\sum_{K=2}^{N+1} J_K \leq min[P_0,M]$$

If we use Little's Law, we see

$$\lambda \sum_{K=2}^{N+1} T_K = \sum_{K=2}^{N+1} E[J_K] \leq min[M,P_0]$$

In summary, we have shown

$$\lambda \leq min \left[\min_{K=0,2,...,N+1} \left[\frac{min[P_0,P_K,M]}{T_K} \right], \frac{P_0}{T_0 + \sum_{K=2}^{N+1} T_K}, \frac{min[M,P_0]}{\sum_{K=2}^{N+1} T_K} \right]$$

4.7.4 Interpretation One intuitive explanation for these bounds is the following. To achieve the upper bound on mean throughput rate, each step of job execution has little fluctuation relative to its mean value, and jobs interleave with one another. The mean throughput rate can be upper bounded via the following mechanisms:

- The total number of jobs circulating in the system is limiting the mean throughput rate; in this regime, as we increase the number of jobs, the mean throughput rate increases in roughly the same proportion

- One stage is executing jobs at its maximum rate, limiting the mean throughput rate; in this regime, as we increase either the speed of each processor at that stage, or the number of processors with the same speed, the mean throughput rate increases in roughly the same proportion

- The constraint on the maximum number of jobs in the system is limiting the mean throughput rate; in this regime, as we increase the allowable maximum number of jobs in the system, the mean throughput rate increases accordingly

To achieve the lower bound on mean throughput rate, each step of job execution has large fluctuations relative to its mean value, so that all jobs in the system are congested at one node. A different way of gaining insight into this lower bound is to replace the service or processing time distribution at each node with a bimodal distribution with the same mean as the old distribution, where $(1-\epsilon_K)$ denotes the fraction of jobs at stage K that are executed in *zero* time and ϵ_K are the fraction of jobs at stage K that are executed in time $1/\mu_K$ such that $T_K = \epsilon_K/\mu_K$. Here in normal operation two things can occur: the mean time for a job to cycle through the network will be roughly zero, since most stages will take zero time, and hence the number of jobs in circulation will limit the mean throughput rate, or one stage of execution will take a time that is much longer relative to all the other times, and hence all but one or two jobs will be congested at one node, thus limiting the mean throughput rate.

4.7.5 Additional Reading

[1] R.W.Conway, W.L.Maxwell, L.W.Miller, **Theory of Scheduling,** Addison-Wesley, Reading, Massachusetts, 1967; Little's formula, pp.18-19.

[2] P.J.Denning, J.P.Buzen, *The Operational Analysis of Queueing Network Models,* Computing Surveys, **10** (3), 225-261 (1978).

[3]   J.D.C.Little, *A Proof of the Queueing Formula L = λ W,* Operations Research, **9**, 383-387 (1961).

[4]   W.L.Smith, *Renewal Theory and Its Ramifications,* J.Royal Statistical Society (Series B), **20(2)**, 243-302(1958).

4.8 A Mean Throughput Rate Upper Bound for Multiple Class Single Resource Models

Now we sketch how to extend the analysis in the previous section that led to an upper bound on mean throughput rate to a system that processes multiple types of jobs, not just one.

4.8.1 Model A computer communication system must execute C classes of jobs. Each job consists of one or more steps, and each step requires a single resource for a mean amount of time. $T_{IK} \geqslant 0$ denotes the total mean amount of time, summed over all steps, that class K job requires resource $I = 1, ..., N$.

The system configuration is $P_I, I = 1, ..., N$ servers or processors for resource I, where $P_I = 1, 2, 3...$ Each resource is fed by a single queue of jobs, i.e., any processor can execute any job.

At any given instant of time, say t, the number of jobs either waiting to be executed or in execution at resource I from class K is denoted by $J_{IK}(t)$. We denote by $\underline{J}(t) \in \Omega$ the vector

$$\underline{J}(t) = [J_{IK}(t), I = 1, ..., N; K = 1, ..., C]$$

where the set of feasible states for $\underline{J}(t)$ is denoted by Ω.

Work is scheduled for each resource such that if a server or processor is idle, it will search the list of jobs ready to be run and execute one if at all possible. This means that at any instant of time the number of busy servers or processors at resource $I = 1, ..., N$ is given by

$$\textit{number of busy servers at node } I = min[P_I, \sum_{K=1}^{C} J_{IK}(t)] \quad I = 1, ..., N$$

We assume that each job type requires a constant amount of storage or memory, denoted by M_K for class $K = 1, ..., C$. This introduces a constraint on the allowable set of states Ω, because only a given number of each type of job can be stored in the system at any one time. For example, if there is a pool of memory of M blocks, then this constraint takes the form

$$\sum_{I=1}^{N} \sum_{K=1}^{C} M_K J_{IK} \leqslant M$$

while if we dedicate say M_K units of memory to each type of job, then this constraint takes the form

$$\sum_{I=1}^{N} M_K J_{IK} \leqslant M_K \qquad K=1,...,C$$

4.8.2 Analysis The previous discussion implies that the set of feasible mean throughput rates for each type of job, $\lambda_K, K=1,...,C$ forms a convex set. In fact, this convex set is a simplex, with the extreme points yielding the maximum possible mean throughput rate vectors. One way to explore the geometry of this model is to fix the *mix* of job types, say $F_K, K=1,...,C$ is the fraction of jobs of type K, and hence the mean throughput rate for job type K is

$$\lambda_K = \lambda_{total} F_K \qquad K=1,...,C$$

where λ_{total} is a scalar denoting the total mean throughput rate of jobs through the system. In order to find the largest such permissible λ_{total}, we would start at zero and increase λ_{total} until we would violate one of the state space or mean value constraints; the point at which this occurs would be the largest possible λ_{total}.

4.9 Voice Message Mail and Electronic Mail Storage System

A digital system is designed to store two different types of messages

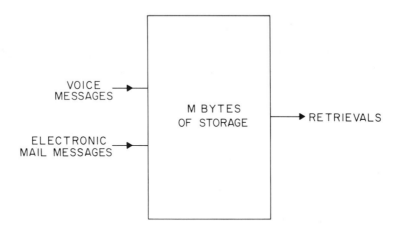

Figure 4.14.Integrated Communication Storage Subsystem Block Diagram

- Voice messages originate at a rate of λ_V messages per unit time, are stored for an average of T_V time units before being removed, and require B_V bytes of storage

- Electronic mail messages originate at a rate of λ_E messages per unit time, are stored for an average of T_E time units, and require B_E bytes of storage

The storage subsystem has a capacity of M bytes. What evidence is there that the storage is adequate?

We denote by $m(t)$ the number of bytes of storage filled with either a voice or electronic mail message at time t. If we ask what the mean amount of occupied storage is, we see

$$mean\ storage = \lim_{T \to \infty} \frac{1}{T} \int_0^T m(t)\,dt$$

Over an interval of duration T we will find N messages total of either type in the storage subsystem. We denote by $B(K)$ the amount of storage (in bytes) of the Kth message, and $T(K)$ denotes the storage time of the Kth message. Given the above, we see

$$\frac{1}{T} \int_0^T m(t)\,dt = \frac{1}{T} \sum_{K=1}^N B(K)T(K) = \frac{N}{T} \frac{1}{N} \sum_{K=1}^N B(K)T(K)$$

We identify the total mean throughput rate of messages over the observation interval with N/T and we identify the other term with the mean number of byte-seconds per message:

$$\lambda = \frac{N}{T} \quad mean\ byte-seconds\ per\ message = \frac{1}{N} \sum_{K=1}^N B(K)T(K)$$

However, we know that the total mean throughput rate equals the sum of the two types of messages:

$$\lambda = \lambda_V + \lambda_E$$

Next, we realize the mean byte-seconds per message is given by the fraction of arrivals of each type weighted by the mean byte-seconds per each message type:

$$mean\ byte\ seconds\ per\ message = F_V B_V T_V + F_E B_E T_E$$

The fraction of messages of each is simply the fraction of arrivals of each type:

$$F_V = \frac{\lambda_V}{\lambda_V + \lambda_E} \quad F_E = \frac{\lambda_E}{\lambda_E + \lambda_E}$$

Combining all this, we see

$$M \geqslant \frac{1}{T} \int_0^T m(t)\,dt = \lambda_V B_V T_V + \lambda_E B_E T_E$$

Notice we have generalized Little's Law here: the jumps up and down in $m(t)$ are no longer all of size one, but equal the amount of storage associated with each arrival or departure. As in the previous case, we might wish to choose M larger than this mean value due to fluctuations about the mean.

EXERCISE: Plot upper and lower bounds on mean throughput rate and mean delay for this system as a function of total mean arrival rate for a given mix of voice and data arrivals.

4.10 Multiple Processor/Multiple Memory Systems

A hardware block diagram of a multiple resource system is shown in the figure below.

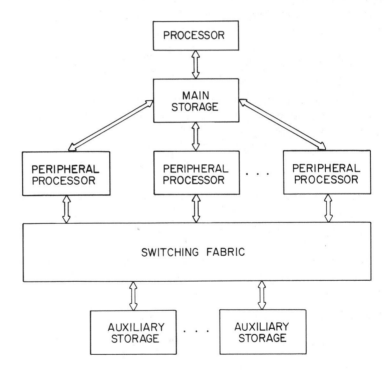

Figure 4.15. Hardware Block Diagram of Record Processing System

Records are retrieved from auxiliary storage, processed, and stored. The system consists of one processor, and main storage capable of holding R records simultaneously. Main storage is connected to P peripheral processors. Each peripheral processor is connected to a switching fabric, as are all the auxiliary storage devices. Each peripheral processor can be connected to any of A auxiliary storage devices via the switching fabric, but only one peripheral processor can access one auxiliary storage device at a time. Each access to an auxiliary storage device retrieves one block of data; each record comprises an integral number of blocks. For simplicity, we assume that all records are one block in size from this point on.

The steps involved in processing a transaction with the associated resources are summarized in the table below:

Table 4.1.Step Resource Table

Step	Processor	Buffer	Peripheral	Aux Storage	Time
Input	0	1	1	1	T_{input}
Processing	1	1	0	0	T_{proc}
Output	0	1	1	1	T_{output}

The time required for input or output is the time required to access or transfer the data from auxiliary storage, transfer it to or from a buffer, with the associated time required for controlling these actions via the peripheral processor; this total mean time is denoted by T_{input} and T_{output}, for input and output respectively. The mean time involved in record processing on the processor is T_{proc}.

Since a job can be in one of three steps, we denote by $\underline{J}$ the three tuple whose elements denote the number of jobs in execution in each step:

$$\underline{J} = (J_{input}, J_{proc}, J_{output})$$

How do the finite resources limit the admissible state space? Since we have only one processor, we see

$$J_{proc} \leqslant 1$$

Since we have P peripheral processors with A auxiliary storage devices, the lesser of these two will limit the total number of transactions involved in input or output:

$$J_{input} + J_{output} \leqslant \min(P, A)$$

Finally, we have a total of R records, and hence

$$J_{input} + J_{proc} + J_{output} \leqslant R$$

The state space Ω is the admissible set of *integer* valued components of $\underline{J}$ that satisfy these constraints. The *convex hull* of the state space Ω, denoted $C(\Omega)$, is the set of *real* valued three tuples that satisfy these constraints. If we substitute into these constraints, if the processor is the bottleneck, then an upper bound on mean throughput rate λ is given by

$$\lambda T_{proc} \leqslant 1$$

On the other hand, if the peripheral processor or auxiliary storage is the bottleneck, then an upper bound on mean throughput rate λ is given by

$$\lambda(T_{input} + T_{output}) \leqslant min(P,A)$$

$$\lambda(T_{input} + T_{proc} + T_{output}) \leqslant R \quad \textit{buffer bottleneck}$$

Summarizing all this, we see

$$\lambda \leqslant min\left[\frac{1}{T_{proc}}, \frac{min(P,A)}{T_{input} + T_{output}}, \frac{R}{T_{input} + T_{proc} + T_{output}}\right]$$

Four configurations are under investigation

- Main memory capacity of one record, with one peripheral processor and one auxiliary storage unit resulting in no concurrency between the processing and input/output

- Main memory capacity of two records, with one peripheral processor and one auxiliary storage unit with the potential for processor/input or processor/output concurrency

- Main memory capacity of two records, with two peripheral processors and two auxiliary storage units, with the potential for processor/input, processor/output, or processor/input-output concurrency

- Main memory capacity of three records, with two peripheral processors and two auxiliary storage units, and the potential for input/output, processor/input, processor/output concurrency

For each configuration, our goal is to calculate an upper bound on mean throughput rate of completing transactions, and to describe the set of parameter values that achieves this upper bound on mean throughput rate.

For the first configuration, we see

$$\lambda \leqslant \frac{1}{T_{input} + T_{output} + T_{proc}}$$

For the second configuration, we see

$$\lambda \leqslant \frac{1}{max[T_{proc}, T_{input} + T_{output}]}$$

For the third configuration, we see

$$\lambda \leqslant \frac{1}{\frac{1}{2}[T_{proc} + max(T_{proc}, T_{input} + T_{output})]}$$

For the fourth configuration, we see

$$\lambda \leqslant \frac{1}{max[T_{proc}, \frac{1}{2}(T_{input} + T_{output})]}$$

EXERCISE: Show that the third configuration is least sensitive to the workload assumptions.

4.11 Transaction Processing System

In a transaction processing, clerks spend a given mean amount of time reading, thinking and typing a transaction via a terminal and then wait for the system to respond before repeating this process. Transaction processing involves:

- Input data validation and logical consistency checking

- Data base management access to modify records appropriately

4.11.1 System Configuration The system hardware configuration consists of C clerks at terminals, one terminal per clerk, plus a single processor and a single disk.

4.11.2 Steps Required Per Transaction The steps and resources required for each step of transaction processing are summarized below:

Table 4.2. Resources Required Per Step of Transaction Processing

Step	Clerk	Processor	Disk	Mean Time
1	Yes	No	No	T_{think}
2	No	Yes	No	T_{input}
3	No	Yes	No	$T_{proc,dbm}$
4	No	No	Yes	$T_{disk,dbm}$

All the steps involved in transaction processing that require the data base manager have been aggregated into two steps, with one step involving only the processor, and the other step involving only the disk.

4.11.3 System State Space The state at a given instant of time, say t, is given by a tuple denoted by $\underline{J}(t)$ where

- $J_{clerk}(t)$ denotes the number of clerks busy with reading, thinking and typing transactions

- $J_{input}(t)$ denotes the number of jobs either waiting for the processor or running on the processor

- $J_{proc,dbm}(t)$ denotes the number of jobs requiring data base management activity either waiting or running on the processor

- $J_{disk,dbm}(t)$ denotes the number of jobs requiring data base management activity either waiting or running on the disk

The system state space is given by Ω which is the set of all admissible $\underline{J}(t)$ tuples:

$$\Omega = \{\underline{J}(t) \,|\, J_{clerk}(t), J_{input}(t), J_{proc,dbm}(t), J_{disk,dbm}(t) = 0,1,2...\}$$

We wish to assess the impact of two different modes of operation, involving different structuring of application software:

- In the first mode, a clerk waits for the transaction submitted to be completely executed before entering the next transaction. This results in a constraint on the admissible values of $\underline{J}(t)$, because the total number of transactions *anywhere* in the system at any given instant of time is given by the total number of clerks:

$$\Omega \ \{\underline{J}(t) | J_{clerk}(t) + J_{input}(t) + J_{proc,dbm}(t) + J_{disk,dbm}(t) = C\}$$

- In the second mode, a clerk waits for the transaction data validation stage to be completed, before entering the next transaction; a clerk can have a maximum number of transactions, say S transactions, in the data validation phase of system operation at any one time. If this threshold is exceeded, then that clerk is blocked from submitting a new transaction until less than S transactions are in the input validation stage. In practice, S would be chosen to be no impediment on a clerk under normal operations, while under heavy loading, when the system performance becomes unacceptable, S would be a throttle or limit on the maximum amount of work that could ever be in the system, a type of overload control. The design problem is to find an appropriate value of S. This results in a different type of state space constraint:

$$\Omega = \{\underline{J}(t) | J_{clerk}(t) + J_{input}(t) \leqslant S\}$$

4.11.4 Mean Resource Utilization Transactions are executed by the system at a total mean rate of λ transactions per unit time. On the average, we will find the mean number of clerks busy reading, thinking and typing given by

$$E[min(J_{clerk}(t),C)] = \lambda T_{think}$$

The fraction of time the processor is busy is given by

$$E[min(J_{input}(t) + J_{proc,dbm}(t),1)] = \lambda(T_{input} + T_{proc,dbm})$$

The fraction of time the disk is busy is given by

$$E[min(J_{disk,dbm}(t),1)] = \lambda T_{disk,dbm}$$

4.11.5 Upper Bounds on Mean Throughput Rate To calculate an upper bound on mean throughput, we examine each resource:

- If the clerks are completely busy, then an upper bound on mean throughput rate is

$$C \geqslant E[min(J_{clerk}(t),C)] = \lambda T_{think} \rightarrow \lambda \leqslant \frac{C}{T_{think}}$$

- If the processor is completely busy, then an upper bound on mean throughput rate is

$$1 \geqslant E[min(J_{input}(t)+J_{proc,dbm}(t),1)] = \lambda(T_{input} + T_{proc,dbm}) \rightarrow \lambda \leqslant \frac{1}{T_{input} + T_{proc,dbm}}$$

- If the disk is completely busy, then an upper bound on mean throughput rate is

$$1 \geqslant E[min(J_{disk,dbm}(t),1)] = \lambda T_{disk,dbm} \rightarrow \lambda \leqslant \frac{1}{T_{proc,dbm}}$$

- If the policy of demanding that a clerk wait until a transaction is completely executed until entering a new transaction is the bottleneck, then

$$C = \lambda(T_{think} + T_{input} + T_{proc,dbm} + T_{disk,dbm})$$

The mean throughput rate is upper bounded by

$$\lambda \leqslant \frac{C}{T_{think} + T_{input} + T_{proc,dbm} + T_{disk,dbm}}$$

- If the policy of allowing a clerk to enter a maximum of S transactions into the system, with only the data input validation being completed before control is under, is the bottleneck, then

$$SC \geqslant E[J_{clerk}(t) + J_{input}(t)] = \lambda(T_{think} + T_{input}) \rightarrow \lambda \leqslant \frac{SC}{T_{think} + T_{input}}$$

4.11.6 Interpretation Let's substitute some numbers to gain insight into what all this means:

Table 4.3.Illustrative Numerical Values

T_{think}	*15 sec*
T_{input}	*0.1 sec*
$T_{proc,dbm}$	*0.5 sec*
$T_{disk,dbm}$	*0.75 sec*
C Clerks	*10*
S Job Limit	*5*

The upper bounds on mean throughput rate are as follows:

- If clerks are the bottleneck then

$$\lambda \leqslant \frac{10}{15 \ sec} = 0.6667 \ jobs/sec$$

- If the processor is a bottleneck then

$$\lambda \leqslant \frac{1}{0.1 \ sec + 0.6 \ sec} = 1.4286 \ jobs/sec$$

- If the disk is a bottleneck then

$$\lambda \leqslant \frac{1}{0.75 \ sec} = 1.3333 \ jobs/sec$$

- If the policy of demanding a clerk wait for a transaction to be completely executed before entering a new transaction is the bottleneck then

$$\lambda \leqslant \frac{10}{15 \ sec + 0.1 \ sec + 0.6 \ sec + 0.75 \ sec} = 0.6079 \ jobs/sec$$

- If the policy of allowing a clerk to enter a maximum of five (S=5) transactions into the system, with control being returned after data input, is the bottleneck then

$$\lambda \leqslant \frac{10 \times 5}{15 \ sec + 0.1 \ sec} = 3.3112 \ jobs/sec$$

Demanding that a clerk wait for a transaction to be completely processed before entering a new transaction results in the mean throughput rate being upper bounded by

$$\lambda \leqslant 0.6079 \ jobs/sec$$

Here, the bottleneck is the work scheduling policy.

Allowing a clerk to immediately enter a transaction after the data input and validation phase is completed, up to a maximum of five, results in the mean throughput rate being upper bounded by

$$\lambda \leqslant 0.6667 \ jobs/sec$$

We have changed the bottleneck from the policy of work scheduling to the clerks as the limit on maximum mean throughput rate.

If we put twenty clerks on the system ($C=20$) rather than ten clerks ($C=10$), then after substituting into the above formulae we find the policy of demanding a clerk wait for a transaction to be completely executed before allowing a new transaction to enter the system results in a maximum mean throughput rate of

$$\lambda \leqslant 1.2160 \ jobs/sec$$

while if we allow each clerk to enter a maximum of five ($S=5$) transactions into the system, with control being returned after the data input phase, then the bottleneck is now the clerk's:

$$\lambda \leqslant 1.3333 \ jobs/sec$$

Finally, if we put thirty clerks on the system ($C=30$) then we find that the disk is the bottleneck, not the scheduling policy or number of clerks.

4.12 A Distributed Data Communications System

A communications system receives messages from two sources labeled A and B, and transmits them to a common source, labeled C. The system configuration consists of four subsystems, each with its own processor and communications facilities, labeled *1,2,3,4* respectively. A block diagram is shown below.

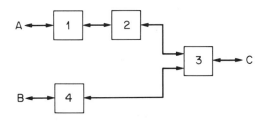

Figure 4.16.Distributed Data Communications System Block Diagram

Conceptually each processor receives messages from a source, and copies them into output buffers. A queueing network block diagram of the system is shown below:

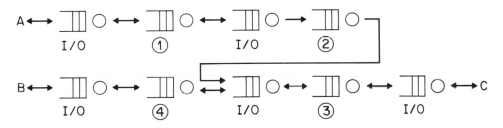

Figure 4.17.Queueing Network Block Diagram

The operation of the system is as follows:

- Processor 1 receives messages from external source A and buffers them into an internal buffer; it then copies the messages into a set of buffers shared with processor 2. In order that no records be lost in copying because a buffer is not available, critical region code governed by two semaphores *P* and *V* is used.

  The pseudo code executed by processor 1 is shown below:

  initialize records(1)=buffer(1),space(1)=0 /*B$_{1,max}$ =buffer(1)*/

process 1
loop

> P(records(1)) /*test if records(1)>0;
> yes->decrement by one; no->wait*/
> P(space(2)) /*test if space(2)>0;
> yes->decrement by one; no->wait*/
> copy(space(1),space(2)) /*copy contents of space(1)
> into space(2)*/
> V(records(2)) /*increment records(2) by one*/

end loop

- Processor 2 receives messages from processor 1 and copies them into a set of buffers shared with processor 3 and processor 4. The pseudo code executed by processor 2 is shown below:

initialize records(2)=buffer(2), space(2)=0 /$B_{2,max}$=buffer(2)*/*

process 2
loop

> P(records(2)) /*test if records(2)>0;
> yes->decrement by one; no->wait*/
> P(space(3)) /*test if space(3)>0;
> yes->decrement by one; no -> wait*/
> copy(space(2),space(3)) /*copy contents of space(2)
> into space(3)*/
> V(records(3)) /*increment records(3) by one*/

end loop

- Processor 4 receives messages from external source B and copies them into a set of buffers shared with processor 3 and with processor 2. The pseudo code executed by processor 4 is shown below:

initialize records(4)=buffer(4), space(4)=0 /$B_{4,max}$=buffer(4)*/*

process 4
loop

> P(records(4)) /*test if records(4)>0;
> yes->decrement by one;no->wait*/
> P(space(3)) /*test if space(3)>0;
> yes->decrement by one;no->wait*/
> copy(space(4),space(3)) /*copy contents of space(4)
> into space(3)*/

$V(records(3))$ /*increment records(3) by one*/
end loop

- Processor 3 receives messages from processors 2 and 4 and copies them into an external buffer shared with external sink C. The pseudo code executed by processor 3 is shown below:

initialize records(3)=buffer(3),space(3)=0 /*$B_{3,max}$=buffer(3)*/

process 3
loop

    $P(records(3))$ /*test if records(3)>0;
    yes->decrement by one;no->wait*/
    $P(space(5))$ /*test if space(5)>0;
    yes->decrement by one;no->wait*/
    copy(space(3),space(5)) /*copy contents of space(3)
    into space(5)*/
    $V(records(5))$ /*increment records(5) by one*/

end loop

The steps and resources required at each step are summarized in the table below:

Table 4.4.Resources Required for Each Step of A->C Transmission

| Step | Processor | | | Buffer | | | Time |
Number	1	2	3	1	2	C	Interval
1	Yes	No	No	Yes	No	No	T_1
2	No	Yes	No	Yes	Yes	No	T_2
3	No	No	Yes	No	Yes	Yes	T_3

Table 4.5.Resources Required for Each Step of B->C Transmission

| Step | Processor | | Buffer | | Time |
Number	3	4	2	C	Interval
1	No	Yes	Yes	No	T_4
2	Yes	No	Yes	No	T_3

4.12.1 System State Space What is the state of this system at any given time instant, say t? We denote by $M_K(t),K=1,2,3,4,C$ the number of messages either waiting to be transmitted or being transmitted at station K at time t, while we let $B_K(t),K=1,2,3,4,C$ denote the number of buffers filled with a message at node K. The stage space Ω is given by

$$\Omega = \{M_K(t)=0,1,2,...;B_K(t)=0,1,...,B_{max,K};K=1,2,3,4,C\}$$

4.12.2 Long Term Time Averaged Utilization of Resources The fraction of time we will find processor K busy, averaged over a suitably long time interval (we will denote the average by $E()$) is simply the mean arrival rate of messages to processor K, denoted by λ_K, multiplied by the mean time spent copying a message, denoted by T_K:

$$E[min(M_K(t),1)] = \lambda_K T_K \quad K=1,2,3,4,5$$

The mean number of buffers we will find filled with a message at node K, averaged over a suitably long time interval, is the mean arrival rate of messages to the buffer pool, denoted by $\tilde{\lambda}_K$, multiplied by the mean time spent copying a message into the buffer and out of the buffer, denoted by $\tilde{T}_K$:

$$E[min(B_K(t),B_{K,max})] = \tilde{\lambda}_K \tilde{T}_K \quad K=1,2,3,4,C$$

4.12.3 Upper Bounds on Mean Throughput Rate Two types of bottlenecks can arise, one due to the processors becoming completely busy copying messages, the other due to the buffers becoming completely filled. How can we quantify these ideas?

First we focus on processor bottlenecks:

- Processor 1 can be completely utilized:

$$1 \geqslant E[min(J_1(t),1)] = P\lambda T_1 \quad \lambda \leqslant \frac{1}{PT_1}$$

- Processor 2 can be completely utilized:

$$1 \geqslant E[min(J_2(t),1)] = P\lambda T_2 \quad \lambda \leqslant \frac{1}{PT_2}$$

- Processor 4 can be completely utilized:

$$1 \geqslant E[min(J_4(t),1)] = (1-P)\lambda T_4 \quad \lambda \leqslant \frac{1}{(1-P)T_4}$$

- Processor 3 can be completely utilized:

$$1 \geqslant E[min(J_3(t),1)] = \lambda T_3 \quad \lambda \leqslant \frac{1}{T_3}$$

Next, we concentrate on potential buffer bottlenecks:

- The buffer pool connecting processor 1 to processor 2 can become completely filled:

$$B_{1,max} \geqslant E[min(B_1(t),B_{1,max})] = P\lambda(T_1+T_2) \quad \lambda \leqslant \frac{B_{1,max}}{P(T_1+T_2)}$$

- The buffer pool connecting processors 2 and 4 to processor 3 can become completely filled:

$$B_{2,max} \geqslant E[min(B_2(t),B_{2,max})] = P\lambda(T_2+T_3)+(1-P)\lambda(T_3+T_4)$$

$$\lambda \leqslant \frac{B_{2,max}}{P(T_2+T_3) + (1-P)(T_3+T_4)}$$

- The buffer pool connecting processor 3 to output sink C can become completely filled:

$$B_{3,max} \geqslant E[min(B_3(t),B_{3,max})] = \lambda(T_3+T_C) \quad \lambda \leqslant \frac{B_{3,max}}{T_3+T_C}$$

The mean throughput rate is upper bounded by finding the minimum of the upper bound on the processor bounds and the minimum of the upper bound on the buffer bounds:

$$\lambda \leqslant min[\lambda_{processor,max} , \lambda_{buffer,max}]$$

$$\lambda_{processor,max} = min\left[\frac{1}{PT_1},\frac{1}{PT_2},\frac{1}{(1-P)T_4},\frac{1}{T_3}\right]$$

$$\lambda_{buffer,max} = min\left[\frac{B_{1,max}}{P(T_1+T_2)},\frac{B_{2,max}}{P(T_2+T_3)+(1-P)(T_3+T_4)},\frac{B_{3,max}}{T_3+T_C}\right]$$

4.12.4 Special Cases Two cases are of interest:

- Single buffering messages so $B_{K,max}=1$ which is a test of the logically correct operation of the system. Can you see that the *buffers* will *always* be the bottleneck, and *never* the processors?

- Double buffering messages to allow for concurrent operation of a transmitter and receiver pair, so that $B_{K,max}=2$. Depending upon the time spent in copying messages into and out of shared buffers, either a processor or a buffer pool may be the bottleneck

4.13 Different Data Structures for Multiple Processors and Multiple Memories

In this section we examine the performance of a computer system with multiple processors and multiple memories interconnected via a high speed bus, that must execute one application program that can have two different data structures. From this point on, we will assume the time the bus is used to transfer bits to and from the processors and memories is negligible compared to the processing time required.

The two different types of data structures are labeled *1* and *2*. To be concrete, we will fix the hardware configuration at seven units of memory and three processors. For data structure 1, four units of memory and (1/19) seconds of execution time are required on one processor, on the average. For data structure 2, two units of memory and (1/10) seconds of execution time are required on one processor. Put differently, data structure 1 uses more memory than data structure 2, but takes less time to execute. The table below summarizes this information:

Table 4.6. Resources Required For Each Data Structure

Type	Processor	Memory	Mean Time
1	1	4	1/19
2	1	2	1/10

The state of the system is given by an ordered pair (J_1, J_2), where $J_K, K=1,2$ is the total number of jobs in execution at a given instant of time using data structure K. Due to the hardware configuration constraints, we see

$$4J_1 + 2J_2 \leqslant 7 \quad \textit{memory constraint}$$

$$J_1 + J_2 \leqslant 3 \quad \textit{processor constraint}$$

$$J_K = 0,1,2,...;K=1,2 \quad \textit{nonnegative integers constraint}$$

The state space, Ω, is given by

$$\Omega = \{(J_1, J_2) \,|\, (0,0),(1,0),(0,1),(1,1),(0,2),(0,3)\}$$

The mean number of jobs in execution, averaged over a suitably long time interval, is denoted by $E(J_K), K=1,2$. The total mean throughput rate of executing jobs is

$$\textit{mean throughput rate} = \lambda = 19E(J_1) + 10E(J_2)$$

Suppose we wish to maximize the mean throughput rate of completing jobs: *which data structure do we choose?*

The fraction of time the system is in state (J_1, J_2), averaged over a suitably long time interval, is denoted by $\pi(J_1, J_2)$. We have six possible states, and we would attempt to maximize the mean throughput rate subject to the constraint

$$\sum_{(J_1,J_2)\in\Omega} \pi(J_1,J_2) = 1 \quad \pi(J_1,J_2) \geqslant 0 \quad (J_1,J_2)\in\Omega$$

If we do so, by direct substitution we find

$$\lambda \leqslant 30 \quad \textit{when } J_1 \equiv 0, J_2 \equiv 3$$

At this point, all three processors are completely busy, while we only have six out of seven memory units busy; based on this evidence, one might naively expect that the processors are a *bottleneck,* i.e., the processors are completely utilized but not memory.

As an aside, it is interesting to note that the point $(J_1=1, J_2=1)$ results in a *local* optimum for the mean throughput rate as we explore all of its nearest neighbors, but this is not the *global* optimum for the mean throughput rate. To see this, we evaluate the mean throughput rate of completing jobs at state

$(J_1=1,J_2=1)$, and compare this mean throughput rate with that for all its nearest neighbors. Unfortunately, the state $(J_1=0,J_2=3)$ is *not* a nearest neighbor, and this state results in a higher mean throughput rate. This suggests that we might be forced to exhaustively enumerate all system states in much more complicated (realistic) systems, and evaluate the mean throughput rate in order to determine an upper bound on mean throughput rate. The time required to carry out this type of analysis, even with a high speed digital computer, can easily become excessive relative to our willingness to pay for this type of analysis.

On the other hand, what if we allow the values for $J_K, K=1,2$ to be continuous, not simply integer valued? This would allow us to apply linear programming techniques, where once we find a *local* maximum we are done, because this is also a *global* maximum. If we do so, we find the maximum mean throughput rate is *higher* (we have dropped the constraint that the pairs (J_1,J_2) be integers, so fewer constraints presumably *increase* the maximum mean throughput rate), and in fact is

$$maximum\ mean\ throughput\ rate = 37\ 3/4 = \max \lambda \geqslant \lambda$$

$$E(J_1) = 7/4 \qquad E(J_2) = 0$$

At this maximum, memory is completely utilized, and we have (5/4) processors idle on the average. This suggests that memory is the *bottleneck*, not the *processors*. This is *completely* different from what we just saw.

Notice that we can get *diametrically* opposite answers depending upon our assumptions: using the assumption that the mean number of jobs must be continuous leads to using only data structure 1, not data structure 2, while assuming that the mean number of jobs must be discrete leads to employing data structure 2, not data structure 1.

What happens if we increase memory from seven to eight units? For this case, keeping three processors, we find that the maximum mean throughput rate is the same whether we assume $J_K, K=1,2$ is continuous or discrete, with

$$maximum\ mean\ throughput\ rate = 38 = \max \lambda \geqslant \lambda$$

which occurs at $J_1=2, J_2=0$.

Since the maximum mean throughput rate *increases* as we add memory, we would say naively that memory was a bottleneck. On the other hand, we can remove one processor now: we cannot use it! For the seven unit memory configuration, we saw that either processors or memory could be a bottleneck, but adding one unit of memory (to relieve the bottleneck) led to only two thirds processor utilization (i.e., we can get rid of a processor).

4.14 Two Types of Jobs

A single processor computer system must execute two different types of jobs, submitted by two different people. The first person spends a mean amount of time reading, and thinking, and typing, with a mean duration of $T_{think,1}$, and then waits for a response before repeating this process. The second person spends a different amount of time reading, and thinking, and typing, with a mean duration of $T_{think,2}$, and then waits for a response before repeating this process. The mean processing times for a job submitted by person $K=1,2$ are denoted by $T_{proc,K}$. Our goal is to determine the mean rate of executing jobs submitted by each person.

4.14.1 Analysis   The system at any instant of time can be in the following states:

[1]   Both operators actively thinking, reading and typing, with no work being processed

[2]   Operator one is waiting for a response while operator two is still reading and thinking and typing

[3]   Operator two is waiting for a response while operator one is still reading and thinking and typing

[4]   Both operators are waiting for a response; the job submitted by operator one is being executed, while the job submitted by operator two is being queued until the processor becomes available

[5]   Both operators are waiting for a response; the job submitted by operator two is being executed, while the job submitted by operator one is being queued until the processor becomes available

We will index the states by $J=1,2,3,4,5$. The system spends a total amount of time T_J in state J during a measurement interval of duration T. The fraction of time the system spends in state J is denoted by $\pi(J)$ where

$$\pi(J) = \frac{T_J}{T} \geqslant 0 \qquad \sum_{J=1}^{5} \pi(J) = 1$$

The mean throughput rate of executing jobs for person $K=1,2$ is denoted λ_K. Little's Law allows us to relate the mean throughput rate to the fraction of time spent in each state.

First, the fraction of time clerk one is reading and thinking and typing is

$$\lambda_1 T_{think,1} = \pi(1) + \pi(3)$$

Next, the fraction of time clerk two is reading and thinking and typing is

$$\lambda_2 T_{think,2} = \pi(1) + \pi(2)$$

Next, the fraction of time the processor is busy executing jobs submitted by operator one is given by

$$\lambda_1 T_{proc,1} = \pi(2) + \pi(4)$$

Finally, the fraction of time the processor is busy executing jobs submitted by operator two is given by

$$\lambda_2 T_{proc,2} = \pi(3) + \pi(5)$$

If we add the first and third equations, we see

$$\lambda_1 (T_{think,1} + T_{proc,1}) = \pi(1) + \pi(2) + \pi(3) + \pi(4) \leqslant 1$$

while if we add the second and fourth equations we see

$$\lambda_2 (T_{think,2} + T_{proc,2}) = \pi(1) + \pi(2) + \pi(3) + \pi(5) \leqslant 1$$

On the other hand, if we add the last two equations, we see

$$\lambda_1 T_{proc,1} + \lambda_2 T_{proc,2} = \pi(1) + \pi(2) + \pi(3) + \pi(4) + \pi(5) \leqslant 1$$

This defines a convex set, with boundaries determined by the upper bounds on λ_1, λ_2.

On the other hand, if we add the first two equations plus twice the third plus twice the fourth equation, we find

$$\lambda_1 (T_{think,1} + 2T_{proc,1}) + \lambda_2 (T_{think,2} + T_{proc,2}) = 2 + \pi(2) + \pi(3) \geqslant 2$$

This gives us a lower bound on the admissible mean throughput rate. All of this is summarized in the figure below.

4.14.2 An Alternate Approach An alternative approach to this is to attempt to maximize the total mean throughput rate λ subject to the constraints implied by Little's Law.

4.15 Multiple Class Multiple Resource Mean Value Analysis

We close with an analysis of an upper bound on mean throughput rate for a system processing multiple types of jobs, with each job requiring multiple resources for a mean duration for each step.

4.15.1 Model There are C types of jobs to be executed. A job consists of $S(J), J=1,...,C$ steps. Each step is defined as requiring a *fixed* set of resources for a certain average or mean amount of time.

The system resources available are given by a vector $\underline{R}$ which has M components, one for each type of resource, with each component denoting the *number* of resources of each type available:

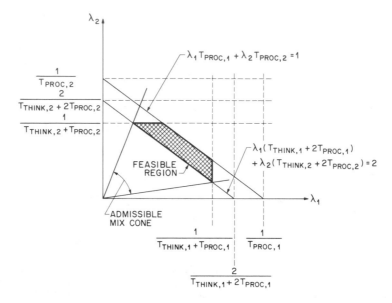

Figure 4.18. Admissible Mean Throughput Rates

$$\underline{R} = (R_1,...,R_M) \quad R_K = amount \ of \ resource \ K, K=1,...,M$$

For a given job step of a class $J=1,...,C$ job, say step $I, 1 \leqslant I \leqslant S$, a set of resources is demanded, denoted by $D_{IJ}(K)$, where $K=1,...,M$ denotes the amount of resource K. The mean duration of step I for jobs in class J is denoted by T_{IJ}.

In what follows we let $N_{IJ}(t)$ denote the number of jobs in class J in the system at time t in step $I=1,...,S(J)$.

The system state space is denoted by Ω with elements denoted by $\underline{N}$ with each element denoting the number of type $J=1,...,C$ jobs in step $I=1,...,S(J)$. Not all states are feasible; states must be nonnegative integers, subject to the constraint that the amount of resources of each used at every instant of time must be less than the total available amount of that resource:

$$\Omega = \{N_{I,J}|N_{I,J}=0,1,...;1 \leqslant J \leqslant C;1 \leqslant I \leqslant S(J);$$
$$\sum_{J=1}^{C} \sum_{I=1}^{S(J)} N_{IJ}D_{IJ}(K) \leqslant R_K, K=1,...,M\}$$

4.15.2 Analysis Little's Law allows us to write that the mean number of jobs in execution equals the mean throughput rate of each job type multiplied by the mean execution time:

$$E[N_{IJ}] = \lambda_{IJ} T_{IJ} \quad 1 \leqslant J \leqslant C; 1 \leqslant I \leqslant S(J)$$

Rather than deal with the individual mean arrival rates of each type of job, we will denote by F_{IJ} the fraction of jobs of type I,J while λ denotes the *total* mean throughput rate of jobs:

$$\lambda F_{IJ} = \lambda_{IJ} \quad 1 \leqslant J \leqslant C; 1 \leqslant I \leqslant S(J)$$

The system will spend a given fraction of time $\pi(\underline{N})$ in each state $\underline{N} \in \Omega$.

Which states will maximize the total mean throughput rate for a fixed set of resources over all possible job mixes F_{IJ}? Substituting into the above, it follows that

$$\frac{1}{\lambda} = \frac{F_{IJ} T_{IJ}}{\sum_{\underline{N} \in \Omega} \pi(\underline{N}) N_{IJ}} \quad 1 \leqslant J \leqslant C; 1 \leqslant I \leqslant S(J)$$

must be maximized over all F_{IJ}:

$$F_{IJ} \geqslant 0 \quad \sum_{J} F_{IJ} = 1$$

and subject to the state space constraint on $\underline{N}$.

If resource K is a bottleneck, then

$$\lambda \leqslant \max_{K} \frac{R_K}{D_{IJ} F_{IJ} T_{IJ}}$$

Let $U_K(t), K=1,...,M$ denote the total amount of type K resources allocated at time t so that it follows that

$$E[U_K(0,T)] = \frac{1}{T} \int_0^T U_K(t) dt = \textit{time averaged value of } U_K(t) \textit{ in } (0,T) \quad K=1,...,M$$

Over the time interval of duration T a total of N_J jobs of type $J=1,..,C$ are executed, so that

$$E[U_K(0,T)] = \sum_{L=1}^{N_J} F_{KJ} D_{KJ} T_{KJ} = \frac{N_J}{T} \frac{1}{N_J} \sum_{L=1}^{N_J} F_{KJ} D_{KJ} T_{KJ}$$

$$= \lambda_J E[D_{KJ} T_{KJ}] \quad K=1,...,M; J=1,...,C$$

Put differently, an upper bound on the mean throughput rate is given by

$$\lambda_J = \frac{E[U_K(0,T)]}{E[D_{KJ} T_{KJ}]}$$

The numerator is the utilization of resource K, while the denominator is the cross product or cross correlation of the demand for resource K by job type J with the holding time of resource K by job type J. To maximize the mean throughput rate for job type J, the utilization must be increased, while the cross correlation must be decreased.

Problems

1) A computer system consists of N clerks at terminals. Each clerk spends a constant amount of time T_{think} reading and typing and thinking to submit a job. The system executes one job at a time, and each job requires T_{system} time units to be completely executed.

A. Assume all clerks begin to read and think and type at time zero. For $N=1,2,3$ draw time lines of the activity of each clerk through three job submission cycles.

B. What is the mean throughput rate for executing jobs beyond the first job submission cycle? What is the mean response time each clerk experiences beyond the first job submission cycle?

C. If $T_{think}=15\ sec$ and $T_{system}=1\ sec$, what is the breakpoint number of clerks? What is the mean response time for $N=10$ and for $N=20$? What is the mean throughput rate for $N=10$ and $N=20$?

2) An interactive transaction processing system handles one type of transaction. A clerk submits transactions and waits for the system to respond before submitting the next transaction. There is a single processor that must execute each transaction. The following data were reported during a four hour time interval of operation:

• Six clerks were signed on during the measurement interval

• The mean *think* time for a clerk was twenty (20) seconds

• $F(K)$ denotes the fraction of time that K clerks are simultaneously waiting for a transaction to complete, and is summarized below

Table 4.7.Number of Clerks vs F(K)

K	0	1	2	3	4	5	6
F(K)	0.40	0.25	0.15	0.10	0.05	0.03	0.02

Estimate the mean transaction processing throughput rate and the mean response time for a transaction.

3) A widget retailer wishes to purchase an online point of sale computer communications system which will

• Check the credit at the point of sale of each potential customer

- Update and control inventory at the point of sale

The retailer wishes to purchase a system capable of handling one transaction per minute per terminal, with a total of two hundred (200) terminals attached to the system. The hardware configuration that the retailer can afford consists of one processor and one disk controller for a single spindle. Each transaction goes through the following steps:

[1] At the start of each transaction, a log file is updated to show that a transaction has entered the system; this is useful for recovery and accounting

[2] A credit check is made by first retrieving a regional customer index and then an accounts receivable index to find the location of the customer accounts receivable file

[3] An application program processes the credit check information and sends an approval or disapproval signal to the point of sale terminal originating the transaction; from this point on we assume the fraction of transactions that are not approved is negligible

[4] An application inventory control program first accesses a model index and then a color index to determine if the widget is in stock. From this point on we assume all but a negligible fraction of items are in stock

[5] An application program generates an order for the appropriate item and has it spooled for subsequent printing at the appropriate warehouse

[6] An application program updates an inventory file

[7] An audit trail file is written

[8] A log file is written showing the final status of the transaction. This is useful for recovery and accounting

The total mean time per disk access is fifty milliseconds. The total mean time the processor is busy per transaction is two hundred fifty milliseconds.

Is this design feasible? Will the system meet its performance goals? You might wish to structure your answer as follows:

A. Make a table showing the resources consumed at each step of execution. What is the total mean amount of each type of resource consumed per transaction?

B. What are the bottlenecks in the system? What is the maximum mean throughput rate of each bottleneck?

C. Two operating systems are under investigation. One operates in a mode of executing one transaction at a time from start to finish, while the second allows concurrent processor and disk activity. What is the maximum number of terminals the system can support for either operating system?

D. What if the system is configured with two disk spindles, not just one?

4) An interactive transaction processing system handles one type of transaction. A clerk submits transactions and waits for the system to respond before submitting the next transaction. The clerical reading and thinking and typing time interval has a mean of thirty (30) seconds. There is a single processor and a single input/output controller for one or more disks. A transaction involves some processing followed by some input/output followed by some processing and so forth until completion. For each configuration below we assume the software (application code and operating system) is unchanged, and we wish to investigate the performance of various hardware configurations on total system traffic handling characteristics. We assume each transaction requires twenty (20) accesses to secondary disk storage. For simplicity, assume the disk controller requires zero time to transfer data to and from disks.

- For each configuration below, clearly state what hardware resource reaches complete utilization first (this is called the *bottleneck* resource) as the number of clerks is increased toward infinity.

- For each configuration below, plot upper and lower bounds associated with the mean throughput rate of completing transactions and the mean response time versus the number of clerks on the system; clearly label each plot.

Here are the different configurations under consideration:

A. The hardware consists of a slow processor with a single slow speed disk. The total mean processor time per transaction is 2.0 seconds. The slow speed disk requires seventy (70) milliseconds to execute one disk access to one block of data.

B. The hardware consists of a slow processor with a special purpose *cache* memory attached, and a single slow speed disk. The total mean processor time per transaction is reduced to 1.25 seconds due to the attached cache.

C. The hardware consists of a slow speed processor with a cache memory, and a single medium speed disk. The medium speed disk requires fifty (50) milliseconds to execute one disk access to one block of data.

D. The hardware consists of a high speed processor with a single medium speed disk. The total mean processor time per transaction is 0.60 seconds.

E. The hardware consists of a high speed processor with either two medium speed disks or a single high speed disk. The high speed disk requires thirty (30) milliseconds to execute one disk access to one block of data.

5) An online transaction processing consists of hardware, a set of application programs, and an operating system that manages resources. The hardware configuration consists of a single processor, a disk controller that controls half duplex communication between the processor and disks, and three disk spindles. The steps involved in transaction processing are

[1] Wait for the disk arm on the requisite spindle to become available

[2] Initiate a head seek to the proper disk cylinder

[3] Wait for the channel to become available

[4] Wait for the proper block to rotate under the head

[5] Read from one file on one disk spindle and release the channel

[6] Process the transaction in the processor

[7] Complete the transaction by following one of the following two branches

    A. Update the file and unlock the disk spindle

    B. Do not update the file and unlock the disk spindle

The following information is available

- Six (6) milliseconds is required for every read or write transfer over the half duplex communication network arbitrated by the disk controller.

- Twenty five per cent (25%) of the file accesses are to the first disk spindle, forty per cent (40%) of the file accesses are to the second disk spindle, and thirty five per cent (35%) of the file accesses are to the third disk spindle.

- Each disk access involves time to move the head to the correct cylinder, called *seek* time, followed by time for the correct file to rotate around to the head, called *rotational latency time*. The seek time is uniformly distributed from forty (40) to one hundred twenty (120) milliseconds. The rotation time is uniformly distributed from zero (0) to thirty four (34) milliseconds.

- The processing time of a transaction in the single processor is uniformly distributed from four (4) to fourteen (14) milliseconds.

- Seventy five per cent (75%) of the transactions require a file update.

Answer the following questions:

A. What is the step resource table for transaction execution?

B. What are upper bounds on the mean throughput rate of executing transactions for each resource? What are the bottlenecks?

C. The degree of multiprogramming is defined as the mean number of jobs in execution at any one instant in time. What is the maximum degree of multiprogramming for this system?

D. What if the disk accesses are equally balanced among all the spindles? What if all the disk accesses are intended for one spindle?

6) Here is a model of a *link level flow control* protocol for exchanging information from a transmitter to a receiver. A data link consists of a transmitter, a receiver, a full duplex noiseless channel (consisting of two one way channels, one from the transmitter to the receiver, and one from the receiver to the transmitter) and a limited amount of memory for buffering messages at the receiver. After initialization procedures, the transmitter can send at most B unacknowledged messages. Every time the transmitter sends a message, it decrements a counter which is initialized at B by one, and if this counter is at zero the transmitter can send no messages. Every time the transmitter receives an acknowledgement, it increments this same counter by one, up to a maximum value of B. The maximum value B associated with this counter is sometimes called a *window* because it portrays the maximum number of unacknowledged messages streaming through the channel at any given instant of time, i.e., it is a window on the message stream. Here are the steps involved in message transmission:

[1] The transmitter decrements its buffer counter by one, hence reserving a buffer at the receiver, and transmits the message; this step requires a mean T_T. If all available buffers are reserved, i.e., if the counter is at zero, the transmitter waits until one becomes available.

[2] The message is transmitted over the link from the transmitter to the receiver; this step requires a mean time T_{T-R} and only involves the time for a message to propagate from the transmitter to the receiver.

[3] The receiver processes the message, empties the buffer and sends an acknowledgement back; this step requires a mean time T_R.

[4] The message is transmitted over the link from the receiver to the transmitter; this step requires a mean time T_{R-T} and only involves the time for a message to propagate from the receiver to the transmitter.

[5] The transmitter processes the acknowledgement; this step requires a mean time T_A and the transmitter marks the appropriate message buffer available or free for new messages, i.e., the counter is incremented by one.

A. Make a table showing the resources required at each step of message transmission and the mean time to hold these resources.

B. Find an upper and lower bound on the mean throughput rate of successfully transmitting messages over this system, as a function of the number of buffers B at the receiver, and other model parameters. Plot these upper and lower bounds vs B assuming $T_T=T_R$ and $T_{T-R}=T_{R-T}$ for three cases: $T_T=T_{T-R}/10$, $T_T=T_{T-R}$, and $T_T=10T_{T-R}$.

C. Suppose that $T_{T-R}=T_{R-T}=0$. What is the change in the upper and lower bounds on mean throughput rate in going from $B=1$ to $B=2$ to $B=\infty$ for $T_T=T_R$? Repeat the above but now assume $T_R=10T_T$.

7) A transaction processing system retrieves a record from one disk spindle, processes it, and stores it back on a second disk spindle. The hardware configuration consists of a central processor connected via a switch to multiple direct memory access disk controllers, with one spindle or moving head disk per controller. The processor has a limited amount of main memory (so called buffers) for storing records. S denotes the number of system buffers. Each buffer can hold one record. The total mean time to retrieve a record is T_{input}, the total mean time to process a record is T_{proc}, and the total mean time to store a record is T_{output}.

A. Make a table showing the resources used at each step of transaction processing and for what mean amount of time.

B. What is the state space for this sytem?

C. If $T_{proc}=1$, $T_{input}=T_{output}=2$, what is the maximum mean throughput rate for $S=1$ versus $S=2$ versus $S=3$?

D. Repeat the above for $T_{proc}=5$, $T_{input}=T_{output}=1$, and $S=1$ versus $S=2$ versus $S=3$?

E. Repeat the above for $T_{proc}=T_{input}=T_{output}=1$ for $S=1$ versus $S=2$ versus $S=3$?

F. The mean time to execute a record is $T_{input}+T_{proc}+T_{output}$. With no concurrency, the mean throughput rate is the reciprocal of this:

$$mean\ throughput\ rate_{no\ concurrency} = \frac{1}{T_{input}+T_{proc}+T_{output}}$$

Compute the reciprocal of the maximum mean throughput rate for each of the above parts, normalized by the mean throughput rate with no concurrency (this displays the gain due to concurrency).

G. Compute the degree of multiprogramming for each of the above configurations, where this is defined as the mean number of tasks simultaneously in execution, assuming the system is executing work at its maximum mean throughput rate.

8) A transaction processing system retrieves a record from storage on one disk spindle, processes it, and stores it on a second disk spindle. The hardware configuration consists of a single central processor connected via a switch to two direct memory access disk controllers, with one spindle for each controller; the direct memory access capability allows the central processor to execute work while the disk controller is busy accessing a record. All of the text required to process records is resident in main memory. The processor can buffer at most S blocks of data at a time. Each disk accesses retrieves or stores one block at a time. N denotes the number of records per block. Each record consists of B bytes. T_{access} denotes the mean time to move the disk head from an arbitrary point to the start of a block. $T_{transfer}$ denotes the mean time to transfer one byte of data from an input/output device to a disk controller. T_{proc} denotes the mean processor time per record.

A. What are the steps and resources held and time to execute each step of each job?

B. Find an expression in terms of model parameters and plot it for the maximum mean throughput rate (records per unit time) versus the number of records per block.

C. Find the ratio of the reciprocal of the maximum mean throughput rate divided by the mean time to process a record from start to finish (this is the reciprocal of the mean throughput rate with no concurrency).

D. What are the bottlenecks in this system?

E. Suppose that the following numbers specify the model parameters:

Table 4.8. Model Parameters

Disk Access Time	T_{access}	50 msec
Disk Transfer Time	$T_{transfer}$	1 microsecond
Buffer Size	B	4096 bytes
Processor Time/Record	T_{proc}	30 msec
Processor Buffers	S	8

For $N=1,2,4,8$ what is the numerical value of the maximum mean throughput rate in records per unit time?

9) Two types of jobs arrive at random instants to be executed by a computer system. The first type of job requires one processor and one memory partition, and will hold these two resources for a mean time of T_{small} to complete its execution with no interruptions. The second type of job requires one processor and two memory partitions, and will hold these resources for a mean time of T_{big} to complete its execution, again with no interruptions. The system consists of P processors and M memory partitions connected by a switching system. The time involved with data transfers through the switching system is assumed to be negligible compared to the time associated with holding a processor and one or more memory partitions.

A. At any given instant of time, there are $J_{small}(t)$ small jobs and $J_{big}(t)$ big jobs in execution in the system. Find the set of feasible pairs $(J_{small}(t), J_{big}(t))$ for this system, which defines the *state space* of operations.

B. We denote by λ_{small} and λ_{big} the mean throughput rate of each type of job. Find the set of feasible mean throughput rates $(\lambda_{small}, \lambda_{big})$. Clearly label all set boundaries in terms of model parameters.

C. List all the potential bottlenecks. For each bottleneck in the system, what is an upper bound on its mean throughput rate?

D. We now fix the *mix* or *fraction* of jobs executed of each type, denoted by F_{small}, F_{big} respectively, where

$$0 \leqslant F_{small} \leqslant 1 \quad 0 \leqslant F_{big} \leqslant 1 \quad F_{small} + F_{big} = 1$$

The mean or average time to process a job is denoted by $T_{average}$ and is given by

$$T_{average} = F_{small} T_{small} + F_{big} T_{big}$$

The mean arrival rate for each type of job is given by

$$\lambda_{small} = \lambda F_{small} \quad \lambda_{big} = \lambda F_{big}$$

where λ is the *total* mean throughput rate of executing jobs. Find upper and lower bounds on the total mean throughput rate λ as a function of model parameters for the following cases

[1] Two processors $P=2$ and two memory partitions $M=2$

[2] Two processors $P=2$ and three memory partitions $M=3$

[3] Three processors $P=3$ and three memory partitions $M=3$

For each case, compare your calculation with the maximum mean throughput rate for a system that has a *processor* bottleneck, i.e., where each processor can execute one job every $T_{average}$ seconds on the average, and memory is *not* a bottleneck. What interactions arise between the processor and memory?

10) We consider an abstraction of a communications system consisting of a transmitter (or producer) and receiver (or consumer). The transmitter generates a record, stores it in an internal transmitter buffer, and tests to see if a buffer from a pool of buffers shared by the transmitter and receiver is available. If a buffer is not available, it waits until a buffer is available, and stores the record in a buffer. The transmitter increments the number of records outstanding, waiting to be handled by the receiver, by one, and repeats the entire process. The receiver tests to see if a record is waiting to be read; if not, the receiver waits until a record is available, and removes it from its buffer in the shared buffer pool into an internal receiver buffer. The receiver then decrements the number of records outstanding, and processes it, and repeats the entire process. There are two processes each in their own physical processor, one for the producer and one for the consumer, plus a pool of buffers of size B records, i.e., one record can fit into one buffer. In order to insure that no records are lost due to a speed mismatch between the producer and consumer, there is a semaphore with P and V primitives. The $P()$ primitive involves testing its argument to see if it is positive; if it is, access to the associated field is locked, and if it is not, wait until it becomes nonzero. The $V()$ primitive involves testing its argument to see if it is nonzero; if it is, the argument is decremented by one, and access is allowed to the associated array; if it is not, wait. The pseudo code (with comments) shown below gives a succinct description of system operation:

initialize space=B, records=0 /*initialize empty buffers=B,ready records=0*/

process producer
loop
 generate record
 P(space) /*test to see if space>0; if so, decrement space by 1; if not wait*/
 deposit record /*deposit record in available space*/
 V(records) /*increment number of records by one*/
end loop{producer}

process consumer
loop
 P(records) /*test to see if records>0; if so, decrement records by 1; if not wait*/
 read record
 V(space) /*increment amount of space by one*/
 process record
end loop{consumer}

The mean time to execute each of these actions without contention on the respective processors is as follows:

- $T_{generate}$ --mean time to generate a record

- $T_{deposit}$ --mean time to deposit a record in a buffer

- T_{read} --mean time to read a record

- $T_{process}$ --mean time to process a record

We assume that the P and V primitives require zero processor time to be executed.

A. Make a table showing the resources required at each step.

B. The pair $J_{producer}(t), J_{consumer}(t)$ denote the number of messages at the producer and consumer respectively at an arbitrary time t. Find the set of admissible values for these pairs, which is called the state space of this system.

C. What are potential bottlenecks limiting the maximum mean throughput rate?

D. What is the maximum mean throughput rate as a function of model parameters?

11) An online transaction processing consists of hardware, a set of application programs, and an operating system that manages resources. The hardware can be configured in two ways

[1] High performance configuration--One high speed processor, disk controller, and high speed disk at a total system cost of two hundred thousand dollars

[2] Low performance configuration--One low speed processor, disk controller, and low speed disk at a total system cost of one hundred thousand dollars

Clerks enter transactions into the system and wait for the system to respond before entering the next transaction. Each clerk is paid a total salary of twenty five thousand dollars per year, fully burdened to reflect salary, benefits, and general and administrative overhead.

The steps involved in a transaction are as follows

[1] A clerk reads an order form, and types this into the system from a terminal; this step has a mean time of thirty seconds

[2] A front end screen manager checks the data and formats it for the next step of processing; this step has a mean time of T_{fe}

[3] A scheduler logs the transaction and passes it onto the next step; this step has a mean time of T_{sched}

[4] A data base manager accepts the transaction and the data base is modified accordingly; this step has a mean time of T_{db}

[5] The scheduler logs the transaction and passes it onto the next step; the mean duration of this step is T_{sched}

[6] A back end transmits a message to another system; the mean time for this step is T_{be}

[7] The scheduler logs the transaction and closes it out; the mean duration of this step is T_{sched}

A prototype system was constructed and benchmarked on the high performance hardware configuration, with the results tabulated below:

Table 4.9. Benchmark Summary

Transaction Step	Processor Time Application	System	Disk Accesses
Front End	0.75 sec	0.25 sec	5
Scheduler	0.05 sec	0.05 sec	0
Data Base Manager	2.10 sec	0.40 sec	25
Scheduler	0.05 sec	0.05 sec	0
Back End	0.50 sec	0.50 sec	10
Scheduler	0.05 sec	0.05 sec	0

The difference in performance between the two hardware configurations is summarized below:

Table 4.10. Hardware Performance Summary

Type	Processor Speed	Time/Disk Access
High Performance	0.7 MIPS	30 msec
Low Performance	0.5 MIPS	50 msec

MIPS refers to *millions of assembly language instructions executed per second* by a single processor.

The following configurations are under investigation:

[1] One high performance configuration

[2] One low performance configuration

[3] Two low performance configurations running identical application programs and operating system code

[4] Two low performance configurations, one running operating system code and one running application programs

[5] Two low performance configurations running the same operating system code, with one running all application programs except data base management, the other running data base management

For each configuration

A. Plot upper and lower bounds on mean throughput rate and mean delay or response time versus number of clerks. Clearly label the breakpoint number of clerks for the upper bound on mean throughput rate and lower bound on mean delay.

B. Assuming the breakpoint number of clerks, calculate the mean throughput rate for executing jobs per hour.

C. Calculate the total cost to operate each configuration for five years, and the ratio of the cost divided by throughput. Use a straight line five year depreciation for the hardware, assume a fifty per cent tax rate with no tax shelters, and assume the software is developed at a cost of two hundred and fifty thousand dollars with a support cost of one and a half per cent per month of the development cost over the five year period.

12) A virtual memory system consists of a processor with attached memory plus a much larger external memory. We assume that there is a nonempty queue of jobs waiting for access to this system, so that whenever one job completes execution and departs, another job immediately takes its place. There is only one type of job, and each job requires a certain number of *pages* of memory for execution on the processor. If a program is in execution in the processor and finds that all the required pages are not present in the attached memory of the processor, a page fault is said to occur, and a request is made to the external memory to load the missing page. The mean time to load one page is $T_{external\ storage}$ and equals ten (10) milliseconds. We measure the behavior of an individual program in this system by gathering measurements for the mean time between page faults with the main processor memory configured for a given number of pages, and we then repeat this process for a different number of pages. The total number of jobs in execution in the system we call the *degree of multiprogramming* of this system. Our goal is to determine the mean throughput rate of completing jobs for a given total number of memory pages and degree of multiprogramming and other parameters.

We let K denote the degree of multiprogramming and M denote the total number of memory pages. Hence, each job has an average of M/K pages available to it at any time. The mean time between page faults for an individual program can be approximated by AK^2, where $A = 9\ \mu sec$.

Answer the following questions:

A. What is the state space for this system?

B. Find an upper bound on the mean time the processor is busy as a function of the degree of multiprogramming K. For $M=100$, plot this versus K. Interpret your results.

13) Twenty five operators at terminals carry out interactive work with a computer system. The computer system also executes batch work. The hardware configuration for the computer system is one processor and one disk. Each operator at a terminal undergoes the same basic cycle: some time is spent reading and thinking and typing, followed by some time waiting for the system to respond. The thinking time has a mean of thirty seconds, denoted by T_{think}. The response time has a mean of R. Each interactive job undergoes some processing and some disk access activity over and over until each job is completely executed. The mean processor time per visit to the processor for each interactive job is ten milliseconds, and each interactive job visits the processor ten times on the average. The mean disk access time for each interactive job is ninety milliseconds, and each interactive job requires ten disk accesses on the average. Each batch job on the other hand requires one disk access followed by one second of processing time, on the average.

The following measurements are carried out on the system in operation:

• The processor is found to be completely busy or saturated throughout the measurement interval

• The mean response time for interactive jobs is four seconds

Answer the following questions:

A. Make a table showing the resources held by each step of each job and the mean time for each step

B. What is the bottleneck?

C. What is the mean throughput rate of executing batch jobs?

D. What is the disk utilization due to interactive and to batch work?

E. Suppose a new processor replaces the old processor, and is found to be five times as fast as the old processor. Answer the following questions:

  • What is the bottleneck now?

  • What is the disk utilization due to interactive and to batch work?

  • What is a lower bound on the mean response time for interactive work?

- What is an upper bound on mean throughput rate for interactive work?

14) A computer system consists of a CPU, a drum with a direct memory access (DMA) controller, and eight pages of memory. A sequence of jobs is executed on this system. The mean throughput rate of executing jobs is denoted by λ, measured in jobs per millisecond. Each job consists of a sequence of steps, with each step of each job indexed by K=1,2,3,4. A job need not execute every step; however, the average number of type K steps per job, denoted by V_K, is given in the table below:

Table 4.11.Mean Number of Steps/Job

Symbol	Steps/Job
V_1	4/3
V_2	8/15
V_3	2
V_4	1

The resource requirement table for the four steps are shown in the table below:

Table 4.12.Resources/Step and Mean Holding Time/Step

Step	CPU	Drum	Pages	Time
1	1	0	4	10 msec
2	0	1	4	20 msec
3	1	0	2	30 msec
4	0	1	2	20 msec

Answer the following questions:

A. Define the state space of this system for *running* jobs. How many states are in the state space?

B. Use Little's Law to write the conservation equations relating the mean throughput rate λ to state space averages.

C. Find an upper bound λ_{max} on the mean throughput rate λ. What resource is the bottleneck if $\lambda=\lambda_{max}$?

D. Assuming that $\lambda=\lambda_{max}$, what is the

- Percentage of time the CPU is busy

- Percentage of time the drum is busy

- Average memory utilization

for *running* jobs?

15) A transaction processing system retrieves a record from storage on one disk spindle, processes it, and stores it on a second disk spindle. The hardware configuration consists of a single central processor connected via a switch to two direct memory access disk controllers, with one spindle for each controller; the direct memory access capability allows the central processor to execute work while the disk controller is busy accessing a record. All of the text required to process records is resident in main memory. The processor can buffer at most S blocks of data at a time. Each disk access retrieves one block at a time. N denotes the number of records per block. Each record consists of B bytes. T_{access} denotes the mean time to move the disk head from an arbitrary point to the start of a block. $T_{transfer}$ denotes the mean time to transfer one byte of data from an input/output device to a disk controller. T_{proc} denotes the mean processor time per record.

A. Find an expression in terms of model parameters and plot it for the maximum mean throughput rate (records per unit time) versus the number of records per block.

B. Find the ratio of the reciprocal of the maximum mean throughput rate divided by the mean time to process a record from start to finish (this is the reciprocal of the mean throughput rate with no concurrency).

C. What are the bottlenecks in this system?

D. Suppose that the following numbers specify the model parameters:

Table 4.13.Model Parameters

Attribute	Symbol	Time
Disk Access Time	T_{access}	50 msec
Disk Transfer Time	$T_{transfer}$	1 μsec
Buffer Size	B	4096 bytes
Processor Time/Record	T_{proc}	30 msec

For $N=1,2,4,8$ what is the numerical value of the maximum mean throughput rate in records per unit time?

16) A computer systems consists of a central processing unit (CPU), processor memory, and two disks (labeled I and II). Each disk is connected to the CPU by its own channel (DMA controller). A hardware monitor is available for measuring the system performance, which has as output three signals, $X_{CPU}(t)$ for the processor, $X_I(t)$ and $X_{II}(t)$ for disks I and II respectively, where

$$X_{CPU}(t) = \begin{cases} 1 & \text{if } CPU \text{ busy at time } t \\ 0 & \text{otherwise} \end{cases}$$

$$X_K(t) = \begin{cases} 1 & \text{if } channel\ K\ busy\ at\ time\ t \\ 0 & otherwise \end{cases} \qquad K=I,II$$

The following measurement data is available concerning the execution of workload over a time interval beginning at time $t=0$ and ending at time $t=T$:

$$X_{CPU}(t) + X_I(t) + X_{II}(t) > 0 \quad 0 < t < T \tag{i}$$

$$\int_0^T X_{CPU}(t)\,dt = 100\ seconds \tag{ii}$$

$$\int_0^T X_I(t)\,dt = 100\ seconds \tag{iii}$$

$$\int_0^T X_{II}(t)\,dt = 125\ seconds \tag{iv}$$

$$\int_0^T X_{CPU}(t)X_I(t)\,dt = 50\ seconds \tag{v}$$

$$\int_0^T X_{CPU}(t)X_{II}(t)\,dt = 25\ seconds \tag{vi}$$

$$\int_0^T X_I(t)X_{II}(t)\,dt = 75\ seconds \tag{vii}$$

$$\int_0^T X_{CPU}(t)X_I(t)X_{II}(t)\,dt = 25\ seconds \tag{viii}$$

Answer the following questions:

A.   What is the fraction of time the CPU is busy during $(0,T)$?

B.   Evaluate

$$\frac{1}{T}\int_0^T [X_{CPU}(t) + X_I(t) + X_{II}(t)]\,dt$$

C.   What fraction of the *potential* speedup was in fact realized?

17) Terminals are connected over data links to a front end processor to a computer system. Each terminal has its own dedicated three hundred bit per second line. Each operator at a terminal does the same job over and over again: each operator spends a certain amount of time reading and thinking and typing, denoted T_{think}, and then strikes a *send* key. At that point the screen data is transmitted over the link to the front end processor; on the average four

hundred bits of data are input. The front end processor is connected to the computer system by a very high speed data link. Each job enters a staging queue where it waits until it can enter the main computer system for processing. The computer system can hold at most five jobs at any one time: if there are less than five jobs in the system, a job in the staging queue will enter the system immediately, otherwise jobs are queued for entry in order of arrival. The system consists of a single processor and a single disk, and each job requires an average of $T_{proc}=2$ seconds of processor time and $N_{disk}=30$ disk accesses, with each disk access requiring a fifty millisecond access time. Once the job completes execution, it is transmitted back over the high speed link to the front end processor, and the terminal displays the output. On the average each screen has 4800 bits of information for output. Assume that the time for signals to propagate from the terminal to the front end processor and back are negligible compared to any other time interval. Assume that the time for signals to propagate to and from the system and the front end processor are negligible compared to any other time interval.

A. Make up a table showing each step of processing a job and the resources required for that step and the mean time duration of that step.

B. What is the bottleneck resource in this system for $N=1$ terminals? What is the bottleneck resource in this system as $N \rightarrow \infty$?

C. Plot an upper bound on the mean throughput rate versus the number of active terminals. Clearly label all regions and breakpoints in terms of model parameters.

D. Mean response time is defined as the time interval from when the operator initiates transmission of a screen of data until the start of output on the screen. Plot a lower bound on mean response time versus the number of active terminals. Clearly label all regions and breakpoints in terms of model parameters.

E. Repeat all the above assuming that the system can now hold twenty jobs at once, not just five.

F. Suppose that the terminals' links are replaced with 56,000 bits per second links connected to a front end that is now connected to a space satellite earth station. The propagation time of signals between the terminals and front end is negligible compared to all other time intervals. The one way propagation time of signals from the front end to the computer system is one fourth second. Repeat all the above.

18) A packet switching system consists of $N=10$ identical nodes connected in a ring, with index $K=0,...,N-1=9$. Each node transmits to only one other node, and each node receives from only one other node; all nodes are connected by

identical one way transmission links with transmission rate $C=10^6$ bits per second. All packets are routed counterclockwise around the ring. Packets can arrive at any node and are transmitted to any of the other remaining $N-1$ nodes, and thence depart from the system. All packets are fixed in size at $B=1000$ bits. The fraction of the *total* network packet load entering at node $I=0,...,N-1$ and departing at a node that is J nodes away (counterclockwise) is denoted by $F_{I,I+J}$ with the sum $I+J$ being modulo N. We assume that

[1]   All stations are statistically identical or symmetric, i.e., $F_{I,I+J}$ is independent of I.

[2]   No station sends packets to itself (i.e., $F_{II}=0, I=0,...,N-1$).

[3]   All packets are sent to *some* node:

$$\sum_{I=0}^{N-1}\sum_{J=1}^{N-1} F_{I,I+J} = 1$$

The total mean packet arrival rate to the system, i.e., summed over all nodes, is denoted by λ.

A.   If $F_{I,I+J} = 1/N(N-1)$ find an upper bound on the maximum mean packet switching rate for this system.

B.   What choice of $F_{I,I+J}, 0 \leqslant I,J \leqslant N-1$ permits the largest mean packet switching rate?

C.   What choice of $F_{I,I+J}$ permits the smallest mean packet switching rate?

Offices provide a concrete example of the principles needed to understand the performance of computer communication systems. In offices, there is a great interest in measuring and improving productivity, coupled with trends of rising personnel costs and falling solid state electronic circuitry costs, just as there is in computer communication systems.

5.1 Why Offices?

An office is an example of a distributed information processing system where a variety of tasks are executed asynchronously and concurrently. These activities are typical of any data communication systems, and comprise data gathering, data manipulation, data communication, data analysis and display, and decision or policy making. Office systems are fundamentally *complex,* making it quite important to be systematic in order not to overlook anything. This requires controlled experimentation and measurement, coupled with the formation of hypotheses or models to explain behavior, as well as analysis.

Perhaps the fundamental idea in office automation is to move *ideas* or *information* to *people* and **not** vice versa. This means the office workers, secretaries and managers, do not physically move (walk, drive, fly, take a train) as much with automation, but rather communicate their ideas to one another with a variety of telecommunications systems (involving data, voice, facsimile, graphics and video output, delivered when desired).

5.1.1 Additional Reading

[1] Montgomery Phister, Jr. **Data Processing: Technology and Economics,** Second Edition, Digital Press, Bedford, Massachusetts, 1979.

5.2 Telephone Tag

You telephone a colleague, the colleague is not at the telephone, and a secretary takes your message asking your colleague to return your call. Later, your colleague gets your message and telephones, but now you are not in, and a secretary takes the message that your call has been returned. You call back, and the process repeats itself, until eventually you both talk to one another via telephone. This is called *telephone tag* because you and your colleague are tagging one another with telephone messages. Figure 5.1 summarizes the work flow.

5.2.1 Workload What are the resources here? We have two managers, you and your colleague, labeled one and two from this point on. Each of the managers has a secretary, labeled one and two for the respective manager. The

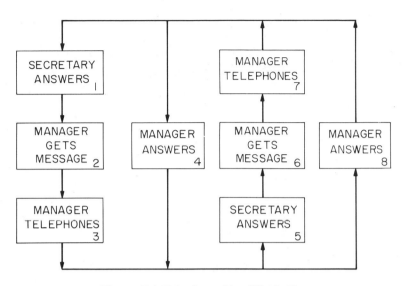

Figure 5.1.Telephone Tag Work Flow

resources required at each step are

[1] Manager two and secretary one talk for a mean time of $T_{sec,1}$ in order to leave a message for manager one

[2] Manager one at some point receives the message and picks up the telephone to return the call, with all this taking a mean time of $T_{mess,1}$

[3] Manager one makes the telephone call to manager two: this requires looking up the telephone number, getting to a telephone and so forth, with a total mean time of $T_{tel,1}$

[4] Manager one and manager two talk with one another via the telephone for a mean time of $T_{ans,1}$

[5] Manager one and secretary two talk for a mean time of $T_{sec,2}$ in order to leave a message for manager two

[6] Manager two at some point receives the message and picks up the telephone to return the call, with a total mean time of $T_{mess,2}$ passing

[7] Manager two makes the telephone call to manager one, with a mean time of $T_{tel,2}$ elapsing

[8] Manager two and manager one talk with one another via the telephone for a mean time of $T_{ans,2}$

The table below summarizes the resources required for each step, and the mean time interval the resources are held:

Table 5.1.Telephone Tag Step/Resource Summary

Step	Manager 1	Secretary 1	Manager 2	Secretary 2	Time
1	0	1	1	0	$T_{sec,1}$
2	1	0	0	0	$T_{mess,1}$
3	1	0	0	0	$T_{tel,1}$
4	1	0	1	0	$T_{ans,1}$
5	1	0	0	1	$T_{sec,2}$
6	0	0	1	0	$T_{mess,2}$
7	0	0	1	0	$T_{tel,2}$
8	1	0	1	0	$T_{ans,2}$

Where did the tag go? We can have multiple visits to the branches for leaving messages, but only one visit to the branch to return the call. To account for this, we denote the mean number of visits to the secretary answering branch for the second manager by $V_{tag,1}$ while the mean number of visits to the secretary branch for the first manager is denoted by $V_{tag,2}$

5.2.2 State Space What might be one appropriate state space to describe the operation of this system? At any instant of time, we could choose a five tuple $\underline{J}$ where

$$\underline{J} = \{J_{sec,1}, J_{man,1}, J_{sec,2}, J_{man,2}, I\}$$

where $J_{sec,1}$ is either zero or one to show that secretary one is not or is busy with telephone call activity, and so forth, and I denotes the step. Not all combinations are feasible: we denote by F the set of feasible states, where

$$F = \{(1,0,0,1,1),(0,1,0,0,2),(0,1,0,0,3),(0,1,0,1,4)$$

$$(0,1,1,0,5),(0,0,0,1,6),(0,0,0,1,7),(0,1,1,0,8)\}$$

5.2.3 Analysis We monitor the system for a time interval of duration T minutes. Over that time interval, the system is in state I for a total time of T_I minutes. For each feasible $\underline{J}$ we denote by $\pi(\underline{J})$ the *fraction* of observation time that the system was in state $\underline{J}$. We see

$$\frac{T_I}{T} = \pi(\underline{J}) \geqslant 0 \quad \underline{J} \in F \quad \sum_{\underline{J} \in F} \pi(\underline{J}) = 1$$

from these definitions. If the observation interval becomes sufficiently large (days, weeks, months) so that the number of calls in progress at the start and end of the observation interval is negligible compared to the total number of calls that start and finish during the observation interval, we will use Little's Law to show that the mean number of calls in each step (eight here) equals the mean throughput rate for each step multiplied by the average duration of each step:

average number of calls in process in state I = $|\underline{J}|_I$

= *(average throughput rate in step I)×(average duration of step I)*   *I,1,2,...,8*

Formally, we can write this as

$$\sum_{\underline{J} \in F} J_I \pi(\underline{J}) = \lambda T_I \quad I=1,2,...,8$$

Our measure of productivity is the mean rate of completing useful telephone calls. Substituting into the relationships, we see

$$\pi(1,0,0,1,1) = \lambda V_{tag,1} T_{sec,1} \quad \pi(0,1,1,0,5) = \lambda V_{tag,2} T_{sec,2}$$

$$\pi(0,1,0,0,2) = \lambda V_{tag,1} T_{mess,1} \quad \pi(0,0,0,1,6) = \lambda V_{tag,2} T_{mess,2}$$

$$\pi(0,1,0,0,3) = \lambda V_{tag,1} T_{tel,1} \quad \pi(0,0,0,1,7) = \lambda V_{tag,2} T_{tel,2}$$

$$\pi(0,1,0,1,4) = \lambda T_{ans,1} \quad \pi(0,1,0,1,8) = \lambda T_{ans,2}$$

If we add up all of these, we see

$$\sum_{\underline{J} \in F} \pi(\underline{J}) = \lambda T_{loop} \leqslant 1 \;\rightarrow\; \lambda \leqslant \frac{1}{T_{loop}}$$

$$T_{loop} = V_{tag,1}[T_{sec,1} + T_{mess,1} + T_{tel,1}] + T_{ans,1} + V_{tag,2}[T_{sec,2} + T_{mess,2} + T_{tel,2}] + T_{ans,2}$$

Let's substitute some illustrative numbers to see what the impact of tag might be. We assume that the time spent leaving the message with the secretary has a mean of two minutes, the time until the message is picked up and read has a mean of thirty minutes, the time to telephone is fifteen seconds, and the time to actually talk is ten minutes:

Table 5.2. Illustrative Telephone Tag Step/Time Numerical Example

Time	Amount
$T_{sec,1}=T_{sec,2}$	2 Minutes
$T_{mess,1}=T_{mess,2}$	30 Minutes
$T_{tel,1}=T_{tel,2}$	1/4 Minutes
$T_{ans,1}=T_{ans,2}$	10 Minutes

If we assume the mean number of tags is two, so that it takes two calls on the average for you and your colleague to talk, then

$$V_{tag,1} = V_{tag,2} = 2$$

then we see that the maximum mean throughput rate is

$$\lambda \leqslant \frac{1}{139 \; minutes}$$

or roughly one telephone conversation lasting ten minutes every two and a half hours! If the mean number of tags increases to three, then the maximum mean throughput rate drops to one call lasting ten minutes every 203.5 minutes!

This is very frustrating for anyone. What can we do to shorten this time to complete one telephone call?

5.2.4 An Alternative: Voice Storage What if we replaced this mode of operation with a voice storage system, where the caller leaves a voice message in a storage system to be retrieved by the callee at convenience, as shown in the figure below

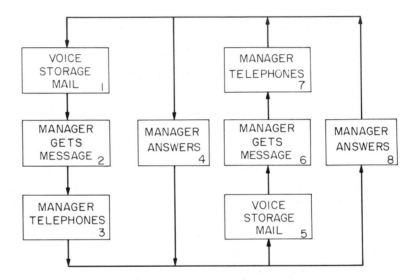

Figure 5.2. Voice Storage Work Flow

The resources required at each step are summarized below

Table 5.3. Voice Storage System Resources/Step

Step	Manager 1	Manager 2	Voice Storage	Time
1	0	1	1	$T_{mess,1}$
2	1	0	0	$T_{delay,1}$
3	1	0	0	$T_{tel,1}$
4	1	1	0	$T_{ans,1}$
5	1	0	1	$T_{mess,1}$
6	0	1	0	$T_{delay,1}$
7	0	1	0	$T_{tel,2}$
8	1	1	0	$T_{ans,2}$

Proceeding as before, and using the same illustrative numbers, but with $V_{tag,1} = V_{tag,2} = 1$, we see that the maximum mean throughput rate is given by

$$\lambda \leqslant \frac{1}{74\frac{1}{2}\ minutes}$$

or roughly one telephone conversation of ten minutes every hour and a quarter, halving the total handling time per call. The gain here is obvious: halving the number of messages for the harried secretary helps enormously! By being systematic, we have quantified the gain for both the secretary and manager. To see if you understand this, ask yourself what happens when the number of tags is greater than two, or if multiple calls are circulating (not just one like here).

5.2.5 Additional Reading

[1] L.H.Mertes, *Doing your Office Over--Electronically,* Harvard Business Review, **59** (2), 127-135 (1981).

5.3 Copying and Reproduction

How many copiers or reproduction machines does an office need for making copies of letters and correspondence, articles of all sorts, bills, contracts, and on and on? More to the point, what are the minimum set of numbers needed to say anything whatsoever that is pertinent to this question?

The figure below is a block diagram of an office with only two entities: secretaries and copiers. The secretaries spend a certain amount of time preparing a paper for reproduction, and then they go to the copying machine and make the copies, collate and staple them, leave, and the process starts all over.

The next figure below is a queueing network block diagram of this system, assuming we have S secretaries and C copiers:

To complete our description, we need to measure or estimate or guess the mean time a secretary requires for preparation of a document for reproduction, denoted by $T_{secretary}$, and the mean time a secretary spends copying a document with all the related steps of collating and stapling, denoted by T_{copy}.

We now have a wealth of information: what do we do next? Let's assume there is only one copier for all S secretaries, before looking at the more general case of $C > 1$ copiers.

With only one copier and one secretary, we see a cycle takes place: the secretary generates the document and then reproduces it, again and again and again. The mean throughput rate of copying documents with one secretary is simply

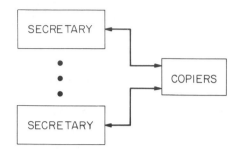

Figure 5.3.Office Copying System Block Diagram

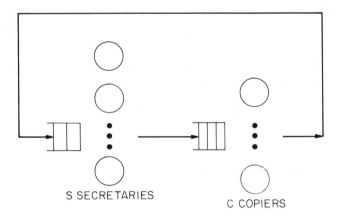

Figure 5.4.Queueing Network of Office Copying System

$$mean\ document\ copying\ rate\ =\ \frac{1}{T_{secretary}\ +\ T_{copy}}\quad one\ secretary, S=1$$

As we add more and more secretaries, the best we can do is to have the mean copying rate grow linearly with the number of secretaries: going from one to two secretaries doubles the document copying rate, and so on:

$$mean\ document\ copying\ rate \leqslant \frac{S}{T_{secretary} + T_{copy}}$$

At some point, the copier will be completely busy reproducing documents, which also upper bounds the mean throughput rate:

$$mean\ document\ copying\ rate \leqslant \frac{1}{T_{copy}}$$

Combining these upper bounds, we see

$$mean\ document\ copying\ rate \leqslant \min\left[\frac{S}{T_{secretary} + T_{copy}}, \frac{1}{T_{copy}}\right]$$

On the other hand, we might find that every time a secretary goes to make a copy, *all* the other secretaries are lined up in front of the copying machine (maybe it is a social gathering, maybe every so often there is a very very big job that all the little jobs have to wait for, and on and on). Now we see that the cycle is for a secretary to generate a document, and then to wait for S documents to be reproduced (S-1 for the other secretaries plus your document):

$$mean\ document\ copying\ rate \geqslant \frac{S}{T_{secretary} + ST_{copy}}$$

Two regimes are evident:

- if the secretaries are the bottleneck (not enough documents are ready to be reproduced) then

$$mean\ document\ copying\ rate \approx \frac{S}{T_{secretary} + T_{copy}}$$

- If the copying machine is the bottleneck, running all the time, then

$$mean\ document\ copying\ rate \approx \frac{1}{T_{copy}}$$

The breakpoint number of secretaries between these two regimes is given by

$$S_{breakpoint} = \frac{T_{secretary} + T_{copy}}{T_{copy}}$$

For example, if each secretary spends one hour in document preparation ($T_{secretary} = 1\ hour$) and five minutes in walking to the copier, making the copies, addressing envelopes, and so forth ($T_{copy} = 5\ minutes$) then the breakpoint number of secretaries is simply

$$S_{breakpoint} = \frac{60 + 5}{5} = 13\ secretaries$$

If we assign ten or fewer secretaries to a copier, the copying machine will rarely be congested; if we assign twenty or more secretaries to a copier, the copying machine will be rarely idle.

What if we add a second copying machine? With two machines completely busy, the upper bound on mean throughput rate is twice that for one machine. However, this will not affect the mean time to make a copy of a document, only the mean delay to get to a copying machine. The upper bound on mean throughput rate is now given by

$$mean\ document\ copying\ rate \leqslant \min\left[\frac{S}{T_{secretary} + T_{copy}}, \frac{2}{T_{copy}}\right]$$

while the lower bound on mean throughput rate becomes

$$mean\ document\ copying\ rate \geqslant \frac{S}{T_{secretary} + \dfrac{S}{2}\,T_{copy}}$$

We summarize all these bounds graphically in the figure below:

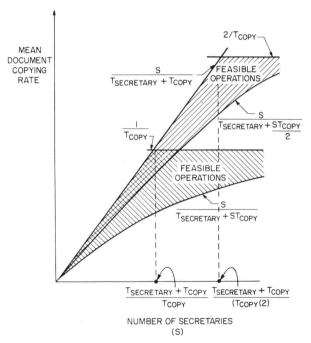

Figure 5.5. Mean Document Copying Rate

Finally, what is the gain in going from one to two copiers? Using the earlier numbers, we see

$$S_{breakpoint} = \frac{T_{secretary} + T_{copy}}{\frac{1}{2} T_{copy}} = \frac{60+5}{5/2} = 26 \; secretaries$$

We have doubled the breakpoint, so that twenty or fewer secretaries could be accommodated by two copiers, with the copiers rarely being a point of congestion, while with thirty or more secretaries the copiers will be congested most of the time.

5.4 Document Preparation

The process of document preparation is undergoing a great change at the present time, again due to computer technology. More and more text is being handled by a digital computer system consisting of terminals that replace typewriters, a storage system (today with moving header magnetic disks, tomorrow with optical laser disks), a printer for generating the physical documents, and a processor for controlling all of these steps. There might be access to a network of other such systems elsewhere. All of this is shown in the figure below:

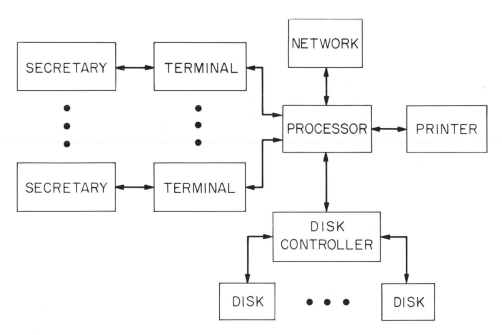

Figure 5.6. Document Preparation System Hardware Block Diagram

Three steps are involved in document preparation

[1]   Entering the document into the system

[2]   Editing the document one or more times

[3]   Reproducing or printing requisite number of copies of the document

The figure below shows a queueing network block diagram of this system:

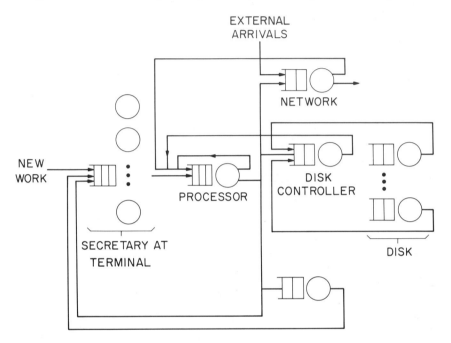

Figure 5.7. Document Preparation Queueing Network Block Diagram

How many secretaries can be active before the congestion inside the document preparation system becomes unacceptable? What numbers do we need to measure or estimate in order to answer this question?

The mean time required for each of the three steps of document preparation is a natural starting point for quantifying performance, along with the resources required at each step of the way; we do so in a hierarchical manner, starting first simply with secretaries using the system, and then breaking down the actions inside the system:

Table 5.4. Document Preparation Step/Resource Table

Step	Secretary	Time	System	Time
Entry	1	$T_{sec,entry}$	1	$T_{sys,entry}$
Edit	1	$T_{sec,edit}$	1	$T_{sys,edit}$
Print	1	$T_{sec,print}$	1	$T_{sys,print}$

Table 5.5. Document Step/Resource Processor Summary

Step Type	Resource and Time	
	Processor	Time
Entry	1	$T_{proc,entry}$
Edit	1	$T_{proc,edit}$
Print	1	$T_{proc,print}$

Table 5.6. Document Resource/Step Disk Summary

Step Type	Resource and Time	
	Disk	Time
Entry	1	$T_{disk,entry}$
Edit	1	$T_{disk,edit}$
Print	1	$T_{disk,print}$

Table 5.7. Document Resource/Step Printer Summary

Step Type	Resource and Time	
	Printer	Time
Entry	0	--
Edit	0	--
Print	1	$T_{printer,print}$

We have done this in two steps to carry out two different levels of analysis, one a coarse aggregate rough sizing, the other a more refined analysis (which needs more information).

In the first level of analysis, simply with secretaries and a system, the rough sizing would be to put one secretary on the system and see how long on the average one document can be generated:

$$T_{doc} = T_{sec,entry} + T_{sys,entry} + T_{sec,edit} + T_{sys,edit} + T_{sec,print} + T_{sys,print}$$

When we examine a system, we see that it is reasonable to assume that the processor or disk time consumed to do document entry and editing is negligible compared with the time required for the processor, disk, and printer to reproduce the requisite hard copy manuscript. On the other hand, the time required for the secretary to do the entry and editing is typically much much greater than the time required to handle work associated with document printing. This is summarized by the following approximations:

$$T_{sec,entry} \gg T_{sys,entry} \quad T_{sec,edit} \gg T_{sys,edit} \quad T_{sys,print} \gg T_{sec,print}$$

The mean throughput rate is upper bounded by

$$mean\ throughput\ rate \leq \min\left[\frac{S}{T_{doc}}, \frac{1}{T_{sys,print}}\right]$$

where we have S secretaries total and using arguments in the earlier sections, and is lower bounded by observing that every time one secretary goes to print a document the other $(S-1)$ secretaries are waiting in line to do exactly the same thing:

$$mean\ throughput\ rate \geqslant \frac{S}{T_{doc} + (S-1)\,T_{sys,print}}$$

A more detailed look is in order concerning the system performance limits, using the additional information we have so laboriously gathered. The resources here are the secretaries, a processor, a disk, and a printer. The state of the system is given by a tuple whose components denote whether each resource is idle or active. The total document preparation system is monitored for a time interval of duration T minutes which is assumed to be sufficiently long that the number of documents that are in preparation at the start and finish of the observation interval is assumed negligible compared to the total number of documents that start and finish during the observation interval. We denote by T_I the total time the system spent in step I during the observation interval T. For each feasible state $\underline{J}$ in the set of feasible states F we denote by $\pi(\underline{J})$ the fraction of observed time that the system spent in that state. We can now apply Little's Law:

$$average\ number\ of\ documents\ in\ state\ I = E[|\underline{J}|_I] = =\lambda_I T_I \quad I=1,2,3$$

$$\lambda_I = mean\ throughput\ for\ step\ I \quad I=1,2,3$$

$$T_I = mean\ duration\ of\ step\ I \quad I=1,2,3$$

$$\sum_{\underline{J} \in F} |\underline{J}|_I \pi(\underline{J}) = \lambda T_I \quad I=1,2,3$$

We wish to maximize λ subject to this constraint, plus meet the following constraints:

$$\frac{T_I}{T} = \pi(\underline{J})_I \quad I=1,2,3$$

$$\sum_{\underline{J} \in F} \pi(\underline{J}) = 1 \quad \pi(\underline{J}) \geqslant 0$$

From our earlier studies, we see that the following regimes can limit the maximum mean throughput rate:

[1] Secretaries cannot generate enough documents and bottleneck the system

$$\lambda_{\max} = \frac{S}{T_{sec,entry} + T_{sec,edit} + T_{sec,print}}$$

[2] The processor is completely busy and is the bottleneck

$$\lambda_{max} = \frac{1}{T_{proc,entry} + T_{proc,edit} + T_{proc,print}}$$

[3] The disk is completely busy and is the bottleneck

$$\lambda_{max} = \frac{1}{T_{disk,entry} + T_{disk,edit} + T_{disk,print}}$$

[4] The printer is completely busy and is the bottleneck

$$\lambda_{max} = \frac{1}{T_{printer,print}}$$

This is basically what we argued earlier, but hopefully makes clearer and less ambiguous the number of assumptions and approximations.

To finish, let's substitute in some typical numbers to get a feel for whether any of this is reasonable. First, a secretary can type fifty words per minute, with each word being five letters. A document consists of two pages typically, with two hundred and fifty words per page, so the initial document typing time is simply ten minutes. We will allow a five minute set up time to be included in this initial document typing time. Next, we get out our stop watch and clip board and measure how long on the average it takes to edit and correct a document: we find this takes five minutes on the average (without a document preparation system whole pages would have to be retyped or rewritten, taking fifteen minutes or more on the average just for the editing). Finally, we need to print the document; two printers are available, one handling twenty five characters per second and the other handling one hundred characters per second. We will need two copies of every document. The slow printer can handle one page every two hundred and fifty seconds, and hence will generate four pages (two pages per document, two copies) in one thousand seconds or sixteen and two thirds minutes. The fast printer can handle this in one fourth the time. The only data we can gather from the computer system suggests that the processor is busy on the average for ten seconds total for each document, while the disk is busy for thirty seconds total for each document. The limits on maximum mean document generation are

[1] Secretaries are the bottleneck

$$\lambda_{max} = \frac{S}{15\ minutes}\ documents/minute$$

[2] The processor is the bottleneck

$$\lambda_{max} = \frac{1}{1/6\ minute} = 6\ documents/minute$$

[3] The disk is the bottleneck

$$\lambda_{max} = \frac{1}{1/2 \; minute} = 2 \; documents/minute$$

[4]   Printers are the bottleneck

$$\lambda_{max} = \frac{1}{16 \; 2/3 \; minutes} \; documents/minute \quad slow \; printer$$

$$\lambda_{max} = \frac{4}{16 \; 2/3 \; minutes} \; documents/minutes \quad fast \; printer$$

Thus, we see that one secretary can keep the slow printer busy, but when we put two secretaries on the system, the printer becomes a bottleneck, and hence we should get a fast printer which can handle up to four secretaries.

Additional Reading

[1]   A.F.Shackil, *Design Case History: Wang's Word Processor,* IEEE Spectrum, **18** (8), 29-33 (1981).

5.6 Local Area Networks

Several years ago a minicomputer was installed in a particular small business for doing billing, accounts receivable and payable, payroll, general ledger activities, quarterly tax reports, and similar types of activities and services. The system consists of several terminals connected to a terminal controller with one processor and one disk.

The trade press is currently full of articles about *local area networks* which suggest that the terminal controller can be replaced with a single local area network, hooking all the terminals and the computer directly together. The two configurations are shown in the figures below:

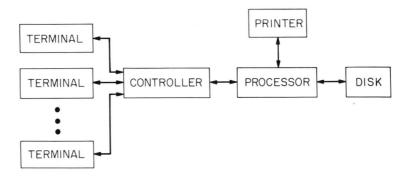

Figure 5.8.Existing Old System Hardware Block Diagram

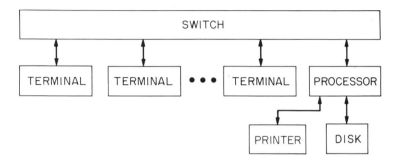

Figure 5.9.Proposed New System Hardware Block Diagram

How much will the local area network affect performance: what numbers do we need to gather or measure or estimate in order to quantify the benefits of the two approaches, the current and proposed?

Let's assume that there is only one type of transaction or job handled by the system, that has the following steps

[1]   Data entry and data validation

[2]   Data base management

[3]   Data retrieval

[4]   Data modification and removal

[5]   Report generation

The resources common to the two systems are the terminals, processor, disk and printer; the old system uses a terminal controller, while the new system uses a local area network to switch messages. The table below summarizes the resources required at each step of job execution

Table 5.8.Transaction Processing Step/Resource Summary

Step	Resource				
Type	Terminal	Processor	Disk	Switch	Printer
Entry	1	1	1	1	0
Execution	0	1	1	1	0
Retrieval	1	1	1	1	1
Modification	1	1	1	1	1
Report	0	1	1	1	1

The mean time required for each resource for each step is denoted by $T_{resource,step}$, where a resource is a terminal, processor or disk or printer, and the step is either data entry or execution or modification or report generation.

The bottlenecks in the system are

[1]   Clerks cannot generate enough load to keep the system busy

$$\lambda_{max} = \frac{C}{\sum_I T_{clerk,I}}$$

[2]   Terminals are completely busy

$$\lambda_{max} = \frac{C}{\sum_I T_{term,I}}$$

[3]   The processor is completely busy

$$\lambda_{max} = \frac{1}{\sum_I T_{proc,I}}$$

[4]   The disk is completely busy

$$\lambda_{max} = \frac{1}{\sum_I T_{disk,I}}$$

[5]   The terminal controller or local area network is completely busy

$$\lambda_{max} = \frac{1}{\sum_I T_{switch,I}}$$

[6]   The printer becomes completely busy

$$\lambda_{max} = \frac{1}{T_{printer,report}}$$

The reason for replacing the terminal controller with a local area network is that the terminal controller is congested or completely busy, which leads to unacceptable delays, and that presumably the clerks at the terminals will become the bottleneck with a local area network in place.

Let's substitute some typical numbers to see if this is reasonable:

Table 5.9.Time/Resource per Step

Resource	Entry	Execution	Retrieve	Modify	Report
Terminal	1.0 sec	0.0 sec	0.5 sec	0.5 sec	0.5 sec
Processor	5.0 sec	7.5 sec	2.0 sec	10.0 sec	2.5 sec
Disk	0.5 sec	10.0 sec	8.0 sec	12.0 sec	5.0 sec
Printer	0.0 sec	0.0 sec	0.0 sec	0.0 sec	100.0 sec
Controller	3.0 sec	0.0 sec	2.0 sec	2.0 sec	0.0 sec
Local Network	0.01 sec	0.0 sec	0.02 sec	0.02 sec	0.02 sec

Finally, we gather statistics on how frequently every hour each transaction type is executed, and summarize them in the table below:

Table 5.10.Frequency of Execution

Entry	10 times/hour
Execute	10 time/hour
Retrieve	100 times/hour
Modify	20 times/hour
Report	2 times/hour

The bottleneck here is the *disk!* Adding a local area network will not significantly improve performance, because the terminal controller is not the point to reach complete utilization first. The best choice from a performance point of view is not the local area network addition, but rather adding more disks.

Additional Reading

[1]   J.M.Kryskow, C.K.Miller, *Local Area Networks Overview--Part I: Definitions and Attributes,* Computer Design, 22-35 (February, 1981), *Local Area Networks Overview--Part II: Standards Activities,* Computer Design, 12-20 (March, 1981).

[2]   B.W.Stuck, *Calculating the Maximum Mean Throughput Rate in Local Area Networks: IEEE Computer Society Project 802 Local Area Network Standards,* Computer, **16**, (5),72-76(1983).

[3]   B.W.Stuck, *Which Local Net Bus Access is Most Sensitive to Traffic Congestion?,* Data Communications, **12** (1), 107-120 (1983).

5.8 Professional Work Station Productivity Gains

In one particular office, professionals do four things

[1]   Work individually on different assignments

[2]   Attend meetings to communicate their findings and learn of others' work

[3]   Telephone others on work related matters

[4]   Document their findings and activities

The office staff manager proposes to provide each professional with a so called *work station* which would have access to all of the documentation via an on line data management system, and which would allow everyone using the system to communicate via either electronic mail (making document distribution much less time consuming for the office staff) and via voice mail (storing telephone calls and filing them when a professional is not available). The work flow of the old system and new system is shown in the figures below:

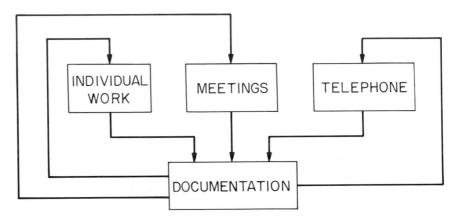

Figure 5.10.Old System Professional Work Flow

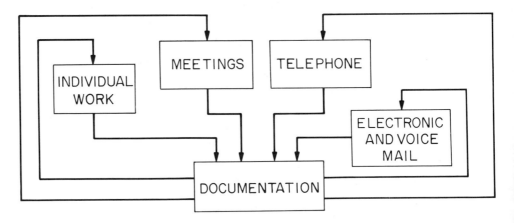

Figure 5.11.New System Professional Work Flow

What would be the impact on productivity for the professional staff? What numbers need to be gathered to quantify these issues? What do we need to measure or estimate or guess?

The resources common to either system are

[1]   The number of professionals P

[2]   The total number of work assignments W

[3]   The total number of simultaneous meetings M

[4]   The total number of documents in preparation D

The resources unique to the old system are

[1]   The total number of telephone calls (including messages) in progress T

The resources unique to the new system are

[1]   The total number of voice storage messages V

[2]   The total number of electronic mail messages E

The mean time required for each action is summarized in the table below

Table 5.11. Time/Job Summary

Job	Mean Time
Work	T_{work}
Meeting	$T_{meeting}$
Telephone	$T_{telephone}$
Document	$T_{document}$
Voice Mail	$T_{voice\ mail}$
Electronic Mail	$T_{electronic\ mail}$

The bottlenecks or resources that can reach complete utilization are

[1]   Professionals are completely busy

$$\lambda_{max} = \frac{P}{T_{work} + T_{meeting} + T_{telephone} + T_{document}} \quad old\ system$$

$$\lambda_{max} = \frac{P}{T_{work} + T_{meeting} + T_{voice\ mail} + T_{electronic\ mail} + T_{document}} \quad new\ system$$

[2]   Work assignments are the bottleneck

$$\lambda_{max} = \frac{W}{T_{work}}$$

[3]   Meetings are the bottleneck

$$\lambda_{\max} = \frac{M}{T_{meeting}}$$

[4]   Document preparation is the bottleneck

$$\lambda_{\max} = \frac{D}{T_{document}}$$

[5]   Messages are the bottleneck

$$\lambda_{\max} = \frac{T}{T_{telephone}} \quad old \ system$$

$$\lambda_{\max} = \min \left[\frac{T}{T_{telephone}}, \frac{V}{T_{voice \ mail}}, \frac{E}{T_{electronic \ mail}} \right] \quad new \ system$$

The work station would help improve office productivity if

[1]   The number of meetings was a bottleneck and could be reduced via voice and electronic mail

[2]   The number of telephone calls was a bottleneck and could be reduced via voice and electronic mail

[3]   Documentation was a bottleneck (filing and gaining access to reports and so on) and could be reduced via electronic and voice mail

Let's illustrate all this with some numbers. The office we'll focus upon has five professionals. In the current system, each professional is working on four different projects simultaneously, and each has ten documents in preparation at any time. There is one conference room. In the current system the total number of telephone calls (including messages) in progress is roughly six per professional. The proposed system can handle roughly one hundred voice storage messages per professional and fifty electronic mail messages per professional. The savings in time are dramatic: the time spent by each professional per assignment will be cut from twenty hours to ten hours, with meeting time cut from five hours per assignment to two hours, telephone time cut from five hours to two hours, and document preparation time cut from twenty hours to five hours. Time spent on voice mail will be roughly fifteen minutes per assignment, while electronic mail will demand forty five minutes per assignment:

Table 5.12. Illustrative Time/Resource Summary

| Job Type | Maximum Jobs | | | Mean Time | |
	Old	New	Symbol	Old	New
Work	20	40	T_{work}	20 hrs	10 hrs
Meeting	1	1	$T_{meeting}$	5 hrs	2 hr
Telephone	30	60	$T_{telephone}$	5 hrs	2 hr
Document	50	200	$T_{document}$	20 hrs	5 hrs
Voice Mail	--	500	$T_{voice\ mail}$	--	1/4 hr
Electronic Mail	--	250	$T_{electronic\ mail}$	--	3/4 hr

For the two systems, the possible bottlenecks are

[1] Professionals are completely busy

$$\lambda_{max} = \frac{5}{20 + 5 + 5 + 20} = 0.1 \ jobs/hr \quad old \ system$$

$$\lambda_{max} = \frac{5}{10 + 5 + 2 + 2 + 1 + 5} = 0.2 \ jobs/hr \quad new \ system$$

[2] Work assignments are the bottleneck

$$\lambda_{max} = \frac{20}{40} = 0.5 \ jobs/hr \quad old \ system$$

$$\lambda_{max} = \frac{40}{20} = 2.0 \ job/hr \quad new \ system$$

[3] Meetings are the bottleneck

$$\lambda_{max} = \frac{1}{5} = 0.2 \ jobs/hr \quad old \ system$$

$$\lambda_{max} = \frac{1}{2} = 0.5 \ jobs/hr \quad new \ system$$

[4] Document preparation is the bottleneck

$$\lambda_{max} = \frac{50}{20} = 2.5 \ jobs/hr \quad old \ system$$

$$\lambda_{max} = \frac{200}{5} = 40 \ jobs/hr \quad new \ system$$

[5] Messages are the bottleneck

$$\lambda_{max} = \frac{30}{2} = 15 \ jobs/hr \quad old \ system$$

$$\lambda_{max} = \min \left[\frac{500}{1/4}, \frac{250}{3/4}, \frac{60}{2} \right] = 30 \ jobs/hr \quad new \ system$$

The bottleneck in either case is the professional staff working all the time; however, by investing in office automation equipment, the staff can handle over twice the workload that the old system could handle. This must be weighed against the capital cost, and a number of other factors before jumping to conclusions, but they are illustrative of the productivity gains possible with such innovations. Substitute in your own numbers to see what the impact is for your office!

5.8.1 Additional Reading

[1] Clarence A. Ellis, Gary J. Nutt, *Office Information Systems and Computer Science,* Computing Surveys **12** (1), 27-60 (1980).

[2] R.P.Uhlig, D.J.Farber, J.H.Bair, **The Office of the Future: Communication and Computers,** North-Holland, Amsterdam, 1979.

5.9 Interactions of Secretaries and Managers

The example office system model we will examine has three types of entities, N managers, N secretaries, and N word processing stations.

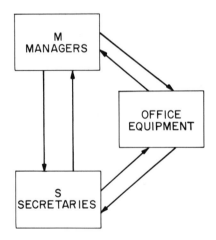

Figure 5.12. Office Block Diagram

The sole function of the office is document preparation. There are three steps involved in document preparation:

[1] A manager dictates a draft to a secretary. This step has a mean duration of T_1 minutes

[2] The secretary enters the draft into a file using a word processor station. This step has a mean duration of T_2 minutes

[3]   The manager originating the document edits and proofs the document at a word processor station until the final corrected version is satisfactory. This step has a mean duration of T_3 minutes

These are shown in the figure below:

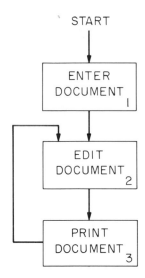

Figure 5.13.Document Preparation Work Flow

Our problem is to determine an upper bound for λ, the mean throughput rate (measured in documents per minute) of document preparation, from start to finish. The first step in the analysis is to construct a state model for the office system behavior. If we imagine observing the office in operation at a given instant of time, say t, we would note at most three kinds of activities, one for each of the three steps. Let the three tuple $\underline{J} = (j_1, j_2, j_3)$ denote the state of the office system, whose components are nonnegative integers. The statement that the office is in state $\underline{J}$ at time t then means that at the time of observation, there were *concurrently* in progress j_1 step one, j_2 step two, and j_3 step three activities. We alert the reader that not all values for $\underline{J}$ are possible. We denote by F the set of $\underline{J}$ vectors which are feasible. As an aid to constructing this set F, we form a step resource requirement table.

Table 5.13. Step Resource Requirements

| Step | Resource | | | Time |
Number	Manager	Secretary	Word Processor	Required
1	1	1	0	T_1
2	0	1	1	T_2
3	1	0	1	T_3

Each column shows the type and quantity of resources required by each step. Since we have a maximum of N units of each resource type, managers and secretaries and word processors, F_1 is the set of three tuples $\underline{J}$ such that

$$j_k \in \{nonnegative\ integers\} \quad k=1,2,3$$

$$j_1 + j_2 \leqslant N \quad manager\ constraint$$

$$j_2 + j_3 \leqslant N \quad secretary\ constraint$$

$$j_1 + j_3 \leqslant N \quad word\ processor\ constraint$$

Now imagine that we monitor the office system for a time interval of T minutes. For each feasible $\underline{J}$ we denote by $\pi(\underline{J})$ the *fraction* of the observation time that the office was in state $\underline{J}$. We then have

$$\pi(\underline{J}) \geqslant 0 \quad \underline{J} \in F \quad \sum_{\underline{J} \in F} \pi(\underline{J}) = 1$$

by definition. Let us denote by λT the number of document preparation completions observed in the time interval $(0, T)$. If T is sufficiently large (so that truncation effects due to partially executed jobs at the ends of the observation interval are negligible), we may apply Little's Law: the mean number of jobs in a system equals the mean rate of jobs flowing through the system multiplied by the mean time per job in the system. Here we have three systems, one for each step of execution:

average number of jobs in execution in step I

$=$ *(average throughput rate for step I)* $\times$ *(average duration of step I)* $I=1,2,3$

More formally, we can write this as

$$\sum_{\underline{J} \in F} j_I \pi(\underline{J}) = \lambda T_I \quad I=1,2,3$$

Before proceeding with the general analysis, let us consider a special case to gain insight, where $N=1$. For this case, it is clear that F consists of just four vectors:

$$F = \{(0,0,0),(1,0,0),(0,1,0),(0,0,1)\}$$

Our earlier expression now becomes

$$\pi(1,0,0) = \lambda T_1 \quad \pi(0,1,0) = \lambda T_2 \quad \pi(0,0,1) = \lambda T_3$$

If we add the left and right hand sides, respectively, of the earlier expression, we find

$$1 \geqslant \pi(1,0,0) + \pi(0,1,0) + \pi(0,0,1) = \lambda(T_1 + T_2 + T_3)$$

This yields the desired upper bound on λ:

$$\lambda \leqslant \frac{1}{T_1 + T_2 + T_3}$$

This is obvious on intuitive grounds: when N=1 only one step may be in progress at any one time, there is no concurrency or parallel execution of tasks, and the total number of minutes required for document preparation is $T_1 + T_2 + T_3$ minutes.

We now examine the general case of an arbitrary positive integer valued N. Our problem is to maximize the mean throughput rate λ over the feasible $\pi(\underline{J}), \underline{J} \in F$:

$$\lambda_{\max} = \underset{\pi(\underline{J}); \underline{J} \in F}{maximum} \quad \lambda$$

This maximization is subject to the following constraints:

$$\sum_{\underline{J} \in F} j_I \pi(\underline{J}) = \lambda T_I \quad I=1,2,3$$

$$\sum_{\underline{J} \in F} \pi(\underline{J}) = 1 \quad \pi(\underline{J}) \geqslant 0$$

A general approach to solving this optimization problem is to rewrite it as a linear programming problem (Omahen, 1977; Dantzig, 1963), and then use one of a variety of standard numerical packages for approximating the solution to such problems. Here, since our problem is simple, we shall proceed analytically rather than numerically, in order to gain insight into the nature and characteristics of the solution. We do so in an appendix to this section, and merely cite the final result before discussing how to interpret this result.

The final result is this upper bound on the maximum mean throughput rate of completed jobs:

$$\lambda \leqslant \min \left(\frac{N}{T_1 + T_2}, \frac{N}{T_2 + T_3}, \frac{N}{T_1 + T_3}, \frac{\left\lfloor \frac{3N}{2} \right\rfloor}{T_1 + T_2 + T_3} \right)$$

As a check, we see that this agrees with the above with N=1.

As an example of how to apply this result, let us assume that $N=2$ and $T_1 = T_2 = T_3 = 15$ minutes. We wish to compare the following two configurations:

[1]   Each manager has his own private secretary and word processor work station, so there are two independent office systems with N=1

[2]   The secretaries and word processor work stations are shared, forming a single pooled office system with N=2

In the first case, the upper bound on λ will be twice that of a single office:

$$\lambda_{max,case\ one} = \frac{2}{45}\ documents\ per\ minute = \frac{8}{3}\ documents\ per\ hour$$

For the second case, using the above relations with N=2 we see

$$\lambda_{max,case\ two} = \frac{3}{45}\ documents\ per\ minute = 4\ documents\ per\ hour$$

Going to N=2 *doubles* total system resources. The second case results in *three* times the maximum mean throughput rate of the N=1 case, while the first case is *twice* the maximum mean throughput rate of the N=1 case. The fifty per cent gain in maximum mean throughput rate of document preparation is entirely due to the policy of pooling (versus dedicating) resources. The intuitive idea for the gain is that more work can be done *concurrently;* put differently, in the first case the *interaction* between the available resources was limiting the maximum mean throughput rate, while in the second case these constraints were relatively less severe.

5.9.1 Appendix From known results (Cairns, p.66, 1966) we observe that a value of λ is possible *if and only if* the point $(\lambda T_1,\lambda T_2,\lambda T_3)$ belongs to the smallest convex set in Euclidean three space containing F, i.e., the *convex hull,* denoted by $C(F)$, of F. Since F is a finite set, $C(F)$ will be a convex polyhedron or simplex. Next, we show that $C(F)$ is defined by the set of points $\underline{X} = (x_1,x_2,x_3)$ where $x_K, K=1,2,3$ that are positive *real* numbers, with

$$x_K \geqslant 0 \quad K=1,2,3$$

$$x_1 + x_2 \leqslant N \quad manager\ constraint$$

$$x_2 + x_3 \leqslant N \quad secretary\ constraint$$

$$x_1 + x_3 \leqslant N \quad word\ processor\ constraint$$

$$x_1 + x_2 + x_3 \leqslant \left\lfloor \frac{3N}{2} \right\rfloor$$

where $\lfloor y \rfloor$ denotes the largest integer less than or equal to y, the so called *floor* function. If we substitute $(\lambda T_1,\lambda T_2,\lambda T_3)$ for (x_1,x_2,x_3) in the above we immediately get the desired result.

5.9.2 Additional Reading

[1]   S.S.Cairns, **Introductory Topology,** Ronald Press, New York, New York (Revised Printing), 1968.

[2]   G.B.Dantzig, **Linear Programming and Extensions,** Princeton University Press, Princeton, New Jersey, 1963.

[3]   K.Omahen, *Capacity Bounds for Multiresource Queues,* J.A.C.M., **24,** 646-663 (1977).

5.10 An Office System Model

We close with a more sophisticated model of an office than what we considered earlier. Although it is more complex, the same techniques discussed in the earlier example still apply. Consider an office with M managers, S secretaries, with each manager having a telephone, each secretary having a typewriter and telephone, and C copiers for the entire staff. There are two types of jobs performed, document preparation (type 1) and telephone call answering (type 2). Document preparation consists of seven steps shown below:

[1]   Step(1,1)--A manager generates a hand written draft of a document. The mean time duration for generating a draft is $T_{1,1}$ minutes.

[2]   Step(1,2)--A secretary produces a typewritten version of the draft and returns it to the originator. The mean duration of this step is $T_{1,2}$ minutes.

[3]   Step (1,3)--The manager corrects the typewritten document. This step has a mean duration of $T_{1,3}$ minutes and is executed an average of $V_{1,3}$ times per document

[4]   Step (1,4)--If after step (1,3) changes are required, a secretary makes the changes and returns the document to the originator. This step has a mean duration of $T_{1,4}$ minutes

[5]   Step (1,5)--If no changes are required after step (1,3), a secretary walks to a copier. The mean time required is $T_{1,5}$ minutes

[6]   Step (1,6)--A secretary reproduces the requisite number of copies. The mean duration of time is $T_{1,6}$.

[7]   A secretary returns the document with copies to the originator. This requires a mean time interval of $T_{1,7}$ minutes

At any given instant of time there are a maximum of D documents in the sum total of all these stages.

The telephone call answering job consists of four steps:

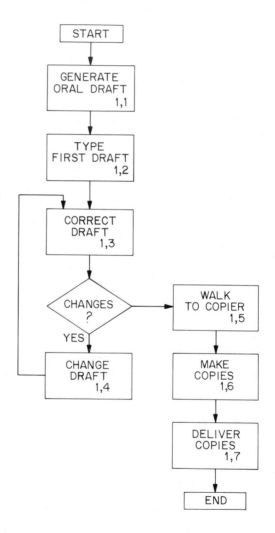

Figure 5.14. Document Preparation Steps

[1]   Step $(2,1)$--A secretary answers a telephone for a manager, talks, and passes the message along to the appropriate manager; this has a mean time of $T_{2,1}$

[2]   Step (2,2)--A secretary answers a telephone for a manager and then passes the caller on to the manager; this has a mean time of $T_{2,2}$

[3]   Step (2,3)--A manager answers a telephone with a mean time of $T_{2,3}$

[4]   Step (2,4)--A manager receives a call that is first handled by a secretary and talks for a mean time $T_{2,4}$

The fraction of calls handled by a secretary alone is $V_{2,1}$, while the fraction handled by a manager alone is $V_{2,3}$ and the fraction handled by a secretary first and then a manager is $V_{2,2}$:

$$V_{2,1} + V_{2,2} + V_{2,3} = \sum_{K=1}^{3} V_{2,K} = 1 \quad V_{2,4} = 1$$

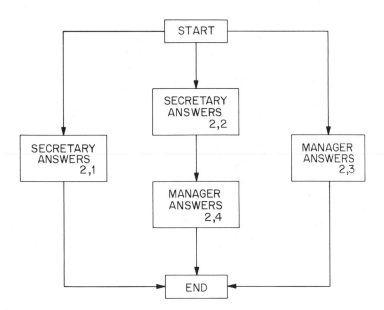

Figure 5.15.Telephone Message Handling Block Diagram

We next construct the step requirements table for this office:

Table 5.14. Document Step Resource Requirements

Step Number	Resource						Time Interval
	Manager	Secretary	Typewriter	Telephone	Copier	Document	
1	1	0	0	0	0	1	$T_{1,1}$
2	0	1	1	0	0	1	$T_{1,2}$
3	1	0	0	0	0	1	$T_{1,3}$
4	0	1	1	0	0	1	$T_{1,4}$
5	0	1	0	0	0	1	$T_{1,5}$
6	0	1	0	0	1	1	$T_{1,6}$
7	0	1	0	0	0	1	$T_{1,7}$

Table 5.15. Telephone Answering Step Resource Table

Step Number	Resource		Time Interval
	Manager	Secretary	
1	0	1	$T_{2,1}$
2	0	1	$T_{2,2}$
3	1	0	$T_{2,3}$
4	1	0	$T_{2,4}$

The documents circulate through the office system, with each document either waiting for one or more resources to become available, or being executed in steps $(1,1)$ through $(1,7)$. It is therefore convenient to append an additional step, $(1,8)$, to our model: step $(1,8)$ is the waiting state of a document, and $T_{wait} \equiv T_{1,8}$ denotes the mean time a document spends waiting for resources. If we denote the mean throughput rate for document preparation, job type 1, by λ_1 jobs per minute, and the mean telephone call answering rate for type 2 jobs by λ_2 jobs per minute, then our goal is to determine upper bounds on λ_1, λ_2 and lower bounds on T_{wait}. The state of the system at any instant of time is represented by a twelve tuple or vector denoted by $\underline{J}$, whose components are nonnegative integers:

$$\underline{J} = (j_{1,1}, j_{1,2}, ..., j_{1,8}, j_{2,1}, j_{2,2}, j_{2,3}, j_{2,4}) \quad j_{I,K} \in \{non\ negative\ integers\}, I=1,2; K=1,...,8$$

From the step requirements table and the discussion we can write that the feasible set of $\underline{J}$ is denoted by F, while the above implies the components of $\underline{J} \in F$ are nonnegative integers such that

$$j_{1,6} \leqslant C$$

$$j_{1,2} + j_{1,4} + j_{1,5} + j_{1,6} + j_{1,7} + j_{2,1} + j_{2,2} \leqslant S$$

$$j_{1,1} + j_{1,2} + j_{1,3} + j_{1,4} + j_{1,5} + j_{1,6} + j_{1,7} + j_{2,3} + j_{2,4} = M$$

$$j_{1,1} + j_{1,2} + j_{1,3} + j_{1,4} + j_{1,5} + j_{1,6} + j_{1,7} + j_{1,8} = D$$

The convex hull of F, denoted $C(F)$, is given by the set of twelve tuples with *real* valued nonnegative entries $\underline{X} = (x_{1,1}, ..., x_{1,8}, x_{2,1}, ..., x_{2,4})$ that satisfy the following constraints:

$$x_{1,1}, x_{1,2}, \ldots, x_{1,8}, x_{2,1}, \ldots, x_{2,4} \geqslant 0$$

$$x_{1,6} \leqslant C$$

$$x_{1,2} + x_{1,4} + x_{1,5} + x_{1,6} + x_{1,7} + x_{2,1} + x_{2,2} \leqslant S$$

$$x_{1,1} + x_{1,2} + x_{1,3} + x_{1,4} + x_{1,5} + x_{1,6} + x_{1,7} + x_{1,8} + x_{2,3} + x_{2,4} \leqslant M$$

$$x_{1,1} + x_{1,2} + x_{1,3} + x_{1,4} + x_{1,5} + x_{1,6} + x_{1,7} + x_{1,8} = D$$

Using Little's Law, we can write that the mean number of managers active in each step of document preparation equals the document arrival rate multiplied by mean document time per step:

$$\sum_{\underline{J} \in F} j_{1,K} \pi(\underline{J}) = \lambda_1 T_{1,K} \quad K=1,2,5,6,7,8$$

The mean number of secretaries busy at each step of document preparation must equal the mean document arrival rate times the mean document time per step:

$$\sum_{\underline{J} \in F} j_{1,3} \pi(\underline{J}) = \lambda_1 V T_{1,3}$$

$$\sum_{\underline{J} \in F} j_{1,4} \pi(\underline{J}) = \lambda_1 (V-1) T_{1,4}$$

Finally, the mean number of telephone calls in each of four steps must equal the telephone call arrival rate multiplied by the mean time per call step:

$$\sum_{\underline{J} \in F} j_{2,K} \pi(\underline{J}) = \lambda_2 V_{2,K} T_{2,K} \quad K=1,2,3,4$$

The relations for steps $(1,3)$ and $(1,4)$ reflect the fact that there are a mean number of $V_{1,3} \geqslant 1$ steps of type $(1,3)$ per job 1 and $(V_{1,3}-1)$ steps of type $(1,4)$ per job 1. The relations for steps $(2,1)$ through $(2,4)$ reflect the fact that there are a mean number of visits $0 \leqslant V_{2,K} \leqslant 1, K=1,..,4$ to each step.

The values $\lambda_1, \lambda_2, T_{wait}$ are possible if and only if the point

$$(\lambda_1 T_{1,1}, \lambda_1 T_{1,2}, \lambda_1 V T_{1,3}, \lambda_1 (V-1) T_{1,4}, \lambda_1 T_{1,5}, \lambda_1 T_{1,6},$$

$$\lambda_1 T_{1,7}, \lambda_1 T_{1,8}, \lambda_2 V_{2,1} T_{2,1}, \lambda_2 V_{2,2} T_{2,2}, \lambda_2 V_{2,3} T_{2,3}, \lambda_2 V_{2,4} T_{2,4})$$

is a member of the convex hull of the feasible set F. Substituting into the above we have

$$\lambda_1 T_{copy} \leqslant C \quad \lambda_1 T_{doc,sec} + \lambda_2 T_{tel,sec} \leqslant S$$

$$\lambda_1 T_{doc,man} + \lambda_2 T_{tel,man} \leqslant M \quad \lambda_1 (T_{doc,man} + T_{doc,sec} + T_{wait}) = D$$

where

$$T_{doc,sec} = T_{1,2} + (V-1)T_{1,4} + T_{1,5} + T_{1,6} + T_{1,7} \qquad T_{tel,sec} = V_{2,1}T_{2,1} + V_{2,2}T_{2,2}$$

$$T_{doc,man} = T_{1,1} + VT_{1,3} \qquad T_{tel,man} = V_{2,3}T_{2,3} + V_{2,4}T_{2,4}$$

$$T_{copy} = T_{1,6}$$

The physical meaning of each of these terms is

- $T_{doc,sec}$ --The mean time a secretary spends on a document

- $T_{tel,sec}$ --The mean time a secretary spends answering a telephone call

- $T_{doc,man}$ --The mean time a manager spends preparing and revising documents

- $T_{tel,man}$ --The mean time a manager spends answering a telephone call

- T_{copy} --The mean time to make copies of a document

Note that there are really only *five* time intervals that we really need: the mean time to make a telephone call for a manager and a secretary, the mean time to handle a document for a manager and a secretary, and the mean time to make sufficient copies of a document. We also need *four* numbers: the total number of managers, secretaries, documents, and copiers. This is the minimum information needed to say *anything* concerning productivity in any quantitative sense. This can be summarized as follows:

$$\lambda_1 \leqslant \min \left[\frac{M - \lambda_2 T_{tel,man}}{T_{doc,man}}, \frac{D}{T_{doc,man}}, \frac{S - \lambda_2 T_{tel,sec}}{T_{doc,man}}, \frac{C}{T_{copy}} \right]$$

$$\lambda_2 \leqslant \min \left[\frac{M - \lambda_1 T_{doc,man}}{T_{tel,man}}, \frac{S - \lambda_1 T_{doc,sec}}{T_{doc,sec}} \right]$$

$$T_{wait} = \frac{D}{\lambda_1} - T_{doc,man} - T_{doc,sec}$$

We remark that the set of feasible points (λ_1, λ_2) form a convex polygon.

For a fixed value of λ_2 ($\lambda_2 < S/T_{tel,sec}$), we can use the above to determine the potential bottlenecks:

[1]   Managers handling documents are the bottleneck

$$\lambda_{1,max} = \frac{M - \lambda_2 T_{doc,man}}{T_{doc,man}}$$

[2]   Secretaries handling documents are the bottleneck

$$\lambda_{1,max} = \frac{S - \lambda_2 T_{tel,sec}}{T_{doc,sec}}$$

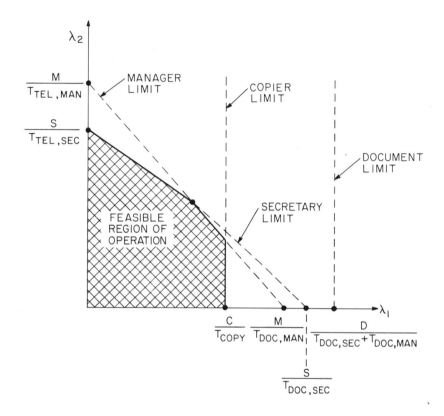

Figure 5.16. Feasible Set of Mean Throughput Rates

[3]   Copiers are the bottleneck

$$\lambda_{1,max} = \frac{C}{T_{copy}}$$

[4]   Documents are the bottleneck

$$\lambda_{1,max} = \frac{D}{T_{document}}$$

[5]   Managers handling telephone calls are the bottleneck

$$\lambda_{2,max} = \frac{M - \lambda_1 T_{doc,man}}{T_{tel,man}}$$

[6] Secretaries handling telephone calls are the bottleneck

$$\lambda_{2,max} = \frac{S - \lambda_1 T_{doc,sec}}{T_{tel,sec}}$$

Where do we want the bottleneck: perhaps managers handling documents? What do you think?

First we illustrate the upper bound on mean throughput rate as a function of the number of secretaries S,

$$S > \max(\lambda_2 T_{tel,sec}, C)$$

in the figure below. The feasible operating regions are also shown.

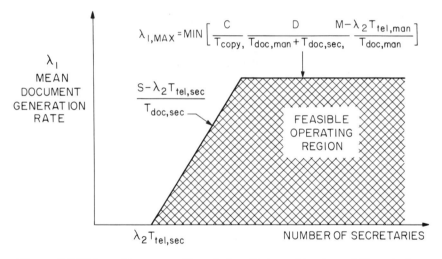

Figure 5.17.Mean Document Completion Rate vs Number of Secretaries

The breakpoint is clearly evident: fewer secretaries than the breakpoint, and the secretaries are the bottleneck, while greater than the breakpoint number and the copies, the number of documents, or the managers are the bottleneck.

This can be completed with the mean document waiting time feasible operating region, shown in Figure 5.18.

The reader hopefully will see the importance of being systematic in approaching such an operation, enumerating all possible states, because nothing will be overlooked.

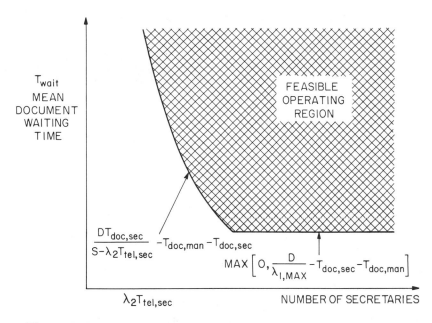

T_{wait}
MEAN
DOCUMENT
WAITING
TIME

FEASIBLE
OPERATING
REGION

$$\frac{DT_{doc,sec}}{S - \lambda_2 T_{tel,sec}} - T_{doc,man} - T_{doc,sec}$$

$$MAX \left[0, \frac{D}{\lambda_{1,MAX}} - T_{doc,sec} - T_{doc,man} \right]$$

$\lambda_2 T_{tel,sec}$ NUMBER OF SECRETARIES

Figure 5.18. Mean Document Waiting Time vs Number of Secretaries

The table below summarizes some illustrative mean times required to do the different aggregate steps:

Table 5.16. Illustrative Mean Times

Job Step	Time (Hr)
$T_{doc,sec}$	1/2
$T_{tel,sec}$	1/30
$T_{doc,man}$	2
$T_{tel,man}$	1/6
T_{copy}	1/3

Suppose we have one copier and one secretary for five managers, with one document per manager in preparation. Where is the bottleneck resource? Let's check one resource at a time:

[1]   Managers handling documents can do a maximum of

$$\lambda_{1,max} = \frac{5}{2} = 2.5 \ documents/hr$$

[2]   Secretaries handling documents can do a maximum of

$$\lambda_{1,max} = \frac{1}{\frac{1}{2}} = 2 \; documents/hr$$

[3]   The copier can handle

$$\lambda_{1,max} = \frac{1}{1/3} = 3 \; documents/hr$$

[4]   The documents in circulation limit us to

$$\lambda_{1,max} = \frac{5}{2 + 1/3 + \frac{1}{2}} = 1 \; 13/17 \; documents/hr$$

[5]   Managers handling telephone calls

$$\lambda_{2,max} = \frac{5}{1/6} = 30 \; calls/hr$$

[6]   Secretaries handling telephone calls

$$\lambda_{2,max} = \frac{1}{1/30} = 30 \; calls/hr$$

The limiting bottleneck here is the *number* of documents in circulation: managers have to have more than one document going at a time. Suppose we double this, so each manager has two documents in the mill at once? What is the new bottleneck? Now it is the secretaries working flat out to keep up with the document load. If we add another secretary to cure this, then the new bottleneck is the managers working full time at document generation.

5.10.1 Additional Reading

[1]   G.H.Engel, J.Groppuso, R.A.Lowenstein, W.G.Traub, *An Office Communications System,* IBM Systems Journal, **18** (4), 402-431, 1979.

[2]   P.C.Gardner, *A System for the Automated Office Environment,* IBM Systems Journal, **20** (3), 321-345 (1981).

Problems

1) Measurements are gathered on clerical work activity during a normal business day both before and after the installation of an online transaction processing computer communications system:

Table 5.17. Clerk Normal Business Day

Work Activity	Fraction of Time Before	After
Telephone	10%	20%
Enter Data	20%	10%
File Data	30%	10%
Retrieve Data	30%	20%
Misc	10%	40%

Answer the following questions:

A. What is the state space for the activities for each clerk?

B. What is the potential gain in productivity, measured in amount of work done per unit time?

C. What is the net percentage change in the number of clerks required to carry out the required work?

2) A secretary does different activities during a normal business day. The table below summarizes the fraction of time spent per activity before and after installation of an office communication system:

Table 5.18. Secretary's Normal Business Day

Work Activity	Fraction of Time Before	After
Face to Face Meetings	10%	20%
Telephone Calls	10%	20%
Typing	35%	40%
Reading/Writing	15%	20%
Mail Handling	10%	5%
Copy Documents	10%	5%
Filing	10%	5%

Answer the following questions:

A. What is the state space for activities for each secretary?

B. What is the gain in productivity, defined as the amount of work done per unit time?

C. What is the percentage change in number of secretaries?

3) A series of measurements are carried out on the activities of professionals in an office environment, both before and after the installation of an office communications system. During a normal business day, the table below summarizes the fraction of time spent in each work activity:

Table 5.19. Professional Normal Business Day

Work Activity	Fraction of Time Before	Fraction of Time After
Face to Face Meetings	50%	25%
Telephone	10%	20%
Read/Write	20%	25%
Misc	20%	30%

Answer the following questions:

A. What is the state space for activities for each professional?

B. What is the gain in productivity, defined as amount of work done per unit time?

C. What is the percentage change in number of professionals?

4) Measurements are carried out on the activities of professionals in an office environment, both before and after the installation of an office communication system. The data are aggregated by the fraction of time spent in a given activity during a normal business day:

Table 5.20.Professionals' Normal Business Day

Work	Fraction of Time	
Activity	Before	After
Search for Data	15%	10%
Input Data	15%	5%
Validate Data	25%	5%
Process Data	15%	5%
Distribute Data	5%	5%
Think	20%	65%
Administration	5%	5%

Answer the following questions:

A. What is the state space for activities for a professional?

B. What is the gain in productivity, defined as amount of work done per unit time?

C. What is the percentage change in number of professionals?

5) A office currently has one secretary for every five professionals. If the professionals are not available, the secretary will answer their telephones and write down any messages. Two different systems are currently being evaluated for reducing the message answering work load on the secretary: one involves electronic mail, where each professional has a special terminal that allows messages to be entered from a key board, displayed, edited, transmitted, filed, archived, retrieved, and deleted as need be. The second involves voice mail, where each professional uses a voice telephone to carry out the same functions. The resources required for each step are summarized in the table below:

Table 5.21.Step/Resource Summary

Job	Resource					Time
Step	Terminal	Port	Processor	Disk	Printer	Interval
Enter	1	1	1	1	0	T_{enter}
Edit	1	1	1	1	1	T_{edit}
Send	1	1	1	1	1	T_{send}
File	0	1	1	1	1	T_{file}
Retrieve	1	1	1	1	1	$T_{retrieve}$
Delete	1	1	1	1	1	T_{delete}

The mean time intervals for each system are summarized below:

Table 5.22.Mean Time Interval/Step

Symbol	Current	Voice Mail	Electronic Mail
Enter	1 Minute	2 Minute	5 Minute
Edit	0 Minute	0 Minute	1 Minute
Send	30 Minute	30 Minute	30 Minute
File	1 Minute	0 Minute	0 Minute
Retrieve	5 Minute	0 Minute	0 Minute
Delete	0 Minute	0 Minute	0 Minute

For the current system, $V_{message}=3$ is the mean number of calls made to actually have one professional talk to another. For either proposed system, $V_{message}=1$ is the mean number of calls required to handle any given matter.

Answer the following questions:

A. What is the state space for each system?

B. Which resource will reach complete utilization first for each system?

C. Plot the mean throughput rate versus number of professionals per one secretary. How many professionals are needed per secretary for each system?

6) A copying machine can be purchased with or without an automatic feeder. When an operator makes one copy of one page, three steps are involved

[1] Set up time denoted by T_{setup} which is the time to set the document properly aligned onto the copier

[2] Copying time denoted by T_{copy} which is the time to make one copy of one page

[3] Clean up time denoted by $T_{cleanup}$ which is the time to remove the document from the copier

For the two configurations, the time intervals are summarized below

Table 5.23.Mean Time/Step

Step	No Feeder	With Feeder
Set Up	5 sec	1 sec
Copy	2 sec	2 sec
Clean Up	5 sec	1 sec

Answer the following questions:

A.   What is the state space for this model?

B.   What is an upper bound on mean throughput rate for each system?

C.   Suppose twenty per cent of the documents are five pages long, while eighty per cent of the documents are one page long: find an upper bound on the mean throughput rate for each system?

7) Two different systems for preparing documents are under consideration. In the first system, one secretary is assigned to ten professionals, and handles all document preparation needs. In the second system, a central text processing center is set up that handles all document preparation needs of all professionals. The main differences in the two approaches are

• Each secretary is given one printer capable of printing thirty characters per second maximum while the central text processing center can afford one high speed printer capable of printing two pages of text (two hundred and fifty words per page, five characters per word) per second maximum

• The central text processing center requires every document be logged in and logged out, while the local system involves much less time consuming procedures for control of documents

We assume each professional generates a two page document every day, and each clerk can type at thirty words per minute. Two minutes are required to log in every document at the central text processing center; fifteen seconds is required for the local secretary to do this.

Answer the following questions:

A.   What is the state space for each system?

B.   Find an upper bound on the mean number of documents per unit time either system can handle?

C.   How many professionals and secretaries are required for either system assuming the upper bound on mean number of documents per unit time is being handled?

8) Two different office communication systems are under consideration. In the current system, people walk to and from offices, copying machines, and typewriters. In the proposed system, a high speed local area network is installed that reduces the need to walk to and from offices, copying machines and typewriters, and secondly reduces the time to transmit information from one place to another. The table below summarizes illustrative time intervals for each job

Table 5.24. Illustrative Time/Step Summary

| Job | | Time Interval | |
Step	Symbol	Current	Proposed
Office to office	T_{office}	5 minutes	2 minutes
Office to copier	T_{copier}	5 minutes	1 minute
Office to printer	T_{print}	10 minutes	2 minutes

Table 5.25. Illustrative Visits/Step Summary

| Job | | Mean Number of Visits | |
Step	Symbol	Current	Proposed
Office to office	V_{office}	5	2
Office to copier	V_{copier}	5	2
Office to printer	$V_{printer}$	2	1

Answer the following questions:

A. What is the state space for each system?

B. Find an upper bound on the mean rate of doing office communication jobs for each system.

C. What is the potential gain, if a job typically requires one hour of other work in addition to communication? What changes if a job requires fifty hours of other work in addition to communication?

9) A charity has an executive office staffed by a director and S secretaries. The current mode of operation involves a great deal of manual work, filing activities with paper index cards, and typing. We wish to compare this mode of operation with a proposed mode of operation, involving conversion to an automated system consisting of work stations, one for each secretary, plus a local network between work stations. The difference in the two modes of operation is the *equipment* available to the secretaries.

Each secretary can do two types of jobs, donor registration (type 1) and telephone call answering (type 2). Donor registration consists of seven steps:

[1] Step $(1,1)$--The donor file is searched to see if the member is already there or not. The mean duration for this step is $T_{1,1}$ minutes.

[2] Step $(1,2)$--The address of the donor is checked against that in the file and appropriate modifications are entered. The mean duration of this step is $T_{1,2}$ minutes.

[3] Step $(1,3)$--A donor number is assigned from a list of available numbers. This requires $T_{1,3}$ minutes on the average.

[4]   Step(1,4)--A donor card is typed. This requires $T_{1,4}$ minutes.

[5]   Step(1,5)--An envelope is addressed and stuffed with the requisite donor card and other written material. This requires $T_{1,5}$ minutes.

[6]   Step(1,6)--The mailing list is updated using a card punch. This requires $T_{1,6}$ minutes.

[7]   Step(1,7)--The new name is entered onto the newsletter mailing list. This requires $T_{1,7}$ minutes.

The telephone call answering job consists of two steps:

[1]   Step(2,1)--A secretary answers a telephone, talks, and determines the purpose of the call. The mean duration of this job is $T_{2,1}$ minutes.

[2]   Step(2,2)--If the secretary can handle the call, this requires $T_{2,2}$ minutes. Otherwise the director handles the call.

The total time to handle each type of job is given by adding up the time to do each step:

$$T_{donor} = T_{1,1} + T_{1,2} + T_{1,3} + T_{1,4} + T_{1,5} + T_{1,6} + T_{1,7}$$

$$T_{telephone} = T_{2,1} + T_{2,2}$$

Answer the following questions:

A.   What is the state space for this model?

B.   The total arrival rate of transactions (both donor gifts and telephone calls) is λ transactions per minute. The fraction of arrivals due to each type is $F_{donor}, F_{telephone}$, and hence the arrival rate of each type of transaction is λF_{donor} and $\lambda F_{telephone}$, respectively. Determine an analytic expression for an upper bound on the total mean number of transactions per minute as a function of the number of secretaries, and plot this versus S, the number of secretaries.

C.   Table 5.26 summarizes the average or mean time to handle each step of donor processing:

Table 5.26.Donor Processing

Step	Current	Proposed
Look Up in File	1 Minute	1/4 Minute
Check/Change Address	1 Minute	1/4 Minute
Assign Donor Number	1/4 Minute	0 Minutes
Prepare Donor Card	1 Minute	1/4 Minute
Address/Stuff Envelope	2 Minutes	1/2 Minute
Update Zipcode List	1 Minute	0 Minutes
Update Newsletter List	1/2 Minute	0 Minutes
Total	6 3/4 Minutes	1 1/4 Minutes

The table below summarizes the mean amount of time required to handle telephone call work:

Table 5.27.Telephone Call Work

Step	Current	Proposed
Answer Telephone	1/4 Minute	1/4 Minute
Answer Query	2 Minutes	1/2 Minute
Total	2 1/4 Minutes	3/4 Minutes

Each secretary works 270 days per year, spending roughly four hours per day handling donor records and telephone calls. For each mode of operation, how many secretaries are needed to handle 100,000 transactions per year, assuming $F_{donor}=0.80$? assuming $F_{donor}=0.20$?

10) Consider an office with M managers, S secretaries, with each manager having a telephone, each secretary having a typewriter and telephone, and C copiers for the entire staff. There are two types of jobs performed, document preparation (type 1) and telephone call answering (type 2). Document preparation consists of seven step:

[1] Step(1,1)--A manager generates a hand written draft of a document. The mean time duration for generating a draft is $T_{1,1}$ minutes.

[2] Step(1,2)--A secretary produces a typewritten version of the draft and returns it to the originator. The mean duration of this step is $T_{1,2}$ minutes.

[3] Step (1,3)--The manager corrects the typewritten document. This step has a mean duration of $T_{1,3}$ minutes and is executed an average of $V_{1,3}$ times per document

[4] Step (1,4)--If after step (1,3) changes are required, a secretary makes the changes and returns the document to the originator. This step has a mean duration of $T_{1,4}$ minutes

[5] Step (1,5)--If no changes are required after step (1,3), a secretary walks to a copier. The mean time required is $T_{1,5}$ minutes

[6] Step (1,6)--A secretary reproduces the requisite number of copies. The mean duration of time is $T_{1,6}$.

[7] A secretary returns the document with copies to the originator. This requires a mean time interval of $T_{1,7}$ minutes

At any given instant of time there are a maximum of D documents in the sum total of all these stages.

The telephone call answering job consists of at most four tasks:

[1] Step (2,1)--A secretary answers a telephone for a manager, talks, and passes the message along to the appropriate manager; this has a mean time of $T_{2,1}$

[2] Step (2,2)--A secretary answers a telephone for a manager and then passes the caller on to the manager; this has a mean time of $T_{2,2}$

[3] Step (2,3)--A manager answers a telephone with a mean time of $T_{2,3}$

[4] Step (2,4)--A manager receives a call that is first handled by a secretary and talks for a mean time $T_{2,4}$

The fraction of calls handled by a secretary alone is $V_{2,1}$, while the fraction handled by a manager alone is $V_{2,3}$ and the fraction handled by a secretary first and then a manager is $V_{2,2}$:

$$V_{2,1} + V_{2,2} + V_{2,3} = \sum_{K=1}^{3} V_{2,K} = 1 \qquad V_{2,4} = 1$$

We next construct the step requirements table for this office:

Table 5.28.Document Step Resource Requirements

Step Number	Resource						Time Interval
	Manager	Secretary	Typewriter	Telephone	Copier	Document	
1	1	0	0	0	0	1	$T_{1,1}$
2	0	1	1	0	0	1	$T_{1,2}$
3	1	0	0	0	0	1	$T_{1,3}$
4	0	1	1	0	0	1	$T_{1,4}$
5	0	1	0	0	0	1	$T_{1,5}$
6	0	1	0	0	1	1	$T_{1,6}$
7	0	1	0	0	0	1	$T_{1,7}$

Table 5.29.Telephone Answering Step Resource Table

Step Number	Resource Manager	Secretary	Time Interval
1	0	1	$T_{2,1}$
2	0	1	$T_{2,2}$
3	1	0	$T_{2,3}$
4	1	0	$T_{2,4}$

The documents circulate through the office system, with each document either waiting for one or more resources to become available, or being executed in steps $(1,1)$ through $(1,7)$. It is therefore convenient to append an additional step, $(1,8)$, to our model: step $(1,8)$ is the waiting state of a document, and $T_{wait} \equiv T_{1,8}$ denotes the mean time a document spends waiting for resources. We denote for the mean throughput rate for document preparation, job type 1, by λ_1 jobs per minute, and for the mean telephone call answering rate for type 2 jobs by λ_2 jobs per minute.

Answer the following questions:

A. What is the state space for this system?

B. What are the bottlenecks in this system?

C. What is the maximum mean throughput rate for document generation?

D. What is the maximum mean throughput rate for telephone call answering?

E. Plot the mean waiting time for document generation versus number of secretaries.

F. The table below summarizes some mean time intervals to handle different steps:

Table 5.30.Illustrative Mean Times/Step

Job Step	Time(Hr)
$T_{doc,sec}$	1/2
$T_{tel,sec}$	1/30
$T_{doc,man}$	2
$T_{tel,man}$	1/6
T_{copy}	1/3

Suppose we have one copier and one secretary for ten managers, with three documents per manager in preparation. Where is the bottleneck resource?

Our goal in this section is to extend the previous performance analysis (based only on mean execution times) to include both fluctuations about mean values as well as ordering constraints or correlations between different steps and different jobs. This demands additional assumptions concerning the job arrival and execution time statistics, as well as the scheduling policy. We focus on a class of Markovian mathematical models where knowing only the present or current state of the system, not the entire history of the system operations, its future statistical behavior is determined. These are called *Jackson queueing networks* in honor of the pioneer researcher who first studied their behavior.

If all possible system states and the associated state transition rates are exhaustively enumerated, oftentimes the *number* of states in such models explodes (into tens of trillions for straightforward applications such as a single terminal word processor system, and into far far greater numbers for more sophisticated applications such as airline reservation systems with hundreds of terminals, tens of communication lines, and upwards of one hundred disk spindles) to far exceed the storage and processing capabilities of the most powerful supercomputers (both available and envisioned!): it can be virtually impossible to extract any analytically tractable formulae or numerical approximations of different measures of performance. The only credible avenues for quantifying system performance for many people for years appeared to be simulation studies or building a prototype (which is another form of simulation, using the actual system but simulating the load).

In a series of seminal papers, Jackson made the *fundamental* observation that for a wide class of Markovian models, the distribution of the number of jobs in each step queued or in service at *each* node in a network could be written as the product of functions, with each function depending only on the workload for that node. This arises in many other areas of mathematics, where the solution to a multivariate set of equations is assumed to be the *product* of functions depending only on one variable, a so called *separation of variables* decomposition. It is also in the spirit of Fourier analysis, where an arbitrary function is approximated as the sum of a number of elementary functions. Because of this property, the long term time averaged distribution for the number of jobs queued or in execution in these Jackson models are often said to obey a *product form* distribution. Just (or more) important than this analysis is the ready availability of efficient and easy to use software packages that numerically approximate a variety of performance measures for these classes of models, and handle both input and output in a flexible manner, allowing different design choices and sensitivity analyses to be quickly carried out*. There is currently a great deal of research activity into both extending this class of models and extending the range of numerical approximations.

6.1 Overview

First we describe the ingredients in a Jackson queueing network model and then we develop the outline of the exposition.

6.1.1 Ingredients The inputs for this type of analysis are a description of the total mean arrival rate for each job, the total mean time each job uses each resource with only one resource used at a time, and a description of how contention for each resource is resolved. The output of this type of analysis is the fraction of time a given *number* of jobs are queued or in execution at each resource. This in turn can be manipulated to determine the utilization of each resource, and the mean throughput rate and mean queueing time (both waiting and execution time) for each job using the techniques developed in the earlier sections. The scheduling policies analyzed here demand that a processor must execute a job if a job is ready for execution: these are called *work conserving* policies because the total backlog of work is independent of the precise details of the scheduling policy at any instant of time. Two examples of work conserving policies are (i) servicing jobs in order of arrival, or (ii) multiplexing a single processor at a high speed among *J* jobs so that each job receives $1/Jth$ the total available processor cycles. The mean value analysis inputs are a subset of these inputs, so we expect the Jackson network outputs to refine the mean value analysis outputs. An example of a policy that does *not* conserve work is found in a system that executes two types of jobs, one with one second execution times and the other with one hour execution times; if it frequently occurs that ten seconds after we begin execution of a one hour job, a short one second job may arrive, then we might wait for eleven seconds after a long job arrives before starting execution, holding the processor idle, to allow short jobs not to be delayed at the expense of long jobs.

6.1.2 Program First we analyze a single parallel group of processors fed from a single queue, for a wide variety of parameter choices. Second we examine an arbitrary network of serially reusable resources where each job migrates from node to node, entering and leaving at different nodes. As a special case, we examine a pipeline of nodes or stages, each with a single processor. All of this

---

*   Efficiency: in one study conducted by the authors for an online transaction processing system with five hundred terminals, ten processors each with two disk spindles, and thirty data links, the entire model (including a graphics library), occupied less than ninety thousand bytes of static main memory, and could produce graphic output for seven hundred and twenty different parameter choices using less than ten seconds of processor time (for both numerical calculations and graphical output) running in a GCOS environment on a H6000.

is done for one type of job, and then extended to multiple types of jobs. These basic cases will form the foundations for a series of case studies and examples in this and subsequent chapters.

Ideas appear here that have not been encountered before. All of these new ideas are expounded for the simplest case, a single parallel group of processors: jobs can be either *delayed* (stored in a buffer) until a processor is available, or *rejected* if no storage space is available. Queueing or buffering jobs might be chosen if it were highly likely that a processor would become available an acceptable time after a job arrival; jobs would be blocked on arrival if this were not the case. A different way of thinking about this is that jobs are blocked or delayed for a finite time from being serviced; in the limit where jobs are blocked or delayed forever, the jobs are lost, i.e., never serviced. In practice, systems are designed so that in normal operation blocking or delay or defection is rare. Many communication systems adopt combinations of loss and delay mechanisms. We choose to first analyze delay alone and then loss alone before attempting to analyze systems combining both these mechanisms.

Finally, special asymptotic limiting cases give us analytic insight into system performance. One such case involves allowing the number of active terminals attached to a computer system to become larger and larger, while the total workload stays constant. As the total number of terminals grows, each terminal contributes less and less to the workload, but the total workload is constant. Another such case involves allowing the number of terminals and processors to become larger and larger, while the ratio of terminals and processors stays fixed. Each terminal contributes the same workload, so as the total number of terminals and processors grows, the total workload grows.

6.1.3 *Additional Reading*

[1]   J.R.Jackson, *Networks of Waiting Lines,* Operations Research, **5,** 518-521 (1957).

[2]   J.R.Jackson, *Jobshop-Like Queueing Systems,* Management Science, **10** (1),131-142(1963).

[3]   F.P.Kelly, *Networks of Queues,* Advances in Applied Probability, **8,** 416-432 (1976).

[4]   F.P.Kelly, **Reversibility and Stochastic Networks,** Wiley, Chichester, 1979.

6.2 A Single Node with P Parallel Processors

Clerks at terminals submit one type of job to a computer system that consists of P processors, then wait for a response before submitting the next job. The processors are fed jobs from a single queue. Jobs are stored in a buffer of capacity M jobs if no processor is available. If a job is submitted with all buffers filled, the job is rejected, and the clerk begins the entire process over again.

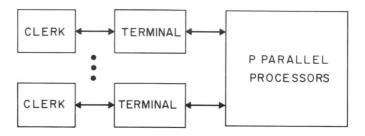

Figure 6.1.System Block Diagram

The mean time spent by a clerk reading and thinking and typing is denoted by T_{think}. The mean processor execution time per job is denoted by T_{proc}. Our goal is to calculate the mean throughput rate λ and the mean delay (waiting plus execution time) that a clerk experiences which we will call the *queueing* time or *flow* time of a job, denoted by $E(T_Q)$.

6.2.1 Functional Operation In order to describe the operation of the system, we need to describe the workload generated by each clerk and the policy for arbitrating contention for shared resources.

The workload is handled first. There are C clerks. There are at least as many clerks as buffer space, $C \geqslant M$. Each clerk spends a mean amount of time T_{think} reading, thinking, and typing and then submits a job for execution. The sequence of times each clerk spends reading and thinking and typing are assumed to be independent identically distributed random variables. Once a job is submitted to the system, if storage space is available, the job is accepted for service; otherwise the job is rejected and returns to the clerk who starts the entire cycle over again. The system is capable of storing a maximum of M jobs. If a job is accepted and there is an idle processor available, that job begins execution immediately. The processor execution times are independent identically distributed random variables with mean T_{proc}.

Next, the arbitration or scheduling policy is described. There are two queues here, one for the clerks and one for the processors.

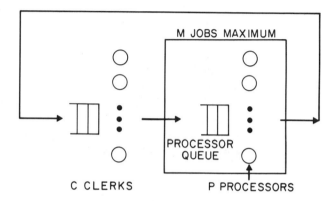

Figure 6.2.Queueing Network Block Diagram

Once a processor finishes executing a job, an idle clerk will enter into the thinking state; since there is one clerk per job, there will never be any jobs waiting in the clerk queue for an idle clerk. The rate at which clerks submit jobs to the system depends upon the number of clerks reading and thinking and typing. Let $\Phi_{clerk}(J_{clerk})$ denote the number of seconds of work done in one second of time. For example, if $\Phi_{clerk}(J_{clerk})=J_{clerk}$, then if $J_{clerk}=0$ then no work is done, while if $J_{clerk}=1$ then one second of work is done in one second, and if $J_{clerk}=2$ then two seconds of work are done in one second, given there are J_{clerk} clerks in the thinking state. More generally, we assume that this function is positive and monotonically increasing with J_{clerk}, and equals zero if $J_{clerk}=0$. We stress that $\Phi_{clerk}(J_{clerk})$ is dimensionless or without any units. The instantaneous (i.e., the instant at which there are J_{clerk} clerks thinking) rate at which jobs are submitted by clerks is given by

$$instantaneous\ job\ submittal\ rate\ =\ \frac{\Phi_{clerk}(J_{clerk})}{T_{think}}\ \ \ \ J_{clerk}=0,1,...,C$$

For example, if we model the clerk behavior by

$$\Phi_{clerk}(J_{clerk}) = min(J_{clerk},C) = J_{clerk}\ \ \ \ J_{clerk}=0,1,...,C$$

note that no jobs will be submitted if $J_{clerk}=0$, i.e., if all clerks are waiting for a response. At the other extreme, if all clerks are reading, thinking and typing, this will be the maximum rate of submitting jobs.

The processor queue operates as follows: if no processor is available, the job is inserted into a buffer, with the lower the index the closer to the head of the queue. We assume the number of buffers is greater than or equal to the number of processors, $M \geqslant P$. If there are J_{proc} jobs in the queue just prior to arrival of a job, the new job is inserted into the queue in position I with probability $\delta(I, J_{proc}+1)$. If a job is inserted in position I, all other jobs are moved to one index higher position. The rate at which all processors execute jobs depends upon the number of jobs in the queue. Let $\Phi_{proc}(J_{proc})$ denote the amount of work done, measured in seconds, during one second of time. For example, if $\Phi_{proc}(J_{proc}) = min[J_{proc}, P=2]$, then for $J_{proc}=0$ no work is done, for $J_{proc}=1$ one second of work is done in one second, for $J_{proc}=2$ two seconds of work are done in one second, and for $J_{proc}>2$ two seconds of work are done in one second. The instantaneous rate at which the processor subsystem is executing jobs is given by

$$processor \; job \; execution \; rate \; = \; \frac{\Phi_{proc}(J_{proc})}{T_{proc}}$$

For example, we might choose

$$\Phi_{proc}(J_{proc}) = min[J_{proc}, P] \quad J_{proc}=0,...,M$$

In words, if there are P or fewer jobs present, then each processor can execute one job at a rate of one job every T_{proc} seconds, while if there are more jobs than processors, then all processors are completely busy executing jobs.

The rate at which job I is executed in the queue when there are J_{proc} jobs total either in execution or waiting is given by $\gamma(I, J_{proc})\Phi_{proc}(J_{proc}) \leqslant 1$, where

$$\sum_{I=1}^{J_\kappa} \gamma_{proc}(I, J_{proc}) = 1$$

We stress that $\gamma(I, J_{proc})$ is measured in seconds of service received during one second of actual time.

From this point on, we assume either of two conditions hold governing the operation of the processor system:

- The processor service time obeys an exponential distribution

  $$fraction \; of \; time \; job \; executed \; in \; X \; seconds \; = \; 1 - exp[-X/T_{proc}]$$

- The service time distribution is arbitrary, and the fraction of time that a job is inserted into position I with J_{proc} jobs in the queue equals the rate at which that job will receive service:

  $$\gamma(I, J_{proc}) = \delta(I, J_{proc})$$

One example of a scheduling rule that meets these conditions is processor sharing, where all jobs are multiplexed by the processor so quickly that effectively each receives a fraction of processor capacity proportional to the number of jobs at the processor queue. If J_{proc} jobs are present, each receives $1/J_{proc}$ the fraction of available processing capacity:

$$\gamma(I,J_{proc}) = \delta(I,J_{proc}) = \frac{1}{J_{proc}}$$

A second example is processor scheduling such that the last arrival is the first to receive service, with subsequent later arrivals preempting the job currently in service, and service is resumed (eventually, after all later arrivals are completely executed) at the point of interruption:

$$\gamma(I,J_{proc}) = \begin{cases} 1 & I=J_{proc} \\ 0 & otherwise \end{cases}$$

A third example is where there is always a processor available to execute a job, so

$$\gamma(I,J_{proc}) = \delta(I,J_{proc}) = 1$$

so that when a job arrives it immediately begins execution.

6.2.2 State Space What is the state of the system? The complete state space would involve specifying the state of each clerk (busy with a transaction or waiting for the system to respond), and the state of each job in the system (where it is in the queue and how much service it had received). Suppose we only keep track of the *total* number of clerks busy with jobs, and the *total* number of jobs in the system? The system state at any instant is given by the pair $\underline{J}=(J_{clerk},J_{proc})$ where $J_{clerk}=0,...,C$ denotes the number of clerks with jobs, i.e., reading, thinking and typing, and $J_{proc}=0,...,M$ denotes the number of jobs in the system, both queued and in execution. A key constraint is that each clerk is either busy reading, thinking and typing, or waiting for a response; put differently, there are always C jobs somewhere:

$$J_{clerk} + J_{proc} = C$$

The state space, the set of admissible pairs $\underline{J}$ is denoted by Ω:

$$\Omega = \{\underline{J}=(J_{clerk},J_{proc})\,|\,J_{clerk}=0,...,C;J_{proc}=0,...,M;J_{clerk}+J_{proc}=C\}$$

In describing the operation of the system, we might measure the following items:

- The times at which jobs are submitted

- Whether a job is accepted or rejected because storage is not available

- The time an accepted job waits without being executed in the system

- The total time an accepted job spends in the system

For each of these, we could summarize the measurements with averages, carried out over a sufficiently long time interval such that the mean values stabilized.

6.2.3 Goals What customer oriented criteria are we interested in here?

- the mean waiting time $E(T_W)$ and mean queueing time $E(T_Q)$

- the fraction of time a task waits at all $PROB[T_W=0]$

- the fraction of time a task waits greater than X time units $PROB[T_W>X]$

- the fraction of time a task has a queueing time greater than X time units $PROB[T_Q>X]$

What system oriented criteria are of interest?

- the mean throughput rate of executing jobs

- the mean number of busy processors

- the fraction of time each processor is busy, its utilization

- the fraction of time more than one processor and more than one clerk are busy

We want to operate in states with acceptable levels of customer and system oriented criteria. States with acceptable customer oriented criteria may result in unacceptable system oriented criteria: delays may be acceptable at the expense of idle processors and low throughput, while high utilization of each available processor and high throughput rates may result in long queues and long delays.

6.2.4 Mean Value Analysis The first level of analysis is based on mean value inputs, with the outputs being mean throughput rate and mean delay. The fraction of attempts that are blocked or rejected because the available storage is filled is denoted by B. The mean throughput rate is

$$\lambda_{offered} = \frac{\lambda_{accepted}}{1 - B} \qquad \lambda_{offered}(1 - B) = \lambda_{accepted}$$

On the other hand, each clerk spends a mean amount of time reading and thinking and typing, T_{think}, and then submits a job; if the job is accepted, i.e., the fraction of attempts that are accepted is $1-B$, then the job will spend a mean time $E(T_Q)$ inside the system either waiting or in execution, and then the cycle starts over again. Since there are C clerks, the mean throughput rate is given by

$$\lambda_{accepted} = \frac{C}{(1-B)E(T_Q) + T_{think}}$$

In order to determine mean throughput rate and mean delay, we need to determine the fraction of requests that are blocked. If there is no blocking, $M=C$, then we can handle this by the methods in the previous sections; if there is blocking, $C>M$, then the earlier analysis will only give a lower bound on mean throughput rate and an upper bound on mean delay.

If $M=C$, the system has three bottlenecks:

- If clerks are limiting the mean throughput rate, then

$$\lambda \equiv \frac{C}{T_{think} + T_{proc}}$$

- If processor time is limiting the mean throughput rate, then

$$\lambda \equiv \frac{P}{T_{proc}}$$

- If storage or buffering is limiting the mean throughput rate, then

$$\lambda \equiv \frac{M}{T_{proc}}$$

Provided that $M=C$, we can write down upper and bounds on the mean throughput rate and mean queueing time:

$$\lambda_{lower} \leqslant \lambda \leqslant \lambda_{upper}$$

$$\lambda_{lower} = \frac{C}{T_{think} + \frac{C}{min[M,C]}T_{proc}}$$

$$\lambda_{upper} = min\left[\frac{P}{T_{proc}}, \frac{C}{T_{think}+T_{proc}}\right]$$

$$max\left[T_{proc}, \frac{C}{\lambda_{upper}} - T_{think}\right] \leqslant E(T_Q) \leqslant \frac{C}{min[M,C]}T_{proc}$$

In order to proceed further, we need to make use of the assumptions outlined earlier concerning arrival and execution time statistics, and scheduling policies.

6.2.5 Jackson Network Analysis Averaged over a suitably long time interval, the fraction of time the system is in a given state is denoted by $\pi(\underline{J})$ which is the product of three terms, one dependent only on clerks, one dependent only on the parallel processor group, and one that normalizes $\pi_C(\underline{J})$ so that the system is in *some* state all the time:

$$\pi_C(\underline{J}) = \frac{1}{G} \ (\textit{clerk dependent term}) \times (\textit{processor dependent term}) \quad \underline{J} \in \Omega$$

$$\sum_{\underline{J} \in \Omega} \pi_C(\underline{J}) = 1$$

and the second factor depends only on the source (here clerks reading and thinking and submitting jobs), while the final factor depends only on the system (which here is a group of parallel processors).

$$\pi_C(\underline{J}) = \pi_C(J_{clerk}, J_{proc}) = \frac{1}{G} \prod_{I=0}^{J_{clerk}-1} \frac{\Phi_{clerk}(I)}{T_{think}} \prod_{K=0}^{J_{proc}} \frac{T_{proc}}{\Phi_{proc}(K)} \quad \underline{J} \in \Omega$$

The function G is also called the *system partition function*, and is chosen such that

$$\sum_{\underline{J} \in \Omega} \pi_C(\underline{J}) = 1$$

The fraction of arrivals that are blocked or rejected is denoted by B, where

$$B = B(M) = \begin{cases} \pi_{C-1}(J_{proc}=M) & C > M \\ 0 & C = M \end{cases}$$

Note that the fraction of time an *arrival* finds J_{proc} jobs in the system is *different* from the long term time averaged distribution of jobs in the system, because when an arrival occurs it *cannot* be in the system, i.e., effectively there are a total of $C-1$ jobs in the system:

fraction of arrivals when system state is $\underline{J} = \pi_{C-1}(\underline{J})$

The fraction of time that a job enters service immediately is given by

$$\textit{fraction of time job enters service immediately} = \frac{\sum_{K=0}^{P-1} B(K)}{1 - B(M)}$$

The mean number of jobs in execution in the system is given by

$$E[min(J_{proc}, P)] = \sum_{K=0}^{M-1} min(K, P) \frac{B(K)}{1 - B(M)}$$

The mean throughput rate is the mean number of jobs in execution divided by the mean time per job:

$$\lambda = \frac{E[min(J_{proc}, P)]}{T_{proc}}$$

The mean queueing time per job, including both waiting and execution, is the ratio of the total mean number of jobs in the processor system divided by the mean throughput rate:

$$E[T_Q] = \frac{E[J_{proc}]}{\lambda} = T_{proc} \frac{E(J_{proc})}{E[min(J_{proc},P)]}$$

The mean queueing time is equal to the mean execution time of a job, multiplied by a stretching factor:

$$stretching\ factor = \frac{E(J_{proc})}{E[min(J_{proc},P)]}$$

If $J_{proc} << P$ then the stretching factor is one, i.e., there is zero mean waiting time, while if $J_{proc} >> P$ then the stretching factor grows as J_{proc}/P.

The difference between the total number of jobs either queued or in execution, J_{proc}, and the number of jobs actually in execution, $min[J_{proc},P]$, is defined as the number of jobs waiting. We can rewrite this as follows

$$J_{proc} - min[P,J_{proc}] = max[0,J_{proc}-P]$$

The mean waiting time per job is the ratio of the mean number of waiting jobs divided by the mean throughput rate:

$$E(T_W) = \frac{E[max(J_{proc}-P,0)]}{\lambda}$$

In general, although we can obtain an expression for the joint distribution of number of jobs at each stage in the system, we do **not** have an expression for the *delay distribution* and must infer mean delay via Little's Law. The exception is where jobs are executed in order of arrival, first come, for one case: jobs are executed in order of arrival, first come, first serve. For this case, when a job arrives it must wait for all jobs ahead of it to be serviced and then it will be executed. For this case, we can explicitly calculate the delay statistics for a job.

$$PROB[T_W > X | job\ accepted] = \frac{\sum_{K=P}^{M-1} B(K)[1-\tilde{E}_{K-P+1}(X)]}{1 - B(M)}$$

$$\tilde{E}_K(X) = 1 - \exp(-X/T_{proc}) \sum_{I=0}^{K-1} \frac{(X/T_{proc})^I}{I!} \quad K=1,2,...$$

EXERCISE. Calculate how quickly the mean value asymptotes are approached, as $P \to \infty$, with all other parameters held constant. Is the rate of convergence exponentially fast? as a power of P?

EXERCISE. Determine the rate of convergence to the mean value asymptotes with $C \to \infty$ but all other parameters fixed. Is the rate of convergence exponentially fast? as a power of C?

6.2.6 Additional Reading

[1]   R.Syski, *Markovian Queues,* pp. 170-227 (Chapter Seven) in **Proceedings Symposium on Congestion Theory,** W.L.Smith, W.E.Wilkinson (editors), 24-26 August 1964, University of North Carolina Press, Chapel Hill, North Carolina, 1965.

6.2.7 Numerical Approximation Just because we have an analytic expression does *not* mean that we can get numbers of interest for engineering actual systems. A key advantage of Jackson network models is that a wide variety of performance measures can be quickly and efficiently (storage and execution time) approximated. This is not to be dismissed lightly: these numbers often suggest design tradeoffs, areas that require further study, in a very short period of time, rather than spending months (or years!) finding out the obvious. Since it does not take long to get numbers, little has been invested, but perhaps a lot is gained!

There exist several classes of algorithms that efficiently use storage for numerically approximating the partition function and related quantities. We will explore these in this and later sections. For the problem at hand, a recursion for approximating the system partition function appears to be most appropriate, provided C is small, e.g., $C < 10$.

We assume the total number of jobs in the system is fixed at M in what follows. The partition function can be viewed as a function of two variables, the total number of nodes N and the total number of jobs inside the system M. For this case, the mean throughput rate λ is given by

$$\lambda = \frac{G(M-1,N)}{G(M,N)} \qquad \sum_{K=1}^{N} J_K = M$$

The fraction of time there are L jobs at node N, i.e., $J_N = L$, is given by

$$\pi(J_N = L) = \sum_{\underline{J} \in \Omega; J_N = L} \pi(\underline{J}) = \frac{G(M-L,N-1)}{G(M,N)} \frac{(T_N)^L}{L!} \prod_{I=0}^{L} \max\left[1, \frac{I}{P_L}\right]$$

Here is an example written in FORTRAN for calculating these recursions:

```
C SYSTEM PARTITION FUNCTION VIA RECURSION
C CLOSED JACKSON NETWORK MODEL
C N NODES, M JOBS IN SYSTEM
C
DOUBLE PRECISION PART(MEAN,PROB,UTIL,IP,N,IC,T)
C
C NODE 1    = CLERK NODE, IC CLERKS = M JOBS
C NODE 2    = SYSTEM PROCESSOR NODE
C T(K)      = MEAN TIME PER JOB AT NODE K,K=1,...,N
```

```
C  IP(K)    = NUMBER OF SERVERS AT NODE K,K=1,...,N
C  MEAN(K)  = MEAN NUMBER OF JOBS AT NODE K,K=1,...,N
C  PROB(K,J) = PROBABILITY J JOBS AT NODE K,K=1,...,N
C
DOUBLE PRECISION PROB,MEAN,SRATE,FRATE,T,G,SUM,TEMP
DIMENSION IP(N),MEAN(N),SRATE(N,IC+1),FRATE(N,IC+1)
DIMENSION PROB(N,IC+1),T(N)
C
C  INITIALIZATION
C
 DO 100 J=1,N
 SRATE(1,J)=1.0d0
 G(1,J)=0.0d0
 DO 110 I=2,IC+1
 G(I,J)=0.0d0
 IMIN=I-1
 IF(IMIN.GT.IP(J))IMIN=IP(J)
 SRATE(I,J)=SRATE(I-1,J)/(DBLE(FLOAT(IMIN))*T(J))
 110 CONTINUE
 110 CONTINUE
C
C  PERMUTATION OF NODE NUMBERS
C  IPERM DENOTES FINAL NODE IN ONE PERMUTATION
C  CYCLIC PERMUTATION: FIRST NODE 1, THEN NODE 2, ON UP
C  TO NODE N CHOSEN FOR FINAL NODE IN RECURSION
C
 IPERM=0
 150 CONTINUE
 IPERM=IPERM+1
 DO 200 J=1,N
 JCOM=J-IPERM
 IF(JCOM.LE.0)JCOM=N+JCOM
 DO 210 I=1,IC+1
 FRATE(I,JCOM)=SRATE(I,J)
 210 CONTINUE
 200 CONTINUE
C
C INITIALIZE FIRST ROW,COLUMN OF PARTITION FUNCTION MATRIX
C
 G(1,1)=1.0d0
 DO 300 I=1,IC+1
 G(I,1)=FRATE(I,1)
 300 CONTINUE
 DO 310 J=2,N
```

```
G(1,J)=1.0d0
310 CONTINUE
C
C FILL OUT BODY OF PARTITION MATRIX
C
DO 400 J=2,N
DO 410 I=2,IC+1
G(I,J)=G(I,J-1)
DO 420 K=2,I
G(I,J)=G(I,J)+FRATE(K,J)*G(I-K+1,J-1)
420 CONTINUE
410 CONTINUE
400 CONTINUE
C
C PROBABILITY DISTRIBUTION OF NUMBER AT NODE IPERM
C
DO 500 K=1,IC+1
PROB(K,IPERM)=FRATE(K,N)*G(IC+1-K+1,N-1)/G(IC+1,N)
500 CONTINUE
TEMP=0.0d0
DO 510 K=1,IC+1
TEMP=TEMP+PROB(K,IPERM)
510 CONTINUE
DO 520 K=1,IC+1
PROB(K,IPERM)=PROB(K,IPERM)/TEMP
620 CONTINUE
C
C MEAN NUMBER AT NODE IPERM
C
MEAN(IPERM)=0.0d0
DO 530 K=1,IC+1
MEAN(IPERM)=MEAN(IPERM)+PROB(K,IPERM)*DBLE(FLOAT(K-1))
530 CONTINUE
C
IF(IPERM.LT.N)GO TO 150
RETURN
END
```

Figure 6.3.Partition Function FORTRAN Program

Two observations are in order:

- The recursion actually involves two aspects, the total number of jobs in the system, and the number of nodes

- The recursion developed here will handle more than two nodes; we will use it later for a three node system.

Here is one way to numerically approximate the following performance measures:

- the fraction of time greater than K jobs are buffered (waiting or in execution) at the processor stage

$$\pi[J_{proc} > K] = \sum_{J_{proc}=K+1}^{C} \pi[J_{clerk}=C-J_{proc}, J_{proc}]$$

- the fraction of time exactly K jobs are at the processor node

$$\pi[J_{proc}=K] = \pi[J_{clerk}=C-K, J_{proc}=K]$$

- the mean queue length at the processor stage

$$E[J_{proc}] = \sum_{J_{proc}=0}^{C} J_{proc}\pi[J_{clerk}=C-J_{proc}, J_{proc}]$$

- the mean number of jobs in execution

$$E[min(J_{proc},P)] = \sum_{J_{proc}=0}^{C} min(J_{proc},P)\pi[J_{clerk}=C-J_{proc}, J_{proc}]$$

- the mean number of jobs waiting

$$E[max(J_{proc}-P,0)] = \sum_{J_{proc}=0}^{C} max(J_{proc}-P,0)\pi[J_{clerk}=C-J_{proc}, J_{proc}]$$

- the fraction of time processors are busy doing work, their utilization

$$U_{processor} = \frac{1}{P}\left[1 - \sum_{K=0}^{P-1}\pi[J_{clerk}=C-K, J_{proc}=K]\right]$$

- the fraction of time both one or more clerks and one or more processors are simultaneously busy

$$\pi[J_{clerk}>0, J_{proc}>0] = 1 - \pi[J_{clerk}=C, J_{proc}=0]$$
$$- \pi[J_{clerk}=0, J_{proc}=C]$$

- the mean throughput rate at the processor stage

$$mean\ throughput\ rate = \sum_{K=0}^{C}\pi[J_{clerk}=C-K, J_{proc}=K]\frac{min[K,P]}{T_{proc}}$$

In the plots below the mean throughput rate and mean delay per transaction as well as upper and lower bounds are calculated versus the number of clerks.

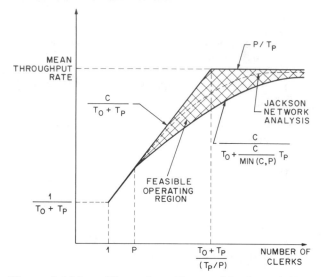

Figure 6.4.Mean Throughput Rate vs Number of Clerks

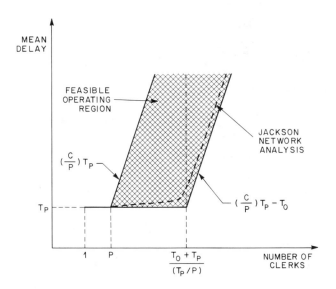

Figure 6.5.Mean Delay vs Number of Clerks

For the numbers chosen here, the mean value upper bound on mean throughput rate and lower bound on mean delay closely approximates the Jackson network analysis. Put differently, the Jackson network analysis refines our earlier analysis, showing in more detail (provided the underlying assumptions are valid) how great contention is for processors or clerks. The mean value bounds arise from *bottlenecks* that have a natural interpretation; oftentimes the designer can choose where the bottleneck should be, or move it from one point to another as needs warrant it. Jackson network analysis results in a smooth curve; mean value analysis results in a piecewise linear function. The *interpretation* of Jackson network analysis results in bottlenecks being identified, just as in mean value analysis. A key contribution of the Jackson network analysis is to provide an independent check on what mean value bounds provide, because the underlying *assumptions* are more stringent or different, and our findings are more robust.

6.2.8 Additional Reading

[1]   S.C.Bruell, G.Balbo, **Computational Algorithms for Closed Queueing Networks,** Elsevier North Holland, NY, 1980.

[2]   J.P.Buzen, *Computational Algorithms for Closed Queueing Networks with Exponential Servers,* C.A.C.M., **16(9),** 527-531 (1973).

[3]   R.B.Cooper, **Introduction to Queueing Theory,** pp.65-77, MacMillan, NY, 1972.

[4]   K.G. Ramakrishnan, D. Mitra, *An Overview of PANACEA: A Software Package for Analyzing Markovian Queueing Networks,* Bell System Technical Journal, **61,** (10), I, 2849-2872 (1982).

[5]   J.McKenna, D.Mitra, *Integral Representations and Asymptotic Expansions for Closed Markovian Queueing Networks: Normal Usage,* Bell System Technical Journal, **61,** (5), 661-683 (1982).

[6]   J.McKenna, D.Mitra, K.G.Ramakrishnan, *A Class of Closed Markovian Queueing Networks: Integral Representations, Asymptotic Expansions, and Generalizations,* Bell System Technical Journal, **60** (5), 599-641 (1981).

6.3 Asymptotics

In order to gain insight into these formulae, we wish to examine two types of special cases. Both arise from examining the formulae presented earlier. In all cases, we assume

$$\Phi_{clerk}\left(J_{clerk}\right) = J_{clerk} \qquad \Phi_{proc}\left(J_{proc}\right) = min[J_{proc},P]$$

In the first type of special case, the total workload offered is fixed, measured in jobs arriving per second, but the number of clerks becomes infinite. This is called an *infinite source* approximation, and it is also called a *Poisson* approximation.

$$\lambda \equiv \frac{C}{T_{think}} = fixed \quad C \rightarrow \infty \quad T_{think} \rightarrow \infty$$

Since $T_{think} \rightarrow \infty$, each clerk spends more and more time reading and thinking and typing, but since we have more and more clerks, the total workload is constant.

A second type of limit is to fix *ratios* C/M and C/P and allow $C \to \infty$, with T_{think} and T_{proc} fixed. Should we have five clerks per processor, or ten clerks for two processors? Should there be three buffers for every five clerks, or six buffers for every ten clerks? Since the mean time intervals T_{think} and T_{proc}, are fixed, the activity of each clerk stays the same, unlike the first case. The advent of inexpensive processors may make this type of analysis of great practical import in times to come.

6.3.1 Infinite Source Asymptotics If we fix $\lambda \equiv C/T_{think}$ and allow $C \to \infty$, then we find that the fraction of time J_{proc} jobs are in the system is given by

$$\pi(J_{proc}) = \frac{1}{G} \frac{(\lambda T_{proc})^{J_{proc}}}{J_{proc}!} \prod_{K=0}^{J_{proc}} \max\left[1, \frac{K}{P}\right] \quad J_{proc} = 0,...,M$$

The distribution of jobs in the system at the instant a job arrives is now *identical* to the long term time averaged number of jobs in the system. If $M = C \to \infty$, the fraction of time that a task must wait greater than X time units is

$$PROB[T_W > X] = \begin{cases} C(P,A)exp[-(1-U)XP/T_{proc}] & A < P \\ \infty & A \geqslant P \end{cases} \quad M \to \infty$$

$$A \equiv E[J_{proc}] = \lambda T_{proc} \quad U \equiv A/P$$

The units of A are called *Erlangs* in honor of the Scandinavian teletraffic engineer A.K.Erlang, who was a pioneer in engineering voice telephone transmission and switching systems. Since A is the mean number of jobs in the processor queue, either waiting to run or in execution, if the mean number of jobs is less than the actual number of processors then the processors can keep up with the work, and otherwise they cannot. U is the fraction of time each processor is busy, its *utilization*.

The expression $C(P,A)$, called *Erlang's delay function* or *Erlang's function of the second kind,* is given by

$$C(P,A) = \frac{A^P/(P-1)!(P-A)}{\displaystyle\sum_{K=0}^{P-1} \frac{A^K}{K!} + \frac{A^P}{(P-1)!(P-A)}}$$

This is a very important function, because we can compute many performance measures directly once we know it:

• The fraction of time a task waits at all is

$$PROB[T_W > 0] = C(P,A) \quad A < P$$

For a single processor, the fraction of time a task waits is the fraction of time the processor is busy; for multiple processors, the fraction of time a task waits at all depends upon finding all the processors busy first, and hence is more complicated.

- The mean waiting time for a task is given by

$$E(T_W) = \frac{C(P,A)T_{proc}}{P-A} = \frac{C(P,A)T_{proc}}{(1-U)P} \qquad A < P$$

- The mean queueing time for a task is the sum of its mean waiting and service time:

$$E(T_Q) = E(T_W) + T_{proc}$$

For one processor, we see

$$C(P=1,A) = A \quad \rightarrow \quad E(T_W) = \frac{AT_{proc}}{1-A} \quad \rightarrow \quad E(T_Q) = \frac{T_{proc}}{1-A}$$

The mean queueing time equals the mean execution time, multiplied by a *stretching* factor of $1/1-A$. Under light loading $A << 1$ the stretching factor is one, while as $A \rightarrow 1$ the stretching becomes larger and larger than one.

6.3.2 Modem Pooling In a dial up online computer system, users dial up the computer over voice telephone lines. Each user will need a modem to connect to the computer. The mean holding time per call is one minute. The mean arrival rate of calls is five calls per minute. We wish to have sufficient modems so that the fraction of time that a user waits at all for a modem is under ten per cent. How many modems are required?

The offered load to the system is given by

$$A = 5 \; calls \; per \; minute \times one \; minute \; per \; call = 5 \; Erlangs$$

We wish to find P such that

$$C(P,A=5) < 0.10$$

If we simply try various numbers, starting with P=5 since we expect to have five busy modems on the average most of the time, we see that eight or more modems is sufficient to meet the delay criterion.

6.3.3 P=M Loss System A typical problem in voice telephony is to determine how many circuits are needed to handle the load. Telephone calls arrive at random instants of time, and will tie up or hold a telephone line for three to five to ten minutes. If all lines are busy, it is highly unlikely a line will become free within the next few seconds, and the new arrival is blocked or rejected. A natural model of this situation is calls or jobs arrive for service at a group of $P=M$ parallel servers or processors, with one buffer per processor. The mean service time of a job is denoted by $E(T_S)$. If all servers are busy when an arrival occurs, the new arrival is rejected or blocked and presumably will retry later.

What goals are to be achieved? From the point of view of a customer, the fraction of time an arrival is rejected should be acceptably low. What system oriented criteria are of interest? The mean number of busy processors, and the fraction of time each processor is busy, its utilization, should be acceptably high.

The interarrival times between jobs are assumed to be independent identically distributed exponential random variables, i.e., the arrival statistics can be modeled by a Poisson distribution. The mean throughput rate of completing tasks is denoted by the carried mean throughput rate, to distinguish it from the offered load, which will be bigger than the carried load because some offered load was rejected. The carried mean throughput rate is

$$\lambda_{carried} = \lambda_{offered}[1 - B(P,A)]$$

where as above A is the mean *offered* load to the system $A = \lambda E(T_S)$ to distinguish it from the *carried (actual)* load $\hat{A}$ given by

$$\hat{A} = A[1 - B(P,A)] = mean\ number\ of\ busy\ servers$$

In some cases, only the carried load can be measured, and then we must work backwards to infer the offered load. As long as the fraction of attempts blocked is negligible, the above expression provides a convenient rough cut for doing so. $B(P,A)$ is called *Erlang's blocking function* or *Erlang's function of the first kind,* and is given by

$$B(P,A) = \frac{A^P/P!}{\sum_{K=0}^{P} A^K/K!}$$

$B(P,A)$ is the fraction of time that all P processors are busy, or it is the fraction of time a new arrival is blocked or rejected.

If a task is accepted, it waits no time at all to be processed. If a task is rejected, it waits forever and is never processed. The queueing time, the sum of the waiting time and the service time, is either equal to the service time if the task is accepted, or is infinite if the task is rejected.

For values of $\lambda_{offered}$ that result in small blocking the mean throughput rate $\lambda_{carried}$ equals $\lambda_{offered}$; for $\lambda_{offered} \rightarrow \infty$ the mean throughput rate approaches $P/E(T_S)$. For intermediate values, the exact expressions must be used. The mean waiting time of accepted tasks is zero, while the mean queueing time of accepted tasks is $E(T_S)$.

6.3.4 Circuit Switching We must configure a data computer communication system with sufficient private communication lines so that the fraction of time call attempts are blocked because no line is available is sufficiently small.

Measurement data suggest a typical call lasts for forty five minutes, with an average of ten calls per hour being attempted. We wish to examine two levels of service, one where a call attempt is blocked no more than ten per cent of the time, and a second where a call attempt is blocked no more than one per cent of the time. How many circuits are needed?

The mean number of calls in progress is

$$A = (3/4) \ hours/call \times 10 \ calls/hour = 7.5 \ calls \ or \ Erlangs$$

Hence, at least 7.5, i.e., eight circuits are needed just to carry the load.

Using an Erlang blocking analysis, in order to meet the goal of calls being blocked no more than ten per cent of the time, we need ten circuits. In order to meet the goal of calls being blocked no more than one per cent of the time, we need fourteen circuits.

6.3.5 Relationships Between Loss and Delay Systems There are many relationships between loss and delay systems. Here is one such formula relating Erlang's loss formula and Erlang's delay formula:

$$C(P,A) = \frac{A \ B(P-1,A)}{P + A[B(P-1,A)-1]}$$

Thus, if we know how to calculate or numerically approximate Erlang's loss formula, we can also numerically approximate Erlang's delay formula.

6.3.6 Numerical Approximation of Erlang's Blocking Function We now present an algorithm for numerically approximating the Erlang blocking function, due to D.Jagerman, that can be readily programmed on a pocket calculator or other machine. The implementation presented here is in FORTRAN, and requires two constants, one for underflow and one for overflow.

```
        DOUBLE PRECISION FUNCTION BERL(N,A)
C
C INPUTS
C
C   P--NUMBER OF PROCESSORS
C   A--OFFERED LOAD IN ERLANGS
C
C OUTPUT
C
C   BERL--ERLANG BLOCKING FUNCTION
C
C ALGORITHM--ITERATE ON THE INVERSE OF BERL
C
```

```
      DOUBLE PRECISION BERL,A,XN,XA,TERM,SUM,DMIN,DMAX
C
C DMIN--CHOSEN TO MACHINE ACCURACY
C DMAX--RECIPROCAL OF SMALLEST BLOCKING OF INTEREST
C
      DMIN=1.0D-10
      DMAX=1.0d9
C
C PARAMETER INITIALIZATION
C
      XN=DBLE(FLOAT(N))
      XA=1.0d0/A
      TERM=XN*XA
      SUM=1.0d0
C
C MAIN LOOP
C
   10 CONTINUE
      SUM=SUM+TERM
      XN=XN-1.0d0
      TERM=TERM*XN*XA
      IF((TERM.LT.DMIN).OR.(SUM.GT.DMAX)) GO TO 20
      GO TO 10
C
C TO REACH HERE MUST HAVE COMPLETED
C
   20 CONTINUE
      BERL=1.0d0/SUM
      RETURN
      END
```

Figure 6.6.Erlang Blocking Function FORTRAN Program

6.3.7 *Additional Reading*

[1]   D.L.Jagerman, *Some Properties of the Erlang Loss Function,* Bell
      System Technical Journal, **53,** (3), pp.525-551, 1974.

6.3.8 *C/M and C/P Fixed, C→∞* The remaining asymptotic case, where the
ratios are fixed for C/M and C/P but $C \to \infty$, is summarized by the following
formulae:

• The fraction of time an attempt is blocked is given by

$$B = 1 - \min\left[1, \frac{C}{T_{think} + \min\left[\dfrac{CT_{proc}}{P} - T_{think}, T_{proc}\dfrac{M}{P}\right]}\right]$$

- The fraction of time a processor is busy is given by

$$U = utilization/processor = \min\left[1, \frac{CT_{think}}{P(T_{think}+T_{proc})}\right]$$

- The mean rate of submitting jobs is given by

$$\lambda_{offered} = mean\ job\ submission\ rate = \frac{PU}{T_{proc}}$$

- The mean throughput rate of jobs is given by

$$\lambda_{carried} = \frac{\lambda_{offered}}{1 - B} = \frac{C}{(1 - B)E(T_Q) + T_{think}}$$

- The mean delay per job is given by

$$E(T_Q) = \max\left[T_{proc}, \min\left[\frac{CT_{proc}}{P} - T_{think}, \frac{M}{P}T_{proc}\right]\right]$$

6.4 Teletraffic Engineering of an Automatic Call Distributor

An automatic call distributor, as the name implies, automatically distributes incoming calls among various available agents. Customers dial a telephone number, and the calls are routed through the voice telephony network to the call distributor. The call distributor either blocks or rejects a call attempt if all incoming circuits or trunks to the call distributor are busy (either with calls waiting for an agent or calls between agents and customers). Customers are queued for service by an agent. If all agents in a given group are busy, the customer is queued for a receiver that plays a recorded message asking the customer to be patient until an agent becomes available; in many cases, music is played while the customer is waiting. After the agent handles the customer request there is often some clean up work associated with that particular task, after which the agent is available for handling the next incoming call.

Automatic call distributors are currently in wide use. Some examples are

- airlines--for handling reservations, time of arrival and departure of flights, travel agent activity, charter and tour operators, charging or billing information, internal administrative use

- hotels and motels--for handling reservations at a nationwide chain, billing questions, travel agent activity

- credit authorization and verification--for a variety of bank credit cards, which require authorization if the purchase price exceeds a given limit

- message service--major companies frequently have a centralized group of agents handle all messages rather than tie up a secretarial pool with this job

6.4.1 Model The model inputs required here would be the mean arrival rate of calls, the mean time a customer would wait for an agent, and the mean time to handle a customer plus any related work (such as logging the result of the customer inquiry).

How can the number of trunks or links and agents be chosen such that the system meets both a given blocking criterion and a mean delay criterion for each customer?

Here is a summary of model parameters for two illustrative cases, one for credit authorization, and one for airline reservations and flight information.

Table 6.1. Model Parameters

Attribute	Credit Authorization	Airline
Announcement Time	10-20 Seconds	20-30 seconds
Talking Time	30-60 seconds	100-200 seconds

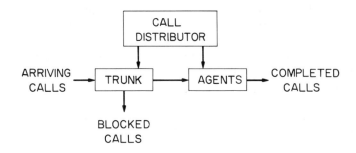

Figure 6.7. Call Distributor Block Diagram

Goals are specified for a peak business hour load. During the first year of operation, the peak business hour mean call arrival rate is four per minute. This will increase to eight calls per minute during the second year, and twenty calls per minute during the third year. Each call that is accepted can wait for

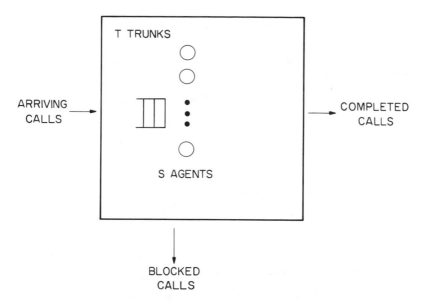

T TRUNKS

ARRIVING CALLS → COMPLETED CALLS

S AGENTS

BLOCKED CALLS

Figure 6.8.Call Distributor Queueing Network

fifteen seconds, on the average, and each inquiry will require a mean of one minute per agent. We denote by T_{wait} the mean waiting time (e.g., to hear an announcement), and T_{talk} the mean time to handle a customer request.

6.4.2 State Space The system state space is denoted by Ω. Elements are integer valued pairs denoted by $\underline{J}=(J_{wait},J_{talk})$, where J_{wait} denotes the number of calls waiting for an agent, and J_{talk} denotes the number of busy agents (busy handling customer requests). Since there are T trunks and S agents, the state space is given by:

$$\Omega = \{(J_{wait},J_{talk})\,|\,J_{wait}+J_{talk}\leqslant T, J_{talk}\leqslant S\}$$

6.4.3 Mean Value Analysis The mean number of trunks held equals the mean arrival rate of accepted calls multiplied by the mean trunk holding time. Since trunks are held for an announcement (if no agent is available), and for handling customer requests, we can write

$$E[min\,(J_{wait}+J_{talk},T)] = \lambda(T_{wait}+T_{talk})$$

The mean number of busy agents is given by

$$E[min\,(J_{talk},S)] = \lambda T_{talk}$$

This suggests the following two bottlenecks:

- If trunks are the bottleneck, then

$$\lambda = \frac{T}{T_{wait} + T_{talk}}$$

For the number here, the required mean number of trunks is summarized in the table below:

Table 6.2.Number of Required Trunks

Year	Trunks
1	5 trunks
2	10 trunks
3	40 trunks

- If agents are the bottleneck, then

$$\lambda = \frac{S}{T_{talk}}$$

For the numbers described above, the mean number of required agents is summarized in the table below:

Table 6.3.Number of Required Agents

Year	Agents
1	4 agents
2	8 agents
3	20 agents

This analysis suggests that 1.25 trunks are required for every agent, i.e., $(T_{talk} + T_{wait})/T_{wait}$ trunks per agent.

6.4.4 Jackson Network Analysis What if we use an Erlang blocking analysis to determine the number of trunks required? This means that we are looking for the largest value of T such that

$$B[T, \lambda(T_{talk} + T_{wait})] \leq \epsilon_{trunk}$$

where ϵ_{trunk} is the fraction of blocked or rejected call attempts. The table below summarizes these calculations:

Table 6.4.Number of Trunks Required

Year	Fraction of Attempts Rejected		
	0.001	0.01	0.1
1	14 trunks	11 trunks	8 trunks
2	21 trunks	18 trunks	13 trunks
3	41 trunks	36 trunks	28 trunks

The interpretation of the data is that during year one 8-14 trunks suffice, during year two 13-21 trunks, and during year three 28-41 trunks. Since trunks may come in bundles or integral multiples of one trunk (such as six trunks or twenty four per trunk group, with all purchases in multiples of trunk groups) economic considerations must be addressed here. For example, two trunk groups of six trunks each would suffice for the first year, four trunk groups for the second year, and seven trunk groups for the third year. On the other hand, the *increment* in carried load is simply the difference in blocking for $T+1$ trunks versus T trunks, multiplied by the carried load.

We next use Erlang's delay formula to calculate the number of agents required to meet a given delay criterion. This means we are looking for the largest value of S such that

$$C(S, \lambda T_{talk}) \leqslant \epsilon_{agent}$$

where ϵ_{agent} is the agent delay criterion. The table below summarizes these calculations:

Table 6.5. Number of Agents Required

Year	Fraction of Time Call Waits > 0		
	0.1	0.2	0.3
1	8 agents	7 agents	6 agents
2	13 agents	12 agents	11 agents
3	22 agents	20 agents	19 agents

This table makes it clear fewer agents are needed than trunks, typically one agent for every 1.1 to 1.5 trunks. In all cases, the number of agents and trunks needed is larger than the mean value analysis suggests. On the other hand, the mean value analysis appears to be a reasonable first cut at answering how many trunks and agents are needed, one that can be refined as additional information comes to light.

6.4.5 Additional Reading

[1] L.Kosten, **Stochastic Theory of Service Systems,** pp.26-40, Pergamon Press, London, 1973.

[2] P.A.Brown, D.W.Clark, *Automatic Call Distribution System-ASDP 162,* Telecommunications Journal of Australia, **29** (3), 245-255 (1979).

6.5 Pooling or Grouping Resources

A voice telecommunications manager can configure a PBX with two groups of six trunks each to the outside voice network, or one single group of twelve trunks. Which should be chosen based on performance alone?

A computer system administrator can configure a packet switching system with two groups of four processors each, or one group of eight processors. Which should be chosen based on performance alone?

One way to quantify this is to use a Jackson network model. For the first problem, the ingredients are the number of trunks in each group, denoted by

$S_K, K=1,2$, the mean arrival rate of calls to each trunk group, denoted by $\lambda_K, K=1,2$ for the two separate trunk groups, and $\lambda_1+\lambda_2$ for the pooled trunk group, and the mean holding time for calls is the same for either case, denoted by T_{talk}. The fraction of time call attempts are blocked to the separate trunk groups is

fraction of time call attempts blocked by group K $= B(S_K, \lambda_K T_{talk})$ $K=1,2$

The total overall blocking is given by weighing the fraction of time a call attempt occurs to group K by the blocking for group K:

$$total\ blocking = \frac{\lambda_1}{\lambda_1+\lambda_2}B(S_1,\lambda_1 T_{talk}) + \frac{\lambda_2}{\lambda_1+\lambda_2}B(S_2,\lambda_2 T_{talk})$$

If there is only one trunk group with S_1+S_2 trunks, and a total mean arrival rate of $\lambda_1+\lambda_2$ call attempts, then the total blocking is given by

$$total\ blocking = B(S_1+S_2, T_{talk}[\lambda_1+\lambda_2])$$

If you substitute in numbers, you will find that the *pooled* group *always* has a lower total blocking than the total blocking for the two separate groups.

For the second question, you need to specify the number of processors $P_K, K=1,2$ for each group, the mean arrival rate of packets to each group $\lambda_K, K=1,2$ and the total mean packet switching time T_{packet}. The mean queueing time for a packet going to group K is given by

$$E(T_{Q,K}) = \left[\frac{C(P_K,\lambda_K T_{packet})}{P_K - \lambda_K T_{packet}} +1\right] T_{packet}   K=1,2$$

The total mean packet queueing time averaged over both groups, is given by

$$E(T_Q) = \frac{\lambda_1}{\lambda_1+\lambda_2} E(T_{Q,1}) + \frac{\lambda_2}{\lambda_1+\lambda_2} E(T_{Q,2})$$

For a pooled group with P_1+P_2 processors and a total mean packet arrival rate of $\lambda_1+\lambda_2$ the total mean queueing time is

$$E(T_Q) = \left[\frac{C(P_1+P_2,T_{packet}(\lambda_1+\lambda_2))}{P_1+P_2 - T_{packet}(\lambda_1+\lambda_2)}+1\right]_{packet}$$

If you substitute numbers in, you will find that the total mean queueing time is *always* smaller for the *pooled* group of processors compared to the two dedicated groups.

Is there an intuitive reason for the benefits of pooling? One explanation is that a job can be blocked or delayed in one dedicated group, while the other dedicated group may have an idle resource. The numerical analysis suggests that the benefits are *better* than might be thought; this is called an economy of scale.

6.5.1 Additional Reading

[1]   D.R.Smith, W.Whitt, *Resource Sharing for Efficiency in Traffic Systems,* Bell System Technical Journal, **60** (1), 39-55 (1981).

6.6 General Single Class Jackson Network Model

Clerks at terminals submit one type of job to a computer communication system.

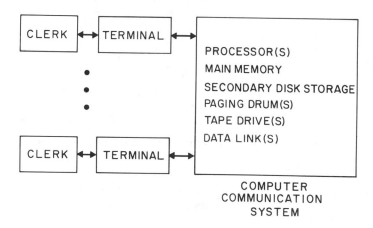

Figure 6.9.System Block Diagram

A queueing network model of this system is as follows: A source submits one type of job to a system. There are a total of P_0 sources. Each job enters a staging queue: if there are less than M jobs in the system, the job immediately enters the system, and otherwise waits for the number of jobs in the system to drop below M. Once a job enters the system, it visits a number of nodes or stations within the network, and after being completely processed exits the system, where the cycle begins anew. The number of processors or servers at node K is denoted by P_K.

6.6.1 State Space The number of jobs either queued or in execution at time t at node $K=1,...,N$ is denoted by $J_K(t)$. Elements $J_K(t)$ are nonnegative integers, and are members of a state space denoted by Ω. The number of sources with a job is denoted by J_0; if there is staging, then

$$number\ of\ jobs\ in\ staging\ queue = min[0, M - J_0]$$

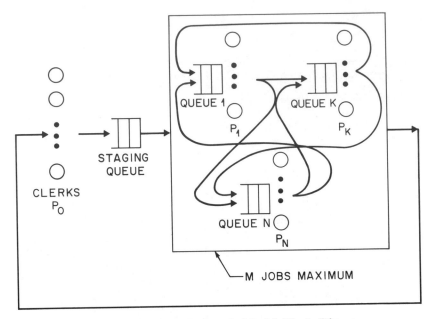

Figure 6.10.Queueing Network Model Block Diagram

Three cases will be dealt with:

[1] Jobs can be submitted to the system sufficiently fast such that the system *always* contains M jobs. The state space for this case is given by

$$\Omega = \{(J_1,...,J_N)\,|\,J_K \geqslant 0, 1 \leqslant K \leqslant N; \sum_{K=1}^{N} J_K = M\}$$

[2] The system always has room for a job, i.e., $M \geqslant P_0$, so there is never a job in the staging queue. The state space for this case is given by

$$\Omega = \{(J_1,...,J_N)\,|\,J_K \geqslant 0, 0 \leqslant K \leqslant N, \sum_{K=0}^{N} J_K = P_0\}$$

[3] One limiting case that is analytically tractable is a so called *open* network, where only the total job arrival rate is known, denoted by $\lambda = P_0/T_0$, with $P_0 \rightarrow \infty$. The state space is now given by

$$\Omega = \{(J_1,...,J_N)\,|\,J_K \geqslant 0, 1 \leqslant K \leqslant N\}$$

It remains to specify the workload in greater precision, and the scheduling or arbitration rule for each node.

6.6.2 Workload The system at any instant of time contains $|\underline{J}|$ jobs, where

$$|\underline{J}| = \sum_{K=1}^{N} J_K$$

Given the system contains $|\underline{J}|$ jobs at time t and that the number of jobs at each node is observed over time, the instantaneous job arrival rate at time t is given by

$$instantaneous\ job\ arrival\ rate = \frac{\Phi_0(|\underline{J}(t)|)}{T_0} > 0$$

Each distinct visit to node K requires a possibly different amount of execution time by a server at that node. The random variable τ_K denotes the service time per visit to node K, which is a sequence of independent identically distributed random variables drawn from a common distribution denoted by $H_K(X)$:

$$PROB[\tau_K \leq X] = H_K(X)$$

The mean of τ_K is denoted by $E(\tau_K)$.

Each job is routed through the network probabilistically: once a job is serviced at node K, it migrates to node J with probability R_{KJ}, where $K=1,...,N$ and $J=0,...,N$, i.e., a job can exit the system and return to the source node when $J=0$. An equivalent description of this process is that each job makes V_K visits to node K, and hence the total mean amount of service at node K, denoted by T_K, is $V_K E(\tau_K)$.

6.6.3 Scheduling Policy for Arbitrating Contention When a job arrives at queue K and finds J_K jobs present, it is inserted into place I with probability $\delta_K(I,J_K+1)$ where $I=1,...,J_K+1$. All tasks in position $I,...,J_K$ are shifted to the position with the next higher index. When a job finishes execution at position I, all jobs at position $I+1,...,J_K$ are shifted to the position with the next lower index.

When J_K jobs are present at node K, work is executed at a total rate (measured in seconds of processing per second, so that it is dimensionless), of $\Phi_K(J_K)$. A job in position I out of J_K at node K is processed at a rate of $\gamma_K(I,J_K)\phi_K(J_K) \leq 1$, again measured in seconds of processing per second, such that

$$\sum_{I=1}^{J_K} \gamma_K(I,J_K) = 1$$

or in words that *some* jobs are receiving *all* the available processing capacity.

We will not allow all possible scheduling rules, but only *two* classes. The first class of rules allows the service time distribution to be *arbitrary* but the scheduling policy must be *balanced* in the sense that

$$\gamma_K(I,J_K) = \delta_K(I,J_K)$$

Examples of scheduling rules that meet these conditions are

- Processor sharing: if J_K jobs are present, each receives $1/J_K$ the fraction of available processing capacity:

$$\gamma_K(I,J_K) = \frac{1}{J_K}$$

- Last come first serve preemptive resume: the last arrival is serviced first, with subsequent arrivals preempting service, and service is resumed at the point of interruption:

$$\gamma_K(I,J_K) = \begin{cases} 1 & I=J_K \\ 0 & otherwise \end{cases}$$

- An infinite server group, i.e., there is always available one server to execute a job, with no waiting or queueing:

$$\gamma_K(I,J_K) = 1$$

The second type of scheduling policy is to allow jobs to be executed in order of arrival, but now the service time distribution must be *exponential*:

$$H_K(\tau_K \leqslant X) = 1 - exp[-X/E(\tau_K)]$$

6.6.4 *Finite Source Arrival Statistics with Staging Analysis* Granted the previous assumptions, the long term time averaged fraction of time the system is in state $\underline{J}$ is denoted by $\pi(\underline{J})$, where

$$\pi(\underline{J}) = \pi(J_1,...,J_N) = \frac{1}{G} \prod_{I=0}^{|\underline{J}|-1} \frac{\Phi_0(I)}{T_0} \prod_{K=1}^{N} \prod_{I=1}^{J_K} \frac{T_K}{\Phi_K(I)}$$

$$\sum_{\underline{J} \in \Omega} \pi(\underline{J}) = 1 \quad \pi(\underline{J}) \geqslant 0$$

If $\Phi_K(I)=min(I,P_K)$, and the system always contains M jobs, this can be written as

$$\pi(\underline{J}) = \frac{1}{G} \prod_{K=1}^{N} \frac{T_K^{J_K}}{J_K!} \prod_{I=0}^{J_K} max\left[1,\frac{I}{P_K}\right] \quad \underline{J} \in \Omega$$

For the case where there is a staging queue with P_0 sources, this can be written as

$$\pi(\underline{J}) = \frac{1}{G} \prod_{K=0}^{N} \frac{T_K^{J_K}}{J_K!} \prod_{I=0}^{J_K} max\left[1,\frac{I}{P_K}\right]$$

6.6.5 *Asymptotics* One natural type of asymptotic analysis is to fix the total arrival rate at λ while allowing the number of sources to become infinite:

$$\lambda \equiv \frac{P_0}{T_0} = \textit{fixed} \quad P_0, T_0 \rightarrow \infty$$

The resulting form of the long term time averaged distribution simplifies:

$$\lim_{\substack{\lambda \text{ fixed}}} \pi(\underline{J}) = \begin{cases} \displaystyle\prod_{K=1}^{N} \prod_{I=1}^{J_K} \frac{\lambda T_K}{J_K!} \prod_{I=0}^{J_K} \max\left[1, \frac{I}{P_K}\right] & \lambda < \min_{K} \frac{P_K}{T_K} = \lambda_{\max} \\ 0 & \lambda \geqslant \min_{K} \frac{P_K}{T_K} = \lambda_{\max} \end{cases}$$

This last condition needs some elaboration: if $\lambda < \lambda_{\max}$, the mean value upper bound on the maximum mean throughput rate, then all nodes can keep up with the workload, and otherwise the number of jobs at the slowest or bottleneck nodes exceeds any threshold. This can be seen from evaluating the partition function: the partition function is finite provided $\lambda < \lambda_{\max}$, and otherwise is infinite.

The total mean queueing delay of a job is the sum of the individual queueing delays at each node:

$$E(T_Q) = \sum_{K=1}^{N} E(T_{Q,K})$$

where the mean queueing delay (waiting plus execution) at node K is given by

$$E(T_{Q,K}) = T_K D(P_K, U_K) \quad K = 1, \dots, N$$

U is the utilization, the fraction of time, *each* server or processor at node K is busy, and $D(P_K, U_K)$ is the *stretching factor* for node K, i.e., it shows how much T_K is inflated or stretched to account for queueing delays.

$$D(P, U) = \frac{C(P, P\,U)}{P(1 - U)} + 1$$

$C(P, P\,U)$ is the Erlang delay function discussed earlier. This can be readily approximated numerically. For $U \ll 1$, light loading, $D(P, U) \approx 1$, i.e., there is virtually no stretching of the execution time, while under heavy loading $U \rightarrow 1$, $D(P, U) \rightarrow \infty$, i.e., the waiting time can swamp the execution time.

What if we plot the mean throughput rate versus the degree of multiprogramming defined to be $|\underline{J}|$? We see for $|\underline{J}| = 1$ the mean throughput rate is simply the reciprocal of the *total* time to complete one job, and hence increasing the degree of multiprogramming will *always* be less than $|\underline{J}|$ times the mean throughput for one job. At the other extreme, as the degree of multiprogramming becomes larger and larger, one or more resources will be completely utilized or busy with work, and we see

$$\lambda = \min_I \left[\frac{P_I}{T_I} \right] \quad |\underline{J}| \to \infty$$

The nodes that reach complete utilization first are called *bottleneck* nodes. The queueing network analysis allows us to interpolate between these two asymptotic regions, as shown in the figure below.

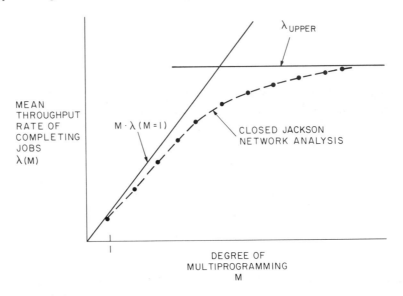

Figure 6.11. Mean Throughput Rate vs Degree of Multiprogramming

One figure of merit discussed earlier is the *stretching factor* which we defined as the ratio of the upper bound on mean throughput rate due to the number of jobs being a bottleneck over the actual mean throughput rate:

$$stretching \ factor = \frac{job \ bottleneck \ mean \ throughput \ bound}{actual \ mean \ throughput \ rate} = \frac{J\lambda(J=1)}{\lambda(J>1)}$$

We want to operate with a stretching factor close to one, i.e., as we add more jobs, the mean throughput rate scales or increases *linearly* with J, and we stay close to the ideal bound. The design question is to intelligently choose the bottlenecks so that this in fact happens!

6.7 Pipeline Processing

The configuration studied here is a pipeline of N processors, one processor per stage. Jobs arrive at the first stage, are processed, and move on to the second stage, until completely executed. What impact might fluctuations have on the performance of such a system?

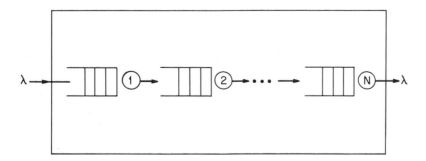

Figure 6.12.Pipeline Queueing Network Block Diagram

6.7.1 Analysis The model ingredients are

- Jobs arrive according to simple Poisson statistics with mean arrival rate λ jobs per unit time

- Each job requires $T_{S,K}$ service at node K, where the service times are independent identically distributed random variables

- Jobs are serviced in order of arrival

If there is no contention at all, to completely execute a job will require on the average $E(T_1) + E(T_2) + ... + E(T_N)$ time units.

We now wish to study the impact that fluctuations about the mean value of the processing times can have on the time required to completely execute a job. First, if the processing times at each stage are exponentially distributed, which might be the case if sometimes one branch were followed and another time another branch were followed, then the mean time that a job is waiting while other jobs are being executed is denoted by $E(T_W)$ and is given by

$$E(T_{W,exponential}) = \sum_{k=1}^{N} \frac{\lambda E^2(T_{S,K})}{1 - \lambda E(T_{S,K})}$$

For example, if $E(T_{S,1}) = ... = E(T_{S,N}) \equiv E(T_S)$, i.e., the processing times at each stage had the same mean value, then

$$E(T_{W,exponential}) = \frac{N \lambda E^2(T_S)}{1 - \lambda E(T_S)} \quad E(T_S) \equiv E(T_{S,1}) = ... = E(T_{S,N})$$

On the other hand, if the processing times at each stage are constant, i.e., no fluctuations about the mean, then the mean time that a job is waiting while other jobs are being executed is denoted by $E(T_{W,constant})$ and is given by

$$E(T_{W,constant}) = \frac{\lambda E^2(T_{S,max})}{2(1 - \lambda E(T_{S,max}))} \qquad E(T_{S,max}) = max(E(T_{S,1}),...,E(T_{S,N}))$$

For example, if $E(T_{S,1}) = ... = E(T_{S,N})$, then

$$E(T_{W,constant}) = \frac{\lambda E^2(T_{S,max})}{2(1 - \lambda E(T_{S,max}))}$$

Note that this can be N/2 times that for the exponential case if the fluctuations about the mean processing times are reduced from the exponential spread to the constant processing time case, with similar much more dramatic payoff if one wishes to cut the ninetieth percentile of the waiting time distribution function, averaged over a long term time interval.

EXERCISE: Show that the result for constant service at each stage is true, by showing that all the queueing or waiting occurs as if all jobs were queued at the stage with the longest service time, independent of the order of nodes in the pipeline.

It is interesting to note that although the delay statistics in pipeline processing can be quite sensitive to the processing time statistics at each stage of execution, the maximum mean throughput rate is the same for either example above:

$$maximum \ mean \ throughput \ rate \ = \ 1/max(E(T_{S,1}), E(T_{S,2}),...,E(T_{S,N}))$$

This means that *small* changes in the mean service rate result in *small* changes in the maximum mean throughput rate but **not** in the mean delay as the underlying execution time distributions at each stage are varied.

6.7.2 An Example Suppose a computer communication system consists of N steps for each job, and each step requires a mean of one second. If jobs arrive at the first stage of the pipeline at the rate of one job every two seconds, then we can compare the performance of this system for different number of stages in the pipeline and to fluctuations about the mean service time, and the results are summarized in the table below:

Table 6.6. Mean Delay with λ=0.5 *jobs/sec*

| Number | Mean Waiting Time $E(T_W)$ | | Mean Queueing Time $E(T_Q)$ | |
of Stages	Constant	Exponential	Constant	Exponential
3	0.5 sec	3.0 sec	3.5 sec	6.0 sec
4	0.5 sec	4.0 sec	4.5 sec	7.0 sec
5	0.5 sec	5.0 sec	5.5 sec	8.0 sec

This makes it evident that the mean waiting grows with the number of stages if the fluctuations are severe. As a check on this study, we allow the first stage to require two units of service, the second stage one half unit of service, and all the rest of the stages require one unit of service, with the calculations summarized below:

Table 6.7.Mean Delay with λ=0.5 *jobs/sec*

Number of Stages	Mean Waiting Time $E(T_W)$		Mean Queueing Time $E(T_Q)$	
	Constant	Exponential	Constant	Exponential
3	2.25 sec	5.67 sec	5.25 sec	8.67 sec
4	2.25 sec	7.67 sec	6.25 sec	10.67 sec
5	2.25 sec	9.67 sec	7.25 sec	12.67 sec

This makes evident that the mean waiting is significantly impacted by the imbalance at the first two stages in the service time, for both the constant and exponential distribution. However, the constant service case is significantly *less* impacted than the exponential case.

6.7.3 Link Level Flow Control Consider a transmitter and a receiver that are connected via a data network of N stages or nodes, with messages at stage K requiring a constant amount of processing, $E(T_{S,K}),K=1,...,N$. In order to insure that no messages are lost along the way, because one stage may be transmitting while the receiving stage may have no storage or buffer space available, a flow control policy regulates message flow between neighboring nodes. Each node has a buffer with two limits, its maximum capacity or *high water mark* and a lower threshold or *low water mark*. When a buffer is filled to its high water mark, the transmitting node is stopped, and the buffer is drained of messages until it reaches its low water mark, at which point the transmitter node can continue to send messages. From the previous discussion, it is straightforward to show that if the high water marks for all nodes are greater than or equal to two messages, then the maximum mean throughput rate is given by

$$maximum\ mean\ throughput\ rate = 1/max(E(T_{S,1}),...,E(T_{S,N}))$$

In other words, the flow control strategy under these assumptions has *no* impact on the maximum data mean throughput rate. No messages will be lost due to buffer space being unavailable, and the slowest stage will be the bottleneck. Furthermore, all of the queueing occurs at the stage with the greatest processing time, and all of the delay analysis sketched earlier carries over immediately.

6.7.4 Additional Reading

[1] Gene M. Amdahl, *Validity of the Single Processor Approach to Achieving Large Scale Computing Capabilities*, AFIPS Spring Joint Computer Conference Proceedings, pp.483-485, 1967.

[2] H.D.Friedman, *Reduction Methods for Tandem Queuing Systems*, Operations Research, **13** (1), 121-131 (1965).

[3] Wolfgang Kramer, *Investigations of Systems with Queues in Series*, Institute of Switching and Data Technics, University of Stuttgart, Report #22(1975).

6.8 One Processor, One Paging Drum, One Moving Head Disk

The hardware configuration of a computer system consists of one processor, one moving head disk, and one paging drum. From the earlier mean value analysis, we know that the best concurrency we might achieve is to keep all three devices simultaneously busy. A job will undergo some processing, some input/output, some processing, and so forth, and then leave, but at the instant it leaves another job will enter to take its place, fixing the total number of jobs in the system at M at all times. Each job accesses the paging drum a mean of seven times, the moving head disk a mean of twice, and has a mean of ten processor visits. The total mean time spent using each resource without contention is:

$$T_{processor} = 280 \ msec \quad T_{drum} = 280 \ msec \quad T_{disk} = 560 \ msec$$

As we increase the total number of jobs, the disk will reach complete utilization first, i.e., the disk is the system bottleneck (why?). It also happens to be the slowest device, but it is really the *total* load per node that determines the bottleneck, not the speed or number of visits individually.

The mean throughput rate for M=1 is

$$\lambda(M=1) = \frac{1}{1120 \ msec} = 0.88 \ jobs/sec$$

The table below summarizes the results of calculating the processor utilization versus M:

Table 6.8. Degree of Multiprogramming vs Utilization

M	1	2	3	4	∞
$U_{processor}$	1/4	4/11	11/23	26/57	1/2

Most of the gain in maximizing mean throughput rate is achieved for increasing M from one to three, and the increase beyond two buys little:

$$mean \ throughput \ rate = \frac{U_{processor}}{T_{processor}}$$

Since we have three devices, the best we could ever do is to keep all three simultaneously busy. For the numbers here, with the disk time per job twice as great as the processor or drum time per job, the disk will reach completely utilization first. If the disk is completely busy, the processor and the drum will each be utilized fifty per cent of the time. Since the mean number of jobs in execution equals the fraction of time each device is busy, the total mean number of jobs in execution with $M \rightarrow \infty$ is *two*, one on the disk, and one half each for the drum and processor. The Jackson network analysis refines this mean value asymptotic analysis, quantifying the mean throughput rate more precisely: 0.3636 jobs per second (M=2) versus 0.4783 jobs per second (M=3), a net gain of 23.9 per cent.

EXERCISE. Graph the mean throughput rate versus M. Plot upper and lower bounds on mean throughput rate versus M that were derived earlier, and compare the results.

6.8.1 Additional Reading

[1]   H.Kobiyashi, **Modeling and Analysis: An Introduction to System Performance Evaluation Methodology,** Addison Wesley, Reading, Mass, 1978.

6.9 Prototype Directory Assistance System Case Study

A prototype of an online directory assistance system was built to handle telephone number directory assistance queries. In a typical cycle of operation, a person at a terminal would be involved in the following steps

[1]   Receive a query from a customer via voice telephone

[2]   Enter the given information into a computer terminal while talking to the customer

[3]   Wait for the system to respond with the answer to the query

[4]   Tell the customer the reply over the voice telephone

[5]   Close out customer interaction

[6]   Wait to receive the next customer query

The hardware configuration for the system consisted of C terminals, a single processor, a single disk controller, and a single disk spindle. An operating system coordinated scheduling and management of these devices, while a set of prototype application programs handled query processing.

Measurements on the prototype system in operation showed that

- The mean time spent by a person talking, reading, and thinking, denoted by T_C, was twenty seconds

- The mean processor time per query was broken down into three sets of application programs

  - The operator interface front end programs consumed 180 milliseconds of processor time per query on the average

  - The index manipulation application programs consumed 420 milliseconds of processor time per query on the average

- The data retrieval application programs consumed 330 milliseconds of processor time per query on the average

- Miscellaneous application programs that were invoked for accounting, system administration, and other purposes consumed one hundred and forty milliseconds (140 msec) per query

Hence, the total mean processor time per query, T_P, was 1.07 seconds

- The mean number of disk accesses per query was twenty six (26), with the disk capable of making one access every twenty five milliseconds (25 msec) which results in a mean time the disk is busy per query, denoted T_D, of six hundred fifty milliseconds (650 msec)

The above measurements on total mean processor time and disk access counts were based on examining the mean resources required for one hundred different queries to the system; the measurement error on the processor time was felt to be under ten milliseconds, while the measurement error on the number of disk accesses was felt to be under one access.

6.9.1 State Space The system state space Ω is given by

$$\Omega = \{\underline{J} = (J_C, J_P, J_D) | J_C + J_P + J_D = C\}$$

J_C clerks are active entering a query, J_P jobs are queued or running on the processor, and J_D jobs are queued or running on the disk.

6.9.2 Mean Value Analysis The upper and lower mean value bounds on mean queueing time or response time are given by

$$\max\left[T_P + T_D, \frac{C}{max[T_P, T_D]} - T_{think}\right] \leqslant E(T_Q) \leqslant C(T_P + T_D)$$

while the associated upper and lower mean value bounds on mean throughput rate are given by

$$\frac{C}{T_C + C(T_P + T_D)} \leqslant \lambda \leqslant \min\left[\frac{C}{T_C + T_P + T_D}, \frac{1}{max[T_P, T_D]}\right]$$

6.9.3 Jackson Network Analysis Provided a Jackson network model adequately fits the data, the distribution of number of jobs at each node is given by

$$\pi(\underline{J}) = \pi(J_C, J_P, J_D) = \frac{1}{G} \frac{T_C^{J_c}}{J_C!} T_P^{J_P} T_D^{J_D}$$

$$G = \sum_{\underline{K} \in \Omega} \frac{T_C^{K_c}}{K_C!} T_P^{K_P} T_D^{K_D}$$

The mean number of jobs inside the computer system is

$$E[J_P + J_D] = \sum_{\underline{K} \in \Omega} [K_P + K_D]\pi(\underline{K})$$

The mean throughput rate is simply the fraction of time the processor is busy multiplied by the maximum rate, in jobs per unit time, that the processor can execute jobs:

$$mean\ throughput\ rate = \sum_{\underline{K} \in \Omega} [1 - \pi(K_C, K_P = 0, K_D)]/T_P = \frac{E[min(1, J_P)]}{T_P}$$

The mean queueing time per job is the mean number of jobs in the system divided by the mean throughput rate:

$$mean\ queueing\ time\ per\ query = \frac{E[J_P + J_D]}{mean\ throughput\ rate}$$

For infinite source arrival statistics, this simplifies:

$$mean\ throughput\ rate = \lambda = \frac{C}{T_C}$$

$$mean\ queueing\ time\ per\ query = \frac{E(T_P)}{1 - \lambda E(T_P)} + \frac{E(T_D)}{1 - \lambda E(T_D)}$$

These bounds are plotted in the figures below, along with observed data gathered over an eight hour time interval with twelve $C=12$ operators and calculations based upon a closed queueing network model with $M=C$ obeying product form type solution. The goodness of fit of the closed queueing network model to actual data was felt to be acceptable for the purposes at hand; the mean value lower bound on mean delay and upper bound on mean throughput rate were also felt to give an indication of performance limitations at an early stage of development, which the data gathering and refinement via a closed queueing network model only strengthened further. Note that the system is achieving a great deal of concurrency, because the actual mean throughput rate is much closer to the upper bound, not the single thread lower bound, as is the mean delay.

6.10 Multiple Class Jackson Network Model

C types of jobs arrive to a system for execution. Each job stream is submitted by P_0 sources. $F_I, I=1,...,C$ is the fraction of job submissions of type I. Each job takes a route through the network, specified by $R_I(M), M=1,...,S(I)$ where M denotes the step for job type I. The job step execution time is denoted by τ_{IK} time units of service at node $K=1,...,N$. The total amount of service required at node K by a type I job is given by aggregating the total service time for each step, denoted by T_{IK}. Each node consists of P_K processors.

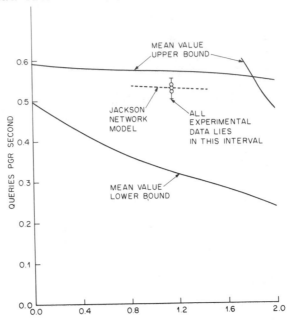

Figure 6.13.Mean Throughput Rate vs Mean Processor Time/Query

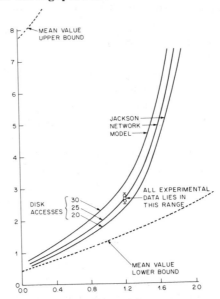

Figure 6.14.Mean Response Time vs Mean Processor Time/Query

6.10.1 State Space The state of the system at any time instant t is denoted by $\underline{J}$ where

$$\underline{J} = (J_{11},...,J_{C1},...,J_{1N},...,J_{CN})$$

with $J_{IK}(t), 1 \leqslant I \leqslant C, 1 \leqslant K \leqslant N$ denoting the number of jobs either waiting or in execution at node K of type I. We denote by J_{K*} the total number of jobs at node K and by J_{*I} the total number of jobs in the system of type I:

$$J_{K*} = \sum_{I=1}^{C} J_{IK} \quad J_{*I} = \sum_{K=1}^{N} J_{IK}$$

Finally, the total number of jobs in the system at time t, denoted by $|\underline{J}(t)|$, is given by:

$$|\underline{J}(t)| = \sum_{K=1}^{N} \sum_{I=1}^{C} J_{IK}(t)$$

6.10.2 *Scheduling Policy* The instantaneous total throughput rate at node K is given by

$$r_K = \frac{\Phi_K(J_{K*})}{\sum\limits_{I=1}^{C} F_I T_{IK}}$$

If the queue discipline is balanced with an arbitrary service time distribution at each node, then the fraction of time the system is in state $\underline{J}$ is given by a product of three terms, a partition function term, a source term, and a term that is the product of one term for each node:

$$\pi(\underline{J}) = \frac{1}{G} \ (source \ term) \times \prod_{K=1}^{N} (node \ K \ term)$$

$$source \ term = \begin{cases} \dfrac{T_0^{J_0}}{J_0!} & J_0 = P_0 - |\underline{J}| \\ 1 & |\underline{J}| = M \\ \lambda^{|\underline{J}|} & \dfrac{P_0}{T_0} = \lambda, P_0 \to \infty \end{cases}$$

$$node \ K \ term = J_{K*}! \prod_{l=1}^{J_K} \frac{1}{\Phi_K(l)} \prod_{I=1}^{C} \frac{(F_I T_{IK})^{J_{IK}}}{J_{IK}!} \quad K = 1,...,N$$

6.10.3 *Infinite Source Asymptotics* For the infinite source case, this can be simplified:

$$\pi(\underline{J}) = \frac{1}{G} \prod_{I=1}^{C} \prod_{K=1}^{N} J_{K*}! \frac{(\lambda F_I T_{IK})^{J_{IK}}}{J_{IK}!}$$

$$
G = \begin{cases}
\displaystyle\prod_{K=1}^{N} \frac{1}{1 - \lambda \displaystyle\sum_{I=1}^{C} F_{IK} T_{IK}} & \lambda < \min_{K} \left[\dfrac{P_K}{\displaystyle\sum_{I=1}^{C} F_I T_{IK}} \right] \\[3em]
\infty & \lambda \geqslant \min_{K} \left[\dfrac{P_K}{\displaystyle\sum_{I=1}^{C} F_I T_{IK}} \right]
\end{cases}
$$

6.10.4 Delay Analysis For either the finite source or infinite source model, the mean queueing delay is simply the sum of the mean queueing delay at each node:

$$
E[T_{I,Q}] = \sum_{K=1}^{N} E[T_{IK,Q}] \quad I=1,..,C
$$

The mean queueing delay at each node is the mean queueing delay for all jobs at that node, apportioned according to the *utilization* of the node by that type of job:

$$
E[T_{IK,Q}] = \frac{F_I T_{IK}}{\displaystyle\sum_{I=1}^{C} F_I T_{IK}} \, E[T_{K,Q}]
$$

where

$$
E[T_{K,Q}] = \frac{E[J_K]}{\lambda} = \left[\sum_{I=1}^{C} F_I T_{IK} \right] \left[D(P,U) \equiv 1 + \frac{C(P,PU)}{P(1-U)} \right]
$$

$C(P,P\,U)$ is the Erlang delay function discussed earlier, and $D(P,U)$ is the stretching factor that multiplies the total mean job execution time at node K. We stress that this can be readily approximated numerically using the Erlang delay numerical approximations discussed earlier. Here the multiple class analysis involves analyzing a *single* class system, with the *total* load on each node apportioned among the different jobs, and then calculating the *multiple* class delays by apportioning the delay at each node according to loading.

6.10.5 An Example As an example, suppose a single processor node $N=1$ executes two types of jobs $C=2$. Jobs arrive according to Poisson statistics, with total job arrival rate λ; F_K denotes the fraction of arrivals of type $K=1,2$. The state space is given by

$$
\Omega = \{(J_{11},J_{21}) \, | \, J_{I1} \geqslant 0, I=1,2\}
$$

The fraction of time the system is in state $\underline{J}=(J_{11},J_{21})$ is given by

$$\pi(J_{11}, J_{21}) = \frac{1}{G} \lambda^{J_{1*}} J_{1*}! \frac{(F_1 T_{11})^{J_{11}}}{J_{11}!} \frac{(F_2 T_{21})^{J_{21}}}{J_{21}!}$$

The partition function is given by

$$G = \frac{1}{1 - \lambda(F_1 T_{11} + F_2 T_{21})}$$

In order to calculate the mean throughput rate, we calculate the mean number of total jobs at the node, $E(J_{1*})$, and then apportion the mean number of each type job according to the workload:

$$E(J_{I1}) = \frac{F_I T_{I1}}{F_1 T_{11} + F_2 T_{21}} E[J_{1*}]$$

If there is only one processor, the mean number of jobs at the node is given by

$$E[J_{1*}] = \frac{\lambda(F_1 T_{11} + F_2 T_{21})}{1 - \lambda(F_1 T_{11} + F_2 T_{21})}$$

The mean throughput rate is λ which equals the total mean number of jobs divided by the total mean execution time per job:

$$\lambda = \frac{E[min(J_{1*}, P_1)]}{F_1 T_{11} + F_2 T_{21}}$$

The total mean delay (waiting plus execution) is given by

$$E[T_Q] = \frac{E[J_{1*}]}{\lambda} = D(P,U)(F_1 T_{11} + F_2 T_{21})$$

which for one processor is simply

$$E[T_Q] = \frac{F_1 T_{11} + F_2 T_{21}}{1 - \lambda(F_1 T_{11} + F_2 T_{21})}$$

The mean throughput rate for each type of job is $\lambda_I = \lambda F_I$. Finally, the total mean delay for each type of job is apportioned according to the load:

$$E[T_{I,Q}] = \frac{F_I T_{I1}}{F_1 T_{11} + F_2 T_{21}} E[T_Q]$$

6.11 Bounds on Mean Throughput Rate in Product Form Network Distributions

Our goal is to obtain upper and lower *bounds* on mean throughput rate *without* explicitly evaluating the mean throughput rate based on the product form formula. These bounds will in general be *tighter* than the mean value bounds obtained earlier, but unfortunately at present are only known for the case where there is *one* processor or serially reusable resource at each step of execution, unlike the mean value bounds which hold for *multiple* processors (and resources) held at each execution step.

6.11.1 Model The mathematical model dealt with here consists of

- One type of job that migrates amongst N stations or stages
- A *single* processor available to execute a job at stage $K=1,...,N$
- M tasks or jobs circulate among the nodes
- T_K denotes the total mean amount of service required by a job summed over all its visits to stage $K=1,...,N$

The system state is denoted by Ω:

$$\Omega = \{(J_1,...,J_N) \mid \sum_{K=1}^{N} J_K = M\}$$

At any given instant of time, the system is in state $\underline{J} = (J_1,...,J_N)$ where $J_K, K=1,...,N$ denotes the number of jobs at node K (both waiting and in execution). The long term time averaged distribution of number of jobs at each node at an arbitrary instant of time can be adequately modeled by *product form* or separation of variables formula

$$PROB[J_1=K_1, \ldots, J_N=K_N] = \frac{1}{G_M}\prod_{I=1}^{N} T_I^{K_I} \quad (K_1,...,K_N) \in \Omega$$

$$G_M = G_M(T_1,...,T_N) = \sum_{\underline{J} \in \Omega}\prod_{I=1}^{N} T_I^{J_I}$$

G_M is the *system partition function* chosen to normalize the probability distribution. Granted these assumptions, we observe that the mean throughput rate of jobs making a complete cycle of the system is given by

$$\lambda = \frac{PROB[J_K>0]}{T_K} = \frac{G_{M-1}(T_1,...,T_N)}{G_M(T_1,...,T_N)}$$

Straightforward manipulations of this expression yield the desired bounds:

$$\frac{M}{\sum_{K=1}^{N} T_K + (M-1)T_{max}} \leqslant \lambda \leqslant min\left[\frac{1}{T_{max}}, \frac{M}{\sum_{K=1}^{N} T_K + (M-1)T_{average}}\right]$$

$$\frac{M}{T_{cycle} + (M-1)T_{max}} \leqslant \lambda \leqslant min\left[\frac{1}{T_{max}}, \frac{M}{T_{cycle} + (M-1)T_{average}}\right]$$

where T_{cycle} is the total mean execution time for a job to cycle through all nodes

$$T_{cycle} = \sum_{K=1}^{N} T_K$$

and $T_{average}$ is the average execution time per node

$$T_{average} = \frac{1}{N} \sum_{K=1}^{N} T_K = \frac{T_{cycle}}{N}$$

and T_{max} is the largest mean execution time per node:

$$T_{max} = \max_{K=1,...,N} T_K$$

If the *average* time per node spent in execution by one job during a cycle and the *maximum* time per node per job are roughly comparable to one another, these bounds will be quite close to one another.

6.11.2 Example The hardware configuration for a computer system consists of a single processor and a single disk. The computer system is assumed to have M jobs resident in main memory at any one time, the so called *degree of multiprogramming*. How should M be chosen to maximize mean throughput rate?

This can be modeled by a two stage queueing network, $N=2$, with the total mean processor time per job denoted by T_{proc} while the total mean number of disk accesses per job multiplied by the mean time per disk access gives the total mean disk time per job, denoted by T_{disk}. The table below summarizes mean value upper and lower bounds on mean throughput rate for this system as a function of M, the degree of multiprogramming, i.e., the number of jobs in the system.

$$\frac{M}{M(T_{proc} + T_{disk})} = \frac{1}{T_{proc} + T_{disk}} \leqslant \lambda \leqslant \min\left[\frac{1}{max[T_{proc},T_{disk}]}, \frac{M}{T_{proc} + T_{disk}}\right]$$

Table 6.9.Mean Value Bounds on λ with $T_{disk}=1.0$

M (Jobs)	$T_{proc}=0.3$		$T_{proc}=1.0$	
	λ_{lower}	λ_{upper}	λ_{lower}	λ_{upper}
1	0.77 jobs/sec	0.77 jobs/sec	0.50 jobs/sec	0.50 jobs/sec
2	0.77 jobs/sec	1.00 jobs/sec	0.50 jobs/sec	1.00 jobs/sec
3	0.77 jobs/sec	1.00 jobs/sec	0.50 jobs/sec	1.00 jobs/sec

All of benefit occurs in increasing the degree of multiprogramming from one to two, because only two resources can be kept busy at any time; going beyond two buys nothing at this level of analysis.

For comparison, Table 6.10 summarizes queueing network upper and lower bounds for the same system:

$$\frac{M}{T_{cycle} + (M-1)T_{max}} \leqslant \lambda \leqslant \min\left[\frac{1}{T_{max}}, \frac{M}{T_{cycle} + (M-1)T_{average}}\right]$$

$$T_{cycle} = T_{proc} + T_{disk} \quad T_{average} = \frac{T_{cycle}}{2} \quad T_{max} = max[T_{proc},T_{disk}]$$

Table 6.10.Queueing Network Bounds on λ **with** $T_{disk}=1.0$

M	$T_{proc}=0.3$		$T_{proc}=1.0$	
(Jobs)	λ_{lower}	λ_{upper}	λ_{lower}	λ_{upper}
1	0.77 jobs/sec	0.77 jobs/sec	0.50 jobs/sec	0.50 jobs/sec
2	0.87 jobs/sec	1.00 jobs/sec	0.67 jobs/sec	0.67 jobs/sec
3	0.91 jobs/sec	1.00 jobs/sec	0.75 jobs/sec	0.75 jobs/sec

The numbers show that the queueing network bounds are considerably tighter than the mean value bounds, for the numbers chosen here. Furthermore, for the case of equal job time balance, $T_{proc}=T_{disk}$, the queueing network upper and lower bounds on mean throughput rate are *identical* and hence equal the *exact* mean throughput rate, something that might not be obvious a priori! Finally, most of the benefit occurs in going from $M=1$ to $M=2$ for the imbalanced case, $T_{proc}=0.3, T_{disk}=1.0$, while the gain for the balanced case in increasing M are much more gradual, provided the Jackson network assumptions are valid. This is a refinement beyond the information provided in the mean value bounds.

6.11.3 Additional Reading

[1]   P.J.Denning, J.P.Buzen, *The Operational Analysis of Queueing Network Models,* Computing Surveys, **10** (3), 225-261 (1978).

[2]   C.Sauer, K.Chandy, **Computer Systems Performance Modeling,** Prentice-Hall, Englewood Cliffs, NJ, 1981.

[3]   J.Zahorjan K.C.Sevick, D.L.Eager, B.Galler, *Balanced Job Bound Analysis of Queueing Networks,* Communications of the ACM, **25** (2), 134-141 (1982).

Problems

1) An online transaction processing system consists of one processor and C clerks at terminals. The mean time a clerk spends reading, thinking and entering the transaction is denoted by T_{think}. The mean time required for the processor to execute the transaction is denoted by T_{proc}.

A. What is the state space for this system?

B. What are the resources required for each step of execution?

C. What are the bottlenecks?

D. Plot bounds on mean throughput rate and mean delay to execute a transaction versus number of clerks using mean value analysis.

E. Plot the mean throughput rate and mean delay versus number of clerks using a closed Jackson queueing network, and compare with the mean value analysis.

F. Suppose the total mean arrival rate of jobs is fixed at λ such that

$$\lambda = constant = \frac{C}{T_{think}} \quad C \to \infty, T_{think} \to \infty$$

which is the infinite source model for this system. Plot the mean throughput rate and mean delay versus arrival rate, and compare with the closed Jackson network analysis and mean value bounds.

2) An online transaction processing system requires dedicated links from front end terminal controllers to back end data base management systems. Each transaction holds a circuit for a mean time interval of one tenth of a second. The arrival statistics are assumed to be simple Poisson. During a normal business hour the system must process ten transactions per second with the fraction of transactions blocked due to all links being busy of less than one transaction in ten thousand. During a peak business hour the system must process thirty transactions per second with the fraction of transactions blocked due to all links being busy of less than one transaction in one hundred.

[1] If all circuits are busy, a transaction will be queued until a circuit becomes available.

  A. How many trunks are needed to meet design goals?

  B. Repeat the above if the mean transaction holding time is one fifth of a second.

C. Repeat the above if the mean transaction holding time is one twentieth of a second.

[2] If all circuits are busy, a transaction is rejected or blocked, and presumably will retry later.

A. How many trunks are needed to meet design goals?

B. Repeat the above if the mean transaction holding time is one fifth of a second.

C. Repeat the above if the mean transaction holding time is one twentieth of a second.

[3] Repeat both A) and B) for the following two new design goals

A. During a normal business hour, no more than one transaction in one hundred is delayed due to trunks not being available. During a peak business hour, no more than one transaction in five is delayed due to trunks not being available.

B. During a normal business hour, no more than one transaction in one million is delayed due to trunks not being available. During a peak business hour, no more than one transaction in ten thousand is delayed due to trunks not being available.

3) Insurance agents dial up through the voice telephone network a central computer, and then use a terminal connected to a modem to query the central computer about different types of insurance policies for potential customers. A five year plan has been proposed. During the first two years of operations, the system should handle five queries per second during a normal business hour, and ten queries per second during a peak business hour. During the next three years, the system should handle twenty queries per second during a normal business hour, and thirty queries per second during a peak business hour. A query session has a mean duration of five minutes. If all ports are busy when a query attempt occurs, a busy tone is generated, and the query is delayed.

[1] Assume all blocked queries are lost or rejected and will retry later:

A. How many modems are needed if the fraction of queries blocked due to no modem being available is no more than one query in ten?

B. Repeat if the criterion is no more than one query in five is blocked?

C. Repeat if the criterion is no more than one query in one hundred is blocked?

    D. Repeat all the above if the mean holding time per query is increased to ten minutes.

[2] Assume all blocked queries are queued or delayed until a port becomes available. Repeat all the above.

4) Jobs arrive for service at a parallel group of P processors. The arrival statistics are Poisson with mean arrival rate λ. The holding time or service time per job forms a sequence of independent identically distributed exponential random variables with mean service time $E(T_S)$. The *offered load* is the mean number of busy servers provided we had an *infinite* number of servers, and this is measured in Erlangs, and denoted by A:

$$A = \lambda E(T_S) = \textit{offered load (Erlangs)}$$

The fraction of time P or more servers are busy with an *infinite* number of available servers is denoted by $F(P,A)$ and is given by

$$F(P,A) = \textit{fraction of time P or more busy servers} = e^{-A} \sum_{K=P}^{\infty} \frac{A^K}{K!}$$

A. Show the following relationships between Erlang's blocking function,

$$B(P,A) = \frac{A^P/P!}{\sum_{K=0}^{P} \dfrac{A^K}{K!}} \quad A = \textit{offered load (Erlangs)} \quad P = \textit{number of servers}$$

which is also called Erlang's function of the first kind and Erlang's delay function,

$$C(P,A) = \frac{A^P/(P-1)!(P-A)}{\sum_{K=0}^{P-1} \dfrac{A^K}{K!} + A^P/(P-1)!(P-A)}$$

which is also called Erlang's function of the second kind:

$$B(P,A) < F(P,A) < C(P,A)$$

Provide a physical interpretation for why this result is reasonable: draw some pictures!

B. Show the following:

$$C(P,A) = \frac{(P/A)B(P,A)}{(P/A)-1+B(P,A)}$$

C. Show the following:

$$C(P,A) = \cfrac{1}{\cfrac{P - A}{A\,B(P-1,A)} + 1}$$

D.   Show the following:

$$B(P,A) = \frac{AB(P-1,A)}{P + A\,B(P-1,A)}$$

E.   Show the following:

$$C(P,A) = \cfrac{1}{1 + \cfrac{P-A}{A}\ \cfrac{P-1-A}{(P-1-A)}\ \cfrac{C(P-1,A)}{C(P-1,A)}}$$

5) The hardware configuration for an online transaction processing system consists of one processor and one disk. Each transaction requires a total mean amount of processor time denoted by T_P and a total mean number of disk accesses N each of which requires τ_D seconds, so the total disk access time per job is denoted by T_D. The system state is given by $\underline{J} = (J_P, J_D)$ where J_P denotes the number of jobs waiting or in execution at the processor queue and J_D denotes the number of jobs waiting or in execution at the disk queue. An infinite source open queueing network is felt to adequately model the distribution of the number of jobs at each queue; if λ is the total mean arrival rate, in transactions per unit time, and $\pi(\underline{J})$ denotes the fraction of time the system is in state $\underline{J}$, then

$$\pi(\underline{J}=(J_P,J_D)) = \frac{1}{G}\ [\lambda T_P]^{J_P}\ [\lambda T_D]^{J_D}$$

A.   Calculate the system partition function G

$$G = \sum_{I=0}^{\infty}(\lambda T_P)^I \ \sum_{J=0}^{\infty}(\lambda T_D)^J$$

B.   Calculate the total mean number of jobs in system from first principles:

$$E[J_P + J_D] = \sum_{J_P=0}^{\infty}\sum_{J_D=0}^{\infty}[J_P + J_D]\pi(J_P,J_D)$$

C.   Show that the mean delay (waiting plus execution time) per transaction equals

$$E[T_{delay}] = \frac{E[J_P + J_D]}{\lambda} = \frac{T_P}{\lambda}\frac{\partial G}{\partial T_P} + \frac{T_D}{\lambda}\frac{\partial G}{\partial T_D}$$

D.   For $N=10,20$ disk accesses, with one processor and one disk, and $\tau_D=50$ *msec* while $\tau_P=300$ *msec*,700 *msec* calculate the mean throughput rate and the mean delay.

6) The hardware configuration for a computer system consists of a single processor and a single disk. The system state at any time is denoted by $\underline{J}=(J_P,J_D)$ where J_P denotes the number of jobs waiting or in execution on the processor, and J_D denotes the number of jobs waiting or in execution on the disk. Each job requires some processor time and some disk access time, in order to be completely executed. The fraction of time a computer system spends in state $\underline{J}$ is denoted by $\pi(\underline{J})$. We are given some mean value or average performance metric $E[PM]$ which is a functional of the system state $\underline{J}$, denoted by $PM(\underline{J})$:

$$E[PM] = \sum_{\underline{J} \in \Omega} PM[\underline{J}]\pi(\underline{J})$$

A. Show that the mean delay per transaction is an example of such a performance metric by exhibiting an explicit formula for $E[PM]$

B. Show that the processor utilization is an example of such a performance metric by exhibiting an explicit formula for $E[PM]$

C. If we wish to assess the sensitivity of the performance metric to a change in *speed* of the processor, show that

$$\frac{\partial E[PM]}{\partial(1/T_P)} = E\left[\frac{\partial PM(\underline{J})}{\partial(1/T_P)}\right] - T_P covar[J_P, PM(\underline{J})]$$

where $covar(I,J)$ denotes the covariance between I,J, and illustrate what this is explicitly for the mean delay and processor utilization performance metrics

D. Suppose that the time per transaction to access the disk is state dependent, such that it equals the product of two terms, the first a disk speed dependent but state independent factor, and the second a state dependent dimensionless function (which accounts for the disk scheduling algorithm):

$$T_D = T_{D,speed}\, f(J_D) \qquad f(J_D) = \begin{cases} 1 & J_D=0 \\ (2J_D-1/J_D) & J_D>0 \end{cases}$$

Write an analytic expression for the fraction of time the system is in state (J_P,J_D), denoted by $\pi(J_P,J_D)$, which is a modification of the expression shown earlier.

E. We wish to assess the sensitivity of changing the *speed* of the disk while keeping the same scheduling algorithm. Show that

$$\frac{\partial E[PM(\underline{J})]}{\partial(1/T_D)} = E\left[\frac{\partial PM(\underline{J})}{\partial(1/T_D)}\right] - T_D covar[J_D, PM(\underline{J})]$$

Evaluate this for a total mean delay performance measure and a disk utilization performance measure

F.   If $T_D=1$ explicitly evaluate all these formulae for $T_P=1,=0.5,=0.2$.

G.   Suppose you can get *one* fast disk or *two* slower disks such that

$$T_{D,one\ fast\ disk} = \tfrac{1}{2}T_{D,one\ slow\ disk}$$

What is the maximum mean throughput rate of the disk for either system? Repeat all of the above (including substitution of numbers into all formulae).

7) The hardware configuration for a computer system consists of a central processor unit (CPU) and two direct memory access (DMA) disk controllers each handling a single spindle. Jobs arrive for execution to this system in such a manner that the staging queue is never empty. The staging queue limits the degree of multiprogramming to a constant level of M jobs always in the system. Measurements are carried out on this system, and are summarized in the table below:

Table 6.11.Measurement Data Summary

Attribute	Symbol	Quantity
Processor Time/Job	T_{proc}	2 sec
Mean Time/Disk Access	T_{access}	50 msec
Mean Number of Disk Accesses/Job:		
To Spindle I	$N_{disk,I}$	50
To Spindle II	$N_{disk,II}$	20

Answer the following questions:

A.   What is the state space for the operations of this system?

B.   Plot upper and lower bounds on mean throughput rate of executing jobs versus M and state what the bottleneck resource is as $M \rightarrow \infty$

C.   Suppose that the long term time averaged fraction of time the system is in a given state can be adequately modeled by a product form distribution. What is an explicit expression for this formula?

D.   Plot the mean throughput rate of executing jobs versus M assuming the product form distribution adequately models the system operation on the same plot as the mean value upper and lower bounds on mean throughput rate.

E.   Plot upper and lower bounds on the mean throughput rate of executing jobs versus M assuming the a product form adequately models system operation. Do this on the same plot as the mean value upper and lower bounds on mean throughput rate.

F. Suppose that the file access load is redistributed so that the mean number of disk accesses per job stays the same but is *equal* to each spindle. Repeat all the above.

8) A data network consists of three nodes, A, B, C. At each node there are two Poisson streams of arriving messages of equal intensity intended for each of the other nodes, with each stream having mean arrival rate λ messages per unit time. Each message consists of a random number of bits with a mean of B bits per message. Each node is connected to every other node by two one way links, with one link for transmission and the other for reception. All links have capacity C bits per second.

A. What is the state space for this system?

B. What is an upper bound on the total number of messages per unit time carried by the network versus the individual message stream arrival rate λ?

C. Assuming a Jackson network model is statistically valid, what is an explicit expression for the fraction of time the system is in a given state?

D. Assuming the validity of a Jackson network model, what is an explicit expression for mean message delay as a function of model parameters?

E. If A can only transmit to C, C can only to transmit to B, and B can only transmit to A, i.e., we have a ring, with each link having capacity $2C$ bits per second, repeat all of the above analysis. Which system should be chosen under what conditions?

9) N clerks each submit a single type of job to a computer system. The hardware configuration for the computer system consists of a single processor and a single disk. Each clerk spends a variable amount of time reading, thinking, and entering the job, and then waits for the system to respond before starting the cycle over again. Each job undergoes processor execution, following by a single disk access, followed by more processor execution, followed by a single disk access, until eventually the processor completes execution of the job. The table below summarizes the quantitative data for this system:

Table 6.12.Measurement Data

Attribute	Symbol	Quantity
Mean Time Thinking	T_{think}	15 sec
Total Processor Time/Job	T_{proc}	3 sec
Probability Job Migrates CPU->Disk	R	360/361
Probability Job Migrates CPU->Clerk	$1-R$	1/361
Mean Time per Disk Access	T_{access}	50 msec

Answer the following questions:

A. What is a suitable state space to describe the operation of this system?

B. What is the mean number of disk accesses per job?

C. Plot upper and lower bounds on mean throughput and mean response time per job versus the number of active clerks.

D. What are the potential bottlenecks in this system?

E. Suppose that the long term time averaged fraction of time the system is in a given state can be adequately modeled by the *product form* probability distribution. What is an explicit expression for this probability distribution in terms of measurement data?

F. Plot the mean throughput rate and mean response time per job versus the number of active clerks assuming the product form distribution adequately models the system operation. Do this on the same plot as the mean value upper and lower bounds.

G. Suppose that the total rate at which jobs are submitted to the system is fixed at $\lambda \equiv N/T_{think}$ while the number of clerks is allowed to become infinite. What is the state space for this system? If a product form distribution adequately models the long term time averaged operational statistics, plot the mean throughput rate and mean response time per job versus the arrival rate λ.

10) Students want to use N terminals attached to a computer system that consists of a single processor. The statistics for students requesting or demanding a terminal are adequately modeled by a Poisson process with mean arrival rate λ which has the numerical value of two (2) sessions per hour. If all terminals are occupied with a student when a request occurs, the requesting student goes away. Once a student gets a terminal, the student keeps the terminal busy for a *session*. Each session consists of a series of interactions between the student at the terminal and the computer. Each interaction consists of a time interval with mean $T_{think} = 4$ *sec* where the student is reading and thinking and typing, and a time interval for the system to respond. With only one student at one terminal using the computer, the mean time for the system to respond is denoted by $T_{system}=2\ sec$. There are a mean number of $I=100$ interactions per student during a session. Once a student completes a session, the student leaves, freeing the terminal for another student.

A. What is the state space for describing the operation of this system?

B. Plot an upper bound on the mean number of sessions per unit time that the system can service versus $N=1,2,3$.

C. If the system statistics for the number of students at terminals and the number of requests in the computer can be adequately modeled by a product form distribution, write an explicit expression for this distribution as a function of N.

D. Using the above product form distribution, plot the fraction of student requests that are blocked or rejected versus $N=1,2,3$.

E. Using the above product form distribution, plot the mean number of sessions per unit time that the system services versus $N=1,2,3$.

F. Plot the mean time per session for students that are not rejected for $N=1,2,3$.

11) A computer system executes one type of job. The system hardware configuration consists of one processor, one fixed head disk (called a drum), and one moving head disk. The file system is configured with some files physically located on the drum and others on the disk. Each job requires some processor time, followed by a secondary storage access, and so on until the job is completely executed. There are N secondary storage accesses, and $N+1$ processor interactions per job. The system holds M jobs at any one time, either waiting or running on the processor, or waiting and accessing secondary storage. The secondary storage subsystem consists of a moving head disk and a fixed head disk (also called a drum). The file system is configured so that a fraction F of the secondary storage requests are made to the drum, and the remainder to the disk. The mean time per processor interaction is T_{cpu}. The mean time for a disk access is T_{disk}, while the mean time for a drum access is T_{drum}. In what follows, use the following numbers:

Table 6.13. Numerical Parameters

T_{cpu}	10 msec
T_{drum}	20 msec
T_{disk}	30 msec
N	25 accesses
M	5 jobs

Answer the following questions:

A.   What is the system state space?

B.   Plot an upper bound on the mean rate of executing jobs as a function of F.

C.   What choice of F maximizes the upper bound on the mean rate of executing jobs?

D.   If the system statistics for the number of jobs queued or in execution at the processor, drum and disk can be adequately modeled by a product form distribution, write an explicit expression for this formula.

E.   Using the above product form formula, plot the mean throughput rate of executing jobs versus F on the same plot as the upper bound.

12) A communication system administrator wishes to determine the benefits of pooling resources. A single type of message holds a link for a mean time interval of two seconds. There are two groups of links that can handle this type of message. The first group has three links and messages arrive at a rate of one message per second. The second group has four links and messages arrive at a rate of three messages every two seconds. The administrator can also pool the links into one group of seven links, with a total message arrival rate of five messages every two seconds.

A.   What is the state space for each configuration?

B.   Based on a mean value analysis, which configuration should be chosen?

C.   If messages are blocked if no link is available, which configuration will achieve the lowest total blocking?

D.   If messages are delayed if no link is available, which configuration will achieve the lowest total mean delay?

CHAPTER 7: JACKSON NETWORKS: APPLICATIONS I

In this section, we examine a variety of communication systems that can be modeled by Jackson networks. We will deal with

- Flow control of a single virtual circuit over a single physical link

- Packet switching network design

- Variable bandwidth circuit switching design

- Circuit switching system design

This list is not exhaustive, but it does hint at the rich variety of phenomena that are amenable to this type of analysis.

7.1 Flow Control over a Single Virtual Circuit on a Single Physical Link

A communications system is composed of a transmitter processor, a receiver processor, a set of B buffers each capable of holding one message at the receiver, and a noiseless communications link. Here are the steps involved in sending a message from the transmitter to the receiver:

[1] The transmitter processes a message. This step has a mean duration T_T at the transmitter, and it requires both the transmitter *and* a buffer at the receiver.

[2] The message propagates over the link from the transmitter to the receiver. This step has a mean duration T_{T-R}.

[3] The receiver processes the message. This step has a mean duration T_R.

[4] An acknowledgement of correct receipt of the message propagates from the receiver to the transmitter. This step has a mean duration T_{R-T}. At the start of this step, the receiver marks the buffer free.

[5] The transmitter processes the acknowledgement. This step has a mean duration of T_A At the end of this step, the transmitter marks the buffer free.

We assume from this point on that the time required by the transmitter to process the acknowledgement is zero. Figure 7.1 shows a hardware block diagram of the system. Figure 7.2 shows a queueing network block diagram of the system.

7.1.1 State Space The system state space is denoted by Ω where

Figure 7.1.Hardware Block Diagram of Communications System

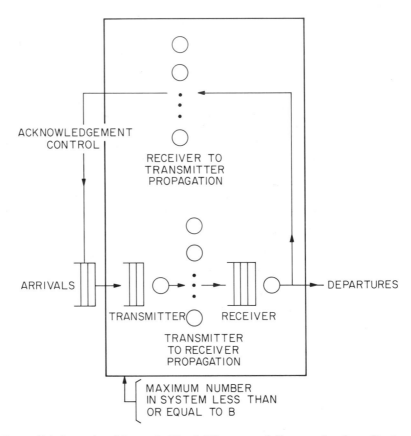

Figure 7.2.Queueing Network Block Diagram of Communications System

$$\Omega = \{(J_T, J_{T-R}, J_R, J_{R-T}) | J_T + J_{T-R} + J_R + J_{R-T} = B\}$$

At any instant of time, the system is in a state given by a four tuple, $(J_T, J_{T-R}, J_R, J_{R-T})$ where each component is nonnegative and integer valued, and the state space constraint is obeyed.

7.1.2 Mean Value Analysis Upper and lower bounds on mean throughput rate
λ are as follows:

$$\frac{B}{BT_T + T_{T-R} + BT_R + T_{R-T}} = \lambda_{lower} \leqslant \lambda$$

$$\lambda \leqslant \lambda_{upper} = \min \left[\frac{1}{T_T}, \frac{1}{T_R}, \frac{B}{T_T + T_{T-R} + T_R + T_{R-T}} \right]$$

The physical interpretation of the upper bound on mean throughput rate is as
follows

- If the transmitter is the bottleneck, then

$$\lambda_{upper} = \frac{1}{T_T}$$

- If the receiver is the bottleneck, then

$$\lambda_{upper} = \frac{1}{T_R}$$

- If the number of buffers is the bottleneck, then

$$\lambda_{upper} = \frac{B}{T_T + T_{T-R} + T_R + T_{R-T}}$$

The physical interpretation of the lower bound is that at most one message at a
time is being handled by the system.

The figures below plot these upper and lower bounds, as well as the results of a
Jackson queueing network analysis for the special case where

$$T_T = T_R \qquad T_{T-R} = T_{R-T}$$

Three different cases are shown, where the propagation delay is much smaller
than , equal to, and much larger than the mean processing time at either end
of the link.

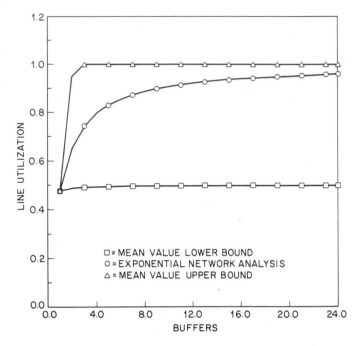

Figure 7.3.Mean Throughput Rate vs Number of Buffers(T_{prop}=0.1)

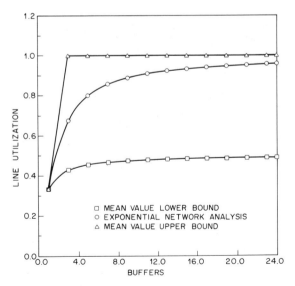

Figure 7.4.Mean Throughput Rate vs Number of Buffers(T_{prop}=1.0)

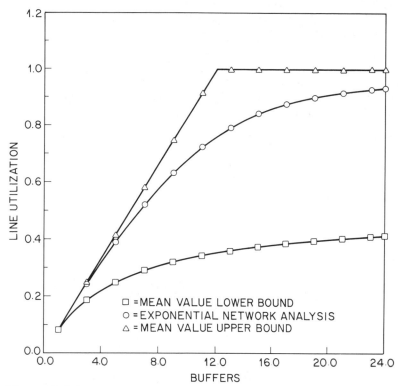

Figure 7.5. Mean Throughput Rate vs Number of Buffers (T_{prop}=10.0)

The fraction of time the Jackson network model predicts the system to be in state $\underline{J}$ is denoted by $\pi(\underline{J})$ where

$$\pi(\underline{J}) = \frac{1}{G} \, T_T{}^{J_T} \frac{T_{T-R}{}^{J_{T-R}}}{J_{T-R}!} T_R{}^{J_R} \frac{T_{R-T}{}^{J_{R-T}}}{J_{R-T}!}$$

where G is the system partition function.

7.1.3 Negligible Link Propagation Delay We now restrict attention to the special case where the propagation delay is negligible compared to the processing at either end of the link, from this point on. For one buffer, the mean throughput rate is upper bounded by

$$\lambda \leqslant \lambda_{upper} = \frac{1}{T_T + T_{T-R} + T_R + T_{R-T} + T_A} = \frac{1}{T_T + T_R}$$

There is no concurrency or parallel execution of messages, and the total time required for message handling is the sum of the individual steps.

For more than one buffer, this will yield an upper bound on the mean throughput rate of simply B times the mean throughput rate for one buffer:

$$\lambda \leqslant \lambda_{upper} = \frac{B}{T_T + T_{T-R} + T_R + T_{R-T} + T_A} = \frac{B}{T_T + T_R}$$

315

On the other hand, as the number of messages increases, then either the transmitter or the receiver (or both) will become completely busy, yielding different upper bounds on mean throughput rate:

- The transmitter is a bottleneck

$$\lambda = \frac{1}{T_T + T_A} = \frac{1}{T_T}$$

- The receiver is a bottleneck

$$\lambda = \frac{1}{T_R}$$

Combining all this, we see

$$\lambda \leqslant \min\left[\frac{1}{T_T + T_A}, \frac{1}{T_R}, \frac{B}{T_T + T_{T-R} + T_R + T_{R-T} + T_A}\right]$$

$$\lambda \leqslant \min\left[\frac{1}{T_T}, \frac{1}{T_R}, \frac{B}{T_T + T_R}\right]$$

Increasing the number of buffers from one to two, $B=1$ to $B=2$, always increases the maximum mean throughput rate, and now we see

$$\lambda \leqslant \min\left[\frac{1}{T_T}, \frac{1}{T_R}\right] \quad B > 1$$

Furthermore, this increase is maximized for $T_T = T_R$, and then the upper bound *doubles* in going from one buffer to more than one buffer. Why is this so? By having more than one buffer, both the transmitter and receiver can simultaneously be filling and emptying a buffer, allowing greater concurrency or parallelism compared with the single buffer case. We also note that allowing more than two buffers, e.g., *infinite* buffers, will not increase the upper bound on the maximum mean throughput rate any further. This is because there are only two serially reusable resources, a transmitter and a receiver, so once they are concurrently busy, no further gains can be achieved.

For the lower bound on mean throughput rate, we see that

$$\lambda \geqslant \lambda_{lower} = \frac{B}{BT_T + BT_R} = \frac{1}{T_T + T_R}$$

which is identical to the upper bound for $B=1$. Why is this so? There may be significant fluctuation about the mean values shown above, and in the limit of one big swing about the mean value all of the messages will pile up at one stage in the network and nothing will be transmitted until buffers become available.

What is the impact of fluctuations about mean values on system performance? Suppose the transmitter processing times are sequences of independent identically distributed exponential random variables with mean T_T. Suppose the receiver processing times are sequences of independent identically random variables with common hyperexponential distribution $G_R(X)$:

$$G_R(X) = (1-\alpha) + \alpha(1 - e^{-X\mu_R})$$

In words, a fraction $1-\alpha$ will require zero processing time at the receiver, while a fraction α will require an exponentially distributed amount of processing time with mean $1/\mu_R$. The parameter α gives us an additional degree of freedom to model fluctuations in the receiver processing times. For this case, we choose to fix the *squared coefficient of variation* denoted by C^2. The squared coefficient of variation is defined as the ratio of the variance to square of the mean (the standard deviation, measured in units of mean value, squared):

$$squared\ coefficient\ of\ variation = \frac{variance\ (X)}{E^2(X)} \equiv C^2$$

When this is zero, the variance is zero, and there is zero fluctuation about the mean. When this is one, we have an exponential distribution, where the standard deviation equals the mean. When this is greater than one, the standard deviation is greater than the mean. For this particular case, we see $0 < \alpha \leqslant 1$ and hence

$$C^2 = \frac{2}{\alpha} - 1 \geqslant 1$$

If the mean is fixed but α is varied from one (the exponential distribution case, where the fluctuations are the order of the mean) to zero (increasing fluctuations about the mean) with most jobs taking zero time but a few taking a very long time, we can gain insight into the impact on performance. Since we have fixed the squared coefficient of variation, the mean is also fixed, since

$$T_R = \frac{\alpha}{\mu_R}$$

The distribution of the number in the receiver subsystem at the completion of processing at the receiver of a message is denoted by $F(K), K = 0, ..., B$. If none are left behind, then the mean time to the next completion epoch is $T_T + T_R$. If more than zero is left behind at the receiver, then the mean time to the next completion epoch is T_R. The mean throughput rate is given by

$$\lambda = \frac{1}{F(0)[T_T + T_R] + [1 - F(0)]T_R} = \frac{1}{F(0)T_T + T_R}$$

$F(0)$ is the fraction of time the system is *empty* of messages at a completion of transmission epoch; $F(0)$ can be approximated numerically or measured empirically.

Illustrative numerical results are plotted in the figures below assuming the transmitter and receiver service times are independent identically distributed exponential random variables.

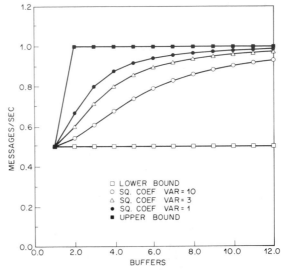

Figure 7.6.Maximum Mean Throughput Rate vs Number of Buffers
$$T_{prop}=0, T_T=1.0$$

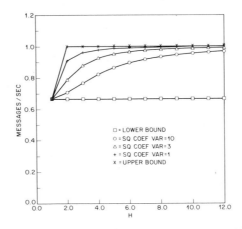

Figure 7.7.Maximum Mean Throughput Rate vs Number of Buffers
$$T_{prop}=0, T_T=0.5$$

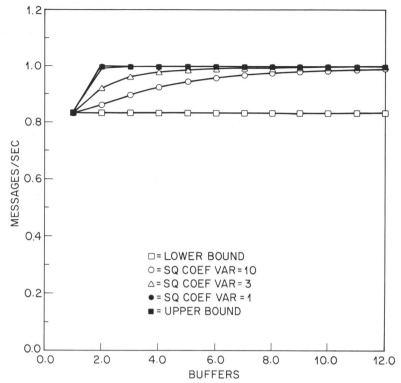

Figure 7.8.Maximum Mean Throughput Rate vs Number of Buffers
$$T_{prop}=0, T_T=0.2$$

Note that for the special case where $T_R=T_T=1$, the mean throughput rate is given by

$$\lambda = \frac{1 + \dfrac{2(B+1)}{C^2+1}}{2 + \dfrac{2(B-1)}{C^2+1}} \quad C^2 \geqslant 1$$

Here we see as $C^2 \to \infty$ that the mean throughput rate approaches the lower bound of ½ arbitrarily closely, i.e., there is no concurrency or gain in going to more than one buffer if the fluctuations are too great. On the other hand, as $B \to \infty$ for C^2 fixed, the mean throughput rate approaches one, which is the best possible. The numerical plots show in which regime which phenomenon (the fluctuations or the buffering and concurrency) dominate the actual mean throughput rate. The impact of speed mismatch (i.e., as the transmitter and receiver mean message execution times start to differ) tends to swamp the impact of fluctuations: the greater the speed mismatch, the greater concurrency achieved, because the exact mean throughput rate approaches the upper bound closer and closer as the speed mismatch between transmitter and receiver increases. The upper bound on mean throughput rate corresponds to a squared coefficient of variation of zero, while the lower bound corresponds to a squared coefficient of variation that becomes infinite.

We now discuss this phenomenon in more detail, because the formulae give only one way of understanding this model. The figure below shows an illustrative sample path generated from a simulation of the model, for a total number of five jobs in the system.

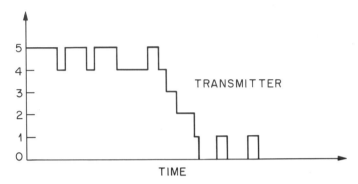

Figure 7.9.A. Transmitter Simulation Results

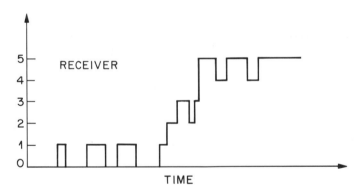

Figure 7.9.B. Receiver Simulation Results

In the initial part of the simulation, the first stage fluctuates between four and five jobs, while the second stage fluctuates between zero and one job; in the final part of the simulation, the situation is reversed; after sufficiently long time, we would return to the first case. When most of the jobs are at one stage, the mean throughput rate is roughly the reciprocal of the time to execute one job from start to finish, and there is no concurrency. The other cases, where there are multiple jobs at each stage, are transient and the system spends relatively little time in these states. As the fluctuations and hence squared coefficient of variation become larger, while the mean time spent at the transmitter and receiver stays fixed, the fraction of time either *all* or *none* of the messages are at the transmitter can be shown to be *arbitrarily* close to one, which is what the simulation result in the figure above shows. At the same time, we see that the mean sojourn time in the state where the receiver is empty is given by

$$mean\ sojourn\ time\ in\ idle\ receiver\ state = \sum_{K=1}^{\infty}(1-\alpha)^{K-1}\alpha K T_T$$

$$= \frac{T_T}{\alpha} \rightarrow \infty \quad \alpha \rightarrow 0$$

Put differently, if one were to measure the operation of this system, the system might be in the receiver idle state for the entire duration of the observation process, and the other state of the receiver having all jobs (which will also become successively longer and longer as $\alpha \rightarrow 0$) will never be observed, or vice versa! In the figure above, this would correspond to gathering data in the first part of the simulation, never in the second part, or vice versa.

7.1.4 Queueing Network Analysis for Negligible Propagation Delay If we calculate upper and lower bounds on mean throughput rate using the Jackson network model, we find:

$$\lambda_{lower} \leqslant \lambda \leqslant \lambda_{upper}$$

$$\lambda_{lower} = \frac{1}{T_T + T_R + max[T_T, T_R]}$$

$$\lambda_{upper} = \frac{1}{T_T + T_R + \frac{1}{2}[T_T + T_R]}$$

The mean value bounds, the queueing network upper and lower bounds, and exact queueing network analysis mean throughput calculations are all plotted in the figures below for $T_R = 1.0$ and $T_T = 1.0, 0.5, 0.2$.

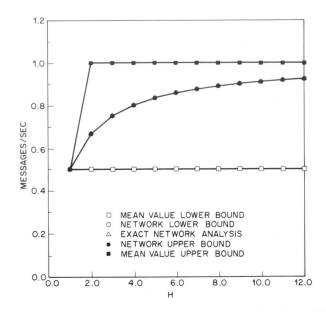

Figure 7.10.Mean Throughput Rate Bounds vs Number of Buffers
$T_R=1.0, T_T=1.0$

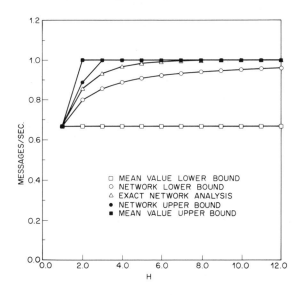

Figure 7.11.Mean Throughput Rate Bounds vs Number of Buffers
$T_R=1.0, T_T=0.5$

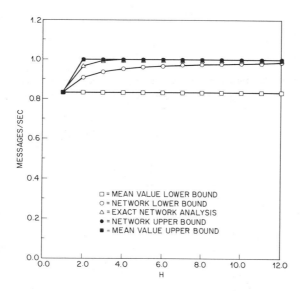

Figure 7.12.Mean Throughput Rate Bounds vs Number of Buffers
$$T_R=1.0, T_T=0.2$$

The queueing network bounds are identical to the exact analysis when the transmitter and receiver execute messages at the same rate. When the transmitter becomes faster than the receiver, the bounds and exact analysis tend to track the upper bound on mean throughput rate; in other words, the speed mismatch is of greater importance than the impact of fluctuations.

7.1.5 Experimental Data In order to test predictions of this analysis against actual operations, a series of experiments were carried out to determine the mean maximum throughput rate of a data communications link constructed with two computers, one transmitting and one receiving, over a data link where the link propagation time was negligible compared to the data communications processing at either end of the link or the data transmission time of a packet over this link. The test described here involved sending 51,200 bytes of data over a 9600 bit per second data link; similar results were found for a 1200 bit per second data link. The source data were encoded into packets containing either thirty two, sixty four, one hundred twenty eight, or two hundred fifty six bytes (one byte equals eight bits) of data. We wish to test the gain in going from start stop or single buffering to double buffering and to greater than double buffering; our previous analysis assumes that a mean value of data communications processing time at the transmitter and receiver adequately characterizes the system performance.

The experiment involved simply measuring the time required to transmit 51,200 bytes of data over each link for each size packet. No processing was done on the data at either the transmitter or receiver other than to do the data communications processing required for correct operation.

The table below summarizes the results of that experiment:

Table 7.1. Maximum Mean Throughput Rate for Transmission of 51,200 Bytes over 9600 BPS Data Link

Number of Buffers	Packet Size	Time (sec)	Maximum Throughput	Link Utilization
1 Buffer	32 bytes	160.0	3200 bps	33%
1 Buffer	64 bytes	125.0	4096 bps	43%
1 Buffer	128 bytes	90.0	5688 bps	59%
1 Buffer	256 bytes	80.0	6400 bps	67%
2 Buffers	32 bytes	80.0	6400 bps	67%
2 Buffers	64 bytes	58.5	8752 bps	91%
2 Buffers	128 bytes	55.5	9225 bps	96%
2 Buffers	256 bytes	55.0	9309 bps	97%
7 Buffers	32 bytes	64.0	8000 bps	83%
7 Buffers	64 bytes	58.0	8827 bps	92%
7 Buffers	128 bytes	55.0	9309 bps	97%
7 Buffers	256 bytes	54.5	9412 bps	98%

The time required to send each of 51,200 bytes of data plus two additional bits (for parity and control) over a serial 9600 bit per second data link is 53.3 seconds; thus, the data link transmission speed and not the transmitter or receiver is limiting data flow here. This can also be seen directly by noting that the link utilization is approaching one hundred per cent in the table above. This table shows that double buffering at the receiver offers substantial improvement in mean message throughput over single buffering, and there is no apparent advantage in terms of throughput in choosing a receiver buffer larger than two (e.g., seven was tried). Finally, this suggests that for this purpose this level of analysis is appropriate, i.e., that other phenomena that are present are in fact negligible for these purposes, as shown by the data.

7.2 Packet Switching Communication Network Analysis

The figure below shows a block diagram of an illustrative computer communication network. Terminals and computers are connected to one another via the network. The communication network consists of four external ports and seven internal channels. In what follows we will assume there are N entry ports and M channels each capable of a maximum transmission rate of C_I bits per second, $I=1,...,M$. There are two classes of policies for allocating transmission capacity

- circuit switching--at the start of a session, address and control information are used to find a path through the network, and network transmission

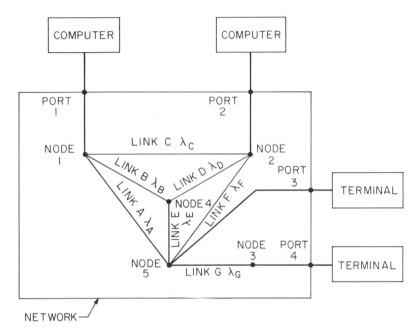

Figure 7.13.An Illustrative Communications System
4 External Ports/5 Internal Nodes/7 Channels or Links

capacity is dedicated to that call for its whole duration; if no paths are available, the call is rejected and presumably will retry later

- packet switching--each interaction contains both address and control information as well as data, each interaction finds its path through the network, and if transmission capacity is not available is buffered at intermediate nodes until transmission is possible

Circuit switching is used in conventional voice telephony, where the set up time is short compared to the call duration. Packet switching is used in data communications, where the set up time is comparable to the time to transmit the data.

7.2.1 Model In the analysis to follow, we assume the switching systems at intermediate nodes are infinitely fast, so there is no queueing for their resources, but the links have finite speeds, and we buffer or queue for each link.

Message lengths are assumed to be independent identically distributed exponential random variables, with a mean of B bits/message:

$$PROB[message \ length \ \leqslant X \ bits] = 1 - exp(-X/B)$$

$$E[message \ length] = B \ bits$$

A static policy is adopted here for routing messages through the network: all messages originating at node J and intended for destination node K follow a route denoted by R_{JK} which is a set of channels connecting J and K

The arrival statistics for messages going from node J to node K are assumed to be Poisson, with mean arrival rate λ_{JK} messages per second.

The mean offered load, in messages per second, on link A, is denoted by γ_A. This will be a function of the topology, routing, and load. Although it is clear what this is intuitively, its analytic expression is more formidable:

$$\gamma_A = \sum_{(J,K)|A \in R_{JK}} \lambda_{JK}$$

We measure performance by the mean time a message spends in the network, averaged over all message types.

In order to pose meaningful design problems, we need one additional constraint:

$$D(C_I) = cost \ in \ dollars \ for \ transmission \ capacity \ C_I$$

and typically we wish to constrain the total cost at D_{total}

$$D_{total} \geqslant \sum_{I=1}^{M} D(C_I)$$

A wide hierarchy of design problems can now be described:

[1] *Capacity Assignment Problem.* Given a fixed routing and network topology, minimize the mean message delay subject to a given cost criterion with respect to channel link transmission rate assignment.

[2] *Flow Assignment Problem.* Given a topology, find a routing R such that the mean message delay is minimized subject to a cost constraint.

[3] *Topology Assignment Problem.* Find a routing R and a topology such that the mean message delay is minimized subject to a constraint on transmission cost.

7.2.2 State Space At any instant of time, the state of the system is given by $\underline{J}$ where $\underline{J}$ is an M tuple with elements being either zero (to show no message is being transmitted) or one (to show that a message is being transmitted):

$$\Omega = \{\underline{J} | (J_1,...,J_M):J_A=0,1; \ A=1,...,M\}$$

7.2.3 Mean Value Analysis The mean number of messages in transmission over link A equals

$$E[\min(1,J_A)] = \lambda_A \, \frac{B}{C_A} \quad A=1,...,M$$

This can be upper bounded by assuming the link is completely busy:

$$\lambda_A \leqslant \frac{C_A}{B} \quad A=1,...,M$$

The mean message delay can be lower bounded by the mean message transmission time, but it can be arbitrarily bigger than this, due to fluctuations about the mean message transmission time. This completes the mean value analysis.

7.2.4 Product Form Analysis If the number in system can be adequately modeled by a *product form* distribution, the long term time averaged distribution for the number of messages at each node in the network is given by

$$\pi[J_1{=}K_1,...,J_M{=}K_M] = \prod_{J=1}^{M} (1{-}\rho_J)\rho_j^{K_J}$$

$$\rho_A = \frac{B\lambda_A}{C_A} = \textit{mean utilization of link } A \quad A=1,...,M$$

In order to calculate the mean message delay, we will use Little's Law. The total mean flow rate into the network is γ_{total} and is given by

$$\gamma_{total} = \sum_{I=1}^{M} \sum_{J=1}^{M} \gamma_{IJ}$$

The total mean queue length is given by

$$E[J_1 + \cdots + J_M] = \sum_{J=1}^{M} \frac{\rho_J}{1{-}\rho_J}$$

Hence, the total mean time in system of a message is

$$T = \frac{1}{\gamma} \sum_{J=1}^{M} \frac{\rho_J}{1-\rho_J} = \frac{1}{\gamma} \sum_{J=1}^{M} \frac{\lambda_J}{\mu C_J - \lambda_J} = \sum_{J=1}^{M} \frac{\lambda_J}{\gamma} T_J$$

These results can be extended in a variety of ways:

- multiple communication links connecting nodes

- multiple message types of differing lengths

- control bit transmission time plus data bit transmission time

- varying length messages as the message moves through the network

7.2.5 Additional Reading

[1]   L.Kleinrock, **Communications Nets: Stochastic Message Flow and Delay,** McGraw Hill, NY, 1964; reprinted, Dover, NY, 1972.

[2]   L.Kleinrock, *Analytic and Simulation Methods in Computer Network Design,* AFIPS Spring 1970 Joint Computer Conference, pp.569-579 (1970).

7.3 Engineering Alternate Routing Trunk Groups

In practice in voice telephony, it is uneconomical to develop a completely connected network. In fact, a hierarchical network is used, with local calls switched by local switching systems, and other calls routed through a high performance long distance or toll network. Typically the local trunks are engineered to have relatively high blocking, say ten to thirty per cent blocking, due to economics. The toll network trunks on the other hand are engineered to have one per cent blocking or less because this is the facility of last resort: if a call cannot be completed with this network, it cannot be completed. Unfortunately, the arrival statistics of calls to the backbone network is anything but Poisson: most of the time there is virtually *no* call switching, because the local network can handle it all, but during a normal or peak busy hour there will be bursts of call attempts. Our intent is to quantify how many trunks are required for a given level of service and for a given level of call attempts that are being alternately routed through the backbone network.

7.3.1 Model L local trunks are offered a load of A erlangs of voice traffic: this means that the arrival statistics to the local trunks are Poisson with mean arrival rate λ, and the mean holding time for a call is $E(T_{talk})$, while $A = \lambda E(T_{talk})$. If a call attempt arrives and a local trunk is available, the call attempt seizes the trunk for the duration of the call. If all local trunks are busy with call attempts when a new call attempt arrives, the new call attempt searches a second group of C overflow trunks. If all local and overflow trunks are busy when a new call attempt arrives, the new call attempt is rejected or blocked from the system.

7.3.2 Equivalent Random Method Analysis The first type of analysis is called the *equivalent random method* in voice telephone traffic engineering. The fraction of time that a call attempt is blocked by all local trunks being busy is $B(L,A)$, where this is the Erlang blocking function with L servers and an offered load of A erlangs. The mean number of busy trunks is $A\,B(L,A)$

$$M \equiv mean\ number\ of\ local\ trunks\ busy = A\,B(L,A)$$

The overflow stream to the toll trunk group will be characterized by two parameters, the mean number of busy trunks for the local trunk group, and the squared coefficient of variation denoted by C^2 which measures the fluctuation about the mean:

$$C^2 \equiv squared\ coefficient\ of\ variation = 1 - M + \frac{A}{L + M + 1 - A}$$

These can be rearranged as follows:

$$M = A \ B \left[A \ \frac{M+C^2}{M+C^2-1} - M - 1, A \right]$$

$$L = A \ \frac{C^2 + M}{M + C^2 - 1} - M - 1$$

The problem is to solve for M and A. Knowing these, the blocking probability for overflow calls is given by

$$overflow \ call \ blocking \ probability = \frac{B(L+C,A)}{B(L,A)}$$

7.3.3 Hayward's Approximation Analysis The equivalent random method is usually used only when the service time distribution for calls on the local trunk group is exponential. For other distributions such as a deterministic or constant holding time distribution, another approximation is widely used due to Hayward:

$$blocking \ probability = B \left[\frac{L}{C^2}, \frac{M}{C^2} \right]$$

To use this requires that C^2 be determined, either from measurement or by analysis.

7.3.4 Numerics Newton's method can be used to accurately numerically approximate A. The fundamental recursion is

$$A_{K+1} = A_K - \frac{A_K B_K - M}{B_K \left[L_K + M + A - A_K - (L_K + M + 1) ln(A_K) \right]} \qquad K=0,1,...$$

$$A_K = M \ C^2 + 3 \ C^2 \ (C^2 - 1)$$

7.3.5 An Example Suppose that $L=15$, $M=10$, and $C^2=3$. Provided that the holding time distribution is exponential, and using the equivalent random method of approximation, we find $A=46.721$ and $X=39.615$. The blocking probability is found to be

$$blocking \ probability \approx \frac{B(54.615,46.721)}{B(39.615,46.721)} = 0.151$$

Using Hayward's approximation, we find

$$blocking \ probability \approx B(5,3.333) = 0.139$$

This is consistent with $\lambda=10$, $A=4$. On the other hand, if the service time distribution is a hyperexponential, with some mass at the origin and the remainder an exponential distribution, then $C^2=4.25$, and hence Hayward's approximation suggests

$$blocking\ probability \approx B\left[\frac{15}{4.25}, \frac{10}{4.25}\right] = 0.187$$

which is significantly greater than the equivalent random method suggests.

7.3.6 Additional Reading

[1] R.Syski, **Introduction to Congestion Theory in Telephone Systems,** Oliver and Boyd, Edinburgh, 1959.

[2] R.I.Wilkinson, *Theories of Toll Traffic Engineering in the U.S.A.,* Bell System Technical Journal, **35** (2), 1956.

[3] L.Y.Rapp, *Planning of Junction Networks in a Multi-Exchange Area, Part I,* Ericsson Technics, **20,** 1964.

[4] J.P.Moreland, *Estimation of Point to Point Telephone Traffic,* Bell System Technical Journal, **57** (8), 2847-2863 (1978).

[5] A.A.Fredericks, *Congestion in Blocking Systems--A Simple Approximation Technique,* Bell System Technical Journal, **59** (6), 805-827 (1980).

7.4 Data Communication Network Design

We wish to build up our intuition design rules for high performance data communications networks. We will do so by means of a variety of examples.

7.4.1 Uncoupled Links, Constraint on Maximum Transmission Capacity

The simplest network we can imagine, shown in the figure below, is one consisting of L links, each of which has a capacity C_K (K=1,...,L) bits per second. There is *no* coupling between the links! Jobs arrive according to simple Poisson statistics with mean arrival rate λ_K to link K. The messages have independent identically distributed exponential lengths, with all messages having the same mean length of B bits. The total network capacity, C_{total}, is the sum of the individual link capacities:

$$\sum_{K=1}^{L} C_K = C_{total}$$

The total mean arrival rate of messages is λ_{total} and is the sum of the individual message arrival rates:

$$\lambda_{total} = \sum_{K=1}^{L} \lambda_K$$

Based on mean value analysis, we require that the individual link capacity be greater than the total offered load:

$$C_K > B\lambda_K \qquad K=1,...,L$$

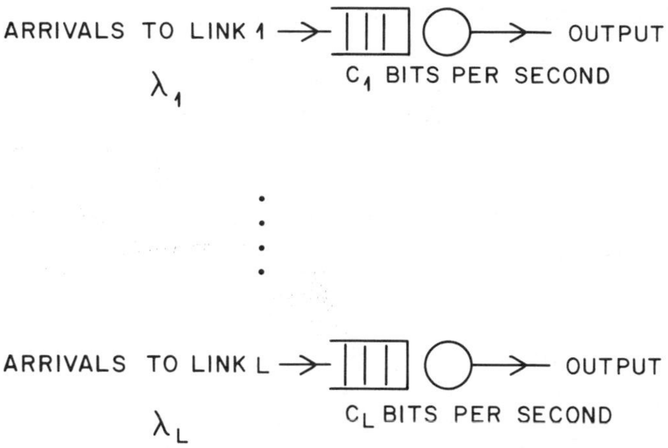

Figure 7.14.L Uncoupled Links

We are given the mean message length and the different mean link arrival rates, and our problem is to choose the link capacities such that the total mean message queueing time is minimized:

$$E(T_Q) = \sum_{K=1}^{L} \frac{\lambda_K}{\lambda_{total}} \frac{B}{C_K - B\lambda_K}$$

We see that each link must be able to keep up with its offered work load, and this will require a minimum amount of transmission capacity:

$$C_{min} = B \sum_{K=1}^{L} \lambda_K = B\lambda_{total}$$

Thus, it makes sense to examine how we will proportion the *excess* transmission capacity:

$$C_{excess} = C_{total} - B\lambda_{total}$$

$$C_K = B \lambda_K + C_{excess,K} \qquad K=1,...,L$$

One way that comes to mind is to proportion the excess capacity proportional to the load for each link:

$$C_K = B\lambda_K + C_{excess} \frac{\lambda_K}{\lambda_{total}} \qquad K=1,...,L$$

This will **not** minimize the mean queueing time of messages! The assignment that does this proportions the excess transmission capacity according to the *square root* of the load for each link:

$$C_{K,min} = B\lambda_K + C_{excess} \frac{\sqrt{B\lambda_K}}{\sum\limits_{J=1}^{L} \sqrt{B\lambda_J}} \qquad K=1,...,L$$

7.4.2 Uncoupled Links, Routing Constraint The network is the same as described above, with one additional constraint: the mean arrival rates are constrained such that

$$\lambda_K \geqslant \alpha_K \qquad K=1,...,L$$

The links are numbered such that

$$\alpha_1 \geqslant \alpha_2 \geqslant \cdots \geqslant \alpha_L$$

In words, the constraints $\{\alpha_K, K=1,...,L\}$ that we are given are due to our desire to make sure each link carries at least a given *minimum* amount of traffic. Put differently, we have a type of *routing* constraint on our traffic, usually for economic reasons. If we wish to minimize the mean queueing time, then it can be shown that

$$\lambda_1 = \lambda_{total} - \sum\limits_{J=2}^{L} \alpha_J \qquad \lambda_K = \alpha_K \qquad K=2,...,L$$

or in other words, we wish to put all of the load on that link that we wish to carry the most messages!

7.4.3 General Network, Constraint on Maximum Transmission Capacity Our third example consists of a network with N ports, and a given offered point to point load of γ_{IJ} messages per second, I,J=1,...,N. This is shown in the figure below. The message arrival statistics are simple Poisson. The message lengths are independent identically distributed exponential random variables with mean B bits per message. The network contains L links, with each link carrying a load of λ_K, K=1,...,L messages per second. We see that the total offered message load is

$$\gamma_{total} = \sum\limits_{I=1}^{N} \sum\limits_{J=1}^{N} \gamma_{IJ}$$

while the total message link load is

$$\lambda_{total} = \sum\limits_{K=1}^{L} \lambda_K$$

From our definitions, we see that the ratio of these two quantities is the mean number of links that a message will traverse inside the network:

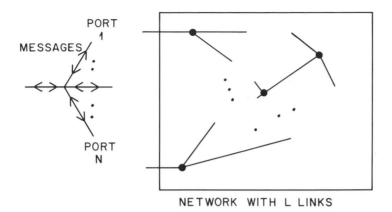

Figure 7.15.General Network with N Ports and L Links

$$\textit{mean number of links traversed per message} = \frac{\lambda_{total}}{\gamma_{total}}$$

Each of the links has a transmission capacity of $C_K, K=1,...,L$ bits per second, and thus we wish to define a quantity analogous to total network link utilization:

$$\sigma = \frac{B\gamma_{total}}{\sum\limits_{K=1}^{L} C_K}$$

We will require $\sigma < 1$ in order for all of the links to keep up with the message load. The total mean queueing time is given by

$$E(T_Q) = \sum_{K=1}^{L} \frac{\lambda_K}{\gamma_{total}} \frac{B}{C_K - B\lambda_K}$$

If we rewrite this as follows

$$E(T_Q) = \frac{\lambda_{total}}{\gamma_{total}} \sum_{K=1}^{L} \frac{\lambda_K}{\lambda_{total}} \frac{B}{C_K - B\lambda_K}$$

and since we are minimizing *exactly* the same function as we did in the second and first examples up to an multiplicative constant, the optimum assignment of excess capacity again obeys a square root proportionality rule:

$$C_{K,opt} = \frac{\lambda_K}{\mu} + C_{excess} \frac{\sqrt{B\lambda_K}}{\sum\limits_{J=1}^{L} \sqrt{B\lambda_J}} \qquad K=1,...,L$$

where

$$C_{excess} = \sum_{K=1}^{L} C_K - B\lambda_{total}$$

while the minimum mean queueing time for messages is given by

$$\min E(T_Q) = \frac{B\lambda_{total}/\gamma_{total} \left[\sum_{K=1}^{L} \sqrt{\lambda_K/\lambda_{total}}\right]^2}{\sum_{K=1}^{L} C_K - (\lambda_{total}/\gamma_{total})\gamma_{total}} > \frac{B}{\sum_{K=1}^{L} C_K - B\lambda_{total}}$$

In words, this suggests that we look for paths that involve the shortest paths through the network, in order to minimize both the mean number of hops traversed per message but also the mean queueing time per message.

7.4.4 General Network, Cost Constraint on Transmission Capacity   We can extend this third example by allowing a cost, say dollars per unit of transmission capacity (dollars per bits per second), denoted by D_K for link K, and we wish to keep the total dollar cost for the network below a given maximum, say D_{max}:

$$\sum_{K=1}^{L} D_K C_K = D \leqslant D_{max}$$

Proceeding as we did in the third example, we see that the assignment of transmission capacity that minimizes the total mean dollar cost is given by a square root assignment of the offered load, weighted by the dollar cost:

$$\min E(T_Q) = \frac{\lambda_{total}}{\gamma_{total}} \sum_{K=1}^{L} \frac{\lambda_K}{\lambda_{total}} \frac{B}{\sum_{J=1}^{L} C_J - B\lambda_K}$$

$$C_{K,opt} = B\lambda_K + \frac{D_{excess}}{D_K} \frac{\sqrt{B\lambda_K D_K}}{\sum_{J=1}^{L} \sqrt{B\lambda_J D_J}}$$

$$D_{excess} = \sum_{K=1}^{L} D_K - \sum_{K=1}^{L} D_K B\lambda_K$$

7.4.5 Tree Network, Constraint on Maximum Transmission Capacity, Two Types of Links   Our fifth and final example is a tree network, as shown in the figure below. This figure shows the mean message arrival rate from each port; since the network is a tree, this defines the point to point offered load. All messages have a mean length of 120 bits. The total transmission capacity available is 4500 bits per second. The table below summarizes the carried link load, the optimum assignment of transmission capacity assuming transmission capacity is available in units of bits per second, as well as the optimum assignment assuming only two speed links are available, 450 bit per second

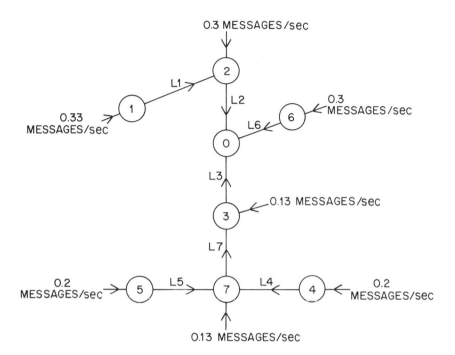

Figure 7.16. An Illustrative Tree Network

links and 900 bit per second links:

Table 7.2. Tree Network Link Load and Capacity Assignment

K	λ_K	$C_{K,opt}$	$C_{K,discrete}$
1	0.33 messages/sec	576 bits/sec	450 bits/sec
2	0.63 messages/sec	819 bits/sec	900 bits/sec
3	0.66 messages/sec	842 bits/sec	900 bits/sec
4	0.20 messages/sec	441 bits/sec	450 bits/sec
5	0.20 messages/sec	441 bits/sec	450 bits/sec
6	0.30 messages/sec	638 bits/sec	450 bits/sec
7	0.53 messages/sec	743 bits/sec	900 bits/sec

The mean queueing delay for the two networks is

$$E(T_Q|optimum) = 0.333 \; seconds \qquad E(T_Q|discrete) = 0.390 \; seconds$$

The penalty paid in having only two speeds of data links available appears to be quite reasonable for the numbers chosen here.

7.4.6 Additional Reading

[1]   L.Kleinrock, **Communications Nets: Stochastic Message Flow and Delay,**
      McGraw Hill, NY, 1964; reprinted, Dover, NY, 1972.

[2]   L.Kleinrock, *Analytic and Simulation Methods in Computer Network
      Design,* AFIPS Spring 1970 Joint Computer Conference, pp.569-579
      (1970).

[3]   S.Lin, B.W.Kernighan, *An Effective Heuristic Algorithm for the
      Traveling Salesman Problem,* Operations Research, **21** (2), 498-516
      (1973).

[4]   S.Lin, *Effective Use of Heuristic Algorithms in Network Design,*
      Proceedings Symposium on Applied Mathematics, **26,** 63-84, American
      Mathematical Society, Providence, RI, 1982.

7.5 A Circuit Switching System

Some important ingredients in a node in a circuit switching system are

- A switching network

- A controller that governs access to the switching network

- A set of receivers that process messages or calls before connection is
  completed

- A controller for governing receiver access

Each call on arrival must find a path through the switching network to an idle
receiver; if no path is available, a decision is made concerning further call
processing. Each call temporarily requires a receiver for message and call
handling services; if no receiver is available, the system decides what
subsequent action is required for that call.

Here a highly simplified tractable model of such a system is studied to gain
insight into performance limitations and shed light on difficulties in extending
analysis to more realistic switching systems.

It is assumed that each call on arrival must be assigned to one of S channels or
paths or links; if no channel is available, the call is blocked or cleared from the
system, and presumably will retry later. Once a call is accepted, it holds a link
and then requires a receiver; if no receiver is available, calls queue until a
receiver is available. Our goal is to determine the *capacity* of the switching
system, which is the *joint* choice of number of links and receivers that allows
the largest possible mean completion rate of calls while still meeting call set up
delay goals. Our purpose is to show that one cannot *independently* choose the
number of links and receivers to achieve a desired capacity, i.e., these numbers
are *coupled.* In fact, we show it is possible to jointly choose the number of

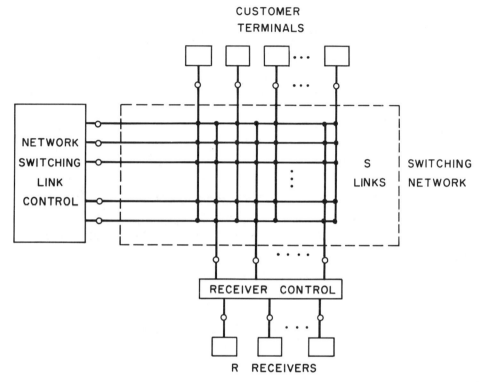

Figure 7.17.Circuit Switching System Hardware Block Diagram

links and receivers to achieve capacity superior to that when each is chosen separately; depending upon numbers and application, this may be significant.

7.5.1 Model Description The model ingredients are

- the admissible set of states comprising the state space

- the arrival process

- the resources required at each stage of execution

- a policy for handling contention for resources

The state of the system at any instant of time is given by an ordered pair *(I,J)*, where the first component *I* denotes the number of calls in the set up stage and the second component *J* denotes the number of calls in the talking stage.

$$0 \leqslant I + J \leqslant S \quad I,J \in \{0,1,...,S\}$$

The arrival statistics of calls are assumed to be Poisson, i.e., the sequence of interarrival times of calls are independent exponentially distributed random variables, with mean arrival rate λ.

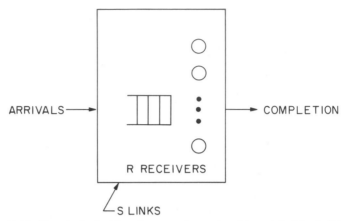

Figure 7.18.Circuit Switching System Queueing Network Block Diagram

The first step of call set up involves holding a link and a receiver for a mean time interval denoted by $T_{control}$. The second step of talking involves holding a link for a mean time interval denoted by T_{talk}.

The space of admissible states is denoted by Ω, where

$$\Omega = \bigcup_{K=0}^{S} \Omega_K$$

where Ω_K denotes the state where there are a total of K calls in the system in both set up and talking:

$$\Omega_K = \{(I,J)\,|\,0 \leqslant I,J \leqslant S, I + J = K\}$$

7.5.2 Mean Value Analysis At any instant of time, the mean number of receivers busy with call set up is

$$\lambda_{accepted}\,T_{control} = E[min(R,I)]$$

The mean number of links or trunks busy with call set up or talking is

$$\lambda_{accepted}\,(T_{control}+T_{talk}) = E[min(S,J)]$$

The mean throughput rate is upper bounded by

$$\lambda_{accepted} \leqslant min\left[\frac{R}{T_{control}}, \frac{S}{T_{control}+T_{talk}}\right]$$

Two bottlenecks arise here.

- If receivers are the bottleneck, then

$$\lambda_{accepted} = \frac{R}{T_{control}}$$

- If links are the bottleneck, then

$$\lambda_{accepted} = \frac{S}{T_{control} + T_{talk}}$$

For voice telephony, $T_{talk} \gg T_{control}$, and we can engineer either links or receivers to be the bottleneck, with receivers engineered according to call set up statistics, and links engineered according to call holding time or talking statistics. For data, $T_{talk} \approx T_{control}$, and there will be very strong coupling between the control and link subsystems.

7.5.3 Jackson Network Analysis Given the previous assumptions, the fraction of time the system is in state (I,J), averaged over a suitably long time interval, denoted by $\pi(I,J)$, is given by

$$\pi(i,j) = \frac{1}{G} \prod_{K=0}^{I} \frac{\lambda T_{control}}{\Phi_{rec}(K)} \prod_{M=0}^{J} \frac{\lambda T_{talk}}{\Phi_{trunk}(M)}$$

$$\Phi_{rec}(K) = \begin{cases} 1 & K=0 \\ min(R,K) & K>0 \end{cases}$$

$$\Phi_{trunk}(K) = \begin{cases} 1 & K=0 \\ min(S,K) & K>0 \end{cases}$$

7.5.4 Long Term Time Averaged Blocking The fraction of time that an arriving call finds all S links occupied and is cleared or blocked from entering the system is called the blocking probability, denoted by *B*. There are two different approaches for calculating blocking probability. The first approach involves calculating the fraction of time the system has all S links occupied (either with call set up or talking)

$$B = \sum_{(I,J) \in \Omega_s} \pi(I,J) = \frac{G_S}{G}$$

$$G_K = \sum_{(I,J) \in \Omega_K} \prod_{M=0}^{I} \frac{\lambda T_{control}}{\Phi_{rec}(M)} \prod_{N=0}^{J} \frac{\lambda T_{talk}}{\Phi_{trunk}(N)} \quad 0 \leqslant K \leqslant S \quad G \equiv \sum_{k=0}^{S} G_k$$

An alternate approach equates the rate at which calls are accepted into the system to the rate at which calls leave the system:

$$\lambda(1 - B) = call\ acceptance\ rate$$

$$\sum_{(I,J) \in \Omega} \frac{J}{T_{talk}} \pi(I,J) = call\ completion\ rate$$

The fraction of time a call is blocked depends upon *all* model parameters and not simply on just the number of links.

7.5.5 Long Term Time Averaged Waiting Time Distribution Let $\pi_{accept}(I,J)$ denote the fraction of time that the system is in state (I,J) and an arriving call is accepted. From earlier definitions, this is given by

$$\pi_{accept}(I,J) = \frac{\pi(I,J)}{1-B} = \frac{1}{(1-B)G_{accept}} \prod_{M=0}^{I} \frac{\lambda T_{rec}}{\Phi_{rec}(M)} \prod_{N=0}^{J} \frac{\lambda T_{talk}}{\Phi_{trunk}(N)} \quad (I,J) \in \Omega_{accept}$$

$$\Omega_{accept} = \bigcup_{K=0}^{S-1} \Omega_K \qquad G_{accept} = \sum_{(I,J) \in \Omega_{accept}} \prod_{M=0}^{I} \frac{\lambda T_{rec}}{\Phi_{rec}(M)} \prod_{N=0}^{J} \frac{\lambda T_{talk}}{\Phi_{trunk}(N)}$$

Let $\pi(I)$ denote the marginal distribution of $p_{accept}(I,J)$:

$$\pi(I) = \sum_{j=0}^{S-1-I} p_{accept}(I,J) \quad 0 \leqslant I \leqslant S-1$$

The random variable T_W denotes the time interval from when an accepted call arrives until it is first attached or assigned a receiver. Recall that calls are processed in order of arrival. If $(R-1)$ or fewer receivers are busy, the accepted call does not wait at all:

$$PROB[T_W=0] = \begin{cases} \sum_{I=0}^{R-1} \pi(I) & R<S \\ 0 & R=S \end{cases}$$

The probability that an accepted calls waits greater than $T>0$ to start receiver processing is given by

$$PROB[T_W>T>0] = \begin{cases} \sum_{I=0}^{R-1} \pi(I) + \sum_{I=R}^{S-1} \pi(I) \left[\frac{R}{R+zT_{rec}} \right]^{I-R+1} & R<S \\ 1 & R=S \end{cases}$$

The total call set up delay, denoted T_Q, is the sum of the waiting time plus the receiver processing time:

$$T_Q = T_W + T_{rec}$$

$$E[exp(-zT_Q)] = \frac{1}{1+zT_{rec}} E[exp(-zT_W)]$$

From Little's Law or by differentiation of this expression and evaluating it at $z=0$ we see that

$$\lambda(1-B)E(T_Q) = \sum_{I=0}^{S} \sum_{J=0}^{S-I} I\pi(I,J)$$

7.5.6 Capacity Determination Given R receivers, S links, with mean set up time T_{rec} and mean call talking time T_{talk}, the problem is to find the *largest* mean arrival rate λ such that the blocking is acceptable, i.e., $B<\delta$ for some threshold δ, and the fraction of time a call waits in set up before it starts processing is acceptable, i.e.,

$$PROB[T_W > T] < \epsilon$$

7.5.7 Asymptotics Before studying system behavior numerically, we want to see how the system behaves asymptotically as various parameters become large, to get further insight.

One way to study behavior under an external overload is to allow $\lambda \to \infty$. In practice, during overload the arrival statistics might change as customer behavior changes due to impatience or retries, as well as for other reasons.

As $\lambda \to \infty$ we see that the long term time averaged distribution becomes concentrated in the states where all S links are always busy (as soon as a call completes, another is ready to seize the link):

$$\lim_{\lambda \to \infty} \pi(I,J) = \begin{cases} 0 & I+J < S \\ \tilde{\pi}(I,J) & I+J = S \end{cases}$$

$$\tilde{\pi}(I,J) = \frac{1}{\tilde{G}} \prod_{M=0}^{I} \frac{T_{rec}}{\Phi_{rec}(M)} \prod_{N=0}^{J} \frac{T_{talk}}{\Phi_{trunk}(N)} \quad (I,J) \in \Omega_S$$

As the arrival rate becomes infinite, the blocking approaches one, i.e., virtually all calls are blocked:

$$B = 1 - \frac{\lambda_{\max}}{\lambda} + \cdots \lambda \to \infty$$

The mean throughput rate of calls is given by

$$mean\ call\ throughput\ rate = \lim_{\lambda \to \infty} [\lambda(1-B)] = \lambda_{\max} = \min \left[\frac{R}{T_{rec}}, \frac{S}{T_{talk} + T_{rec}} \right]$$

For the case where R=S we see that

$$\lambda_{\max} = \frac{S}{T_{talk}} \frac{1}{\dfrac{1}{T_{rec}} + \dfrac{1}{T_{talk}}} \quad R=S$$

In fact, it is also possible for the interaction between links and receivers to limit the maximum mean call completion rate below either of these upper bounds. Because the network or links are used for two purposes, control or call set up and talking or data transfer, it is possible for $\lambda_{\max}$ to be less than S/T_{talk} which would be the limit due to links being a bottleneck.

If the number of receivers is fixed and small, while the number of links is so large that calls rarely are blocked, then for all intents the number of links is infinite. For this case, two regimes arise:

- $R/T_{rec} \leqslant \lambda$ and hence $\lambda_{\max} = R/T_{rec}$, receivers are always busy executing calls

- $R/T_{rec}>\lambda$, receivers can keep up with arriving calls, and the distribution for number of calls in the system is given by manipulations of the earlier expressions (Do this as an exercise!)

The mean waiting time is given by

$$E(T_W) = \frac{C(R,\lambda T_{rec})}{R - \lambda T_{rec}} \, T_{rec}$$

For light loading, $\lambda T_{rec} \ll 1$, the mean waiting time goes to zero. For heavy loading, $\lambda T_{rec} \to R$, the mean waiting time exceeds any finite threshold. Furthermore, the above expression is an *upper* bound on the actual mean waiting time, because for an infinite number of trunks all arrivals are accepted, which can lead to greater waiting than if some arrivals are rejected and this is a finite number of calls waiting.

7.5.8 Telephone Call Switching   The table below is a summary of capacity, chosen such that the blocking of calls occurs less than one per cent of the time and the fraction of time a call waits for a receiver exceeding three seconds occurs less than one per cent of the time:

$$B < \epsilon=0.01 \quad PROB[T_W>3 \ seconds] < \delta=0.01$$

For point of comparison, the case where receivers are infinitely fast is included to show how far off capacity can be:

Table 7.3. Capacity (Voice Telephone Calls/Hr)

Links(S)	$\gamma=0$	R=1	R=2	R=3	R=4	R=5
5	24.7	5.0	21.6	24.0	24.0	24.0
10	80.3	5.0	72.0	78.0	79.0	79.0
15	145.8	5.0	72.0	145.0	145.0	145.0
20	216.4	5.0	72.0	214.0	216.0	216.0
25	290.7	5.0	72.0	260.0	330.0	335.0
30	366.3	5.0	72.0	265.0	330.0	335.0
35	443.7	5.0	72.0	265.0	385.0	426.0
40	522.4	5.0	72.0	265.0	385.0	498.0
45	603.0	5.0	72.0	265.0	385.0	566.0
50	682.2	5.0	72.0	265.0	385.0	599.0

Note that if the actual arrival rate becomes greater than the maximum capacity, performance drops off much faster for large S than for small S. For example, with R=1, when S=2,3,4, doubling the mean arrival rate from 24 to 48 calls per hour results in blocking probability not simply doubling, but increasing by 2.6, 3.6, 6.1 and 10.1 respectively.

In certain cases a graph allows one to assess performance sensitivity to different parameter values more readily than using tables of numbers. The figures below plot the probability of blocking, the mean throughput rate, and the probability of waiting greater than three seconds, for one to ten links and one or two receivers. We have chosen parameters typical of those found in voice telephony: a mean set up or dialing time of ten seconds, and a mean call holding or talking time of two hundred seconds.

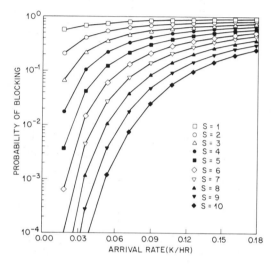

Figure 7.19. Blocking vs Mean Arrival Rate(R = 1)

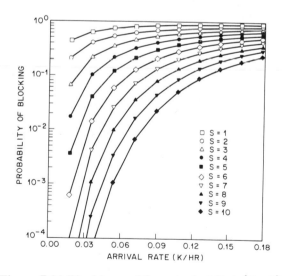

Figure 7.20. Blocking vs Mean Arrival Rate(R = 2)

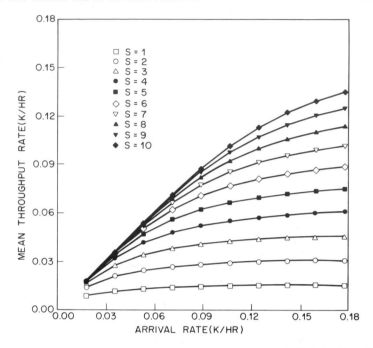

Figure 7.21.Mean Throughput Rate vs Mean Arrival Rate(R = 1)

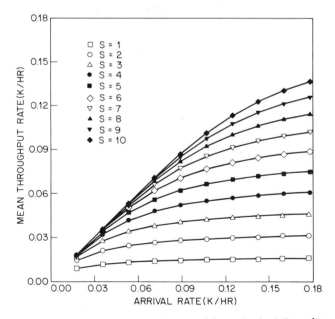

Figure 7.22.Mean Throughput Rate vs Mean Arrival Rate(R = 2)

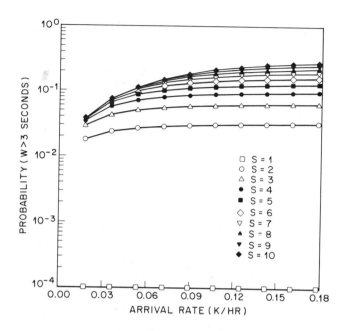

Figure 7.23.PROB[$T_W > 3$] vs Mean Arrival Rate(R = 1)

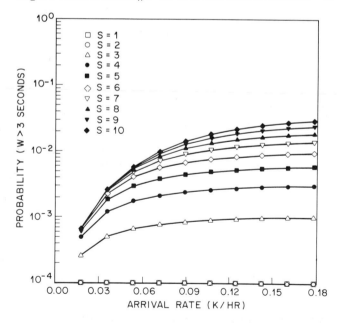

Figure 7.24.PROB[$T_W > 3$] vs Mean Arrival Rate(R = 2)

Several observations can be made based on inspection of these figures:

- For a fixed mean arrival rate, the blocking decreases as the number of links increases. The ninetieth percentile of the waiting time distribution also increases as the number of links increases. This implies there is a subset of values of S (possibly an empty set!) such that for each given mean arrival rate, a given criterion on blocking and waiting time percentile is met.

- For fixed mean arrival rate, blocking is insensitive to choosing the number of receivers, while the waiting time percentiles are *very* sensitive to choosing *both* R and S. This shows that it is **not** straightforward to design the number of links and receivers by studying two limiting cases where receivers are infinitely fast ($1/\gamma=0$) for sizing the number of links and where links are plentiful ($S=\infty$) to size waiting time performance for choosing number of receivers.

7.5.9 Data Transmission Circuit Switching How will this system perform if it must circuit switch data rather than voice? We have simply changed the mean set up time from ten seconds to one second ($\gamma=1$) and the mean holding time from two hundred seconds to one second ($\mu=1$). Performance here means guaranteeing that the probability of waiting does not exceed one second more than ten per cent of the time, while the mean throughput rate is ninety per cent of the offered load, i.e., ten per cent of the arrivals are blocked.

$$PROB[T_W>1 \ second] < \delta = 0.1 \quad B < \epsilon=0.1$$

Note the very strong coupling between performance or capacity and the *joint* choice of R and S, as shown in the table below:

Table 7.4.Capacity(Data Calls per Hour)

Links(S)	$\gamma=0$	R=1	R=2	R=3	R=4	R=5
1	360	200	200	200	200	200
2	2160	760	1050	1100	1100	1100
3	4500	770	2500	2500	2500	2500
4	7280	780	3400	3500	3550	3550
5	10440	800	3800	5000	5200	5250
6	13680	800	3900	6400	6600	6800
7	16920	800	3900	7500	8050	8300
8	20160	800	3900	8300	9500	10000
9	23760	800	3900	8300	11000	11500
10	27180	800	3900	8300	12000	12400

The figures below plot the mean throughput rate, the probability of waiting more than one second, and the fraction of calls blocked:

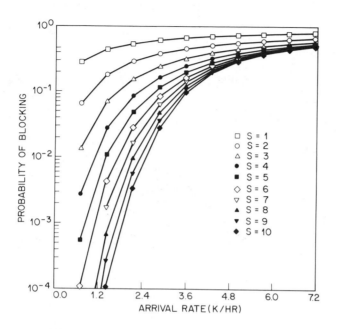

Figure 7.25.Blocking vs Mean Arrival Rate(R = 1)

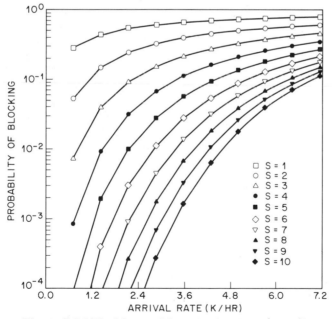

Figure 7.26.Blocking vs Mean Arrival Rate(R = 2)

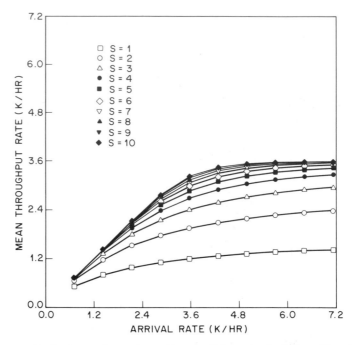

Figure 7.27.Mean Throughput Rate vs Mean Arrival Rate(R = 1)

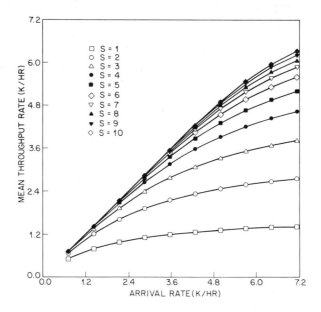

Figure 7.28.Mean Throughput Rate vs Mean Arrival Rate(R = 2)

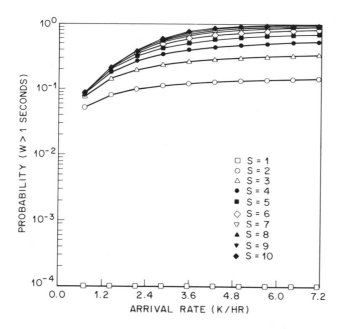

Figure 7.29.PROB[$T_W > 1$] vs Mean Arrival Rate(R = 1)

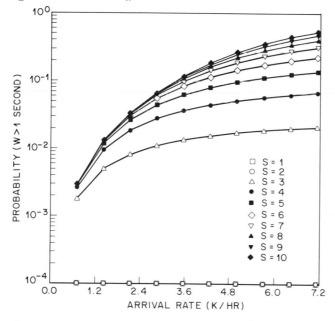

Figure 7.30.PROB[$T_W > 1$] vs Mean Arrival Rate(R = 2)

7.6 Digital Circuit Switching

Voice telephone systems employ circuit switching: at the start of each call, all of the required resources (links and switching system buffers) are allocated for the duration of the call, and otherwise the call attempt is rejected or blocked. Current voice telephony requires 64 kilobits per second of transmission capacity per telephone call from one person to another; computers and terminals require many other data rates, such as multiples of 300 bits per second, as well as many other rates. How many links are required, with what data rate for each link, connected to how many switching systems, in order to handle a given workload with a given acceptable level of performance? Jackson networks are a step in the direction of answering questions like these. Sometimes, it is possible to have *zero* blocking; this is a baseline case which we wish to compare against allowing *some* blocking. Often, for economic reasons, it may be possible to engineer a system with a *small* amount of blocking that costs less to manufacture and operate than a system with *zero* blocking. How much less depends on the designer and available technology!

7.6.1 *Additional Reading*

[1]   C.Clos, *A Study of Non-Blocking Switching Networks,* Bell System Technical Journal, **32,** 406-424 (1953).

[2]   A.A.Collins, R.D.Pedersen, **Telecommunications: A Time for Innovation,** Merle Collins Foundation, Dallas, Texas, 1973.

[3]   T.Feng, *A Survey of Interconnection Networks,* Computer, **14** (12), 12-27 (1981).

7.6.2 An Illustrative Digital Circuit Switching System   Figure 7.31 is an illustrative block diagram of a digital circuit switching system.

One terminal inputs bits to a digital circuit switching system via *input link 1.* Eventually the bits should reach another terminal, that receives bits on *output link L.* The sending terminal can transmit one chunk of bits at a regularly spaced time interval called a *frame.* For simplicity, the input link and output link frame periods are assumed identical, for example 125 μseconds, or 8000 times a second. The input chunks are transmitted in time intervals called *slots* because time is multiplexed, one chunk per slot. In the example shown, terminal two inputs bits during time slot five over link 1. The switch must send these bits out on link L for terminal four during time slot three. How does it do this?

In the example shown here, there are two special purpose hardware subsystems that accomplish this switching function. The first subsystem is called a *time slot interchanger* because it interchanges the time slots that bits come in on and go out on: in the example, bits in time slot five go out in time slot seven. How might this be implemented? the input bits during one frame might be

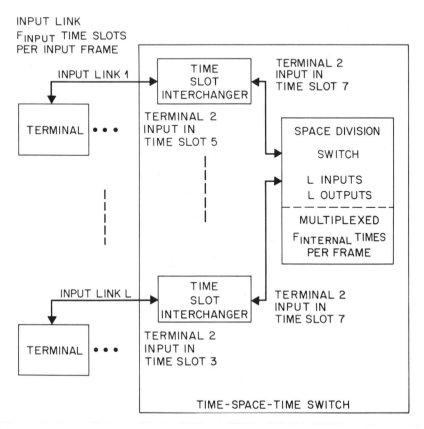

Figure 7.31.Digital Circuit Switching System

stored in one memory location of the time slot interchanger, and are output one frame later. At the start of a circuit session, a set of pointers are initialized in a table, showing which bits in which memory locations are to be input and output. Similarly, bits in time slot seven go out on time slot three via a second time slot interchanger. This requires that the time slot interchanger buffer two frames worth of bits, one for receiving while the second is used for transmitting. In other words, circuit switching employs a very limited amount of buffering, compared to packet switching: enough to buffer one input frame and one output frame. The other special purpose piece of hardware is a space division switch, which consists of L input links and L output links. The input from terminal two in time slot seven goes into the switch on one link during one time slot, and comes out another link on another time slot, with the internal switch multiplexing time slots at $F_{internal}$ frames per second, which must equal or exceed F_{link}. Putting it all together, bits go in from one terminal on one time slot and come out on the other terminal on another time slot. The purpose in using either a time slot interchanger or a space division switch is to get greater connectivity between the terminals than either alone might provide: it may well be that certain patterns of bits going in and coming out, with the space division switch alone, make it *impossible* to connect all inputs to all outputs. The purpose of using the space division switch is to get even greater connectivity than would be possible with just time slot interchangers. Finally, this pattern can be repeated, to allow building multiple stage switching systems out of these basic building blocks.

There are three types of bottlenecks here:

- The transmission capacity of the input link is completely utilized

- The transmission capacity of the time slot interchanger or time division switch is completely utilized

- The transmission capacity of the output link is completely utilized

A related phenomenon here arises from variable bandwidth switching. Digital circuit switching involves assigning a variable number of time slots (e.g., twice as many for a 9.6 KBPS source as for a 4.8 KBPS source), and then rearranging these time slots via time slot interchangers and space division switches to connect the appropriate inputs to the appropriate outputs. Two types of phenomena arise:

- *External* fragmentation, where the number of available time slots per frame is exceeded by the number of competing demands

- *Internal* fragmentation, where a demand requires fewer time slots per request than the system can actually assign (e.g., an attempt demands one time slot per frame but the system requires that two time slots per frame be assigned)

We assume that the internal fragmentation is negligible from this point on, and focus only on external fragmentation or blocking of attempts. Our goal is to quantify performance of such systems, starting from simple examples and building up to more complex cases.

7.6.3 One Input Link, One Output Link Time Slot Interchanger   To begin with, suppose we had one input link and one output link, with no time slot interchanger. Each link has S slots per frame. The state is given by the pair (J,K) where J denotes the number of calls up on the input link and K denotes the number of calls up on the output link; each call is assumed to require one time slot per frame. We assume that the interarrival times of calls are independent identically distributed exponential random variables with mean arrival rate λ. The sequence of call holding times are independent identically distributed random variables drawn from an arbitrary distribution with mean T_{active}. Granted all these assumptions, the long term time averaged fraction of time the system is in state (J,K), denoted by $\pi(J,K)$, is given by

$$\pi(J,K) = \frac{1}{G^2} \frac{(\lambda T_{active})^{J+K}}{J!K!} \qquad J,K=0,...,S$$

$$G = \sum_{L=0}^{S} \frac{(\lambda T_{active})^L}{L!}$$

If there is no time slot interchanger, then the time slot on the input link is identical to the time slot on the output link. The long term time averaged fraction of time a call is blocked is thus given by

$$fraction\ of\ time\ call\ blocked = \frac{1}{G^2} \sum_{J=0}^{S} \sum_{K=S-J}^{S} \frac{\begin{pmatrix} J \\ S-K \end{pmatrix}}{\begin{pmatrix} S \\ S-K \end{pmatrix}} \frac{(\lambda T_{active})^{J+K}}{J!K!}$$

which can be rewritten in terms of Erlang's blocking function $B(S,A)$ as

$$fraction\ of\ time\ call\ blocked = B(S,A)[S+1-A(1-B(S,A))] \qquad A = \lambda T_{active}$$

For numbers of practical interest, $B(S,A) <\!< 1$ and thus

$$fraction\ of\ time\ call\ blocked \approx B(S,A)[S+1-A] \qquad B(S,A) <\!< 1$$

which is $S+1-A$ larger than designing the system based solely on the input links or output links blocking!

7.6.4 Example If the offered load is eight Erlangs per link, we need eight time slots per frame to handle the load, based on a mean value analysis, with complete link utilization. If we desire blocking to occur no more than one call in a hundred, averaged over a suitably long time interval, then eighteen or more time slots per frame per link are required, and the maximum link utilization is four ninths. On the other hand, $B(S=18, A=8)$ is roughly one in one thousand, i.e., the total system blocking could be low by a factor of ten if the interaction between the input and output links is ignored.

What a time slot interchanger is added? Now the long term time averaged fraction of time a call is blocked is

$$fraction\ of\ time\ call\ blocked = B(S,A)[2-B(S,A)] \qquad A = \lambda T_{active}$$

and thus the relative gain in blocking in using a time slot interchanger versus not using it is

$$\frac{blocking\ with\ no\ time\ slot\ interchanger}{blocking\ with\ time\ slot\ interchanger} = 1 + \frac{S-1-A+(A+1)B(S,A)}{2-B(S,A)}$$

$$\approx 1 + \frac{S+1-A}{2} \qquad B(S,A) << 1$$

which can be calculated numerically for a given application. Here the relative gain for $A=8, S=18$ is 6.5.

7.6.5 Sensitivity Analysis How robust are these findings to a change in certain underlying assumptions? For example, what if we change the arrival statistics? N sources can be in one of two states, idle (where no circuit bandwidth is required) and active (which requires one time slot). The mean time in each state is denoted by T_{idle} and T_{active}. Then with no time slot interchanger, the fraction of time the system is in state (J,K) is given by

$$\pi(J,K) = \begin{bmatrix} S \\ J \end{bmatrix} \begin{bmatrix} S \\ K \end{bmatrix} \left[P \equiv \frac{T_{active}}{T_{idle}+T_{active}} \right]^{J+K} \left[1 - P \equiv \frac{T_{idle}}{T_{idle}+T_{active}} \right]^{2S-J-K}$$

The long term time averaged fraction of blocked call attempts with no time slot interchanger is

$$\textit{fraction of time call blocked} = [P(2-P)]^{S-1}$$

With a time slot interchanger, the blocking is given by

$$\textit{fraction of time a call blocked} = ENG(S, A=SP)[2 - ENG(S, A=SP)]$$

where $ENG(S, A=SP)$ is the Engset blocking formula* given by

$$ENG(S, A=SP) = \frac{\displaystyle\sum_{M \in \Omega_{BLOCK}} \pi(M)[N-M]}{\displaystyle\sum_{M \in \Omega} \pi(M)[N-M]}$$

where Ω and Ω_{BLOCK} are the sets of total admissible states and blocking states, respectively.

7.6.6 Variable Bandwidth Traffic Time Slot Interchanger What if not one time slot per frame is required but rather R time slots per frame? Given J time slots occupied on the input link and K time slots occupied on the output link, we see

---

* Named in honor of the voice telephone traffic engineer who pioneered this type of analysis.

$$\pi[R \; TIME \; SLOTS \; AVAILABLE \,|(J,K)] = \frac{\begin{pmatrix} S-K \\ R \end{pmatrix} \begin{pmatrix} K \\ J-R \end{pmatrix}}{\begin{pmatrix} S \\ J \end{pmatrix}}$$

For example, we see

$$fraction \; of \; time \; call \; blocked[I\,|J,K]$$

$$= \sum_{M=0}^{I-1} \frac{\begin{pmatrix} S-K \\ S-K-M \end{pmatrix} \begin{pmatrix} K \\ J+M+K-S \end{pmatrix}}{\begin{pmatrix} S \\ S-J \end{pmatrix}}$$

is the fraction of time that I or fewer time slots are available between source J and destination K, and hence

$$fraction \; of \; time \; call \; blocked\,(I)$$

$$= \sum_{J=0}^{S} \sum_{K=0}^{S} \pi(J,K) fraction \; of \; time \; call \; blocked[I\,|J,K]$$

is the long term fraction of requests demanding I time slots are blocked, averaged over all inputs and outputs. If the input offered load is A_{input} Erlangs per line, and the output offered load is A_{output} Erlangs per line, then

$$\pi(J,K) = \frac{(A_{input}^{J}/J!)\,(A_{output}^{K}/K!)}{\sum_{P=0}^{S} \sum_{Q=0}^{S} (A_{input}^{P}/P!)\,(A_{output}^{Q}/Q!)}$$

EXERCISE: Numerically explore the parameter space for $S=24$, $T_{idle}=300 \; sec$, $T_{active}=100 \; sec$.

7.6.7 L Input Links, L Output Links, One Time Slot Interchanger Next we allow blocking at either an input link, a time slot interchanger, or an output link. L input links are connected to a time slot interchanger capable of supporting M simultaneous calls with L output links. State is specified by (I,J,K) where I is the number of input links and J the number of output links handling calls requiring K time slots per frame. The interarrival times for each call type form a sequence of independent identically distributed exponential random variables, with mean rate given by $\lambda(I,J,K)$. The sequence of holding times are independent identically distributed random variables, $T_{active}(I,J,K)$, drawn from an arbitrary distribution. The admissible state space is denoted by Ω. Different policies for operating links and switches will determine different admissible state spaces. The set of blocking states is denoted by $\Omega_{BLOCK}(K)$.

$$\Omega = \{N(I,J,K)\,|0 \leqslant N(I,J,K) \leqslant S-K; 1 \leqslant I,J \leqslant L\}$$

$$\Omega_{BLOCK}(K) = \Omega_{BLOCK-INPUT}(K) \bigcup \Omega_{BLOCK-SWITCH}(K) \bigcup \Omega_{BLOCK-OUTPUT}(K)$$

$$\Omega_{BLOCK-INPUT}(K) = \{N(I,J,K) \mid \sum_{J=1}^{L} N(I,J,K) > S-K, 1 \leqslant I \leqslant L\}$$

$$\Omega_{BLOCK-SWITCH}(K) = \{N(I,J,K) \mid \sum_{I=1}^{L}\sum_{J=1}^{L} N(I,J,K) > M-K\}$$

$$\Omega_{BLOCK-OUTPUT}(K) = \{N(I,J,K) \mid \sum_{I=1}^{L} N(I,J,K) > S-K, 1 \leqslant J \leqslant L\}$$

The long term time averaged fraction of time the system is in state (I,J,K) is given by

$$\pi(N(I,J,K)=\nu(I,J,K)) = \frac{1}{G} \prod_{(I,J,K)\in\Omega} \frac{(\lambda(I,J,K)T_{active}(I,J,K))^{\nu(I,J,K)}}{\nu(I,J,K)!}$$

$$G = \sum_{(I,J,K)\in\Omega}\prod_{(I,J,K)\in\Omega} \frac{(\lambda(I,J,K)T_{active}(I,J,K))^{\nu(I,J,K)}}{\nu(I,J,K)!}$$

The blocking states are given by Ω_{BLOCK}, and hence

$$B = \sum_{(I,J,K)\in\Omega_{BLOCK}} \pi(N(I,J,K) = \nu(I,J,K))$$

7.6.8 Example Two classes of different types of tasks with different arrival rates and different holding times request transmission capacity.

There are a total of $N(1)$ type one sources and $N(2)$ type two sources. Each source is idle for a random time interval; the idle times are assumed to be independent identically distributed sequences of exponential random variables with mean idle time $T_{idle}(1)$ and $T_{idle}(2)$ for type one and two, respectively. When a source goes from idle to active and is not blocked, it holds a given amount of transmission capacity for a random time interval. The holding times are assuming be mutually independent sequences of independent identically distributed random variables drawn from arbitrary distributions with mean holding time $T_{active}(1)$ and $T_S(2)$ for type one and two respectively.

In order to complete the problem description, we must describe how the calls are handled upon arrival and completion. Each type of call has a dedicated amount of transmission capacity. In addition, there is a shared pool of transmission capacity. If an arrival cannot find available transmission capacity in its dedicated transmission system, it will attempt to find it in the shared pool. If an arrival cannot find the requisite capacity in either place, it is blocked or rejected from the system. Presumably at a later point it will return to retry.

The figure below shows the admissible state space for a set of 2.4 kilo bit per second and 4.8 kilo bit per second data terminals with dedicated and partially

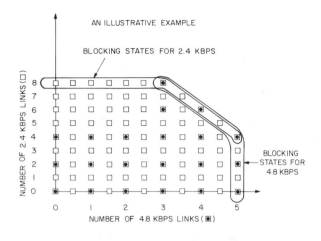

AN ILLUSTRATIVE EXAMPLE

BLOCKING STATES FOR 2.4 KBPS

NUMBER OF 2.4 KBPS LINKS (□)

NUMBER OF 4.8 KBPS LINKS (■)

BLOCKING STATES FOR 4.8 KBPS

ADMISSIBLE STATE SPACE:
9.6 KBPS DEDICATED TO 2.4 KBPS TRAFFIC
14.4 KBPS DEDICATED TO 4.8 KBPS TRAFFIC
9.6 KBPS SHARED TRANSMISSION CAPACITY

Figure 7.32.State Space of Variable Bandwidth 2.4/4.8 KBPS Switch

shared transmission capacity.

7.6.9 Mean Value Analysis Consider the following example, motivated from office communications. Two types of calls or messages are handled by a common link, voice telephony and data communications (e.g., inquiry to a set of data bases, data entry, text processing). Each voice telephone message lasts for a mean of three minutes with a total of twenty voice calls over a six hour day. Each data message lasts for a mean of forty five minutes, and there are four data sessions over a six hour business day. How many slots are required to support a given number of voice and data sessions with given blocking? Should the slots be pooled or dedicated or a mixture of these two policies?

The rough sizing for this example might go as follows: we have a transmission link capable of supporting 24 simultaneous voice calls. The offered load due to voice is 1/6 Erlang per station, and thus we can have 144 telephone stations for voice with complete loading (we must backoff from this in order to achieve lower blocking such as one per cent). The offered load due to data is 4 Erlangs per station, and thus we can assign 6 data stations with complete loading. Note that if we pooled the transmission capacity, it is possible for a small number of data terminals to lock out all the voice for very long time intervals. If we dedicated say half the transmission capacity to voice and half to data, we could support roughly 72 voice stations and three data stations, and we would engineer these separately without worrying about interactions between the two, which might be of great practical import. Finally, if the channels are in fact 64 kilobit per second channels, and each voice call requires a 64 kilobit channel while each data call requires a 2.4 kilobit per second channel, then total sharing results in 144 voice stations or 156 data terminals, while dedicating half the transmission capacity to each results in 72 voice terminals and 76 data terminals respectively. The analysis outlined earlier is a refinement of this crude sizing, and allows us to see how far off from complete utilization we must operate to have adequate service.

7.6.10 Additional Reading

[1] J.M.Aein, *A Multi-User Class, Blocked-Calls-Cleared Demand Access Model,* IEEE Transactions on Communications, **26** (3), 378-385 (1978).

[2] J.S.Kaufman, *Blocking in a Shared Resource Environment,* IEEE Transactions on Communications, **29** (10), 1474-1481 (1981).

7.6.11 Blocking with Balanced versus Unbalanced Loads
How does the effect of load balancing (each station generating the same message load equally likely to any other station) versus load imbalance impact performance?

In the figure below we show a block diagram of a switching system capable of supporting at most two simultaneous calls, and two input/output links each capable of supporting at most one call.

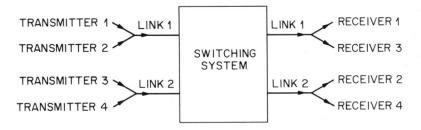

Figure 7.33.Two Input Links/One Switch/Two Output Links

The calling rate per idle source pair is $\lambda(I,J), 1 \leq I,J \leq 2$ and the mean holding time per call is $T_{active}(I,J), 1 \leq I,J \leq 2$. The state space is given by

$$\Omega = \{N(1,1), N(1,2), N(2,1), N(2,2)\} =$$

$$\{(0,0,0,0), (0,0,0,1), (0,0,1,0), (0,1,0,0),$$

$$(1,0,0,0), (1,0,0,1), (0,1,1,0)\}$$

Hence, the long term fraction of time the system is in a given state is

$$\pi(N(1,1),N(1,2),N(2,1),N(2,2)) = \frac{1}{G} \prod_{I=1}^{2}\prod_{J=1}^{2}[\lambda(I,J)\,T_{active}(I,J)]^{N(I,J)}$$

We wish to consider two cases to exhibit the phenomena here: the network offered load and the link offered load is identical, with only the routing patterns of calls different:

- Total balance

$$\lambda(I,J)\,T_{active}(I,J) = fixed \qquad 1 \leqslant I,J \leqslant 2$$

- Fifty per cent mismatch

$$\lambda(1,1)\,T_{active}(1,1) = \lambda(2,2)\,T_{active}(2,2) = (1/2)\,fixed\ constant$$

$$\lambda(1,2)\,T_{active}(1,2) = \lambda(2,1)\,T_{active}(2,1) = (3/2)\,fixed\ constant$$

The results are plotted in the figure below, and show that the heavily loaded links experience *less* blocking than the *lightly* loaded links, and bracket either side of the balanced case. This is reasonable, although perhaps at first sight counterintuitive!

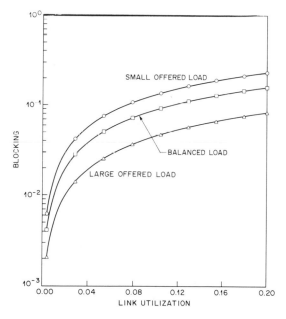

Figure 7.34.Blocking vs Balanced/Unbalanced Load

7.6.12 Variable Bandwidth Digital Circuit Switching The block diagram of the system in the figure below is slightly more general than that above, to emphasize the impact of variable bandwidth traffic on performance. The system consists of transmitters and receivers, with transmitter I sending only to receiver I, $1 \leq I \leq 5$. Each link is multiplexed with two time slots per frame, as is the circuit switch concentrator. Source three requires two time slots per call, while all other calls require one time slot per call. There are two classes of calls, those requiring one time slot per call, indexed by J, and those requiring two slots per call, indexed by K. The system state space is

$$\Omega = \{(J,K) \mid (0,0),(1,0),(0,1),(2,0)\}$$

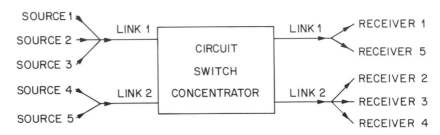

Figure 7.35. Variable Bandwidth Circuit Switch
Two time slots per frame for each link and for switch
Sources 1,2,4,5 require one time slot per call
Source 3 requires two time slots per call

The mean arrival rate of calls requiring I time slots per call is $\lambda(I)$ while the mean holding time of a call requiring I time slots is $T(I)$. The fraction of time the system is in state (J,K) is

$$\pi(J,K) = \frac{1}{G} \binom{4}{J} A(1)^J A(2)^K \quad \lambda(I)T(I) \equiv A(I) \quad (J,K) \in \Omega$$

The mean fraction of call attempts requiring one time slot that are blocked is denoted by $B(1)$ and given by

$$B(1) = \frac{4A(2)+12A(1)^2}{4+12A(1)+12A(1)^2+4A(2)}$$

which shows the interaction of the two call types. The mean fraction of call attempts requiring two time slots that are blocked is denoted by $B(2)$ and given by

$$B(2) = \frac{4A(1)+6A(1)^2}{1+4A(1)+6A(1)^2}$$

which shows that its blocking depends solely on the call statistics of single time slot calls, because only one of these can block a two time slot call. In the figure below we have chosen to fix $A(2)=0.25$ and varied $A(1)$ to illustrate how counterintuitive the blocking behavior can be: blocking *drops* for small offered loads before increasing, because some single slot traffic is blocking the two slot traffic more effectively as load increases, making it more likely for single slot attempts to be successful.

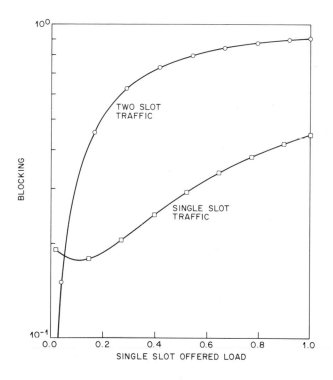

Figure 7.36. Blocking versus Low Bandwidth Offered Load

7.6.13 Additional Reading

[1] V.E.Benes, **Mathematical Theory of Connecting Networks and Telephone Traffic,** Academic Press, NY, 1965.

[2] V.E.Benes, *Programming and Control Problems Arising from Optimal Routing in Telephone Networks,* Bell System Technical Journal, **45** (9), 1373-1438 (1966).

[3] L.Katzschner, R.Scheller, *Probability of Loss of Data Traffics with Different Bit Rates Hunting One Common PCM Channel,* pp.525-1-- 525-8, Eighth International Teletraffic Conference, Melbourne, Australia, 1976.

Problems

1) Jobs arrive for execution by a system according to simple Poisson arrival statistics, mean arrival rate λ. The system consists of a group of parallel servers: once a job begins execution, it executes until finished. If all servers are busy, jobs are queued in order of arrival. The maximum mean throughput rate of executing jobs with J jobs in the system (waiting and executing) can be written as the product of two terms, one speed dependent and the other state dependent:

maximum mean throughput rate $= R \; \Phi(J)$

A. Suppose the system consists of P processors, so that

$$\Phi(J) = min[J,P]$$

Calculate the partial derivative of the total job mean delay with respect to R. Evaluate this for $R=0.5, 1.0, 2.0$. Do you see a pattern?

B. Suppose the system consists of a drum with B blocks per track and a rotational period of T seconds, so that

$$R = \frac{1}{T} \quad \Phi(J) = \frac{2 \, J \, B}{2 \, J + B - 1}$$

Calculate the partial derivative of the total job mean delay with respect to R. Evaluate this for $R=0.5, 1.0, 2.0$. Do you see a pattern?

2) Two processors and two memories share a common bus. On its Kth memory access a processor will retrieve data in M_K sequential locations in memory, starting at address A_K and going through address A_K+M_K-1. The processor executes this data and then repeats this memory fetch process. The memory addresses are assumed to be *interleaved* among the memory modules: memory fetches are made first from one module, then the other, then the first and so on.

The system state at any instant is given by a pair (I,J) where I refers to the number of processors accessing memory module one and J refers to the number of processors accessing memory module two, $I,J=1,2$. We denote by $\pi(I,J)$ the fraction of time, averaged over a suitably long time interval, that the system is in a given state.

A. If the mean number of memory locations fetched per access is $E(M)$ show

$$\pi(0,2) = \pi(2,0) = \frac{1}{2 + E(M)} \quad \pi(1,1) = \frac{E(M)}{2 + E(M)}$$

B. The *unnormalized memory bandwidth* is defined as the mean number of active processors doing memory accesses. Show that this equals

$$unnormalized\ memory\ bandwidth = 2\pi(1,1) + \pi(0,2) + \pi(2,0)$$

C. The maximum number of processors doing memory accesses can be *two,* and hence we can normalize the actual by the maximum memory bandwidth; show that this equals

$$\frac{unnormalized\ memory\ bandwidth}{maximum\ memory\ bandwidth} = \frac{1 + E(M)}{2 + E(M)}$$

D. For interleaved memory accesses, with $E(M) \to \infty$, what is the normalized memory bandwidth?

E. For noninterleaved memory accesses, with $E(M) \to 0$, what is the normalized memory bandwidth?

F. **BONUS:** For a noninterleaved system with P processors accessing M memories via a full crossbar interconnection switch, show via a Jackson network analysis that

$$normalized\ memory\ bandwidth = \frac{M\ P}{M + P - 1}$$

For $P = 4$ plot this versus $M = 1,2,3,4$. What is the incremental gain in going from one to two, two to three, three to four processors?

G. **BONUS:** For a system with P processors and M memories, with *constant* number of memory addresses fetched per memory access, show that

$$unnormalized\ memory\ bandwidth = min(P,M)$$

3) A system consists of C clerks at terminals that submit transactions to an online system. Each clerk is idle for fifteen seconds and then active. The system hardware configuration consists of terminals, processors and disks. Each transaction requires some processor time and some time to access data stored on disk. We wish to compare the following two configurations

[1] One processor and one disk, with the mean processor time per job equal to one second and the mean disk access time per job equal to one second

[2] Two processors and two disks, with the mean processor time per job equal to two seconds and the mean disk access time per job equal to two seconds

Answer the following questions:

A. What is the system state space?

B.   What are the resources per job?

C.   What are upper and lower bounds on mean throughput rate and mean delay?

D.   Plot mean throughput rate and mean delay as well as upper and lower bounds on these quantities versus number of clerks for a closed network. Repeat for an open network.

E.   Which configuration should be chosen? Why?

4) We wish to compare the traffic handling characteristics of three different computer configurations:

- a single input stream feeding one buffer with one processor capable of executing a maximum of one million assembly language instructions per second

- a single input stream feeding one buffer with two processors each capable of executing a maximum of five hundred thousand assembly language instructions per second

- a single input stream that is split into two streams each of half the intensity of the original stream, with each stream feeding its own buffer and own processor, and each processor capable of executing five hundred thousand assembly language instructions per second

Each task involves the execution of an exponentially distributed number of assembly language instructions, with a mean of one hundred thousand assembly language instructions executed per task. The number of instructions executed per task are assumed to be statistically independent.

Plot the following quantities versus the mean arrival rate of tasks for each of the above three configurations:

A.   the mean rate of completing tasks

B.   the mean waiting time per task

C.   the mean queueing time per task

D.   the mean queue length

E.   the fraction of time that a task waits greater than zero

F.   the fraction of time that a task waits greater than T seconds vs T for a fixed processor utilization of 0.1, 0.5, 0.9

5) Jobs arrive for processing by a pipeline of processors: the input stream is handled by stage one, the output of stage one is the input to stage two, and so forth, for a total of N stages. Each job requires a random number of assembly language instructions be executed; we assume the number of instructions per job form a sequence of independent identically distributed exponential random variables with mean *INST* total. Each processor is capable of executing a maximum of *IPS* (*N*) assembly language instructions per second, where we stress that the maximum execution rate of each processor depends on the number of stages in the pipeline as we vary N. In an N stage pipeline, each processor will execute 1/Nth of the total number of instructions per job. The arrival statistics are Poisson; we fix the mean arrival rate at the same value for both systems. We denote by $E(T_Q|N=1)$ the mean queueing time for a one stage system that does exactly the same work as the N stage pipeline. We fix the mean queueing time for either system at twice the mean execution time of the job on the single fast processor. Find the required speed processor for each stage of the N stage pipeline, and plot *IPS* (*N*)/*IPS* (*N*=1) versus N for the above conditions.

6) Two different time slot interchangers are under consideration. The first handles twenty four lines, while the second handles ninety six lines. Each interchanges one eight bit sample on each line eight thousand times a second. The second costs twice as much as the first to initially manufacture, test and assemble; the market measured in terms of number of lines is the same for each. If the design goal is to have blocking occur within the time slot interchanger no more than one ten thousandth of the time, which system should be chosen, based on cost/benefit analysis? Why?

7) A time slot interchanger can interchange six time slots per frame. Two types of message traffic must be switched. Low bandwidth messages require one time slot per frame, while wide bandwidth messages require two time slots per frame. The mean holding time for the low bandwidth one time slot per frame is two time slots, while the mean holding time for the high bandwidth two time slot per frame messages are three frames.

[1]   The total message arrival rate is two messages per frame. Plot the blocking of both types of messages as the mix is varied from all low bandwidth to all wide bandwidth.

[2]   Repeat the above if the total message arrival rate is doubled and halved.

[3]   Repeat the above if the time slot interchanger can switch four slots per frame and eight slots per frame.

8) A variable bandwidth circuit switch consists of

[1] Two input links, each capable of handling two time slots per frame

[2] Two output links, each capable of handling two time slots per frame

[3] A central switch, capable of switching four time slots per frame

Two types of calls are switched, one requiring one slot per frame, the other requiring two slots per frame. The arrival statistics for each call type are simple Poisson. The sequence of call holding times for each call type are independent identically distributed random variables.

A. Assume each call type is equally likely to go from any input link to any output link.

   [1] Plot the blocking for each call type versus the fraction of arrivals that are low bandwidth (varied from zero per cent to one hundred per cent) assuming the two call types have identical call holding times of one frame.

   [2] Repeat the above, assuming the low bandwidth call has a holding time of ten frames, and the high bandwidth call has a holding time of one frame.

   [3] Repeat the above, assuming the high bandwidth call has a holding time of ten frames, and the low bandwidth call has a holding time of one frame.

B. Assume all the high bandwidth calls arrive on one input link, and are destined for one output link. Assume the low bandwidth calls all arrive on the other input link, and are all destined for the other output link. Repeat all the above.

C. Repeat all the above if the switch capacity is increased to eight slots per frame.

D. Repeat all the above if the link capacity is reduced to one slot per frame.

9) A disk storage system must store two types of messages:

• Data messages with a mean of one kilobyte per message and a mean residence time (time from arrival until retrieval) of two hours

• Voice messages with a mean of four kilobytes per message and a mean residence time (time from arrival until retrieval) of four hours

The total message arrival rate is one message per ten seconds.

[1]   The disk can store ten megabytes. Plot the fraction of time data
       messages and voice messages are blocked or rejected if the disk storage
       is shared among the two types of messages as a function of the mix of
       data messages, zero to one hundred per cent.

[2]   Repeat the above if the disk storage is doubled to twenty megabytes.

[3]   Repeat all the above if the mean arrival rate increases by a factor of
       ten, and one hundred.

[4]   Repeat the above if the disk storage is partitioned into a fixed amount of
       storage for data and a fixed amount for voice, with the fraction of each
       type of dedicated storage being in proportion to the ratio of the mean
       arrival rate of each type multiplied by the respective holding time.

CHAPTER 8: JACKSON NETWORKS: APPLICATIONS II

In this section we examine computer applications of Jackson queueing networks. The examples comprise

- A private branch exchange

- A multiple processor packet switching system

- An automatic call distributor

- A hierarchical analysis of a computer system

- A distributed online transaction processing system

These examples are quite lengthy, because the systems themselves are intrinsically complicated, and the requisite analysis of design tradeoffs must be done systematically. Each example involves extensive numerical studies, in order to gain insight into formulae.

8.1 Private Branch Exchange (PBX) Customer Communications Engineering

Customer premises voice switching systems *(private branch exchanges or PBXs)* can be configured with a set of trunks for connecting the local switching system to the outside telephone system. The number of trunks is typically chosen to meet a given grade of service, based on measurements of analysis (e.g., Erlang blocking formula). Currently available customer premises voice switching systems can be configured with two different types of trunks for telephone calls made outside the premises. One type is called *private line* because typically these are special or private facilities that are leased to take advantage of tariffs, and the other type is called *common carrier* because these are offered by a provider of service of the last resort (if all the private line circuits are busy, the common carrier is assumed to have circuits available for completing telephone calls). The figure below shows a hardware block diagram of such a system.

A customer hopes to take advantage of voice calling patterns, and save money, by configuring a PBX with a mix of private line and common carrier facilities. A well engineered PBX most of the time would complete calls with private line trunks, and only rarely (e.g., during a peak business hour) would there be a significant demand for common carrier trunks. Customers need not know which set of trunks were used to complete the call; only the system administrator would have this knowledge. How can this system be engineered to achieve desired performance at an acceptable price? What measurements might be gathered to quantify any statements in this realm? If call attempts

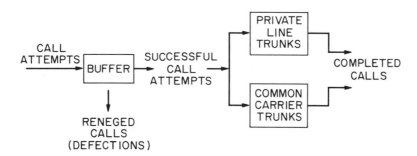

Figure 8.1.Hardware Block Diagram of PBX System

can be buffered, waiting for an available trunk, how many buffers are required? Customers can be impatient, and can hang up, renege, or defect from the buffer, if the time spent waiting (in the buffer) is unacceptable. How does customer impatience impact a design? In a well engineered system, customers will only rarely defect and redial telephone calls; how can we measure how many customers are trying for the first time and how many have tried more than once to check this? These are typical of the questions we wish to address.

8.1.1 Model Figure 8.2 is a queueing network block diagram of the system to be analyzed. Calls arrive and are held in a buffer of maximum capacity B calls; if a call arrives and finds the buffer full, it is blocked and presumably will retry later.

There are S trunks available for calls: if less than S trunks are busy when a call arrives, it seizes a trunk for the duration of the call. If all the trunks are busy when a call arrives, the call is buffered and will either defect or renege if it does not receive some service after a given time interval, or will seize a server from a second group of *infinite* servers for the duration of a call if its waiting time exceeds a threshold.

Calls attempts arrive to a system with the interarrival times being independent identically distributed exponential random variables with mean interarrival time $1/\lambda$.

Call holding times are independent identically distributed exponential random variables with mean holding time $1/\mu$.

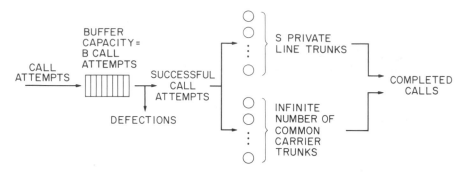

Figure 8.2.Queueing Network Block Diagram of PBX

If a call is buffered because all trunks are busy, the sequence of time intervals until defection, given that no service was received, are assumed to be independent identically distributed exponential random variables with mean $1/\alpha$.

If a call is buffered because all trunks are busy, the sequence of time intervals until a call seizes a common carrier trunk are independent identically distributed exponential random variables with mean time out interval $1/\beta$.

If there are B calls in the buffer, all new arrivals are blocked or rejected. Calls are removed from the buffer in order of arrival.

8.1.2 System State Space The state of the system at any instant of time t is given by $J(t)$, where $J(t)=0,1,2,...,S,S+1,..,B$ is the number of calls in the system, both buffered and in progress.

8.1.3 Mean Value Analysis The mean throughput rate of completing calls is denoted by λ. A call holds a buffer until it defects or until it is assigned a common carrier trunk, whichever occurs first. Hence, the mean time a buffer is held is the minimum of these random variables, which has a mean value $1/(\alpha+\beta)$. The mean number of calls holding buffers is given by

$$E[min(B,J)] = \lambda/(\alpha+\beta)$$

If buffers are the bottleneck, then

$$\lambda = B(\alpha+\beta)$$

The mean number of calls holding a private line trunk is given by

$$E[min(S,J)] = \lambda/\mu$$

If private line trunks are the bottleneck, then

$$\lambda = S\mu$$

Hence, the largest possible mean rate of completing calls is given by

$$\lambda \leqslant \min\left[S\mu, B(\alpha+\beta)\right]$$

Let's subsitute some numbers to interpret this formula. Suppose a typical call lasts for a mean of three minutes, $\mu=1/180\ sec$. The mean time a customer waits until defecting is assumed to be twelve seconds, so $\alpha=1/12\ sec$. The mean time out until a call is completed by the common carrier rather than private link trunk is six seconds, $\beta=1/6\ sec$. This suggests that

$$\lambda \leqslant \min\left[\frac{S}{180}, B(\frac{1}{6}+\frac{1}{12})\right]\ calls/sec$$

Trunks are more expensive than buffers, so we would presumably choose for trunks to be the bottleneck. In order for buffers *not* to be the bottleneck, we would demand that

$$B \leqslant S\ \frac{180}{1/6+1/12} = 9\ S$$

Configuring the system with up to nine times as many buffers as trunks will achieve this goal.

8.1.4 Jackson Network Blocking Analysis The fraction of time the system is in state J is denoted by $\pi(J)$ where

$$\pi(J) = \begin{cases} \dfrac{1}{G}\left[\dfrac{\lambda}{\mu}\right]^{J}/J! & 0 \leqslant J < S \\[4mm] \dfrac{1/G\ S!}{\displaystyle\prod_{I=1}^{J-S}[1+\gamma I/S\mu]} & S \leqslant J \leqslant B \end{cases}$$

where

$$\gamma = \alpha + \beta$$

is the total mean rate at which calls leave the buffer due to either defection or time outs. G is chosen such that

$$\sum_{J=0}^{B}\pi(J) = 1$$

A number of quantities of interest can be found now:

- The fraction of time a call attempt is immediately blocked or cleared because the buffer contains B call attempts:

$$PROB[call\ attempt\ cleared\ immediately] = \pi(B)$$

- The mean rate at which calls are cleared or blocked

$$mean\ rate\ of\ call\ attempts\ cleared = \lambda\pi(B) + \sum_{J=S}^{B}(J-S)\alpha\pi(J)$$

- The mean rate at which call attempts seize common carrier trunks

$$mean\ rate\ of\ seizing\ common\ carrier\ trunks = \sum_{J=S}^{B}(J-S)\beta\pi(J)$$

- The mean rate of completing calls on the private line trunks

$$mean\ rate\ of\ completing\ calls\ on\ private\ line\ trunks = \mu\sum_{J=1}^{B}min[J,S]\pi(J)$$

- The mean number of private link calls in progress

$$mean\ number\ of\ calls\ in\ progress\ on\ private\ lines = \sum_{J=1}^{B}min[J,S]\pi(J)$$

- The mean number of common carrier calls in progress

$$mean\ number\ of\ calls\ in\ progress\ on\ common\ carrier\ trunks$$

$$= [\lambda\pi(B) + \alpha\sum_{J=S}^{B}(J-S)\pi(J)]/\mu$$

This list is merely illustrative of some measures that would be of interest to a PBX administrator.

In a well engineered system, the fraction of time a call attempt is blocked or cleared because all buffers are filled should be negligible:

$$\pi(B) \approx 0$$

The mean rate at which calls are cleared or blocked is given by

$$mean\ rate\ of\ call\ attempts\ cleared \approx \sum_{J=S}^{B}(J-S)\alpha\pi(J)$$

Again, in a well engineered system this should be close to zero.

Since the whole point in this exercise is to use the private line trunks most of the time, the mean rate at which call attempts seize common carrier trunks should be close to zero.

Finally, most of the calls should be completed on private line trunks, so the mean call completion rate is approximated by *mean rate of completing calls on private line trunks* $= \mu\, E[J]$

These can be measured and compared with goals to see if the system is in fact meeting expectations.

8.1.5 Jackson Network Waiting Time Analysis The waiting time distribution for calls that are buffered for private line trunks and are still successfully completed is of interest. Let $G_W(t\,|\,J)$ be the distribution of waiting time of a call that finds $J \geqslant S$ call attempts in the system upon arrival given that it is successfully completed.

$$G_W(t\,|\,J) = PROB[W \leqslant t\,|\,J]$$

When a call arrives and is buffered, the statistics of subsequent call attempts do not matter. Hence, we need to measure the statistics of the time interval moving from the initial state $J > S$ to the state of having $S-1$ trunks available, at which point the call will be completed. The event of a successfully completed call attempt on the private line trunk group is denoted by A_{accept}. On the other hand, while we are waiting for a trunk to become available, the caller could hang up or renege, which we denote by the event A_{defect}. Finally, the call could time out and overflow to the common carrier trunk group, which we denote by the event $A_{overflow}$. For each of these three cases, we find

$$E[e^{-zW} \cap A_{accept}\,|\,J] = \tilde{G}(z+\alpha+\beta)$$

$$E[e^{-zW} \cap A_{defect}\,|\,J] = \frac{\alpha[1 - \tilde{G}(z+\alpha+\beta)]}{z + \alpha+\beta}$$

$$E[e^{-zW} \cap A_{overflow}\,|\,J] = \frac{\beta[1 - \tilde{G}(z+\alpha+\beta)}{z+\alpha+\beta}$$

$$\tilde{G}(z) = \prod_{K=S}^{J} \frac{S\mu+(J-S)(\alpha+\beta)}{z+S\mu+(J-S)(\alpha+\beta)}$$

In all cases, $J=S,S+1,...,B$. Otherwise, the call is completed immediately by the private link trunk group, with no waiting.

In a well engineered system, most calls should wait *zero,* and the mean waiting should be less than the mean time to time out to common carrier facilities or to renege from impatience:

$$PROB[W=0\,|\,successful\ call\ attempt\,] \approx 1$$

$$E[W \cap A_{accept}\,] \leqslant \frac{1}{\beta}$$

8.1.6 Jackson Network Asymptotics Here are a number of tractable special cases.

First, if the buffer capacity equals the number of private line trunks $B=S$, there will be no queueing, and call attempts will be either accepted or rejected.

The fraction of call attempts that are rejected is given by the Erlang blocking function:

$$fraction\ of\ blocked\ call\ attempts\ =\ B(S,\lambda/\mu)\ =\ \frac{(\lambda/\mu)^S/S!}{\displaystyle\sum_{K=0}^{S}(\lambda/\mu)^K/K!}$$

This provides a baseline case for comparing all subsequent studies. In a well engineered system, there should be little waiting, and little reason to have the number of buffers significantly larger than the number of private line trunks.

A second special case is to choose $B\rightarrow\infty$, which effectively means that there is *never* any buffer overflow. For this case, for the system to simply keep up with the work, we must demand

$$\lambda\ <\ S\mu\ +\ \alpha+\beta$$

In words, the arrival rate of calls must be less than the call departure rate (either due to successful completion or defection).

A final special case is to allow $\lambda\rightarrow\infty$, an overload. As $\lambda\rightarrow\infty$ the number of calls in the buffer is always B, and hence

$$\pi(B)\ =\ 1\qquad\pi(K)\ =\ 0,\ K=0,1,...,B-1$$

EXERCISE: What happens if $S\rightarrow\infty$?

8.1.7 Summary For a private branch exchange, under normal conditions there should be no calls queueing for private line trunks: most of the calls should be completed by the private link facilities. Call buffering should occur rarely, and buffer overflow should trigger an alarm that the system is not engineered properly. The time out for overflow to common carrier facilities should be set shorter than the mean time to defect. This suggests measuring the mean number of calls completed by the private line and common carrier facilities, the number of call attempts blocked by either buffers or private line trunks not being available, the number of calls that time out, the number of calls that renege and how long they are in the system, and the time a successful call waits to be completed.

8.2 A Data Packet Switching Node

We analyze traffic handling characteristics of different configurations of a data packet switching system.

8.2.1 Functional Description The figure below shows a hardware block diagram of a multiple processor packet switching system.

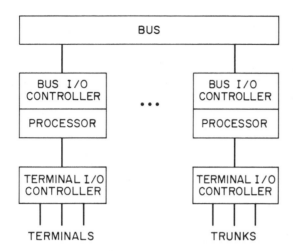

Figure 8.3.Hardware Block Diagram of Packet Switching System

The companion figure below shows a functional block diagram of each step of packet handling.

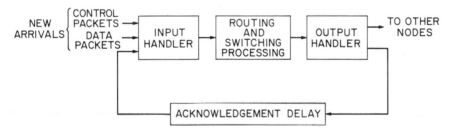

Figure 8.4.Data Flow Block Diagram of Packet Switching System

Two types of transactions arrive from elsewhere in the network to be executed:

- control packets--these carry data describing a portion of the network state, maintenance information, routing information, and other network management data, but do not carry any customer data

- data packets--these carry both control information concerning the sequence number of the packet in a message and actual useful data information supplied by a customer

For control packets, there are three stages of execution:

- input handling--checking the packet to determine whether it is a control or data packet, checking the packet for errors due to transmission anomalies, and formatting it for subsequent execution

- switching and routing--updating various network management files with information on facility status at selected points in the network, modifying routing strategies to account for perceived problem areas

- output handling--formatting the control packet for subsequent transmission to another cluster in the network, adding status information concerning this cluster

For data packets, there are five stages of execution:

- input handling--checking the packet type, checking the packet for errors due to transmission anomalies, and formatting it for execution at the next stage

- switching and routing--determining the next cluster to which the packet will be sent as well as the path through the network

- output handling--formatting the data packet for subsequent transmission to another network cluster

- acknowledgement of correct receipt of the packet at the destination cluster-- the receiver of the packet now sends back a special data packet acknowledging proper receipt of the data packet which is first handled by the input handler

- switching and routing--this module updates appropriate network management files to acknowledge that the packet was correctly transmitted and then releases or discards its copy of the original data packet which was held until this point in case the transmitted packet was unsuccessfully transmitted

In any actual application, there will in fact be lost packets and a variety of failures that must be guarded against. Here we have made the assumption that everything is performing properly which hopefully would be the case in any actual system during normal operation; within this very restricted framework there are still a great many issues to be explored quantitatively.

The hardware configuration is a set of multiple processors connected by a high speed communications network or bus. The operating system allocating resources for this configuration is distributed across the processors, and administers and facilitates communication between the different modules. How many processors are needed? Should there be one processor running all this code, or more than one? Should there be functionally dedicated processors running only one portion of this code, and if so how many of each? How fast should the processors be for adequate performance? What type of delay and throughput will occur for control packets versus for data packets? How much buffering will be required in each processor? For a more detailed exposition of a data communications packet switch the interested reader is referred to the references at the end of this section.

The figure below is a block diagram of a queueing network corresponding to the above verbal description.

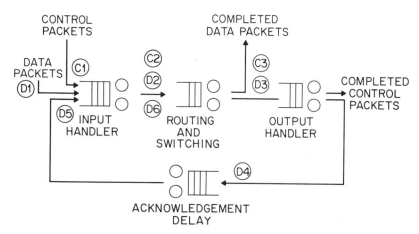

Figure 8.5. Queueing Network Block Diagram of Packet Switching System

Control packets migrate from cluster to cluster via steps C1, C2, C3. Data packets migrate according to steps D1, D2, D3, D4, D5, D6. Should each processor be capable of executing all steps, or should processors be dedicated to steps?

8.2.2 Traffic Handling Requirements   Before determining what this system *could* do, we wish to specify what it *should* do. Our goals are as follows:

- for data packets, in the initial field system we desire a mean throughput rate of one hundred packets per second with a mean delay at a node from arrival until system buffers are flushed of all work related to that packet no larger than one hundred milliseconds during an average business hour and no larger than two hundred milliseconds during a peak business hour; two years after initial deployment we wish to handle two hundred data packets per second with the same delay during an average business hour and a peak business hour

- for control packets, for the initial field system we desire a mean throughput rate of twenty packets per second with a mean delay at a node from arrival until system buffers are flushed of all work related to that packet no larger than ten milliseconds during an average business hour and no larger than twenty milliseconds during a peak business hour; two years after initial deployment we wish to handle forty control packets per second with the same delay as the initial system

The control packet delay criterion is much more stringent than the data packet delay criterion because we wish to minimize delays in controlling the entire data communications network to prevent overload, deadlocking, and so forth. There are a variety of ways to achieve this goal and we will investigate one family of approaches in the following sections.

8.2.3 Mean Value Analysis The fraction of arriving packets that are control and data packets are denoted by F_{con}, F_{data}, respectively.

The tables below summarize the number of assembly language instructions, both application and operating system, that must be executed at each stage of execution. We have included illustrative numerical values for the symbolic parameters in order to make this more concrete.

Table 8.1. Number of Instructions Executed at Each Step per Packet

Control Packets			Data Packets		
Step Number (Fig.8.5)	*Number of Instructions of Assembly Language Symbol*	*Value*	*Step Number (Fig.8.5)*	*Number of Instructions of Assembly Language Symbol*	*Value*
C1	C_{input}	300	D1	D_{input}	300
C2	C_{switch}	1500	D2	$D_{switch}(1)$	5000
C3	C_{output}	200	D3	D_{output}	300
			D4	---	---
			D5	$D_{input}(2)$	300
			D6	$D_{switch}(2)$	750

Next, we must describe the number of processors of each type, and their respective maximum instruction rates.

Table 8.2. Processor Hardware Description

Type	*Number*	*Maximum Instruction Rate*
Input Handling	P_{input}	I_{input} instructions/sec
Switching	P_{switch}	I_{switch} instructions/sec
Output Handling	P_{output}	I_{output} instructions/sec

Our goal is to obtain an upper bound on mean throughput rate. First, we must calculate the total time required per module for each type of transaction. For brevity, we assume we have either one pool of processors doing all packet switching functions or three types of dedicated processors.

The crudest level of sizing is to assume either only control packets or only data packets. Each control packet requires 2,000 lines of assembly language code to be executed, and hence with a processor capable of executing 300,000 lines of code per second, 150 control packets per second can be executed on one processor. Each data packet requires 6,650 lines of assembly language code to be executed, and with the same speed processor 45 packets per second can be executed on one processor.

For a system with three types of processor clusters, it is useful to look at the ratio of number of lines of assembly language code executed for each of the three functions, in order to gain some feel for the approximate ratio of processor types required. Output handling requires the smallest number of lines of code per packet to be executed, and hence we normalize our results by saying that for every one output handler processor, we will require two input handler processors and from eleven processors (for a 80% control packet/20% data packet traffic mix) to eighteen processors (for a 20% control packet/80% data packet traffic mix) for routing and switching.

Table 8.3A. Single Processor Cluster--Total Time per Packet per Module

Control Packets	Data Packets
$\dfrac{C_{input}+C_{switch}+C_{output}}{I_{proc}\times I_{proc}}$	$\dfrac{D_{input}(1)+D_{switch}(1)+D_{output}+D_{input}(2)+D_{switch}(2)}{I_{proc}\times P_{proc}}$

Table 8.3B. Three Functionally Dedicated Processor Clusters
Total Time per Packet per Module

Processor Type	Control Packets	Data Packets
Input	$\dfrac{C_{input}}{I_{input}\times P_{input}}$	$\dfrac{D_{input}(1)+D_{input}(2)}{I_{input}\times P_{input}}$
Switching	$\dfrac{C_{switch}}{I_{switch}\times P_{switch}}$	$\dfrac{D_{switch}(1)+D_{switch}(2)}{I_{switch}\times P_{switch}}$
Output	$\dfrac{C_{output}}{I_{output}\times P_{output}}$	$\dfrac{D_{output}}{I_{output}\times P_{output}}$

We focus on two special cases:

- 20% control packets and 80% data packets--this is typical of what might be encountered in a well designed system during a peak busy hour for example

- 80% control packets and 20% data packets--this is typical of what might be encountered during severe network congestion during a peak busy hour for example

The following tables give the system capacity, in packets per second, for the case of a single cluster of processors versus three clusters of functionally dedicated processors.

**Table 8.4A.Maximum Mean Throughput Rate
for Single Cluster of Processors**

Number of Processors	20% Control 80% Data	80% Control 20% Data
1	52 packets/sec	102 packets/sec
2	103 packets/sec	204 packets/sec
3	156 packets/sec	306 packets/sec
4	209 packets/sec	409 packets/sec
5	261 packets/sec	511 packets/sec

**Table 8.4B.Maximum Mean Throughput Rate for Three Clusters of
Functionally Dedicated Processors/One Input and One Output Processor**

Number of Switching Processors	20% Control 80% Data	80% Control 20% Data
1	61 packets/sec	127 packets/sec
2	122 packets/sec	254 packets/sec
3	183 packets/sec	381 packets/sec
4	245 packets/sec	509 packets/sec
5	306 packets/sec	636 packets/sec

The capacity for the input handling processor with 20% control packets is 429 packets per second, while with 80% control packets it is 750 packets per second. The capacity for the output handling processor is independent of mix, and is 1000 packets per second. Thus, the routing and switching processor cluster is the bottleneck in the three functionally dedicated cluster implementation, and by adding processors to do that task capacity will increase linearly over the above range of values, until the input processor becomes a bottleneck.

The main thrust of traffic studies is to first make sure that the maximum mean throughput rate is well in *excess* of that required for a given application before next turning to meeting delay criteria. This excess margin of throughput will be used to assure that delay criteria are met: since the resources are not fully utilized, there will be less contention and hence shorter waiting times. Determining the maximum mean throughput rate is a necessary but by no means sufficient condition for assuring adequate system performance.

8.2.4 Delay Analysis The mean delay analysis is developed in several steps. First, if we have P identical processors each capable of a maximum instruction execution rate of I_{proc} handling one type of job with a mean of I_{job} instructions, and each processor has mean utilization U, then the mean delay per job is

$$E(T_Q) = \frac{I_{job}}{I_{proc}} \left[D(P,U) = \frac{C(P,P\,U)}{P(1-U)} + 1 \right]$$

where $C(P,P\,U)$ is the Erlang delay function discussed earlier. Second, if we allow the P identical processors to execute two different job types, with the mean number of instructions executed per job being $I_J, J=1,2$ then the mean delay for each job type is

$$E(T_{Q,J}) = \frac{U(J)}{U(1) + U(2)} D(P,[U(1) + U(2)]) \quad J=1,2$$

$$U(J) = \lambda \times F_J \times \frac{I_J}{P \, I_{proc}} \quad J=1,2$$

where F_J denotes the fraction of type J jobs that are executed over a long time interval. Finally, for the case at hand, we can calculate for each of the three workload partitions the mean delay for both control and data packets; we do so only for one case, the case of three functionally dedicated processor clusters, and omit the remaining cases for brevity:

$$E(T_{Q,control}) = \frac{C_{input}}{I_{input}} D(P_{input}, U_{input}) + \frac{C_{switch}}{I_{switch}} D(P_{switch}, U_{switch})$$

$$+ \frac{C_{output}}{I_{output}} D(P_{output}, U_{output})$$

$$E(T_{Q,data}) = \frac{D_{input}(1) + D_{input}(2)}{I_{input}} D(P_{input}, U_{input})$$

$$+ \frac{D_{switch}(1) + D_{switch}(2)}{I_{switch}} D(P_{switch}, U_{switch}) + \frac{D_{output}}{I_{output}} D(P_{output}, U_{output}) + T_{ack}$$

where T_{ack} is the acknowledgement delay.

8.2.5 Illustrative Numerical Results We now present illustrative numerical results for

- different workload partitioning
- different numbers of processors
- different mixes of control and data packets
- different processor speeds

The numbers chosen to generate the curves that follow are those described in the previous section for number of lines of assembly language code per packet.

In the study that follows, we assume that all the processors are identical, and execute either 0.3 or 0.5 million assembly language instructions per second*

---

* One million instructions per second is abbreviated to one *mip* in current common usage.

which is felt to be typical of current technology, based on discussions with numerous knowledgable workers in the field plus a variety of trade publications.

We vary the mix of control and data packets from 20% control and 80% data to 80% control and 20% data.

The following cases are studied:

- One processor cluster executing input handling, switching, and output handling, with from one to five processors in the cluster

- Three processor clusters, one cluster for input handling, one cluster for switching, and one cluster for output handling, with from one to five switching processors and one processor handling input and one processor handling output

The remaining case, one cluster for input and output handling, and one for switching, is omitted for brevity, and its performance should be bounded by the above two extreme points.

Acknowledgement delay is varied from ten to fifty milliseconds.

We wish to calculate or approximate the largest total mean packet arrival rate such that a given set of delay criteria is met. The goals we wish to meet are the mean data packet delay, including acknowledgement, at a given node should not exceed one hundred milliseconds, while the mean control packet delay at a given node should not exceed ten milliseconds.

We first examine the data packet handling characteristics for different values of acknowledgement delay and for different mixes. We tabulate the results below:

Table 8.5A. Maximum Total Mean Arrival Rate with Mean Data Packet Delay Less Than 100 msec--20% Control/80% Data Packets--0.3 MIPS per Processor

Total Number of Processors	Single Cluster Acknowledgement Delay		Number of Switching Processors	Three Clusters Acknowledgement Delay	
	10 msec	50 msec		10 msec	50 msec
1	35 pkts/sec	30 pkts/sec	1	40 pkts/sec	30 pkts/sec
2	85 pkts/sec	80 pkts/sec	2	105 pkts/sec	85 pkts/sec
3	140 pkts/sec	130 pkts/sec	3	165 pkts/sec	140 pkts/sec
4	185 pkts/sec	195 pkts/sec	4	225 pkts/sec	215 pkts/sec
5	235 pkts/sec	250 pkts/sec	5	270 pkts/sec	290 pkts/sec

Table 8.5B. Maximum Total Mean Arrival Rate with Mean Data Packet Delay Less Than 100 msec--80% Control/20% Data Packets--0.3 MIPS per Processor

Number of Processors	Single Cluster Acknowledgement Delay		Number of Switching Processors	Three Clusters Acknowledgement Delay	
	10 msec	50 msec		10 msec	50 msec
1	75 pkts/sec	60 pkts/sec	1	100 pkts/sec	75 pkts/sec
2	180 pkts/sec	155 pkts/sec	2	225 pkts/sec	190 pkts/sec
3	280 pkts/sec	260 pkts/sec	3	360 pkts/sec	400 pkts/sec
4	350 pkts/sec	370 pkts/sec	4	430 pkts/sec	460 pkts/sec
5	450 pkts/sec	470 pkts/sec	5	550 pkts/sec	600 pkts/sec

Inspection of these two tables reveals that

- the workload mix has a definite impact on performance

- adding processors can increase traffic handling faster than one might expect naively because the processors are not completely utilized

We now turn to control packet traffic handling characteristics. The results are tabulated below:

Table 8.6A. Maximum Total Mean Arrival Rate with Mean Control Packet Delay Less Than 10 msec--0.3 MIPS per Processor

Number of Processors	Single Cluster Workload Mix		Number of Switching Processors	Three Clusters Workload Mix	
	20% Control	80% Control		20% Control	80% Control
1	15 pkts/sec	35 pkts/sec	1	25 pkts/sec	50 pkts/sec
2	65 pkts/sec	120 pkts/sec	2	75 pkts/sec	185 pkts/sec
3	110 pkts/sec	215 pkts/sec	3	130 pkts/sec	270 pkts/sec
4	160 pkts/sec	310 pkts/sec	4	185 pkts/sec	370 pkts/sec
5	210 pkts/sec	400 pkts/sec	5	240 pkts/sec	470 pkts/sec

Based on both these tables, we see that the control packet delay criterion and not the data packet delay criterion is limiting performance for the numbers chosen here.

How sensitive is performance if we change the delay criterion? We might design the system for an average control packet delay of ten milliseconds and a peak control packet delay of twenty milliseconds. The numbers are tabulated below:

Table 8.6B. Maximum Total Mean Arrival Rate with Mean Control Packet Delay Less Than 20 msec--0.3 MIPS per Processor

Number of Processors	Single Cluster Workload Mix		Number of Switching Processors	Three Clusters Workload Mix	
	20% Control	80% Control		20% Control	80% Control
1	35 pkts/sec	70 pkts/sec	1	40 pkts/sec	85 pkts/sec
2	85 pkts/sec	165 pkts/sec	2	105 pkts/sec	215 pkts/sec
3	135 pkts/sec	265 pkts/sec	3	165 pkts/sec	330 pkts/sec
4	190 pkts/sec	370 pkts/sec	4	225 pkts/sec	425 pkts/sec
5	235 pkts/sec	475 pkts/sec	5	285 pkts/sec	590 pkts/sec

System engineers can then block out total network performance knowing that data packet delays are one hundred milliseconds or less per node while control packet delays are ten milliseconds or less per node on the average, and twenty milliseconds or less per node during peak loading.

What would happen if a faster processor were available? The tables below summarize the results of one such exercise assuming the maximum instruction rate of each processor is 500,000 instructions per second:

Table 8.7A. Maximum Total Mean Arrival Rate with Mean Data Packet Delay Less Than 100 msec--20% Control/80% Data--0.5 MIPS per Processor

Number of Processors	Single Cluster Acknowledgement Delay		Number of Switching Processors	Three Clusters Acknowledgement Delay	
	10 msec	50 msec		10 msec	50 msec
1	75 pkts/sec	65 pkts/sec	1	65 pkts/sec	55 pkts/sec
2	150 pkts/sec	140 pkts/sec	2	160 pkts/sec	150 pkts/sec
3	250 pkts/sec	235 pkts/sec	3	280 pkts/sec	260 pkts/sec
4	320 pkts/sec	310 pkts/sec	4	380 pkts/sec	355 pkts/sec
5	420 pkts/sec	400 pkts/sec	5	480 pkts/sec	460 pkts/sec

Table 8.7B. Maximum Total Mean Arrival Rate with Mean Data Packet Delay Less Than 100 msec--80% Control/20% Data--0.5 MIPS per Processor

Number of Processors	Single Cluster Acknowledgement Delay		Number of Switching Processors	Three Clusters Acknowledgement Delay	
	10 msec	50 msec		10 msec	50 msec
1	150 pkts/sec	120 pkts/sec	1	175 pkts/sec	155 pkts/sec
2	300 pkts/sec	280 pkts/sec	2	390 pkts/sec	360 pkts/sec
3	480 pkts/sec	455 pkts/sec	3	600 pkts/sec	570 pkts/sec
4	650 pkts/sec	630 pkts/sec	4	800 pkts/sec	270 pkts/sec
5	820 pkts/sec	800 pkts/sec	5	1030 pkts/sec	1010 pkts/sec

Table 8.8A.Maximum Total Mean Arrival Rate with Mean Control Packet Delay
Less Than 10 msec--0.5 MIPS per Processor

Number of Processors	Single Cluster Workload Mix		Number of Switching Processors	Three Clusters Workload Mix	
	20% Control	80% Control		20% Control	80% Control
1	50 pkts/sec	100 pkts/sec	1	60 pkts/sec	120 pkts/sec
2	125 pkts/sec	260 pkts/sec	2	150 pkts/sec	340 pkts/sec
3	210 pkts/sec	425 pkts/sec	3	250 pkts/sec	550 pkts/sec
4	300 pkts/sec	600 pkts/sec	4	350 pkts/sec	750 pkts/sec
5	400 pkts/sec	770 pkts/sec	5	450 pkts/sec	950 pkts/sec

Table 8.8B.Maximum Total Mean Arrival Rate with Mean Control Packet Delay
Less Than 20 msec--0.5 MIPS per Processor

Number of Processors	Single Cluster Workload Mix		Number Switching Processors	Three Clusters Workload Mix	
	20% Control	80% Control		20% Control	80% Control
1	65 pkts/sec	140 pkts/sec	1	85 pkts/sec	180 pkts/sec
2	155 pkts/sec	350 pkts/sec	2	185 pkts/sec	380 pkts/sec
3	245 pkts/sec	425 pkts/sec	3	285 pkts/sec	600 pkts/sec
4	315 pkts/sec	650 pkts/sec	4	375 pkts/sec	800 pkts/sec
5	430 pkts/sec	800 pkts/sec	5	475 pkts/sec	1025 pkts/sec

The benefit in going to a faster processor is greater than just a simple speed scaling! This is because the processors are not completely utilized, and an economy of scale benefit is present.

8.2.6 Summary of Performance Analysis for Data Packet Switch We conclude with a brief summary of the relevant performance parameters for the data packet switch example discussed here.

The switching module is the main bottleneck. To alleviate this problem, designers can

- add more *dedicated* or *shared* processors, making a tradeoff between parallelism achieved by pipelining versus parallelism achieved by multitasking

- fix the number of processors and vary the workload partitioning

- chose different speed processors

- combinations of the above

We can achieve this with either

- three processors in a cluster handling input, routing and switching, and output, assuming all processors execute 0.3 MIPS

- five processors in three clusters, with one in one cluster for input handling, one cluster of three processors for routing and switching, and one for output, assuming all processors execute 0.3 MIPS

- two processors in one cluster, with each processor handling all three tasks, assuming all processors execute 0.5 MIPS

- four processors in three clusters, with one input handling cluster of one processor, one routing and switching cluster of two processors, and one output handling cluster of one processor, assuming all processors execute 0.5 MIPS

If we fix the total workload and the total number of processors, then the greatest gains are to be made **not** by functionally dedicating processors but rather by pooling them to execute packets, if the goal is to minimize the total mean packet delay. The refinement of having some processors for input alone and others for output alone may not be justified in terms of traffic handling capacity alone, based on the numbers at hand. Even dedicating some processors to input and output handling and others to routing and switching is not justified. However, if we wish to minimize the response time for a particular type of packet, then it may prove worthwhile to add dedicated rather than shared processors.

Varying the control and data packet mix or the processor speed can have great impact on system performance for the numbers presented here. A combination of all of the above items appears to offer the greatest potential for traffic performance improvement for the numbers presented here. The tables quantify precisely the amount of gain for each of these factors.

8.2.7 Additional Reading

[1] W.Bux, *Modelling and Analysis of Store and Forward Data Switching Centres with Finite Buffer Memory and Acknowledgement Signalling,* Elektronische Rechenanlagen, **19** (4), 173-180(1977).

8.3 Automatic Call Distributor with Customer Defection

We now return to the automatic call distributor system described earlier, in order to illustrate how to include the phenomenon of *reneging* where customers defect or hang up rather than waiting for service by an agent. Even music while you wait need not keep everyone happy! In a more serious vein, this example illustrates the *versatility* of Jackson queueing network models to handle quite complicated realistic situations, involving interactions between customers, trunks and agents. The power of the method is it makes all this look easy! A variety of models are possible, only one of which is presented here. Finally, this is a standard computer communications system that virtually everyone has encountered everyday, vitally important in daily business. Suppose you were put in charge of managing such a system: the analysis presented here would suggest where to begin to look for coming to grips!

8.3.1 Model The initial ingredients in the model are

- S servers or agents

- T trunks or links

- The arrival statistics of calls

- The service statistics of calls

The arrival statistics are assumed to be Poisson, with total offered mean arrival rate λ. The call service statistics are assumed to be adequately modeled by independent identically distributed exponential random variables with mean $1/\mu$ for the mean service time per call (this includes the time an agent and customer spend talking plus time spent by the agent in call cleanup work with no customer).

After handling this model (always do this first, simply as a check or baseline case for comparison, before doing the more complicated model), we will allow customers to defect after they have been accepted but before an agent has handled them.

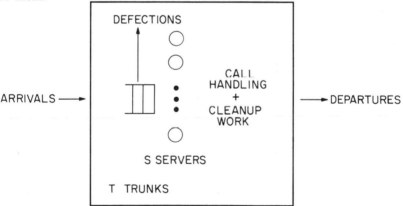

Figure 8.6. Automatic Call Distributor with Customer Defection Queueing Network

8.3.2 State Space The system state space is denoted by Ω which is the set of all integer valued admissible numbers of customers in the system:

$$\Omega = \{K \mid K = 0, 1, \dots, T\}$$

8.3.3 Mean Value Analysis The mean throughput rate of completing calls is denoted by λ. The mean number of occupied trunks is given by

$$E[min(K,T)] = \lambda T_{trunk}$$

where T_{trunk} is the mean trunk holding time for completed calls, including waiting for an agent. We will calculate this in the next section; for now, it suffices to note that if trunks are the bottleneck, then

$$\lambda = \frac{T}{T_{trunk}}$$

The mean number of busy agents is given by

$$E[min(K,S)] = \frac{\lambda}{\mu}$$

If agents are the bottleneck, then

$$\lambda = S\mu$$

Combining all this, we find

$$\lambda \leqslant min\left[S\mu, \frac{T}{T_{trunk}}\right]$$

For the bottleneck to occur at either the trunks or the agents, we must demand that

$$\frac{T}{S} = \mu T_{trunk} \quad trunks/agent$$

If we choose $\mu = 1/30$ *seconds* while $T_{trunk} = 45$ *seconds*, then we need $45/30 = 1.5$ trunks per agent.

8.3.4 Jackson Network Analysis Let K denote the number of customer calls in the system. The long term time averaged fraction of time that K calls are in the system is given by

$$\pi_K = \frac{1}{G} \frac{(\lambda/\mu)^K}{K!} \prod_{I=0}^{K} max\left[1, \frac{I}{S}\right]$$

As before, the system partition function, denoted by G, will determine various measures of performance.

Many call distributors are operated with a blocking of ten to thirty per cent of offered call attempts, in an attempt to have fewer agents and equipment than would be needed for a blocking of one to five per cent. This has an impact on customer arrival statistics. Customers will defect, hang up, or abandon waiting if too much time passes before an agent handles their transaction; this occurs when more call attempts are present rather than agents. Here is one way to quantify this phenomenon, using the modeling techniques developed earlier: the call holding rate is allowed to depend upon the number of calls in the system, such that for S or fewer calls (one per agent) the call holding time is not affected at all, while for greater than S calls, the call holding rate goes up; equivalently, the mean call talking time goes down:

$$\Phi(K) = \begin{cases} K\mu & K \leqslant S \\ S\mu + (K-S)\alpha & K > S \end{cases}$$

The new parameter α is the mean rate at which calls defect or abandon because no agent handles them. How does this impact the distribution of the number in system? We see

$$\pi_K = \frac{1}{G} \prod_{I=0}^{K} \frac{\lambda}{\Phi(K)}$$

8.3.5 Blocking We first deal with the case of no defection. The fraction of time that all T trunks are busy is given by

$$blocking = \frac{G_T}{\sum\limits_{K=0}^{T} G_K} \quad G_K = \sum_{J=0}^{K} \prod_{I=1}^{J} \frac{\lambda/\mu}{\Phi_{agent}(J)} \quad K=0,...,T$$

$$\Phi_{agent}(J) = \begin{cases} 1 & J=0 \\ min(S,J) & J>0 \end{cases}$$

It is instructive to rewrite this in terms of Erlang's blocking function to see how the number of agents as well as the number of trunks enters into determining the blocking:

$$blocking = \frac{\rho^{T-S} B(S,a)}{1 + \rho B(S,a)[1 - \rho^{T-S}]}$$

$$B(S,A) = \frac{\frac{A^S}{S!}}{\sum\limits_{K=0}^{S} \frac{A^K}{K!}} \quad \rho \equiv \frac{A}{S}$$

$\rho < 1$ denotes the fraction of time each *agent* is busy (either talking with a customer or doing cleanup work). Since this is less than one, the blocking can be approximated (why?) by

$$blocking \approx \frac{\rho^{T-S} B(S,A)}{1 + \rho B(S,A)} \approx \rho^{T-S} B(S,A) \quad \rho < 1$$

Thus the blocking can be significantly less (why?) than we might expect based on an Erlang blocking analysis alone.

Finally, how do we include defection? We simply replace G_K in the initial expression with the appropriately modified expression, and the method for calculating the blocking is still valid (although the numbers are different!) To emphasize this, we denote by $P_K, K=0,...,T$ the fraction of time there are K calls in the system.

The mean call completion rate is given by

$$\lambda(1-B) = \mu \sum_{K=1}^{T} min(K,S) P_K$$

8.3.6 Waiting Time   Suppose that calls cannot defect. The fraction of time that a call waits greater than X seconds, given that it is accepted and not blocked upon arrival, is given by

$$PROB[T_W > X | accepted] = \frac{1}{G} \frac{(\lambda/\mu)^S/S!}{1-B} \sum_{J=0}^{T-S-1} \rho^J \sum_{K=0}^{J} e^{-S\mu X} \frac{(S\mu X)^J}{J!}$$

The mean waiting time of an accepted call is the mean number of calls divided by the mean call completion rate, given that a call is not blocked:

$$E[T_W | accepted] = \frac{1}{G} \frac{(\lambda/\mu)^S/S!}{\lambda(1-B)} \sum_{J=1}^{T-S-1} J\rho^J$$

Next, we allow for defection of accepted calls. The fraction of time a customer is blocked is P_T, which is the fraction of time all trunks are busy. The fraction of time that a calling customer waits without defecting and without being blocked is given by

$$PROB[T_W > X | no\ blocking, no\ defection] =$$

$$= \frac{1}{1-P_T} \sum_{K=S}^{T-1} P_K \left[\frac{\alpha+\mu S}{\mu S} \right]^{K-S+1} \int_X^{\infty} e^{-\tau(\alpha+\mu(K-S+1))} \frac{[\tau(K-S+1)]^{K-S+1}}{(K-S)!} d\tau$$

8.3.7 Closing Comment   In a well engineered call distributor, approximating the blocking by the Erlang B analysis and analyzing delay by Erlang C analysis should be the starting point for virtually any performance analysis. This analysis is very sophisticated compared to the much more rudimentary Erlang analysis. In any event, either analysis should be confirmed by data from an actual automatic call distributor, before doing anything else. As an exercise, try and determine for what set of parameters the mean value or Erlang analysis will give misleading insight compared with the analysis developed here.

8.3.8 Additional Reading

[1]   J.W.Cohen, *Basic Problems of Telephone Traffic Theory and the Influence of Repeated Calls,* Telecommunications Review, **18** (2), 49-100 (1957)

8.4 Hierarchical Analysis

Our intent in this section is to describe a hierarchical performance analysis of a model of a computer communication system. The bottommost level is processor and memory interaction. Outputs of an analysis of this subsystem will feed the next level, operating system critical region contention. Outputs of this analysis in turn feed the next level, paging for memory management to drums and file accesses to moving head disks. Finally, outputs of that analysis feed in turn the topmost level, clerks at terminals interacting with the multiple disk spindle, multiple processor computer system.

An implicit assumption in this type of analysis is that each subsystem is in a steady state. On the other hand, the time scales for each subsystem (or layer) can be and are radically different. The processor and memory contention occurs on a time scale of tens of microseconds. The operating system critical region contention occurs on a time scale of tens of milliseconds; this means that many processor and memory interactions occur relative to any operating system critical region activity. The paging memory contention and file system access activity occurs on a time scale of hundreds of milliseconds to seconds; this means that many accesses to the operating system table occur for every page or I/O related activity. Finally, human interaction and response times have a time scale of one to ten seconds, so that many page faults and file accesses occur for every human interaction.

The figure below is a block diagram of the processor memory subsystem.

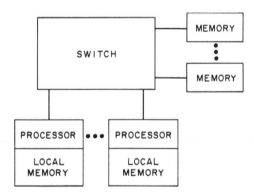

Figure 8.7.Processor/Memory Hardware Block Diagram

At the hardware system level, P processors are connected to M memory subsystems via a crossbar switch, i.e., any processor can access any memory. Each processor has a local cache memory that it checks first; if the instructions or data are not in the cache, the processor accesses the appropriate memory. Execution of that job is resumed when the appropriate memory retrieval is finished. Contention arises when more than one processor demands access to the same memory subsystem.

The figure below is a block diagram of processors contending for a serially reusable operating system kernel table: At the operating system kernel level, only one logical abstraction of a processor (a so called *process)* at a time can access an operating system table. This is done to insure logically correct

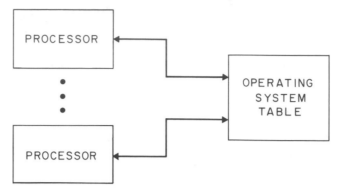

Figure 8.8.Process Contention for Operating System Table

operation, e.g., the operation of table access is atomic and irreversible. Contention arises when more than one process demands access to this table.

The figure below is a block diagram of the memory paging subsystem:

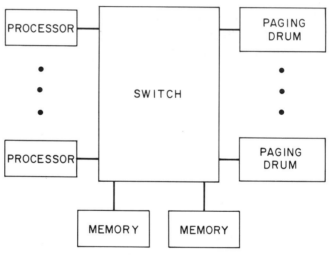

Figure 8.9.Memory/Drum Subsystem Block Diagram

Each application process is segmented into *pages* of memory. At any given instant of time, only a subset of all the pages associated with a given application process need be in main memory. A fixed head disk or *drum* stores all pages that cannot fit into main memory. How large should main memory be to insure that the delay due to waiting for pages to be moved into and out of secondary storage is acceptable?

The figure below is a block diagram of operators interacting with the computer system. Operators at terminals use the system. Each operator submits the same type of job to the system, with each job consisting of a sequence of steps involving some processing time and some input/output to moving head disks. How many operators can the system support with acceptable delay with a given processor, memory, drum and moving head disk configuration?

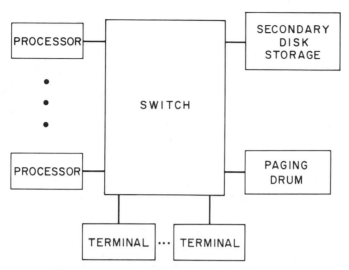

Figure 8.10.Clerk/System Block Diagram

8.4.1 Additional Reading

[1] P.J.Kuehn *Approximate Analysis of General Queuing Networks by Decomposition,* IEEE Transactions on Communications, **27** (1), 113-126 (1979).

[2] P.J.Kuehn, *Analysis of Switching System Control Structures by Decomposition,* Archiv fuer Elektronik und Uebertragunstechnik, **34,** 52-59 (1980).

8.4.2 Processor/Memory Model Each job requires a mean total of I instructions to be completely executed by P identical processors. No job can execute in parallel with itself, i.e., at any instant of time each job is in execution on at most one processor. Each job executes on a processor with a local cache memory: the processor checks the local memory to see if the appropriate text and data are present, and if they are, executes work. If local memory does not contain the appropriate text or data, it is fetched from one of M distinct memories. Each job involves two time intervals, one for execution out of cache memory and one for waiting for memory fetches to be completed. If all the instructions and data are in cache memory, a job will execute in a mean time T_{cache}; if none of the instructions or data are in cache memory, a job will execute in a mean time T_{memory}. The fraction of time a job executes out of cache memory is denoted by Q_{cache}; the fraction of time a job executes out of main memory is denoted by $Q_{memory} = 1 - Q_{cache}$. If there are J_P active processors, where $0 \leqslant J_P \leqslant P$, then the mean job execution rate of the *system* denoted by $I(J_P)$ is given by

$$I(J_P) = \frac{J_P}{Q_{cache}T_{cache} + Q_{memory}[T_{wait}(J_P)+T_{memory}]}$$

where $T_{wait}(J_P)$ is the mean waiting time for a memory box. A different way of thinking about this is that a processor executes an average of I_{cache} instructions before a memory fetch is made, and that while executing out of cache the processor completes ν instructions per second, so T_{cache} is the total mean time to execute a job, multiple time intervals each of mean duration νI_{cache}.

All processors are fed jobs from a single ready job queue, i.e., all jobs in the queue hold all requisite resources (e.g., files, memory, buffers) except for a processor. If a processor is idle, a ready job begins execution on the idle processor. Each job will make a fraction of $F_K, K=1,...,M$ accesses to memory K in its execution. Because there is contention for memory, as more and more processors are added the mean throughput rate of executing jobs will not scale linearly with the number of processors, but will increase at a slower rate. The total number of jobs, summed over all memories, equals all processors:

$$\sum_{I=1}^{M}[J_{memory,I}+J_{cache,I}] = J_P \ processors \quad J_P=1,2,...,P$$

$J_{memory,I}, J_{cache,I}$ denotes the respective numbers of jobs executing out of cache and out of main memory directly. T_{wait} and T_{memory} are related by

$$T_{wait}+T_{memory} = T_{memory} \times stretching \ factor$$
$$stretching \ factor = \frac{E_K[J_1 + \cdots + J_M]}{E_K[min(1,J_1) + \cdots + min(1,J_M)]}$$

If there is no contention for memory, the stretching factor is one (why?), while if there is memory contention, the stretching factor can be greater than one (why?).

If we refine this analysis by using a Jackson network model, then the state space is given by

$$\Omega = \{\underline{J}|J_C + \sum_{K=1}^{M}J_K = J_P\}$$

The fraction of time the system is in state $\underline{J}$ is given by

$$\pi_{J_P}(J_C,J_1,...,J_M) = \frac{1}{G_{J_P}}\frac{(Q_{cache}T_{cache})^{J_{cache}}}{J_{cache}!}\prod_{K=1}^{M}\left[Q_{memory}F_K T_{memory}\right]^{J_K}$$

This can be used to explicitly calculate the stretching factor. A mean value analysis would only allow us to bound the stretching factor. A different way of thinking about this is to determine the *effective* number of processors, denoted by $\Phi(J_P)$. Even though there are P processors, the memory contention will reduce this below P. The effective number of processors is given by

$$\Phi(J_P) = \frac{G_{J_P-1}}{G_{J_P}} T_{cache} \leqslant \min[J_P,P]$$

This is simply the mean throughput rate multiplied by the mean time to execute a job out of cache memory.

8.4.3 Additional Reading

[1] J.Bell, D.Casaent, C.G.Bell, *An Investigation of Alternative Cache Organizations,* IEEE Transactions on Computers, **23** (4), 346-351 (1974).

[2] W.F.Freiberger, U.Grenander, P.D.Sampson, *Patterns in Program References,* IBM J.Research and Development, **19** (3), 230-243 (1975).

[3] A.J.Smith, *Multiprocessor Memory Organization and Memory Interference,* Communications of ACM, **20** (10), 754-761 (1977).

[4] A.J.Smith, *Cache Memories,* Computing Surveys, **14** (3), 473-530 (1982).

8.4.4 Operating System Table Model There are a total of J_P active processors. There are J_U processors executing unlocked reentrant code and J_L processors either waiting or executing locked nonreentrant code, with

$$J_P = J_U + J_L$$

The nonreentrant code is serially reusable. A total of I_U and I_L instructions are executed in each state, respectively. The output of the memory/processor interference analysis enters into the operating system contention at this point. The rate at which jobs execute unlocked code is given by

$$\alpha_U(J_U) = \frac{J_U}{I_U[J_U + \min(1,J_P - J_U)]} \Phi[J_U + \min(1,J_P - J_U)]\,\nu$$

The rate at which jobs execute locked code is given by

$$\alpha_L(J_L) = \frac{\min[1,J_L]}{I_L(J_P - J_L + \min[1,J_L])} \Phi[J_P - J_L + \min(1,J_L)]\,\nu$$

The fraction of time the system is in state J_U,J_L is given by $\pi(J_U,J_L)$, where

$$\pi(J_U,J_L) = \frac{1}{G_{J_A}} \prod_{I=1}^{J_U} \frac{1}{\alpha_U(I)} \prod_{K=1}^{J_L} \frac{1}{\alpha_L(K)} \quad J_U+J_L=J_A$$

The effective mean number of active processors is denoted by $\Phi'(J_A)$ and is given by

$$\Phi'(J_A) = \Phi\left[E\left(J_U + min\left(1, J_A - J_U\right)\right)\right]$$

This will be even lower than what we found for memory contention (why?).

8.4.5 Drum/Disk/Memory Paging Model   Each job makes an average of F file system accesses, with an associated mean time per access denoted by T_{access}. A job stores its text and data in memory pages; at any instant of time, only a subset of all the memory pages associated with a job needed for execution. Those pages that are not needed can be stored on a secondary storage device, a fixed head disk called a *drum*. A page fault is said to occur when the desired next page is not in main memory but is stored on the drum and must be moved into main memory before execution can resume. The mean number of page faults per job is a function of the mean number of pages per job: the mean number of page faults per job will decrease monotonically as we increase the mean number of pages per job. We assume that we can measure the mean number of page faults per job as a function of J_A. We denote this function by $PF(J_A)$. The mean time to service a page fault is denoted by T_P.

The page fault also requires execution of additional memory management operating system code. A job requires I_E instructions to be executed, assuming *no* page fault activity, and I_{PF} instructions to be executed per page fault, so the total mean number of instructions executed per job is given by

$$mean \ number \ of \ instructions \ per \ job = I_E + I_{PF}PF(J_A)$$

The fraction of time a processor is doing useful work is the ratio of the mean number of useful nonpaging instructions executed per job I_E divided by the total mean number of instructions executed per job. The mean number of effective processors divided by the total mean number of instructions per job is the rate at which jobs are executed. The product of these two terms is the completion rate of executing jobs, denoted by $\beta(J_A)$ and is given by

$$\beta(J_A) = \frac{I_E}{I_E + I_{PF}PF(J_A)} \ \frac{\Phi'[J_A]}{I_E + I_{PF}PF(J_A)}$$

Finally, we need to specify the disk activity. Each job makes an average of N_K disk accesses to disk $K = 1, ..., D$. Each disk access requires a mean time of T_D. There is only one paging drum. The system state at any instant of time is given by $\underline{J}$ where J_P jobs are waiting or in execution at the processors, J_{PF} jobs are waiting or in page fault activity at the drum, and $J_K, K = 1, ..., D$ jobs are waiting or in access to disk K. The state space constraint is that the total number of active jobs J_A must equal the total number of jobs in each activity:

$$J_P + J_{PF} + \sum_{K=1}^{D} J_K = J_A$$

The fraction of time the system is in $\underline{J}$ is denoted by $\pi(\underline{J})$:

$$\pi(\underline{J}) = \frac{1}{G_{J_A}} \prod_{K=1}^{J_P} \frac{I_E v}{\beta(K)} (T_{PF})^{J_{PF}} \prod_{I=1}^{D}\prod_{J=1}^{J_I}(T_D N_J)^J$$

The mean throughput rate of executing jobs is given by

$$mean\ throughput\ rate = \frac{G_{J_A-1}}{G_{J_A}}$$

8.4.6 Additional Reading

[1]   P.J.Denning, *Virtual Memory,* Computing Surveys, **2** (3), 153-189.

[2]   P.J.Denning, G.S.Graham, *Multiprogrammed Memory Management,* Proceedings of the IEEE, **63** (6), 924-939 (1975).

8.4.7 Clerk/System Model   There are C clerks at terminals. Each clerk spends a mean amount of time T_C reading and thinking and typing, and then waits for the system to respond. There are D disks. The mean processor time per job will be inflated due to execution of memory management paging code. The mean number of drum accesses per job will be inflated due to paging. Each job has a dedicated amount of memory for its own pages. The system state at any instant of time is given by J_C, the number of clerks reading and thinking and typing, J_P, the number of jobs waiting or in execution on the processors, J_{PF}, the number of jobs waiting or servicing a page fault on the drum, and $J_K, K=1,...,D$, the number of jobs waiting or servicing an access to disk K. The total number of jobs must equal the number of clerks:

$$J_P + J_{PF} + \sum_{K=1}^{D} J_K = C$$

The fraction of time the system is in state $\underline{J}$ is denoted by $\pi(\underline{J})$, and is given by

$$\pi(J_P,J_1,...,J_D) = \frac{1}{G_C}\frac{T_C^{J_C}}{J_C!} \prod_{K=1}^{J_P} \frac{v/I_E}{\beta(K)} (T_{PF})^{J_{PF}} \prod_{K=1}^{D}(T_D N_K)^{J_K}$$

8.4.8 Additional Reading

[1]   J.Abate, H.Dubner, S.B.Weinberg, *Queueing Analysis of the IBM 2314 Disk Storage Facility,* Journal of the ACM, **15** (4), 577-589 (1968).

[2]   J.P.Buzen, *I/O Subsystem Architecture,* Proceedings of the IEEE, **63** (6), 871-879 (1975).

8.4.9 Summary   In a well engineered system, there should be little contention for resources:

• Processors execute most of the time out of local cache memory, while contention for main memory should be rare

- Processors should contend rarely for a common operating system table

- Paging should occur rarely because most jobs should fit into memory

- Clerks should contend rarely for common files and processor cycles

EXERCISE: Plot the effective number of processors versus J_P, the mean number of jobs waiting or in execution for one of P processors, on the same plot, for

A. The mean value analysis $min[J_P, P]$

B. With memory contention

C. With memory contention and operating system critical region lockout

D. With memory contention, operating system critical region lockout, and secondary storage activity for paging and for file I/O

E. With memory contention, operating system critical region lockout, secondary storage activity for paging and for file I/O, and with clerks submitting jobs at random instants of time

Interpret your results.

8.4.10 Additional Reading

[1] A.A.Fredericks, *Approximations for Customer Viewed Delays in Multiprogrammed, Transaction Oriented Computer Systems,* Bell System Technical Journal, **59** (9), 1559-1574 (1980).

[2] J.C.Browne, K.M.Chandy, R.M.Brown, T.W.Keller, D.F.Towsley, C.W.Dissly, *Hierarchical Techniques for the Development of Realistic Models of Complex Computer Systems,* Proceedings of the IEEE, **63** (6), 966-975 (1975).

8.5 On Line Transaction Processing

The motivation for this section was taken from what is widely known as online transaction processing:

- Attendants or clerks receive telephone calls from customers

- Information is entered into and retrieved from an online data base by clerks talking with customers

- Workers who do not have direct customer access fill the customer order again by interacting with the online system

This particular system is involved with handling telephone repair transactions, but the principles encountered here could just as well be applied to banking, finance, distribution, transportation, or other market segments. In fact, one of the first applications of this type of system was found in the airline industry, and the hard won lessons there have been applied in numerous other applications.

The system must execute four different types of transactions:

[1]   Trouble Entry (TE)--The telephone number of the problem telephone is entered into the system, and the clerk waits for the system to respond with a list of past problems associated with that telephone plus customer information plus a list of potential times and dates when a service call can be made (if necessary)

[2]   Trouble Report (TR)--A more detailed description of the problem is entered into the system for use later on, or in some cases for closing out the problem

[3]   Trouble Tracking (TT)--Customers and service staff interrogate the system to find the status of a particular job

[4]   Testing--Actual repair staff testing, either remotely or on premises, of the facilities in question

The figures below are a representative hardware configuration and a queueing network block diagram for this system:

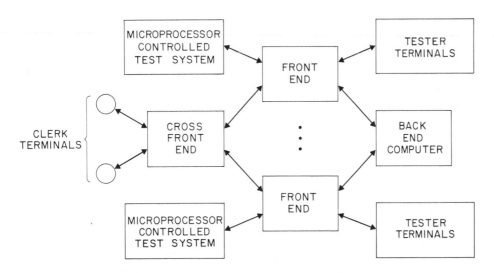

Figure 8.11.Hardware Configuration

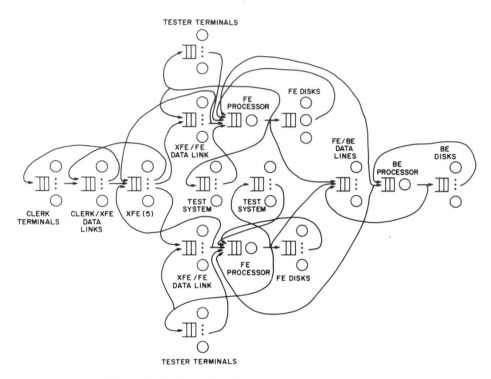

Figure 8.12. Queueing Network Block Diagram

8.5.1 System Traffic Performance Goals The table below is a representative set of mean value arrival rates and mean response time goals for each type of transaction:

Table 8.9. Traffic Goals

Transaction Type	Interarrival Frequency	Response Time
Trouble Entry	1 per clerk per two minutes	5 seconds
Trouble Report	1 per clerk per two minutes	10 seconds
Trouble Tracking	1 per clerk per minute	15 seconds
Testing	1 per clerk per five minutes	45 seconds

These goals are intended for a peak busy hour: if they are met, performance is adequate. As a refinement, we might wish to specify these goals at two different points, say during a normal business day (10-11 AM or 2-3 PM), as well as during a peak busy hour (busiest day in the month, quarter, year), in order to assess sensitivity to fluctuations in offered load.

The figure below plots the total mean time to complete one customer contact (both a trouble entry and trouble report) transaction as a function of the mean number of lines that each attendant must handle. We have assumed one order per line per year, and two hundred fifty business days per year. We might wish to assign staff to this type of job for only part of a day, say two or four hours, rather than for eight hours a day, and have plotted the impact on system performance in this figure for these three choices.

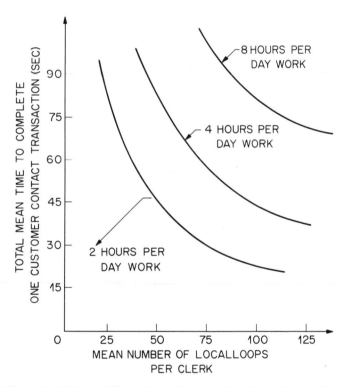

Figure 8.13.Mean Throughput Rate vs Number of Lines/Clerk

We complement this plot with a second plot showing mean customer delay vs number of lines per clerk, shown below.

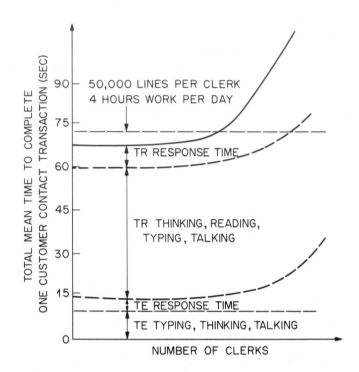

Figure 8.14.Mean Customer Delay vs Number of Lines/Clerk

8.5.2 Resources Required Per Transaction What are the resources required for each step of each transaction? First, we show the workflow and resource used at each step for each transaction type in the figures below:

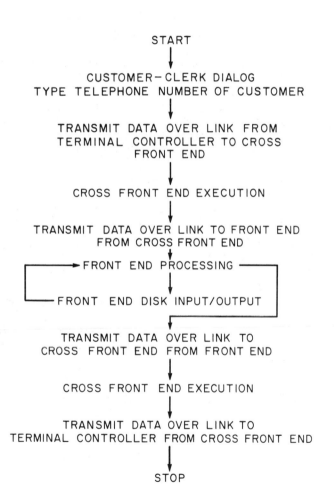

Figure 8.15. Trouble Entry Work Flow

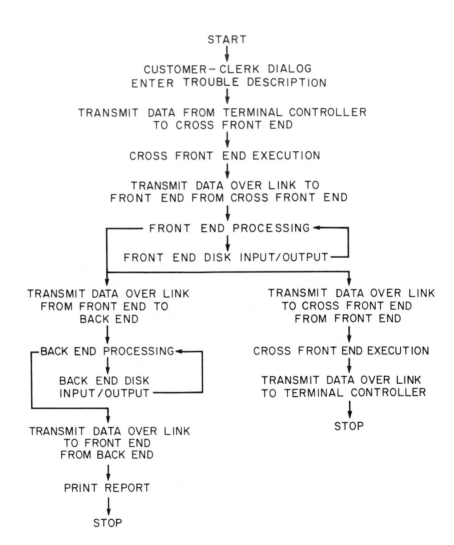

Figure 8.16.Trouble Report Work Flow

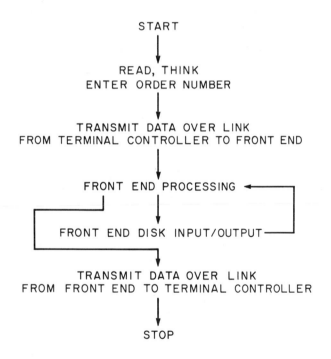

START

READ, THINK
ENTER ORDER NUMBER

TRANSMIT DATA OVER LINK
FROM TERMINAL CONTROLLER TO FRONT END

FRONT END PROCESSING

FRONT END DISK INPUT/OUTPUT

TRANSMIT DATA OVER LINK
FROM FRONT END TO TERMINAL CONTROLLER

STOP

Figure 8.17.Trouble Tracking Work Flow

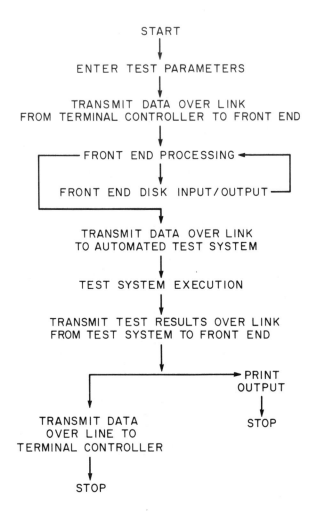

Figure 8.18. Testing Work Flow

The tables below summarize the mean time required to hold these resources at each step of execution of each transaction:

Table 8.10. Trouble Entry Work Flow Resources

Task	Mean Time
Transmit 30 Bytes Data from Terminal to XFE	80 msec
XFE Switching	250 msec
Transmit Data from XFE to FE	80 msec
Front End Processor	500 msec
Front End Disk Access (5 Accesses)	125 msec
Transmit Mask (800 Bytes) from FE to XFE	250 msec
XFE Switching	250 msec
XFE to Terminal Transmission (800 Bytes)	250 msec
Total	2.785 sec

Table 8.11. Trouble Report Work Flow Resources

Task	Mean Time
Data Transmission from Terminal to XFE (500 Bytes)	1.25 sec
XFE Switching	250 msec
XFE to FE Data Transmission	1.25 sec
Front End Processor Execution	750 msec
Front End Disk Access Time (12-15 Accesses)	300-375 msec
FE to XFE Data Transmission	125 msec
XFE Switching	250 msec
XFE to Terminal Data Transmission (50 Bytes)	125 msec
Total	4.3-4.375 sec

Table 8.12. Tester Work Flow Resources

Task	Mean Time
Data Transmission from Terminal to FE (150 Bytes)	750 msec
FE Processor Time	100 msec
FE Disk Access Time (2 Disk Accesses)	100 msec
Data Transmission from FE to MLT (150 bytes)	750 msec
MLT Execution	20-30 sec
MLT to FE Data Transmission (300 Bytes)	1.5 sec
FE Processor Time	100 msec
FE Disk Access Time (2-3 Disk Accesses)	100-150 msec
Print Output (900 characters, 30 char/sec)	30 sec
Total	53.4-63.45 sec

Table 8.13.Trouble Tracking Work Flow Resources

Task	Mean Time
Terminal to FE Data Transmission(200 Bytes)	1.0 sec
FE Processor Time	500 msec
FE Disk Access Time(5 Accesses)	250 msec
Transmit Data to Terminal(200 Bytes)	1.0 sec
Total	1.75 sec

8.5.3 Delay Analysis We choose to fix the background workload and vary the number of clerks at terminals handling TE and TR transactions. The background load we fix is

- Two hundred forty trouble status transactions per hour

- Sixty tester transactions per hour per front end

The remaining parameters that can be varied are

- Number of cross front end processors

- Number of front end subsystems

- Number of disks per front end

- Number of data links between the clerks' terminals and XFE

- Number of data links between each FE and XFE

- Work balance per FE

We begin with the simplest case, doing a single type of transaction, TE. If performance is inadequate here, it will presumably be worse with multiple transactions being executed. This also gives us a natural starting point for more detailed studies, a baseline comparison case. The table below summarizes the mean number of trouble entry transactions per hour that can be handled with a mean response time of four seconds or less, assuming

- Six front ends

- Two cross front ends

- Six terminal to XFE data links

- Two disks per FE

- 50 msec per disk access per transaction

- 250 msec FE processor time per transaction

**Table 8.14. Trouble Entry Mean Throughput Rate
with Mean Response Time 4 Seconds or Less
with No Other Types of Transactions Executed**

XFE Time	FE Disk Access/TE	
per TE	5 Disk Accesses	25 Disk Accesses
0.10 sec	>29,647 TE/HR	22,235 TE/HR
0.20 sec	>29,647 TE/HR	21,176 TE/HR
0.30 sec	19,059 TE/HR	17,470 TE/HR
0.40 sec	13,764 TE/HR	12,706 TE/HR
0.50 sec	10,588 TE/HR	9,529 TE/HR
0.60 sec	8,470 TE/HR	7,941 TE/HR

Each trouble entry transaction is switched twice by the XFE, once going in, once going out, and requires 250 msec per switch, so the current system is operating at a maximum of roughly ten thousand TE transactions per hour with no other work going on.

What if we include the three other transaction types? How will this impact the system performance? The table below summarizes calculations for that exercise:

**Table 8.15. Trouble Entry Mean Throughput Rate
with Mean Response Time 4 Seconds or Less
with Other Transactions Concurrently Executed**

XFE Time	FE disk Access/TE	
per TE	5 Disk Accesses	25 Disk Accesses
0.10 sec	28,059 TE/hr	18,000 TE/hr
0.20 sec	23,294 TE/hr	16,941 TE/hr
0.30 sec	15,353 TE/hr	13,765 TE/hr
0.40 sec	11,118 TE/hr	10,059 TE/hr
0.50 sec	8,470 TE/hr	7,412 TE/hr
0.60 sec	6,882 TE/hr	5,823 TE/hr

This impact is roughly twenty per cent: the system TE handling capability drops from 10,588 or 9,529 TE/hr to 8,470 or 7,412 TE/hr

What if the XFE were replaced with a high speed bus, i.e., such as *ETHERNET* or any of a wide number of variants? This would move performance down to the regime where the XFE time per message is under ten milliseconds, increasing capacity to 18,000 TE/hr at the worst! Note that the total system capacity increases by roughly a factor of two to three if the XFE is *infinitely* fast, because the XFE is no longer the bottleneck limiting performance.

What if we vary the number of CRSAB-XFE data links? The table below summarizes the impact on performance in going from four to six links, with five disk accesses per TE:

**Table 8.16. Trouble Entry Mean Throughput Rate
with Mean Response Time 4 Seconds or Less
5 Disk Accesses/TE**

| XFE | 25 msec/disk access | |
Time/TE	4 CRSAB-XFE Links	6 CRSAB-XFE Links
0.10 sec	29,647 TE/hr	29,647 TE/hr
0.20 sec	29,647 TE/hr	29,647 TE/hr
0.30 sec	19,059 TE/hr	19,059 TE/hr
0.40 sec	13,765 TE/hr	13,765 TE/hr
0.50 sec	10,588 TE/hr	10,588 TE/hr
0.60 sec	8,470 TE/hr	8,470 TE/hr

Hence, we see that going from four to six CRSAB-XFE data links has *negligible* impact on performance at this level of analysis.

What is the impact on performance due to file system layout? One way to quantify this is to vary the disk access time from twenty five milliseconds per access to fifty milliseconds per access:

**Table 8.17. Trouble Entry Mean Throughput Rate
with Mean Response Time 4 Seconds or Less
Four CRSAB-XFE Data Links**

| XFE | 5 Disk Accesses/TE | |
Time/TE	25 msec/Disk Access	50 msec/Disk Access
0.10 sec	18,529 TE/hr	18,529 TE/hr
0.20 sec	18,529 TE/hr	18,000 TE/hr
0.30 sec	14,823 TE/hr	14,823 TE/hr
0.40 sec	10,588 TE/hr	10,588 TE/hr
0.50 sec	8,470 TE/hr	8,470 TE/hr
0.60 sec	6,682 TE/hr	6,682 TE/hr

This shows that at this level of analysis, varying the file system layout has virtually no impact on performance.

What if we go from one to two XFE systems? The table below is a summary of calculations for one such exercise:

Table 8.18.Trouble Entry Mean Throughput Rate
with Mean Response 4 Seconds or Less
5 Disk Access/TE--4 CRSAB-XFE Data Links

XFE Time/TE	One XFE	Two XFEs
0.10 sec	18,529 TE/hr	18,529 TE/hr
0.20 sec	13,235 TE/hr	18,000 TE/hr
0.30 sec	6,882 TE/hr	14,823 TE/hr
0.40 sec	4,765 TE/hr	11,117 TE/hr
0.50 sec	3,176 TE/hr	8,470 TE/hr
0.60 sec	2,647 TE/hr	6,882 TE/hr

This table makes clear the traffic handling capability of the *system* is roughly doubled in going from one to two XFEs, because this is the bottleneck!

What if we drop the mean response time criterion from four seconds to three seconds? The table below is a summary of one such set of calculations:

Table 8.19.Trouble Entry Mean Throughput Rate
vs XFE Time per TE
5 Disk Accesses/TE--Two XFEs

XFE Time/TE	Maximum Mean Response Time	
	3 Seconds	4 Seconds
0.10 sec	18,000 TE/hr	18,529 TE/hr
0.20 sec	17,470 TE/hr	18,000 TE/hr
0.30 sec	14,291 TE/hr	14,823 TE/hr
0.40 sec	10,059 TE/hr	11,118 TE/hr
0.50 sec	7,941 TE/hr	8,470 TE/hr
0.60 sec	5,823 TE/hr	6,682 TE/hr

This suggests that the total system traffic handling capability is sensitive to the mean response time goal, since going from three to four seconds increases the mean throughput rate by ten per cent.

Additional studies can be carried out varying

- The amount of front end processor time per TE

- The number of front end processors

- The tester workload distribution (uniformly distributed across all front ends versus all focused on one front end)

8.5.4 Buffering Analysis What type of buffering might be employed in the XFE? Most of the time a transaction demands a buffer, a buffer should be available: the fraction of time a buffer is not available should be negligible. As an exercise, show that the fraction of time no buffer is available, given

B_{buffer} buffers for a P_{XFE} processor XFE configuration is given by

$$\text{fraction of time no buffer available} = \frac{P\ U^{B_{buffer}+1-P_{XFE}}B_{Erlang}(P,P\ U)}{P(1-U)(1-B_{Erlang}(P,P\ U))}$$

where $B_{Erlang}(P,A)$ is the Erlang blocking function:

$$B_{Erlang}(P,A) = \frac{A^P/P!}{\sum_{K=0}^{P}A^K/K!}$$

and U is the fraction of time each XFE processor is busy, its utilization.

The table below summarizes one set of calculations for number of buffers for either one or two XFE processors (i.e., the calculation was not sensitive to the number of XFEs):

Table 8.20.Minimum Number of Buffers

Processor Utilization	Fraction of Time All Buffers Filled		
	0.001	0.0001	0.00001
0.50	11	14	17
0.60	14	19	23
0.70	20	27	33
0.80	32	42	52
0.90	66	88	110

In practice, it is important to *dedicate* buffers to different FE processors rather than to *pool* buffers for all FE processors, because one FE will typically be congested, and will hold its buffers for much longer than all the other FE systems, effectively locking out or hogging resources.

8.5.5 Summary First we developed a systematic description of the flow of control and data throughout the system, the resources required for each step of each job, and the mean time for each job step. Second we used this to determine bottlenecks. What are the bottlenecks? The candidates are

- The XFE processor is a bottleneck
- The FE processor is a bottleneck
- The FE disk is a bottleneck
- The MLT is a bottleneck
- The data links between the attendants and XFE are a bottleneck
- The XFE to FE data links are a bottleneck

The numbers here suggested that for virtually any scenario, under light load, the attendants are the bottleneck, while under heavy load, the XFE is the bottleneck. If the XFE is replaced by a much higher speed local area network or switch, then the FE (either processor or disk) becomes the bottleneck.

Third, we carried out sensitivity studies, that showed that

- If the system executed TE transactions alone, then the current mean throughput rate is 10,000 per hour, while if a representative mix of TE, TR, Tracking and Testing transactions are executed, then this drops to 7,500 transactions per hour.

- Once the XFE-CRSAB has four or more data links, the data links are not a significant bottleneck.

- If the file system layout is changed on the FE disk, this has virtually no impact on performance.

- Doubling the number of XFEs more than doubles the number of TEs per hour with acceptable mean response time (3,000 TE/hour with one XFE, 8,000 TE/hour with two XFEs). The reason it *more* than doubles is that the XFE is *not* executing jobs at its maximum rate, plus there is an *economy of scale* in going from one to two XFEs.

- Changing the acceptable mean response time from four to three seconds had negligible impact on performance.

8.5.6 Additional Reading

[1]   R.L.Martin, *System Architecture of the Automated Repair Service Bureau,* Bell System Technical Journal, **61** (6), Part 2, 1115-1130 (1982).

[2]   J.P.Holtman, *The Context-Sensitive Switch of the Loop Maintenance Operations System,* Bell System Technical Journal, **61** (6), Part 2, 1197-1208 (1982).

Problems

1) Terminals are connected to one of four computers. The computers are connected in a network: link A connects computers 1 and 2, link B connects computers 2 and 3, link C connects computers 3 and 4, and link D connects computers 4 and 1. The links allows the computers and terminals to send messages back and forth. The message lengths are independent identically distributed exponential random variables, with the mean message length one thousand (1000) bits. Each computer wishes to send six (6) messages per second to every other computer. The total transmission capacity available is two hundred kilobits (200,000 bits) per second, apportioned amongst all the links. The routing strategy adopted is to send all messages clockwise around the network.

A. Write out the explicit routing path for all messages from computer i to computer j, i,j=1,2,3,4.

B. Calculate the mean message rate for each of the four links.

C. Find an assignment of transmission capacity that minimizes the total mean message queueing time (time in system)

D. Find the minimum total mean message queueing time.

Repeat the above exercise for a shortest path routing policy.

A complete answer must exhibit:

[1] the routing paths

[2] the mean message rates on each link

[3] the capacity assignment

[4] the minimum mean message delay

2) An automatic call distributor will have to handle one hundred calls during a normal business hour, and two hundred calls during a peak business hour. The mean duration of each call is two minutes, with thirty seconds of after call cleanup work done by the attendant.

A. How many trunks and agents are required to achieve a trunk blocking of no more than one per cent during a normal business hour, and no more than five per cent during a peak business hour, with a mean waiting time of no more than ten seconds during a normal business hour, and no more than thirty seconds during a peak business hour?

B.   Repeat if the mean call duration is reduced to thirty seconds with no after call cleanup work

C.   Repeat if the mean call duration is increased to five minutes with one minute of after call cleanup work

D.   Repeat for each of the above if the goals are changed to no more than ten per cent trunk blocking during a normal business hour, and no more than thirty per cent trunk blocking during a peak business hour

E.   BONUS: Repeat for each of the above if one quarter of the calls that get accepted defect or renege before an agent handles them

3) A transmitter sends data to a receiver over a serially reusable link. The propagation time of data from transmitter to receiver and back is negligible. The transmitter spends a mean amount of time T_{trans} processing each message. The receiver spends a mean amount of time T_{rec} processing each message. We choose to fix $T_{rec}=1.0$ and vary $T_{trans}=1.0, 0.5, 0.2$.

A.   Plot the mean throughput rate of message through the system versus the total number of messages in the system using these numbers for

   • An exponential closed queueing network model

   • An exponential open queueing network model

   • An exponential distribution for the transmitter processing time and a hyperexponential distribution for the receiver processing time

   • A hypoexponential distribution for the transmitter processing time and an exponential distribution for the receiver processing time

B.   Suppose that we attempt to replace the two stage pipeline by one queue with one server: what is the service rate of the server versus the number of messages in the system? Plot the mean throughput rate versus the number of messages in the system using an exponential queueing network model and compare with that in the previous section.

4) * A data communications system consists of two subsystems

---

*   P.J.Schweitzer, S.S.Lam, *Buffer Overflow in a Store and Forward Network Node,* IBM J.Research and Development, **20** (6), 542-550 (1976)

- The first stage examines each arriving message, and determines whether it is a new message or an acknowledgement of a properly received previously transmitted message. If it is a new message, it is stored in a buffer until an acknowledgement is received. If it is an acknowledgement, the buffer with the message is flushed. For each new message, a header is added that contains a checksum and associated control information. This requires a mean time of T_{new} for each new message and T_{ack} for each acknowledgement.

- The second stage involves transmitting each message over a link. There are only two output links. Each message is transmitted and then held in a system buffer until an acknowledgement of receipt of the message is received. This effectively increases the message transmission time by a factor of V_{ack} over what it would be if no acknowledgement were required.

The total number of system buffers is fixed at B. The entire system is modeled as a queueing network with a memory constraint of B messages inside it. For each of the following parts, we wish to plot the mean throughput rate versus number of buffers assuming a closed exponential queueing network, and compare this with upper and lower bounds on mean throughput rate using mean value information only and using queueing network bounds.

A. The initial new message handling time is $T_{init} = 500\ \mu\ sec$, while the acknowledgement message handling time is $T_{ack} = 100\ \mu\ sec$. The output speeds of both lines are identical, and are fixed at 9.6 KBPS. The inflation of the message transmission time due to waiting for an acknowledgement is a factor of twenty, i.e., $V_{ack}=20$. Plot the mean throughput rate versus the number of buffers, for B=1 to 100, for three cases

    [1]   Fifty per cent of the total message arrivals go to line one

    [2]   Twenty per cent of the total message arrivals go to line one

    [3]   Eighty per cent of the total message arrivals go to line one

B. Repeat the above with the line speed 19.2 KBPS

C. Repeat the above with the line speed 56 KBPS

D. Repeat the above with line one at 9.6 KBPS and line two at 56 KBPS

E. Repeat the above with $V_{ack}=1$

5) C clerks at terminals submit one type of transaction for execution by a computer system. Each clerk spends a given amount of time reading, thinking and typing to enter the transaction, denoted by T_{clerk}, and then waits for the system to respond, with the execution time of a transaction with no contention

denoted by $T_{transaction}$. The mean time to execute one transaction is fixed at one time unit, $E(T_{transaction})=1$.

A. If T_{clerk} and $T_{transaction}$ are deterministic or constant, what is the mean throughput rate of work through the system? What is an upper bound on the mean throughput rate of work through the system?

B. If T_{clerk} is an exponentially distributed random variable, and $T_{transaction}$ is hyperexponentially distributed, what is a lower bound on the mean throughput rate of work through the system?

C. The squared coefficient of variation for the distribution of T_{clerk} is given by

$$C^2_{clerk} = \frac{var(T_{clerk})}{E^2(T_{clerk})}$$

If $T_{transaction}$ is exponentially distributed and T_{clerk} is hyperexponentially distributed with its mean fixed at ten, then plot the mean throughput rate versus the number of clerks C for $C=1,...,10$ for $C^2_{clerk}=0,1,2,4,8$

D. Repeat the above with T_{clerk} hyperexponentially distributed with a mean of five.

6) A system consists of a single central processor, plus two disk controllers each handling one disk, plus five fixed head disks or drums. The system handles one type of job, which requires T_{proc} mean amount of processor time, N_{drum} accesses to the drums, and N_{disk} disk accesses. The table below summarizes representative disk access times:

Table 8.21. Disk Access Time Summary

Disk Type	Mean Access Time
Slow Speed	100 msec
Medium Speed	50 msec
High Speed	20 msec

The table below summarizes representative drum access times:

Table 8.22. Drum Access Time Summary

Drum Type	Mean Access Time
Slow Speed	5 msec
High Speed	1 msec

Answer the following questions:

A. Assume that N_{disk}=20 and N_{drum}=100. For a configuration consisting of only slow speed drums and disks, plot the mean throughput rate versus number of jobs in the system using a queueing network analysis as well as upper and lower bounds. What is the resource that reaches complete utilization first?

B. Repeat for a configuration consisting of only high speed drums and disks. What is the resource that reaches complete utilization first?

C. Repeat both of the above if the processor is replaced by a processor that is four times as fast.

D. Suppose that $N_{terminal}$ terminals are connected to this system, with a mean time per transaction at the terminal due to reading and thinking and typing of thirty seconds. Plot the mean throughput rate and mean delay versus number of terminals for each of the above parts.

7) M jobs circulate in a closed system consisting of a processor and a paging drum. The mean processor time per transaction is the sum of two terms, one due to actual processing, $T_{processor}$, where $T_{processor}$ equals two hundred eighty milliseconds (280 msec) and one due to processor time to handle page faults, T_{page}. The mean processor time due to page fault handling is the product of the number of drum accesses per job, N_{drum}, and the mean time for the processor to handle one page fault, T_{fault}, where T_{fault} equals one millisecond. The mean number of drum accesses per job depends on model parameters via the following expression:

$$N_{drum} = 9 + 2 \times max\,(0, M - 2)$$

so for $M \leqslant 2$ this equals nine, and otherwise increase by two beyond this point. The mean time for the drum to fetch a page is forty milliseconds.

A. Plot the mean number of paging drum accesses versus M.

B. Plot the mean throughput rate of completing jobs versus M,

$$mean\ throughput\ rate = \frac{U_{processor}}{T_{processor} + N_{drum} \times T_{fault}}$$

where $U_{processor}$ is the processor utilization, the fraction of time the processor is busy doing work.

C. Find that value of M that maximizes the mean throughput rate.

8) An online transaction processing system consists of C clerks at terminals

with a single processor and a single disk. The mean time each clerk spends per transaction reading, thinking and typing is fifteen seconds. The total mean amount of processor time per transaction is five hundred milliseconds. Each transaction makes a mean of twenty five disk accesses, and each disk access requires a mean time to complete of fifty milliseconds.

A. What is the bottleneck in the system for five clerks? for ten clerks? for twenty clerks?

B. Plot the mean rate of executing transactions per second for the entire system versus the number of clerks, using a closed queueing network with exponentially distributed service times at each node as well as upper and lower bounds on mean throughput rate from Little's Law

C. If the file system layout is changed, the mean time per disk access is reduced to twenty milliseconds. What changes in the above analysis?

D. If the mean time a clerk spends reading, thinking and typing is increased to thirty seconds, what changes in the above analysis?

E. If additional features are added so the mean processor time per transaction is increased to eight hundred milliseconds per transaction, what changes in the above analysis?

9) A packet switching system has a design goal of handling two hundred packets per second during a normal business hour, and five hundred packets per second during a peak business hour. Each packet requires the following steps:

Table 8.23. Packet Operations

Step	Function	Instructions
1	Generate Interrupt	50
2	Strip Old Header	250
3	Access Routing Tables	100
4	Add New Header	300
5	Generate Interrupt	50
6	Transmit Packet	100
7	Generate Interrupt	50
8	Process Acknowledgement	150
9	Log Packet Statistics	300

A set of single board computers are employed with a high speed backplane bus. The bus is assumed to be infinitely fast compared with the speed of packet processing.

[1]   Each processor can execute 500,000 assembly language instructions per second

    A.   How many processors are needed if each processor will handle all packet processing functions?

    B.   How many processors are needed if some processors handle input/output while others handle routing and still others log packet statistics?

[2]   Repeat if each processor can execute 1,000,000 assembly language instructions per second

10) A data switching system employs fast circuit switching. Each message upon arrival is executed in the following manner

Table 8.24.Data Switching System

Step	Function
1	Seize Circuit
2	Route Message
3	Release Circuit
4	Record Statistics

The resources and mean time for each step are as follows:

Table 8.25.Resource/Step Summary

Step	Circuit	Processor	Time
1	1	0	1 msec
2	1	1	5 msec
3	1	1	1 msec
4	0	1	2 msec

If all available circuits are busy, arrivals are blocked or rejected and are assumed to retry later. If all processors are busy, messages are buffered until a processor becomes available. The message arrival statistics are assumed to be simple Poisson. During a normal business hour, the system is intended to switch one hundred messages per second. During a peak business hour, the system is intended to switch five hundred messages per second.

[1]   During a normal business hour, no more than one message in ten can be blocked due to no circuit available, and no more than one message in one hundred can be blocked due to no processor available. How many circuits and processors can meet normal business hour design goals?

[2] During a peak business hour, no more than one message in two can be blocked due to no circuit available, and no more than one message in ten can be blocked due to no processor available. How many circuits and processors can meet peak business hour design goals?

11) An online airline reservation system handles transactions from operators at terminals:

- Status inquiry: Flight arrival, departure, time/date/airport

- Sell: Purchase a ticket for a particular flight

- Passenger data: How many seats are available for a given flight? Is a given person listed as a passenger for a given flight?

- Cancel: Delete a given item.

The hardware configuration consists of a processor with a given amount of memory, and a disk controller that can handle up to four disk spindles. Each transaction involves both processing and input/output from and to disks. The arrival rate of each type of transaction and the mean amount of processor time and input/output is summarized in the table below:

Table 8.26. Workload Summary

Transaction Type	Arrival Rate	Mean Processor Time/Transaction	Mean Number of Disk Accesses/Transaction
Inquiry	26,000/day	10 msec	2 disk accesses
Sell	32,000/day	35 msec	3 disk accesses
Passenger Data	47,000/day	9 msec	2 disk accesses
Cancel	7,000/day	55 msec	8 disk accesses

The amount of time spent per disk access is summarized in the table below:

Table 8.27. Disk Access Time Statistics

Revolution time	25 msec
Data record length	1/10 of a track
Mean access time	85.5 msec
Controller time	2 msec

A. What is the mean utilization of the processor, disk controller, and each disk?

B. Plot the mean throughput rate and mean delay for each type of transaction versus the total mean arrival rate.

C. If a mean delay of one second or less is desirable, can the system meet its design goal?

D. What is the largest number of transactions that are active in the system when the mean delay per transaction is one second or less?

E. Suppose it is possible to purchase a system with two processors, each of which is half the speed of that proposed here. What is the largest total mean arrival rate of transactions to that system that will meet a design goal of a mean transaction delay of one second or less?

12) A private branch exchange consists of a buffer capable of holding five simultaneous calls at most, two private line trunks, and access to common carrier trunks. Call holding times are independent identically distributed exponential random variables with mean holding time of one hundred seconds. If a call is buffered because all trunks are busy, that call will defect in a mean time of ten seconds. If a call is buffered because all trunks are busy, that call will be assigned to a common carrier trunk in a mean time of fifteen seconds.

A. What is the state space for describing the operation of this system?

B. What is the maximum mean throughput rate for completing calls based on a mean value analysis alone?

C. What is the fraction of call attempts blocked based on a Jackson network analysis?

D. What is the mean rate of completing calls on the private line trunks based on a Jackson network analysis?

E. What is the mean rate at which calls seize common carrier trunks based on a Jackson network analysis?

F. What are the mean number of calls in progress on the private line and common carrier calls?

G. What fraction of successful call attempts wait for less than five seconds to get serviced?

Up to this point we have concentrated on analyzing the mean throughput rate for multiple resource systems, and the mean throughput rate and mean delay bounds for networks of single resource systems. We saw that for many different types of systems typically *one* single type of resource is limiting the maximum mean throughput rate. The avenues available for improving system performance are to add more resources (perhaps moving the bottleneck resource elsewhere) or *scheduling* the single resource in an effective manner. In this section we will focus on different techniques for scheduling a single resource, in order to meet delay criteria. In practice a system cannot be exercised continuously at its maximum mean rate of completing work, but rather must complete work at some lower rate in order to meet delay criteria of different types. How much below complete utilization this one resource can operate is the subject of this section (and the realm of *queueing theory* as a branch of applied mathematics).

Rather than focusing on simply a mean value analysis, we now worry about other phenomena:

• *fluctuations* about a mean value and

• *correlations* among the fluctuations.

Intuitively, the more regular (the less the fluctuations) or constant and the more predictable the fluctuations (the correlations in the fluctuations), the easier it will be to meet delay criteria, and vice versa. Since more detailed questions are asked, more detailed information must be given to describe system operation. In any queueing system there are three main ingredients:

• a characterization of the arrival statistics of each transaction type

• a characterization of the resources required at each stage of execution of each transaction type

• a policy arbitrating contention for resources (remember there is only a limited amount of each resource type!)

In the previous sections, we used mean values to characterize the arrival statistics (e.g., a rate) and resources required at each stage of execution, for a given policy. In analyzing the mean throughput rate and mean delay in earlier sections, when we fixed the mean time for execution at each stage of each job, we saw that the best performance was obtained when the mean times for each stage of execution were *constant* or *deterministic* while the worst performance was obtained when the fluctuations about the mean times became larger and larger. Here, we expect to see similar phenomena. Remember: all the systems we deal with are *deterministic* in their functional operation, but they are sufficiently complex that we choose a *statistical* or *probabilistic* characterization of the arrival and service statistics, in order to summarize with a very small number of parameters what in fact is a very large number of parameters whose detail may be overwhelming.

9.1 Time Scale of Interest

What time scale is of interest? In order to adequately characterize a system statistically, we expect the measurements we take to stabilize at some (small!) range of values if measurements are carried out over a sufficiently long time interval. How long is long enough? There is no simple answer here. For example, if the disk subsystem is capable of making a disk access every thirty milliseconds, and the processor is capable of doing useful work every ten milliseconds, then if we gather measurements over a time scale one hundred or one thousand times as long as these smallest time intervals, for example, every ten or every thirty seconds, then this is a long time interval during which there is a reasonable possibility that the system has stabilized. On the other hand, it is easy to produce counterexamples in which this need not be the case. The problem is studied in the realm of time series analysis and we will drop it from further consideration here. Our intent is merely to point out that this is a real problem that must be dealt with in actual systems. Queueing systems have both an initial or transient behavior and a long term time averaged behavior. The long term time averaged behavior will occupy all of our attention here, but the transient behavior is clearly of great interest in many applications. When measurements are presented on any system, always check to see at what point transients have died out and at what point long term time averaged behavior appears to set in. Unfortunately, since we wish to study behavior with congestion, as load builds, transients take longer and longer to die out, and we need more and more data to see the demarcation between the two regimes!

9.2 Workload Arrival Statistics

How do we characterize the arrival statistics? Suppose we observed N arrivals in an interval of duration T time units starting at time zero, and we recorded the arrival time epochs as $t_K, K=1,...,N$ which may possibly be the empty set. One way to characterize the arrival statistics would be by a cumulative distribution function

$$distribution\ function = PROB[t_1 \leqslant T_1, \ldots, t_N \leqslant T_N]$$

for each value of N, or the interarrival time distribution for each value of N. In practice, this becomes very unwieldy, so in the next section we introduce additional restrictions on the arrival process that are very often met in practice yet are analytically tractable.

9.2.1 Finite Source Arrival Statistics We first turn to the type of arrival statistics that we used to model clerks at terminals submitting transactions in earlier sections. Since we only have a finite number of clerks and terminals, the population is *finite* and the arrival statistics are due to a *finite set of sources* which leads to the title of this section. The sequence of times from the completion of the last transaction until the submission of the next transaction fluctuate; the time intervals are called *random variables* because they vary and because the fluctuations, while due to many diverse causes, are so complex that we simply summarize all of this by calling them random. Every sequence of time intervals is different from every other, because the precise combination of events leading to that set of times is highly likely to be duplicated exactly.

Example. Ten clerks submit one hundred transactions each to an online transaction processing system. The time interval between the completion of the last transaction and submission of the next transaction is recorded, and the results summarized in the table below:

Table 9.1.One Hundred Transactions/Each of Ten Clerks

Intersubmission Time	Number of Transactions
0-2.5 seconds	150
2.5-5.0 seconds	135
5.0-7.5 seconds	110
7.5-10.0 seconds	90
10.0-12.5 seconds	80
12.5-15.0 seconds	65
15.0-17.5 seconds	60
17.5-20.0 seconds	45
20.0-25.0 seconds	75
25.0-30.0 seconds	55
> 30 seconds	135

We want to summarize all this information with *one* parameter, the *average* or *mean* intersubmission time. We compute this by multiplying the *fraction* of transactions with a given mean intersubmission time by the *maximum* intersubmission (e.g., 0-2.5 seconds means we assume all jobs had an intersubmission time of 2.5 seconds), and then summing the resultant terms:

$$E(T_{idle}) = 2.5(.150) + 5.0(.135) + 7.5(.110) + 10(.09) + 12.5(.08) + 15(.065)$$
$$+ 17.5(.06) + 20(.045) + 25(.075) + 30(.055) + 45(.135)$$
$$= 14.425 \; seconds \approx 15 \; seconds$$

Note that we have assumed that *all* intersubmissions greater than thirty seconds were *arbitrarily* forty five seconds.

In summary, we can summarize *all* the data by its average or mean value of approximately fifteen seconds, and if we wish to assess sensitivity to this parameter we can change it to ten seconds or to twenty seconds or to whatever value is felt to be appropriate.

We now make even stronger assumptions:

- The sequence of intersubmission times are independent from transaction to transaction and operator to operator (no coffee breaks, no ganging up at the water cooler)

- The sequence of intersubmission times are identically distributed random variables (all operators and transactions lead to identical intersubmission time statistics)

- The intersubmission times are exponentially distributed random variables.

This last statement, the choice of an *exponential* distribution to summarize *all* the intersubmission time statistics, is a key assumption. In words, this says the fraction of intersubmission times that is less than a given threshold, say X seconds, is approximated by an exponential distribution:

$$\textit{fraction of intersubmission time interval} \leqslant X =$$

$$1 - exp[-X/E(T_{idle})] = 1 - e^{-\lambda_{idle}X} \quad \lambda_{idle} \equiv \frac{1}{E(T_{idle})}$$

To test this goodness of fit, the figure below shows a quantile quantile plot of empirical or data quantiles versus exponential model quantiles.

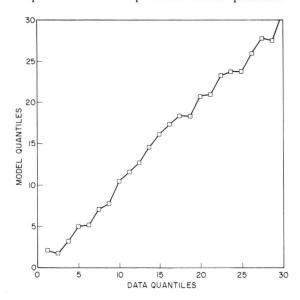

Figure 9.1. Empirical Quantiles vs Exponential Model Quantiles

Since the plot is approximately a straight line, the goodness of fit is felt to be acceptable, and we can use the exponential model with as much confidence as we place in our data and its analysis.

The fraction of time one clerk is idle less than or equal to X is given by

$$PROB[T_{idle} \ for \ one \ clerk \ \leqslant \ X] = 1 - exp[-X/E(T_{idle})] = 1 - e^{-\lambda_{idle}X}$$

The probability or fraction of time that we have J submissions by N clerks in an interval of duration T is given by

$$PROB[J \ submissions \ by \ N \ clerks \ in \ interval \ \leqslant \ X]$$

$$= \begin{pmatrix} N \\ J \end{pmatrix} \left[1 - exp(-X\lambda_{idle}) \right]^J \left[exp(-X\lambda_{idle}) \right]^{N-J} \quad J = 0,1,...,N$$

Many times the moment generating function of a distribution is easier to work with (analytically or numerically) than the actual distribution. Here the moment generating function is given by

$$E[X^J] = \sum_{J=0}^{N} Y^J PROB[J \ submissions \ by \ N \ clerks] =$$

$$\left[exp(-X\lambda_{idle}) + Y(1 - exp(-X\lambda_{idle})) \right]^N$$

This can be differentiated to find the mean number of submissions in a given time interval, and hence the mean arrival rate:

$$\frac{d}{dY}E[Y^J]|_{Y=1} = E(J) = N[1 - exp(-\lambda_{idle}X)]$$

The total mean arrival rate of work is thus given by the mean rate at which each clerk submits work multiplied by the mean number of clerks in the idle state, reading, thinking, typing, and so on:

$$total \ mean \ arrival \ rate = mean \ number \ of \ idle \ clerks \ \times \ \lambda_{idle}$$

As we add more and more clerks, the mean number *idle* (as well as the mean number waiting for response) will grow without bound over any threshold we set. What we want to do is fix the *total mean arrival rate* and increase the total number of clerks; this means the total mean number of idle clerks will grow without bound, while the total mean arrival rate is fixed, so the *mean idle time per transaction* must also grow without bound:

$$N \times \lambda_{idle} = \frac{N}{E(T_{idle})} = total \ mean \ arrival \ rate \equiv constant = \lambda$$

If we do this, we see that the mean number of arrivals in an interval of duration X seconds is given by

$$\lim_{N \to \infty} \begin{bmatrix} N \\ J \end{bmatrix} \left[1 - exp\left(-X\lambda_{idle} \right) \right]^{J} \left[exp(-X\lambda_{idle}) \right]^{N-J} = \frac{(\lambda X)^{J}}{J!} e^{-\lambda X} \quad J=0,1,2,...$$

Note that each terminal or source is contributing less and less arriving work, because the individual mean arrival time is growing without bound, and hence we call this the *infinite* population limit $(N \to \infty)$ of the finite population arrival process, the so called *Poisson* arrival process, which is the subject of our next section.

9.2.2 Infinite Source Poisson Process Now we assume the interarrival times are independent identically distributed exponential random variables, or, that the arrival statistics are *Poisson* distributed. This means that the interarrival times obey the following relationship:

$$PROB[t_{K+1} - t_{K} \leqslant X] = 1 - exp\left(-X/E[T_{A}] \right) = 1 - e^{-\lambda X} \quad K=1,2,3,...,N-1$$

$$E[t_{K+1} - t_{K}] = E[T_{A}] = \frac{1}{\lambda} \quad K=1,2,...,N-1$$

Numerous real life situations can in fact be adequately modeled by Poisson statistics. Why should this be a reasonable fit to actual data? Because whenever there is a superposition of a number of independent sources of arrivals, no one of which dominates, then under a variety of assumptions it can be shown that as the number of sources approaches infinity the superposition or sum of all the arrival streams converges to a Poisson process (this is the so called generalized *Central Limit Theorem* of probability theory). Another reason why the Poisson process matches actual data is that it has two properties that are often met in practice:

- the number of arrivals in disjoint time intervals are *independent* random variables

- the number of arrivals is proportional to the duration of the observation time interval

These are properties that are *unique* to the Poisson process, and for all these reasons make it a worthy candidate first cut model of arrival statistics in many applications.

What are some analytic properties of the Poisson process that might be useful in modeling?

- the superposition or sum of Poisson processes is Poisson, with mean arrival rate being the sum of the individual arrival rates: if we add two processes, the rates add and the new process is Poisson

- the randomized thinning of a Poisson process is a Poisson process, whereby at each arrival epoch we flip a coin and with probability P include the arrival epoch while with probability $(1-P)$ we discard it, i.e., we thin the arrival stream, with mean arrival rate P times that of the original process's arrival rate

The moment generating function of the interarrival time distribution is given by

$$E[exp(-z(t_{K+1}-t_K))] = \int_0^\infty e^{-zX} d_X[1-e^{-\lambda X}] = \frac{\lambda}{\lambda + z}$$

and this can be used to find moments of all integral order by the identity

$$E[T_A{}^K] = (-1)^K \frac{d^K}{dz^K}\left[\frac{\lambda}{\lambda + z}\right]\Big|_{z=0} \quad K=1,2,3,...$$

For example, the second moment of the interarrival time distribution of a Poisson process is given by

$$E(T_A{}^2) = \frac{2}{\lambda^2} \rightarrow var(interarrival\ time) = E(T_A{}^2) - E^2(T_A) = E^2(T_A) = \frac{1}{\lambda^2}$$

A related quantity is the number of arrivals in a time interval of duration T, denoted $N(T)$. Assuming the arrivals arc Poisson we see

$$PROB[N(T) = K] = \frac{(\lambda T)^K}{K!} exp(-\lambda T) \quad K=0,1,2,3,...$$

The moment generating function is given by

$$E[X^{N(T)}] = \sum_{K=0}^\infty X^K e^{-\lambda T} \frac{(\lambda T)^K}{K!} = e^{-\lambda T(1-X)}$$

This can be differentiated to find all factorial moments using this identity:

$$E[N(T)[N(T)-1][N(T)-2]...[N(T)-K+1]] = \frac{d^K}{dX^K} e^{-\lambda T(1-X)}\Big|_{X=1}$$

This has mean value

$$E[N(T)] = \lambda T$$

while the second factorial moment is given by

$$E[N(N-1)] = (\lambda T)^2$$

9.2.3 General Interarrival Time Statistics What if the interarrival time distribution is arbitrary, i.e., not finite or infinite source processes? One way to characterize the interarrival time distribution is by its first two moments, for example. One measure of the fluctuations in the interarrival time sequence is to measure the variance in units of the mean interarrival time (squared), with the result called the squared coefficient of variation:

$$squared\ coefficient\ of\ variation\ =\ \frac{var\,(interarrival\ time)}{E^2(interarrival\ time)}$$

Three cases arise:

$$squared\ coefficient\ of\ variation\ = \begin{cases} <1 & more\ regular\ than\ Poisson \\ 1 & Poisson \\ 1 & more\ irregular\ than\ Poisson \end{cases}$$

9.2.4 Message Switching System A message switching system must handle two different types of messages. Twenty per cent of the messages have a mean interarrival time of 320 microseconds, while eighty per cent of the messages have a mean interarrival time of 1024 microseconds. What is the squared coefficient of variation? First we calculate the mean interarrival time:

$$mean\ interarrival\ time\ =\ E\,(T_A)\ =\ 0.20{\times}32\ +\ 0.80{\times}1024\ =\ 825.6\ microseconds$$

Next, we calculate the variance of the message interarrival time distribution:

$$variance\ of\ message\ interarrival\ time\ distribution\ =\ var\,(T_A)$$

$$=\ 0.20{\times}[32{-}E\,(T_A)]^2\ +\ 0.80{\times}[1024{-}E\,(T_A)]^2$$

$$=\ 157450.24\ microseconds^2$$

Finally, we calculate the squared coefficient of variation for the message interarrival time distribution:

$$squared\ coefficient\ of\ variation\ =\ \frac{var\,(T_A)}{E^2(T_A)}\ =\ \frac{157450.24}{(825.6)^2}\ =\ 0.23099$$

This shows that the fluctuations are not as severe as would be encountered with an exponential message interarrival time distribution. In practice, we might choose to be *pessimistic* (fluctuations can presumably only make things worse) by using an exponential interarrival time distribution rather than using a constant interarrival time distribution.

9.2.5 Additional Reading

[1] M.B.Wilk, R.Gnanadesikan, *Probability Plotting Methods for the Analysis of Data,* Biometrika, **55** (1), 1-17 (1968).

[2] H.Heffes, *A Class of Data Traffic Processes--Covariance Function Characterization and Related Queuing Results,* Bell System Technical Journal, **59** (6), 897-929 (1980).

9.3 Service Time Distribution

The sequence of service or processing times can be characterized by their joint distribution. Rather than do so, we assume the processing times are independent identically distributed random variables, because in many cases this is a reasonable match of data, and because it is analytically tractable and allows many sensitivity studies to be readily performed.

9.3.1 Exponential Service Time Distribution A program executes one hundred times on the same hardware configuration with different inputs. The following statistics summarize how long the program executed:

Table 9.2.Execution Time Summary

0-1000 machine cycles	28 runs
1001-2000 machine cycles	21 runs
2001-3000 machine cycles	16 runs
3001-4000 machine cycles	10 runs
4001-5000 machine cycles	9 runs
5001-10,000 machine cycles	13 runs
10,001-15,000 machine cycles	2 runs
>15,000 cycles	1 run
Total	100 runs

We wish to summarize all this data with *one* easy to work with statistic, such as the mean number of machine cycles per run. Here the mean number of machine cycles executed per run is roughly 6,630 machine cycles (check this!). We might use 5,000 to 7,500 machine cycles per job to bracket this estimate in further analysis. What about the distribution of machine cycles per job?

If we test this data against an exponential distribution model using a quantile-quantile plot, the results are plotted in the following figures.

Since the graph is approximately a straight line, the goodness of fit of the data to the exponential distribution model is felt to be adequate.

Because of this data analysis, we assume that the distribution of machine cycles can be summarized by

$$PROB[execution\ time \leqslant X] = 1-exp(-\mu X) = 1-exp(-X/E(T_S))$$

$$E(T_S) \approx \frac{6,630\ machine\ cycles}{machine\ clock\ rate}$$

Hence, the mean rate of executing work is μ jobs per unit time, while the mean time per job to completely execute it is $1/\mu = E(T_S)$. The moment generating function of this distribution is given by

$$E[e^{-zT_s}] = \frac{\mu}{\mu + z} = \frac{1}{zE(T_S) + 1}$$

The second moment and variance are given by

$$E[T_S{}^2] = 2E^2[T_S] \quad var(T_S) = E^2(T_S)$$

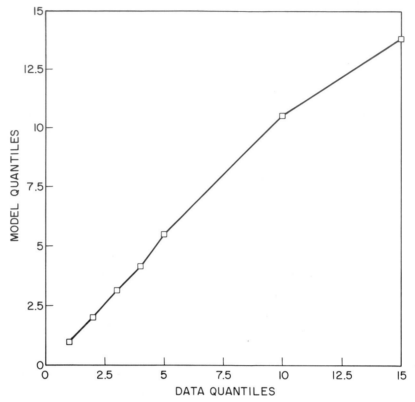

Figure 9.2. Empirical Quantiles vs Exponential Model Quantiles

9.3.2 Constant Service Time Distribution If all the runs for a given program require virtually the same amount of time, irrespective of the input, the service times are deterministic or constant, and

$$PROB[execution\ time \leqslant X] = \begin{cases} 1 & X > E(T_S) \\ 0 & X \leqslant E(T_S) \end{cases}$$

The moment generating function for this distribution is

$$E[e^{-zT_S}] = e^{-zE(T_s)}$$

The second moment and variance is given by

$$E[T_S{}^2] = E^2[T_S] \quad var(T_S) = 0$$

9.3.3 Erlang Service Time Distribution Suppose that we have a pipeline of K processors, with each processor executing only one program. Each program and each processor is identical. The operation of a single program on a single processor is measured, and is found to be exponentially distributed. Thus, the total execution time is the sum of the execution time of each stage:

$$T_{S,total} = \sum_{J=1}^{K} T_{S,J}$$

Since each stage is identical, the total mean execution time is K times the mean execution time for any one stage:

$$E(T_{S,J}) = \frac{E(T_{S,total})}{K} \quad J=1,...,K$$

The moment generating function for the total time to execute a job is:

$$E[e^{-zT_{S,total}}] = \left[\frac{1}{\dfrac{zE(T_{S,total})}{K}+1} \right]^K \quad K=1,2,3,...$$

This is called an *Erlang* distribution in honor of the great Danish teletraffic engineer who laid the foundations for much of modern queueing theory and analysis of congestion.

EXERCISE. Check that this has mean $E(T_S)$ for all K.

For $K=1$ this is the exponential distribution, while for $K>1$ this is a more complicated expression. The second moment of this distribution is

$$E[T_S^2] = E^2(T_S)\frac{K+1}{K}$$

and hence the squared coefficient of variation is given by

$$squared\ coefficient\ of\ variation = \frac{1}{K}$$

For $K=1$ this is the exponential distribution, while for $K\rightarrow\infty$ this is approaching the constant or deterministic distribution, and hence models fluctuations in between these extremes.

9.3.4 Hyperexponential Service Time Distribution A processor executes any one of N types of jobs. Once a job begins execution, it runs to completion. Measurements are gathered on the system in operation.

- The fraction of jobs of each type are measured; $F_K, K=1,...,N$ denotes the fraction of jobs that were executed that were type K

- The execution time statistics of each job are measured, and are felt to be adequately modeled for each and every job type by an exponential distribution but with a different mean depending upon the job type: $E(T_{S,K}), K=1,...,N$ denotes the mean execution time of job type K

This type of distribution is called the *hyperexponential* distribution which is a mixture or sum of two or more exponential distributions.

The chart below shows one method for generating hyperexponential random variables: For two distributions, we see

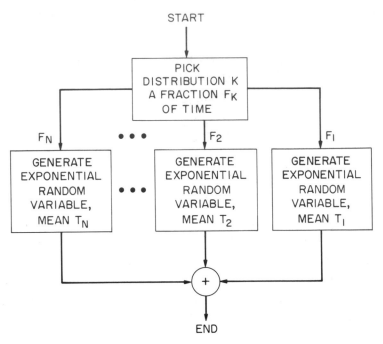

Figure 9.3. Hyperexponential Random Variable Generation

$$PROB[T_S \leq X] = F_1(1 - e^{-X/E(T_{s,1})}) + F_2(1 - e^{-X/E(T_{s,2})}) \quad F_1 + F_2 \equiv 1$$

If we fix the mean, we can make the squared coefficient of variation greater than one, and hence model fluctuations greater than those encountered for the exponential distribution case.

Exercise: Find the moment generating function of the hyperexponential distribution.

Solution: From the definition, we see

$$E[exp(-zX)] = \int_0^\infty exp(-zX)\,dG(X)$$

$$= \sum_{K=1}^{N} F_K \int_0^\infty exp(-zX)\frac{1}{E(T_{S,K})}exp(-X/E(T_{S,K}))\,dX = \sum_{K=1}^{N} F_K \frac{1}{zE(T_{S,K}) + 1}$$

9.3.5 Hypoexponential Distribution A job is decomposed into N tasks, with each task executed by a single processor. Measurements are gathered on

- The fraction of arriving jobs due to each type of task, denoted by $F_K, K = 1,...,N$

- The execution time statistics of each task which are exponentially distributed with mean $E(T_{S,K}), K = 1,..,N$ for stage K

The chart below summarizes work flow.

434

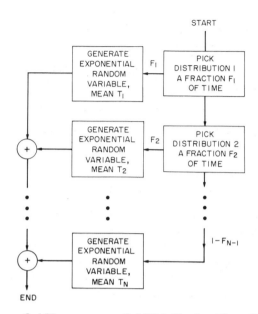

Figure 9.4. Hypoexponential Distribution Flow Chart

This type of execution time statistics is called the *hypoexponential* distribution which generalizes the Erlang distribution. One way to generate random variables from this type of distribution is to first generate an exponential random variable, and then allow a fraction F_1 of jobs to have this distribution while the rest of the jobs require not only this service but additional service which is generated from a second exponential distribution with possibly different mean, and we can repeat this process again and again.

Exercise: Show the Erlang distribution is hypoexponential.

Solution: A random variable from the Erlang distribution can be generated by using N exponential random number generators each with the same mean in a pipeline, with the output from one stage feeding the input to the next stage.

9.3.6 Single Link Flow Control One transmitter receives messages from a variety of sources and transmits them over a data link to a single receiver. The following steps are involved in message transmission:

[1]   The transmitter adds source and destination header to the message, adds start and end of message delimiters, adds an appropriate cyclic redundancy check to the message, and transmits the message; this requires a time interval $T_{transmitter}$

[2]   The receiver buffers the message, strips off the start and end delimiters, checks the cyclic redundancy check to see if errors might be present, passes the message on to the proper destination, and if all is correct

transmits an acknowledgement of proper transmission to the transmitter; this requires a time interval $T_{receiver}$

[3] The transmitter processes the acknowledgement, and flushes the message from its buffer

The transmitter and receiver can operate at widely disparate speeds:

- The transmitter might be an electromechanical terminal and the receiver a computer

- The transmitter might be an intelligent disk controller and the receiver a microprocessor controlled electronic funds transfer automatic teller

In order to insure that no messages are lost due to speed mismatching, because the *receiver* has limited and *finite* buffering or storage of messages, a maximum of **B** unacknowledged messages can be transmitted from the transmitter to the receiver; beyond this point, the transmitter waits to receive an acknowledgement. This is called *flow control* because the flow of data over the link is paced or controlled by this mechanism.

We now consider the case where the propagation effects are negligible compared to the transmitter and receiver message execution times. This will be the case in a local area network, with terminals and computers interconnected over a distance of a few kilometers or less, for example. Since we only have *one* transmitter and *one* receiver, the greatest amount of concurrency or parallelism possible is to have both resources executing messages. Thus, we consider the case where at most two unacknowledged messages can be outstanding (B=2) at the transmitter at any one time. For this special case, we also show an illustrative timing diagram of system operation.

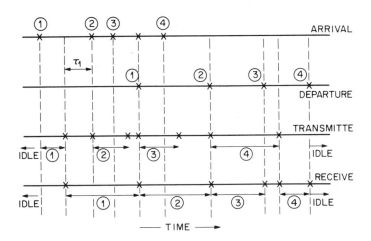

Figure 9.5.Illustrative Operation with Negligible Propagation Time

Note that after the initial idle to busy transient condition, the transmitter and receiver are very strongly coupled in their operation. A race condition can occur if the transmitter finishes before the receiver or the receiver before the transmitter and two messages have to be acknowledged. If we ignore the startup transient, the time required to transmit a message, denoted by $T_{message}$, by inspection of the figure, is given by

$$T_{message} = max(T_{trans}, T_{rec}) + T_{rec}$$

The mean message transmission time is given by

$$E(T_{message}) = E[max(T_{trans}, T_{rec})] + E(T_{rec})$$

The message handling time is not simply the sum of the individual message handling times. What is the distribution of the message handling time distribution? To find this, we need to find the distribution of the maximum of the transmitter and receiver message handling time distributions:

$$PROB[max(T_{trans}, T_{rec}) \leqslant X] = PROB[T_{trans} \leqslant X]PROB[T_{rec} \leqslant X]$$

On the other hand, rather than work with this complicated expression directly, we might be satisfied with simply *bounds* on the message handling time:

$$max[E(T_{trans}, T_{rec})] \leqslant E[max(T_{trans}, T_{rec})] \leqslant E(T_{trans}) + E(T_{rec})$$

Check this! How do we interpret these two bounds?

- The lower bound says that the slower of the transmitter and receiver will be the system bottleneck

- The upper bound says that if fluctuations are sufficiently great about the mean values, the mean message handling time will be approximately the same mean time as if the receiver could only buffer *one* message at a time, with no parallelism or concurrency possible

Here is a different way of understanding this phenomenon:

- The transmitter can be much slower than the receiver:

$$E(T_{trans}) \gg E(T_{rec})$$

and hence there will never be any queueing at the receiver, or the receiver can be much slower than the transmitter:

$$E(T_{rec}) \gg E(T_{trans})$$

and hence there will always be two messages at the receiver. This case is called *speed mismatch*

- Fluctuations about the mean transmitter and receiver times can be severe:
  - If the transmitter and receiver message service times are *constant,* then

$$E(T_{message}) = max[E(T_{trans}), E(T_{rec})] + E(T_{rec})$$

- If the transmitter and receiver message service times are *exponential* random variables, then

$$E(T_{message}) = \frac{E(T_{trans})E(T_{rec})}{E(T_{trans}) + E(T_{rec})} + E(T_{rec})$$

The figures below plot the ratio of the mean of the maximum of the transmitter and receiver message handling times divided by the single message at a time, assuming the transmitter and receiver have *identical* distributions with identical squared coefficients of variation.

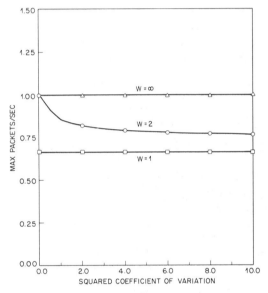

Figure 9.6.Mean Throughput Gain of Double vs Single Buffering

When the speed of the transmitter and receiver are roughly equal, and the squared coefficient of variation is close to zero, then the gain approaches fifty per cent. When the speeds of the transmitter and receiver are mismatched by a factor of two or more, or the fluctuations become significant (squared coefficient of variation greater than one), or both, the gain is roughly ten per cent or less.

9.4 Resource Allocation Policy

At each arrival epoch and each completion epoch, a decision must be made for which task(s) are processed. What are some of the means for resolving contention for a processor?

- At each arrival epoch, we could use the arrival time as a priority index. The smaller the index, the higher the priority leads to the policy of service in order of arrival, or first come, first served.

- At each arrival epoch, we could use the arrival time as a priority index, but now the larger the index the higher the priority! If we decide that we will execute jobs to completion once they begin to execute, i.e., to execute *nonpreemptively,* then our work discipline is service in reverse order of arrival, last come, first serve, nonpreemptive. If we decide that we will make scheduling decisions at job arrival instants, i.e., to execute *preemptively,* then we could choose to preempt a job and either *resume* processing at the point of interruption or *repeat* processing from the beginning, or any of a number of other points.

- At each arrival epoch, we could use a given label on the job as a priority index. Jobs would be executed according to priority index; jobs with the same index would be executed in order of arrival. At least two options are available, *preemptive resume* scheduling where higher priority jobs interrupt lower priority jobs upon arrival and execution is resumed at the point of interruption, and *nonpreemptive* scheduling where once a job begins to execute it runs to completion.

- At each arrival epoch, we could use both the arrival time and a second quantity which is the desired execution time window of that job to determine priority: we simply add the arrival time to the window, and execute jobs according to highest priority. This is called *deadline* scheduling because the arrival time plus window is called the *deadline* for that job.

- At each arrival epoch, we could use the processing time of the job to determine its priority. If we schedule jobs nonpreemptive, then one such rule is to execute that job with the *shortest processing time* at all times; if we schedule jobs preemptive resume, then one such rule is to execute that job with the *shortest remaining processing time* at all times.

Many more policies are known, as well as variations on those above. We will not deal with all of these, but only wish to give the reader some idea of how rich the policy space in fact is. One way of classifying these policies is by the labels *static* and *dynamic:* a *static* policy depends only upon the attributes of a job that do not change with time, while a *dynamic* policy does allow the priority or urgency of a job to depend on time.

9.5 Measures of Congestion

Broadly speaking, there are two types of congestion measures, those oriented toward the *customer* and those oriented toward the *system.* For each type, we might associate a cost, and then attempt to trade off among them: as we improve customer oriented measures, system oriented measures degrade, and vice versa!

Customer oriented criteria deal with the *mean throughput rate* and the *delay statistics* for each type of task. We characterize delay by

- queueing time or flow time or time in system of a task, denoted T_Q

- waiting time, the time interval from arrival until a task first receives service, denoted T_W

System oriented criteria deal with

- *mean number of jobs in execution in the system,* defined as

$$mean\ number\ of\ executing\ jobs = \frac{mean\ service\ time}{mean\ interarrival\ time}$$

which follows from Little's Law

- utilization, defined as

$$utilization = fraction\ of\ time\ resource\ busy$$

- distribution of number of tasks in the system (at arrival epochs, completion epochs, or *arbitrary* time epochs)

This list is not complete. Our goal will be to calculate these different measures given certain arrival statistics, service time statistics, and policies for arbitrating contention.

9.5.1 Additional Reading

[1] R.B.Cooper, **Introduction to Queueing Theory,** Chapters 1-3, Macmillan, NY, 1972.

[2] H.Kobayashi, **Modeling and Analysis: An Introduction to System Performance Evaluation Methodology,** Chapter 2, 3.1-3.5, Addison-Wesley, Reading, Mass. 1978.

[3] L.Kleinrock, **Queueing Systems, Volume I: Theory,** Chapters 1-2, Wiley, NY, 1975.

9.6 Approximation of the Inverse of a Laplace Transform

We have already introduced and used the concepts of moment generating function and Laplace transform. These transforms are often easier to manipulate and work with, rather than working directly with probability distributions. Furthermore, since we are demanding additional distributional information concerning the workload, we would like to get more out of this input than simply a mean value: what fraction of the time does a transaction take longer than T seconds to spend either waiting or executing? what point in time in system will result in ninety per cent or ninety five per cent or ninety nine per cent of the transactions being completed? This suggests numerical methods for approximating the inverse of the moment generating function or Laplace transform.

The properties that we wish to preserve with our numerical methods are

- Nonnegativity--Certain types of approximations result in *negative* probabilities in exactly the region of interest, the *tail* of the distribution, the point at which ninety five per cent of the jobs have been completely executed; our goal here is to have a nonnegative class of approximations

- Monotonicity--Certain types of approximations, such as those based on Fast Fourier Transform methods, result in oscillations and waves in the region of interest (not surprising, if the approximation is a sum of sinusoidal waves); we wish to preserve monotonic behavior

In summary, we will approximate a distribution function by another distribution function.

9.6.1 Description of Basic Approximating Algorithm Consider a function $g(x)$ for which the Laplace transform, denoted $\tilde{g}(z)$, defined by

$$\tilde{g}(z) = \int_0^\infty e^{-zx} g(x) dx$$

exists for all $Re(z) > \beta$ where β is the *abscissa of convergence* of the transform. We will assume that $g(x)$ drops off exponentially fast in x, which will occur with the problems we will encounter.

$$\lim_{x \to \infty} g(x) e^{\gamma x} = \begin{cases} \infty & \gamma < \beta \\ constant & \gamma = \beta \\ 0 & \gamma > \beta \end{cases}$$

We now define a sequence of linear functionals that will approximate $g(x)$, denoted by $L_n, n = 0, ..., \infty$, given by

$$L_n[g(x)] = g_n(x) = \frac{(-1)^n}{n!} z^{n+1} \frac{d^n \tilde{g}(z)}{dz^n} \Big|_{z + \frac{n+1}{z}}$$

It can be shown that

$$\lim_{n \to \infty} g_n(t) = g(t)$$

The zeroth order approximation is given by

$$L_0[g(x)] = z\tilde{g}(z) \Big|_{z = \frac{1}{x}}$$

while the first order approximation is given by

$$L_1[g(x)] = -z^2 \frac{d\tilde{g}(z)}{dz}\bigg|_{z=\frac{2}{x}}$$

The reason for choosing this type of approximation is that the resulting approximation is nonnegative. Other methods, such as those based on Fast Fourier Transform techniques, do not preserve positivity. This is not free: if we go from the nth order approximation to the 2nth order approximation, the error will only halve, while using other methods (such as those based on Fast Fourier Transform techniques) result in the error being quartered.

9.6.2 An Example To illustrate all of this, we try a probability distribution function of the form:

$$PROB[T>x] = g(x) = \tfrac{1}{2}e^{-x} + \tfrac{1}{2}e^{-3x}$$

This is convenient and easy to work with analytically, to illustrate our points. The Laplace transform of this function is given by

$$\tilde{g}(z) = \int_0^\infty g(x)e^{-zx}dx = \tfrac{1}{2}\left[\frac{1}{z+1} + \frac{1}{z+3}\right]$$

The abscissa of convergence here is one, i.e., the minimum of three and one.

The zeroth and first order approximation to $g(x)$ is given by

$$g_0(x) = \tfrac{1}{2}\left[\frac{1}{1+x} + \frac{1}{3x+1}\right] \quad g_1(x) = \tfrac{1}{2}\left[\frac{1}{(\tfrac{1}{2}x+1)^2} + \frac{1}{(3x/2+1)^2}\right]$$

The tables below summarizes numerical studies as a function of approximation parameters:

Table 9.3. $\alpha=0$

x	g	g_{50}	g_{100}
2	0.06891	0.07203	0.07048
4	0.00916	0.01064	0.00990
8	0.00017	0.00030	0.00023

Table 9.4. $\alpha=1$

x	g	$g_{50,1}$	$g_{100,1}$
2	0.06891	0.06911	0.06901
4	0.00916	0.00916	0.00916
8	0.00017	0.00017	0.000017

Since the abscissa of convergence of the Laplace transform of $g(x)$ is one, $\alpha=1$ is the appropriate value to use here.

The error is halved in going from fifty to one hundred terms, as expected. The effect of $\alpha=1$ is greater for larger values of t since the exponential term which is being tracked becomes dominant.

A different type of example is shown in the figure below. The total mean arrival is fixed at 0.5 arrivals per second, with each arrival requiring a mean service of one second. Jobs are executed in order of arrival. The final parameter is the second moment of the service time distribution; this allows fluctuation about the mean.

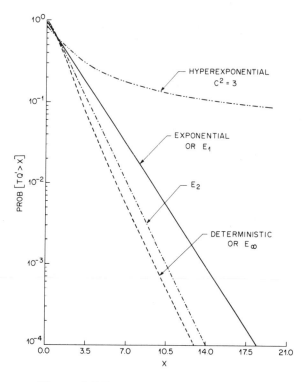

Figure 9.7. Fraction of Time $T_Q > X$ vs X

For example, ninety per cent of the jobs are executed within four seconds of their arrival if there is *no* fluctuation in the service time distribution, while for the exponential distribution ninety per cent of the jobs are executed within six seconds of their arrival.

9.6.3 *Additional Reading*

[1]   D.Jagerman, *An Inversion Technique for the Laplace Transform with Application to Approximation,* Bell System Technical Journal, **57** (3), 669-710(1978).

9.7 Kendall's Queueing System Notation

Kendall has introduced a notation for characterizing queueing systems:

$$ARRIVAL/SERVICE/NUMBER \ OF \ SERVERS/CAPACITY$$

These terms are as follows:

- *ARRIVAL*--the interarrival time distribution

- *SERVICE*--the service time distribution

- *NUMBER OF SERVERS*--the number of processors or servers

- *CAPACITY*--the total system capacity for tasks (if this is infinite, this term is often omitted)

The following abbreviations are often used to characterize these different interarrival and service time distributions:

- M--exponential (Markovian) distribution

- D--deterministic or constant distribution

- E_K--Erlang-K distribution, a type of gamma distribution

- H--hyperexponential distribution (linear combination of two or more exponentials)

- G--general or arbitrary distribution (as distinct from the above highly structured distributions)

Many other abbreviations have crept into use than just those above. Here are some examples of this nomenclature:

- $M/M/1$--a single server queue with exponential interarrival times and exponential service times

- $M/G/1$--a single server queue with exponential interarrival times and arbitrary or general service times

- $G/E_K/3/7$--a three server queue with capacity seven with arbitrary or general interarrival time distribution and Erlang-2 service time distribution

This nomenclature is widely used, and we will adopt it from this point onward.

9.7.1 Additional Reading

[1] D.G.Kendall, *Some Problems in the Theory of Queues,* J.Royal Stat.Society (B), **13,** 151-173, 1951.

[2] P.Kuehn, *Delay Problems in Communications Systems: Classification of Models and Tables for Application,* IEEE International Conference on Communications, **1,** 237-243, Chicago, Illinois, 1977.

9.8 Single Server Queues with Poisson Arrivals and General Service Times

We wish to assess the impact on performance when the arrival statistics are Poisson but the service times for jobs are arbitrary. This allows us to quantify the impact on delay statistics for jobs that have different processing time requirements and also different delay goals: often we wish to execute short jobs that have stringent delay criteria much more quickly than long jobs whose delay criteria are much more loose, and this class of models allows us to quantify the gain due to scheduling to achieve these goals. For example, we might be interested in how variable size packets impact congestion in a packet switching system, so we might choose to fix the *mean* packet length but allow the *distribution* or *variance* to fluctuate to see how performance is affected.

9.8.1 Mean Value Analysis In what follows, we are interested in mean throughput rate and queueing and waiting time statistics. Our mean value analysis allows us to plot the mean throughput rate versus the mean arrival rate, as shown in the figure below.

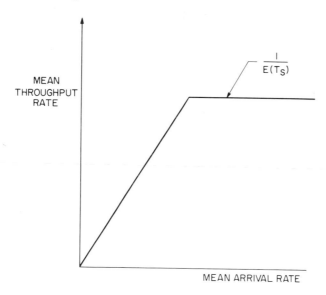

Figure 9.8. Mean Throughput Rate vs Mean Arrival Rate

As long as the mean arrival rate is less than the maximum rate at which jobs can be serviced, the mean throughput rate equals the mean arrival rate, i.e., the arrival rate is limiting the mean throughput rate. On the other hand, the mean delay can be *anything* from the mean service time on up to infinity, i.e., we can say *nothing* about the mean delay at this level of analysis. Different scheduling policies will lead to different delays.

Once the mean arrival rate exceeds the maximum rate of executing jobs, the single serially reusable resource is a bottleneck. Furthermore, delays will exceed any threshold, because the resource cannot keep up with arrivals, i.e., buffers overflow and so forth.

9.8.2 The M/G/1 Queue with Service in Order of Arrival The benchmark against which we will judge all of our different scheduling policies is the policy of service in order of arrival. We now present one result from the general theory of the $M/G/1$ queueing system. The moment generating function of the waiting time distribution is given by

$$E[exp(-zT_W)] = \frac{z(1 - \rho)}{z - \lambda[1 - E[exp(-zT_S)]]}$$

which has mean value given by

$$E(T_W) = \frac{\lambda E(T_S{}^2)}{2(1 - \rho)}$$

$E(T_S{}^2)$ is the *second* moment of the service time distribution, or, in other words, the *first* moment of the waiting time distribution depends on *more* than just the first moments of the interarrival and service time distributions. If we adopt the previous definition of squared coefficient of variation, we see

$$E(T_W) = \frac{\lambda E^2(T_S)[1+C_S{}^2]}{2(1 - \rho)}$$

$$C_S{}^2 = \frac{variance \ of \ service \ time \ distribution}{(mean \ of \ service \ time \ distribution)^2}$$

A different way of expressing the mean waiting time is

$$E(T_W) = \frac{\rho}{1 - \rho} \frac{E[T_S{}^2]}{2E[T_S]}$$

In words, the mean waiting time is the product of two factors, one that depends only on the fraction of time the server is busy, ρ, and one that depends on the fluctuations in the service times for jobs, which is the ratio of the second moment over twice the first moment. Under light loading, $\rho \rightarrow 0$, the mean waiting time is negligible, while under heavy loading, $\rho \rightarrow 1$, the mean waiting time is inflated or stretched by $1/(1 - \rho)$ and can dominate the mean queueing time.

The queueing time (or time in system) moment generating function is given by

$$E[exp(-zT_Q)] = E[exp(-zT_W)]E[exp(-zT_S)]$$

which has mean value

$$E(T_Q) = E(T_W) + E(T_S) = \frac{\lambda E(T_S{}^2)}{2(1-\rho)} + E(T_S)$$

Several special cases are of interest:

- exponential service, $C_S{}^2 = 1$:

$$E(T_W) = \frac{\lambda E^2(T_S)}{1-\rho}$$

- deterministic or constant service, $C_S{}^2 = 0$:

$$E(T_W) = \frac{\lambda E^2(T_S)}{2(1-\rho)}$$

which is one half the mean waiting time of that of the exponential case

- hyperexponential service, where one might encounter $C_S{}^2 = 100$ for example:

$$E(T_W) = \frac{101 \times \lambda E^2(T_S)}{2(1-\rho)}$$

The random variable N denotes the number of jobs in the system (including the job in execution), and this has moment generating function given by

$$E[X^N] = E[exp(-T_Q[\lambda(1-X)])]$$

From Little's Law, we recall that the mean number in system equals the mean arrival rate multiplied by the mean time in system:

$$E(N) = \lambda E(T_Q)$$

We have summarized these formulae graphically in the following plots of mean queueing time, waiting time, and number in system versus the fraction of time the single server is busy, with the squared coefficient of variation of the service time distribution varied from the deterministic case of zero through the hypoexponential case of one half, through the exponential case of one, and on into the hyperexponential case of one and a half, two, and two and a half. In all cases, the mean service time of a job is one time unit. Two plots are presented, one for utilization varied out to one, and the second for the more typical loading case where the utilization varies up to one half. These plots are useful for assessing transients: if the system is normally loaded to thirty to forty per cent utilization, but suddenly a workload surge raises this to seventy per cent, then the mean values can be see to roughly double or triple in all cases. This suggests doubling system design margins to allow for these longer times and greater amount of storage.

The fraction of time the waiting time and queueing time exceed X is plotted in Figure 9.9, assuming an exponential service time distribution.

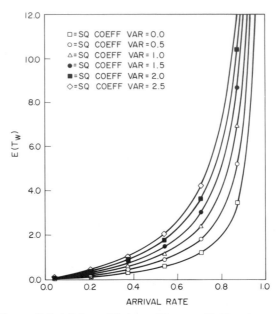

Figure 9.9.A.Mean Waiting Time vs Utilization $\rho \leqslant 1$

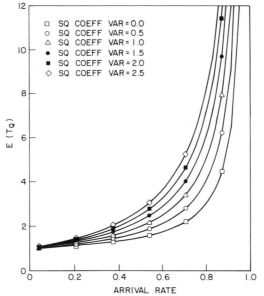

Figure 9.9.B.Mean Queueing Time vs Utilization $\rho \leqslant 1$

This figure shows that under light loading, $\rho = 0.1$, the fraction of time a job waits greater than one service time is under ten per cent, while as the loading increases, $\rho \rightarrow 1$, the fraction of time a job waits ten or more service times becomes larger and larger.

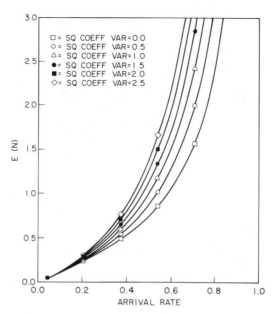

Figure 9.9.C. Mean Number in System vs Utilization $\rho \leqslant 1$

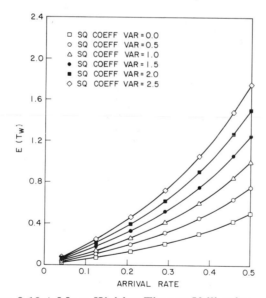

Figure 9.10.A. Mean Waiting Time vs Utilization $\rho \leqslant 0.5$

Finally, the random variable T_B denotes the duration of a busy period; the processor is busy, idle, busy, idle, and so on. The moment generating function for the busy period distribution is given implicitly by

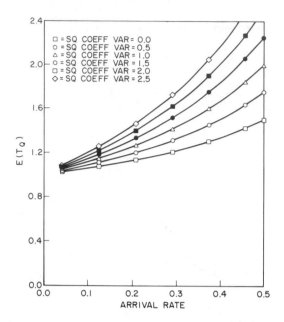

Figure 9.10.B.Mean Queueing Time vs Utilization $\rho \leqslant 0.5$

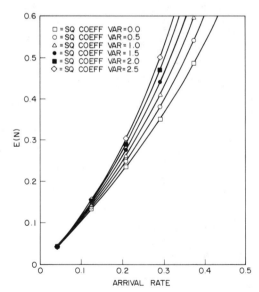

Figure 9.10.C.Mean Number in System vs Utilization $\rho \leqslant 0.5$

$$E[exp(-zT_B)] = E[exp(-T_S(z+\lambda-\lambda E[exp(-zT_B)]))]$$

and hence the mean duration of a busy period is

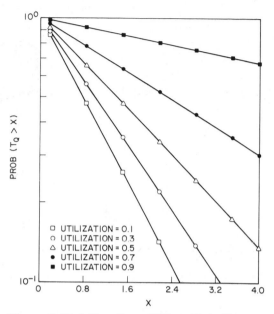

Figure 9.11.A.Fraction of Time $T_Q > X$ versus X

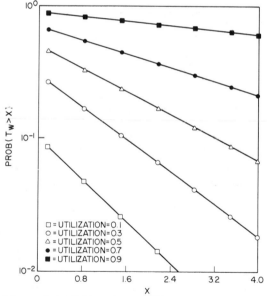

Figure 9.11.B.Fraction of Time $T_W > X$ versus X

$$E(T_B) = \frac{E(T_S)}{1 - \lambda E(T_S)}$$

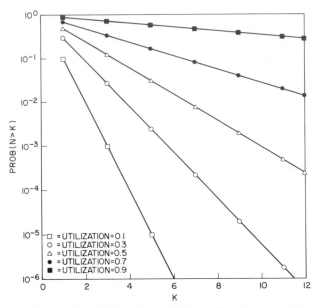

Figure 9.11.C.Fraction of Time $N > K$ versus K

9.9 The FS/G/1 Queue with Service in Order of Arrival

What if the arrivals are generated from a finite rather than infinite population? Our model is as follows:

- N identical stations attempt to execute jobs; each station is either idle or is active (either waiting to execute or executing). The idle times for all stations form a sequence of independent identically distributed exponential random variables with mean idle time $1/\lambda$

- the execution times for each station form a sequence of independent identically distributed random variables, with associated transmission time T_S which has an associated moment generating function $\gamma_{T_s}(z)$ defined by

$$E[exp(-zT_S)] = \gamma_{T_s}(z)$$

- jobs are executed in order of arrival

The mean rate of executing jobs is simply the fraction of time the server is busy executing jobs divided by the mean time to execute one job. We denote by ρ the server utilization, while $E(T_S)$ is the mean job execution time, and see

$$mean\ throughput\ rate = \frac{\rho}{E(T_S)}$$

Since each station is either idle or active, the mean cycle time for one station to go from idle to active and back to idle is simply

$$mean\ station\ cycle\ time = E(T_{idle}) + E(T_{delay})$$

and by definition the mean throughput rate is the number of stations divided by the mean cycle time per station:

$$mean\ throughput\ rate = \frac{N}{E(T_{idle}) + E(T_{delay})}$$

Equating these two expressions, we see

$$E(T_{delay}) = \frac{N\ E(T_S)}{\rho} - E(T_{idle})$$

The mean utilization is given by

$$\rho = \frac{\sum_{J=0}^{N-1} \binom{N-1}{J} \prod_{K=0}^{J} [E[exp(\lambda(K\ T_S))]-1]}{1 + \sum_{J=1}^{N} \binom{N}{J} \prod_{K=0}^{J-1}[E[exp(\lambda(K\ T_S))]-1]}$$

Note that we are computing the moment generating function of the job execution time distribution at evenly spaced points. This means that the mean delay depends on *more* than just the mean message length.

EXERCISE: Compute the mean delay versus N for $T_{idle}=1$ and $E(T_S)=0.3$, for exponential and deterministic service time distributions, for a finite source model. Compare these calculations with those from an infinite source model with arrival rate $\lambda=N/T_{idle}$.

9.10 M/G/1 Last Come, First Serve

In this section we examine a different policy for administering a single serially reusable resource: service in reverse order of arrival. Two cases are possible here:

- Upon arrival, the job in service is preempted and the arrival will seize the resource

- Upon arrival, the job in service is not preempted but finishes execution, and the latest arrival then seizes the resource and is completely executed

For the case of preemption, we will only examine the case where service is resumed for the preempted task(s) at the point of interruption. A different case might be to start execution anew or afresh for a preempted job, which we will not deal with here.

Why deal with this policy? Many computer systems employ a hardware device called a *stack* which conceptually is a single serially reusable resource that operates according to a policy of the last arrival is served first.

9.10.1 Nonpreemptive Last Come, First Serve When a job arrives, it will either execute immediately because the system is idle, or it must wait, because one job is in execution. If the job must wait, other jobs may arrive after it but before the first job finished execution, and all of these jobs will be executed before the job of interest is executed. The time in system is given by

$$T_Q = \begin{cases} T_S & \text{with probability } 1 - \rho \\ \tilde{T}_S & \text{with probability } \rho \end{cases}$$

The moment generating function is given by

$$E[exp(-zT_Q)] = (1 - \rho)E[exp(-zT_S)] + \rho E[exp(-z\tilde{T}_S)]$$

If the system is busy upon arrival, a job must wait until the current job in execution is finished, which we denote by $\hat{T}_S$

$$E[exp(-z\hat{T}_S)] = \frac{1 - E[exp(-zT_S)]}{zE(T_S)}$$

If we stretch $\hat{T}_S$ to account for arrivals after the job in question, we find $\tilde{T}_S$:

$$E[exp(-z\tilde{T}_S)] = E[exp(-y\hat{T}_S)]$$

$$y = z + \lambda - \lambda E[exp(-zT_B)]$$

$$E[exp(-zT_B)] = E[exp((z + \lambda - \lambda E[exp(-zT_B)]T_S)]$$

The mean queueing time is given by

$$E(T_Q) = E(T_S) + \frac{\lambda E(T_S^2)}{2(1 - \rho)}$$

This is identical to that for service in order of arrival. The reason is that no preemption is allowed, so when a job completes, another starts (the last one or the first one), and hence the mean number of jobs in the system either waiting to execute or in execution is the same for either policy. Little's Law tells us that the mean queueing time must be the same for the same mean arrival rate.

9.10.2 Preemptive Resume Last Come, First Serve If we allow preemptive resume service, then as soon as a job arrives it begins execution, irrespective of whether the processor or server is busy. However, this job can be preempted by later arrivals. Hence, we see

$$E[exp(-zT_Q)] = E[exp(-yT_S)]$$

$$y = z + \lambda - \lambda E[exp(-zT_B)]$$

$$E[exp(-zT_B)] = E[exp(-(z + \lambda - \lambda E(exp(-zT_B)))T_S)]$$

The mean queueing time is given by

$$E(T_Q) = \frac{E(T_S)}{1 - \rho}$$

This is the same form as the mean queueing time for an M/M/1 system with service in order of arrival, except that here we have arbitrary service and preemptive resume service in reverse order of arrival. By switching the scheduling policy, the mean value behaves as if the service time were exponentially distributed.

9.10.3 Example The distribution of number of clock cycles per assembly language instruction is measured and found to be adequately modeled by an constant distribution with a mean of two cycles per instruction. We wish to compare the impact on performance using a stack with either nonpreemptive or preemptive resume arbitration versus a fifo or first in, first out buffer discipline. The table below summarizes the mean number of clock cycles per instruction (including both execution and waiting):

Table 9.5.Mean Execution Time $E(T_Q)$

	FIFO	LCFS	
Utilization	Policy	Nonpreemptive	Preemptive Resume
0.1	2.1 cycles	2.1 cycles	2.2 cycles
0.5	3.0 cycles	3.0 cycles	4.0 cycles
0.9	11.0 cycles	11.0 cycles	20.0 cycles

The impact due to fluctuations for preemptive resume versus nonpreemptive scheduling is severe as the load grows.

BONUS: What is the variance about the mean for each of these policies?

9.10.4 Graphical Comparisons For the special case of deterministic or constant service time, we can explicitly calculate the exact distribution of T_Q. This is plotted in Figure 9.12 assuming Poisson arrivals with mean arrival rate of one job every two seconds, while the mean service time for each job is one second, so the processor is fifty per cent utilized. In addition, we have plotted the zeroth and first order approximations to the exact solution, plus the modified approximations assuming the fraction of time $T_Q > X$ drops off exponentially as $\exp^{-\alpha X}$. The approximation $g_{0,\alpha}(X)$ is within ten per cent of the exact solution, while $g_{1,\alpha}(X)$ is within five per cent of the exact solution.

By way of comparison, if we change the service time distribution from constant to exponential, and keep everything else the same, then the results are plotted in Figure 9.13. For example, for the constant service time distribution case, ninety nine per cent of the jobs are serviced within ten seconds while the corresponding number for exponential service is seventeen seconds.

Finally, what if we vary the policy, but fix the Poisson arrival rate at one job every two seconds, with each job requiring a constant one second of service.

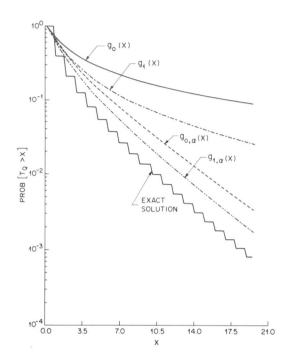

Figure 9.12.Last Come First Served Preemptive Resume/Constant Service

Figure 9.14 summarizes numerical approximations:

Ninety per cent of the jobs are executed within four seconds for first in first out service, while this grows to six seconds for nonpreemptive last in first out service, and to seven seconds for preemptive resume last in first out service. The corresponding results for exponential service is shown as follows: Ninety per cent of the jobs are executed within six seconds for first in first out service, while this grows to nine seconds for nonpreemptive last in first out service, and to twelve seconds for preemptive resume last in first out service. Note that this is significantly greater than the constant service case.

9.11 The M/G/1 Queue with Processor Intervisits

As a useful variation on the above example, we consider the following system

- Arrivals obey simple Poisson statistics with mean arrival rate λ

- The service times of jobs are independent identically distributed random variables with T_S denoting the processing time random variable

- Jobs are serviced in order of arrival

- The buffer for work has infinite capacity

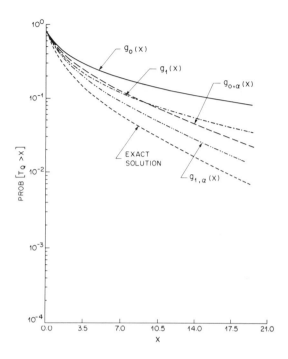

Figure 9.13.Last Come First Served Preemptive Resume/Exponential Service

- The processor executes all jobs until the system is completely empty of work, and then leaves for a random time interval called an *intervisit* time; the sequence of intervisit times are independent identically distributed random variables with V denoting the intervisit time random variable. If the processor arrives from an intervisit to find the system empty, it immediately leaves to begin another intervisit time.

In many digital systems, the processor is multiplexed amongst a number of jobs, and hence is not available all the time to handle one job type. From the point of view of any one job, the processor is busy handling its type of work, and then is absent (doing work elsewhere), so this is often a much more realistic model than the model of the previous section (remember: always check *your* particular application to see what assumptions are valid!).

Let's examine a special case of this to gain insight: $T_S \equiv 0$. This situation is not uncommon in digital systems: often no one job requires a great amount of service, but the processor must handle so many different types of jobs that the time it is absent (doing jobs elsewhere) is much much longer than the time it is present handling any one job type. If the mean time between intervisits is denoted by $E(V)$, then many people would claim that the mean waiting time is simply one half the duration of a mean intervisit time interval, because on the average a job arrives half way through a mean intervisit interval. *This is false!*

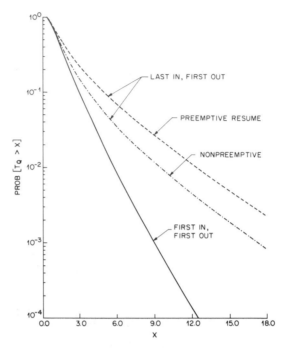

Figure 9.14.A.Poisson Arrivals/Constant Service/Different Policies

In fact, the mean waiting time and also the mean queueing time (since the service time is zero) is given by

$$E(T_Q) = E(T_W) + [E(T_S)=0] = \frac{E(V^2)}{2E(V)} = \tfrac{1}{2}E(V)\left[1 + C_V^2\right]$$

$$C_V^2 = squared\ coefficient\ of\ variation\ of\ intervisit = \frac{var(V)}{E^2(V)}$$

Only if the intervisit times are constant will the mean waiting time be one half of a mean intervisit time: if there are severe fluctuations about the mean, such as with an exponential distribution where the squared coefficient of variation is one, then the mean waiting and queueing time will lengthen (for the exponential distribution the mean waiting and queueing time will be *twice* that of the constant distribution).

This is a very subtle phenomenon: in words, if there is a severe fluctuation about the mean, the impact on congestion will be much worse than might be expected: work will continue to arrive, and the system will take longer and longer to process this work by passing it off to other queues (where it is absent most of the time anyway), compounding the process in a regenerative or positive feedback manner. Some refer to this phenomenon as *length biasing:* arrivals are much more likely to occur during long intervisit time intervals than

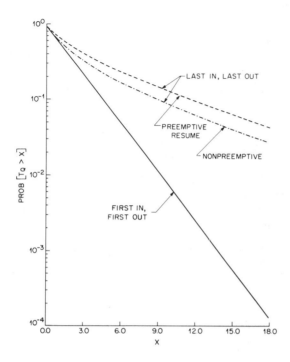

Figure 9.14.B.Poisson Arrivals/Exponential Service/Different Policies

during short intervisit time intervals, and so on.

How do we show this? Let us denote by t_K the arrival instants of jobs, $K=1,2,....$ The probability that the waiting time at some time instant say t is less than or equal to some threshold say X is given by

$$PROB[T_W(t) \leqslant X] = \sum_{K=1}^{\infty} PROB[t < t_K \leqslant t + X < t_{K+1}]$$

$$= \sum_{K=1}^{\infty} \int_{t}^{t+X} [1-G_V(t+X-u)]dG_A[t_K \leqslant u]$$

In words, at least one arrival must occur during $(t,t+X]$ and this event can occur in several mutually exclusive ways, since the last arrival in the time interval $(t,t+X]$ may be the first, the second, the third, and so on. The mean number of arrivals during the time interval $(0,t]$ is equal to

$$E[T_A(0,t)] = \sum_{K=1}^{\infty} PROB[t_K \leqslant t] = \frac{t}{E(V)}$$

Using this, we see

$$PROB[T_W(t) \leqslant X] = \frac{1}{E(V)} \int_t^{t+X} [1-G_V(t+X-u)]du = \frac{1}{E(V)} \int_0^X [1-G_V(y)]dy$$

which is independent of t. The moment generating function of this distribution is given by

$$E[exp(-zT_Q)] = \frac{1-E[exp(-zV)]}{E(V)}$$

If we use the earlier identity, we can determine all moments of integral order.

What about if $T_S \neq 0$? Now we see that the mean waiting time is simply the sum of an intervisit time interval plus the time required to complete the backlog of work that is present when a given arrival occurs, the virtual workload described earlier:

$$T_W = V + W \rightarrow E[exp(-zT_W)] = E[exp(-zV)]E[exp(-zW)]$$

The queueing time is the sum of the waiting time plus the service time:

$$T_Q = T_V + T_W + T_S$$

$$\rightarrow E[exp(-zT_Q)] = E[exp(-zT_V)]E[exp(-zT_W)]E[exp(-zT_S)]$$

The mean waiting time is given by

$$E(T_W) = \frac{E(V^2)}{2E^2(V)} + \left[\frac{\lambda E(T_S^2)}{2(1 - \lambda E(T_S))} = \frac{\lambda E(T_S)}{1 - \lambda E(T_S)} \frac{E[T_S^2]}{2E[T_S]} \right]$$

We have deliberately rewritten the mean waiting time as the product of a term dependent only on mean utilization $\lambda E(T_S) \equiv \rho$ and the randomized mean service time. The mean queueing time is given by

$$E(T_Q) = E(T_W) + E(T_S)$$

As an example of this phenomenon, let's look at the Laplace transform of the waiting time distribution of an M/G/1 queueing system with service in order of arrival:

$$E[exp(-zT_W)] = \frac{(1 - \rho)z}{z + \lambda - \lambda E[exp(-zT_S)]}$$

$$= (1 - \rho) \sum_{K=0}^{\infty} \rho^K E^K[exp(-z\tilde{T}_S)]$$

$$E[exp(-z\tilde{T}_S)] = \frac{1 - E[exp(-zT_S)]}{zE(T_S)}$$

For light loading, $\rho \ll 1$, we see

$$E(T_W) = (1 - \rho) + \rho E(\tilde{T}_S) + \cdots$$

$$E(\tilde{T}_S) = \frac{E(T_S{}^2)}{2E(T_S)}$$

In words, this says that on the average, under light loading, an arrival will not wait at all a fraction of the time $1 - \rho$, and will wait for one job a fraction of the time ρ with the waiting time being $E(\tilde{T}_S)$, and other terms are negligible (proportional to $\rho^K, K > 1$).

9.11.1 Additional Reading

[1] L.Takacs, **Introduction to the Theory of Queues,** pp.10-11, Oxford University Press, New York, 1962.

9.12 Synchronous Data Link Control

A widely used data link control procedure is called *Synchronous Data Link Control (SDLC)* and its international standard cousin (HDLC). Compared with previous widely used data link control procedures, it offers a number of advantages:

- It is insensitive to the actual character set being used, because it deals with bit streams, and knows nothing about character sets

- The encoding and buffering is simplified because it is done on the fly, as bits arrive

- A very high link efficiency is achievable compared with other widely used approaches

This does not come for free. Its disadvantages include

- Variable lengths of messages or frames, which leads to complicated buffering strategies compared to earlier approaches

- The overhead is dependent on the pattern of ones and zeros in the data

- Certain types of single bit errors are undetectable; how often these errors occur can determine how suitable this is in a given application

How does SDLC function? Data arrives at a link controller, is encoded with appropriate address, control field, and error detecting and/or correcting cylic redundancy checking (CRC) coding, and then transmitted over a link. Each frame begins and ends with a unique bit pattern called a *flag* that delimits frames from one another.

Contention for the link is arbitrated using a nonpreemptive priority policy: data has highest priority, while at the lower priority level a flag is always present to be sent. If there is no data, a flag is transmitted. At the end of each flag transmission, the controller checks to see if any data is ready to be transmitted, and if so, begins transmission; otherwise, a flag is transmitted, and the process

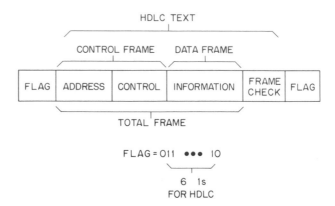

Figure 9.15.SDLC Frame Format

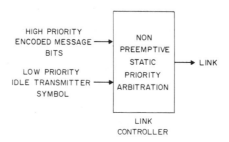

Figure 9.16.Priority Arbitration Queueing Network Block Diagram

repeats itself.

Flags delimit the start and finish of data transmission: a flag is inserted at the beginning and appended to the end of every data transmission. The flag consists of R+2 bits: a leading zero bit, R+1 successive one bits, and a trailing zero bit. It is mandatory that the flag pattern *not* appear in the middle of the data. Special circuitry in the link encoder monitors the total data transmission: if a zero is followed by R successive ones, the special circuitry at the transmitter inserts a zero immediately after the R successive ones, i.e., it stuffs a bit into the data, and hence is called a *bit stuffer*. At the receiver all stuffed bits are removed by an analogous process. Figure 9.17 illustrates a thirteen bit data stream with a four bit flag (a leading zero, two ones, and a zero) that leads to an encoded stream of nineteen bits: two flags of four bits each, thirteen data bits, and two inserted or stuffed bits.

In the following example, a single bit channel error in bit position five results in the received frame being a flag, which would be undetected by the controller described here (but presumably would be caught by other protocol levels). There are D data bits per message, with a mean of $E(D)$ data bits and a variance of $var(D)$ $bits^2$ per message. There are $A=8$ address bits, $C=8$

UNENCODED MESSAGE DATA BITS

OOIOIIOIIIIIO   I3 BITS TOTAL

ENCODED MESSAGE BITS (4 BITS/PACKET)

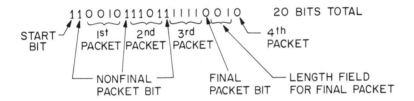

ENCODED MESSAGE BITS (4 BIT FLAG)

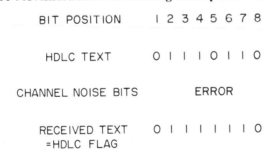

Figure 9.17. Illustrative Bit Stuffing Example: D = 13, R = 2

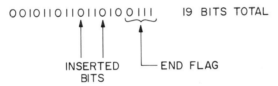

BIT POSITION	I 2 3 4 5 6 7 8
HDLC TEXT	O I I I O I I O
CHANNEL NOISE BITS	ERROR
RECEIVED TEXT =HDLC FLAG	O I I I I I I O

Figure 9.18. Illustrative Spurious Flag from Single Bit Error

control bits, and $CRC=16$ error coding bits associated with each message. The total number of bits to be encoding by bit stuffing is $B=D+32$ bits. Figure 9.19 summarizes both the frame encoding, bit stuffing encoding, and link arbitration.

If P and $Q=1-P$ denote the fraction of D bits that are ones and zeros, respectively, then the mean and variance of the number of data bits between inserted or stuffed bits is

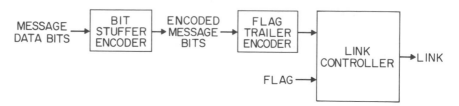

Figure 9.19. SDLC Link Controller Block Diagram

$$mean\ number\ of\ bits\ between\ bit\ stuffs \approx \frac{B}{\mu}$$

$$variance\ of\ number\ of\ bits\ between\ bit\ stuffs \approx \frac{B}{\mu}\frac{\sigma^2}{\mu^2} + \left[\frac{B}{\mu}\right]^2 var(D)$$

$$\mu = \frac{1-P^R}{Q\ P^R} \qquad \sigma^2 = \frac{1}{(Q\ P^2)^2} - \frac{2R+1}{q\ P^R} - \frac{P}{Q^2}$$

SDLC employs a one byte flag: $R=5$ with the flag consisting of a zero, six ones, and a zero. For $P=Q=\frac{1}{2}$, i.e., equal fractions of ones and zeros, the mean number of bits that are transmitted before a bit stuffing occurs is sixty two bits, $\mu=62\ bits$. Put differently, the mean overhead is one bit out of every sixty three bits, or 1.5873 %. For $P=2/3$, i.e., two thirds of the bits are ones, one bit is stuffed on the average every 19.78 bits, for a bit stuffing overhead of 4.812%; for $P=1/3$, i.e., one third of the bits are ones, one bit is stuffed on the average every 363 bits, resulting in bit stuffing overhead of 0.274%. This makes it clear that the bit stuffing overhead incurred by this type of encoding uses relatively few bits to achieve a *transparent* encoding of a bit stream: note that there are no special control characters with this encoding strategy, unlike other approaches such as *Binary Synchronous Communications*. Furthermore, the overhead is relatively insensitive to the proportion of ones and zeros in a frame.

BONUS: What is the overhead per frame for a four bit flag, $R=1$ as a function of $0<P<1$? Repeat for a two byte flag, $R=13$.

A *frame* consists of a leading flag, an address field, a control field, a data field, a CRC field, and a trailing flag. The mean number of bits per frame is given by

$$mean\ number\ transmitted\ bits/frame = 2(R+3) + B\left[1 + \frac{1}{\mu}\right]$$

The first term is due to the two flags, the term B is due to the control and data bits, and the final term B/μ is due to bit insertions among the control and data bits. The variance of the number of bits in a frame is given by

$$variance\,(number\;bits\;transmitted/frame) = \sigma_{frame}^2 = \frac{B}{\mu}\frac{\sigma^2}{\mu^2} + \frac{var\,(D)}{\mu^2}$$

The maximum rate at which the link can transmit the frame is given by

$$\lambda_{max} = \frac{link\;data\;rate\,(bits/sec)}{mean\;number\;bits/frame}$$

The table below summarizes the mean and variance of the number of bits per frame transmitted (including control bits and inserted or stuffed bits) assuming equal fractions of ones and zeroes in the data bits, with parameters being the mean number of data bits per frame, and the squared coefficient of the number of data bits per frame (denoted C_{data}^2):

Table 9.6.Bits Transmitted/Frame Statistics(Rounded up to Nearest Integer)

Mean Data Bits/Frame	Mean Bits Transmitted/Frame	σ_{frame} $C_{data}^2=0$	$C_{data}^2=1$
500	589	3	9
1000	1097	5	13
2000	2113	6	33

This numerical summary shows that this encoding method incurs a small amount of overhead beyond the needed seventy two bits per frame for flags, address and control fields, and CRC coding, and that the fluctuations about the mean measured in units of standard deviations are relatively modest.

If the message arrival statistics to the controller can be adequately modelled by a Poisson process with rate λ, then the mean delay, including bit stuffing and transmission, from when the first bit of the message arrives until the last bit is transmitted is the sum of three terms:

- a term accounting for the delay in waiting for the last flag to be transmitted, and since each flag consists of a fixed number of $R+3$ bits each frame will be delayed on the average by $\frac{1}{2}(R+3)$ bit transmission times

- a term accounting for the delay while the backlog due to previously arrived frames is transmitted

- a term due to transmitting the frame

Combining all this, we find:

$$mean\;frame\;delay\; = E[T_Q]= E[T_{frame}] + \frac{1}{2}T_{flag}$$

$$+ \begin{cases} \dfrac{\lambda E[T_{frame}]}{1 - \lambda E[T_{frame}]} \dfrac{variance\,(number\ of\ bits/frame}{2(mean\ number\ of\ bits/frame)^2} & \lambda < \lambda_{max} \\ \infty & \lambda \geqslant \lambda_{max} \end{cases}$$

$$E[T_{frame}] = \frac{mean\ number\ of\ bits/frame}{link\ data\ rate\,(bits/sec)} \qquad T_{flag} = \frac{R+3\ bits/flag}{link\ data\ rate\,(bits/sec)}$$

EXERCISE: Plot the mean frame delay versus message arrival rate for 500, 1000, and 2000 data bits per frame with a four, eight, and sixteen bit flag, assuming $P=\frac{1}{2}$ and $P=2/3$.

9.12.1 Additional Reading

[1]   R.J.Camrass, R.G.Gallager, *Encoding Message Lengths for Data Transmission,* IEEE Transactions on Information Theory, **24** (4), 495-496 (1978).

[2]   R.L.Donnan, R.Kersey, *Synchronous Data Link Control: A Perspective,* IBM Systems Journal, **13** (2), 140-161, 1974.

[3]   J.S.Ma, *On the Impact of HDLC Zero Insertion and Deletion on Link Utilization and Reliability,* IEEE Transactions on Communications, **30** (2), 375-381 (1982).

Problems

1) The arrival times (using a decimal clock!) are monitored for tasks handled by a point of sale terminal over an hour, starting at time zero. The measurement data are summarized in the table below.

Table 9.7. Arrival Times

0.475	0.148	0.853	0.154	0.126
0.785	0.936	0.999	0.610	0.960
0.350	0.312	0.084	0.318	0.387
0.572	0.270	0.651	0.601	0.133

A. Plot the cumulative distribution of interarrival times of tasks

B. Compute the mean and median of the interarrival time distribution

C. Compute the variance and standard deviation and twenty fifth and seventy fifth percentiles of the interarrival time distribution

D. Plot data quantiles vs quantiles from a uniform distribution, i.e., a distribution given by

$$PROB[X \leqslant Y] = \begin{cases} 0 & Y < 0 \\ X & 0 \leqslant Y < 1 \\ 1 & Y > 1 \end{cases}$$

2) What is the squared coefficient of variation of the number of arrivals in a time interval of fixed duration T for a finite source arrival process? Repeat for a Poisson process.

3) A front end processor to a transaction processing system handles one particular type of job. The arrival statistics are assumed to be Poisson. The sequence of processing times are assumed to be independent identically distributed exponential random variables. Each job requires ten thousand (10,000) assembly language instructions on the average to be executed. Jobs are executed in order of arrival. During a normal business hour, seven (7) jobs per second arrive to be executed. We wish to study the impact on performance for three different types of peak business hour overloads:

- a peak business hour overload of twenty (20) per cent, with the mean arrival rate of jobs being 8.4 jobs per second

- a peak business hour overload of ten (10) per cent, with the mean arrival rate of jobs being 7.7 jobs per second

- a peak business hour overload of five (5) per cent, with the mean arrival rate of jobs being 7.35 jobs per second

Two different delay criteria must be met:

- During a normal business hour, the fraction of time a job is in the system (its queueing time, the sum of its processing and waiting time) more than one (1) second must be less than five per cent

- During a peak business hour, the fraction of time a job is in the system more than one (1) second must be less than ten per cent

For each of the three different peak business hour overloads, answer the following questions and summarize your results in a table.

[1]   Find the *minimum* speed processor needed to meet the above performance goals. Measure the processor speed in the maximum number of assembly language instructions per second that can be executed.

[2]   Find the processor utilization during a normal business hour of this minimum speed processor.

[3]   Find the fraction of jobs executing on this minimum speed processor during a normal business hour that wait zero before beginning execution

4) An online computer system processes three different types of tasks. Each type of task arrives according to independent Poisson statistics. Type I tasks have a mean arrival rate of 0.5 tasks per second, with a constant or deterministic processing or service time of 0.5 seconds each. Type II tasks have a mean arrival rate of 0.1 tasks per second, and an exponentially distributed processing time of 2.0 seconds each. Type III tasks arrive at the rate of 0.03 tasks per second, and each Type III task has an Erlang-5 distribution of processing times with a mean processing time of 5.0 seconds each. If the tasks are processed in order of arrival, first in, first out, find

- A.   the utilization of the processor

- B.   the mean waiting time for each type of task

- C.   the mean queueing time for each type of task

D.   the mean number of tasks in the system

E.   the probability that each type of task has to wait at all

BONUS: Repeat the above assuming a static nonpreemptive priority arbitration rule is used, with I highest priority, II second highest, and III lowest.

5) We wish to compare the traffic handling characteristics of three different computer configurations:

- a single input stream feeding one buffer with one processor capable of executing a maximum of one million assembly language instructions per second

- a single input stream feeding one buffer with two processors each capable of executing a maximum of five hundred thousand assembly language instructions per second

- a single input stream that is split into two streams each of half the intensity of the original stream, with each stream feeding its own buffer and own processor, and each processor capable of executing five hundred thousand assembly language instructions per second

Each task involves the execution of an exponentially distributed number of assembly language instructions, with a mean of one hundred thousand assembly language instructions executed per task. The number of instructions executed per task is assumed to be statistically independent.

Plot the following quantities versus the mean arrival rate of tasks for each of the above three configurations:

A.   the mean rate of completing tasks

B.   the mean waiting time per task

C.   the mean queueing time per task

D.   the mean queue length

E.   the fraction of time that a task waits greater than zero

F.   If we require that the mean queueing time be less than SCALE times the mean processing time per task, find the maximum mean throughput rate of tasks for each of the above configurations for SCALE equal to ten (e.g., during a normal business hour) and for SCALE equal to twenty (e.g., during a peak business hour).

BONUS: Repeat the above if the number of assembly language instructions per task is constant, with the same mean, versus hyperexponential with squared coefficient of variation ten, with the same mean.

6) Messages are generated from a set of sources, and must be transmitted over a single link. The messages are of fixed length. The arrival statistics are Poisson distributed.

A. Twenty messages per second arrive; all messages are 64 bytes long (eight bits per byte). What is the minimum line speed needed to achieve a mean delay per message (waiting time plus transmission time) equal to five times a message transmission time? Three times a message transmission time? One millisecond mean delay?

B. Plot the minimum line speed versus the mean arrival rate for 64 byte messages, with a mean delay equal to three times a message transmission time.

C. Plot the minimum line speed versus the mean arrival rate for 1024 byte messages with a mean delay equal to five times a message transmission time.

D. What changes in the previous sections if the messages are no longer constant length, but have an exponentially distributed length with the above mean value?

E. What changes in the previous sections if the messages are no longer constant length, but have an Erlang-2 distributed length with the above mean value?

7) An inventory control transaction processing system employs a data base management system. A typical transaction uses the data base as follows:

[1] A part number table is accessed

[2] A warehouse table is accessed

[3] An inventory table is accessed

The time to hold each of these resources and the execution time statistics are summarized below:

Table 9.8. Execution Time Statistics

Table	Distribution	Mean Time
Part Number	D	100 μsec
Warehouse	M	250 μsec
Inventory	E_2	150 μsec

In order to insure correct logical operation, each table is locked for the duration of a transaction.

A. What are the steps and resources held at each step?

B. What is the state space describing system operations?

C. What is the effective distribution of execution time for each transaction using the data base management system?

D. What is the maximum mean throughput rate of the data base management system?

E. Repeat all of the above if each step is a *constant* service time of 100 μ seconds, and an *exponential* service time of 100 μ seconds.

8) A single processor executes work from a single queue. The arrival statistics are felt to be adequately modeled as Poisson. The execution time of each job has a mean of one second, and is deterministic or constant. Plot the variance of queueing time versus the utilization of a processor for

• Service in order of arrival

• Service in reverse order of arrival, nonpreemptive scheduling

• Service in reverse order of arrival, preemptive resume scheduling

BONUS: Repeat for exponentially distributed execution time statistics.

9) P processors access a common shared memory. Only one processor at a time is allowed to access the memory. The mean memory access time is two clock cycles. The mean time interval between memory access requests for a given processor is five clock cycles.

A. Each memory access time is assumed to be constant and equal to two clock cycles. Plot the mean memory access delay versus the number of processors, for one to four processors, using a finite source arrival process model. Repeat for an infinite source arrival process model, and compare results.

B. Repeat if the memory access times are drawn from an exponential distribution with a mean of two clock cycles.

C. Repeat if the memory access times are drawn from a hyperexponential distribution with a mean of two clock cycles and with a squared coefficient of variation of ten.

CHAPTER 10: **PRIORITY SCHEDULING II**

The previous chapter laid the groundwork for analyzing priority system performance. In this chapter we will focus on the following topics:

- Static priority scheduling of a single serially reusable resource

- Performance comparisons of different priority scheduling policies

- Overload control of a single serially reusable resource

- Priority scheduling of voice and data over a single digital link

- Sliding window link level flow link level flow control

10.1 Examples

A wide variety of examples motivate interest in this subject.

10.1.1 Static Priority Scheduling of a Single Processor Figure 10.1 shows the tasks that must be executed and the order for a single processor packet switching system. Jobs typically arrive in bursts or clumps: there is nothing, or there is a pile of jobs waiting to be executed. Each task of each job must be done in the order shown, i.e., there is correlation between tasks. Each job and perhaps each task generates at its arrival an *interrupt* of the processor. Both these phenomena must be included when calculating performance. The conventional assumption in the previous chapter of purely random arrivals (simple independent Poisson streams) may result in unduly optimistic performance projections.

In general purpose computer systems, the servicing of a job requires the execution of several tasks with different urgencies. At a minimum, the processing of a job will usually require two different types of work modules, the invocation of a *request type* module followed by the appropriate *service type* module. In addition, at the completion of a job, various tables and pointers must be reset before processing the next job. A second source of clustering in arrival patterns occurs in computer communication networks, where jobs are serviced in batches and arrivals and departures tend to clump. Each task of each job is assigned a priority. At any instant of time the processor executes the highest priority task. How should priorities be assigned to achieve desired performance? What is the penalty paid in mean throughput rate and mean queueing time if the arrival stream is more bursty than just Poisson? How is performance impacted by interrupt handling and operating system calls?

10.1.2 Voice and Data Multiplexing over a Single Digital Link A digital transmission link is clocked at a repetitive time interval called a *frame*. Each frame consists of S time intervals called slots, with F frames per second.

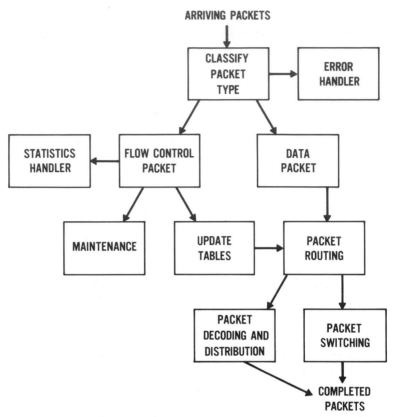

Figure 10.1.Packet Switching System Work Flow

During each time slot one packet or chunk of information can be transmitted. Two types of requests bid for use of the link. The first type is voice telephone calls. Each call requires one time slot for the duration of a call; if a slot is available, it is held for the call duration, while if no slot is available, the call is rejected and will try later. The second type is data generated from low speed terminals and computers. Each data transmission attempt requires one or more time slots to be transmitted; if no transmission capacity is available, the attempts are buffered or delayed until capacity is available. In order to provide adequate voice service, only a fraction of the time slots will carry voice on the average, e.g., sixty to eighty per cent, and hence the remaining transmission capacity is available for data. How much voice and data can be handled?

10.1.3 Sliding Window Link Level Flow Control A transmitter wishes to send a message to a receiver over a communications channel. The receiver only has a limited amount of buffering available for messages. If all the receiver buffers are filled with messages, and the transmitter sends another message, some message will be lost. A *sliding window flow control* policy paces the transmitter: the transmitter can send up to a maximum of W (the window)

474

messages before an acknowledgement is required; if no acknowledgement is received, the transmitter stops sending packets, and hence delay increases and mean throughput rate drops. What is the penalty of using a sliding window flow control policy in terms of mean throughput rate and mean delay versus infinite buffering or versus a buffer capable of holding only one message? How does the speed mismatch of the transmitter and receiver impact this system?

10.2 The CP/G/1 Queue with Static Priority Arbitration

In the previous chapter, the arrival streams of jobs were uncorrelated from one another, and there was no way to explicitly model the bursty nature of the work load. Here we allow tasks to arrive according to *compound Poisson (CP)* statistics. More than one job can arrive at a time, and each job consists of one or more tasks. This gives us a rich enough class of models to capture the correlated bursty nature of the work load.

10.2.1 Arrival Process A job consists of one or more tasks. Jobs arrive at N infinite capacity buffers according to a vector valued compound Poisson *(CP)* process. The buffers are assumed to be capable of holding all arrivals, i.e., there is never any buffer overflow. The arrival process sample paths or realizations may be visualized as follows: the arrival epochs' interarrival times form a sequence of independent identically distributed exponential random variables. At each arrival epoch, a random number of tasks of each of the N types of jobs arrive. We assume the interarrival times are independent of the number of tasks arriving at each arrival epoch. Multiple jobs of the same or different type can arrive simultaneously. The first case to be investigated in any design may well be the case of independent streams to each buffer. These streams can be perturbed from simple to batch or compound Poisson to study the effect on system performance of bunching of arrivals.

A second case is to assume that a job is actually a sequence of tasks that must be done in a specified order. Here we model this by having a simultaneous arrival of each type of task to each buffer, and we can measure performance as the distribution of time interval from when the task arrives with the highest priority until the task with the lowest priority is completely processed, and take a look at distributions of the intermediate task flow times. The main requirement is that the partial ordering on the sequence of performing the jobs must be consistent with the priority indices. Note that in effect we allow the task to migrate from buffer to buffer. We emphasize that the migration problem may well be the more realistic case, especially if the priority ordering is not consistent with the partial ordering; we give up an element of realism in order to analyze something tractable.

A third case is to assume that the highest priority work models overhead incurred by the operating system in handling interrupts, while the lower level priorities are dedicated to application programs.

One final case is to assume that the lowest level task is so called maintenance or diagnostic checking work, where the operating system is called to check both its own integrity as well as various hardware items. Here we model this by assuming that the single processor can keep up with work in all but the lowest levels, so that instead of the system ever becoming idle, it goes into a maintenance state, which will be concluded when tasks at any higher priority level arrive to be processed.

10.2.2 Processing Time Distribution Arrivals to each particular buffer are assumed to require independent identically distributed amounts of processing. Note that the type of processing is quite arbitrary. In many dedicated applications, certain types of tasks require processing times that lie within narrow bounds, while other types of tasks require processing times that may fluctuate wildly.

10.2.3 Processor Work Discipline We confine attention to nonpreemptive and preemptive resume static priority work disciplines. For a nonpreemptive schedule, once a task begins execution, it is the highest priority task in the system, and will run to completion. For a preemptive resume schedule, a job in execution may be preempted by the arrival of a higher priority task; the state of the task that is interrupted is saved, and once all higher priority tasks are executed, execution of the interrupted task is resumed at the point of interruption.

Once a task arrives it is assigned to one of N queues. The processor visits the queues according to a static priority scheduling rule:

[1] Each queue is assigned a unique index number. The smaller the value of the index, the higher the priority of tasks in that queue over tasks with larger indices.

[2] Tasks within the same priority class are served in order of arrival.

10.2.4 Nonpreemptive Static Priority Arbitration The figure below shows a queueing network block diagram for a nonpreemptive static priority scheduler. At the lowest priority level a scheduler job is always ready to be executed. Once it completes execution, the processor scans the queues in downward priority order to find work; if work is present, it is executed, and the scheduler is invoked once again at completion of execution of the highest priority job. Put differently, the scheduler is a *loop,* and hence the processor is always busy, either executing jobs at priority levels K=1,...,N or executing scheduler work.

10.2.5 Controlled Nonpreemptive Scheduling One variant on nonpreemptive scheduling is so called *controlled* nonpreemptive scheduling. One problem with nonpreemptive scheduling is that once a job begins execution, it cannot be interrupted. One way to provide *some* responsiveness is as follows. Each job consists of one or more tasks, with no task capable of executing more than a

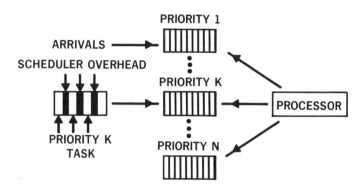

Figure 10.2.Nonpreemptive Static Priority Scheduling

maximum number of processor seconds. Once a task finishes execution, the scheduler is invoked, and the processor scans the ready list for the highest priority task. In effect, no job can be locked out of execution for more than the maximum length of time of any task, but a task might have to be split into multiple tasks (artificially) in order to meet this design constraint. The scheduler will run at the lowest priority level in the system if no work is present:

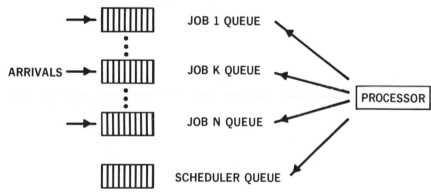

Figure 10.3.Controlled Nonpreemptive Scheduling

10.2.6 Multiple Level Downward Migration In many systems jobs that require a short amount of execution are delayed by jobs that require a large amount of execution. One scheduler that gives short jobs priority at the expense of long jobs is a quantum multiple level feedback scheduler. Each job receives some service at the highest priority level, and either finishes or migrates to the next lowest priority level. The maximum amount of service at each priority level is called the *quantum* for that priority. In practice, most jobs should finish in one quantum, i.e., short jobs should run to completion, while long jobs can migrate to lower priority levels, because long jobs take a

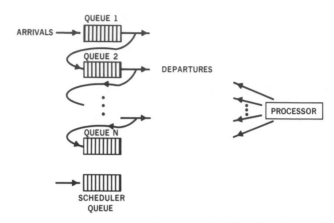

Figure 10.4.Multiple Level Downward Migration Scheduling

long time.

10.2.7 Interrupt Driven Preemptive Resume Scheduling In order to be responsive, the processor should respond at the arrival of a job. Each job consists of two tasks, an interrupt task or trap handler, followed by a useful work task. Once the processor is interrupted, the context of the current task is saved, and will be restored for execution at the point of interruption once all higher priority work (including subsequent interrupts) are executed.

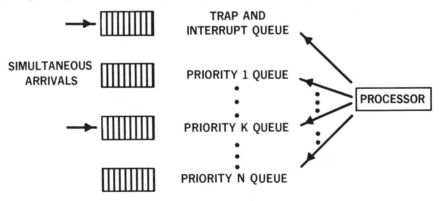

Figure 10.5.Interrupt Driven Preemptive Resume Scheduling

10.2.8 General Static Priority Scheduling The most general case dealt with here consists of decomposing each job into three tasks: an interrupt or trap handling task executed at highest priority level, a useful work task executed at priority level K=1,2..., and a cleanup task executed at the highest priority level. At any instant of time there are wait queues, holding tasks that have received no service, and active queues each capable of buffering one task at most, with tasks that have begun execution but not yet finished in the active set of queues.

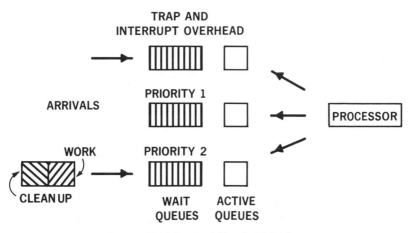

Figure 10.6.General Static Priority

Each job upon arrival consists of a setup task, arriving at the highest priority level, plus tasks arriving at lower priority levels. Tasks at these lower levels consist of a work task followed by a cleanup task. All tasks have two priority indices upon arrival, a nonpreemptive or dispatching index and a preemptive index. Initially tasks are entered into the various system buffers according to their dispatching index, in what will be called a wait list. Tasks that have received some processing are stored in what will be called an active list, where there are at most N entries on the active list, each indexed from 1 to N. We assume there is a single job type; if there are multiple job types, we assume an arbitration rule exists for deciding which tasks from which job are entered into the system buffers when jobs of different types arrive simultaneously. Any partial ordering within the tasks are assumed consistent with the dispatching priority index ordering. The processor scans the active list, and services that task with the lowest index first, according to a preemptive resume work discipline, until this list is empty. The processor next scans the wait list and services that task with the lowest index and earliest arrival epoch; once this task receives some service, it is removed from the wait list and entered on the active list, but it moves to that entry on the active list specified by its preemptive index, assumed here to be less than or equal to the dispatching or nonpreemptive index. Note that if the two indices are equal for all tasks, then we have a pure preemptive resume work discipline, while if the second index is set to one, i.e., the preemptive index is as high as possible, then that task, once it starts execution, cannot be interrupted. In effect, we have changed the priority of a task, artificially raising it to insure that when it accesses some *logical* resource, such as an operating system table, the integrity of this resource is assured; since we do this by a *physical* resource, i.e., the processor, we see that we are actually treating a multiple resource scheduling problem, where we use the priority indices for both controlling system responsiveness and system integrity. This practice is quite common in modern operating system design in practice. A little thought will show that if we wish to control a

479

resource, we might simply construct a queue or buffer for that resource, which would be managed in such a way to maximize performance. The method described here is quite popular at present, but does not appear to be the only method for restricting access to a resource.

This particular labeling scheme also clarifies the concepts of mixing preemptive resume and nonpreemptive work disciplines, which on close inspection is much more complex than at first sight (try a three buffer system, with the first buffer operating preemptive resume and the second two nonpreemptive, and study the waiting and flow time of tasks arriving at the middle buffer).

With this pair of priority indices, we can now simply model the processor work involved at the completion of a job by setting its preemptive priority index to unity, guaranteeing it will not be interrupted. In many computer applications there is a third list in addition to the wait list and active list, where tasks that are blocked from further processing (due to waiting for the completion of another task, or attempting to access a critical table while another task is doing so, for example) are stored.

Finally, we cannot handle the arbitrary case where the preemptive index is greater than the nonpreemptive index.

10.2.9 Summary of Results   The waiting time of a task is the time interval between the arrival epoch of this task and the instant at which processing starts on the task. The queueing or flow or response time of a task is the time from when a task arrives until it is completely processed and leaves its buffer. Granted this, we can quantify what levels of work load result in no more than five per cent of the arrivals in priority class seven experiencing waiting times in excess of three seconds, or flow times in excess of ten seconds.

Our method for evaluating the waiting and flow time distributions involves tracing a job through the system. The waiting time is the sum of two time intervals, with the first due to work in the system at arrival that must first be processed, and the second due to work of higher priority that arrives at the same time. Both these time intervals can be stretched by the time required to execute subsequent arrivals of higher priority work. The flow time of a task is the sum of two time intervals, with the first due to waiting time, while the second is due to processing time (the time from when processing is started until it is completed: in preemptive resume work disciplines the processing time interval could involve interruptions due to servicing of a newly arrived higher priority task). The detailed expressions for these transforms as well as numerical studies are given in subsequent sections. The claim is often made that one would like to schedule the processor with a preemptive resume work discipline in order to gain maximum control over responsiveness, but the penalty paid in overhead on the processor for each interrupt rules this out. With a nonpreemptive work discipline the processor overhead can be simply lumped into the service required for each job, but one might have to wait for the processor to finish a low priority slowly running task before more urgent high priority work can be handled. Because of this, one finds that the most urgent work in applications is scheduled using preemptive resume, while less urgent work uses a nonpreemptive work discipline.

10.3 Analysis of the CP/G/1 Queue with Static Priority Arbitration

We now summarize our analysis with formulae and examples.

10.3.1 Arrival Process Tasks arrive at N infinite capacity buffers according to a vector valued compound Poisson arrival process, $\underline{A}(t)=(A_1(t),...,A_N(t)$. $A_K(t),1\leqslant K\leqslant N$ denotes the number of arrivals to buffer K in the time interval $[0,t)$. c denotes the mean rate of arrival epochs, i.e., the interarrival times between arrival epochs are independent identically distributed exponential random variables with mean $1/c$. The random variable $\underline{A}(t)$ is defined as the sum of M independent random variables with a given probability distribution H, where M is the number of arrival epochs in the interval $[0,t)$, and H is the probability distribution governing the number of arrivals at each arrival epoch. The probability generating functional of $\underline{A}(t)$ is given by

$$\eta_A(t,x_1,...,x_N)=E\left[\prod_{K=1}^{N}x_K^{A_K(t)}\right]\quad |x_K|<1,K=1,...,N$$

$$\eta_A(t,x_1,\ldots,x_N)=exp[-ct(1-\eta(x_1,\ldots,x_N))]\quad t\geqslant 0;|x_K|<1;K=1,...,N$$

where $\eta(x_1,...,x_N)$ is the probability generating function of the arriving batch size distribution H,

$$\eta(x_1,...,x_N)=\sum_{\underline{J}}\left[\prod_{K=1}^{N}x_K^{j_K}\right]H(j_1,\ldots,j_N)\quad |x_K|<1;K=1,...,N$$

The rate of arrival of tasks with priority index K, denoted λ_K, is then given by

$$E[A_K(t)]=ct\frac{\partial\eta}{\partial x_K}\Big|_{x_I=1-}=\lambda_K t\quad I=1,...,N;K=1,...,N$$

$$\lambda_K=c\frac{\partial\eta}{\partial x_K}\Big|_{x_I=1-}=cE[j_K]\quad I=1,...,N$$

10.3.2 An Example of Correlated Arrivals Packets of digital data arrive at a packet switching node in a data communications network. Each packet requires two processing operations, validity checking (protocol processing) and routing processing for subsequent transmission. For simplicity of analysis, the arrival epochs are assumed to occur according to Poisson statistics with intensity c, and the probability distribution for the number of packets in a group is given by $\overset{\rightharpoonup}{H}(.)$. Let validity checking be the type one task and communication routing processing the task with priority index two (with type one having higher priority over type two). Then

$$\eta(x_1,x_2)=\eta_{\tilde{H}}(x_1 x_2) \quad |x_1 x_2|<1$$

where $\eta_{\tilde{H}}$ is the probability generating function of $\tilde{H}(.)$,

$$\eta_{\tilde{H}}(y)=\sum_{k=1}^{\infty}\tilde{H}(k)y^k \quad |y|<1$$

and $\tilde{H}(0)$ is assumed here to be zero. Let $E_{\tilde{H}}(k)$ denote the expected number of packets in each arrival group. Then the rate of arrival of tasks of priority one and priority two is given by

$$\lambda_1=\lambda_2=cE_{\tilde{H}}(k)$$

10.3.3 An Example of Correlated Arrivals Digital data arrives from different types of peripheral devices to a central processor in a dedicated application, e.g., in a petrochemical refinery, in a telephone switching center, or in a data communications network switching node. For simplicity of analysis, the arrival epochs are assumed to occur in accordance with a Poisson process of intensity c, and we further assume there are only two different types of peripheral devices. Whenever a task arrives, it must be checked by the processor to see if it should be acted upon; we assume the processor interrupts whatever work it is doing, checks the arrival to see whether or not it must be acted upon, and then resumes processing the interrupted task at the point it was at. Each type of arrival consists of a random number of jobs, which together make up the task. We let the highest priority level, one, denote the interrupt handling overhead associated with the tasks, i.e., the work involved in checking each arrival to see where it must be assigned. We let levels two and three denote the actual work tasks, where the lower the index the higher the priority. For example, in a switching node in a data communications network, level two might correspond to checking parity on the received data packet, while level three might represent the work associated with reformatting the received messages for further transmission. Let $\eta(.)$ denote the generating function associated with the joint multivariate distribution for the number of arriving jobs at each arrival epoch, denoted $H(j_1,j_2,j_3)$,

$$\eta(x_1,x_2,x_3)=x_1\tilde{\eta}(x_2 x_3)$$

where $\tilde{\eta}$ is the joint moment generating function associated with arrivals at levels two and three. For example, if the arrival streams are simple Poisson, then $\tilde{\eta}$ can be given explicitly by

$$\tilde{\eta}(x_2,x_3)=\frac{\lambda_2}{\lambda_1}x_2+\frac{\lambda_3}{\lambda_1}x_3 \quad \lambda_1\equiv\lambda_2+\lambda_3$$

In the general case, the mean arrival rates are given by

$$\lambda_1 = c \quad \lambda_K = c \frac{\partial \tilde{\eta}}{\partial x_K}\Big|_{x_1 = x_2 = x_3 = 1} \quad K = 2,3$$

10.3.4 Two Examples of Bursty Arrivals Jobs arrive according to compound or batch Poisson arrival statistics for execution by a single processor. The interarrival times between job batches are independent identically distributed exponential random variables with mean time $1/c$. At each arrival epoch a geometrically distributed number of jobs arrive:

$$H(K) = (1 - \alpha)\alpha^K \quad K=1,2,... \quad \eta(X) = \sum_{K=1}^{\infty} X^K H(K) = \frac{(1 - \alpha)X}{1 - \alpha X}$$

The *total* mean arrival rate of jobs is given by

$$\lambda = c \frac{\partial \eta(X)}{\partial X}\Big|_{X=1} = c\eta'(1) = c \sum_{K=1}^{\infty} K\, H(K) = \frac{c}{1 - \alpha}$$

By way of contrast, if a *constant* number of jobs, say D, arrived at each arrival epoch, then

$$H(K) = 1 \quad K=D \qquad H(K)=0 \quad K \neq D \qquad \eta(X) = X^D$$

The *total* mean arrival rate of jobs is given by

$$\lambda = c \frac{\partial \eta(X)}{\partial X}\Big|_{X=1} = cD$$

10.3.5 An Illustrative Example of Correlated Bursty Arrivals The job interarrival times are independent identically distributed exponential random variables with mean time $1/c$. At each arrival epoch a geometrically distributed number of jobs arrive. Each job consists of two tasks, an interrupt handling task and a work task. The interrupt handling task is executed at priority level 1, while the work task is executed at priority level $K=2,...,N$. The distribution of jobs at each arrival epoch is given by

$$H(K) = (1 - \alpha)\alpha^K \quad K=1,...; \ \eta(X) = \sum_{K=1}^{\infty} X^K H(K) = \frac{(1 - \alpha)X}{1 - \alpha X}$$

The generating function for number of tasks at each arrival epoch is given by

$$E\left[\prod_{K=1}^{N} X^{J_K}\right] = \frac{(1 - \alpha)Y}{1 - \alpha Y} \quad Y = X_1 \sum_{K=2}^{N} X_K F_K$$

where F_K are the fraction of arrivals of type K.

10.3.6 Processing Time Distribution P_{Kr} denotes the time required to process the rth arrival to buffer K, independent of the arrival process. For each K, the sequence $\{P_{Kr}:r=1,2,...\}$ is an independent identically distributed set of random variables. The joint distribution function and its Laplace Stieltjes transform for the priority class K arrivals will be denoted by $G_{P_K}(.)$ and $\hat{G}_{P_K}(.)$, respectively, where

$$G_{P_K}(t) = Pr[P_{Kr} \leq t], \ G_{P_K}(0) = 0 \quad \text{for } r = 1,2..; K = 1,...,N; t \geq 0$$

$$\hat{G}_{P_K}(y) = \int_0^{\infty} e^{-yt} dG_{P_K}(t) \quad Re(y) \geq 0$$

10.3.7 Processor Work Discipline There is a single processor which operates in accordance with the following static priority scheduling rule:

[1] Each buffer is assigned a unique index number. The smaller the index, the higher the priority of tasks in that buffer. Tasks in this set of infinite capacity buffers will be said to be on the wait list. In addition to this set of buffers, there is a second set of finite capacity buffers, numbered from 1 to N, each of which can hold at most one task. The smaller the value of the index, the higher the priority of the task in this finite buffer over all other tasks in the other finite capacity buffers with larger indices. Tasks in this set of finite capacity buffers are said to be on the active list.

[2] Tasks within the same buffer (same priority class) on the wait list are served in order of arrival.

[3] The processor scheduling decision epochs are arrival epochs and completion epochs of tasks. At each decision time epoch, the processor first scans the active list, and services the highest priority task in that list. If the active list is empty, the processor scans the wait list, and chooses the task with the earliest arrival time that has the highest priority. Each task in the wait list thus has received no processing at all. Associated with each task is a multi-index (K,I), where K refers to the wait list priority, and I refers to the order of the task within a job. When the processor begins to service a task, the task is moved from the wait list to the active list, and inserted into buffer $1 \leq \nu_{KI} \leq K$ on the active list. By construction this position must be empty of work. If we allowed the number of tasks composing each job to become infinite, while keeping the mean amount of service per task constant, then for a pure nonpreemptive work discipline, in the limit as the number of tasks became infinite, in this sense we would approach a pure preemptive resume work discipline. Here such a limiting process does not result in a preemptive resume work discipline (why?).

[4] We now differentiate between nonpreemptive and preemptive resume scheduling:

   • For nonpreemptive arbitration, when a task of type I arrives to find the processor occupied with a type J task (where we assume $1 \leq I < J \leq N$), the processor does *not* interrupt the processing of the lower priority task. The higher priority task enters buffer I and waits for the lower priority task to complete.

- For preemptive resume arbitration, when a task arrives to find the processor occupied with a type J task, it will interrupt the processing of that task if and only if $J > I$.

For special cases, e.g., $v_{KI}=1$, the preemptive index is set as high as possible, and such a task cannot be interrupted by any other task. This allows us to model at one stroke both processor scheduling overhead associated with interrupt handling as well as task completion scheduling overhead.

10.3.8 Load Process Let $L_K(t)$ denote the total processing time required for the arrivals to buffers 1 through K inclusive in the time interval [0,t). For each K, $\{L_K(.)\}$ is a stationary independent increment process. The moment generating functional for $\{L_K(.)\}$ is denoted by $\hat{G}_{L_K}(t,y)$, where

$$\hat{G}_{L_K}(t,y)=E[e^{-yL_K(t)}]=exp[-t\Phi_K(y)] \quad Re(y)\geqslant 0;\ t\geqslant 0;\ 1\leqslant K\leqslant N$$

$$\Phi_K(y)=c[1-\eta(\hat{G}_{P_1},\hat{G}_{P_2},...,\hat{G}_{P_K},1,1,...,1)] \quad Re(y)\geqslant 0;\ 1\leqslant K\leqslant N$$

It is convenient to adopt the convention

$$\Phi_0(y)\equiv 0$$

By differentiating these expressions, we see

$$E[L_K(t)]=U_K t \quad t\geqslant 0; 1\leqslant K\leqslant N$$

$$U_K=\frac{d\Phi_K(y)}{dy}\Big|_{y=0}=\sum_{I=1}^{K}\lambda_I E[P_I]<\infty \quad 1\leqslant K\leqslant N$$

U_K is the fraction of time the processor is busy in order to keep up with the work arriving in buffers 1 through K inclusive, with the letter U a mnemonic for *utilization*. If $U_N<1$, the processor can keep up with its workload, i.e., the processor will go idle, and no job will be locked out forever from execution. If $U_N\geqslant 1$ the system is always busy.

For each K ($1\leqslant K\leqslant N$), realizations of the load process are nondecreasing, constant except for positive jumps occurring at random time epochs, where the jumps epochs obey Poisson point process statistics with mean positive rate c_K

$$c_K=\Phi_K(\infty)<\infty$$

Let $\{S_{Kr}; r=1,2,..\}$ be the sequence of independent, identically distributed, positive random variables representing the jump amplitudes in $\{L_K(.)\}$ where r indexes the arrival or jump epoch. The joint distribution of the $\{S_{Kr}\}$ is denoted by $G_{S_K}(.)$ which has associated Laplace Stieltjes transform $\hat{G}_{S_K}(y)$,

$$Pr[S_{Kr} \leqslant t] = G_{S_{\kappa}}(t), \ G_{S_{\kappa}}(0) = 0 \quad t \geqslant 0$$

$$\hat{G}_{S_{\kappa}}(y) = \int_0^\infty e^{-yt} dG_{S_{\kappa}}(t) = 1 - \frac{\Phi_K(y)}{c_K} \quad Re(y) \geqslant 0$$

10.3.9 Summary of Results The waiting time of a task is the time interval between the instant of arrival of this task and the instant at which processing starts on the task. The flow or response time of a task is the sum of the waiting time and the processing time of a task. For each $k(1 \leqslant K \leqslant N)$, let the sequence of waiting times and flow times encountered by tasks of priority K be denoted $\{W_{Kr}; r=1,2,...\}, \{F_{Kr} \equiv W_{Kr} + P_{Kr}; r=1,2,...\}$, respectively, where $\{P_{Kr}; r=1,2,...\}$ denotes the processing times required by the sequence of arrivals of priority K. The $\{P_{Kr}\}$ are exogenous variables of the system, while the $\{W_{Kr}\}$ are endogenous variables which determine system performance. The moment generating functions associated with the waiting and queueing time distributions are given as follows:

$$\hat{G}_{W_{\kappa}}(y) = \int_{0-}^\infty e^{-yt} dG_{W_{\kappa}}(t) \quad \hat{G}_{F_{\kappa}}(y) = \int_{0-}^\infty e^{-yt} dG_{F_{\kappa}}(t) \quad Re(y) \geqslant 0$$

For nonpreemptive priority arbitration, $U_N < 1$, these transforms are given by

$$\hat{G}_{W_{\kappa}}(y) = \hat{G}_{V_{\kappa}}(\zeta_K(y)) \hat{G}_{D_{\kappa}}(\zeta_K(y)) \quad Re(y) \geqslant 0; 1 \leqslant K \leqslant N \quad U_N < 1$$

$$\hat{G}_{F_{\kappa}}(y) = \hat{G}_{W_{\kappa}}(y) \hat{G}_{P_{\kappa}}(y) \quad Re(y) \geqslant 0; 1 \leqslant K \leqslant N \quad U_N < 1$$

$$\hat{G}_{V_{\kappa}}(y) = \frac{(1-U_N)y + \sum_{I=K+1}^{N} \lambda_I [1 - \hat{G}_{P_I}(y)]}{y + c_K - c_K \hat{G}_{S_{\kappa}}(y)} \quad U_N < 1$$

$$\hat{G}_{D_{\kappa}}(y) = \frac{\Phi_K(y) - \Phi_{K-1}(y)}{\lambda_K [1 - \hat{G}_{P_{\kappa}}(y)]} \quad U_N < 1$$

$$\zeta_K(y) = y + c_{K-1} - c_{K-1} \hat{G}_{B_{\kappa-1}}(y) \quad U_N < 1$$

B_K denotes the *busy* period associated with doing work at level $1,...,K$. $\hat{G}_{B_{\kappa}}(y)$ is the moment generating function associated with B_K, and is the unique root inside the unit circle of

$$\hat{G}_{B_{\kappa}}(y) = \hat{G}_{S_{\kappa}}(y + c_K - c_K \hat{G}_{B_{\kappa}}(y)), \ \hat{G}_{B_0} = 1 \quad U_N < 1$$

If $U_{L-1} < 1, \ U_L \geqslant 1 \ (L=1,...,N)$, then for $K < L$

$$\hat{G}_{W_{\kappa}}(y) = \hat{G}_{V_{\kappa}}(\zeta_K(y)) \hat{G}_{D_{\kappa}}(\zeta_K(y)) \quad U_N \geqslant 1$$

$$\hat{G}_{F_{\kappa}}(y) = \hat{G}_{W_{\kappa}}(y) \hat{G}_{P_{\kappa}}(y) \quad U_N \geqslant 1$$

$$\hat{G}_{V_K}(y) = \frac{\sum_{I=K+1}^{L-1} \lambda_I[1-\hat{G}_{P_I}(y)] + \frac{1-U_{L-1}}{U_L-U_{L-1}} \lambda_L[1-\hat{G}_{P_L}(y)]}{y + c_K - c_K \hat{G}_{S_K}(y)} \qquad U_N \geqslant 1$$

where $\hat{G}_{D_K}(y), \varsigma_K(y), \hat{G}_{B_K}(y)$ are as given for $U_N < 1$, while if $K \geqslant L$,

$$G_{W_K}(t) = 0 \qquad G_{F_K}(t) = 0 \qquad 0 \leqslant t < \infty$$

10.3.10 Example We return to the earlier example of communications processing to illustrate these results. We first obtain the moment generating functional of the load process:

$$E[exp(-yL_K(t)] = exp[-t\Phi_K(y)] \quad K = 1,2 \quad where$$

$$\Phi_1(y) = c[1 - \eta_{\tilde{H}}(\hat{G}_{P_1}(y))]$$

$$\Phi_2(y) = c[1 - \eta_{\tilde{H}}(\hat{G}_{P_2}(y))]$$

where we assume $Re(y) \geqslant 0$. Since $\tilde{H}(0) = 0$, and the mean service times were both assumed finite, we see that

$$c_1 = \Phi_1(\infty) = c_2 = \Phi_2(\infty) = c$$

$$\hat{G}_{S_1}(y) = \eta_{\tilde{H}}[\hat{G}_{P_1}(y)] \qquad \hat{G}_{S_2}(y) = \eta_{\tilde{H}}[\hat{G}_{P_1}(y)\hat{G}_{P_2}(y)]$$

$$\lambda_1 = \lambda_2 = cE_{\tilde{H}}(k)$$

$$U_1 = \lambda_1 E[P_1] \qquad U_2 = \lambda_1 E[P_1] + \lambda_2 E[P_2]$$

If $U_2 < 1$, then we can write

$$\hat{G}_{V_1}(y) = \frac{(1-U_2)y + \lambda_2(1-\hat{G}_{P_2}(y))}{y + c - c\eta_{\tilde{H}}[\hat{G}_{P_1}(y)]}$$

$$\hat{G}_{V_2}(y) = \frac{(1-U_2)y}{y + c - c\eta_{\tilde{H}}[\hat{G}_{P_1}(y)\hat{G}_{P_2}(y)]}$$

$$\hat{G}_{D_1}(y) = \frac{c[1 - \eta_{\tilde{H}}(\hat{G}_{P_1}(y))]}{\lambda_1[1 - \hat{G}_{P_1}(y)]}$$

$$\hat{G}_{D_2}(y) = \frac{c[\eta_{\tilde{H}}(\hat{G}_{P_1}(y)) - \eta_{\tilde{H}}(\hat{G}_{P_1}(y)\hat{G}_{P_2}(y))]}{\lambda_2[1 - \hat{G}_{P_2}(y)]}$$

$$\varsigma_1(y) = y \qquad \varsigma_2(y) = y + c - c\hat{G}_{B_1}(y)$$

where $\hat{G}_{B_1}(y)$ is the unique root inside the unit circle of

$$\hat{G}_{B_1}(y) = \hat{G}_{S_1}[y + c - c\hat{G}_{B_1}(y)]$$

After substituting all this into the appropriate formulae, we finally obtain the desired results:

$$\hat{G}_{W_K}(y) = \hat{G}_{V_K}(y)\,\hat{G}_{D_K}(y) \qquad K=1,2$$

$$\hat{G}_{F_K}(y) = \hat{G}_{W_K}(y)\hat{G}_{P_K}(y) \qquad K=1,2$$

EXERCISE. Compute an explicit analytic formula for the mean waiting time and mean flow or queueing time for each type of task.

10.3.11 Preemptive Resume Arbitration Now we turn to preemptive resume arbitration, with $U_N < 1$. The formulae are analogous to the nonpreemptive case. The key differences are that the backlog of work is only due to work at the same or higher priority level, and the processing of a job must be stretched to account for interruptions by higher priority work:

$$\hat{G}_{W_K}(y)=\hat{G}_{V_K}(\hat{G}_{\zeta_K}(y))\hat{G}_{D_K}(\zeta_K(y)) \quad Re(y)\geqslant0; 1\leqslant K\leqslant N \quad U_N<1$$

$$\hat{G}_{F_K}(y)=\hat{G}_{W_K}(y)\hat{G}_{P_K}(\zeta_K(y)) \quad Re(y)\geqslant0; \ K=1,...,N \quad U_N<1$$

$$\hat{G}_{V_K}(y)=\frac{(1-U_K)y}{y-c_K[1-\hat{G}_{S_K}(y)]} \quad U_N<1$$

$$\hat{G}_{D_K}(y)=\frac{\Phi_K(y)-\Phi_{K-1}(y)}{\lambda_K[1-\hat{G}_{P_K}(y)]}$$

$$\hat{\zeta}_K(y)=y+c_{K-1}-c_{K-1}\hat{G}_{B_{K-1}}(y)$$

$\hat{G}_{B_K}(y)$ is the unique root inside the unit circle of

$$\hat{G}_{B_K}(y)=\hat{G}_{S_K}(y+c_K-c_K\hat{G}_{B_K}(y)), \ \hat{G}_{B_0}=1$$

EXERCISE. Substitute into the expressions given earlier for both nonpreemptive and preemptive resume scheduling. Assume $N=3$, with interrupt handling at level one, and work at levels two and three. Every job includes a cleanup phase. Assume λ is the *total* job arrival rate. The fraction of type K arrival is fixed at $F_2=0.25, F_3=0.75$. The arrival statistics are varied from independent simple Poisson streams, to correlated simple Poisson streams where at each arrival either a type one and type two or a type one and type three arrive, independent bursty Poisson streams with either geometric or constant batch size distributions, and correlated bursty Poisson streams. The service time distributions are either constant or exponential, the mean interrupt handling service time equals one second, the mean service time at levels $K=2,3$ equals three and ten, respectively, and the cleanup service time to equal one tenth second. Plot the mean queueing time versus the total arrival rate of jobs. Write an expression for the queueing time Laplace Stieltjes transform, plot its approximate numerical inverse for $U_3=0.5$.

10.3.12 Numerical Studies In order to numerically study the performance of a static priority arbitration system we must specify

- The fraction of arrivals of each job type

- The bursty character of the job arrival stream

- The tasks that make up each job:

  - For a nonpreemptive scheduler, each job includes a series of tasks: some tasks involving useful work time followed by some cleanup or context switching time.

  - For a preemptive resume scheduler, each job includes a series of tasks: some interrupt handling work followed by some clumps of tasks, with each task clump involving some useful work time followed by some cleanup or context switching time.

- The execution time statistics of each task: constant, hypoexponential, hyperexponential, arbitrary.

- The scheduling policy:

  - For a nonpreemptive scheduler, a scheduler task is always ready to execute at the lowest priority level, i.e., the scheduler is a loop. At the completion of each task, the list of ready tasks is scanned, and the processor executes the highest priority task to completion without interruption.

  - For a preemptive resume scheduler, the highest priority task is executed at any instant of time. If a task arrives of higher priority than the task in execution, the task in execution has its context saved, and the processor begins execution of the higher priority task. Once all higher priority tasks have been executed, the interrupted task resumes execution at the point of interruption.

We might not have all this information available. On the other hand, we can postulate all this information, and see how sensitive performance might be to parameters that we do not in fact know.

10.3.13 Example A processor executes only two types of jobs. The fraction of time the processor is doing useful work is assumed to be fifty per cent; so $U_2 = 0.5$. The mean work service time for type one tasks is fixed at one second, $E(T_{S1}) = 1$, while the mean work service time for type two tasks is varied from one to three to five seconds, $E(T_{S2}) = 1, 3, 5$. For one extreme, we assume arrivals are simple Poisson streams, no batching of arrivals, with each task requiring a *constant* amount of execution time, and *no* time required to execute the scheduler in the background or for cleanup. This extreme would be the *best* possible performance: if this is unacceptable, then the design has to be redone. The other extreme for *worst* possible performance would be geometric batching of arrivals ($\alpha{=}0.25$), with each task requiring an *exponentially* distributed amount of execution time, and a background scheduler that requires one half second of execution time, plus a cleanup task associated with each work task of one half second of execution time. These two cases are plotted in the following figures:

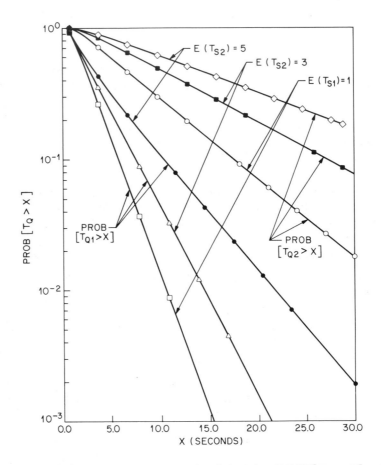

Figure 10.7.Best Case Nonpreemptive Scheduler: PROB[$T_Q > X$] vs X

How can this data be interpreted?

- The fraction of time a one second priority one job is executed within ninety per cent of the time varies from four to eight seconds for the best case, while it varies from six to eleven seconds for the worst case. In other words, ninety per cent of the time a high priority job spends one second in

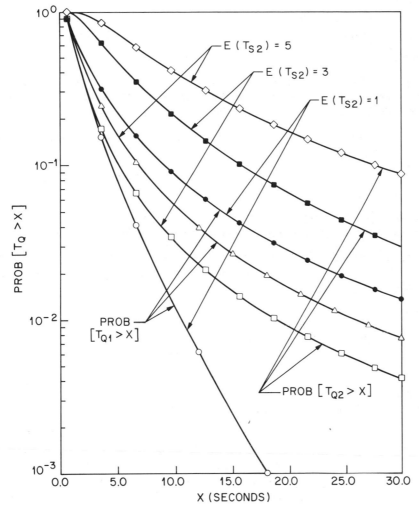

Figure 10.8. Worst Case Nonpreemptive Scheduler: PROB[$T_Q > X$] vs **X**

execution and from three to ten seconds waiting to be executed.

- The fraction of time a one second priority two job is executed within ninety per cent of the time varies from five to twenty eight seconds for the best case, while it varies from eighteen to thirty seven seconds for the worst case. In other words, ninety per cent of the time a low priority job spends from one to five seconds in execution, and from zero to thirty six seconds waiting to be executed.

In order to go beyond this analysis, more precise numbers are needed for each task execution step. On the other hand, this is exactly what computers can readily do, if appropriately instrumented. Put differently, this set of data should be gathered anyway simply to confirm the implementation of any priority scheduler.

10.4 Packet Switch Delay Analysis

A single processor is multiplexed amongst several different types of tasks that arise in switching a packet of information through a communications system. We first discuss the problem in more detail, and then the method of analysis.

10.4.1 Problem Statement The processor uses a static priority nonpreemptive work discipline as follows:

- at any given instant of time, the highest priority task in the system is being executed

- a message upon arrival generates an interrupt, and then is executed by input handling routines, routing and switching routines, and output routines

- interrupt handling is done at the highest priority level, followed by output handling, routing and switching, input handling, and background maintenance tasks

- within each priority class, tasks are executed in order of arrival

- at the completion of the input handling, routing and switching, and output handling there is some process overhead involved in switching from one task to the next

In order to complete the description of the model, we must describe the arrival statistics and the processing required by each task.

The interarrival times between message groups are assumed to be independent identically distributed exponential random variables. The number of messages arriving in each group are assumed to form a sequence of independent identically distributed random variables; here we cover two cases, although others are possible, a geometric batch size distribution and a constant batch size distribution, with the mean arrival batch size fixed. The case of constant batch size could be the result of one flow control strategy, while the geometric arrival batch size could be the result of a different flow control policy.

In order to complete the model description, we assume that the processing times at each priority level are constant, within the following ranges:

- interrupt handling--0.5-1.0 msec per interrupt

- maintenance--2.5 msec per task

- routing and switching--5.0-7.5 msec

- input and output handling--1.0-2.0 msec (assumed symmetrical)

- context switching--0.5-1.0 msec per context switch

- system call for sanity checking--0.5-1.0 msec per call

The last item warrants additional comment. One of the dangers of priority scheduling is the so called *insane* process, a process that grabs control of the processor and never relinquishes it. In order to combat this, we choose to make a given number of system calls at evenly spaced points throughout the execution of a message to return control to the process scheduler; this incurs additional overhead, which we can quantify, showing its impact on throughput and delay characteristics.

In order to assess performance, it seems worthwhile to demand as a benchmark that the total processor message delay cannot exceed a mean value of one hundred milliseconds during a normal busy hour and two hundred milliseconds during a peak busy hour, as a first cut at capacity estimation. Some such goal or set of goals is needed to interpret the results. This can then be modified as additional information comes to light.

10.4.2 Mathematical Analysis Our goal is to calculate the long term time averaged flow time distribution of a packet, where the flow time is the time interval from packet arrival to departure. The sequence of processing times is

- $P_{trap,in}$--trap handling at the input

- P_{input}--input handling

- $P_{input-route}$--context switching from input handling to routing

- P_{route}--routing

- $P_{route-output}$--context switching from routing to output handling

- P_{output}--output handling

- $P_{trap,out}$--trap handling at the output

We denote by $\hat{G}_P(y) = E(exp(-yP))$ the moment generating function of the appropriate processing distribution. The moment generating function for the number of packets arriving in a batch is given by $\eta(x)$, while the interarrival times between batches are independent identically distributed exponential random variables with mean $1/c$. Thus, the amount of work brought into the system by a packet, denoted by the random variable S, has moment generating function $\hat{G}_S(y)$ where

$$\hat{G}_S(y) = \eta \left[\hat{G}_{trap,in} \hat{G}_{input} \hat{G}_{input-route} \hat{G}_{route} \hat{G}_{route-output} \hat{G}_{output} \hat{G}_{trap,out} \right]$$

The backlog of work that must be completed by the processor before it can start an arriving packet is denoted by the random variable V, which has the associated moment generating function $\hat{G}_V(y)$ given by

$$\hat{G}_V(y) = \frac{(1-cE(S))y}{y-c(1-\hat{G}_S(y))}$$

In addition, during the execution of this backlog of work, additional work arrives with associated trap handling, and thus we must stretch the packet flow time to account for this. We denote by B the random variable for the busy period of the processor solely concerned with input trap handling work. Its moment generating function is denoted by $\hat{G}_B(y)$ and is given implicitly by

$$\hat{G}_B(y) = \eta\left[\hat{G}_{trap,in}(y+c-c\hat{G}_B(y))\right]$$

In addition, a packet is delayed by the execution of packets that arrive with it in its arrival batch but are executed ahead of it. We assume that the packets are chosen randomly for execution within an arrival batch, and the batch delay random varible, T_{batch}, has associated moment generating function

$$\hat{G}_{T_{batch}}(y) = \frac{1-\eta(\hat{G}_{work}(y)\hat{G}_{overhead}(y))}{\eta'(1)(1-\hat{G}_{work}(y)\hat{G}_{overhead}(y))}$$

$$\hat{G}_{work}(y) = \hat{G}_{input}(y)\hat{G}_{route}(y)\hat{G}_{output}(y)$$

$$\hat{G}_{overhead}(y) = \hat{G}_{input-route}(y)\hat{G}_{route-out}(y)\hat{G}_{trap,out}(y)$$

with the terms *work* and *overhead* having the obvious meanings.

Combining all this, the moment generating of the packet queueing or flow time distribution is given by

$$E(exp(-zF)) = \hat{G}_F(y) = \hat{G}_V(y)\hat{G}_{T_{batch}}(y)\hat{G}_{overhead}(y)\hat{G}_{work}(y)\hat{G}_{trap,out}(y)$$

$$y = z - c + c\hat{G}_B(z)$$

We can numerically approximate the inverse of this generating function via several techniques, or we can simply compute a mean value.

10.5 The M/G/1 Queue with Processor Sharing

Instead of first come, first service for arbitrating contention, we adopt a different policy: if N tasks are present, each will receive (1/N) of the effective processing time of the processor, i.e., the processor will be quickly multiplexed amongst the different tasks. Why do this? One of the problems with service in order of arrival is that if there is a wide disparity in the service time required, i.e., a large squared coefficient of variation, then the waiting time for *all* tasks is severely inflated, even those tasks that require little processing relative to many other tasks. The problem is that tasks with large processing time requirements tend to lock out or hog the processor relative to those with small processing time requirements. If we could multiplex the processor quickly among all the tasks present, the short tasks could finish quickly (figuratively speaking) while the long tasks would finish after a long time, as expected.

The key result here is that the mean time in system, the mean queueing time, for a task that requires X seconds of processing, is

$$E(T_Q | \text{task requires } X \text{ seconds of processing}) = \frac{X}{1 - \rho}$$

Note that this is *independent* of the *shape* of the service time distribution!

The figure below is a plot of the mean queueing time versus the service required for a job for processor sharing and for service in order of arrival, first in first out.

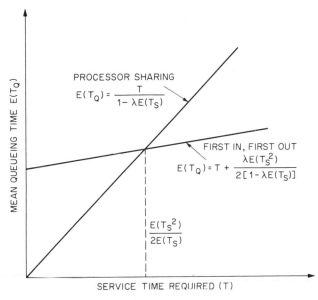

Figure 10.9.Mean Queueing Time vs Service Time Required

If the service required is less than $E(\tilde{T}_S)$, then processor sharing enjoys lower mean queueing time than first come first serve. If the service required is greater than $E(\tilde{T}_S)$, then first come first serve enjoys lower mean queueing time. In words, if the service required is less than the randomized mean service time, these jobs can be executed more quickly by processor sharing than service in order of arrival. On the other hand, if the service required is greater than the randomized mean service time, service in order of arrival executes these jobs more quickly than processor sharing. For example, if all jobs take a *constant* amount of service, than service in order of arrival enjoys the lower mean queueing time.

10.5.1 Additional Reading

[1] L.Kleinrock, **Queueing Systems, Volume II: Computer Applications,** Chapter 4.4, Wiley, NY, 1976.

[2] S.F.Yashkov, *A Derivation of Response Time Distribution for a M/G/1 Processor Sharing Queue,* Problems of Control and Information Theory, **12** (2), 133-148 (1983).

10.6 Comparisons of Scheduling Policies with Fixed Workloads

Our goal in this section is to quantitatively compare different policies for arbitrating contention for a single serially reusable resource.

10.6.1 Performance Measures What will be the measures of performance used?

- The mean queueing time of a task, averaged over a long time interval

- The mean waiting time of a task, averaged over a long time interval

- The variance of the queueing time of a task, averaged over a long time interval

- Percentiles of the queueing time and waiting time distributions, averaged over a long time interval

- The fraction of time that tasks with a given urgency meet their associated deadline

- The fraction of tasks that exceed their associated deadline

- The behavior of the system under transient overloads of many sorts, such as encountering a step function increase in the number of arrivals per unit time over a given time interval that then subsides

10.6.2 M/G/1 with FIFO, LIFO, and RANDOM Service Policies The first comparison is

- service in order of arrival, first come, first served

- last come, first served, with or without preemption

- random service: at the completion of each task, any task of those remaining is equally likely to be serviced

For this set of policies, we see that the mean number in system is identical, and the mean throughput rate is identical, so from Little's Law the mean time in system is identical. Hence, we know the mean time in system for each of these policies:

$$E(T_Q) = \frac{\lambda E(T_S{}^2)}{2(1 - \rho)} + E(T_S)$$

$$E(T_W) = \frac{\lambda E(T_S{}^2)}{2(1 - \rho)}$$

What about second moments? It can be shown that

$$E_{LCFS,nonpreempt}(T_W{}^2) = \frac{1}{1-\rho}\,E_{FCFS}(T_W{}^2)$$

while under the assumption of exponential service times

$$E_{RANDOM}(T_W{}^2) = \frac{1}{1-\frac{1}{2}\rho}\,E_{FCFS}(T_W{}^2)$$

Thus, as we increase the arrival rate or offered load, the second moment is smallest for first come, first served, next smallest for random, and largest for last come, first served.

10.6.3 M/G/1 with Priority Arbitration Policies Now we build on the above studies. We wish to compare some of the facets required in assessing what policy is adequate for attaining desired performance of a single server queueing system. We focus on

- FCFS--first come, first serve, or service in order of arrival

- PS--processor sharing, where if N tasks are present, each receives 1/Nth of the total processor time

- Nonpreemptive static priority--two classes, shorter processing time at higher priority level, breakpoint chosen to minimize total mean queueing time

- Preemptive resume static priority--two classes, shorter processing time at higher priority level, breakpoint chosen to minimize total mean queueing time

- SPT--shortest processing time nonpreemptive static priority

- SRPT--shortest remaining processing time preemptive resume static priority

What about a general comparison of several of these policies for fixed mean service time but different service time distributions and different policies? Here we choose to compare service in order of arrival, processor sharing, nonpreemptive shortest processing time, and preemptive resume shortest remaining processing time against a two class nonpreemptive (NP) or preemptive resume (PR) scheduling policy where the jobs are sorted such that short jobs run at high priority and long jobs at low priority, with the point that determines the priority chosen to *minimize* the total mean queueing time of jobs in the system. Those results are summarized below:

Table 10.1.Total Mean Queueing Time vs Utilization

Utilization	Exponential Service Time, $E(T_S)=1$					
	FCFS	PS	NP	PR	SPT	SRPT
0.3	1.4	1.4	1.4	1.3	1.4	1.2
0.5	2.0	2.0	1.8	1.5	1.7	1.4
0.7	3.3	3.3	2.5	2.1	2.3	1.9
0.9	10.0	10.0	5.3	4.6	4.2	3.6

Table 10.2.Total Mean Queueing Time vs Utilization

Utilization	Uniform (0,2) Service Time, $E(T_S)=1$					
	FCFS	PS	NP	PR	SPT	SRPT
0.3	1.3	1.4	1.3	1.2	1.2	1.2
0.5	1.7	2.0	1.6	1.5	1.5	1.4
0.7	2.6	3.3	2.2	2.0	2.1	2.0
0.9	7.0	10.0	5.0	4.9	4.6	4.4

As can be seen, the gain in going to two classes apparently buys most of the benefit, and the refinement of the *optimal* policies of shortest processing time and shortest remaining processing time buy relatively little compared to the rough cut. In practice, since the distributions are not known precisely in many cases, this may be the best design compromise available, in order to allow short tasks to finish quickly at the expense of delaying long tasks. Note that a simple two class priority arbitration policy does much better than the processor sharing discipline for the numbers chosen here.

10.6.4 Impact due to Fluctuation in Service Time Distribution The table below summarizes the impact of varying the shape of the distribution on system performance:

Table 10.3.Mean Queueing Time

Number of Phases	Erlang K, (K Phases), Utilization$=0.9E(T_S)=1.0$		
	FCFS	PS	SPT
∞	5.5	10.0	5.5
10	5.6	10.0	4.2
5	6.4	10.0	4.1
3	7.0	10.0	4.1
2	7.8	10.0	4.2
1	10.0	10.0	4.2

This shows quantitatively that the gain can be dramatic, especially if there is a mixture of short and long tasks. Note that the more irregular the distribution, the fewer the number of phases in the Erlang distribution, the *better* the processing sharing discipline performs relative to the rest. On the other hand, the more knowledge we have, the more regular the processing time statistics of tasks, the *worse* the processing sharing discipline performs relative to service in order of arrival or other priority arbitrary schemes that take advantage of this knowledge. This is because processor sharing discriminates against long jobs in favoring short jobs, but if there is no significant spread or *mean squared coefficient of variation* greater than unity then these other disciplines can outperform it.

Finally, what about higher order moments? The variance of the queueing time is tabulated below for two different distributions and two different policies:

Table 10.4. Variance of Total Mean Queueing Time

Utilization	Exponential Service		Erlang-2 Service	
	FCFS	*SPT*	*FCFS*	*SPT*
0.3	2.0	1.9	1.0	1.0
0.5	4.0	3.6	2.1	2.2
0.7	11.1	12.3	5.9	8.0
0.9	100.0	222.2	55.1	186.2

Here we see that service in order of arrival does much better than the priority arbitration rule. Put differently, the criterion we are addressing might involve both a mean and a variance, and the choice may not be so clear cut in practice!

10.6.5 Other Scheduling Policies Many other types of scheduling policies are possible. One such class of policies are called *policy driven* schedulers because the user or system manager defines a *desired* policy for executing work and then the system dispatches work in an attempt to meet this goal. The figure below shows one example of a desired set of policies for two tasks, denoted 1 and 2, respectively. The policy is defined by giving a trajectory for each type of task depicting cost versus time in system. In the example shown in the figure, type 1 tasks incur a linear cost versus time in system initially, then the cost is constant versus time in system, then increases linearly versus time, and at some final time becomes infinite; a similar scenario holds for type 2 tasks. The user must define the breakpoints and the costs at each end of the different time in system intervals. Some reflection shows that this is exactly what deadline scheduling does: the execution time windows are the different breakpoints in executing a job.

10.7 Optimum Scheduling Policies

Very little is known about scheduling policies to minimize or maximize various performance measures for an M/G/1 queueing system. Here is a sampling of what is known:

- service in order of arrival minimizes the long term time averaged variance of queueing time over all other policies. In addition this policy minimizes the maximum lateness and maximum tardiness assuming all tasks have the identical execution time window

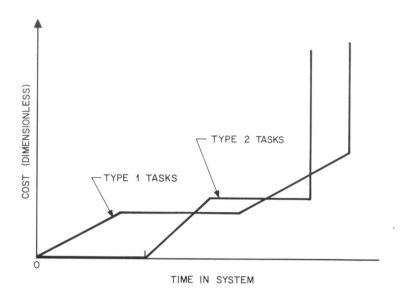

Figure 10.10.Illustrative Cost Functions versus Time
For a Two Class Policy Driven Scheduling Policy

- shortest processing time minimizes the long term time averaged mean queueing time over all other static priority nonpreemptive policies

- shortest remaining processing time minimizes the long term time averaged mean queueing time over all other scheduling policies; this can be seen intuitively using Little's Law, because in order to minimize the total mean queueing time we must have on the average the smallest number of jobs in the system at any one time, independent of arrival and service time statistics.

- deadline scheduling minimizes the maximum tardiness and lateness over all job classes and arrival statistics

- if we use nonpreemptive scheduling, where the job streams have independent Poisson arrival statistics but different independent identically distributed arbitrary service times, then the vector space of admissible mean queueing and waiting times, averaged over a long time interval, is a *convex* set. If we wish to minimize a linear combination of the mean waiting or queueing times we should use a policy at the extreme points of this space; it can be shown under a variety of assumptions that these extreme points are achieved by *static priority* nonpreemptive scheduling. The figure below shows the admissible set of mean waiting time vectors for a system with two different types of tasks with arbitrary processing time statistics, and independent Poisson arrival streams for each job type.

What are some open questions in this realm?

500

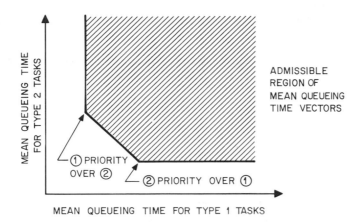

**Figure 10.11.Admissible Region of Mean Waiting Time Vectors
for Nonpreemptive Scheduling of One Processor and Two Task Types**

- Find the set of admissible mean queueing and waiting times for preemptive resume scheduling

- Find the *distribution* of queueing time for each class for deadline scheduling

10.7.1 Additional Reading

[1]   R.W.Conway, W.L.Maxwell, L.W.Miller, **Theory of Scheduling,** Chapters 8-4--8-7, 9, 11, Addison-Wesley, Reading, Massachusetts, 1967.

[2]   H.W.Lynch, J.B.Page, *The OS/VS2 Release 2 System Resources Manager,* IBM Systems Journal, **13** (4), 274-291 (1974).

[3]   W.W.Chiu, W. Chow, *A Performance Model of MVS,* IBM Systems Journal, **13** (4), 444-462 (1974).

[4]   U.Herzog, *Optimal Scheduling Strategies for Real Time Computers,* IBM Journal of Research and Development, **19** (5), 494-504 (1975).

[5]   H.M.Goldberg, *Analysis of the Earliest Due Date Scheduling Rule in Queueing Systems,* Mathematics of Operations Research, **2** (2), 145-154 (1977).

[6]   T.Beretvas, *Performance Tuning in OS/VS2 MVS,* IBM Systems Journal, **17** (3), 290-313 (1978).

[7]   D.P.Heyman, K.T.Marshall, *Bounds on the Optimal Operating Policy for a Class of Single Server Queues,* Operations Research **16** (6), 1138-1146 (1968).

[8]   D.P.Heyman, *Optimal Operating Policies for M/G/l Queuing Systems,* Operations Research, **16** (2), 362-382 (1968).

[9]   M.Ruschitzka, *An Analytical Treatment of Policy Function Schedulers,* Operations Research, **26** (5), 845-863 (1978).

[10]   M.Ruschitzka, *The Performance of Job Classes with Distinct Policy Functions,* Journal of the ACM, **29** (2), 514-526 (1982).

10.8 Controlling Overload

The main reason for focusing on a single resource is that it is often a bottleneck in limiting system traffic handling capabilities. What happens if the resource becomes overloaded? Here probably the most important thing is to *think* how to handle the problem and what consequences of overload might be, and then do *something* rather than nothing to safeguard against this possibility.

The maximum mean throughput rate, denoted $\lambda_{capacity}$, is defined to be the maximum job completion rate for which all delay requirements can be met. What is an overload? An overload can be of two types

- An external overload is due to a surge of work beyond the design limits of the system; this we have no control over and will occur when the arrival rate exceeds $\lambda_{capacity}$

- An internal overload is due to allowing so much work into a system that delay criteria are violated; this we can control

There are two basic mechanisms for controlling overload:

- Rejecting work when the load becomes too great

- Smoothing the arriving work stream to make it more regular and less bursty

In normal operation, virtually no work would be rejected and the arrivals would enter and leave the system with no delay other than the execution delay. In overload operation, the converse would be true.

We choose to tackle this in two stages:

- First we size up the mean throughput rate, because if a fraction L of arrivals are rejected or lost out of a total mean arrival rate of λ jobs per unit time, then the mean throughput rate is

$$mean\ throughput\ rate = \lambda(1-L)$$

Under normal operation $L << 1$ while under overload we expect the mean throughput rate to saturate at some limit:

$$\lim_{\lambda \to \infty} mean\ throughput\ rate = constant$$

- Second, with the mean throughput rate properly sized, we must investigate delay characteristics.

We will examine two cases of overload control, one due to static priority scheduling, the other due to designing a control valve.

10.8.1 Static Priority Scheduling Overload Control A single resource has N types of jobs, each with its own static priority. At any given instant of time, the job with the highest priority is being executed. If an overload occurs, the single resource will spend more time executing high priority jobs and less time executing low priority jobs, and the low priority jobs may begin to miss delay goals. On the other hand, these jobs were chosen to be low priority for a reason: they really are not as urgent as higher priority jobs. One often hears that this type of scheduling is not *fair,* and a variety of different policies are proposed for overcoming the problem of not giving all job classes *some* service *all* the time (which requires a very great conceptual leap to determine what delays are acceptable and not acceptable, but that is not our problem). Here is one such argument: we propose to poll all job classes exhaustively, first taking one job class and emptying the system of all that work, then the next, and so on in a logical ring manner. This will avoid the *lock out* of low priority work by high priority work since the job class with highest priority changes with time. What happens now? Let's look at an example from our earlier discussion: two class of jobs, one with a mean execution time of one second and one with a mean execution time of ten seconds. If we have a surge of work, we will spend a larger fraction of time doing jobs with ten second average execution time, and a smaller fraction of time doing jobs with one second average execution time. In fact, the delay criterion for the jobs with one second execution time may very well be violated, in our attempt to be *fair* (whatever that means), rather than simply giving the shorter jobs higher priority *all* the time over the longer jobs. **Moral:** Be careful in jumping to conclusions!

10.8.2 Overload Control Valve Design Suppose we designed our system with a first stage queue that *every* task must enter followed by a second set of queues that tasks will migrate amongst once they pass through the first stage. The first stage would be a valve, and would control the amount of work that would get into the system in two ways:

- The first stage queue has a *finite* capacity of Q jobs; when an arrival occurs and Q jobs are present in the input queue, *one* job gets rejected or lost and presumably will retry later

- When the single server visits the first stage queue, a maximum number of jobs, say S tasks, will be removed per visit

Under *normal* operation, only rarely would jobs be rejected, and all jobs would be removed on each server visit. Under *overload* operation, the input queue would always be full with jobs, and the maximum allowable number would be removed per server visit.

The size of the first stage queue and the maximum number of jobs removed per visit would be chosen in order that the largest number of jobs could be handled by the *total* system, i.e., the mean throughput was as large as possible while still meeting delay criteria. In this sense, the first stage is a control valve, preventing the *internal* overload from occurring at other stages when an *external* overload occurs.

First we calculate the mean throughput rate. The server is either present at the input valve or not present, and we denote these two time intervals be $T_{present}$ and T_{absent}. The server alternates back and forth, either present or absent, and hence the mean cycle rate is simply the reciprocal of the total mean cycle time. The fraction of time the server is present at the input queue is simply the ratio of the time it is present over the total cycle time:

$$fraction\ of\ time\ server\ present\ at\ input\ queue = \frac{E(T_{present})}{E(T_{present}) + E(T_{absent})}$$

The mean throughput rate is simply the fraction of time the server is present, multiplied by the rate at which the server can execute input jobs:

$$mean\ rate\ server\ can\ execute\ jobs\ at\ input\ queue = \frac{1}{E(T_{input,S})}$$

$$mean\ throughput\ rate = \frac{E(T_{present})}{E(T_{present}) + E(T_{absent})} \frac{1}{E(T_{input,S})}$$

Under overload, the input queue will always have more than S jobs, and hence the mean time spent at the input queue will be

$$E(T_{present}) \approx SE(T_{input,S}) \quad overload$$

On the other hand, the *total* cycle will in any reasonable design be dominated by the time the server is doing useful work elsewhere, and hence

$$E(T_{absent}) \gg E(T_{present})$$

This suggests the following approximation for the mean throughput rate under overload (for the input queue only, but once jobs clear the input queue they sail through the rest of the system):

$$mean\ throughput\ rate \approx \frac{SE(T_{input,S})}{E(T_{absent})} \frac{1}{E(T_{input,S})} = \frac{S}{E(T_{absent})}$$

What does this say in words?

- As we make S larger, as we remove more jobs, the mean throughput rate increases

- If we get a faster server or processor, the time spent elsewhere, absent, will drop, and hence the mean throughput rate increases

- If we fix the mean throughput rate, then we have chosen to fix the *ratio* of the maximum number removed from the input queue and the mean time the server is absent from the input queue

Next, how do we size up the delay statistics for this system? Under light loading, the mean time spent by a job in the input queue will simply be

$$E(T_Q) \approx \frac{E(T^2_{absent})}{2E(T_{absent})} = \frac{1}{2}E(T_{absent})[1+C^2(T_{absent})] \quad light \ load$$

We want to have the absent times have a small squared coefficient of variation, little variability, in order for this to be close to one half a mean intervisit time.

Under overload, the input buffer will always be full when the server visits it. Let's look at two policies for running the input buffer:

- Latest arrival cleared--If the input buffer is full when a job arrives, the latest arrival is rejected or cleared

- Earliest arrival cleared--If the input buffer is full when a job arrives, the earliest arrival is rejected or cleared

Why look at these two extremes? In the first approach, latest arrival cleared means that under load Q jobs are present in the input queue and S are removed per visit, so

$$E(T_Q) \approx \frac{Q}{S} SE(T_{input,S}) = QE(T_{input,S}) \quad heavy \ load, \ latest \ arrival \ cleared$$

On the other hand, for earliest arrival cleared, what happens? All jobs always enter the input queue, but only *some* of them get serviced, and some get rejected. The amount of jobs that are rejected for *either* policy is the same: whenever the input queue is full and there is a new arrival, *one* job (either the arrival or the one in the input queue for the longest time) gets rejected. Which job do we wish to reject: the one that is closest to missing its delay goals, which is the job that has been in the system the longest time. Jobs that get serviced with the earliest arrival cleared policy are jobs that spend little time in the input queue, which is exactly what we want.

What is the mean queueing time for jobs in the first stage with the earliest arrival cleared policy? Here we use Little's Law again. We denote by T_{reject} the time a rejected job spends in the input queue under earliest arrival cleared. Since a fraction L of the arrivals are lost, with the total arrival rate denoted by λ, we see that the mean number of jobs in the input queue for latest arrival cleared under heavy load is given by

$$E(N_{input}) = (1-L)\lambda E(T_Q) \approx (1-L)\lambda QE(T_{input,S}) \quad \textit{latest arrival cleared}$$

On the other hand, the mean number of jobs in the input queue for earliest arrival cleared is the sum of the mean number of jobs that will be rejected and jobs that will be serviced:

$$E(N_{input}) \quad (1-L)\lambda E(T_Q) + L\lambda E(T_{reject}) \quad \textit{earliest arrival cleared}$$

For either policy, the mean number of jobs must be the same, and hence we see

$$E(T_Q) = QE(T_{input,S}) - \frac{L}{1-L}E(T_{reject}) \quad \textit{earliest arrival cleared, heavy load}$$

This shows that the mean delay will *always* be smaller for earliest arrival cleared versus latest arrival cleared! In fact, under earliest arrival cleared, during a heavy overload, jobs that get serviced would spend virtually *zero* time in the input buffer (why?).

How would we implement earliest arrival cleared? By using a circular buffer, with a pointer to the job at the head of the queue; as we overload, the point will move around the buffer and begin to overwrite or clear earlier arrivals, as desired.

10.8.3 Additional Reading

[1]   E.Arthurs, B.W.Stuck, *Controlling Overload in a Digital System,* SIAM J.Algebraic and Discrete Methods, **1** (2), 232-250 (1980).

10.9 Multiplexing Voice and Data over a Single Digital Link

In this section we analyze the performance of a digital link multiplexer handling synchronous (e.g., voice) and asynchronous (e.g., data) streams.

Two types of sources use the link for communications: *synchronous* sources that generate messages at regularly spaced time intervals, and *asynchronous* sources that do so at irregular points in time. Figure 10.12 is a block diagram of a model of a link level multiplexer we wish to analyze. The fundamental logical periodic time unit is called a *frame*. A frame is subdivided into *slots* and each slot is available for transmission of a *chunk* of bits. The design question is to decide which slots will be assigned to synchronous and which to asynchronous message streams. Figure 10.13 shows a representative frame. Three cases arise.

10.9.1 Dedicating Time Slots to Each Session The first policy is dedicating time slots during a frame to each session so that each message stream has its own digital transmission system. Each transmission system can be engineered separately with no interaction between different types of message streams. This allows sharing and hence a potential economy of scale of hardware, software,

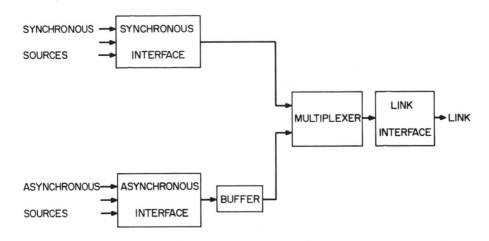

Figure 10.12. Link Level Multiplexer

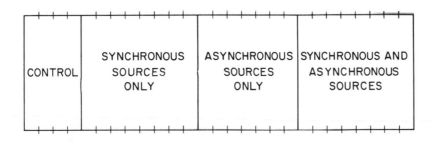

Figure 10.13. An Illustrative Frame

and maintenance costs. Synchronous sources can be multiplexed by a generalization of circuit switching: one or more slots per frame can be dedicated to a communication session, while conventional circuit switching has only one slot per frame per session. For example, with a frame rate of 1200 frames per second, four slots per frame, and two bits per slot, one 2400 bit per second terminal would require one slot per frame, while one 4800 bit per second terminal would require two slots per frame. In order to transmit data from asynchronous sources via synchronous transmission facilities, one common practice is to always transmit an idle character if no data character is present, so that the asynchronous stream has the transmission characteristics of a synchronous bit stream.

10.9.2 Sharing Time Slots Among All Sessions   Allowing all sessions equal access to any time slot within a frame is a different policy. This allows sharing and hence a potential economy of scale for hardware, software, and maintenance costs, as well as the transmission costs. A priority arbitration rule is employed to determine which message stream gains access to the link. The priority might be chosen according to the urgency of the message stream.

10.9.3 Dedicating Time Slots to Some Sessions and Sharing the Remainder The remaining case, a hybrid of the previous two, involves dedicating some transmission capacity to each session, with a common shared transmission capacity pool that is used by all sources in the event that the dedicated capacity is completely exhausted.

10.9.4 Overview   Our purpose is to study the most difficult case for analysis: totally shared transmission capacity for all communication sessions. Because the message streams can have radically different characteristics, which will have a profound impact on our analysis, we digress to discuss each traffic in more detail.

10.9.5 Synchronous Message Streams   First, we focus on a very common type of synchronous message stream, a voice telephone call. In practice, analog voice signals are sampled, encoded into a digital bit stream, and then transmitted over a link. The voice samples are delivered at regularly spaced time intervals for each conversation, with at least one and at most two sampling intervals (due to clock jitter and skew) between successive samples. All the samples must be buffered and transmitted before the next arrivals. This suggests inserting a fixed delay, hopefully negligible compared to voice time scales, which is the time required to load and unload a voice sample during a conversation. Typically voice conversations last for one hundred to three hundred seconds, while the initiation and completion lasts for one to five seconds; this suggests attempting to dedicate transmission capacity for the duration of a conversation, and if no capacity is available at the instant a telephone call is attempted, new arrivals or attempts should be blocked or rejected, because it is highly unlikely that transmission capacity would become available within the next few seconds. Voice bit stream utilization per conversation is typically on the order of thirty to fifty per cent, a further argument for demanding that transmission capacity be dedicated to each conversation for the duration of a call, because it is quite likely that the transmission capacity will in fact be needed. These conditions are felt to be sufficient for high quality speech reproduction, but may be unduly conservative when compared with other alternatives.

10.9.6 Asynchronous Message Streams Second, we focus on data traffic generated by interactive terminals and computer systems. Messages within each conversation or session arrive at very irregularly spaced time intervals. In applications representative of online computer systems for support of telephone company operations activities, the authors have found traffic is typically one to two bytes per second per session for a stream generated by a terminal interacting with a computer, with the interarrival times between samples being much less regular than voice. Furthermore, the utilization of a typical dedicated link for one terminal interacting with a computer is often well under one per cent. Since the message arrival statistics are highly irregular, and the link utilization is quite low, this suggests pooling or buffering messages from a number of sources (with the pooling strategy based on the statistics of the message streams and their urgencies) for subsequent transmission over a link. This allows both the transmitter and the link to be simultaneously busy, and hence offers a higher total mean throughput rate, at the expense of additional storage. Communication session initiation and completion cleanup times can be comparable to data transmission message times, unlike for the synchronous message stream. If a controller is capable of setting up and taking down a circuit in a time much shorter than the session, this type of switch might be chosen: less time would be spent in overhead versus in useful communications. If this is not the case, then a packet switch might be the choice. In addition, a variety of control bits are required to govern flow control, addressing, error handling, and so forth, that must be transmitted along with the actual data bits, further reducing link utilization.

10.9.7 Outline In the next section we present a *naive* analysis of the benefits of *total* sharing of transmission capacity that leads to completely *erroneous* insight into the gain of such a policy. The reason for the error is that a mean value analysis of first order statistics for the arrival rates and holding times of voice and data conversations ignores secondary statistics such as *fluctuations* about the mean values and more importantly *correlations* from one frame to the next, which *cannot* be ignored here. The following section gives a more rigorous analysis that quantifies these statements. Great care is required in engineering a transmission system that pools messages from sources with radically different characteristics. The closing section summarizes our findings and presents a number of options or alternatives for effective use of a single link by both synchronous (e.g., voice) and asynchronous (e.g., data) message streams.

10.9.8 Problem Statement Information is transmitted over a digital link in repetitive time intervals called frames. Frame $n=1,2,...$ consists of S_n slots. Each slot contains a fixed number of bits. Messages arrive from synchronous sources and are either accepted or rejected, and presumably will retry later. The synchronous message streams that have been accepted for transmission demand V_n time slots in frame $n=1,2,....$ From this point on, in the interest of brevity, we will refer to the synchronous message stream as *voice*. Each remaining slot within a frame can be used to transmit messages from asynchronous sources. Asynchronous messages arrive during frame $n=1,2,...$ and require D_n time slots of transmission capacity. From this point on, in the interest of brevity, we will refer to the asynchronous message stream as *data*. S_n-V_n is the amount of transmission capacity (measured in time slots) available during frame $n=1,2,...$ for transmission of asynchronous traffic. The random variable R_n denotes the amount of asynchronous chunks waiting to be transmitted at the start of frame n. From this discussion, R_n is governed by the following recursion:

$$R_{n+1} = max\,(0,R_n+D_n+V_n - S_n) \quad n=0,1,2,...$$

In the interest of brevity we fix $S_n=S$. If we allowed the number of available slots to vary from frame to frame, this would correspond to the case of partially shared transmission capacity for synchronous and asynchronous message streams. Our goal is to study the statistics of R_n as a function of the statistics of D_n and V_n for a given choice of S.

Granted that $D_n+V_n-S_n$ obeys Markovian statistics, our analysis shows that the long term time averaged distribution of $R_n,n\rightarrow\infty$, is a weighted sum of geometric distributions. The weights and modes of the different geometric distributions are dependent upon the particular modeling assumptions for the arrival and holding time statistics for the synchronous and asynchronous message streams as well as the policy for allocating time slots within a frame. One of the modes of the long term time averaged distribution for $R_n,n\rightarrow\infty$ will decay more slowly than all the other modes, and will dominate the asynchronous traffic delay and buffering requirements under load. The geometric decay parameter for the most slowly decaying mode of the distribution of $R_n,n\rightarrow\infty$ will be called the *critical exponent* because it will be critical in determining the fraction of time the buffer contains greater than a given amount of data chunks.

10.9.9 Summary of Results   From an engineering point of view, knowing that the long term time averaged distribution for data decays geometrically suggests that the most slowly decaying mode of all the distributions should be measured. In a well engineered system, this should be close to zero, i.e., there should be relatively little data buffering. If this mode is close to one, then there is a *potential* for buffering significant amounts of data. If voice and data are multiplexed together over a common link, the analysis presented here suggests that the voice can demand all the transmission capacity for a period of time that is brief relative to the duration of a voice telephone call, yet is much longer than typical data transmission times. Effectively voice locks out data for time intervals unacceptable to data. This suggests that prudence is required in assessing the benefits of dedicating transmission capacity versus totally sharing transmission capacity for each type of message stream. Engineering practice based on mean values, average loadings and the like appear to give excellent insight into traffic handling characteristics for *dedicated* transmission systems handling only *one* type of service. When transmission capacity is *shared* average loading and mean value analysis can be misleading, and much greater caution and sophistication is required. Here timing between stations is quite controlled and regular; other schemes have been proposed that involve uncontrolled and irregular timing, and hence should do *worse* than the approach described here for handling data.

10.9.10 A Naive First Cut Analysis Consider the following example: $S=24$ time slots are transmitted eight thousand times per second, with each time slot containing eight bits. Each voice call requires one slot per frame, or 64 KBPS. Suppose that the link is engineered to handle sufficient voice telephone calls such that no more than one per cent of the voice traffic is blocked or rejected. Using standard Erlang blocking analysis techniques, we find the link will handle on the average 15.3 voice telephone calls, i.e.,

$$PROB[all \ S=24 \ slots \ filled \ with \ voice] = B(S,A) < 0.01 \rightarrow S=24, A=15.3$$

where $B(S,A)$ is the Erlang blocking function for S servers and an offered load of A erlangs. This implies we have $S-A=24-15.3$ or 8.7 time slots per frame available for data, or 557 KBPS. If we only use 64 KBPS for data, for example, always transmit one byte of data every frame, then the total (both voice and data) link utilization will be (16.3/24) or 67.9%; the data delay may be roughly two frames, or 250 μsec, and hence the mean data buffering may be 64 KBPS multiplied by 250 μsec or 16 bits.

The table below summarizes the mean number of time slots filled with voice out of twenty four ($S=24$) for a given level of blocking B, the transmission capacity that is idle for handling surges of voice and data:

Table 10.5.Time Slots/Frame, 8000 Frames/Sec Transmission Rate

Fraction of Attempts Blocked	Mean Number of Voice Filled Slots	Mean Number of Idle Slots	Excess Transmission Capacity for Data
0.001	12.1 Slots	11.9 Slots	762 KBPS
0.002	13.0 Slots	11.0 Slots	704 KBPS
0.005	14.3 Slots	9.7 Slots	621 KBPS
0.010	15.3 Slots	9.3 Slots	557 KBPS
0.020	16.7 Slots	7.3 Slots	467 KBPS
0.050	19.0 Slots	5.0 Slots	320 KBPS
0.100	20.7 Slots	3.3 Slots	211 KBPS

This type of analysis is based on mean values. Unfortunately, this chain of reasoning ignores *both* the *fluctuations* of the voice and data about their mean values, and the *correlation* present from one frame to the next for voice. The combination of these phenomena makes the mean value analysis sketched here *much* too optimistic: we will need *much* greater buffering for data than expected, data delays will be *much* greater than expected, with *much* less margin for overload surges.

The reason for this is clear on physical grounds: voice telephone calls last for two to three minutes, or one hundred to two hundred seconds. Data messages can last for one to ten milliseconds. The time scale for voice is hundreds of seconds, which is four to five orders of magnitude greater than that for data. A relatively short surge of voice traffic might last for one to ten seconds, but this short surge may demand *all* the available transmission capacity, i.e., none is available for data. As far as data is concerned, the link has just *failed:* no messages can be transmitted. With the link engineered for a voice service grade of one per cent blocking, this will occur one per cent of the time during an hour, or a total of thirty six seconds, scattered throughout the hour: five seconds here, two seconds there, ten seconds there. Data will be arriving throughout the time when all the transmission capacity is dedicated to voice, potentially leading to thousands of data packets arriving during such an interval. Once this occurs, the validity of the model is now in question: higher level data communications protocols, which are ignored here, come into play, flow control procedures are invoked, timeouts occur, retries and reinitialization of link control procedures take place, compounding the data delay even more. The figure below is an illustrative simulation of this phenomenon: an illustrative sample path of the stochastic processes we wish to study, that is typical of that encountered in simulation studies.

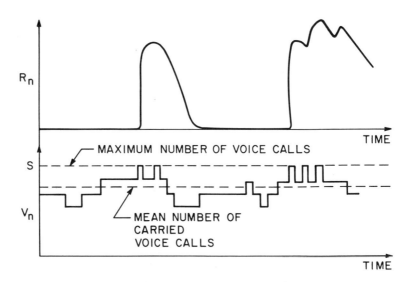

Figure 10.14.Illustrative Simulation Sample Path

The voice traffic rarely surges to seize all the available transmission capacity. Once the voice blocks all data transmission, enormous data queues arise, that persist long after the voice blocking has ended. Put differently, most of the time the data is *not* delayed at all, but if the data is delayed, it is delayed a *long* time.

10.9.11 A More Sophisticated Analysis In order to get more insight into the behavior of the example in the previous section, we study in greater detail the statistical behavior of the voice loss system. The sequence of nonblocked voice telephone calls holding times are assumed to be independent identically distributed exponential random variables with mean $1/\mu$. The modeling assumptions here are that the duration of a voice call is much longer than a frame, and that we require a geometrically distributed number of frames to be dedicated to each telephone call. The figure below shows states and transition rates for the voice telephone calls.

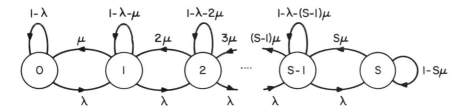

Figure 10.15. Voice Telephone Call States/Transition Rates

We denote by $\lambda \equiv \lambda_{offered}$ the mean arrival rate of the *offered* voice traffic load, while $\lambda_{carried}$ is the mean throughput rate of the *carried* voice traffic load, given by

$$\lambda_{carried} = \lambda_{offered}[1 - B(S, A = \lambda_{offered}/\mu)]$$

A level is fixed, denoted by L, for the maximum number of simultaneous active voice telephone conversations. When the number of calls in progress exceeds L, newly arriving voice calls will be rejected or blocked. Hence, $0 < L \leqslant S$. $\pi(K), K = 0,...,S$ denotes the fraction of time there are K simultaneously active voice calls in progress. The rate of entering the state of having L calls in progress from the state of having $L-1$ calls in progress is denoted by $r_{L-1,L}$. This implies using standard techniques that

$$r_{L-1,L} = \lambda_{offered}\,\pi(L-1)$$

In words, the fraction of time there are $L-1$ simultaneous voice telephone calls multiplied by the total arrival rate of voice calls yields the rate of entering state L from state $L-1$.

$T_{L,L-1}$ denotes the mean time to move from state L to state $L-1$, i.e., to move out of the blocking state of having L simultaneously active voice telephone calls. This implies

$$r_{L-1,L} \, T_{L,L-1} = \sum_{K=L}^{S} \pi(K)$$

In other words, to find the mean time to move from the state of L to $L-1$ active telephone calls, the total fraction of time the Markov process modeling voice calls is in state $K=L,...,S$ must be divided by the rate of entering state L from $L-1$:

$$T_{L-1,L} = \frac{\displaystyle\sum_{K=L}^{S} \pi(K)}{\lambda_{offered}\,\pi(L-1)}$$

Choosing $L=S$ simplifies all of this:

$$r_{S-1,S} = \lambda_{offered}\,\pi(S-1) = \mu\, S\, B[S,\lambda_{offered}/\mu]$$

For example, with $S=24$ time slots per frame, and with $1/\mu=100$ *seconds* for a voice call holding time of one hundred seconds, and the voice call blocking engineering to be no more than one per cent of the time $(B(S,A)=0.01)$ the mean time to enter the state of having all $S=24$ time slots filled from the state of having of having $S-1=23$ time slots filled with voice, is given by

$$\frac{1}{r_{S,S-1}} = \frac{1}{\mu S B\,(S,\lambda_{offered}/\mu)} \approx 416\frac{2}{3} \; seconds \quad S=24 \; slots/frame$$

In words, on the average every four hundred and sixteen and two thirds seconds the link will be completely filled with voice calls in progress. How long will this last on the average? For a mean time denoted by $T_{S,S-1}$, where

$$T_{S,S-1} = \frac{1}{\mu S} \approx 4.16667 \; seconds \quad S=24$$

As far as the data is concerned, on the average, every four hundred and sixteen and two thirds seconds the voice will demand all the transmission capacity for a mean time interval of four and one sixth seconds. If data arrives at an average rate of 64 KBPS, then at least 256K bits of data on the average must be buffered when the link is busy handling nothing but voice, or 32K bytes. Furthermore, the transmission capacity for data once the system leaves the voice blocking state is now only 64 KBPS, which only keeps up with arriving data but does *not* empty the buffer, and the very strong correlation suggests that the link might block within the next second or two with nothing but voice, as before.

The table below is a summary of similar calculations for the same parameters described in the earlier section:

Table 10.6. Time Slots/Frame, 8000 Frames/Sec Transmission Rate

Fraction of Attempts Blocked	Mean Excess Transmission Capacity Available for Data	Mean Time to Enter Voice Blocking State
0.001	762 KBPS	4166.67 sec=69.44 min
0.002	704 KBPS	2083.33 sec=34.72 min
0.005	621 KBPS	833.33 sec=13.89 min
0.010	557 KBPS	416.67 sec=6.94 min
0.020	467 KBPS	208.33 sec=3.47 min
0.050	320 KBPS	83.33 sec=1.39 min
0.100	211 KBPS	41.67 sec=0.69 min

The sojourn time in the all blocking state is 100/24 seconds or 4.16 seconds. Would a customer choose a system with voice blocking only one per cent of the time, while 557 KBPS of idle transmission capacity is available, knowing that on the average every 6.94 minutes the idle transmission capacity would drop to *zero* for an average of 4.16 seconds? Many knowledgeable engineers would argue that it is difficult enough to get such systems to work at all, without having to handle *interactions* between different services like voice and data such as this is.

10.9.12 A Lower Bound on Critical Exponent Here is a *lower* bound on the critical exponent ω that illustrates the impact that correlation can have on performance. This is much much easier to calculate than carrying out an exact analysis, and the techniques are felt to be of general interest and hence should be popularized. To simplify notation, we define a new random variable, Y_n, which is the difference between the voice and data arriving in frame n and the total available transmission capacity, in slots: $Y_n = D_n + V_n - S$. We model correlation by assuming that Y_n is modulated by a Markov chain. This means that there is an underlying Markov chain with state σ_n for frame n taking values in a discrete state space denoted by Ω, and with transition probability generator for the voice and data given by $H_{lk}(i,j)$:

$$H_{lk}(i,j) = PROB[D_n=i, S-V_n=j, \sigma_{n+1}=k \mid \sigma_n=l]$$

As one example, we assume the voice traffic is generated by a birth and death process, with λ denoting the probability of an arrival and $i\mu$ denoting the probability of a departure given there are i active voice calls. The state of the underlying Markov chain associated with the start of frame n is denoted by σ_n. Given these assumptions, we see that

$$R_{n+1} = max(0, R_n + Y_n) \quad n=0,1,2,...$$

From this recursion, we can rewrite the fraction of time that $R_n, n \rightarrow \infty$ exceeds a finite threshold, say K:

$$\lim_{n \to \infty} PROB[R_n > K] = \sum_{J=0}^{S} \pi(J) PROB[\sup_n [Y_1 + Y_2 + ... + Y_n] > K | \sigma_0 = i]$$

If we focus only on the state where the synchronous traffic has seized all available time slots, i.e., and drop the other $(S-1)$ states from consideration, then we obtain a *lower* bound on our expression of interest:

$$\lim_{n \to \infty} PROB[R_n > K] > \pi(S) PROB[Y_1 + Y_2 + ... + Y_m > K | \sigma_0 = S]$$

Since the process is Markovian, the holding time distribution in this state is *geometric*, with the number of time slots in this state, say M, having a moment generating function given by

$$E[X^M] = \frac{X(1 - S\mu)}{1 - SX\mu}$$

The lower bound on the fraction of time $R_n, n \to \infty$ exceeds K can be written as

$$\lim_{n \to \infty} PROB[R_n > K] = \pi(S) PROB[D_1 + ... + D_M > K | \sigma_0 = S]$$

For example, with one data chunk arriving every frame, $D_n = 1(a.s.)$,

$$\lim_{n \to \infty} PROB[R_n > K] > \pi(S)(1 - S\mu)^K$$

where

$$\pi(S) = B(S, \lambda/\mu) = \frac{(\lambda/\mu)^S / S!}{\sum_{k=0}^{S} (\lambda/\mu)^k / k!}$$

and hence

$$\omega > 1 - S\mu$$

which is independent of the arrival rate. For example, choosing $S = 24$ and one hundred second voice holding time, so $\mu = 1/(100 \ seconds)(8000 \ frames/sec)$, we find

$$\omega > 1 - \frac{24}{100 \times 8000} = 1 - \frac{1}{40000} = 0.999975$$

On the other hand, if D_n obeys a geometric distribution, so as $n \to \infty, D_n \to D$,

$$E\left[x^D\right] = \frac{(1-\alpha)x}{1-\alpha x}$$

then the same chain of arguments can be used to show

$$\omega > 1 - (1 - S\mu)(1 - \alpha) > 1 - (1 - S\mu)$$

which is even closer to unity than ignoring the bursty nature of the data arrivals, i.e., the shape of the data arrival distribution statistics matter!

As a second example of how to use this model, what if we wish to multiplex data during speech silence intervals, e.g., in between words and pauses in conversation? Again, we can refine the above argument as follows: let (i,j) denote i active calls and j calls actively talking at a given time epoch, where $i=0,...,S; j \leqslant i$. We model this via a Markov chain as follows:

$$PROB[i+1,j+1|i,j] = \lambda \qquad 0 \leqslant i < S$$

$$PROB[i,j+1|i,j] = \beta(i-j) \qquad 0 < i \leqslant S, j < i$$

$$PROB[i,j|i+1,j+1] = \mu(j+1) \qquad 0 \leqslant i < S$$

$$PROB[i,j|i,j+1] = \gamma(j+1) \qquad 0 \leqslant i \leqslant S$$

Then paralleling the previous arguments we see that the fraction of time the long term time averaged amount of data buffered exceeds a threshold K is lower bounded by

$$\lim_{n \to \infty} PROB[R_n > K] = \pi(S,S) PROB[D_1 + ... + D_m > K]$$

where the random variable m is drawn from a geometric distribution,

$$PROB[m=J] = \gamma S (1-\gamma S)^{J-1} \qquad J > 0$$

and hence

$$\omega > 1 - S\gamma$$

To summarize both these exercises, granted these assumptions, we have shown

$$\omega > 1 - \frac{Number\ of\ slots/frame}{Mean\ holding\ time\,(in\ slots)/call}$$

which is independent of the arrival rate. As the arrival rate approaches zero, it is not the exponent that approaches zero but rather the constant multiplying the exponential term that approaches zero.

10.9.13 Numerical Comparison of Bounds and Exact Analysis How close is the bound to that of an exact analysis? To answer this, we choose the following parameters: a frame consists of two time slots, each capable of holding eight bits. The frame repetition rate is eight thousand times per second, so each frame is one hundred and twenty five microseconds. Voice calls require one time slot per call for the duration of the call, and are generated according to simple Poisson statistics. Voice calls last for a geometrically distributed number of frames. Eight bits of data *always* arrives every frame. If all available transmission capacity is filled with voice calls, new voice calls are blocked or rejected. If all available transmission capacity is filled with voice calls, data is buffered or delayed until capacity becomes available.

The figure below shows the bound on the critical exponent as well as the *exact* critical exponent for different levels of blocking, as a function of mean voice holding time. When the voice holding time exceeds ten milliseconds, the agreement between the bound and the exact analysis is excellent.

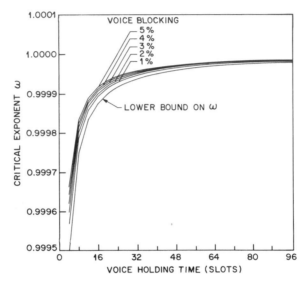

Figure 10.16.Exact Critical Exponent and Bound vs Mean Voice Holding Time

Since in reality voice telephone calls last for hundreds of seconds, for all practical purposes there is no numerical difference between the bound and the exact analysis.

What about the constant? Maybe this is close to zero, while the exponent is close to one, with the net result being small data delay. The figure below shows the fraction of time data is delayed at all versus the fraction of time voice is blocked (which will occur when all time slots are filled with voice, $V=S$). To complement this, we plot the mean data delay versus the fraction of time voice is blocked. For these numbers, with the mean voice holding time being ten to fifty slots per frame, the fraction of time that data is delayed at all can be made small. On the other hand, the mean data delay can be in excess of one millisecond. As the voice holding time increases, the mean data delay will increase, even for relatively low levels of voice blocking. This confirms our intuition: most of the time the data is transmitted immediately, but when it is delayed, it is delayed for a very long time (tens and hundreds of milliseconds).

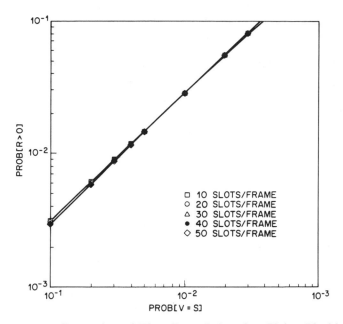

Figure 10.17.Fraction of Time Data Delayed vs Voice Blocking

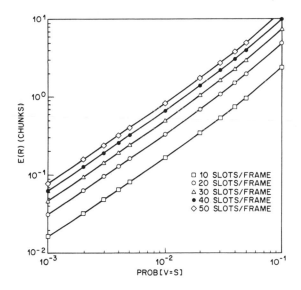

Figure 10.18.Mean Data Delay vs Voice Blocking

10.9.14 Summary and Closing Comments Our goal was to study properties of the statistics of R_n, the amount of data waiting to be transmitted at the start of frame n, which was governed by the recursion

$$R_{n+1} = max[0, R_n + D_n + V_n - S]$$

Two phenomena are present which can impact traffic handling characteristics:

- fluctuations in D_n, V_n or, in other words, the *shape* of the distribution

- correlation from frame to frame of D_n, V_n or, in other words, the relative *time scale* of the different types of traffic

Under certain specific assumptions, it can be shown that

$$\lim_{n \to \infty} PROB[R_n > k] \approx CONSTANT \times \omega^k$$

The constant and ω can be evaluated. The transient behavior of the system is related to time scales of the order of $1/\omega$ which is also of great interest.

How can we combat the phenomena here? There are a variety of methods. One approach is to dedicate a given amount of transmission capacity to voice and a given amount to data, and engineer these two systems separately. The voice transmission capacity could be chosen to meet a lost calls cleared grade of service, while the data transmission capacity could be chosen to meet a delayed message grade of service. The problem in the example here was the transmission capacity was shared or pooled, and the voice swamped the data. A second approach is as follows: In many applications, the amount of bits transmitted due to voice is much much greater than that due to data: rather than demand the relatively small amount of data be delayed by the relatively large amount of voice, why not reverse the priorities? Simply give the data higher priority over the voice, and if there is a surge in voice, drop the voice bits and not the data bits. This is possible because *people* are generating the voice, and will detect problems (clicks, unusual sounds, spurious signals, and so on) and will retry ("What did you say?" or "Could you repeat that, we seem to have a bad connection!")

Our point here is totally sharing transmission capacity for voice and data with *fixed* bandwidth appears to offer no benefit over dedicating bandwidth to each service. Adding enough bandwidth to handle each separately appears to offer significant benefits.

10.9.15 Additional Reading

[1] P.T.Brady, *A Statistical Analysis of On-Off Patterns in 16 Conversations,* Bell System Technical Journal, **47** (1), 73-91 (1968).

[2] K.Bullington, I.M.Fraser, *Engineering Aspects of TASI,* Bell System Technical Journal, **38** (3), 353-364 (1959).

[3] S.I.Campanella, *Digital Speech Interpolation,* Comsat Technical Review, **6** (1), 127-158 (1976).

[4] J.G.Gruber, *Delay Issues in Integrated Voice and Data Transmission,* IEEE Transactions on Communications, **29** (6), 786-800 (1981).

[5] N.S.Jayant, S.W.Christensen, *Effects of Packet Losses in Waveform Coded Speech and Improvements Due to an Odd/Even Sample Interpolation Procedure,* IEEE Transactions on Communications, **29** (2), 101-109 (1981).

[6] D.H.Johnson, G.C.O'Leary, *A Local Access Network for Packetized Digital Voice Communication,* IEEE Transactions on Communications, **29** (5), 679-688 (1981).

[7] K.Kuemmerle, *Multiplexer Performance for Integrated Line and Packet Switched Traffic,* Second International Computer and Communications Conference, pp.505-515, Stockholm, Sweden, 12-14 August 1974.

[8] B.Maglaris, M.Schwartz, *Performance Evaluation of a Variable Frame Multiplexer for Integrated Switched Networks,* IEEE Transactions on Communications, **29** (6), 800-807 (1981).

[9] B.Maglaris, M.Schwartz, *Optimal Fixed Frame Multiplexing in Integrated Line- and Packet-Switched Communication Networks,* IEEE Transactions on Information Theory, **28** (2), 263-273 (1982).

[10] C.Weinstein, M.Malpass, and M.J.Fischer, *Data Traffic Performance of an Integrated Circuit and Packet Switched Multiplex Structure,* IEEE Transactions on Communications, **28** (6), 873-878 (1980).

10.10 Flow Control of a Single Virtual Circuit over a Single Link

We wish to study the traffic handling characteristics of a policy for pacing the flow of information from a transmitter to a receiver over a logical abstraction of a physical circuit (a so called *virtual* circuit) within a local area network. The transmitter formats a message into one or more packets. If the receiver has only a limited amount of storage, and the transmitter is faster than the receiver, packets can be transmitted and blocked or rejected by the receiver because no room is available. A protocol is used for controlling the flow of information to insure that no packet is lost due to no room being available, as well as for other reasons. The transmitter must be turned on and off to insure no packet are lost. What is the penalty in mean throughput rate and packet delay statistics as a function of receiver buffering and transmitter and receiver processing speeds? We analyze a model for a class of protocols, so called *sliding window** protocols, for controlling the flow of information between a

---

*   As far as the transmitter is concerned, there is a *window* on the packet stream: some packets have been transmitted but not yet acknowledged. The window *slides* from the start of the packet stream to the end.

transmitter and receiver. If the time for a packet to propagate from the transmitter to the receiver and back is negligible compared to the transmitter and receiver packet processing times, such as in local area network applications, it is possible to engineer a virtual circuit to achieve predictable performance. This protocol is representative of a great many protocols currently in use, each of which differs in detail in terms of error handling, but not in terms of pacing the flow of packets between the transmitter and receiver.

10.10.1 Problem Statement Messages arrive for execution to a transmitter. The transmitter buffer has infinite capacity. Each message is composed of one or more packets: The packet arrival statistics are compound Poisson, i.e., the packet group interarrival times form a sequence of independent identically distributed exponential random variables, and the number of packets arriving at each arrival epoch forms a sequence of independent identically distributed random variables. The transmitter executes packets in order of arrival, with the transmitter processing times forming a sequence of independent identically distributed arbitrary random variables. The receiver has capacity W packets, with the packets being executed at the receiver in order of arrival, and the receiver processing times forming a sequence of independent identically distributed arbitrary random variables. The transmitter will not execute packets between the time interval when the receiver buffer is filled with W packets until the receiver buffer is filled with B packets. The transmission propagation times between the transmitter and receiver are assumed to be zero.

We fix notation for the following random variables:

- $T_{T,k}$--the communications processing time at the transmitter for the kth packet; the sequence of packet processing times are assumed to be independent identically distributed random variables

- $T_{R,k}$--the communications processing time at the receiver for the kth packet; the sequence of receiver processing times are assumed to be independent identically distributed random variables

- A_j--the interarrival time between the jth and (j+1)th batch of packets; the sequence of interarrival times are assumed to be independent identically distributed exponential random variables with mean $1/\lambda$

- B_j--the number of packets arriving at the jth arrival epoch; the sequence of batch sizes are assumed to be independent identically distributed random variables with associated moment generating function $E[x^B] = \eta(x)$ and Q_J denotes the probability an arrival batch contains $J \geqslant 1$ packets

- F_k--the time interval from the arrival to the departure of packet k

10.10.2 Summary of Results The long term time averaged message flow time distribution for the start stop (W=1) protocol has a moment generating function given by

$$\lim_{k \to \infty} E[e^{-zF_k}] =$$

$$\frac{[1-\lambda E(B)E(T_T + T_R)]z\hat{G}_{T+R}(z)}{z - \lambda + \lambda\eta[\hat{G}_{T+R}(z)]} \quad \frac{1 - \eta[\hat{G}_{T+R}(z)]}{E(B)[1 - \hat{G}_{T+R}(z)]}$$

For the double buffering protocol for (W=2) the moment generating function for the message flow time distribution is given by

$$\lim_{k \to \infty} E[e^{-zF_k}] =$$

$$\frac{1-\lambda E(B)E(T_M)}{1 + \lambda E(T_I - T_M)} \quad \frac{z\hat{G}_I(z) + \lambda[\hat{G}_M(z) - \hat{G}_I(z)]}{z - \lambda + \lambda\eta[\hat{G}_M(z)]} \quad \frac{1-\eta[\hat{G}_M(z)]}{E(B)[1-\hat{G}_M(z)]} \hat{G}_R(z)$$

We have used the following notation:

$$\hat{G}_T(z) = E[exp(-zT_T)] \quad \hat{G}_R(z) = E[exp(-zT_R)] \quad \hat{G}_{T+R}(z) = \hat{G}_T(z)\hat{G}_R(z)$$

$$\hat{G}_M(z) = E[exp(-z\ max(T_T,T_R))] \quad \hat{G}_I(z) = E[exp(-z\ max(T_T,T_R-A))]$$

Here are the expressions for mean message delay for the special case of constant packet processing times at the receiver and transmitter. First, for W=1, the long term time averaged mean packet delay is given by

$$\lim_{k \to \infty} E(F_k) = \frac{\lambda E((T_T+T_R)^2)}{2(1-\lambda E(T_T+T_R))} + E(T_T+T_R)$$

assuming $\lambda E(T_T+T_R) < 1$.

Next, for W=2, the long term time averaged mean packet delay is given by

$$\lim_{k \to \infty} E(F_k) = \frac{\lambda E(T_M^2)}{2(1-\lambda E(T_M))} + E(T_T+T_R) + \frac{E(e^{-\lambda(T_M-T_T)})}{(1+E(e^{-\lambda(T_M-T_T)}))(1-\lambda E(T_M))}$$

assuming $\lambda E(T_M) < 1$ where $T_M = max(T_T,T_R)$. Finally, for $W \to \infty$, the long term time averaged mean message delay is given by

$$\lim_{k \to \infty} E(F_k) = \frac{\lambda E(T_M^2)}{2(1-\lambda E(T_M))} + E(T_T+T_R)$$

assuming $\lambda E(T_M) < 1$, where $T_M = max(T_T,T_R)$. The insight in the earlier section is that double buffering appears to achieve most of the benefit of infinite buffering, in the face of speed mismatches and fluctuations in processing times.

The extension to compound Poisson arrival statistics is handled as follows: The Laplace Stieltjes transform for the flow time distribution is given by

$$\hat{G}_F(z) = \frac{E\left[\sum_{K=1}^{N} e^{-zF_K}\right]}{E(N)}$$

where the random variable N is the number of packets serviced in a busy period. The mean number of packets served during a busy period equals the mean number of packets arriving in a batch multiplied by the mean number of groups of packets serviced during a busy period. The first group of packets serviced during a busy period contributes to the numerator of the flow time Laplace Stieltjes transform

$$first\ group\ contribution = \sum_{J=1}^{\infty} Q_J[\hat{G}_I(z)[I + \hat{G}_M(z) + \cdots + \hat{G}_M(z)^{J-1}]]$$

$$= \hat{G}_I(z)\ \frac{1 - \eta[\hat{G}_M(z)]}{1 - \hat{G}_M(z)}$$

If a group is the Kth group during a busy period $(K>1)$, and the first packet of a group has to wait W_K time units, then the Kth group contributes a term of the form

$$nonfirst\ group\ contribution = E[e^{-zW_K}] \sum_{J=1}^{\infty} Q_J[\hat{G}_M(z) + \cdots + \hat{G}_M(z)^J]$$

$$= E[e^{-zW_K}]\ \hat{G}_M(z)\ \frac{1 - \eta[\hat{G}_M(z)]}{1 - \hat{G}_M(z)}\quad K>1$$

to the numerator of the flow time distribution Laplace Stieltjes transform. Combining all this, we see

$$\hat{G}_F(z) = \frac{1}{\eta'(1)E[\gamma]} \left[\hat{G}_I(z) + \hat{G}_M(z)E[\sum_{K=2}^{\gamma} e^{-zW_K}] \right] \frac{1 - \eta[\hat{G}_M(z)]}{1 - \hat{G}_M(z)}$$

where the random variable γ denotes the number of groups of packets serviced during a busy period,

$$E[\gamma] = 1 + \frac{\lambda[E[T_I] + [\eta'(1) - 1]E[T_M]}{1 - \lambda\eta'(1)E[T_M]}$$

and $\eta'(1)$ is the derivative of the moment generating function of the arrival batch distribution evaluated at one, i.e., the mean number of packets arriving in a batch.

$$E[\sum_{K=2}^{\gamma} e^{-zW_K}] = \frac{\lambda}{\hat{G}_M(z)}\ \frac{\hat{G}_M(z) - \hat{G}_I(z)\eta[\hat{G}_M(z)]}{z - \lambda + \lambda\eta[\hat{G}_M(z)]}$$

The figure below plots mean packet delay versus mean packet arrival rate, assuming simple Poisson arrival statistics, for the receiver and transmitter processing times being exponentially distributed, with the mean receiver processing time per packet fixed at one second, while the mean transmitter processing time per packet is fixed at one second.

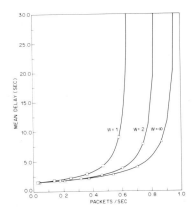

Figure 10.19.Mean Packet Delay vs Mean Packet Arrival Rate.
Exponential Transmitter/Receiver Times, $E(T_T)=E(T_R)=1.0$

The companion figure does so for the transmitter and receiver packet time transmission distributions constant, with mean $E(T_T)=E(T_R)=1.0$:

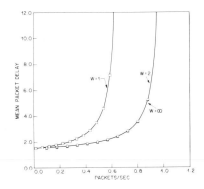

Figure 10.20.Mean Packet Delay vs Mean Packet Arrival Rate
Constant Transmitter/Receiver Times, $E(T_T)=E(T_R)=1.0$

The following figure is a segment of the above plots, covering only the lower range of mean packet arrival rates, in order to make it graphically clear that for normal operating regions the difference in mean delay for infinite window size versus double buffering is practically speaking *negligible* and considerably smaller than start stop buffering.

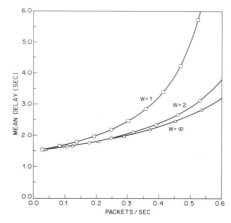

Figure 10.21.Mean Packet Delay vs Mean Packet Arrival Rate Exponential Transmitter/Receiver Times,$E(T_T)=E(T_R)=1.0$

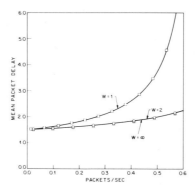

Figure 10.22.Mean Packet Delay vs Mean Packet Arrival Rate Constant Transmitter/Receiver Times,$E(T_T)=E(T_R)=1.0$

The case of exponentially distributed packet processing times is highly pessimistic; a constant distribution for packet processing times is more common in practice, because there is little data dependency or looping or fluctuations in many applications. Even for this very pessimistic set of assumptions, there is remarkably little difference in the performance of infinite buffering and double buffering versus the single buffering case.

Problems

1) A packet switching system handles two types of packets, control packets and data packets. The system consists of a single processor that executes the highest priority job in the system at any point in time. The total arrival statistics are Poisson distributed. The fraction of arrivals that are control packets is twenty per cent under normal operations, and is eighty per cent under overload. The packet execution times are given in the table below:

Table 10.7.Packet Execution Times

Type	Distribution	Mean
Control	D	100 μsec
Data	M	500 μsec

Under normal conditions, the processor is thirty per cent utilized. Under overload conditions, the processor is seventy per cent utilized. The design goal is to process a control packet within 200 μsec during normal operations, and 1000 μsec under overload, ninety per cent of the time for both cases. What is the largest mean throughput rate of data packets that the system can handle if we schedule work according to

  A. Service in order of arrival

  B. Service in reverse order of arrival, nonpreemptive

  C. Service in reverse order of arrival, preemptive resume

  D. Static priority nonpreemptive scheduling, with control higher priority than data

  E. Static priority preemptive resume scheduling, with control higher priority than data

2) A local area network is used for multiplexing voice and data over a common shared bus. The following information is measured on system operation:

- Each user will be involved with five telephone calls per peak business hour. Each telephone call will last for a mean of three minutes. Each telephone call involves converting speech to digital bits, for transmission at 64 KBPS over the bus

- Each user is involved with twenty five data transactions during a peak busy hour. Each transaction involves one thousand bytes (eight bits per byte) of data being input to the system, and two thousand bytes of data being output to the user.

All bits are encoded into a two thousand byte fixed length packet for transmission over the bus. Plot the mean data delay versus bus transmission speed, from the range 10 KBPS to 10 MBPS, for each of the two policies below:

A. Voice has higher priority than data with nonpreemptive scheduling

B. Data has higher priority than voice with nonpreemptive scheduling

3) P processors access a common shared memory. Only one processor at a time is allowed to access the memory. The mean memory access time is two clock cycles. The mean time interval between memory access requests for a given processor is five clock cycles.

A. Each memory access time is assumed to be constant and equal to two clock cycles. Plot the mean memory access delay versus the number of processors, for one to four processors, using a finite source arrival process model. Repeat for an infinite source arrival process model, and compare results.

B. Repeat if the memory access times are drawn from an exponential distribution with a mean of two clock cycles.

C. Repeat if the memory access times are drawn from a hyperexponential distribution with a mean of two clock cycles and with a squared coefficient of variation of ten.

4) A processor executes two types of jobs. Each job consists of three tasks: a setup task, an execution task, and a cleanup task. The setup phase requires a constant time of one tenth of a second. The execution phase requires a mean time of one second. The cleanup phase requires a mean time of two tenths of a second. Jobs arrive according to batch Poisson statistics, with a total mean arrival rate of $\lambda_K, K=1,2$ jobs per second, and a bimodal distribution of jobs at each arrival epoch: with probability P one job arrives at an arrival epoch, and with probability $1-P$ five jobs arrive at an arrival epoch.

A. What is the largest rate at which type one jobs and type two jobs can be executed, if jobs are executed in order of arrival?

B. What is the largest rate at which type one jobs and type two jobs can be executed, if the setup is executed at priority zero, the work at priority K, and the cleanup at priority zero, with a preemptive resume work discipline?

C. What is the largest rate at which type one jobs and type two jobs can be executed, if the setup, work, and cleanup are all executed at priority K for job type K, with a nonpreemptive priority work discipline?

D. Plot the mean queueing time for each task versus the total mean arrival rate, assuming a mix of 20% type one and $P=0.5$. Repeat if the mix is 80% type one. Repeat all the above if $P=0.1$ and $P=0.9$.

5) A local area network has a data clock rate of 10 MBPS. Both voice and data packets are transmitted over the network. Voice packets are 512 bits long, the total voice bit rate for a telephone call is 64 KBPS, and a voice telephone call lasts for three minutes. Data packets are 8192 bits long. Assume that voice telephone calls and data packets are generated according to Poisson statistics with mean arrival rate λ_{voice} and λ_{data} respectively.

A. What is the largest possible value of λ_{voice} such that no more than one call in one million is blocked? No more than one call in ten thousand? No more than one call in one hundred?

B. How often does the voice traffic lock out the data? For how long on the average?

C. If a voice surge ties up all available transmission capacity, what is the maximum number of data packets that must be buffered?

D. If the system is engineered so that 64 KBPS of transmission capacity is available for data all the time, i.e., the number of simultaneous voice calls is always one less than the maximum possible number, what changes in the above discussion?

E. What changes if voice is transmitted at 32 KBPS? 16 KBPS?

6) A transmitter employs a sliding window flow control policy to send packets to a transmitter. The mean number of instructions executed by the transmitter is one hundred assembly language instructions, while for the receiver it is two hundred assembly language instructions. The transmitter and receiver employ different microprocessors and each microprocessor can execute one hundred thousand assembly language instructions per second. The transmitter and receiver are connected via a local area network, with a constant network propagation delay of 50 μ seconds per packet.

A. What is the maximum mean throughput rate for transmitting packets assuming the window size is one packet? an infinite number of packets? two packets with constant execution times at the transmitter and receiver? two packets with exponentially distributed execution times at the transmitter and receiver?

B. What is the mean packet queueing time for the above versus the total packet arrival rate?

C. Repeat all the above if the microprocessors can execute one million assembly language instructions per second. What changes for ten million assembly language instructions per second?

7) A single processor can execute one hundred thousand assembly language instructions per second. We wish to design an overload control for this processor that has the following design parameters:

• The mean loss must be one per cent or less of arriving jobs

• The mean overload control delay must be one hundred microseconds or less.

• The mean time the processor is elsewhere than handling input, i.e., executing work, cannot be greater than one millisecond.

The arrivals statistics are measured and felt to be Poisson distributed. The number of instructions executed in overload control input handling is felt to be constant and independent of the job. For each of the cases below, how many assembly language instructions can be executed by the processor doing overload control input handling?

A. A static priority arbitration scheme

B. A first in, first out buffer

C. A circular buffer

D. What changes if the processor can execute one million assembly language instructions per second?

8) A job consists of a mean number of Q tasks. The number of tasks per job is initially fixed at $Q=3$. Each task requires one second to be executed on a single processor. Jobs arrive according to simple Poisson statistics, with mean arrival rate λ. Plot the mean queueing time for a job versus mean arrival rate for

A. Execution in order of arrival

B. Processor sharing

C. Downward migration priority arbitration, where initially the job receives up to one second of processing time at the highest priority level and it either finishes or migrates to the next highest priority level, until eventually it finishes.

D. Repeat all the above if the number of tasks per job is geometrically distributed with a mean of Q tasks per job.

E. Repeat all the above if the number of tasks per job is bimodally distributed with three quarters of the jobs consisting of one task and the remainder consisting of a fixed number of tasks such that the total mean number of tasks per job is fixed at $Q=3$.

F. Repeat all the above if each task requires one tenth of a second to be executed on a single processor.

What is a *local area network?* A local area network is a switching system that

- Employs digital rather than analog transmission

- Transmits bits serially rather than in parallel

- Employs typical clock rates of one to twenty million bits per second

- Is relatively noise free compared to analog voice communication lines: Bit error rates of one bit in one billion are typical

- Switches packets or frames of bits rather than holding transmission bandwidth for the duration of a communication session

- Has a geographic extent of one to ten kilometers at most

- Can have a wide variety of devices attached (e.g., sensors, thermostats, security alarms, process control devices, low speed data terminals, voice, facsimile, computer high speed I/O, video) offering multiple services

A key design consideration in local area networks is that for typical applications with packet lengths of five hundred to ten thousand bits, at most *one* packet will be in transit at any time, in contrast to long haul terrestrial or space satellite networks where more than one packet (perhaps ten to one hundred packets) may be in transit at any time.

11.1 Traffic Handling Characteristics of Local Area Networks

Topologically, any local area network appears to be a set of stations connected to a common hub or pincushion. This suggests two different traffic handling regimes:

- One regime where the local area network is lightly loaded, the transmission medium has a low utilization, message delays are acceptable, because the workload generated by the stations is too low to cause unacceptable congestion in the network, and

- A second regime where the local area network is heavily loaded, the transmission medium has a high utilization, message delays are unacceptable, because the workload generated by the stations does cause unacceptable network congestion.

The purpose of traffic analysis is to determine the demarcation between the lightly and heavily loaded regions; in any such system it will always be present, the only question is *where?* Here is a different way of thinking about this:

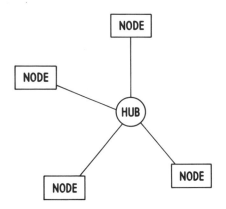

ONE HOP LOCAL AREA NETWORK TOPOLOGY

Figure 11.1.Topology of a Local Area Network

Where would a designer choose to operate a local area network? Since there are more than enough problems getting these systems to work at all, let alone with congestion, many designers would choose to operate in the lightly loaded regime.

11.1.1 Traffic Analysis Inputs In order to say *anything* about the traffic handling characteristics of a local area network, we must specify two ingredients, the *workload* (how many devices are attached, how often does each device generate each type of message, how many bits per message), and the *policy* for arbitrating contention for the shared but serially reusable local area network transmission medium.

11.1.2 Traffic Handling Goals What are desirable properties of a given policy or access method?

- Packet delay should be acceptable under light load

- The transmission medium should be efficiently utilized under heavy load

- For a fixed workload, packet delay should be *insensitive* to how the workload is generated among the devices since in practice this will *not* in fact be known with any precision.

We will judge traffic handling performance by examining mean packet delay and mean packet throughput rate for a fixed workload. The figure below is an illustrative plot of mean delay versus load: Since we are employing *distributed* control, presumably the delay under light load is *greater* than for central

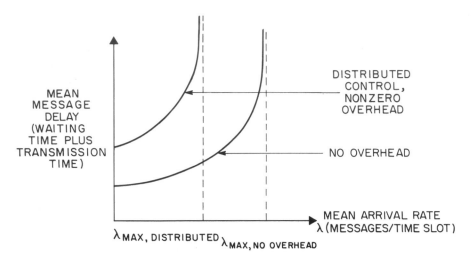

Figure 11.2.Mean Packet Delay vs Mean Packet Arrival Rate

control, and the *maximum* mean throughput rate is *lower*. We want to quantify precisely how much worse these measures can be, for a variety of access methods or scheduling policies for arbitrating local area network access.

We stress that the link level access method is only *one* factor that must be addressed in total communication system performance.

11.1.3 Additional Reading

[1]   P.Baran, *On Distributed Communication Networks,* IEEE Transactions on Communications, **12,** 1-9 (1964).

11.2 Local Area Network Topology

A local area network might have a variety of topologies. One example is a *star* topology, where all nodes are connected to a central hub. This might be implemented with circuit switching, such as in a private branch exchange, where transmission capacity is dedicated for the duration of a communication session at the start of the session, and if there is none available a new attempt is blocked or rejected. It might be implemented with packet switching, where messages are broken into packets and buffered internally until transmission and switching resources become available. Both these approaches employ *central* control or arbitration of resources.

In contrast to these, a *broadcast* medium or *bus* might be employed, with either *central* or *distributed* control. The transmission attempt of any station is received by all stations. A different type of topology that can employ

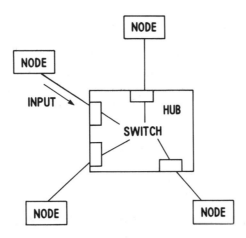

Figure 11.3. Circuit Switching Local Area Network

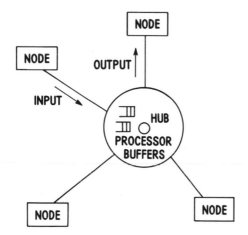

Figure 11.4. Packet Switching Local Area Network

distributed control is a *ring,* where each station receives messages from only one station and transmits to only one station. This taxonomy by no means exhausts the design alternatives. These topologies are currently the most popular, and we will confine attention to them from this point on.

11.2.1 Additional Reading

[1]   J.H.Saltzer, D.D.Clark, K.T.Pogran, *Why a Ring?,* Proceedings Seventh Data Communications Symposium, pp.211-217, 27-29 October 1981, Mexico City, Mexico, ACM 533810, IEEE 81CH1694-9.

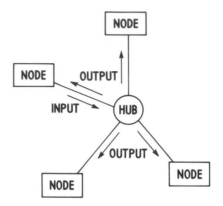

Figure 11.5.Broadcast Bus Local Area Network

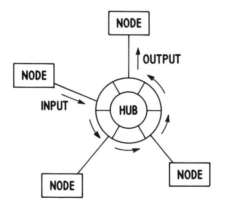

Figure 11.6.Ring Local Area Network

11.3 Bus or Broadcast Medium Model

In this section we focus attention on a bus or broadcast medium local area network, while in subsequent sections other variants are explored. Here, a set of stations are geographically separated, and send and receive messages on a common broadcast medium called a *bus*. What are the states of the bus?

- *Idle--* No transceiver is active, and all transceivers recognize this within a given time unit

- *Transmit--* Exactly one transceiver is actively transmitting a message successfully

- *Collide*-- Two or more transceivers are simultaneously active attempting to transmit, causing interference or a *collision* between transmission attempts and all messages involved in the collision must be retransmitted later.

Arbitration policies dealt with here encompass

- *Token passing access* where control is passed via a token from one station to the next, and the station with the token is the only one allowed to transmit. Collisions are rare events here (initialization of the system, loss of token, generation of multiple tokens, and so forth), and for purposes of traffic or congestion are ignored from this point on. Each station can be polled either explicitly (from a central station) or implicitly (via distributed control)

- *Carrier sense collision detection access* where, roughly speaking, all stations sense the transmission medium to scc if carrier energy is present; if no carrier is sensed, a station will attempt to seize the transmission medium and transmit its message; if carrier is sensed, a station will defer its attempt to a later time; if two or more stations attempt to seize the transmission medium within a given time interval, a *collision* is said to occur, and this must be *detected* by all stations involved and the next attempt deferred to a later time. The mechanism for determining the retry time intervals involves spreading retransmission attempts out farther and farther in time, in order to maximize bus utilization at the expense of message delay

- *Decision tree access* which looks like carrier sense collision detection access under light load and like token passing or polling under heavy load. It achieves this by a priority arbitration retry policy in event of a collision, interrogating *groups* (subtrees) of stations such that at most one station in a group has a packet to send. Carrier sense collision detection assumes that at most *one* station out of *all* stations has a packet, while token passing assumes that *every* station has a packet.

The transmission medium is used for both control and data transmission. The time spent using the transmission medium for control should be negligible compared with the time spent transmitting data. Polling achieves this under heavy loads, while carrier sense collision detection achieves this under light loads. Decision tree arbitration does so under virtually *all* loads.

11.3.1 Additional Reading

[1] J.E.Donnelley, J.W.Yeh, *Interaction Between Protocol Levels in a Prioritized CSMA Broadcast Network,* Computer Networks, **3**, 9-23 (1979).

[2] O.Spaniol, *Modelling of Local Computer Networks,* Computer Networks, **3** (5), 315-326 (1979).

11.4 Token Passing Access via a Bus

The figure below shows illustrative operation of a token passing or distributed polling system; stations zero, one, four and seven have messages to transmit.

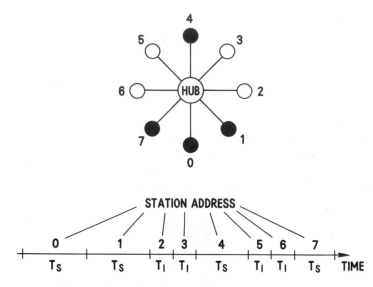

Figure 11.7.Illustrative Token Bus Operation

In the scenario shown in the figure, station zero transmits, then passes control to station one, station one transmits and passes control to station two, and so forth. The mean time to transmit a message is denoted by T_M, and it includes both data bits and framing bits. The mean time to pass the token from one station to another is denoted by T_{TOKEN}.

What are the salient features of distributed polling or token passing transmission medium access? Stations are logically organized in a ring; this allows *separation* or *dedication* of transmission capacity to different types of services, by simply assigning a given number of visits per polling cycle to each service. For example, if a work station offered both 9.6 KBPS data service and 64 KBPS voice service, the voice port could be visited eight times (we have rounded upward from the smallest integer greater than 64/9.6 to get eight) as often as the data port, i.e., we are dedicating eight times the transmission capacity to voice as to data.

Load balancing is possible via two mechanisms: First, token passing can control the number of visits per polling cycle per station (if one station has twice the load of the other stations, visit it twice as often). Second, token passing can control the maximum number of frames transmitted per visit; if one station has a lot of traffic (e.g., a printer, a gateway, or a disk) while the remainder of the stations generate messages rarely (e.g., work stations or low speed data terminals), the one station with a lot of messages will transmit for a long time if there is no limit on the number of frames transmitted per visit, and all the other stations must wait for it to finish. This can lead to unacceptable delays, but the bus can be very efficiently utilized. If a limit is set on the maximum number of frames that can be transmitted per visit, then each of the terminals or work stations will get access just as under light load, while the one station with lots of messages will be delayed (but it will be delayed anyway since it has so much to transmit, the only question is how much!).

Overhead time per transmission is bounded by a linear function of the number of transceivers (typically this is a constant due to bus propagation and circuitry transients plus a linear term due to the transceiver processing) because control must be passed to each station at least once in a ring or polling cycle.

Under heavy load high throughput is achieved because in this regime the transmission medium will be busy transmitting messages under load, not passing the token from station to station.

Under light loading on the local area network, the mean waiting time of a station that is ready to transmit a packet or frame equals the time for the token to circulate through one half of the total number of stations N, on the average:

$$T_W = \tfrac{1}{2} \, T_{TOKEN} \, N \quad \text{one out of } N \text{ stations active}$$

This immediately gives us the maximum mean message throughput rate for one out of N stations always active:

$$\text{mean throughput rate} \leqslant \frac{1}{N T_{TOKEN} + T_M} \quad \text{one out of } N \text{ stations active}$$

With every station (all N) active, the mean waiting is given by:

$$T_W = N T_{TOKEN} + (N-1) T_M \quad \text{all } N \text{ stations active}$$

This in turn gives us an upper bound on the mean throughput rate:

$$\text{mean throughput rate} = \frac{1}{T_{TOKEN} + T_M} \quad \text{all } N \text{ stations active}$$

Suppose the fraction of time the transmission medium is busy transmitting data, the bus utilization, is fixed. As the number of stations is increased so that the amount of data per message per station decreases toward zero, the mean waiting time or delay experienced by any station in transmitting a message will increase above any fixed threshold, because more and more time will be spent passing the control token from one station to another rather than transmitting data. In this sense, token passing is said to be *unstable*.

If we fix the utilization, the fraction of time the bus is busy with data transmission, and increase the number of stations, each station will be less and less likely to have a message to transmit, but we will still pass the token through each station, increasing the total message waiting time. What is the point? Utilization of the local area network transmission capacity may be an inadequate or incomplete measure of system loading: we must also describe how many stations are attached, and how active each of them is, in order to say anything concerning the traffic handling characteristics of such a system.

11.5 Token Passing Mean Value Analysis

This section deals with several limiting cases in order to gain insight into bounds on the mean throughput and delay.

11.5.1 One Message Always at Every Station Assume one message is **always** ready for transmission at each station. Every station is continually offering work, and the system is never idle.

First, we fix notation. $R_{max}(K)$ denotes the maximum mean throughput rate of messages from source $K, K=1,...,N$. $T_M(K)$ denotes the mean amount of time required for a message to be transmitted from source $K, K=1,...,N$ once the serially reusable channel is seized by that source. Source K, $K=1,...,N$ is visited $V(K)$ times per polling cycle.

First, we assume there is no overhead incurred in token passing, to bound the best possible performance. The fraction of time this serially reusable resource is busy handling requests from source K is simply the mean throughput of that source times the mean service time for that source:

$$U(K) = R_{max}(K) \times T_M(K)   K=1,...,N$$

where $U(K)$ is the utilization or fraction of time source K is active. In order to insure that the system can keep up with its work, we demand the fraction of time the serially reusable resource is busy must be less than one:

$$\sum_{K=1}^{N} U(K) = \sum_{K=1}^{N} R_{max}(K) \times T_M(K) \leqslant 1$$

Now we include polling overhead. During a polling cycle, the link is assumed to be busy either executing work from a source or busy doing overhead work in switching from one source to another. We denote by T_O the **total** mean time interval that the system is busy executing overhead work during one polling cycle, i.e., the sum of times to move from a source through all the other sources in a cycle and return, with no station transmitting any messages at all. We denote by C_{max} the maximum duration of one complete polling period or cycle. Since every source is assumed to always have a message, we are computing the worst case performance under congestion. Since we assume that the system is busy either doing useful work or doing overhead, the polling cycle must satisfy

$$C_{\max} = T_O + \sum_{K=1}^{N} T_M(K) \times V(K)$$

Since we assume that each source always has a message to be sent, the mean throughput rate for source $K, K=1,...,N$ is

$$R_{\max}(K) = \frac{V(K)}{C_{\max}} = \frac{V(K)}{T_O + \sum_{K=1}^{N} T_M \times V(K)} \qquad K=1,...,N$$

11.5.2 Polling Stations that are Idle and Active Assume the system is always busy with polling overhead or message transmission, but the sources may be busy or idle. In the previous section, we calculated the maximum mean throughput rate and the maximum cycle time; here we see

$$R(K) \leqslant R_{\max} \quad K=1,...,N \quad C \leqslant C_{\max}$$

Since there is only one reusable message transmission medium, the fraction of time the system spends in the overhead and message states must sum to one.

$$\frac{T_O}{C} + \sum_{K=1}^{N} R(K) \times T_M(K) = 1$$

Solving for C, we get

$$C = \frac{T_O}{1 - \sum_{K=1}^{N} R(K) \times T_M(K)}$$

The duration of a polling cycle is proportional to T_O at all traffic rates: measure this to see if your actual system is performing as expected (doubling the mean overhead time should double the mean cycle time, for a fixed workload). If each source is polled once in a polling cycle, the reciprocal of the polling cycle is an upper bound on the mean throughput rate for each source. More generally,

$$R(J) \leqslant \frac{V(J)}{C} \qquad J=1,...,N$$

$$R(J) \leqslant V(J) \times \frac{1 - \sum_{K=1}^{N} R(K) \times T_M(K)}{T_O}$$

The figure below plots an illustrative feasible region of mean throughput rates for the special case of two sources. This is a convex set, with the convex hull given by the static priority policies.

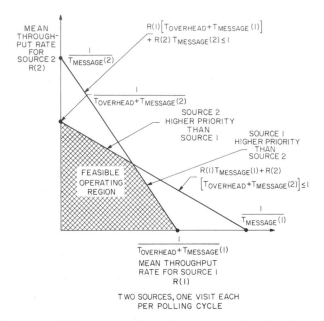

Figure 11.8.Illustrative Mean Throughput Feasible Region

11.5.3 All Sources Generate Identical Workload If the sources have identical traffic characteristics, so that

$$R(K) = R \qquad T_M(K) = T_M \;\rightarrow$$

$$R \leqslant \frac{1-N \times R \times T_M}{T_O}$$

$$R \leqslant \frac{1}{T_O + N \times T_M}$$

Now let us examine the mean delay for each source here. We observe that each source is busy (either queued or transmitting data) for a mean time interval denoted T_D, or is idle for a mean time interval T_I. The mean throughput rate for each source, by definition, is simply the reciprocal of the sum of these two time intervals:

$$R = \frac{1}{T_D + T_I}$$

If we rearrange this, we see that

$$T_D = \frac{1}{R} - T_I$$

Using the earlier upper bound on throughput for identical sources,

$$T_D \geqslant T_O + (N \times T_M) - T_I$$

In practice, T_O may be a constant dependent on the round trip propagation time plus a term proportional to the number of source visits per cycle

$$T_D \geqslant C_0 + [N \times (C_1 + T_M)] - T_I$$

The figure below shows an illustrative feasible region of mean delay for a given source.

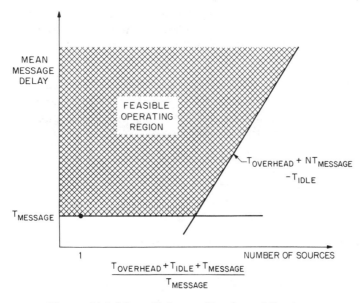

Figure 11.9. Mean Delay vs Number of Stations

There are two regions evident:

- Light loading--the serially reusable resource is lightly loaded, so the mean delay is simply the time required to transmit data, with virtually no queueing; the different sources are the bottleneck in this regime, not the serially reusable resource! The different sources cannot generate enough message to congest the link.

- Heavy loading--the serially reusable resource is heavily loaded, so the mean delay, queueing plus data transmission, increases linearly with each additional source; the serially reusable resource is the bottleneck

If we poll a given source more frequently, the throughput for that source would increase, and the slope of $T_D(K)$ would decrease in the heavily loaded region. However, this might be accomplished at the expense of increasing the polling period, thereby reducing the upper bound on throughput for other sources.

A key concept is that of *load balancing*. The idea here is to configure the system so that the fraction of time spent per visit per station during a polling cycle is roughly equal or balanced. For example, if there are three stations, and during heavy loading one station typically has two messages per cycle while the other stations have one message per cycle, then we could allow each station to transmit a maximum of one message per cycle, and visit the heavily loaded station twice per cycle. Put differently, if we put no limit on the maximum amount of messages that a station can transmit per visit or poll, then any station can drive the system to complete utilization, but the delay might be unacceptable for some stations. If we put a limit on the maximum amount that any station can transmit per poll, then no station can drive the link to complete utilization, but the delay might be made acceptable.

11.5.4 Finite Source Mean Throughput and Mean Delay Asymptotes What if we have one terminal or source on the system, i.e., N=1? Then we see that the source is idle or active, and the active time is the time to gain access to the channel plus the message transmission time.

$$T_O + T_M + T_I = C \quad \textit{one terminal}$$

The reciprocal of this mean cycle time is the mean throughput rate

$$R = \frac{1}{T_O + T_M + T_I} \quad \textit{one terminal}$$

If N is greater than one, and each source has a message to transmit on each visit, then

$$N \times T_O + N \times T_M + T_I = C \quad \textit{N terminals}$$

$$\rightarrow R = \frac{N}{N \times T_O + N \times T_M + T_I} \quad \textit{N terminals}$$

which for large N and fixed T_I will approach that of a single source!

A different type of insight is gained if we start with our fundamental identity:

$$\frac{U}{T_M} = \frac{N}{T_I + T_D}$$

We now fix the quantity $N/T_I \equiv \lambda$ at a constant but allow the number of stations and the mean idle time per station to approach infinity together:

$$\lim_{N \to \infty} \frac{U}{T_M} = \frac{U_{\max}}{T_M} \quad \lambda = \textit{constant} = \frac{N}{T_I}$$

where $U_{\max}$ is the maximum utilization of the serially reusable resource. All mean throughput and mean delay studies are devoted to calculating $U_{\max}$ for different workload statistics, and access policies.

EXERCISE: Can you calculate a lower bound on mean throughput rate and a corresponding upper bound on mean delay?

11.6 Exhaustive Polling of Two Queues with Switching Overhead

Here is a case study to illustrate the complexity of analyzing the traffic handling characteristics of exhaustive polling of two stations, which is a case that can be completely handled. The model ingredients are:

- The message arrival statistics--Each station has simple Poisson arrival statistics with mean arrival rate λ_K to station K=1,2.

- The message length statistics--The sequence of message lengths for either station are independent identically distributed random variables, denoted by B_K bits for station K=1,2.

- The scheduling policy--Each station is polled to exhaustion upon visiting a station; messages are queued in order of arrival for transmission.

We are also given the link transmission speed, BPS, measured in bits per second, and the total time to switch from one queue to another and back again given that no message is present at either queue, denoted $T_{overhead}$.

The mean queueing time at queue one, including both waiting and message transmission time, is

$$E(T_{Q1}) = \frac{\lambda_2 E(B_2^2/BPS^2)(1-U_1)^2 + \lambda_1 E(B_1^2/BPS^2)U_2^2}{2(1-U_1)(1-U_1-U_2)(1-U_1-U_2+2U_1U_2)} + \frac{\lambda E(B_1^2/BPS^2)}{2(1-U_1)}$$

$$+ \frac{(1-U_1)T_{overhead}}{2(1-U_1-U_2)} \qquad U_K = \lambda_K E(B_K)/BPS \qquad K=1,2$$

By interchanging indices one and two, a similar expression follows for the mean queueing time at queue two.

In order to gain engineering insight into the behavior of this system, we vary the following parameters:

- The fraction of total arrivals to the system that arrive at queue one $F(1)$

- The mean number of bits per message at queue one and queue two

- Fluctuations in the message length about its mean value for queues one and two, measured via the *squared coefficient of variation* which is the ratio of the variance divided by the mean squared, so it measures fluctuations (standard deviation about the mean) in units of mean message length; zero squared coefficient of variation is no variation at all, squared coefficient of variation of one is the exponential distribution, and so forth

Our goal is to plot the mean delay of messages from queue one and queue two as a function of the total utilization of the transmission medium. Not surprisingly, these figures show that the station with the greater utilization, i.e., the station that is busy the greater fraction of time, will monopolize the

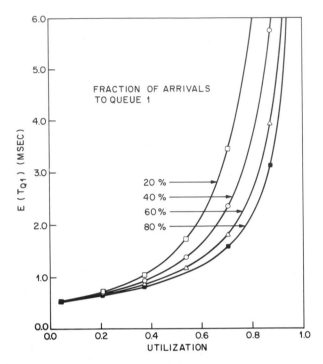

Figure 11.10. $E\,(T_{Q1})$ **vs Total Bus Utilization**
10 μsec Switching Overhead per Poll, Eight Bit Header/Packet
1 MBPS Transmission Speed, 500 Bits/Packet for Queue 1 and 2
Squared Coefficient of Variation Packet Length: Queue 1=1, Queue 2=2

transmission medium, and the delays encountered by messages from the station with lighter utilization will be higher than if the other station were not present. This is presented to show that even for something supposedly as *simple* as two queues, we should measure

- The arrival statistics

- The packet length statistics

- The packet header and overhead time per poll

11.6.1 Additional Reading

[1] J.S.Sykes, *Simplified Analysis of an Alternating Priority Queueing Model with Set Up Times,* Operations Research, **18** (6), 1182-1192 (1970).

[2] M.Eisenberg, *Two Queues with Changeover Times,* Operations Research, **19** (2), 386-401 (1971).

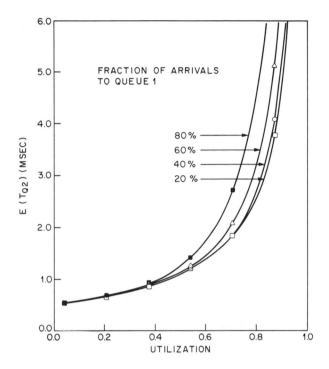

Figure 11.11. $E\,(T_{Q2})$ **vs Total Bus Utilization**
10 μsec Switching Overhead per Poll, Eight Bit Header/Packet
1 MBPS Transmission Speed, 500 Bits/Packet for Queue 1 and 2
Squared Coefficient of Variation Packet Length: Queue 1 = 1, Queue 2 = 2

11.6.2 Model Here is one model for analyzing performance of a token passing
or polling system:

- N stations each generate messages according to simple Poisson arrival
  statistics, with mean message interarrival time $1/\lambda$ (each station generates
  messages with the *same* arrival statistics)

- The messages form a sequence of independent identically distributed
  random variables drawn from an arbitrary distribution with message
  transmission time denoted by T_M (each station generates messages with the
  same message length statistics)

- The stations are visited in a cyclic manner; after all messages are removed
  from the buffer at one station, i.e., the service is exhaustive, a time interval
  of duration T_O passes doing overhead work before reaching the next station;
  all messages are removed from that next station, including both messages
  present at the arrival to that station and messages that arrive during the
  transmission of the initial workload; finally, the next overhead time interval
  is entered

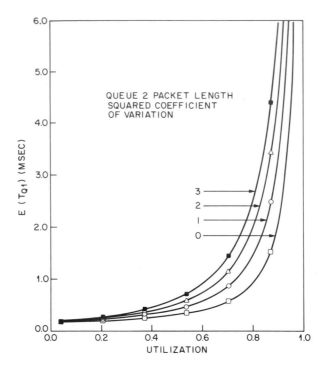

Figure 11.12. $E(T_{Q1})$ **vs Total Bus Utilization**
10 μsec Switching Overhead per Poll, Eight Bit Header/Packet
3 MBPS Transmission Speed, 500 Bits/Packet for Queue 1 and 2
20% Total Arrivals to Queue 1; Queue 1 Packet Length Sq Coef Var = 1

Granted these assumptions, it can be shown that the mean waiting time (the time a message is delayed due to waiting for the token plus waiting for all earlier arrivals to be transmitted) is given by

$$E(T_W) = \frac{N\lambda E(T_M{}^2)}{2(1 - N\lambda E(T_M))} + \tfrac{1}{2}E(T_O)\,\frac{1 - \lambda E(T_M)}{1 - N\lambda E(T_M)}$$

The mean waiting with zero overhead, with messages transmitted in order of arrival, gives a *lower* bound on the mean waiting time with polling:

$$E_{polling}(T_W) = E_{order\ of\ arrival}(T_W) + E_{overhead}(T_W) \geqslant E_{order\ of\ arrival}(T_W)$$

$$E_{order\ of\ arrival}(T_W) = \frac{N\lambda E(T_M{}^2)}{2(1 - N\lambda E(T_M))}$$

$$E_{overhead}(T_W) = \tfrac{1}{2}E(T_O)\,\frac{1 - \lambda(T_M)}{1 - N\lambda E(T_M)}$$

The first term depends on both the first and second moments of the message length statistics, as claimed. The second term in the mean waiting time expression using polling is due to irregularities or fluctuations in the cycle

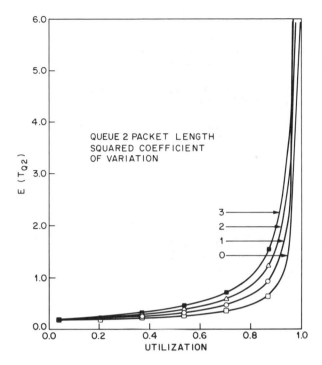

Figure 11.13. $E(T_{Q2})$ **vs Total Bus Utilization**
10 μsec Switching Overhead per Poll, Eight Bit Header/Packet
3 MBPS Transmission Speed, 500 Bits/Packet for Queue 1 and 2
20% Total Arrivals to Queue 2; Queue 1 Packet Length Sq Coef Var = 1

times.

The mean delay, queueing plus transmission, is given by

$$E(T_D) = E(T_W) + E(T_M)$$

This analysis is useful for developing a great deal of insight into the behavior of communication systems.

11.6.3 An Example: N Stations Generating Identical Message Traffic A communication system consists of a single serially reusable resource, a serial bus, shared by N stations. The bus utilization or offered load is fixed, measured in the fraction of time that the transmission medium is busy transmitting data, and excluding the fraction of time the transmission medium is used for token passing control. As the number of stations is increased so that the amount of data per message per station decreases toward zero, then the mean waiting time or delay experienced by any station in transmitting a message will increase above any fixed threshold, because more and more time will be spent passing the control token from one station to another rather than transmitting data. In this sense, token passing is said to be *unstable*. The figure below plots mean message waiting time (excluding message transmission time) for twenty to one hundred stations, as a function of bus utilization. The remaining parameters are summarized in the table below.

Table 11.1.Model Parameters

Bus Clock Rate	10 MBPS
Token Header	96 Bits
Round Trip Propagation	20 μsec
T_{token}	29.6 μsec

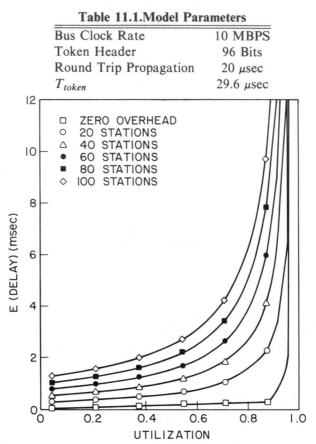

Figure 11.14.Mean Message Waiting Time vs Bus Utilization

Under light loading on the bus, a station will have to wait for the token to circulate through one half of the total number of stations N before it will be allowed to transmit:

$$T_W = \tfrac{1}{2}\, T_{token}\, N \quad light\ loading$$

Each message is assumed to be one thousand bits long, and hence requires one hundred microseconds to be transmitted, T_M. This determines the maximum mean throughput rate:

$$maximum\ mean\ throughput\ rate = \frac{1}{T_{token} + T_M} \quad messages/sec$$

If we fix the utilization, the fraction of time the bus is busy with data transmission, and increase the number of stations, each station will be less and less likely to have a message to transmit, but we will still pass the token through each station, increasing the total message waiting time.

What have we learned? The utilization of the serially reusable resource, the link or bus, may be an inadequate or incomplete measure of system loading: we must also describe how many stations are attached, and how active each of them is, in order to say anything concerning the traffic handling characteristics of such a system. Stating that a network is fifty per cent loaded, does *not* imply than congestion delays will be negligible. More information concerning *how* the network is being used, how *many* stations are doing what sorts of things are required.

11.6.4 Polling Stations with Different Workloads What about different stations generating different message loads? Some stations generate and receive more messages than other stations. One way to handle this is to think of bounding two extreme cases:

- All the messages are generated by one station, which will be the *best* possible delay performance

- All the messages are generated equally by all stations, which will be the *worst* possible delay performance

To do the best case, we assume an intervisit model where the token is passed to $(N-1)$ other stations and then to the station with all the work.

To handle the worst case, we use the formula given in the earlier part of this section.

Combining these two analyses, we plot the mean message queueing time versus bus utilization below using ten megabit transmission speed, and typical protocol header bits, and bus propagation time. Always plot these graphs to see how important imbalance is *first* before jumping to conclusions! For twenty stations, for practical purposes the two bounds are identical; for one hundred stations, the two bounds *can* be far apart. For twenty stations, no more analysis may be needed; for one hundred, more data should be gathered on message traffic.

11.6.5 Terminal Polling vs Host Computer Polling Measurements are carried out on a communication system. First, the frequency of arriving messages per terminal is measured:

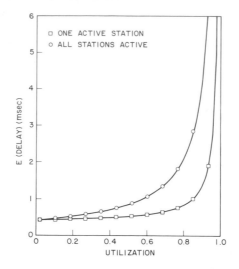

Figure 11.15.A.Mean Message Queueing Time vs Data Link Utilization, 20 Stations

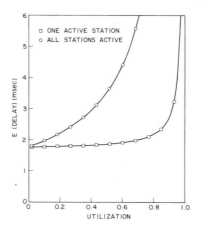

Figure 11.15.B.Mean Message Queueing Time vs Data Link Utilization, 100 Stations

Table 11.2.Terminal Arrival Statistics

Messages per Hour	Interarrival Time(sec)	Messages per Hour	Interarrival Time(sec)
10	360	30	120
15	240	35	103
20	180	40	90
25	144	45	80

The terminal transmission statistics are given by the following distribution:

Table 11.3.Terminal to Computer Transmission Statistics

Percentage	Number of Eight Bit Characters
40%	80 characters
20%	81-320 characters--mid range 200 characters
20%	321-700 characters--mid range 510 characters
20%	701-1500 characters--1100 characters

The distribution of the number of characters received by each terminal is given in the table below:

Table 11.4.Computer to Terminal Transmission Statistics

Percentage	Number of Eight Bit Characters
20%	80-240 characters--mid range 160 characters
20%	241-480 characters--mid range 360 characters
20%	481-720 characters--mid range 600 characters
20%	721-1440 characters--mid range 1080 characters
20%	1441-1920 characters--mid range 1680 characters

We are interested in the mean number of characters transmitted (both ways) per polling visit to an active station, and its variance; this is simply the sum of the means and variances, respectively, of the total number of characters transmitted both ways per polling visit.

$$C_S{}^2 = \frac{variance\ of\ number\ of\ transmitted\ characters}{[mean\ number\ of\ transmitted\ characters]^2}$$

Note that the message distribution may be adequately modeled by an Erlang 3 distribution (why?). Generate a quantile-quantile plot to check this!

For the numbers of interest here, using the above distributions, we see

mean number of transmitted characters = 1176 *characters*

variance of number of transmitted characters = 447,968 *characters*^{2}

squared coefficient of variation = 0.3272

Thus, the fluctuations are not nearly as great as an exponential distribution would generate, based on this criterion.

We now combine all this information to determine the desired number of terminals.

- Two configurations are considered, one with host computers alone, one with terminals alone

- The mean interarrival time of messages from terminals (30 seconds) or from host computers (30 msec)

- The transmission speed of the link (one, three and ten megabits per second)

- The number of characters required to interrogate a given terminal to determine if it has a message or not, called a flag (eight to twenty four bits)

- The one way propagation time of a bit (one to ten microseconds)

- Message length statistics: mean value of one thousand to two thousand bits per message, with a squared coefficient of variation of zero or one. The one way propagation time was fixed at five microseconds.

The tables below summarize the results of various calculations for such a system:

Table 11.5.Maximum Number of Sources with Mean Response 10 msec or Less

Interarrival Time	*One Megabit/Sec Line Speed--Mean Message Size=1000 Bits Squared Coefficient of Variation for Message Length=0*			
	Number of Bits of Overhead/Source			
	0 bits	*8 bits*	*16 bits*	*24 bits*
30 sec	29,995	2,093	1,085	732
30 msec	30	30	30	29

Table 11.6.Maximum Number of Sources with Mean Response 10 msec or Less

Interarrival Time	*Three Megabit/Sec Line Speed--Mean Message Size=1000 bits Squared Coefficient of Variation for Message Length=0*			
	Number of Bits of Overhead/Source			
	0 bits	*8 bits*	*16 bits*	*24 bits*
30 sec	89,973	6,708	3,484	2,353
30 msec	90	89	88	87

Table 11.7.Maximum Number of Sources with Mean Response 10 msec or Less

Interarrival Time	*Ten Megabit/Sec Line Speed--Mean Message Size=1000 bits Squared Coefficient of Variation for Message Length=0*			
	Number of Bits of Overhead/Source			
	0 bits	*8 bits*	*16 bits*	*24 bits*
30 sec	299,910	22,858	11,882	8,028
30 msec	300	297	293	290

In addition, the mean message length was varied to two thousand bits per message, which halved all the above numbers, the squared coefficient of variation was varied to one, which changed the above numbers by at most hundredths of a percent, the threshold was varied to twenty milliseconds with virtually no change on the above numbers, and the one way propagation time was varied from zero to thirty microseconds with virtually no impact.

The numbers chosen here show that

- The terminal interarrival time per message, line speed, and mean message size are significant in determining traffic handling characteristics

- The overhead per source visit, the threshold chosen, and the one way propagation time have less of an impact on system behavior

Again, we stress that a variety of other factors, such as the hardware and software design for the communications interface, can and must be considered in assessing this approach for a given application.

11.6.6 Additional Reading

[1] R.B.Cooper and G.Murray, *Queues Served in Cyclic Order*, Bell System Technical Journal, **48** (3), 675-689 (1969).

[2] R.B.Cooper, *Queues Served in Cyclic Order: Waiting Times*, Bell System Technical Journal, **49** (3), 399-413 (1970).

[3] A.G.Konheim, B.Meister, *Waiting Lines and Times in a System with Polling*, J.A.C.M., **21** (3), 470-490 (1974).

[4] P.J.Kuehn, *Multiqueue Systems with Nonexhaustive Cyclic Service*, Bell System Technical Journal, **58** (4), 671-698 (1979).

11.7 Carrier Sense Collision Detection

The figure below shows illustrative operation of a carrier sense collision detection system; stations zero, one, four and seven have messages to transmit, just as in the token passing polling case. In the scenario shown there, two collisions occur, and stations seven and four transmit earlier than in the token passing access. In the illustrative scenario shown, stations zero and one attempt to seize the channel simultaneously within a collision window; both schedule retransmissions for a later point in time, and so forth until all messages are transmitted.

Almost immediate media access is possible under light traffic. Put differently, the waiting time is zero under light load, and hence

$$T_W = 0 \quad one \ out \ of \ N \ active \ \rightarrow mean \ throughput \ rate = \frac{1}{T_M}$$

If a station can exhaustively transmit, then the utilization of the transmission medium can be driven to one hundred per cent. However, this can lead to unacceptable delays as some stations are locked out by other stations. Traffic can be controlled by limiting the maximum number of frames transmitted per local area network access by each station; this allows stations that rarely generate messages a chance to access the local area network, while delaying those stations with a lot of message traffic. On the other hand, the utilization of the transmission medium cannot be driven to one hundred per cent. Time required to resolve conflicts is unbounded because *no* station is successful in

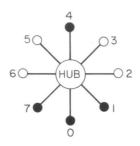

Figure 11.16.Illustrative Operation of CSCD

transmitting its message when a collision occurs (positive feedback!). If the total offered load (bits per unit time) is fixed but the number of stations is increased, more and more collisions will take place to transmit one message, hence the mean delay and message waiting time will increase above any threshold. Utilization is not a complete measure of the loading on a carrier sense collision detection local area network, and more information must be given about the number of stations and what each station is doing in order to say *anything* concerning delay. The mean waiting time to transmit a message grows faster than any linear function of the number of stations attached to the local area network.

A fundamental parameter in a carrier sense collision detection local area network is the *slot time* (denoted here by T_{slot}) which roughly speaking is the worst case time required for a signal to propagate from one end of the network to another, plus account for circuitry transients. A variety of theoretical analyses for carrier sense collision detection access for a local area network have suggested that if N identical stations are connected to the bus, with each station always idle, the maximum mean throughput rate of this system is

$$mean\ throughput\ rate \leqslant \frac{1}{T_M + (2e-1)T_{slot}}$$

In words, there will be roughly 2e=5.43.. collisions for every successful message transmission. This has *not* been validated by controlled experimentation on actual networks. A great deal of evidence (both analytical and simulation) suggest this is in fact a very reasonable first cut sizing of maximum mean

556

throughput rate.

What about mixing voice and data with such an access policy? Again, there are no publicly available and independently reproducible results to date, but there is a body of evidence that suggests the following scenario is quite plausible. We will assume voice will require 64 KBPS of transmission capacity for the duration of a voice telephone call, say one hundred seconds. With a 10 MBPS transmission speed, we can have at most the following number of simultaneous voice telephone calls:

$$maximum \ number \ of \ simultaneous \ voice \ telephone \ calls = \frac{10 \ MBPS}{64 \ KBPS} \approx 156$$

For virtually any scenario proposed to date involving digital voice and low speed data transmission, the total number of bits transmitted will be predominantly voice: check this yourself. People typically make three to six telephone calls per peak business work hour, lasting two to three minutes each on the average, which generates a lot of voice bits relative to the amount of data bits each person might generate.

If we have much less than this maximum number of simultaneous voice telephone calls in progress, then it may be possible for the data messages to be interleaved with voice packets. If we have much more than this number of simultaneous voice telephone calls in progress, because we have many many more voice packets than data packets the voice packets will be more much more likely to be successfully transmitted (this is the nature of the access method), voice packets will swamp the transmission capacity, and data packets will be locked out from using the local area network.

Suppose we have much less than the maximum number of simultaneous voice telephone calls in progress, say 100 simultaneous voice telephone calls during a peak business work hour. Rarely, say one per cent of the time, there will be a surge or fluctuation about this mean value, and we will have *all* the available transmission capacity occupied with voice packets. There are thirty six hundred seconds in one hour, so one per cent of the time, or thirty six seconds out of the hour, the local area network will be completely busy with voice: as far as data is concerned, the local area network will have failed, i.e., there is no transmission capacity for data. Furthermore, the duration of these surges of voice will be ten seconds here, five seconds there, fairly unpredictable, throughout a business hour. Remember there are higher level protocols for flow control with timeouts: these additional control mechanisms were not designed for handling voice and data, only data, and as far as data is concerned, the local area network has failed at this point. The question is not *will* this occur but rather *how often* will this occur: in order to answer that, we clearly need to be more specific about the voice services and data services, but the phenomenon we have just described must be present: the time scale for voice is tens of seconds, while the time scale for data is tens of milliseconds, and hence a short fluctuation in voice load looks like it lasts for a very very long time in the world of data.

At the present time, our understanding of carrier sense collision detection access is relatively incomplete compared with that for token passing access: we understand how one station loads the system, and how an infinite number of stations load the system, but we have no idea of any intermediate (such as *two* stations) case, either in terms of simulations or analysis or data (best of all), for one service or a mix of services.

11.8 Carrier Sense Access Loss Model Analysis

We will analyze two modes of operation, one without any synchronization between stations and one with a clock synchronizing station message transmission attempts. The basic period of the clock is called a *time slot,* and hence the two analyses are for *unslotted* and *slotted* operation, respectively.

11.8.1 Unslotted Operation with Loss   All attempts are assumed to obey simple Poisson arrival statistics with mean arrival rate of messages λ. Since there is no synchronization between source arrivals, i.e., they occur randomly in time, this mode of operation is called *unslotted*. The message transmission types are independent identically distributed random variables drawn from an arbitrary distribution denoted by $G_{T_M}(X) = PROB[T_M \leqslant X]$ with associated Laplace Stieltjes transform $\hat{G}_{T_M}(z)$. If a source has been listening to the channel for at least T_{OV} time units, and the channel is busy with another message over that time, then the attempt from that source is rejected or lost, and presumably will retry later. The moment generating function for the random variable for the time interval between successful message transmission completion epochs, denoted T_S, is given by, from these definitions

$$E[exp(-zT_S)] =$$

$$\frac{\lambda}{\lambda + z} \left[e^{-\lambda T_o} \hat{G}_{T_M}(z) + \int_0^{T_o} \lambda e^{-\lambda X} dX e^{-zX} \hat{G}_\Delta(z) E(exp(-zT_S)) \right]$$

where Δ is the smallest value of t such that the backward recurrence time from an arrival epoch of a Poisson process with rate λ is T_O. For example, the mean duration of time between successful message transmissions is

$$E(T_S) = E(T_M) - T_O + \frac{e^{2T_o\lambda}}{\lambda}$$

The mean utilization of the channel is denoted by U, where

$$U = \frac{E(T_M)}{E(T_S)}$$

This reaches its maximum value when $2 \lambda T_O = 1$:

$$\max U = \frac{E(T_M)}{E(T_M) + T_O(2e - 1)}$$

The interpretation of this is that for every successful message transmission, under maximum link utilization, there will be $2e - 1 \approx 5.39$ collisions for every successful transmission. By way of contrast, in a space satellite link, we would choose $E(T_M)$ equal to T_O, i.e., each message will take as long to transmit as it takes to propagate from the transmitter to the receiver, so

$$\max U = \frac{1}{2e} \quad E(T_M) = T_O$$

As an example, suppose that a number of asynchronous terminals can all transmit over a shared 9.6 KBPS channel to a central computer, and if the terminal packet is received without error the central computer broadcasts back to all the terminals over a separate 9.6 KBPS channel an acknowledgement. If no acknowledgement is received, the terminal will try again. An operator at a terminal can type one to two key strokes per second, or ten to twenty bits per second; we will split the difference and call it fifteen bits per second. How many terminals can the link support? If the link is a radio link, with a slot time of 50 μ seconds, then

$$\max U = \frac{15 \ bits / 9600 \ bps}{15 \ bits / 9600 \ bps + 50 \ \mu sec \ (2e - 1)} \approx 85.3\%$$

With perfect scheduling, each terminal demands 15 bps of bandwidth, and hence the largest possible number of terminals is $(9600/15) = 640$ terminals. In fact, we can only utilize the channel 85.3% at most, and so the largest number of terminals this could support is 85.3% of 640 terminals, or 545 terminals. How do we interpret this number? If we never have more than two hundred terminals actively using the system, this is fine; most terminals will simply transmit a keystroke and receive an acknowledgement, with little load on the link. If we have one thousand or more terminals simultaneously using the system, most terminals will experience unacceptable delays.

11.8.2 Slotted Operation with Loss In a slotted system there is a common clock or measure of time for all stations. Time is broken up into equal length time intervals called time slots, and all attempts are made at the start of a slot. For this case,

$$\max U = \frac{E(T_M)}{E(T_M) + T_O(e - 1)}$$

The interpretation of this is that under maximum link utilization, there are

$e-1 \approx 1.71$ collisions for every successful message transmission. For the space satellite application with $E(T_M) = T_O$, we see

$$\max U = \frac{1}{e} \qquad E(T_M) = T_O$$

In our example of terminals generating fifteen bits per second of traffic over a 9600 bps link, with a 50 μ second overhead time, we see that the maximum link utilization can be increased to

$$\max U = \frac{15 \; bits/9600 \; bps}{15 \; bits/9600 \; bps \; + \; 50 \; \mu sec \, (e-1)} = 94.2\%$$

The maximum number of terminals the link can support is increased from 545 with unslotted or unsynchronized operation to 603 with slotted or synchronized operation. Is it worth it? This must be addressed relative to many other factors: link access performance is only one consideration.

11.8.3 Aloha Mean Throughput Rate Analysis Here is an analysis based on a different set of *assumptions* that leads to the same conclusions as the previous section.

Messages arrive to be transmitted over a serially reusable link according to simple Poisson arrival statistics, with mean arrival rate λ. The sequence of message transmission times are independent identically distributed random variables drawn from a common distribution $G_{T_M}(X)$ with $\hat{G}_{T_M}(z)$ denoting the associated moment generating function $E[exp(-zT_M)]$. If a message transmission attempt is made, and no other attempts are made for the duration of the message transmission, then the message transmission is successful. If two or more attempts to seize the channel are made during a message transmission, all attempts are unsuccessful or lost and will presumably retry later.

The fraction of time the transmission medium is idle is denoted by π_0, the fraction of time no message transmission attempts are being made, which must equal

$$\pi_0 = e^{-\lambda E(T_M)}$$

On the other hand, the mean transition rate out of this idle state, denoted R_0, multiplied by the mean sojourn time in this state, denoted $1/\lambda$, must equal the fraction of time the transmission medium is idle:

$$\pi_0 = \frac{R_0}{\lambda}$$

Next, we observe that the transition rate out of the idle state must equal the transition rate into the state where one message is being transmitted, denoted R_1:

$$R_1 = R_0$$

Finally, the rate of successfully transmitting messages is simply the rate of entering state of one active transmission and no other messages arriving during that transmission, denoted $\hat{G}_{T_M}(\lambda)$

$$R_S = R_1 \, \hat{G}_{T_M}(\lambda)$$

Combining all this, we see

$$R_0 = R_1 = \lambda e^{-\lambda E(T_M)}$$
$$R_S = \lambda e^{-\lambda E(T_M)} \hat{G}_{T_M}(\lambda)$$

For the special case where the message transmission time distribution is deterministic, we see

$$R_S = \lambda e^{-2\lambda E(T_M)}$$

If we maximize the mean throughput rate over the message arrival rate, we find that

$$\max_{\lambda} R_S \approx \frac{1}{2e} \frac{1}{E(T_M)}$$

which is what we found in the earlier section, under different assumptions.

11.8.4 Additional Reading

[1] N.Abramson, *The Throughput of Packet Broadcasting Channels,* IEEE Transactions on Communications, **25,** 117-128 (1977).

[2] G.T.Almes, E.D.Lazowska, *The Behavior of Ethernet-Like Computer Communications Networks,* Proceedings of Seventh Symposium on Operating Systems Principles, pp.66-81, Asilomar Grounds, Pacific Grove, California, 10-12 December 1979.

[3] D.R.Boggs, R.M.Metcalfe, *Ethernet: Distributed Packet Switching for Local Computer Networks,* Communications ACM, **19** (7), 395-404 (1976).

[4] A.B.Carleial, M.E.Hellman, *Bistable Behavior of ALOHA-Type Systems,* IEEE Transactions on Communications, **23** (4), 401-410 (1975).

[5] M.Kaplan, *A Sufficient Condition for Nonergodicity of a Markov Chain,* IEEE Transactions on Information Theory, **25** (4), 470-471 (1979).

[6] L.Kleinrock, S.S.Lam, *Packet Switching in a Multiaccess Broadcast Channel: Performance Evaluation,* IEEE Transactions on Communications, **23** (3), 410-422 (1975).

[7]   O.Spaniol, *Analysis and Performance Evaluation of HYPERchannel Access Protocols,* Performance Evaluation, **1**, 170-179 (1981).

[8]   F.Tobagi, *Multiaccess Protocols in Packet Communication Systems,* IEEE Transactions on Communications, **28** (4), 468-488 (1980).

11.9 Performance Analysis of Slotted P-Persistent Carrier Sense Access

Here is an analytically tractable model for CSCD that bounds not only mean throughput rate but also delay statistics.

11.9.1 Model   A set of stations are connected via a bus. Each station continuously senses the transmission medium to see if carrier is present. A clock synchronizes the actions of all stations, with the clock period called a time slot. A time slot is chosen equal to the worst case time for energy to propagate from one station to another plus allow all electronic transients to decay to acceptable levels. All transmission attempts begin at the start of a time slot, and all messages transmitted are an integral number of time slots. If a station has a message to transmit, it first attempts to seize the transmission medium by transmitting a preamble equal to one time slot in duration; if the preamble is transmitted without distortion (e.g., due to another station transmitting its preamble, which is called a collision), then the station proceeds to transmit its message. If the preamble is distorted, then a collision is said to occur, and each station involved in the collision will retry at a later point in time to go through the same process. In a local network, the preamble transmission time or time slot is typically small compared to the message transmission time. As the transmission speed increases, the slot time or time required to resolve contention becomes relatively more important compared to the mean message transmission time. The retry policy adopted here is called *p-persistent* because if station becomes active, and the transmission medium is busy (with either a message transmission or a collision), the station will wait (or persist) until the transmission medium becomes idle. The parameter p denotes the probability that a station involved in a collision will retry in the next time slot, or with probability $(1-p)$ repeat this retry process in the subsequent time slot.

Messages arrive according to a very particular pattern which is practical to implement as a test procedure or diagnostic in such systems: all but one of the stations always have a message to transmit. The remaining station generates message transmission attempts according to Poisson statistics. This will bound the delay for any one station, i.e., this is a *worst* case analysis. Furthermore, this analysis is *sharp* or *achievable,* and hence provides a simple check on operations.

11.9.2 Message Arrival Statistics   N stations are connected to a common transmission medium or bus. A clock signal with period T_{slot} is transmitted over the bus. Every station but one, i.e., a total of $(N-1)$ stations, always has a message to transmit. The final station has messages arrive for transmission according to simple Poisson arrival statistics with mean arrival rate λ.

11.9.3 Message Length Statistics The message length statistics are identical for all stations, with the message lengths forming a sequence of independent identically distributed random variables. The message transmission time T_M has moment generating function $E[e^{-zT_M}]$ given by

$$E[e^{-zT_M}] = \sum_{K=1}^{\infty} F(K)e^{-zKT_{slot}} \qquad \sum_{K=1}^{\infty} F(K) = 1, \ 0 \leqslant F(K) \leqslant 1$$

$F(K), K = 1, \dots$ is the fraction of messages requiring $K \geqslant 1$ time slots to be completely transmitted.

11.9.4 Station Buffering Policy Each station can buffer an infinite number of messages. Messages are transmitted in order of arrival from each station.

11.9.5 Transmission Medium Access Policy The transmission medium is a serially reusable resource. Contention for this shared resource is arbitrated as follows:

• All stations sense the state of the transmission medium at all times to see if it is busy

• If the transmission medium is not busy, then with probability p a station that has a message to transmit will attempt to transmit in the next time slot, and with probability $1-p$ will wait until the subsequent time slot and repeat this process

• If one station successfully seizes the transmission medium for one time slot, it will hold it for the duration of the message transmission

• If two or more stations attempt to seize the transmission medium during one time slot, neither will succeed, and both will retry according to the above policy

11.9.6 Goals We wish to calculate the mean throughput rate and delay statistics of D, the message delay statistics encountered by messages at one station, with all the other stations always having a message to transmit.

11.9.7 Analysis The probability that a given station is successful in seizing the transmission medium, given that a total of K stations actually have messages to transmit is given by Q_K:

$Q_K = PROB[a \ given \ station \ successfully \ seizes \ a \ time \ slot] = p(1-p)^{K-1}$

The sequence of time intervals that the server is absent (handling message transmissions and collisions) are independent identically distributed arbitrary random variables called intervisit times. The random variable for the delay in this model is the sum of three random variables

[1] The time interval from when a message arrives at a station until the local area network becomes idle, denoted $\tilde{V}$, the forward recurrence time of the intervisit time

[2] W, the time spent waiting to transmit all messages queued in the buffer of a station that arrived ahead of a given arrival

[3] $\tilde{T}_M$, the time measured from the start of the first transmission attempt until the message is successfully transmitted; this includes the time waiting for collisions and for other successful attempts by other stations attempting to use the channel, plus the time to actually transmit the message, T_M

Symbolically, this is written as

$$D = \tilde{V} + W + \tilde{T}_M$$

All of these random variables on the right hand side are statistically independent of one another:

- The forward recurrence time of the intervisit distribution depends on the load at the other stations and the arrival statistics of messages at the final station; the other stations always have a message to transmit

- The waiting time to transmit messages ahead of a given arrival depends only on the number of messages ahead of a given arrival, and not on the intervisit time statistics or the message transmission statistics of the given arrival

- The transmission time statistics depend only on the activity of the other stations and the access method, not on the intervisit statistics or waiting time statistics

The moment generating function of D is the product of the individual moment generating functions:

$$E[e^{-zD}] = E[e^{-z\tilde{V}}]E[e^{-zW}]E[e^{-z\tilde{T}_M}]$$

We now calculate each of these three individual moment generating functions.

11.9.8 Forward Recurrence Time Distribution Moment Generating Function
The moment generating function for the intervisit time V follows from decomposing an intervisit into two distinct events with different probabilities:

[1] The transmission medium is busy transmitting a message from one of the other $(N-1)$ stations

[2] The transmission medium is busy with a collision between two or more stations

The moment generating function of the intervisit time distribution is given by

$$E[e^{-zV}] = (N-1)Q_{N-1}E[e^{-zT_M}] + [1-(N-1)Q_{N-1}]e^{-zT_{slot}}$$

The moment generating function for the forward recurrence time distribution is given by

$$E[e^{-z\tilde{V}}] = \frac{1-E[e^{-zV}]}{zE(V)}$$

11.9.9 Waiting Time Distribution Moment Generating Function The waiting time moment generating function is given by

$$E[e^{-zW}] = \frac{z[1-\lambda E(\tilde{T}_M)]}{z-\lambda[1-E(e^{-z\tilde{T}_M})]} \qquad \lambda E[\tilde{T}_M] < 1$$

In words, we demand that the mean arrival rate of messages be less than the total time required to successfully transmit a message $(\lambda E(\tilde{T}_M) < 1$.

11.9.10 Moment Generating Function of Inflated Transmission Time Distribution The final moment generating function, for the message transmission time, involves taking into account three distinct events:

[1] With probability Q_N the last station will succeed and hold the transmission medium for an interval of duration T_M

[2] With probability $(N-1)Q_N$ one of the other $(N-1)$ stations will succeed and hold the transmission medium for an interval of duration $\tilde{T}_M$ and then the last station will succeed and hold the transmission medium for an interval of duration T_M

[3] With probability $1-NQ_N$ there will be a collision consuming a time slot of duration T_{slot} followed by a time interval of duration $\tilde{T}_M$.

Combining all these terms, the moment generating function for $\tilde{T}_M$ is given by

$$E[e^{-z\tilde{T}_M}] =$$

$$Q_N E[e^{-zT_M}] + (N-1)Q_N E[e^{-zT_M}]E[e^{-z\tilde{T}_M}] + [1-NQ_N]E[e^{-z\tilde{T}_M}]e^{-zT_{slot}}$$

$$E[e^{-z\tilde{T}_M}] = \frac{Q_N E[e^{-zT_M}]}{1-(N-1)Q_N E[e^{-zT_M}] - [1-NQ_N]e^{-zT_{slot}}}$$

The mean or first moment of the delay process is given by

$$E(D) = E(\tilde{V}) + E(W) + E(\tilde{T}_M)$$

$$E(\tilde{V}) = \frac{(N-1)Q_{N-1}E(T_M^2) + T_{slot}^2[1-(N-1)Q_{N-1}]}{2(N-1)Q_{N-1}E(T_M) + 2T_{slot}[1-(N-1)Q_{N-1}]}$$

$$E(W) = \frac{\lambda E(\tilde{T}^2{}_M)}{2(1-\lambda E(\tilde{T}_M))}$$

$$E(\tilde{T}_M) = NE(T_M) + \frac{T_{slot}(1-NQ_N)}{Q_N}$$

$$E(\tilde{T}^2{}_M) =$$

$$NE(T^2{}_M) + (N-1)E(T_M)E(\tilde{T}_M) + \frac{1-NQ_N}{Q_N}[T^2_{slot}+2T_{slot}E(\tilde{T}_M)]$$

There are two regions of operation:

- Light loading, $\lambda \rightarrow 0$, where the mean delay is dominated by the mean of the forward recurrence time of the intervisit time plus the mean of the inflated message transmission time

$$E(D) \approx E(\tilde{V}) + E(\tilde{T}_M) \quad \lambda \rightarrow 0$$

- Heavy loading, $\lambda \rightarrow 1/E(\tilde{T}_M)$, where the mean delay is dominated by the mean waiting time to transmit messages

$$E(D) \approx E(W) \quad \lambda \rightarrow \frac{1}{E(\tilde{T}_M)}$$

$E(\tilde{T}_M)$ equals a term proportional to each station transmitting a message plus a term that is dependent on controlling access to the channel. The mean or first moment of message delay depends not only on the *first* but also the *second* moment of the message transmission time distribution. Thus, knowing only the mean message length only allows the maximum mean throughput rate to be determined, but *nothing* can be said concerning mean delay unless information about fluctuations about the mean message transmission time is available.

There is still one degree of freedom left: how do we choose p? One way to choose p is to maximize the mean throughput rate, i.e., to choose p such that we have the largest mean arrival rate to one queue that still results in a nondegenerate statistical equilibrium distribution. This results in choosing $p=1/N$. In words, each station that is competing for access is equally likely to gain control of the transmission medium when it becomes available. For sufficiently many stations, $N \gg 1$, the condition for statistical equilibrium becomes

$$N\lambda < \frac{1}{E(T_M)+T_{slot}(e-1)} \quad N \gg 1$$

A different way of interpreting this result is to consider the channel in one of two states. The first state is due to arbitration or controlling access, and has mean duration $(e-1)T_{slot}$. The second state is due to successful data transmission, and has mean duration $E(T_M)$. The maximum mean throughput rate, which we identify with $N\lambda$, is the reciprocal of the sum of the mean time spent in each state. The mean access time is controlled by the worst case propagation of energy from one end of the transmission medium to the other, while the mean message transmission time is controlled by the mean message size (measured in bits) and the data transmission rate (measured in bits per second). One way to understand the interaction of these parameters is to see when $(e-1)T_{slot}$ equals $E(T_M)$, because at this point half of the time is spent in message transmission and half is spent in controlling channel access. A different type of insight is that for high maximum mean throughput rate we wish to design the system so that little time is spent in controlling access and most of the time is spent in data transmission, i.e., $E(T_M)$ must be much greater than $(e-1)T_{slot}$. This can occur by increasing the message length (in bits) or decreasing the data transmission rate (in bits per second), holding all other parameters fixed.

11.9.11 Illustrative Numerical Studies We now turn to an illustrative case study to numerically explore design consequences.

11.9.12 Parameters The model ingredients are

- Arrival statistics

  - Number of stations--20, 40, 60, 80, 100 stations

  - Arrival rate of messages at each station--All but one station always has a message, while the final station has messages arriving according to Poisson statistics with rate λ

- Message length statistics

  - Message length distribution (in bits)-- Exponentially distributed and constant length messages, with means of 500, 1000, and 2000 bits per message

  - One way propagation time of energy from one end to the other-- ten or twenty microseconds

  - Transmission rate, measured in bits per second-- One, three or ten megabits per second

11.9.13 Maximum Mean Throughput Rate The figures below plot the carried data transmission rate versus the actual data transmission rate for these parameters. If the channel were used for data transmission alone, this would be a straight line with slope one; since the channel is used for control and data transmission, the result is a curve that lies below the zero overhead straight line. The distance from the straight line zero overhead case to the actual curve shows the amount of transmission capacity devoted to controlling channel access.

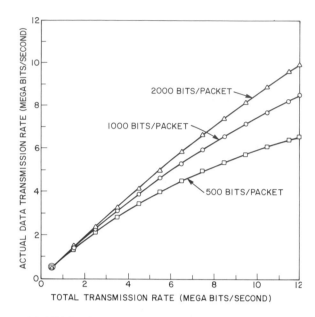

Figure 11.17.Maximum Mean Throughput Rate vs Clock Rate

11.9.14 Message Delay Statistics Next, we fix the mean fraction of time the transmission medium is busy transmitting data, which is called the *utilization,* and equals the mean arrival rate of messages multiplied by the mean message transmission time; since the mean message length is fixed, this fixes the mean arrival rate. The figures below plot illustrative upper bounds on mean delay versus line utilization due to data transmission alone for the numbers described above. The parameter p is chosen to the reciprocal of the number of stations in all cases.

For example, with fifty per cent utilization, one hundred stations, ten megabits transmission speed, one thousand bits per constant length message, ten microseconds one way propagation time (one hundred bit transmission times), the mean delay is upper bounded by over 1.4 seconds. If we halve the message length to five hundred bits, the upper bound on mean message delay does *not* halve, but drops to 0.9 seconds; if we double the message length to two thousand bits, the upper bound on mean message delay does *not* double, but increases to 2.3 seconds. If we increase the slot time from ten to twenty microseconds, with one thousand bits per constant length message, and a transmission rate of ten megabits per second, the upper bound on mean message delay increases to 1.8 seconds. Finally, changing the shape of the message length distribution by going from constant to exponentially distributed message lengths, has negligible impact on the upper bound on mean delay.

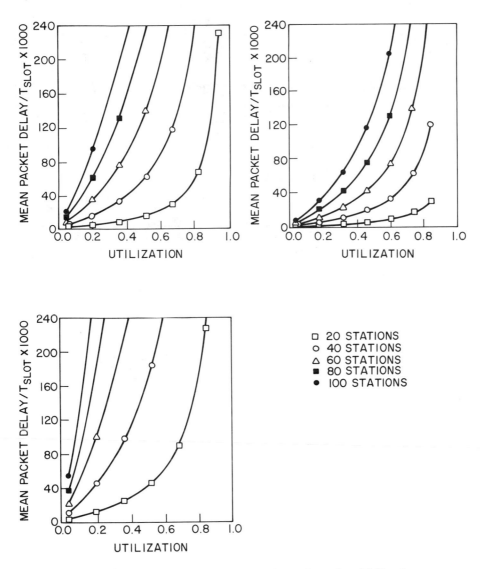

Figure 11.18.Mean Message Delay Upper Bound vs Utilization
1000 Bits/Packet; Constant Packet Size; $T_{prop}=10\mu sec$
Lower Left: 1 MBPS; Upper Left: 3 MBPS; Upper Right: 10 MBPS

11.9.15 Interpretation   These numerical plots quantify the following phenomena:

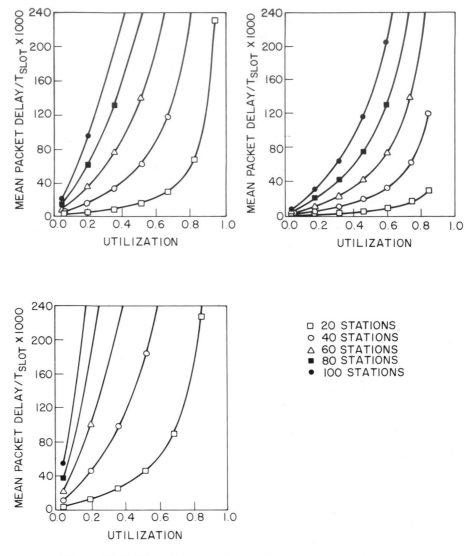

Figure 11.19.Mean Message Delay Upper Bound vs Utilization
1000 Bits/Packet; Exponential Packet Size Distribution; $T_{prop}=10\mu sec$
Lower Left: 1 MBPS; Upper Left: 3 MBPS; Upper Right: 10 MBPS

- As the slot time increases, with all other parameters fixed, the mean delay upper bound increases and the maximum bandwidth available for data transmission decreases.

- As the mean packet length increases, with all other parameters fixed, the mean delay upper bound increases and the maximum bandwidth available for data transmission increases.

- As the fluctuations about mean packet length increase from constant to exponential distribution, the mean delay upper bound increases and the maximum bandwidth available for data transmission is not affected.

- As more and more stations are added, with all other parameters fixed, in particular with the mean utilization of the link due to data transmission fixed, the maximum bandwidth available for data transmission is not affected, but the mean delay upper bound increases.

11.10 Reservation Decision Tree Access via a Bus

Reservation decision tree access is the least studied access method of the proposed bus access methods. The figure below shows illustrative operation of a reservation decision tree access policy, where the station addresses are used to determine retry priorities for stations involved in message collisions.

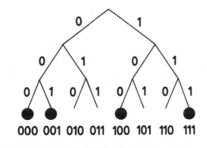

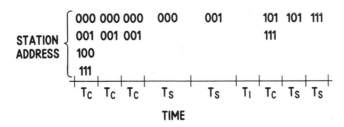

Figure 11.20. Reservation Decision Tree Access

An illustrative scenario begins at the start of a frame, when all stations that have a message to transmit go active and collide. The retry policy involves a controlled priority arbitration among all stations active at the start of the frame, with the station addresses used to determine or control the retry priorities.* After the first collision, only those stations whose most significant address bit is a zero can retry, and all other stations are silent: stations zero and one will attempt to transmit in the next time slot, and stations four and seven will defer transmission attempts. Once more, stations zero and one transmit during the same time slot, and now all stations whose first two leading address bits are zero will attempt to transmit in the next slot, and all other stations will defer: stations zero and one will attempt to transmit, while stations four and seven will defer transmission attempts. Once more stations zero and one transmission attempts collide in the next time slot, and now only those stations with three leading address bits all zero will attempt to transmit in the next time slot: only station zero will retry, and stations one, four and seven will defer. In the next time slot, station zero succeeds in transmitting. Now we allow all stations whose leading address bits are two zeroes followed by a one to transmit in the next time slot: station one will transmit then, with stations four and seven deferring. Now all stations with a leading zero and one address bit are allowed to transmit in the next time slot: this would be stations two and three, neither of which has a message, and hence the time slot is an idle time slot. All stations whose address begins with a zero have been allowed to transmit and have successfully transmitted a message, if they had one at the start of the frame. Now we repeat the process: all stations with a leading address bit of one, stations four and seven, attempt to transmit in the next time slot, and their attempts collide. In retrying, all stations with a leading address bit sequence of one followed by zero, which is only station four, attempt to transmit in the next time slot: station four is successful. Finally, all stations with leading address bits of one followed by one, which is only station seven, attempt to transmit in the next time slot: station seven is successful. The figure is a graphical summary of this process.

Why does this look like carrier sense collision detection under light load? Because if only one station has a message, it will transmit it immediately. Why does this look like token passing or polling under heavy load? Because if every station has a message, we will have 2^N-1 collisions for 2^N stations, hence we will effectively pass a token 2^N-1 times among 2^N stations. The key observation here is that we wish to interrogate groups of stations once a collision occurs, with at most one station in each group having a message. By controlling the retry process, making it quite predictable and regular, we gain in traffic handling capability over irregular retry and retransmission.

---

* Those familiar with algorithms will recognize this as a topological binary tree sort, with the nodes of the tree being searched depth first, and then left to right; station retry priorities determine the graph.

The figure below shows illustrative operation of a related policy, where the messages are transmitted in order of arrival using the message arrival time to determine priority ordering; the next figure shows the associated decision tree used to arbitrate contention.

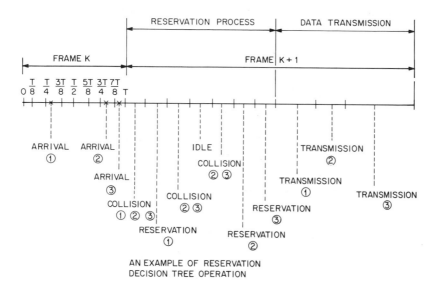

AN EXAMPLE OF RESERVATION
DECISION TREE OPERATION

Figure 11.21.Reservation Tree Access Order of Arrival Transmission

For this example we assume all stations have a clock available for determining the duration of each frame, unlike the previous example. The parameter T shown in the figure above is the duration of the *previous* frame: each station uses its clock to determine if it became active during the previous frame or not, and then each station refines this to determine in which half of the previous frame it became active, and then iterates. These are just two examples of the many possible policies that can be realized by this policy class.

Here are highlights of reservation access:

- Transceivers are logically organized into a tree, with the leaves of the tree determining the urgency of message transmission.

- After a collision, all messages involved in a collision are successfully transmitted before any subsequent arrivals are transmitted.

- All of the traffic handling hooks in polling can still be used (multiple visits per logical frame, maximum number of frames transmitted per visit, dedicating transmission capacity to each service).

We stress the following points:

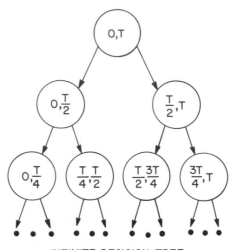

INFINITE DECISION TREE
TRANSMISSION IN ORDER OF ARRIVAL

Figure 11.22. Decision Tree for Order of Arrival Transmission

• Mean time required to resolve collisions per transmission is bounded by a logarithmic function of the number of ready transceivers (here for eight ready stations in the finite tree we need on the order of three collisions to the first successful transmission).

• Maximum time required to resolve collisions per transmission is bounded; the example for the finite tree shows that for eight stations at most seven collisions occur.

• Mean waiting is linearly proportional to the number of active stations: each station active at the start of each frame is guaranteed of being able to successfully transmit its message within each frame, and there are at most 2^N stations.

• There is roughly one control overhead time slot interval for every one successful message transmission, just as in central control (cf. the above examples). What is more subtle is that the variance of the overhead time per successful message transmission only grows *linearly* with the number of stations attempting to transmit at the start of a frame, just as in central control.

If we return to the first example, we see that an additional degree of freedom is available: at what priority level do we attempt to start our retry arbitration: using the most significant address bit of each station, or the two most significant address bits of each station, or so forth? One way to quantify our intuition on this is to examine the number of steps required (idle, collision, and transmission) as a function of the number of bits used for retry arbitration. This is summarized in the table below:

Table 11.8.Number of Steps vs Number of Bits for Initial Retry Priority

Number of Steps	Number of Bits for Initial Retry Priority			
	0	1	2	3
Idle	1	1	1	4
Collision	4	3	1	0
Transmit	4	4	4	4
Total	9	8	6	8

Hence, for this example, the optimum number of bits to use for starting the retry arbitration would be two bits. Under light traffic, the optimum level to start is zero bits just as in carrier sense collision detection. Under heavy traffic, the optimum level to start is three bits, just as in polling. Under light load, no control is needed on the number of retry bits; as load builds, we should start to use more and more station address bits in the priority arbitration retry process, because it is more and more likely stations are active.

One key feature of reservation decision tree access is its *transient* behavior: when a station is added or turned off, or fails in a wide variety of ways, the access policy, since it is carrier sense collision detection, is quite *robust* to these types of failures, and will recover within a finite time interval, at most one frame transmission time. The key difference between carrier sense collision detection access and reservation access is the retry policy: each station using reservation access must keep track of *two* parameters in counters, with one counter keeping track of the total tree frame (for synchronization of the start and end of frames) and the other keeping track of the subtree that is currently involved in collision resolution. In comparison, carrier sense collision detection requires a random number generator plus a counter, so the complexity of the two approaches on the surface may be comparable (at this level of analysis). In reservation access, the key identity for each frame for updating the counters is

number of messages transmitted + number of idle time slots =

number of collisions during a frame + 1

Hence, the global frame counter for all stations is set at one at the start of a frame, and is incremented by one every time a collision occurs and decremented by one every time a successful message transmission or idle time slot occurs; when this strikes zero, the frame has ended, and the process repeats. The same process occurs for a subtree counter. The table below shows the state of the two counters, frame synchronization (Frame) and transmission control (Control), for every station involved in transmission for the above example at the conclusion of each step, as well as whether the station is active (A) or idle (I) for the next step.

Table 11.9.Station States at Conclusion of Step in Decision Tree

Step Number	Station 0 Frame	Station 0 Control	Station 0 All	Station 1 Frame	Station 1 Control	Station 1 All	Station 4 Frame	Station 4 Control	Station 4 All	Station 7 Frame	Station 7 Control	Station 7 All
0	1	0	A	1	0	A	1	0	A	1	0	A
1	2	1	A	2	1	A	2	1	I	2	1	I
2	3	1	A	3	1	A	3	2	I	3	2	I
3	4	1	A	4	1	I	4	3	I	4	3	I
4	3	0	I	3	1	A	3	2	I	3	2	I
5	2	0	I	2	0	I	2	1	I	2	1	I
6	1	0	I	1	0	I	1	0	A	1	0	A
7	2	1	I	2	1	I	2	1	A	2	1	I
8	1	0	I	1	0	I	1	0	I	1	0	A
9	0	0	I	0	0	I	0	0	I	0	0	I

At each step, each station consults its priority index (the station address for the first example, the arrival time within the frame for the second example) and its transmission control and frame synchronization counter state. If a station becomes active during a frame, it will defer transmission attempts until the start of the next frame, when its frame synchronization counter strikes zero.

11.10.1 Decision Tree Search Access Performance Analysis Here are the results of a traffic analysis for the decision tree arbitration policy.

First we must specify the arrival statistics:

- The message interarrival times are independent identically distributed exponential random variables

- Message lengths are independent identically distributed arbitrary random variables with associated moment generating function $\hat{G}_M(x)$

Next the access method must be specified:

- Basic transmission time unit is a time slot. A frame is made up of a variable number of time slots

- Messages that arrive during a frame will be transmitted during the next frame

- Initial time slots within a frame are devoted to determining which sources have a message to transmit

- Final time slots within a frame are devoted to data transmission from active sources

The process $L_N, N > 0$ denotes the number of time slots consumed for reservation by N sources at the start of a frame. Its moment generating function is given by

$$\eta_N(x) = E[x^{L_N}]$$

It can be shown that

$$\lim_{N\to\infty} \frac{E(N)}{N} = \alpha = \frac{2}{\log_e(2)} \approx 2.88542...$$

$$\text{if } \lambda < \frac{1}{\alpha + E(T_{message})}$$

The mean message delay, including transmission plus waiting, is given by

$$E(T_{delay}) = E(T_{message}) + \frac{1 + \lambda E(T_{message})}{2\lambda} \times$$

$$\frac{\sum_{K=1}^{\infty} K(K-1)\pi_K}{\sum_{K=1}^{\infty} K\pi_K} + \frac{\sum_{K=1}^{\infty} \pi_K KE(L_K)}{\sum_{K=1}^{\infty} K\pi_K}$$

Note that the mean delay involves first and second moments of L_N. In some cases it may prove easier to work with upper and lower bounds on the first and second moments rather than the statistics of L_N. The tightest possible bounds known to the authors are

$$\underline{a}\,K + \underline{b} \leqslant E(L_K) \leqslant \bar{a}\,K + \bar{b}$$

$$\underline{c}\,K^2 + \underline{d}\,K + \underline{e} \leqslant E(L_K^2) \leqslant \bar{c}\,K^2 + \bar{d}\,K + \bar{e}$$

The best known coefficients for these bounds at the present time are

$$2.8810K - 1 \leqslant E(L_K) \leqslant 2.28965K - 1$$

$$8.300K^2 + 0.4880K + 1 \leqslant E[L_K(L_K-1)]$$

$$\leqslant 8.333K^2 + 0.5175K + 1$$

These expressions have been found to be useful in practice for rough sizing of system performance and to guide refinements of this analysis.

11.10.2 Additional Reading

[1] E.H.Frei, J.Goldberg, *A Method for Resolving Multiple Responses in a Parallel Search File*, IRE Transactions on Electronic Computers, **10** (4), 718-722 (1961).

[2] N.Pippenger, *Bounds on the Performance of Protocols for a Multiple-Access Broadcast Channel*, IEEE Transactions on Information Theory, **27** (2), 145-151 (1981).

[3]   I.Rubin, *Synchronous and Channel-Sense Asynchronous Dynamic Group-Random-Access Schemes for Multiple-Access Communications* IEEE Transactions on Communications, **31** (9) 1063-1077 (1983).

[4]   R.Seeber, A.B.Lindquist, *Associative Memory with Ordered Retrieval,* IBM J.Research and Development, **6** (1), 126-136 (1962).

11.11 Token Passing Access via a Ring

Token passing access via a ring is logically identical to that for a bus. We will only dwell on differences here between a bus and a ring. The physical topology of a ring is that each station transmits to only one station and receives from only one station. The token is a unique bit pattern that circulates around the ring. When it is transmitted to a station ready to send a packet, that station changes the token bit pattern on the fly, i.e., destroys the token, and then appends its packet. The packet circulates around the ring, to the intended receiving station, and then returns to the transmitting station to acknowledge complete successful transmission around the ring. Because of the geographic extent of the local area network, at most *one* packet can be circulating about the ring at any one time.

Since this is a variant on polling, a number of traffic load balancing mechanisms are available. *Separation* or *dedication* of transmission capacity to different types of services is still possible. The number of visits per polling cycle per station can be controlled, and the maximum number of frames transmitted per visit can be set. Overhead time per transmission is bounded by a linear function of the number of transceivers (typically this is a constant due to ring propagation and circuitry transients plus a linear term due to the transceiver processing) because control must be passed to each station at least once in a ring or polling cycle; this will typically be *much* smaller for a ring than for a bus, because the propagation is now only from station to station, not worst case from one end of the bus to the other, and because the transceiver token processing can be done in parallel (except for a delay on the order of one bit transmission time per interface). Typical numbers for token passing from station to station over a ring are one microsecond, while a bus requires ten times this typically. This improves delay access under light load, where typically we must wait for the token to be passed through half the stations, and it improves the maximum mean throughput rate under heavy load, since less time is spent in token passing versus message transmission. High throughput under heavy load is achieved because most of the time the transmission medium will be busy transmitting messages under load, not passing the token from station to station. Mean message delay time that is linear in the number of stations is achievable because if each station has a message to transmit then the waiting time at any one station is simply the time required for all other stations in the polling cycle to transmit.

11.11.1 Additional Reading

[1]   W.D.Farmer, E.E.Newhall, *An Experimental Distributed Switching System to Handle Bursty Computer Traffic,* Proc.ACM Symp.Problems in the Optimization of Data Communication Systems, pp.1-34, Pine Mountain, GA, October 1969.

11.12 Comparisons

What types of questions do we wish to answer in comparing different access methods? First, let's deal with mean value measurements and statistics, before turning to more sophisticated second order statistics involving fluctuations and correlation:

• What fraction of transmission capacity is devoted to control versus data transmission?

• What is the impact on transmission speed versus throughput and delay?

• How sensitive is system performance to a change in workload, such as changing the message length, or having voice and data services instead of just data?

• How do protocol parameters (length of header, carrier sense collision detection jam time or interframe gap time) influence traffic handling characteristics?

Two workloads are used to bound performance. In Figure 11.23, one station out of one hundred is always actively transmitting a message, while in Figure 11.24 one hundred out of one hundred stations are active attempting to transmit messages. All messages are four thousand bits long. The horizontal axis or abscissa in either case is the raw data transmission speed of the network (the clock rate), while the vertical axis or ordinate is the actual carried data rate, the rate at which data bits are successfully transmitted. The ideal case is to use zero transmission capacity for network access control, which would be a straight line with slope unity. The deviation from this straight line shows the penalty paid using the same network to control access as well as transmit messages.

Figure 11.25 is a plot of lower bound on message delay versus number of active stations, assuming each station goes idle for a mean amount of time T_I and then active in order to transmit a message.

The best available evidence today is:

• Token passing via a ring is the least sensitive to workload, and offers short delay under light load and controlled delay under heavy load.

• Token passing via a bus has the greatest delay under light load and under heavy load cannot carry as much traffic as a ring and is quite sensitive to

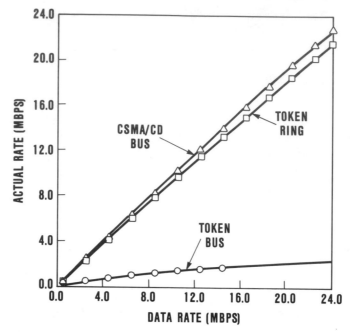

Figure 11.23.Maximum Mean Data Rate vs Clock Rate

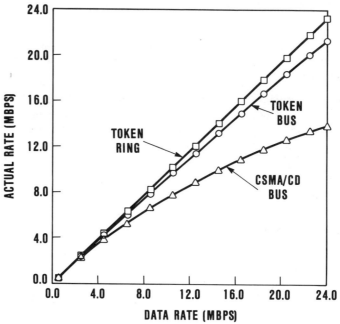

Figure 11.24.Maximum Mean Data Rate vs Clock Rate

the bus length (through the propagation time for energy to traverse the bus).

- Carrier sense collision detection may offer the shortest delay under light load, or a ring may do better if the ring is sufficiently short, while it is quite

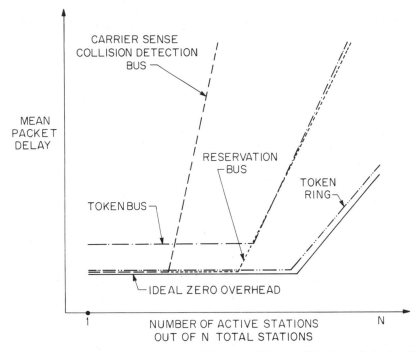

Figure 11.25. Lower Bound on Mean Message Delay vs Number of Active Stations

sensitive under heavy load to the workload and is sensitive to the bus length (the shorter the bus the better it performs) and to message length (the longer the packet the better it does).

Numerous caveats and disclaimers are in order:

- This evidence is currently being examined by those involved in actually building local area networks. No experimental data is available to confirm these plots independently. It is hoped that others will study this and subject it to independent tests.

- The scenario of one hundred stations active out of one hundred, with each generating the same workload, is possibly the *worst* congestion scenario for any system, and may in fact *never* occur in practice.

What about the impact of fluctuations, correlation, and multiple services? A great deal of work has been done in this area, and it has been summarized in earlier sections. Many argue that we should check the mean value measurements and models first, before jumping to more complicated situations. In fact, congestion analysis has had little actual impact on local area network design. However, it may have greater impact in the marketplace, where paying customers want to know how many devices of what type can be interconnected before congestion through the network becomes unacceptable. Best currently available evidence is that increasing the local area network bandwidth offers an excellent avenue for reducing transmission medium congestion. A common theme heard again and again is that it is probably better to deploy these

581

systems and see how people really wish to use them, gathering and analyzing traffic measurements, before doing anything else.

11.12.1 Additional Reading

[1] E.Arthurs, B.W.Stuck, W.Bux, M.Marathe, W.Hawe, T.Phinney, R.Rosenthal, V.Tarassov, *IEEE Project 802 Local Area Networks Standards Traffic Handling Characteristics Committee Report Working Draft,* 1 June 1982, IEEE Computer Society, Silver Spring, Maryland.

[2] D.D.Clark, K.T.Pogran, D.P.Reed, *An Introduction to Local Area Networks,* Proceedings IEEE, **66** (11), 1497-1517 (1978).

[3] J.F.Hayes, *Local Distribution in Computer Communications,* IEEE Communications Magazine, **19** (2), 6-14(1981).

[4] IEEE Computer Society, *IEEE Project 802 Local Area Network Standards, Draft D 802.2 (Logical Link Control), Revision D 802.3 (CSMA/CD Access Method and Physical Layer Specification), Draft D 802.4 (Token-Passing Bus Access Method and Physical Layer Specification)* IEEE Computer Society, Silver Spring, Maryland (1983).

Problems

1) A communications system must poll two different types of sources for work. The arrival statistics for each source are independent Poisson processes, with the same mean arrival rate of 0.3 tasks per second. The service statistics for each source are independent identically distributed Erlang-2 random variables, with mean service time 1.0 seconds per task. Each source is served by a single processor as follows: the processor empties all of the work from source one in order of arrival, switches instantaneously to the other source, empties all of the work from source two in order of arrival, switches instantaneously to the other source, and so forth. Find

A.   the utilization of the processor

B.   the probability that a task must wait at all

C.   the mean number of tasks in the system

D.   the mean queueing time for a task

BONUS: Repeat the above if there is an overhead of 0.1 seconds to switch from one queue to the other.

BONUS: Repeat all of the above assuming *all* the work is generated at one queue versus equally balanced load

2) A multidrop communication system has multiple drops or taps from a common bus to different devices. We are given the following parameters:

- Transmission speed of 10 **MBPS**

- Time for energy to propagate from end of the bus to other worst case 20 μsec

- Time for each station to detect carrier and do polling protocol processing 100 μsec

- Fraction of time bus is busy transmitting data bits is 0.5

- Fifty stations connected to the communication system

We wish to examine two cases:

[1]   All the messages are generated by one station

[2]   Each station generates the same workload

For each of these cases

A. Calculate the mean message delay for each of the above cases, assuming constant, Erlang-2, and exponential message length distributions.

B. Repeat the above if the number of stations is changed to twenty stations and to one hundred stations.

C. Repeat all of the above if the utilization changes to 0.9.

3) A four story office building has two corridors per floor, with two rows of offices per corridor. Each office is fifteen feet by fifteen feet square. Each office has two local area network sockets on each of the two walls perpendicular to the wall with the door to the corridor. Each office has a nine foot ceiling with a false hung ceiling one foot below the actual ceiling. Each floor has a wiring closet at the northeast corner. Assuming wiring or cable or optical fiber can be run only in the walls and ceiling, estimate the number of feet of cabling required for

A. A star configuration for each floor connecting each office to the closet via three pairs of wire, and each closet connected by a vertical riser of coaxial cable.

B. A coaxial cable bus with a drop from the ceiling to each outlet of four pairs of twisted wires.

C. A fiber optic ring that connects each outlet to the wiring closet, and each closet is connected by a vertical fiber optic riser.

4) A coaxial cable is used in a local area network. Electromagnetic energy propagates through the cable at a speed of 200 meters/μsec. The bus is one kilometer long. The clock transmission rate is ten million bits per second. Each station transmits a 1000 bit packet, which includes both control bits and data bits.

A. If the cable is used as a token passing bus, with the electronics at each station requiring 5 μsec per token pass, how long does it take to pass the token through one hundred stations, if no station has a packet to transmit? if every station has a packet to transmit?

B. If the cable is used as a token passing ring, with the electronics delay at each station requiring one bit transmission time per token pass, how long does it take to pass the token through one hundred stations, if no station has a packet to transmit? if every station has a packet to transmit?

C. Repeat if the clock transmission rate is one hundred million bits per second.

D. Repeat all the above if the packet size is changed to 10,000 bits per packet.

E. Repeat all the above if the bus is ten kilometers long.

5) Four stations are interconnected via a token passing bus. The mean arrival rate of messages to each station is denoted by $\lambda_K, K=1,2,3,4$. Stations one, two and three transmit a one thousand bit frame if they have any message to send; station four transmits a four thousand bit frame if it has a message to send. The token passing bus clock rate is one million bits per second. The time to pass the token from one station to another is ten microseconds.

A. If each station is visited only once during a token passing polling cycle, and each station transmits until it empties its buffers, what is the admissible region of mean throughput rates?

B. If each station is visited only once during a token passing polling cycle, and each station transmits up to one thousand bits per visit, what is the admissible region of mean throughput rates?

C. If stations one, two and three are visited only once during a token passing polling cycle, while station four is visited four times during a token passing polling cycle, and each station can transmit up to two thousand bits per visit, what is the admissible region of mean throughput rates? Repeat if each station can transmit up to one thousand bits per visit. Repeat if station four is visited two times during a token passing polling cycle.

D. Repeat if the token passing overhead is zero, or is twenty microseconds.

6) A carrier sense collision detection local area network bus is operated as a loss system: if carrier is absent, a station attempts to transmit, and is either successful or garbles its transmission with that of one or more other stations. Transmission attempts are generated according to Poisson statistics with mean arrival rate λ. Each message has a constant length of one thousand bits. The bus clock rate is one million bits per second.

A. What is the largest arrival rate that results in no more than one in one million packets undergoing a collision? No more than one in one thousand packets undergoing a collision? No more than one in ten packets undergoing a collision?

B.   Repeat if the packet mean length is fixed at one thousand bits, but the packet length statistics fit an exponential distribution.

C.   Repeat if the bus clock rate is ten million bits per second.

7) N stations are connected to a local area network bus. Each station generates packets with a mean length of one thousand bits. The local area network bus clock rate is one million bits per second. Electromagnetic energy can propagate from one end of the bus to the other worst case in 20 μ seconds, which we call a slot time, denoted T_{slot}. The bus access method is slotted P-persistent collision detection: If the previous time slot was idle, a ready station begins to transmit. If the station successfully seizes the transmission medium for one slot time, it continues to transmit the message to completion. If the station is not successful in seizing the transmission for one slot time, it ceases transmission and will retry in the next time slot with propability P and otherwise defer to the next slot time and repeat the decision process all over again.

A.   What is the maximum data transmission rate versus the bus clock rate?

B.   Suppose all but one station always have a message to transmit, and the final station generates messages according to Poisson statistics with mean arrival rate λ. What is the largest value of λ such that the mean packet queueing time (both transmission and waiting) is under ten milliseconds for twenty stations total? for one hundred stations total? Repeat if the bus clock rate is ten million bits per second. Repeat if the bus clock rate is one hundred million bits per second.

8) Eight stations are connected to a local area network bus. The bus can be in one of three states: idle, collision, and successful message transmission. The mean time in the idle state and collision state are equal to 20 μ seconds. The mean time in the successful message transmission state equals the time to transmit a one thousand bit packet. A binary decision tree is used to determine station retry priorities.

A.   The bus clock rate is one million bits per second. If the station addresses are encoded into three bits, what is the worst case and best case time to the first successful packet transmission? What is the worst case and best case time to allow every station to transmit one packet?

B.   Repeat if the bus clock rate is ten million bits per second.

C.   Repeat if the bus clock rate is one hundred million bits per second. Plot the maximum mean data rate versus the clock rate.

D. Repeat if the number of stations is increased to one hundred and twenty eight.

E. Repeat for the case where the total number of packets transmitted per frame is fixed, but instead of each station generating a packet, only one station generates all the packets.

9) A local area network bus interconnects one hundred stations. Each station is either idle for a mean time of 10 milliseconds, or active waiting to transmit or transmitting a constant length 1000 data bit packet. Each packet also has one hundred control bits associated with addressing, sequencing, and error detection. The bus transmission rate is ten million bits per second. The bus can be accessed in three different ways:

[1] Token passing: each station passes the token to the next station with an overhead time of 10 μ seconds for propagation plus five microseconds per station (to allow electronics to quiesce).

[2] Carrier sense collision detection: each station waits for the transmission medium to be idle, and then transmits; if the transmission is successful within a slot time equal to two one way propagation times (20 microseconds) plus five microseconds per station (to allow electronics to quiesce) then the transmission continues, and otherwise it is aborted and will be attempted at a later point in time. The station enters back into its idle state and the process starts anew.

[3] Decision tree: each station waits for the start of a variable length frame, and then transmits. If the transmission is successful within a slot time equal to two one way propagation times (20 microseconds) plus five microseconds per station (to allow electronics to quiesce), then the transmission continues, and otherwise it is aborted and is retried according to the station binary address (lower addresses have higher priority).

Answer the following questions:

A. Plot a lower bound on mean delay versus number of stations for each access method.

B. Repeat if the bus transmission speed is ten million bits per second. Repeat if the bus transmission speed is one hundred million bits per second.

CITATION INDEX

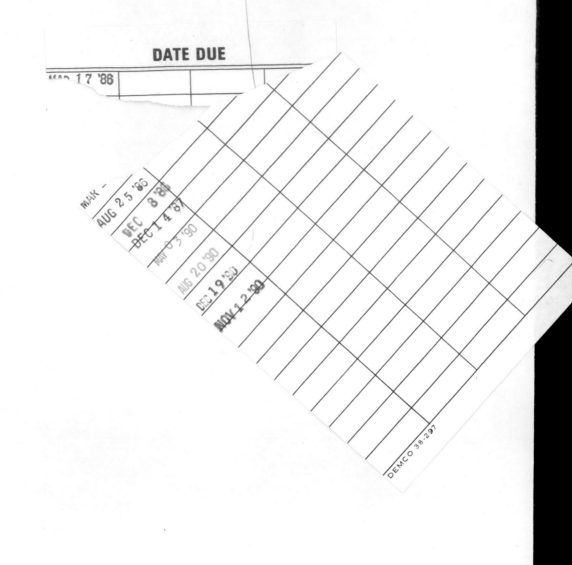